OFF THE BEATEN TRACK • OFF THE BEATEN TRACK • OFF THE BEATEN TRACK • OFF THE BEATEN TRACK • OFF THE BEATEN TRACK

OFF THE BEATEN TRACK

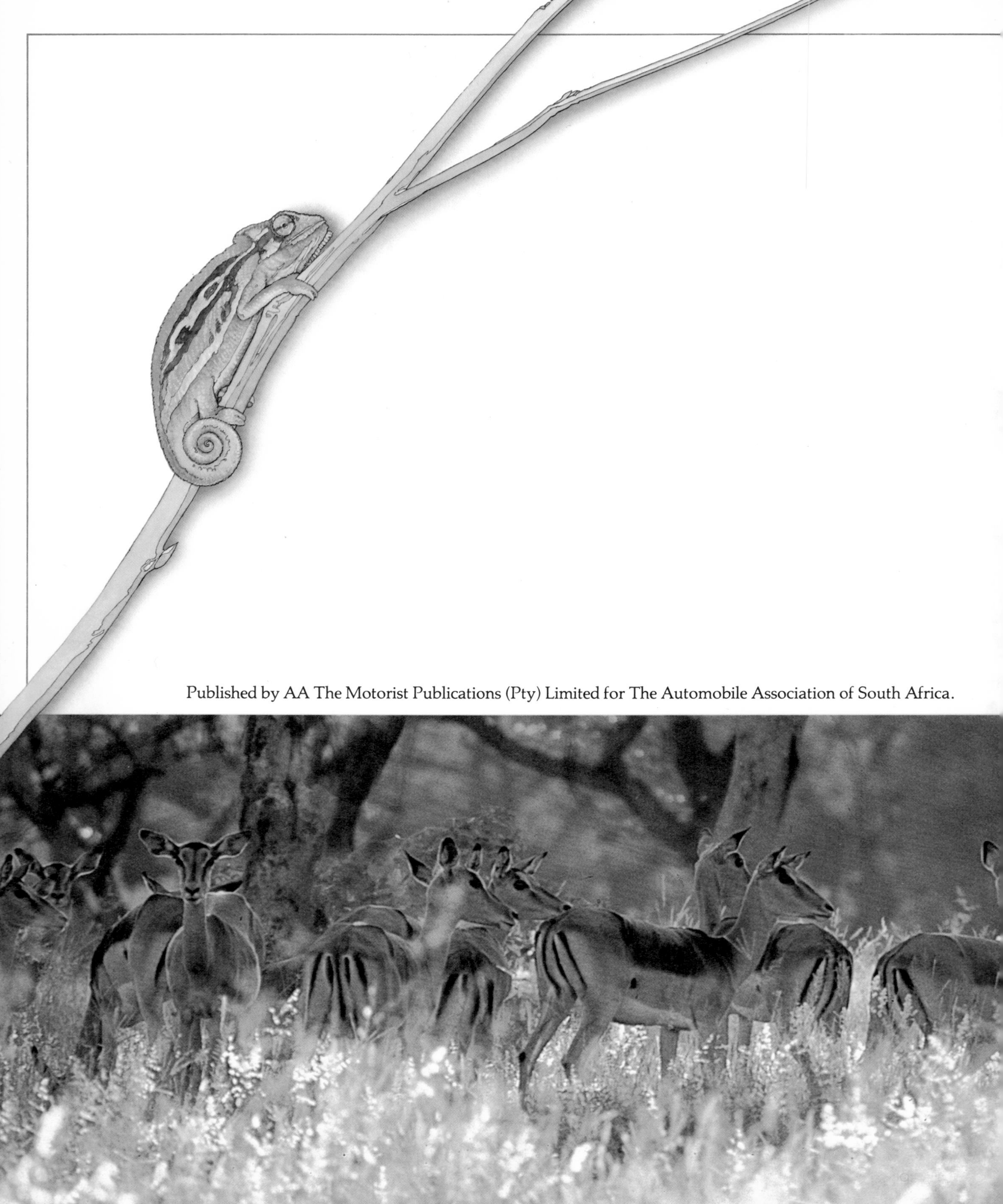

Published by AA The Motorist Publications (Pty) Limited for The Automobile Association of South Africa.

OFF THE BEATEN TRACK

SELECTED DAY DRIVES IN SOUTHERN AFRICA

Printed and bound by CTP Book Printers, Cape

OFF THE BEATEN TRACK was edited and designed at AA The Motorist Publications (Pty) Ltd, 130 Strand Street, Cape Town 8001.

Information from official maps reproduced under Government Printer's Copyright Authority 8472 of 3 January 1986.

ISBN 0 947008 25 X

FRONT COVER: *A trout-filled lake in Natal's Kamberg Nature Reserve.* (Photograph: Walter Knirr)
BACK COVER: *The calm, translucent waters of the Cape Peninsula's Clifton Beach.* (Photograph: Jean Morris)
INTRODUCTORY PAGE: *The richly hued rock strata of Meiringspoort.* (Photograph: David Steele)
TITLE PAGE: *Sunlight catches a herd of impala in a typical Lowveld setting.* (Photograph: Gerald Cubitt)
UPPER RIGHT: *The sparkling waters of a mountain stream in Giant's Castle Game Reserve.* (Photograph: Walter Knirr)
RIGHT: *The sinking sun adds a blush of pink to a coast of golden sands.* (Photograph: Anthony Bannister)

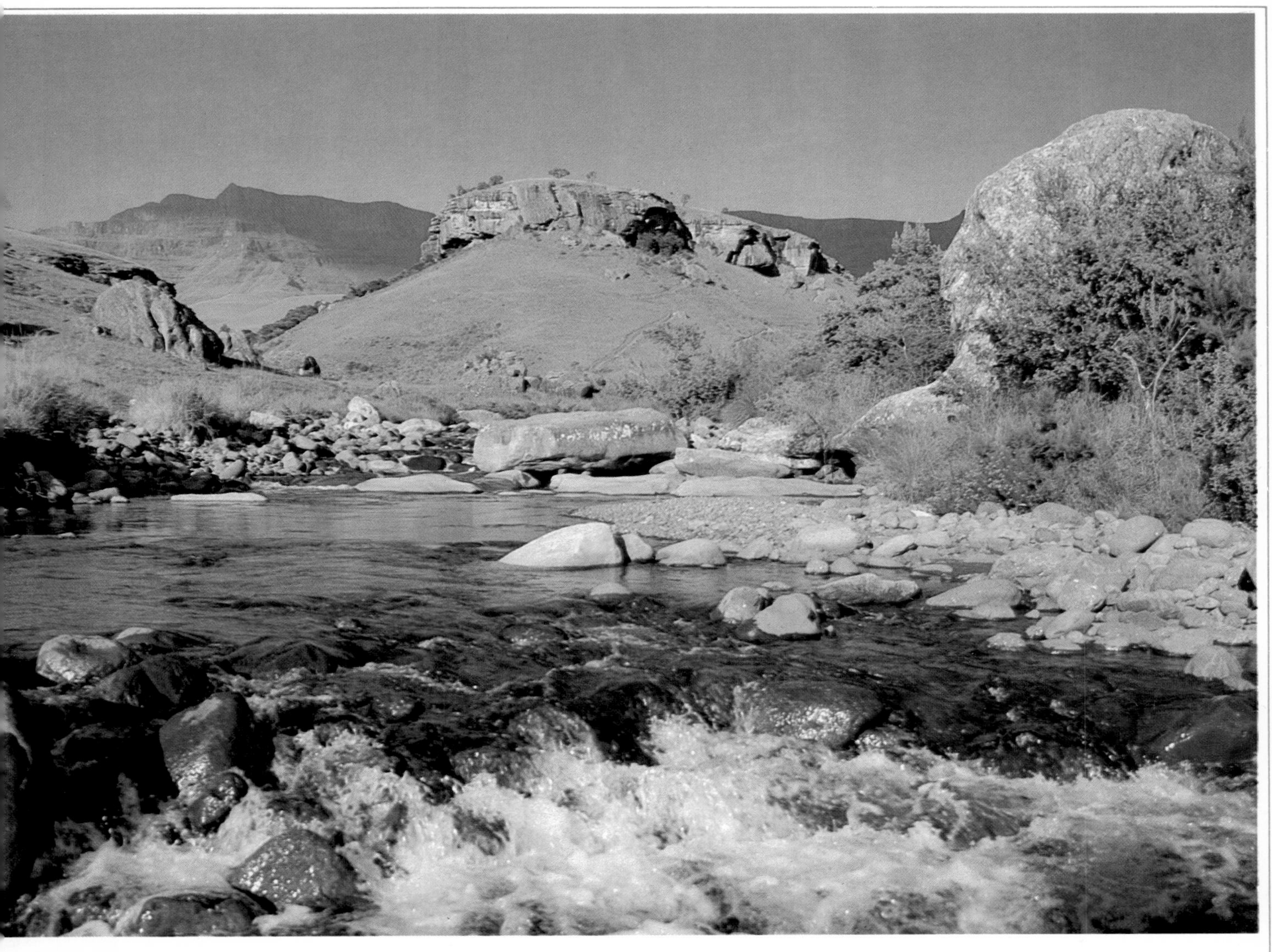

COMPOSITION OF DRIVES George Maclay

ART EDITOR Neville Poulter

EDITOR Alfie Steyn

PRINCIPAL WRITER Brian Johnson-Barker

RESEARCH EDITOR Judy Beyer

PROJECT CO-ORDINATORS Carol Kleinhans, Zaidah Abrahams

REGIONAL AND SPECIALIST CONTRIBUTORS Leo Braack, Alan Duggan, Monica Fairall, Christabel Hardacre, Rob McCallum, Charles Norman, Tim O'Hagan, Charles Riddle, Charlotte Siebert, Anne Turner, Jacqueline Veening

ILLUSTRATIONS Tobie Beele

PRODUCTION ARTISTS Clarence Clarke, Felicity Harris

TYPESETTING Mary Lacey, Elizabeth Brookes, Dalene Newbould

PROOFREADER Jack Early

PICTURE LIBRARIAN Dominique Davis

INDEX Ethleen Lastovica

CARTOGRAPHY Institute for Cartographic Analysis, University of Stellenbosch; Chris Vlok, Janine Blaauw

How to use this book

This book is divided into two parts. The first provides a selection of THROUGH ROUTES that criss-cross the country; the second contains an extensive collection of interesting and scenic DAY DRIVES — which either branch off from the through routes or lead out of the country's major urban centres.

The THROUGH ROUTES given in the first part of the book include the major highways that link the country's principal cities, and also a number of attractive alternative routes that offer different scenery and less traffic, and which, in place of a familiar, often-travelled route, present a fresh and fascinating new way to reach your destination — allowing you to explore parts of the country you might not have seen before.

With each of these routes, in addition to detailed instructions and a map, interesting information is given relating to the countryside you will be travelling through and the towns that you visit. Also supplied are cross-references to the day drives that start from the towns you pass through — enabling you to add two or three days to your journey and turn it into an adventurous holiday.

The DAY DRIVES comprise the second and larger part of the book, beginning on page 70. Each day drive is a carefully constructed one-day tour, designed to guide you to a selection of the most fascinating and beautiful places in a given region.

All but a few of these drives are circular, bringing you back to your starting point at the end of the day. Each drive may be undertaken as a one-day outing from the town or city that serves as its starting point, or you may link several drives together to create a motoring holiday through a particular region of the country. Here and there, where the natural attractions of the region merit it, a special feature has been included alongside a drive — telling you more about the landscape you are exploring, or perhaps giving you a guided walk through one of the old towns in the area.

Start the day early

An important point to keep in mind when undertaking any of the day drives is to start early. Read through the route in advance, prepare the night before (which includes filling the car with petrol and checking that everything is in working order) then make an early start before the morning traffic fills the roads. To have designed each drive for a more leisurely holiday-maker who wishes to set out in mid-morning would have resulted in a far less varied and interesting day for those who desire the full adventure. If circumstances give you no choice but to start a drive late, you will need to omit some part of the route.

The distances given in the route instructions are as accurate as possible. You will find discrepancies, because the odometers of different cars give slightly varying measurements, and readings are affected by such factors

Key to maps for Through Routes and Day Drives

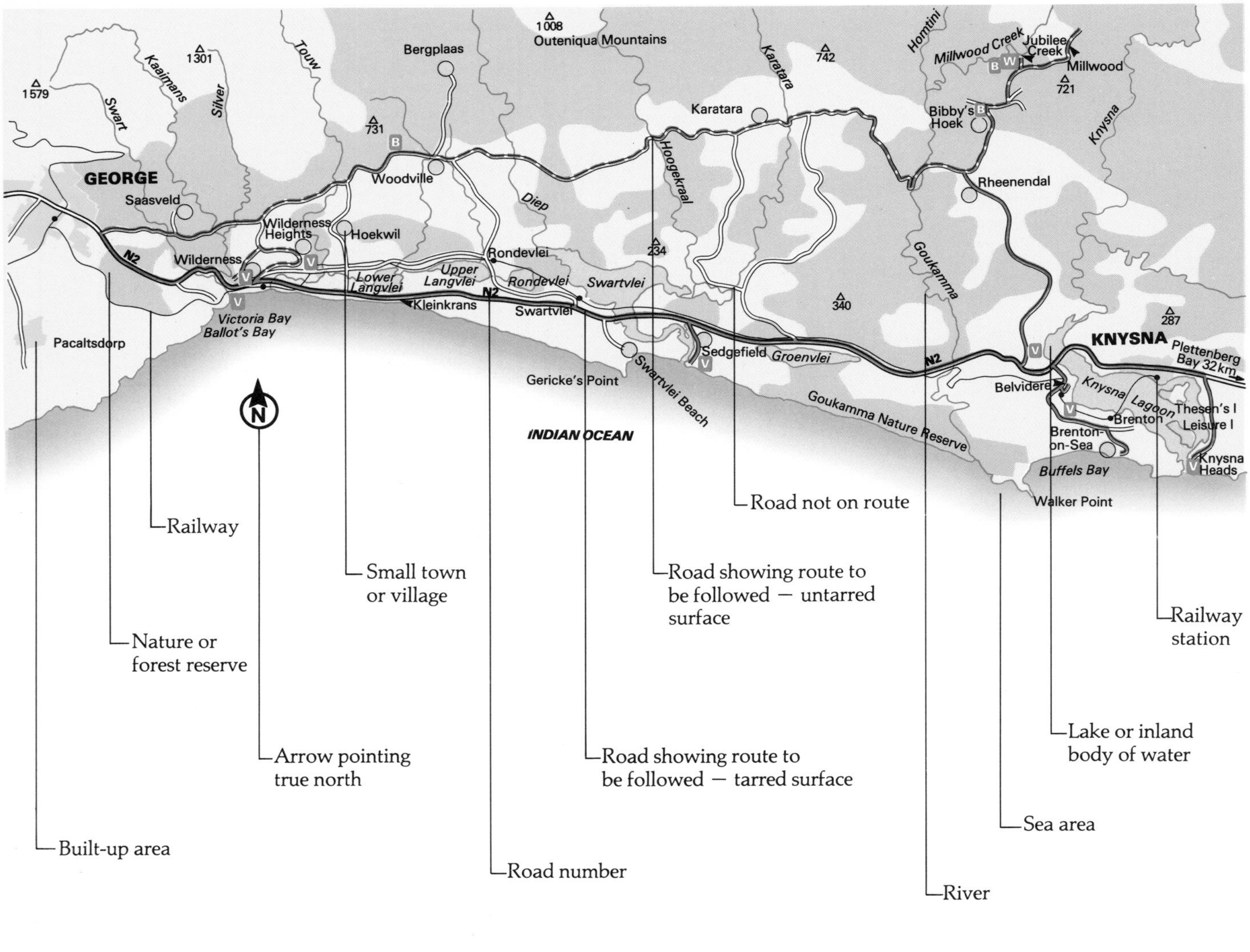

as the hardness or softness of a car's tyres, but every distance given is an actual recording, or the median between two measurements recorded by two different vehicles. (Throughout the route instructions the phrase 'after 10,7 km', for example, would refer back to the last point at which you were asked to note your kilometres, unless the context clearly indicates some other point of reference. Where a route includes an opportunity for a short walk, the phrase 'allow 40-60 minutes' would refer to the total time — there and back.)

For further information

With each drive, at the end of the route instructions, you will find an information panel containing several valuable addresses and telephone numbers. Use these to inquire into the state of the roads, to get up-to-the-minute information relating to restaurants along the route, to find out about overnight accommodation in the area, and generally to answer any further query you might have. (Are dogs allowed into a particular area? Is the museum still closed on Sundays?)

Until recently many of South Africa's beaches, restaurants and holiday resorts have been strictly reserved for use by one or another race group. This is changing rapidly, but more rapidly in some parts than in others. The drives provided here have been designed to show the traveller the finest scenery and the most interesting places that a region contains, ignoring artificial social conventions and regulations. If there is any likelihood that your day might be spoilt by such restrictions, contact one of the organisations listed to discover what regulations apply.

Many of the drives include scenic mountain or river-valley passes that are not suitable for vehicles towing trailers or caravans. If you are towing, contact the AA office given in the information panel to confirm that the route you plan to take is suitable. (Remember also to check what documents are needed before crossing international borders.)

Confirm your route in advance

Bear in mind that the roads on which you are travelling are being altered continually — gravel surfaces are tarred, old roads are re-routed. With the passage of time, the route instructions will inevitably become incorrect here and there. Where such alterations have occurred, you will need to follow whatever new signs are erected, and you will need to refer to both the route instructions and the accompanying map to make the most appropriate adjustment. A sensible precaution, before setting out on a drive, is to contact the AA office given in the panel and ask whether there have been any important alterations to the roads in the area — or whether the route needs to be modified in any other way. (A picnic area might have closed, or a new game reserve might offer an interesting detour.)

The information collected in this volume represents several years of research and over 100 000 kilometres of driving on roads and tracks throughout the country. Great care has been taken to ensure that the information and the directions given are correct in every detail. However, the publishers cannot accept responsibility for any loss, damage or inconvenience that might result, either directly or indirectly, from the use of the instructions or the maps provided here ●

Key to maps for Town Walks and Nature Reserves

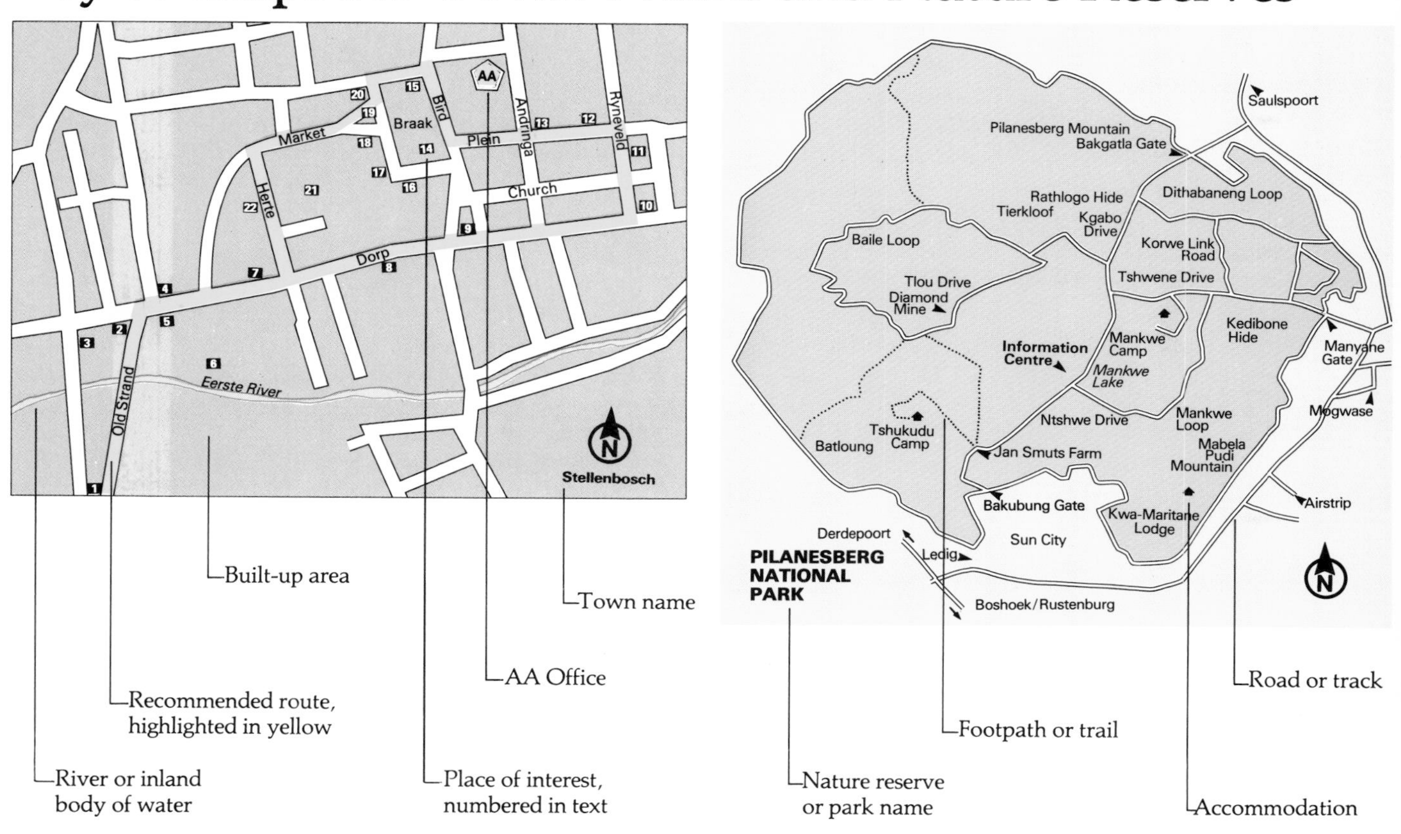

Additional symbols

V	Viewsite	R	Restaurant/hotel		Marsh
B	Braai/barbecue facilities	RR	Restaurants/hotels	○	Small town (Through Routes)
P	Picnic facilities		International boundaries	○	Small town (Day Drives)
W	Drinking water available		Provincial boundaries	1579	Mountain (height in metres)

CONTENTS

Introduction to Through Routes 10

Introduction to Day Drive Regions 70

Northern Transvaal 72

Eastern Transvaal & Swaziland 84

Southern Transvaal 118

Orange Free State & Lesotho 140

Natal 154

Transkei 194

Eastern Cape 204

Southern Cape 244

South-Western Cape 260

Northern Cape 304

Touring Tips: 318

Index 326

Solid and moody, the mighty wall of the Transvaal Drakensberg looks down on a party of modern explorers approaching the scenic Abel Erasmus Pass.

THROUGH ROUTES

FEW COUNTRIES ON EARTH can rival the beauty and grandeur of the South African landscape — range after range of mountains, hazy in the distance, beckon the traveller on through sunburned deserts to explore deep forests, fruit-filled valleys, and idyllic coastal hideaways where lazy rivers spill into shimmering blue lagoons. The following pages, from 12 to 69, contain a complete collection of 'through routes' that traverse this giant canvas.

These include the most direct routes between the country's major urban centres, and also an assortment of alternative routes, which link the same points but lead through different, less-travelled parts of the country — showing you magnificent scenery and places of interest that lie 'off the beaten track'.

Some of the longer routes have been divided into separate sections for convenience, and are described on two or even three consecutive double-page spreads. Each section of a route that has been divided in this way is roughly a full day's drive, but it is not necessary to break your journey at exactly the same points — in fact it is recommended that you give yourself more time, in order to explore the fascinating places you pass through, and to follow some of the side-trips that are described.

Within the route instructions you will also find cross-references to day drives that begin and end at the towns you pass through. If possible, you should add several days to your journey so that you can stop at these points and use the day drives to discover the most interesting and scenic places in each region.

The variety offered by these alternative routes across the country, when read in conjunction with the day drives that lead off from them, makes it possible to construct an almost infinite number of 'tailor-made' touring holidays.

Johannesburg/Pretoria - Pietersburg - **Messina 12-3**
Johannesburg/Pretoria - Nelspruit - **Komatipoort 14-5**
Johannesburg/Pretoria - Lydenburg - **Skukuza 16-7**
Johannesburg/Pretoria - Pietersburg - Tzaneen - **Letaba 18-9**
Punda Maria - Louis Trichardt - Blyde River Canyon - **Johannesburg 20-1**
Johannesburg/Pretoria - Bethal - Ermelo - **Mbabane 22-3**
Johannesburg/Pretoria - Harrismith - Pietermaritzburg - **Durban 24-5**
Johannesburg/Pretoria - Piet Retief - Eshowe - **Durban 26-7**
Durban - Greytown - Volksrust - **Johannesburg/Pretoria 28-9**
Durban - Eshowe - Vryheid - Mbabane - **Skukuza 30-1**
Pretoria/Johannesburg - Kroonstad - Bloemfontein - **Colesberg 32-3**
Colesberg - Three Sisters - Beaufort West - Worcester - **Cape Town 34-5**
Pretoria/Johannesburg - Klerksdorp - Kimberley - **Three Sisters 36-7**
Pretoria/Johannesburg - Bethlehem - Ladybrand - **Aliwal North 38-9**
Aliwal North - Graaff-Reinet - Oudtshoorn - **Cape Town 40-1**
Bloemfontein - Aliwal North - Queenstown - **East London 42-3**
Colesberg - Middelburg - Graaff-Reinet - Uitenhage - **Port Elizabeth 44-5**
Cape Town - Clanwilliam - Calvinia - Kenhardt - **Upington 46-7**
Upington - Kuruman - Vryburg - Zeerust - **Pretoria/Johanneburg 48-9**
Durban - Port Shepstone - Kokstad - Umtata - **East London 50-1**
East London - King William's Town - Port Elizabeth - **Knysna 52-3**
Knysna - Mossel Bay - Swellendam - Caledon - **Cape Town 54-5**
Cape Town - Ladismith - Oudtshoorn - Uniondale - **Graaff-Reinet 56-7**
Graaff-Reinet - Middelburg - Molteno - Dordrecht - **Elliot 58-9**
Elliot - Maclear - Kokstad - Pietermaritzburg - **Durban 60-1**
Durban - Harrismith - Winburg - N1 to **Cape Town 62-3**
Pretoria/Johannesburg - Wolmaransstad - Upington - **SWA/Namibia 64-5**
Vioolsdrif - Grünau - Keetmanshoop - Mariental - **Windhoek 66-7**
Cape Town - Clanwilliam - Garies - Springbok - **Vioolsdrif 68-9**

The Great North Road through the bushveld and the Soutpansberg to the lazy Limpopo River

This is the principal route to the north from Johannesburg and Pretoria, known to generations of hunters and missionaries as the 'Great North Road'. The route leads through typical bushveld, crosses the Soutpansberg range, then cuts through mopane and baobab forest to reach the Limpopo River — South Africa's border with Zimbabwe.

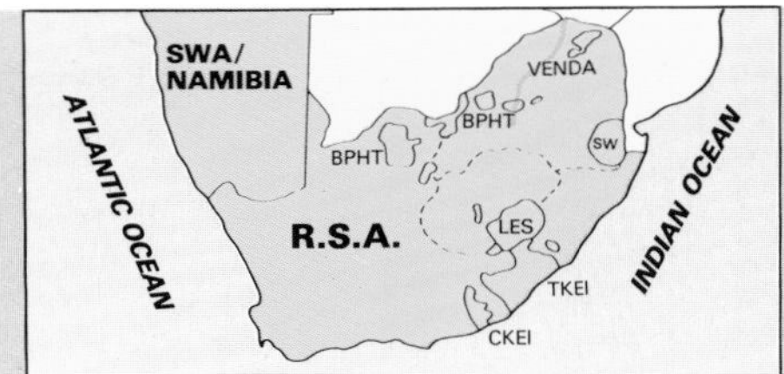

AA Office AA House, 66 De Korte Street, Braamfontein, Johannesburg 2001 Tel. (011) 4035700
AA Office AA House, 395 Schoeman Street, Pretoria 0002 Tel. (012) 283829
AA Office Talmot Building, 53 Schoeman Street, Pietersburg 0700 Tel. (01521) 71442
SA Tourism Board Cnr Vorster & Landdros Maré Streets, Pietersburg 0700 Tel. (01521) 3025
Louis Trichardt Tourist Information Public Library, Krogh Street, Louis Trichardt

Johannesburg (544 km) - Pretoria (490 km) - Warmbad - Potgietersrus - Pietersburg- Louis Trichardt - **Messina**

DRIVE NORTH OUT OF JOHANNESBURG on the N1. Roughly two-thirds of the way to Pretoria, at the Brakfontein interchange, take the off-ramp to your left in order to stay on the N1 (to continue straight would take you into Pretoria on the R28). The section of the N1 that you are now on is known as the Danie Joubert Freeway and also as the Eastern Bypass. As it passes through the eastern outskirts of Pretoria, it crosses the N4, which leads east to Komatipoort. Continue north on the N1, but note your kms as you pass the entry-ramp from the N4. (If you are starting your journey from Pretoria, drive east out of the city on Schoeman Street, which becomes the N4, then turn left onto the N1, noting your kms.)

Roughly 38 km from Pretoria you pass the turn-off to Hammanskraal on your left, and 54 km after this you reach the end of the freeway. Take the exit road (R516) for Pietersburg and Warmbad (hot bath — referring to the hot springs that occur here). After 8 km turn right at the T-junction, and at the next T-junction, in front of the hotel in Warmbad, turn right again. Note your kms as you leave Warmbad on what is now the N1 again, the old 'Great North Road', for Potgietersrus and Pietersburg.

There are many roadside stalls along this route, selling hand-made baskets, vegetables and fruit — especially oranges in the season.

Warmbad to Pietersburg

Soon after leaving Warmbad you pass a prominent hill on your right, known as Buyskop after the notorious outlaw Coenraad de Buys, and 9 km from Warmbad you pass a road on your left leading to Groot Nylsoog — the source of a river that early Voortrekkers believed to be the Nile. A further 15 km brings you to the pretty little town of Nylstroom (Nile stream) on the banks of one of the 'Nile's' tributaries. The N1 passes straight through Nylstroom and after 40 km you reach the busy little town of Naboomspruit (see below).

Stay on the N1, which passes straight through Naboomspruit, and note your kms as you leave the town. After 6 km you pass a road on your right to Tobias Station. In the distance ahead, you can now see the Strydpoortberge (battle gorge mountains), and away to your left are the Waterberg (water mountain) ranges. Cotton is one of the crops grown in this region of the Transvaal, and you will see a few fields of it alongside the road. Roughly 37 km from Naboomspruit you come to a fairly large clearing on your right. In the clearing, under two spreading camel-thorn trees, is the Moorddrif Monument (see below).

9 km after the monument you enter Potgietersrus on Voortrekker Street. You pass the town's museum on your left, at the corner of Retief Street. (To view the ana trees — see below — turn left into Potgieter Street and continue straight ahead. After 7,9 km turn left onto the R518 for Marken. You reach the clump of trees on your left after a further 6,3 km.)

Sparkling blue waters of the mineral spa at Warmbad.

David Livingstone camped under these ana trees near Potgietersrus.

The monument at Moorddrif.

THE TRAGEDY OF MOORDDRIF

Beneath the stone monument at Moorddrif (murder drift), close to the roadside, are buried the remains of a party of Voortrekkers killed as a result of a feud, or possibly a misunderstanding, between their leader Hermanus Potgieter and the Tlou chiefs Makapan and Mapela. The Voortrekkers were attacked while they had outspanned from their wagons in the shade of the camel-thorn trees, during a break in their journey from Schoemansdal to Marico. The party of Voortrekkers was wiped out, and it is said that the children in the party had their skulls smashed against the trunks of the trees (the trees are a proclaimed part of the monument). The incident led to the Tlou being besieged at Makapansgat by a force of Voortrekkers seeking terrible revenge, resulting in the deaths of at least 1 500 of the Tlou people.

The Makapansgat site is not open to the public, although permission may be obtained from the University of the Witwatersrand to join an occasional guided tour.

'LIKE A TREE' STREAM

The site of the town of Naboomspruit was once known as Kaufmann's store. There were stables and a small trading post here in the days when horse-drawn mail coaches plied between Pretoria and Pietersburg. The town's present name is derived from the *Euphorbia ingens* and a nearby spruit (stream). *Euphorbia ingens* is a large succulent that grows to a height of 9 metres. At first glance it resembles a tree — hence its Afrikaans name *naboom*, meaning 'like a tree'.

At the northern end of Voortrekker Street a Class 19D steam locomotive is displayed on the left, at the municipal caravan park. Directly opposite, on the right side of the road, is the entrance to the nature reserve and breeding station run by the National Zoological Gardens of South Africa. This makes an ideal spot for a picnic lunch, with braai places, water and toilets, and a large variety of both indigenous and exotic animals that are readily visible.

Leave Potgietersrus by continuing north along Voortrekker Street, which becomes the N1 for Pietersburg. Note your kms as you pass under the railway bridge. The country through which you now pass has been called 'the cradle of man in South Africa', and many valuable archeological finds have been made at Makapansgat.

25 km after leaving Potgietersrus, turn right onto a gravel road to visit Eersteling, scene of the first gold-crushing operation in the Transvaal in modern times (see below). Note your kms as you turn off the tar. Turn right after 4,7 km, and take the widest of the several gravel roads after the cattle grid — leading straight down the hill. Drive slowly, as there are prominent humps across the road at irregular intervals. After 5,7 km on the gravel, keep straight where a road on your left leads up a small hill. You reach the tall chimney on your right 200 m later. The road up the hill leads to a turning circle after roughly 100 m, with a view of the old workings and the entire valley.

Return to the N1 and turn right, noting your kms. After 23,6 km the road becomes a double carriageway, and after a further 4 km you enter the built-up area of Pietersburg (see pages 18-19). Stay in the left lane, and keep straight at the first set of traffic lights. At the second set of lights, turn left into Landdros Maré Street. (The offices of the South African Tourism Board are on your right, just before you turn.)

Continue out of town on Landdros Maré Street, passing on your left an outdoor display of old vehicles and farming implements. Note your kms as you pass the entrance to the air force base on your left. A few hundred metres out of town you pass a short grey tower, also on your left, commemorating the disastrous trek by Louis Trichardt and his party from the Soutpansberg to Lourenco Marques (now Maputo). A flight of steps leads to the top of the tower, where a bronze map illustrates the area, and from where there is a good view over the route traversed by the Voortrekkers.

Pietersburg to Messina

Roughly 54 km after leaving Pietersburg you cross the Tropic of Capricorn, and you can see the Soutpansberg (salt pan mountain) range rising from the plains ahead of you.

Roughly 100 km from Pietersburg you pass the town of Louis Trichardt on your left (see pages 20-21, and day drive, pages 74-77). You pass through two four-way stop streets here — note your kms at the second. Immediately after this the road begins to climb the Soutpansberg through the Hanglip Forest Reserve. After 8,7 km there is a picnic site on your left, with good views over Louis Trichardt and the wide plains to the south.

You drive through the Soutpansberg by way of the scenic Wyllie's Poort, and the road enters the first of the two Hendrik Verwoerd Tunnels 20,5 km from Louis Trichardt. Immediately after this first tunnel there is a parking area on your left, with a commemorative plaque and good views of the mountains. From here you can also see below you the old road through the poort, closely following the course of the small stream that carved the route.

North of Wyllie's Poort the character of the vegetation changes to mopane forest, with a sprinkling of baobabs. 55 km after leaving Louis Trichardt you pass through a crossroads, where the road on your right leads to the Honnet Nature Reserve and the hot-springs resort of Tshipise. 89 km from Louis Trichardt you reach the northernmost town in South Africa, Messina, surrounded by baobab trees.

Messina is a hot but attractive town, where bougainvillea and daisies make a colourful display in late winter and spring, and the garden of the railway station frequently wins awards. The town's information bureau is in the main street, with an old steamroller standing outside. The N1 continues through Messina, crossing the railway twice, and after 14 km reaches the Beit Bridge over the Limpopo River, the border between South Africa and Zimbabwe ●

Hendrik Verwoerd Tunnel in the Soutspansberg.

1871 — GOLD IN THE TRANSVAAL

In 1871 Edward Button, in partnership with William Pigg, discovered gold on the farm Eersteling. A stamp battery and steam engine were ordered from England, and Button imported Aberdeen granite with which to build the chimney for his power plant. The total cost of the chimney is said to have been around R40 000, and today it is all that remains of this first modern gold-mining operation in the Transvaal. The very first ore-crushing was carried out on the nearby rocky outcrop by means of a large boulder — ridden as a seesaw by two men, while a third man fed in pieces of ore beneath. The boulder is now in the museum of the Geological Survey in Pretoria.

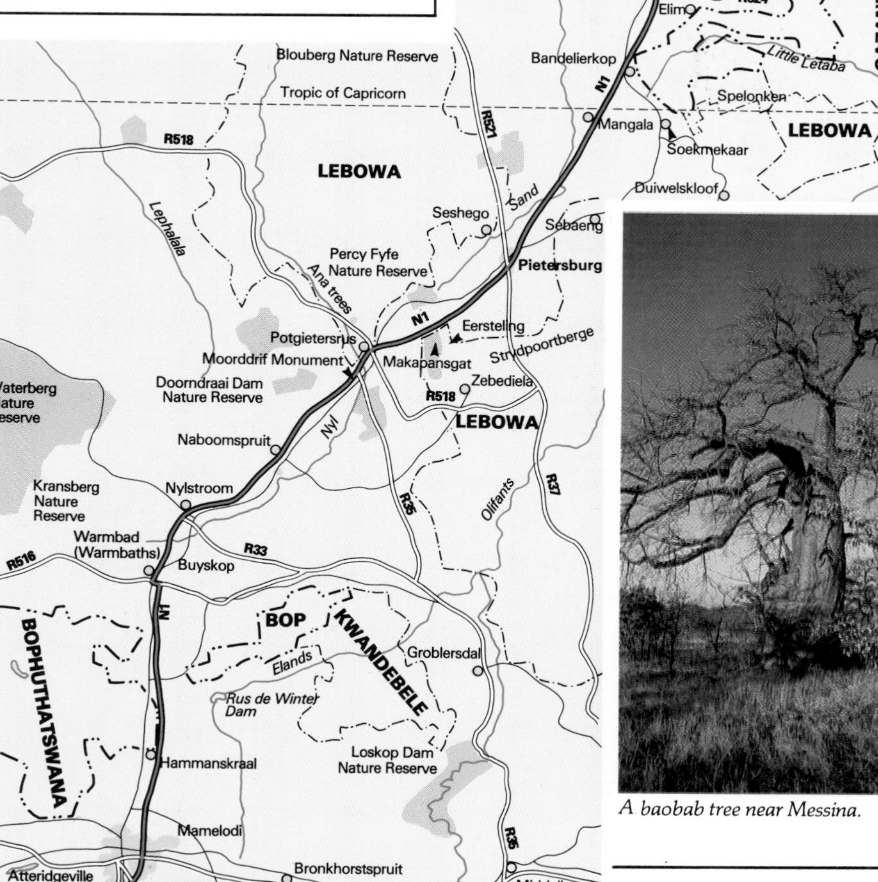

A baobab tree near Messina.

Scenic holiday route to the Lowveld that follows the 'railway of death'

The thousands of tourists who annually drive from Pretoria and the Witwatersrand to the scenic holiday wonderland of the Eastern Transvaal and Lowveld follow a road rich in memories and suffering. This is the route chosen by the builders of the original railway between Pretoria and the sea; a route that claimed a life for every sleeper laid.

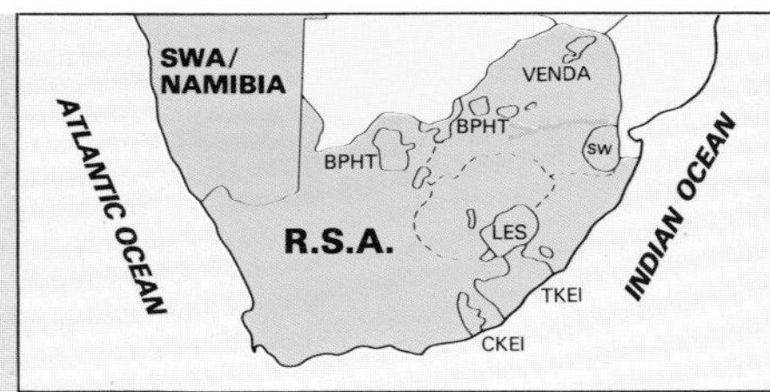

AA Office AA House, 66 De Korte Street, Braamfontein, Johannesburg 2001 Tel. (011) 4035700
AA Office AA House, 395 Schoeman Street, Pretoria 0002 Tel. (012) 283829
AA Office 56 Brown Street, Nelspruit 1200 Tel. (01311) 24631
SA Tourism Board 4th Floor, United Building, cnr Brown and Paul Kruger Streets, Nelspruit 1200 Tel. (01311) 23443

Johannesburg (Pretoria) - Witbank - Middelburg - Waterval-Boven - Nelspruit - **Komatipoort (480—490 km)**

IF YOU ARE STARTING your journey from Johannesburg, drive east on the R22. Shortly after passing Witbank on your left you join the N4, heading towards Middelburg. If you are starting from Pretoria, drive east along Schoeman Street, which becomes the N4, and continue on the N4 to Middelburg.

You enter Middelburg on Kerkstraat. Turn right into Jan van Riebeeck Street for 'Nelspruit/Kruger National Park', then keep straight through several sets of traffic lights. Note your kms as you pass beneath a rail bridge.

The road passes through a flat landscape of grainfields and silos, with far on the right the great power stations of Hendrina and Arnot. At 59 km an access road leads left to Belfast, and at 64,4 km a gravel road leads right for 200 m to the Bergendal monument (toilets and picnic sites — see opposite).

Note your kms at this turn-off. Three kilometres further, a road on the right leads to the rail siding of Dalmanutha, as the battle of Bergendal is sometimes known.

Machadodorp to Nelspruit

The road descends gently with wide views of rolling hills and fields. At 15,9 km a road on the right leads into Machadodorp which, after the fall of Pretoria, was the seat of the republican Transvaal government for more than two months in 1900. Note your kms as you pass this road. 7,4 km later you pass the R36 to Lydenburg on your left, and after a further 4,4 km you pass a road leading right into Waterval-Boven.

Three kilometres past Waterval-Boven the road crosses the Elands River, and 200 m later the old NZASM railway tunnel comes into view to the left of the modern tunnel (see opposite). There is a large parking area on the left where you can stop to explore the tunnel.

Five kilometres beyond the tunnel look out for another parking area on the left. Stop the car (remembering to keep it locked) and walk back toward the old five-arch bridge. Go through the gate on your right and walk for about two minutes to reach a good position from which to view the river below, and the stone bridge.

The road continues downward, and at the second crossing of the Elands River, 800 m from the parking area, the original railway bridge — on stone piers — can be seen on your left, next to the present bridge.

2,3 km from the parking area a road leads on the right to Waterval-Onder. Here, in the grounds of a hotel, stands Krugerhof, the last residence in the Transvaal (other than railway carriages) of President Paul Kruger before his departure for Europe in October 1900.

Note your kms as you pass this road. From here you begin to see candelabra-like naboom trees dotted among the hills. After 42,5 km you reach the first of four crossings of the Elands River, after which the road winds towards a junction with the R539. Opposite this junction turn right, drive in front of the petrol station, then turn right and pass several houses to reach a small parking area — from where a footpath leads to fine views of the Montrose Falls.

Continue on the N4, which crosses the Crocodile River just above the falls. Shortly after this, at about 50 km, there is a good view back and to the right of the road you have followed, winding its way up among the hills. Slow down for a steep descent 1 km later, and pass the R539 to the Sudwala Caves on your left at 53 km.

At 76 km you reach Nelspruit, nestling among bare granite outcrops and citrus orchards. Keep straight on Louis Trichardt Street, following the signs for 'N4/Komatipoort'. 500 m after the second set of traffic lights, go right at the fork and note your kms. The road is now lined by palm trees, and soon you pass the R538 to White River on your left — as the road winds among stern, granite hills.

Nelspruit to Komatipoort

At around 21 km the road crosses Gould's Salvation Spruit, with the Crocodile River 500 m further on. You are now in the rocky Crocodile Gorge, with the river on your right. There are several places on your right where you can pull off the road for a view of the boulder-strewn river bed below. The gorge ends after some 14 km, when the road again crosses the river. At 37 km you pass on your right the R38 to Barberton, and a few hundred metres later you pass a road leading left to Kaapmuiden. 4 km after passing Malelane, the R570 leads left to the Malelane Gate of the Kruger National Park.

Canefields and citrus estates line the road near Hectorspruit, said to have been named after the favourite dog of an early hunter. After Hectorspruit the road runs through fairly dense bush for 26 km to reach a crossroads 4,5 km from the Lebombo border post with Mocambique (to reach the border continue straight ahead). Turn left here for the 2 km drive to Komatipoort, then continue straight for a further 11 km if you wish to reach the Crocodile Bridge Gate to the Kruger National Park ●

NZASM tunnel entrance, Waterval-Boven.

Five-arch bridge on the NZASM railway.

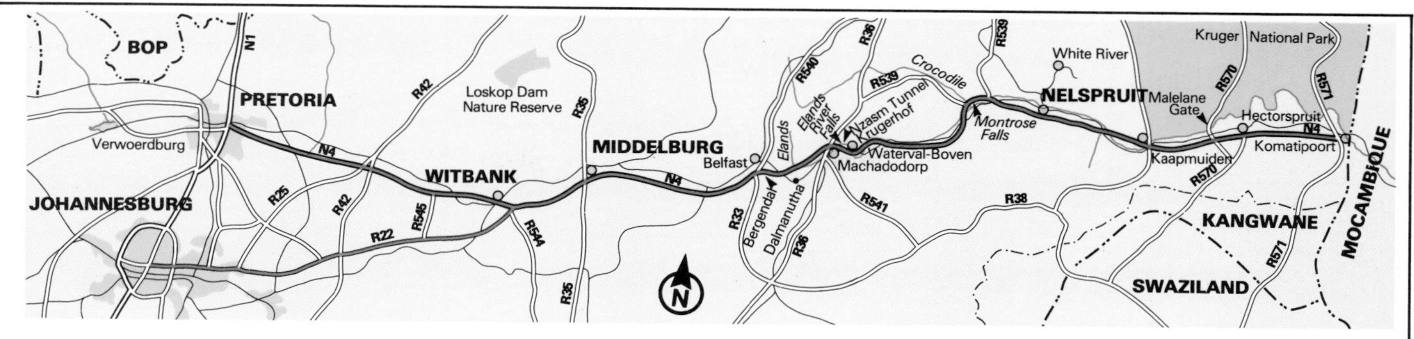

'DEATH RAILWAY' TO THE SEA

A death for every sleeper laid. This was the claim made in 1894 when the Nederlandsche Zuid-Afrikaansche Spoorweg-Maatschappij (NZASM) opened the first rail link between the Transvaal and the sea at Delagoa Bay.

In seven years an army of workers had overcome terrible gradients, ravines and disease to complete the railway. But no one will ever know just how many workers died: a monument in Dutch on the station at Waterval-Boven is dedicated to their memory. Some of the sections were so steep that special 'rack' rails had to be built — and these can still be seen at Waterval-Boven and at the nearby NZASM tunnel. In 1908 the line was taken over by the Central South African Railways.

THE LAST BOER BATTLE

The last pitched battle of the Anglo-Boer war took place in August 1900 at Bergendal near Belfast. Here 20 000 British troops attacked an outnumbered Boer force that included a detachment of Zarps (members of the South African Republic's police force).

To halt the British advance, General Louis Botha formed a thin line extending some 80 kilometres, and General Sir Redvers Buller, quite fortuitously, directed his attack against one of its gaps, inadequately covered by the Zarps. After a three-hour artillery bombardment, men of the Rifle Brigade and Inniskilling Fusiliers advanced. The Zarps kept firing to the last before they were eventually overrun.

The 90 m plunge of the Elands River Falls near Machadodorp.

The cycad Encephalartos ferox *in the Lowveld Botanical Gardens, Nelspruit.*

MACHADO'S HAPPINESS

Machadodorp is named after Joaquim Machado, a Portuguese engineer who first surveyed the railway route between Delagoa Bay and Pretoria in 1876. He later became Governor General of Mocambique. The town was established on the farm Geluk (happiness), and for a few months following the British occupation of Pretoria during the Anglo-Boer War was the Seat of the Transvaal Government.

The sulphur springs in the town are said to have healing powers.

TOWN ON THE 'RIVER OF COWS'

The Komati River — the river of cows — breaks through the Lebombo Mountains through a gorge (poort) on its way to Delagoa Bay, where it is known as the Incomati. When the NZASM railway reached this point from the coast in 1891, the town of Komatipoort was established as a supply-base for further construction work. Not far from the town is the border post with neighbouring Mocambique.

Komatipoort is one of the hottest towns in the Transvaal, with temperatures of 35°C common in January and February. During the Anglo-Boer War it was the base of Steinacker's Horse, one of several irregular units, derisively known as 'the forty thieves'.

Left: *Massive boulders litter the valley of the Elands River.*

President Kruger's last Transvaal residence at Waterval-Onder.

Heading for the cool forests of the eastern Transvaal and the sun-drenched Kruger National Park

The first leg of this route from the southern Transvaal to Skukuza is described on pages 14-5. This second section starts at Belfast, climbs to Dullstroom and Lydenburg, then takes the scenic Long Tom Pass to Sabie. From Sabie we descend through forests to the Lowveld, and enter the Kruger National Park through the Paul Kruger Gate.

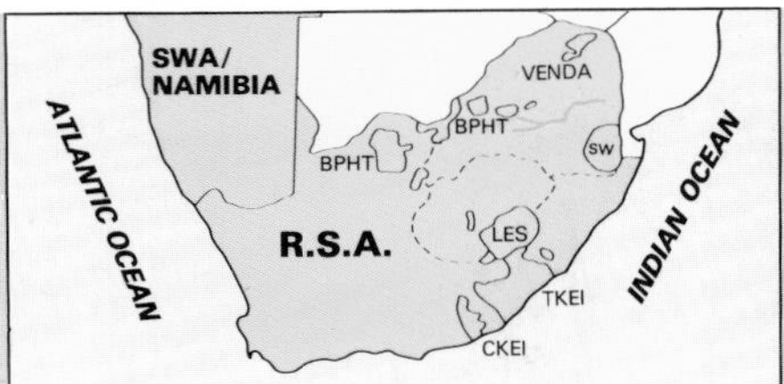

AA Office AA House, 66 De Korte Street, Braamfontein 2001 Tel. (011) 4035700
AA Office AA House, 395 Schoeman Street, Pretoria 0002 Tel. (012) 283829
Belfast Municipality Voortrekker Street, Belfast 1100 Tel. (0132512) 291
Sabie Forestry Museum Ford Street, Sabie 1260 Tel. (0131512) 54
Lydenburg Municipality cnr Voortrekker and Viljoen Streets, Lydenburg 1120 Tel. (01323) 2121

Johannesburg (480 — 500 km)/Pretoria (450 — 470 km) - Middelburg - Belfast - Lydenburg - Sabie - **Skukuza**

THE FIRST PART of this route (roughly 120 km) is identical to the first part of the route from the southern Transvaal to Komatipoort described on pages 14-5. For Skukuza, turn left (off the N4) 59 km after leaving Middelburg, following the signs to Belfast.

After 1,4 km you enter Belfast on Vermooten Street. Continue straight ahead at the intersections with Duggan Street and Fitzgerald Street, and turn right at the next stop street for Dullstroom and Lydenburg, noting your kms. On your left you pass an old steam-roller which stands in the park-like grounds of the town hall. (The municipal offices here can supply information about the town and its surroundings — see opposite.) This road you are now travelling on, which becomes the R540, is lined with attractive gardens full of roses in the summer.

After 11,7 km you cross the Lakesvlei bridge, and after 16 km you pass the Long Tom railway siding on your left. At 19,6 km you pass a road on your left leading to Palmer, where there is an important kaolin (china clay) mine. After 25,4 km you pass another railway siding, this one named Tuisbly (stay at home) by a frustrated commuter who kept missing his train through being unable to read the timetable.

After 31 km you enter Dullstroom, noted for having the highest railway station in South Africa (2 076 m above sea level). Dullstroom is also one of the coldest towns in the country. Dutch settlers led by Wolterus Dull, after whom the town was named, planted large numbers of elm and beech trees here, and trout fishing in the local streams is a major attraction.

Leave Dullstroom by continuing on the R540, and note your kms as you pass the speed de-restriction sign on the outskirts of the town. Some 200 m later you cross the Crocodile River, with the old bridge visible below you on your left. You now pass through an area thick with pine and eucalyptus plantations. After 16,7 km you reach a clearing on your left in which a marble cross inscribed 'Honour the Brave' commemorates British soldiers of the Manchester regiment who were killed in January 1901.

Continue on the R540, with wide views over cultivated valleys to your left, and fields and hills to your right. After 26,6 km you pass on your right the railway siding of Marmerkop (marble hill) where marble is quarried. After roughly 30 km you cross the Dorpsrivier (town river) several times, and after 50,4 km you reach a T-junction with the R36. Turn left here onto the R36, and 300 m later you enter Lydenburg (see pages 94-5).

Lydenburg to Skukuza

Turn right at the traffic lights into Voortrekker Street. You pass under a pedestrian bridge, and shortly after this you pass under a railway bridge — note your kms here. After 600 m you pass a road on your right leading to the aquarium and hatchery of the Department of Inland Fisheries. You are now travelling on the R37, and you climb steeply for several kms before the road levels, offering grand views on both sides over wild, rugged valleys. Eventually you round Mauchsberg and begin to descend the magnificent Long Tom Pass (see pages 94-97).

The Long Tom Pass follows the historic Hawepad (harbour road) which once linked the land-locked Transvaal to the sea at the port of Lourenco Marques (now Maputo). Sections of the old road are indicated by signs, as are a

Lydenburg's imposing Voortrekker Church.

From the Long Tom Pass — rolling hills blanketed with man-made forests stretch towards the Lowveld.

number of other historical features such as the Long Tom Shellhole, and the last-known position from which the great gun was fired. After driving about 20 km from Lydenburg you pass several viewsites on your left, offering breathtaking vistas over the valley of the Sabie River (see below). Eventually the road winds gently down into the town of Sabie, roughly 50 km from Lydenburg.

You enter Sabie on Main Street. Turn right at the T-junction in the town centre onto the R536 for Hazyview, noting your kms. 500 m later, as you leave the town, you pass on your right the R537 leading to White River. After 3,2 km you cross Spitskopspruit, winding through extensive forestry plantations. The road here is lined with jacarandas, which make a splendid display when in flower. After 31,5 km you cross the Sabaan River and from here on you pass through large plantations of citrus and bananas. After 42 km turn right at the T-junction onto the R40/R536 for Hazyview and White River, and 400 m later you enter Hazyview. After 500 m, turn left at the crossroads, where the road to the right leads to Hazyview Business Centre — and note kms.

Watch for stray livestock on this section of the road (which is still the R536). After 9,5 km you pass Hazyview Station on your right, and after a further 500 m you cross the Sand River. After 17 km, continue straight at the crossroads where the road left leads to Bosbokrand and the road right leads to Mkhuhlu. After 28 km you cross the Saringwa River and pass over a number of small bridges. Continue straight, passing after 36 km a road leading left to Mala Mala, and after 38,2 km a road leading right to Sabie Park. 1 km after passing this road to Sabie Park you reach the Paul Kruger Gate into the Kruger National Park. A further 12 km through the park brings you to Skukuza ●

SKUKUZA — THE POACHER'S ENEMY

Colonel James Stevenson-Hamilton, the first warden of the Kruger National Park, was known to his assistants as siKhukhuza (he who sweeps clean) because of his ruthless vendetta against poachers. He devoted most of his working life to establishing and protecting the park, and keeping its borders intact.

To commemorate this extraordinarily energetic man, the first rest camp and administrative centre of the park was named after him. Skukuza remains the largest of the camps in the park and has among its facilities a well-stocked shop, an open-air cinema, a library and a museum — and a restaurant and reception complex said to have the largest thatched-roof area in the world. Indigenous plants are cultivated and sold here, including cycads and baobabs.

An ancient baobab tree in the Kruger National Park.

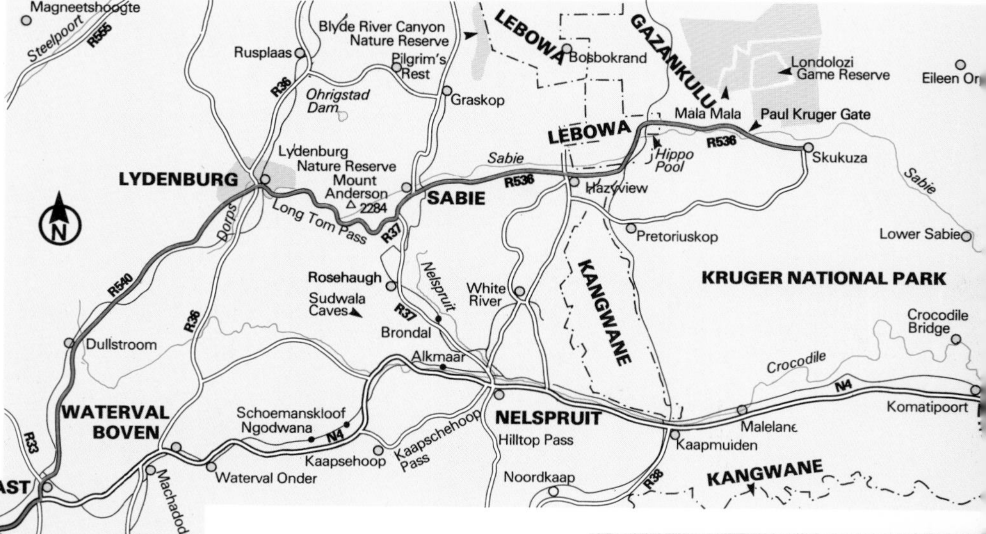

BELFAST

The town of Belfast originated in 1890 on land belonging to a farmer, John O'Neill. O'Neill named the town after his grandfather's birthplace in Ireland, and today it is the busy centre of a region renowned for its sheep and dairy farms. Clay and kaolin are mined in the district, and large quantities of chrome have been found. Tulips grow well in this area, and in late September/early October their brightly-coloured blooms are at their most attractive. The clear, cold streams in the district offer good trout fishing. The town is located in the eastern Highveld 2 025 metres above sea level.

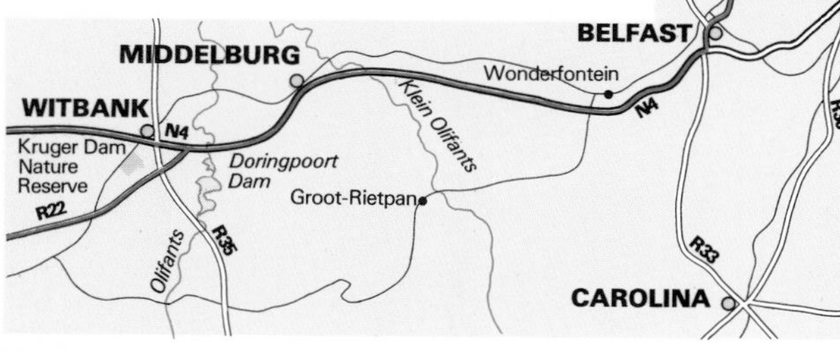

The deep ravine of the Sabie Falls on the outskirts of Sabie.

CHANGING MOODS OF THE SABIE RIVER

The Sabie River rises on the historic slopes of the Mauchsberg (see pages 94-7) and Mount Anderson. Numerous tributaries rush down the many ravines of the Long Tom Pass, forming cool cascades and tumbling waterfalls. The river flows east, changing from a rushing mountain stream into a lazy, moody river, meandering through the sun-drenched Lowveld. For 45 kms it forms the western border of the Kruger National Park, then it runs through the heart of the park for some 60 km. Situated on its banks is the main rest camp and administrative centre of Skukuza (see above). Finally the Sabie joins the Komati River in Mocambique.

The name of the river is said to come from the Shangane word uluSaba, meaning a fearful river — presumably because of the crocodiles and floods in its lower reaches.

The best known town on the river is Sabie, founded by hunter H T Glynn in 1895 after gold was discovered in the area.

One of the 140 000 impala in the Kruger National Park

To the Lowveld and Letaba through the deep green forests of Magoebaskloof

The first leg of this route from the southern Transvaal to Letaba is described on pages 12-13. This second section begins at Pietersburg, passes through Lebowa, then winds down through the beautiful Magoebaskloof into the Lowveld. From Tzaneen we pass the ghost town of Leydsdorp to Phalaborwa and the Kruger National Park.

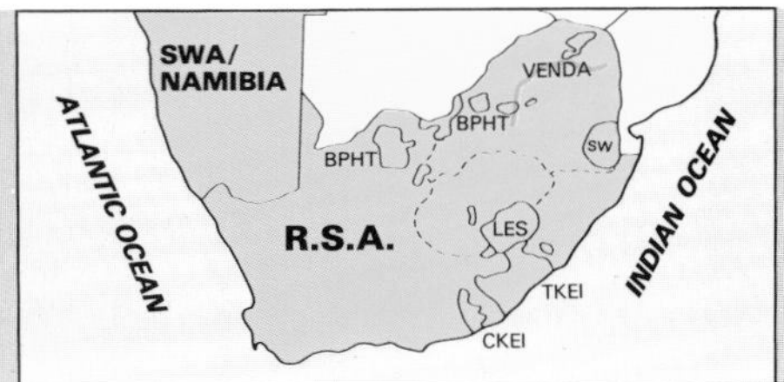

AA Office AA House, 66 De Korte Street, Braamfontein, Johannesburg 2001 Tel. (011) 4035700
AA Office AA House, 395 Schoeman Street, Pretoria 0002 Tel. (012) 283829
AA Office Telmot Building, 53 Schoeman Street, Pietersburg 0700 Tel. (01521) 71442
Kruger National Park Chief Director, Reservations, National Parks Board, Box 787, Pretoria 0001

Johannesburg (580 — 600 km)/Pretoria (530 — 550 km) - Nylstroom - Pietersburg - Tzaneen - Phalaborwa - **Letaba**

THE FIRST PART of this route (as far as Pietersburg) is identical to the first part of the route from the southern Transvaal to Messina, which is described on pages 12-13. For this route to Letaba via Tzaneen and Phalaborwa, turn right in Pietersburg from Landdros Maré Street into Grobler Street, noting your kms as you turn.

As you leave Pietersburg on this road (R71) you pass on your left the R526 to Duiwelskloof, and after roughly 22 km you pass a small urban area in Lebowa. After 24,5 km you pass a road on your left to Houtbosdorp, and at 28 km you pass another road on your left leading to Turfloop and the University of the North.

After 39 km you pass a gravel road on your right that leads into the Wolkberg Wilderness Area, and from this point the road begins to undulate through bushy country, passing rural settlements and sawmills. After 48 km the road begins to climb through a series of sharp curves — lasting for roughly 4 km. At roughly 50 km from the turn in Pietersburg you reach an attractive viewsite and picnic site on your left.

Industrial art on display in the busy town of Pietersburg.

PIETERSBURG

The bustling northern Transvaal town of Pietersburg owes its existence to a battle between the Voortrekkers and the Venda in 1867. The Venda forced the Europeans to abandon their northern capital of Schoemansdal and seek a new seat of local government elsewhere. After an initial move to Marabastad, the defeated Voortrekkers favoured a site on the banks of the Sterkloop (strong flow) River. Here in 1884 they established the town of Pietersburg — named after Commandant-General Piet Joubert, hero of the Battle of Majuba.

Compensation Street takes its name from the fact that plots were granted to former residents of Schoemansdal as compensation for their earlier loss.

During the Anglo-Boer War, Pietersburg was the temporary capital of the Transvaal Republic. Today it is the commercial, farming and educational centre of the northern Transvaal.

'FRENCH BOB'S' CAMP

When gold was discovered in the Murchison Range in the 1880s, one of the first diggers to reach the new field was the French prospector Auguste Robert. Robert was known to the diggers in Barberton as 'French Bob', and the new field in the Murchison Range was known for the first few years of its existence as 'French Bob's Camp'. The settlement was proclaimed a town in 1890, and was then named after the Transvaal State Secretary, W J Leyds.

After 15 years the gold ran out and the diggers drifted away, many to the Witwatersrand, leaving Leydsdorp to become a ghost town. A few forlorn buildings still stand, and on the road to the town there is still the great baobab tree where thirsty diggers refreshed themselves at a bar that operated from its hollow trunk — about ten men can fit inside.

A tea plantation makes a sea of green on the hillsides near Tzaneen.

The road now begins its long descent from the Highveld, and you pass the small settlement of Haenertsburg on your right. Immediately after this you pass on your right the R528 into George's Valley, then cross the upper reaches of the Great Letaba River. At 62 km you pass a road on your right that leads to the Ebenezer Dam (see pages 82-3) and a little over 2 km later you pass the Magoebaskloof Hotel.

After passing the hotel you begin the winding, scenically breathtaking descent through the kloof (valley). The road is lined by thick pine and eucalyptus forests which sweep away over the hills as far as the eye can see. At 68 km there is a good viewsite on your right, and 1 km later you come to a shaded picnic site on your right. (This area is described in detail on pages 80-83.)

As you reach the floor of the valley you pass a gravel road on your left that leads to the spectacular Debengeni Falls. This is a worthwhile side-trip if you can afford the time — simply follow this gravel road for 3 km, then turn right and drive down the hillside to the falls. Note that the great smooth rock surfaces at the falls are dangerous to walk on. (There are picnic and braai sites here, and toilets nearby.)

Continuing on the R71 beyond the Debengeni Falls turn-off you pass the attractive Magoebaskloof Dam, then the road leads through bright green tea plantations — to arrive eventually at a T-junction with the R36. Turn right here onto the R36, and note your kms. After 3 km you cross the Great Letaba River again, with good views of the river to your left. At 4,2 km take the exit-ramp left for Tzaneen, and at the top of the ramp turn left to the town.

Tzaneen to Letaba

Drive through the town, following the signs for Kruger National Park and Phalaborwa, and note your kms as you cross the Great Letaba River once again on the outskirts of the town. You are now travelling on the R71 again.

The road leads through bush-covered hills, and passes extensive plantations of bananas and mangoes. After 26 km you cross the Great Letaba again, and the low hills of the Murchison Range come into view shortly before you enter Gravelotte — a little over 50 km from Tzaneen (see below). 100 m after entering the town, turn right to visit the giant baobab and the ghost town of Leydsdorp. Note your kms as you turn.

This gravel road leads among the hills of the Murchison Range, and after 3,4 km you reach the turn-off to the baobab tree on your right. The tree is 370 m along this side-road (and there are picnic sites nearby). After visiting the giant tree, drive back to the main gravel road and turn right to continue along it — noting your kms. After 6,5 km turn left for Leydsdorp, whose abandoned buildings you reach after roughly 500 m (see opposite).

Retrace your route to Gravelotte, and turn right onto the R71. 300 m later turn left, and note your kms. After 9 km you pass the Consolidated Murchison Mine on your left, and 11 km later you pass a group of Zimbabwe-style buildings on your right. Roughly 44 km after leaving Gravelotte the hills known as the Tweeling (twins) come into view, and at 50 km the road passes between them.

At 54 km you reach a four-way stop-street, with the road on your right leading into the centre of Phalaborwa (see below). Continue straight ahead here on Kruger Park Road, and after a further 3,5 km you reach the Phalaborwa Gate into the Kruger National Park.

The gate into the park closes at 17h30 (April to August), 18h00 (March, September, October) and 18h30 (November, December, January, February) — but note that you should pass through the gate in good time to reach Letaba before the camp closes. The distance from Phalaborwa Gate to Letaba is 51 km, and camp closing times (which also change through the year) are given on pages 106-7. Bear in mind that you should have an overnight booking at the camp before proceeding into the park. For more information, see pages 106-117 ●

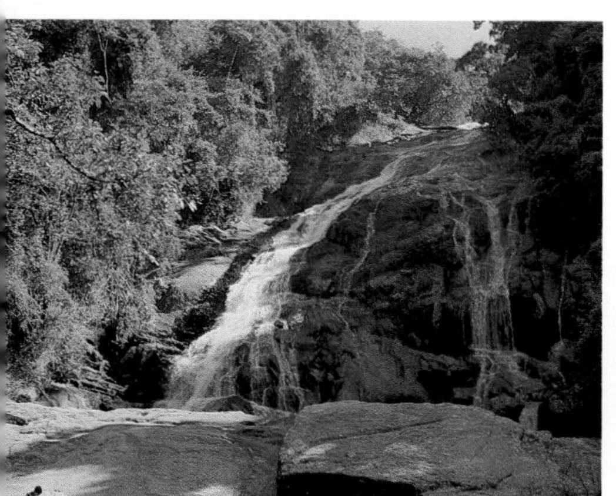

Foaming waters of the Debengeni Falls.

Phalaborwa's koppie is a national monument.

EMERALDS AND ANTIMONY

The gold that first attracted prospectors to the valleys of the Murchison Range has long since ceased to be a paying proposition, but a variety of other underground treasures have taken its place — including emeralds and antimony. The centre of this mining activity is Gravelotte, believed to have been named by Fritz Reuter, a Prussian dragoon who had taken part in the Battle of Gravelotte during the Franco-Prussian War.

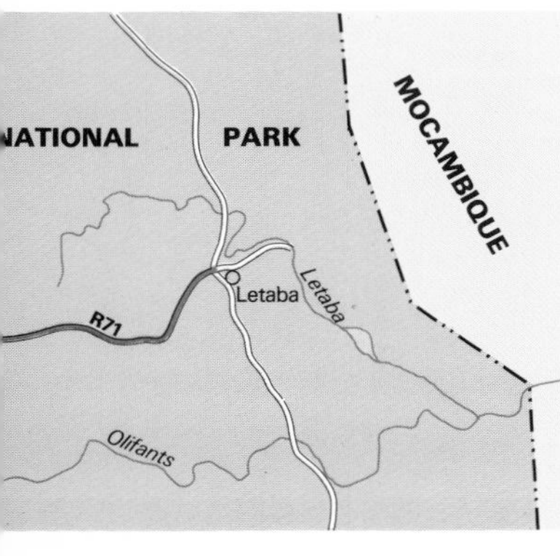

A TOWN WITH TWO SUMMERS

Traces of mining activity at Phalaborwa date back many centuries to the iron-age miners who won copper and iron from the twin hills of Sealene and Kgopolwe (now national monuments). Phalaborwa was founded in 1955, after rich phosphate-bearing ore was discovered on the hill known as Loole Kop. Like Colesberg Koppie at Kimberley, Loole Kop has vanished before the onslaught of men and machines, and is now an open-cast mine. The phosphates are used extensively in the manufacture of agricultural fertiliser, while the same mine also provides all of South Africa's copper requirements. Tours of the mine may be arranged by telephoning (01524) 2211 (tours commence at 12h30 on Fridays). Phalaborwa, noted for its many attractive gardens and lawns, is sometimes known as 'the town with two summers' — the average winter temperature is a warm 26°C, not far below its summer average of 31°C.

Right: *Giraffe in Kruger Park.*

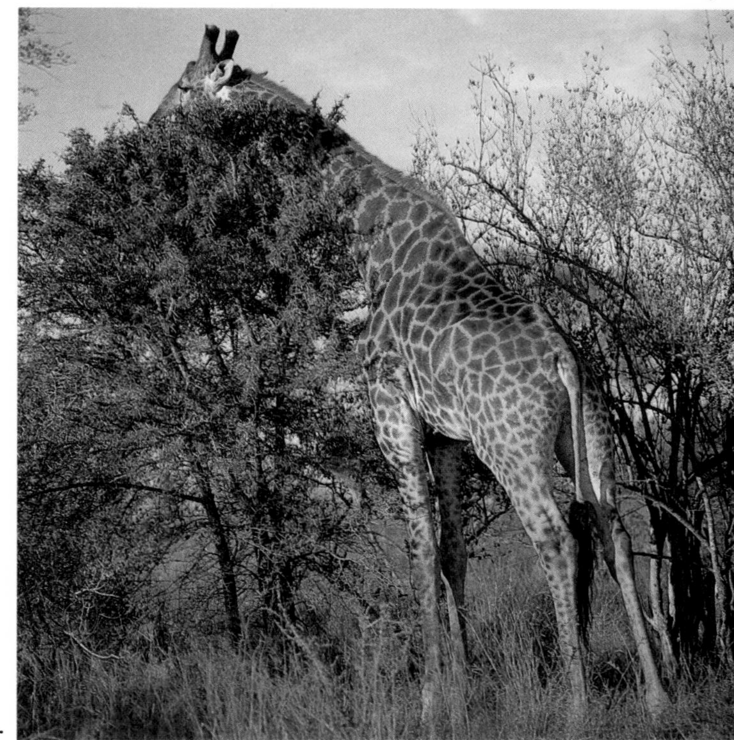

South from Punda Maria along the crest of the Drakensberg escarpment

This route leads from the Kruger National Park's Punda Maria gate to Pretoria and Johannesburg — taking not the shortest route, but a leisurely scenic meander along the Transvaal's Drakensberg escarpment. We recommend that you give the trip three days, or allocate more time and enjoy several of the day drives that branch off from this route.

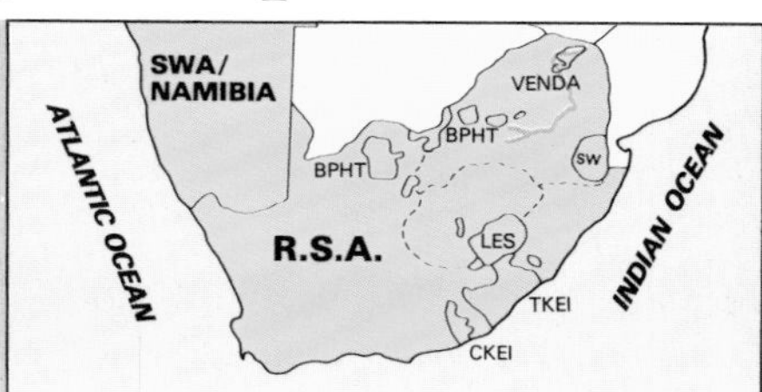

Tzaneen Municipal Tourist Office Agatha Street, Tzaneen 0850 Tel. (015236) 20132
Graskop Information Office Louis Trichardt Street, Graskop 1270 Tel. (0131522) 6
AA Office AA House, 395 Schoeman Street, Pretoria 0002 Tel. (012) 283829
AA Office AA House, 66 De Korte Street, Braamfontein, Johannesburg 2001 Tel. (011) 4035700

Punda Maria - Tzaneen - Blyde River Canyon - Pilgrim's Rest - Lydenburg - **Pretoria (800 — 820 km) Johannesburg (810 — 830 km)**

NOTE YOUR KMS AS you leave the Kruger National Park through the Punda Maria gate. From here the road (R524) crosses flat, bushy country, dotted with rural settlements. After roughly 40 km you cross the Levubu River and enter Venda, and 27 km later you pass a road on your right leading to Sibasa and the Venda capital of Thohoyandou (see pages 74-9). After a further 1 km you pass the Venda Arts and Crafts Centre on your right — note your kms again here. You pass three roads leading left to the tropical-fruit farming centre of Levubu, and after roughly 65 km you reach an intersection with the N1 on the outskirts of Louis Trichardt (see pages 74-9). Turn left onto the N1, noting your kms.

After roughly 1 km, drive straight through the intersection and continue on the N1. You now enter a stretch of flat bushveld studded with raised granite outcrops, and here and there you pass small patches of cultivated fields. After some 38 km on the N1, turn left onto the R36 for Soekmekaar and Tzaneen. (To continue on the N1 will bring you to Pretoria or Johannesburg much more quickly, but this direct route on the N1 is far less scenic — see pages 12-13 for map.)

After some 22 km on the R36 turn left for Soekmekaar, where the road ahead leads to Munnik — noting your kms at this turn. Drive straight through the little town of Soekmekaar (search for one another) and continue on the R36 towards Duiwelskloof.

You now enter countryside covered with eucalyptus plantations. A little over 18 km after noting your kms you cross the Middle Letaba River, and the northernmost heights of the Drakensberg can be seen ahead of you. Some 7 km later, go left at the Y-junction to stay on the R36 (where the R526 leads right towards Pietersburg).

Some 2 km after the Y-junction you cross the Koedoes River, and immediately after this you cross a bridge over the railway line. On both sides of the road here are extensive orchards of mangoes. 12 km after the Y-junction you pass a road leading left to Ga-Kgapane and Modjadji, and 5,5 km later you enter the town of Duiwelskloof (see pages 80-1).

Follow the main road as it winds through the town and then continues south through the forested kloof from which the town took its name. Some 12 km after leaving the outskirts of Duiwelskloof you cross the Politsi River, and 4 km later you cross the Great Letaba River. After a further 1 km you reach a road leading left into Tzaneen — turn left here if you wish to stop in Tzaneen (see day drives, pages 80-3), or continue straight ahead on the R36 if you wish to by-pass the town.

Driving south from Tzaneen on the R36 you pass through fields and plantations of subtropical fruit, and away to your right are the towering slopes of the Drakensberg. After travelling roughly 14 km from Tzaneen, keep straight at the crossroads (where the road left leads to Letaba Station and the road right leads to the Letsiteli Valley). 28 km later, at another crossroads, keep straight again (where left leads to Leydsdorp and right leads to Ofcolaco).

The road now runs parallel to the Drakensberg escarpment on your right, and after some 20 km you can see ahead of you the high cliffs of the Abel Erasmus Pass and the impressive buttresses that tower over the Blyde River Canyon. After a further 26 km you cross the Olifants River, and 1 km later you reach a T-junction with the R531. Turn right here for Ohrigstad, noting your kms as you turn.

Abel Erasmus Pass to Pilgrim's Rest

You are still travelling on the R36, and after 7,5 km you begin to climb the Abel Erasmus Pass (see page 87). A little over 1 km later you reach a parking area on the right that offers a fine view over the Olifants River, and 1,5 km after this there is another parking area at the entrance to the J G Strijdom Tunnel. At the far end of the tunnel is a parking area offering quite different views. There is a striking waterfall to be seen here, cascading over a tufa-formation that it has created (see page 89 column 2). Note your kms as you leave this parking area.

You now pass several picnic sites as the road continues to climb over the pass. 22 km after noting your kms, turn left onto the R532. (If you continue straight here, you will reach a gravel turn-off to the Echo Caves after 1,1 km.) The R532 crosses the Ohrigstad River and winds through rolling countryside towards the scenic crest of the Drakensberg. You pass the F H Odendaal Public Resort on your left, and after 22 km on the R532 you cross the Kadishi (Kadisi) River. 1,8 km later, turn left onto a 3 km side-road to the Three Rondavels viewsite.

Return to the R532 (which appears suddenly at the top of a rise) and turn left onto it, noting your kms. After 4,7 km turn left and follow another side-road for 400 m to reach the Lowveld viewsite. Return to the R532 and turn left onto it, noting your kms again. 9 km now brings you to Bourke's Luck (see pages 86-7).

Continue on the R532, noting your kms as you leave Bourke's Luck. After 500 m you cross the Blyde River, and at 2,3 km and 5 km you cross and re-cross the Treur River. At just over 9 km you pass a cairn on your left commemorating the Voortrekkers (see pages 88-9). Roughly 22 km after leaving Bourke's Luck you cross the Watervalspruit. 4,8 km later, turn right onto a gravel road to visit the Berlin Falls.

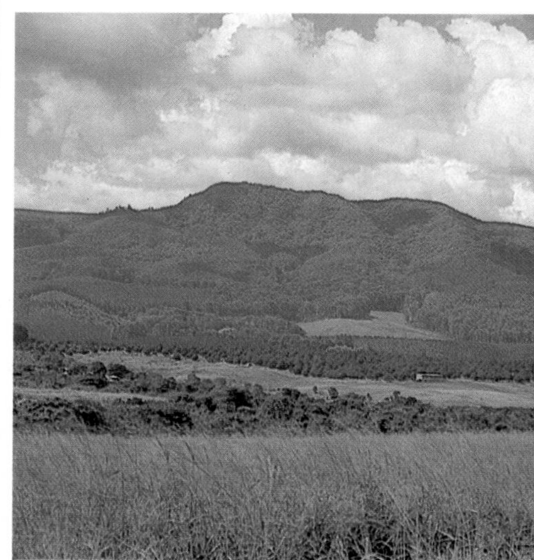

THE MYSTERY OF SWANN'S RACE
Miners of alluvial gold need water to wash their gravel, and a channel or 'race' would be dug to carry water to the claim-site from the nearest stream. In the late 1870s John Swann, who claimed to have found an exceptionally rich strike, brought enough gold into town to finance four years of digging and blasting his race across the hillsides. Unfortunately Swann died before his race was completed, and nobody knew the point it was intended to reach — to this day the site of Swann's miraculous find remains a mystery.

After 1,1 km on the gravel you pass a road leading left, and 800 m later turn left. A further 300 m brings you to a parking area, from where a path (slippery when wet) leads to a viewsite near the edge of the gorge.

Return to the R532 and turn right, noting your kms. After 1,2 km turn left onto the R534. (Continue on the R532 first if you wish to view the Lisbon Falls — see pages 90-1.) You pass several signposted viewsites on your left, overlooking the Lowveld. After 7 km on the R534 you reach Wonderview, followed by God's Window and The Pinnacle (see pages 90-1).

After 16 km on the R534 you rejoin the R532 at a T-junction. Turn left here onto the R532, to enter Graskop on Hugenotestraat. Turn right into Louis Trichardt Street, and 500 m later turn left into Hoofstraat (Main Street). Turn right at the four-way stop street to leave Graskop on Pilgrim's Road (R532/R533). Roughly 1 km after leaving Graskop there is a parking area on your left near to a small natural bridge, and some 3 km later you reach a Y-junction at the base of a rocky outcrop known as The Bonnet. Go right here, on the R533 to Pilgrim's Rest. (The road left, the R532, leads to the Mac-Mac Falls and Sabie — see pages 86-7, 90-1.)

Pilgrim's Rest to the Witwatersrand

You now climb over the Bonnet Pass, and after descending on the western side you drive through the old gold-mining town of Pilgrim's Rest (see below, and pages 92-3). Note your kms as you cross the Blyde River on the historic Joubert Bridge at the lower end of the town, and 1 km later turn left to stay on the R533 for Lydenburg — noting your kms again.

You now climb over Robber's Pass (see below) and there are several places where you can pull off the road for good views. After roughly 25 km you reach a T-junction with the R36 — turn left here for Lydenburg, which you enter 27 km later on De Clerq Street (see pages 94-7). Turn left into Voortrekker Street, and later turn right into Viljoen Street, which leads out of town. Roughly 2 km after leaving the town, turn right onto the R540 for Dullstroom — noting your kms. The R540 leads through high-lying grasslands whose cold streams are renowned for their trout-fishing. After roughly 55 km you cross the Crocodile River and pass the town of Dullstroom. Some 13 km later you pass large kaolin works at Palmer Siding, and a further 20 km brings you into the town of Belfast.

Turn left in Belfast into Vermooten Street, and 3 km later turn right onto the N4 for Middelburg — which you enter on Jan van Riebeeck Street after a further 59 km (see pages 120-1). Turn left into Kerk (Church) Street, and follow the signs onto the N4 for Pretoria and Johannesburg. A little over 10 km after leaving Middelburg the N4 becomes a double carriageway. If you are heading for Pretoria, stay on the N4; if you are heading for Johannesburg, take the well-signposted exit onto the R22 shortly before Witbank ●

The Entabeni State Forest.

Blyderivierspoort Dam — heart of the Blyde River Canyon.

ROBBER'S PASS

The coaches of the old Zeederberg company, which transported gold from the mining towns, were robbed only twice, the first in 1899, when two bars of gold were stolen. The second robbery was less successful, but stranger and more memorable. Tom Dennison, the village barber from Pilgrim's Rest, held up the coach on its way *to* the mines — when he must have known it carried no gold. All he came away with was £129 in half-crown coins. After robbing the coach Dennison returned to Pilgrim's Rest and began paying off his debts, but he was well-known in the village and was promptly arrested. After serving five years in jail he returned to Pilgrim's Rest and opened the 'Highwayman's Garage'.

Above: *The restored village of Pilgrim's Rest.*
Left: *The approach to the Abel Erasmus Pass.*

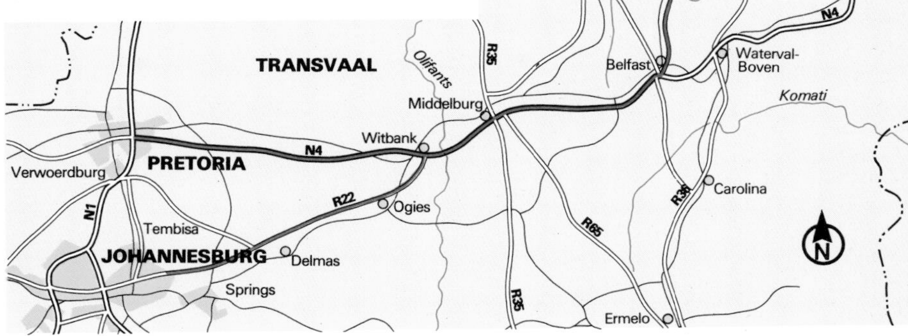

From the grassy Highveld to 'Bitter River' and the 'Place of Heaven'

This route leads from the densely populated centres of the southern Transvaal through the coal country of the eastern Highveld and into the fascinating Kingdom of Swaziland. Note that the Oshoek/Ngwenya border post closes at 22h00, and that passports are required for entry into Swaziland. (Overseas visitors may need visas.)

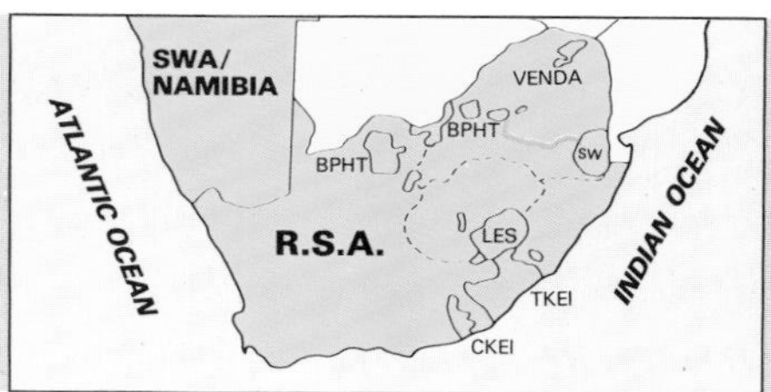

AA Office AA House, 66 De Korte Street, Braamfontein, Johannesburg 2001 Tel. (011) 4035700
AA Office AA House, 395 Schoeman Street, Pretoria 0002 Tel. (012) 283829
AA Office 9 Trust Bank Arcade, Joubert Street, Ermelo 2350 Tel. (01341) 3255
Ermelo Information Office Civic Centre, Taute Street (off Kerk Street), Ermelo 2350 Tel. (01341) 2112
Swaziland Tourist Office Swazi Plaza, Allister Miller Street, Mbabane Tel. (0194) 42531

Johannesburg (370 km)/Pretoria (420 km) - Springs - Bethal - Ermelo - Oshoek - **Mbabane**

IF YOU ARE STARTING your journey from Johannesburg, drive east on the R22 (North Rand Road) towards Witbank, and note your kms as you cross over the R21. If you are starting from Pretoria, drive south-east on the R21 (Maria Van Riebeeck Avenue) and after passing Jan Smuts Airport on your left, exit onto the R22 for Witbank — noting your kms.

After travelling 18 km on the R22 from the R21/R22 intersection, take the exit for 'R51/Springs/Pretoria'. Note your kms when you come to the stop sign, and turn right, crossing over the R22 and travelling south towards Springs. You are now on the R51 (Kingsway Road, changing to Paul Kruger Highway). All around you now are mine dumps, recalling the days when Springs was the world's largest single gold producer (see below).

Secunda — electricity generating powerhouse of southern Africa.

POWER FROM 'BLACK GOLD'

It is no wonder that the Sasol 1 and Sasol 2 oil-from-coal plants and three of the largest thermal power stations in the southern hemisphere (Matla, Kriel and Duvha) are sited around Secunda. All are insatiable coal-devouring monsters, and must be fed with the 'black gold' 24 hours a day. The R6 billion Sasol projects are expected to supply fully half of South Africa's fuel needs and consume a third of the country's coal output. To feed them are the eastern Highveld coalfields, 20 of which are situated in the Bethal district.

White-faced whistling ducks at Mlilwane Wildlife Sanctuary.

Lush greenery surrounds Swaziland's Mantenga Falls.

THE ORIGINAL 'RAND TRAM'

The first railway in the Transvaal, the 'Rand Tram', was built in 1890 to carry coal to Johannesburg from the mines around Springs. But Springs, once inhabited by Welsh Miners, has an unhappy coal-mining history. The coal was of a type that ignited spontaneously when exposed to air, and a fire in one colliery in 1899 resulted in the mine having to be sealed off forever. In 1907 a major subsidence at the Great Eastern colliery formed a hole that swallowed the houses of two mine officials — killing one of the mine captain's children. Mining in the area switched gradually from coal to gold, and Springs for a while became the world's leading gold producer.

SANCTUARY FOR WILDLIFE

South of Mbabane, in the Ezulwini Valley, lies the 5 000 hectare Mlilwane Wildlife Sanctuary — 'mlilwane' means 'embers', and refers to the glow of the scattered cooking fires that could be seen covering the floor of the valley at night. The sanctuary contains about 100 km of gravel roads, from which visitors may view white rhino, hippo, crocodile, giraffe, wildebeest and various smaller buck species. Roughly 240 different species of birds can be seen, including the magnificent Black Eagle. There are also guided pony treks and walks through the sanctuary.

A small museum illustrates Swaziland's wildlife heritage.

9,2 km after noting your kms, turn left at the traffic lights into 4th Avenue (at the sign for 'R29/Secunda/Springs Centre'). Continue along 4th Avenue as it curves to the right, and shortly after passing the Central Fire Station on your left, at 11,5 km, turn left into 1st Avenue (also known as Ermelo Road) for 'R29/Secunda'. You are now travelling south-east on the R29. You pass some quaint old buildings and mine headgear, then the scene changes to typical Highveld maize-farming country.

Springs to Ermelo

The R29 passes the small towns of Devon (where there is a large military base on your left) and Leandra, and then reaches Kinross, which is the centre of one of South Africa's most advanced maize, potato and cattle farming regions, as well as being a major producer of gold and coal.

Kinross lies on the crest of South Africa's watershed — rain falling to the east of the town will eventually make its way to the Indian Ocean, while rain falling to the west of the town runs off into the South Atlantic.

16 km after Kinross, still on the R29, you pass through Trichardt — with the Sasol 1 and Sasol 2 oil-from-coal projects nearby at Secunda. Also nearby are Matla, Kriel and Duvha, three of the largest coal-fired power stations in the southern hemisphere (see opposite).

Stay on the R29 through Bethal, to enter Ermelo on Joubert Street. Ermelo was razed to the ground by the British during the Anglo-Boer War, but rebuilding began at the end of the war in 1902, and the town is now the busy hub of the eastern Highveld. Turn left into Kerkstraat (church street), then take the fourth turn right into Fourie Street, which changes its name to Everard Street and becomes the R39 for Chrissiesmeer. (The longest stone-arched bridge in the Transvaal, the Begin der Lijn bridge, straddles the Vaal roughly 30 km south of Ermelo. It dates from 1898, when it marked the old border with Swaziland, and is 124 m long. To visit it, turn right out of Joubert Street into Kerkstraat, and drive south on Kerkstraat, which becomes the R36 for Volksrust.)

Ermelo to Mbabane

About 5,5 km beyond Ermelo turn right to remain on the R39 for Chrissiesmeer (Lake Chrissie). The lake from which the village takes its name lies a short distance to the south. After good rains, this is the largest natural body of inland water in South Africa (9 km by 3 km). In times of drought, the lake is reduced to a few muddy pools, inhabited by hundreds of flamingoes. To view the lake, turn right in the village at the 'Koolbank' sign onto a gravel road — this leads around the lake's north-eastern shore.

Return to the R39, heading north-east for Warburton. The grassy Highveld now becomes more hilly, and trees begin to dot the landscape. You pass the small towns of Warburton and Lochiel, and arrive eventually at the Oshoek/Ngwenya border post between South Africa and Swaziland. The border post is open from 07h00 to 22h00 each day, and passports must be shown. Visitors from overseas may also need visas. (Motorists in Swaziland should keep a lookout for semi-permanent speed traps and roadblocks. Always ask permission before taking photographs of the Swazis.)

Note your kms as you leave the border post. You now pass many stalls selling woodcarvings, basketwork, bright clothing and curios. After roughly 19 hilly and scenic kilometres, the road forks. Take the left road, which passes the Swaziland College of Technology, then leads into Mbabane on Gilfillan Street (see opposite, and pages 102-5).

Mbabane has a picturesque setting in the green Dlageni Hills, and some of the finest curios and craftwork in Africa can be found in its Swazi Market. To reach the market, continue to the end of Gilfillan Street, turn right into Allister Miller Street, then park as close to the end of Allister Miller Street as possible — lock your car here, and walk down into the market.

From Allister Miller Street, the main road continues south into the beautiful Ezulwini (place of heaven) Valley, passing hotels, casinos and nightspots on the road to Manzini. Along the way are the scenic Mantenga Falls, the Mlilwane Wildlife Sanctuary, and Lobamba — site of the Royal Residence and the Parliament building ●

MBABANE

The capital of Swaziland, Mbabane, owes its name to the nearby Mbabane (bitter) River. During the 1888 gold rush, a former British Army gunner, Michael Wells, set up a trading store here, and at the end of the Anglo-Boer War the growing settlement was proclaimed by the British as their administrative capital for the region.

Recent archeological research has shown that Mbabane lies in one of the oldest continuously settled areas in southern Africa — having been inhabited since the Stone Age. Swazi tradition tells of at least 24 kings who have ruled the country through the ages, and the bodies of some of these kings lie in caves in the Mdimba Mountains, which form the eastern wall of the Ezulwini Valley. (See also pages 102-5.)

One of the most important tourist attractions in the town is the lively Swazi Market selling handcrafts at its southern end.

Riverside scene between Mbabane and Manzini.

A thick-tailed bushbaby at the Mlilwane Wildlife Sanctuary.

Holiday highway from the Highveld to the coastal playgrounds of Natal

The N3 between the Highveld and the sea is one of the busiest roads in the country, linking the southern Transvaal to the subtropical Natal coast. This 'holiday highway' leads hundreds of thousands of visitors a year past the soaring Drakensberg, and through a land where Briton and Boer once fought and died under a relentless sun.

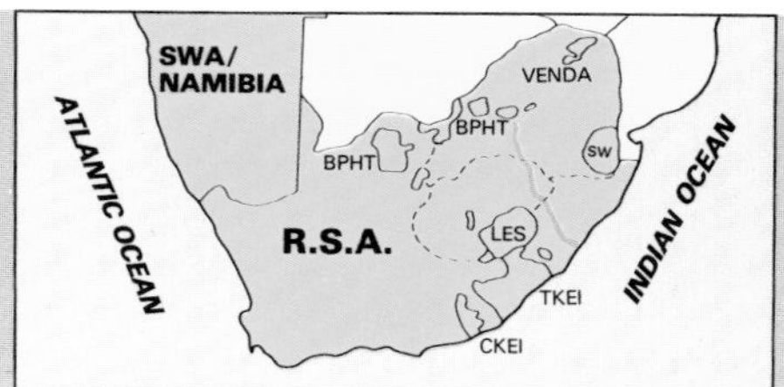

AA Office AA House, 395 Schoeman Street, Pretoria 0002 Tel. (012) 283829
AA Office AA House, 66 De Korte Street, Braamfontein, Johannesburg 2001 Tel. (011) 4035700
AA Office NBS Building, 174 Murchison Street, Ladysmith 3370 Tel. (0361) 26875
AA Office NAU Building, cor Buchanan and Carbineer Streets, Pietermaritzburg 3201 Tel. (0331) 20571
AA Office AA House, 537 Smith Street, Durban 4001 Tel (031) 3010341

Pretoria (650—670 km) - Johannesburg (600—620 km) - Heidelberg - Harrismith - Ladysmith - Pietermaritzburg - **Durban**

IF YOU ARE STARTING YOUR journey from Pretoria, drive south on the Ben Schoeman Highway (R28) and continue straight onto the N1 at the Brakfontein interchange. At the Buccleuch interchange, exit left onto the N3 (the Eastern Bypass around Johannesburg) following signs for 'Germiston N3' and later 'Heidelberg N3'. If you are starting from Johannesburg, drive east on the M2, then turn south onto the N3 for Heidelberg.

42 km after the M2 joins the N3 you have a choice: you can stay on the N3 and by-pass Heidelberg, or you can turn onto the R42 for a short stop in the town — which contains many old buildings and a fascinating Transport Museum (see opposite).

Heidelberg to Harrismith

Continuing south from Heidelberg on the N3, you pass on your left, after roughly 7,5 km, a turn-off onto the R23 for Standerton. (This offers an alternative route that rejoins the N3 at Ladysmith, and which is recommended if you are towing.)

From here the N3 now crosses wide, flat plains, and passes enormous fields of maize — as well as the gentle hills of the Suikerbosrand (sugar-bush ridge). About 35 km south-east of Heidelberg you pass the large Grootvlei power station on your left, and 32,5 km later you cross the Vaal River and enter the Orange Free State. Shortly after crossing the river you pass Villiers on your right — a small town in the heart of the maize country, dominated by its enormous grain silos.

Some 62 km after Villiers you pass on your left the R34 to Vrede, named in 1863 after the peace (vrede) that followed serious arguments over the best possible site for the town. A further 47 km then brings you to the town of Warden — named after Charles Warden, a late 19th century landdrost (magistrate) of Harrismith, and son of the founder of the Free State capital of Bloemfontein.

As you continue southwards from Warden towards Harrismith, you can see ahead of you the outline of Platberg (flat mountain), which towers above Harrismith. On its summit there is a blockhouse built during the Anglo-Boer War, and laid out in stones on its slopes (visible on your left as you pass Harrismith) are the badges of two British regiments — the sphinx of the Gloucestershires and the knot of the Staffordshires. The town of Harrismith was named in honour of the jovial and energetic Cape Governor, Sir Harry Smith, who managed to retain the respect of many Voortrekkers despite political differences.

Sir Henry (Harry) Smith and his lady... an enduring love affair.

The Platberg (flat mountain) above the town of Harrismith. A British blockhouse is situated on the summit.

HEROIC SIR HARRY

Sir Henry George Wakelyn Smith was the very stuff of the British Empire, whether battling against the Spanish in South America, the French in Spain, the Sikhs in India or the Boers in South Africa. Wherever trouble flared Sir Harry was there: cool, courageous, magnanimous, and usually victorious.

It was at one such desperate fight, the defeat of the French at the Spanish city of Badajoz in 1812, that 24-year-old Harry rescued the 14-year-old daughter of a nobleman, Juana Maria de los Doloros de Leon. A few days later he married her — the start of a long and blissfully happy union. The spirited young girl followed Harry throughout the tough war against Napoleon, culminating in the Battle of Waterloo. She then accompanied him to India and South Africa — where he scored victories against the Sikhs, the Xhosa, and the Boers at the Battle of Boomplaats.

It was following this battle in 1848 that the town of Harrismith was founded as the centre of the newly created district of Vaal River. Sir Harry favoured the name Vrededorp (peace town) but Harrismith, named after Sir Harry himself, was the popular choice.

Harrismith to Durban

South of Harrismith the N3 draws close to the Drakensberg, and offers spectacular mountain views on both sides. About 30 km from Harrismith you pass through the little village of Van Reenen, then begin the descent of Van Reenen's Pass into Natal (see opposite). The summit of the pass is marked by a sign showing the altitude as 1 680 m above sea level. About 600 m beyond the summit there is a 1 km road on your right leading to the Windy Corner viewsite, from where there are grand views over mountains and valleys.

Roughly 27 km from the foot of the pass, the road crosses the Klip (stone) River on the outskirts of Ladysmith — named after the Spanish wife of Harry Smith (see above), and the scene of a prolonged siege during the Anglo-Boer War (see pages 168-9). The bungled campaign to relieve the town earned the British commander Sir Redvers Buller the nickname 'Sir Reverse Buller'.

25 km after passing Ladysmith you cross the Tugela River, then pass the town of Colenso on your left. You now drive through an area where much bitter fighting took place during the attempts to relieve Ladysmith. 4,5 km after crossing the Tugela you pass on your right the Clouston Garden of Remembrance, containing the bodies of British soldiers killed in a disastrous attempt to cross the river. Among the dead was Lieutenant Frederick Roberts, son of Field Marshal Lord Roberts, who was about to be appointed to the command of all British forces in South Africa. Both father and son were holders of the Victoria Cross. Lieutenant Roberts was buried not at Clouston but in the military cemetery at Chieveley Station — which can be reached by following a 1,2 km gravel road on your left, 5 km after passing Clouston Koppie.

A TOWN OF WHEELS

The Transvaal town of Heidelberg is the home of one of the country's foremost transport museums situated in the town's picturesque, step-gabled stone railway station. The collection of vehicles ranges from a Louis XV sedan chair to a class 16C steam locomotive gleaming in honourable retirement after 55 years of work on the rails of South Africa.

The evolution of the bicycle is displayed, from the Boneshaker or Velocipede of the 1860s to the modern, slim-tyred speedsters of today. One interesting exhibit is a Mercedes Benz of 1935, built as a car for the working man — to rival Dr Ferdinand Porsche's Volkswagen. The museum is closed on Sundays and Mondays.

Mercedes at Heidelberg Transport Museum.

A TOWN FOR SIR HARRY'S LADY

Like Ladismith in the Cape, this important growth centre is named after Lady Juana Maria Smith, wife of Sir Harry Smith. Established in 1847 as Windsor, after a local trader, George Windsor, it was given its present name three years later. The town is best remembered for its long siege during the Anglo-Boer War. This is recalled in the Siege Museum, partly housed in the historic Town Hall, where a section of the clock tower was blasted away by a direct hit from a shell fired by one of the Boers' Creusot 'Long Tom' guns.

Surrounding hills are dotted with monuments and the graves of men who died during the siege, and the All Saints Church in the town lists the names of more than 1 000 British soldiers who died. Built into the church is a Boer shell that demolished the porch of the building.

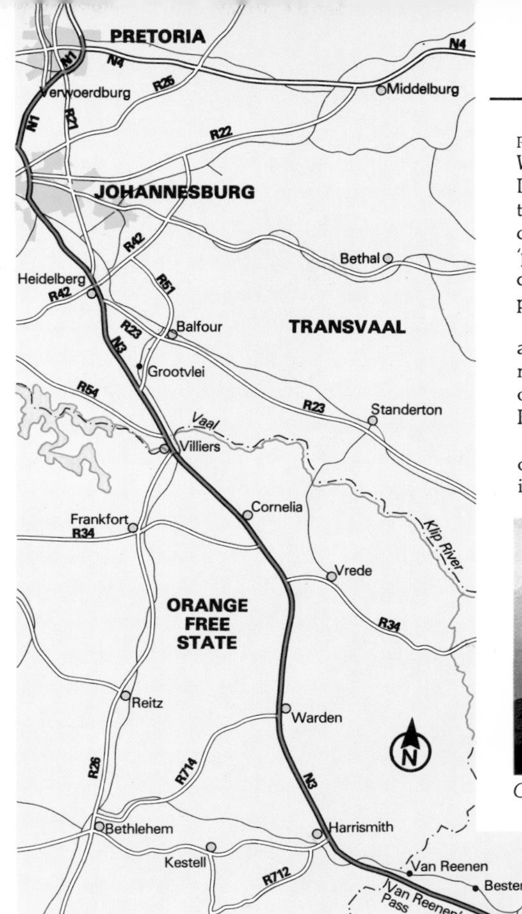

Ladysmith's historic town hall.

9,5 km after passing Chieveley Station the N3 becomes a freeway, and you by-pass the town of Estcourt. (The town was named Bushman's River Post when it was laid out in 1848, but was renamed in honour of a British parliamentarian who sponsored the emigration of settlers to Natal. It now serves as the commercial centre of a large cattle-farming district.)

Beyond Estcourt the road traverses attractive hilly country, and you pass the town of Mooi River on your right. In winter this stretch of the N3 is subject to heavy hailstorms and occasional falls of snow. After passing the town of Howick on your left and the Midmar Dam on your right, you begin the descent of Town Hill — a long and picturesque entrance into Pietermaritzburg, the administrative capital of Natal (see pages 172-7).

From Pietermaritzburg the N3 freeway descends gradually to the coast through a landscape of rolling hills. Follow the signs for Durban — the toll road is the quickest ●

PASS TO THE 'PROMISED LAND'

When the Voortrekkers reached the lip of the Drakensberg above Natal in 1837, they faced the difficult problem of getting their wagons down from the high country into the 'promised land' of Natal below. The first crossing is believed to have been down the present-day Oliviershoek Pass.

With the growth in trade between Natal and the Orange Free State, a more practicable route was sought, and was eventually based on a track used by a farmer, Frans van Reenen, to drive his cattle inland to market.

The first pass suitable for traffic was opened in 1856, and a railway pass was built in 1891.

Granite outcrop near Van Reenen's Pass.

End of the road: Hotels and apartment blocks overlook the Indian Ocean at Durban's North Beach.

From the Witwatersrand to Natal's holiday coast through historic Vryheid and Eshowe

For holiday-makers heading from the southern Transvaal to Natal's south coast, here is an alternative to the busy N3. This route is longer, but it is relatively traffic-free, more scenic, and makes a change if you have travelled the N3 many times before. The route leads east across the Highveld, then south through Vryheid.

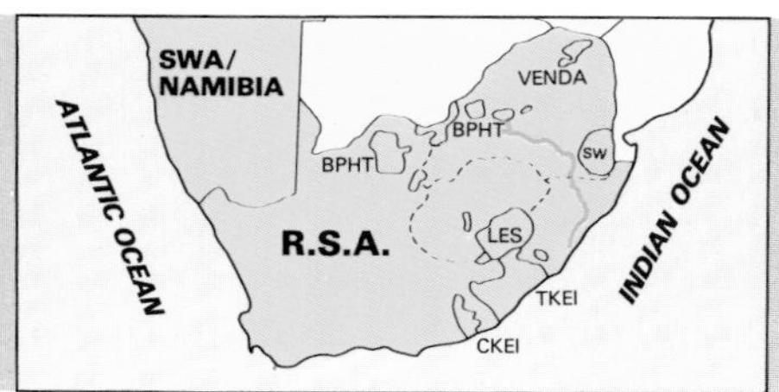

AA Office AA House, 66 De Korte Street, Braamfontein, Johannesburg 2001 Tel. (011) 4035700
AA Office AA House, 395 Schoeman Street, Pretoria 0002 Tel. (012) 283829
Public Library cnr Hoog and Mark Streets, Vryheid 3100 Tel. (0381) 2133
AA Office AA House, 537 Smith Street, Durban 4001 Tel. (031) 3010341

Johannesburg (790 — 800 km)/Pretoria (840 — 850 km) - Ermelo - Piet Retief - Vryheid - Eshowe - **Durban**

IF YOU ARE STARTING your journey from Johannesburg, drive east on the R22 (North Rand Road) towards Witbank, and note your kms as you cross over the R21. If you are starting from Pretoria, drive south-east on the R21 (Maria Van Riebeeck Avenue) and after passing Jan Smuts Airport on your left, exit onto the R22 for Witbank — noting your kms.

After travelling 18 km on the R22 from the R21/R22 intersection, take the exit for 'R51/Springs/Pretoria'. Note your kms when you reach the stop sign, and turn right, crossing over the R22 and driving south towards Springs. You are now on the R51, which is called Kingsway Road initially, but which changes its name to Paul Kruger Highway. You are now surrounded by mine dumps, recalling the days when Springs was the world's largest single gold producer.

9,2 km after noting your kms, turn left at the traffic lights into 4th Avenue (at the sign for 'R29/Secunda/Springs Centre'). Continue along 4th Avenue as it curves to the right, and at 11,5 km, turn left into 1st Avenue (also known as Ermelo Road) for 'R29/Secunda'. You are now travelling south-east on the R29. You pass some quaint old buildings and mine headgear, then the scene changes to typical Highveld maize farming country.

Kinross to Piet Retief

The R29 takes you past the small towns of Devon (where there is a large military base on your left) and Leandra, and then reaches Kinross, which is the centre of one of South Africa's most advanced maize, potato and cattle-farming regions, as well as being a major producer of gold and coal. Kinross lies on the crest of South Africa's watershed — rain falling to the east of the town will eventually make its way to the Indian Ocean, while rain falling to the west runs off into the South Atlantic.

16 km after Kinross, still on the R29, you pass through Trichardt — with the Sasol 2 oil-from-coal project nearby at Secunda.

Also nearby are Matla, Kriel and Duvha, three of the largest coal-fired power stations in the southern hemisphere.

Follow the signs for the R29 through Bethal, and roughly 58 km after Bethal you enter Ermelo on Joubert Street. In the centre of the town, turn right into Kerk (Church) Street. Shortly after passing the Civic Centre on your left, turn left to stay on the R29 for Piet Retief — noting your kms as you turn.

Roughly 15 km later you pass on your right the massive Camden power station. After this you leave the maize-farming and coal-mining area, and enter huge wattle and pine plantations. Some 100 km from Ermelo you enter Piet Retief — named after the Voortrekker leader who was murdered by Zulu impis in 1838.

Piet Retief to Eshowe

Continue straight through Piet Retief on the R29/R33. When these two roads part, a short distance from the town, take the R33 — leading south towards Paulpietersburg. 40 km after leaving Piet Retief you cross the border into Natal at the Phongola River.

17 km after crossing into Natal you enter Paulpietersburg. Turn left, following the sign for 'R33/Vryheid', and right after the town. After a further 48 km you enter Vryheid — once the capital of 'The New Republic', an area that included northern Natal and part of Zululand (see opposite, and day-drive, pages 156-7). You enter Vryheid on Emmett Street. Turn left into Kerk (Church) Street, and follow the signs for 'North Coast/Durban' right into Oos Street.

After travelling roughly 130 km on the R34 you pass through Melmoth, and enter country-

Johannesburg Stock Exchange and Anglo-American building.

ESHOWE

Eshowe was established in 1860 when the Zulu chief Cetshwayo built a village on the cool hills surrounding the silent Dlinza Forest. He named his new headquarters Eziqwaqweni (abode of robbers) and retreated here during the hot, humid summer months. Missionaries established a mission station nearby and it was here that a British force was besieged for over two months at the beginning of the Anglo-Zulu War in 1879. The mission station was later destroyed by fire.

The name Eshowe is said to represent the sound of the wind rushing through the trees, but it is probably derived from the *xysmalobium* or 'shongwe' shrubs that grow here. The town was established as the capital of Zululand, and today it serves as an administrative centre for KwaZulu.

The endless horizons of KwaZulu tempt the motorist to venture deep into the heart of the interior.

PIET RETIEF

This attractive town lying high in the mist belt on the edge of the Highveld is the centre of a flourishing tobacco and paper industry, and is surrounded by huge forests of wattle. It is named after the Voortrekker leader who was killed by the Zulu king, Dingane.

Retief was born near Wellington in 1780, and he later settled in the Eastern Cape. Then in 1837 he joined other Boers led by Gert Maritz and Andries Hendrik Potgieter in their Great Trek northwards to escape British rule at the Cape. Retief felt that their future lay in Natal, and he crossed the Drakensberg at a point known today as Retief's Pass to negotiate with the Zulu king, Dingane. Dingane at first accused the Boers of stealing cattle, but later, when this disagreement appeared to have been resolved, he invited them to visit the royal kraal. Retief and his followers arrived, and were initially treated with great hospitality, but were then suddenly attacked by Dingane's warriors.

The town was established after a proclamation in 1882 authorised that a township be built on the farms Osloop and Geluk, provided that the town was named after a Voortrekker leader.

VRYHEID

In 1884 Vryheid (liberty) was made the capital of De Nieuwe Republiek (The New Republic) by a group of Boer and British mercenaries who had helped Dinuzulu — son of Cetshwayo — defeat his rival Zibebu for succession to the Zulu throne. In exchange for their help, Dinuzulu had promised farming land to the mercenaries, but when the promised area was measured out it was discovered that the Zulu nation would be left homeless. It was British intervention that ensured that some of Zululand be left to the Zulus. In July 1888 De Nieuwe Republiek became incorporated with Paul Kruger's Transvaal Republic, and at the end of the Anglo-Boer War the entire area was annexed to Natal.

Today Vryheid is a centre for coal mining and ranching. A small museum, containing relics from the days of the new republic, is housed in the building once used as the republic's council chamber.

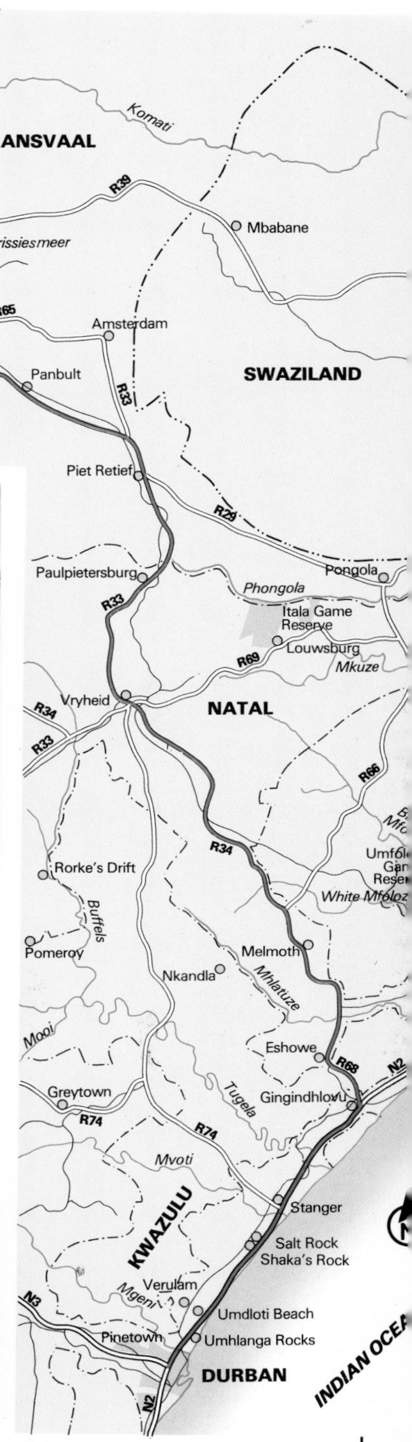

A cluster of huts dots the hillside north of Melmoth.

A lighthouse towers above the shore at Umhlanga Rocks.

side typical of coastal Natal — rolling fields of thick green sugar-cane, tangled sub-tropical bush and colourful flowers. Some 27 km after passing through Melmoth, bear right onto the R68 for Eshowe where the R34 leads left to Empangeni. After a further 20 km you pass the road leading to Eshowe, the administrative capital of KwaZulu (see opposite).

Eshowe to Durban

21 km after passing Eshowe the R68 intersects with the N2 near Gingindhlovu — known to the British troops of last century as 'Gin, Gin, I love you'. Turn right onto the N2, noting your kms as you turn. A little over 23 km later you cross the Tugela River on the John Ross bridge. After a further 27 km you pass a road leading left to Blythdale Beach and another leading right to Stanger. Now predominantly Indian, Stanger used to be called the capital of the Zulu nation. It was here that Chaka was assassinated by his two half-brothers, Dingane and Mhlangane, on 22 September 1828.

Continue on the N2, which follows the coast south to Durban with frequent glimpses to your left of the Indian Ocean ●

Below: *Night falls on Durban.*

From Durban to the Witwatersrand on a scenic route through Natal

This route from the holiday resorts of the southern Natal coast to the major population centres of the Transvaal offers a scenic alternative to the N3. We drive through sugar-cane country and the Tugela River valley to Dundee and Newcastle, and continue through Volksrust and Standerton to join the N3 near Heidelberg.

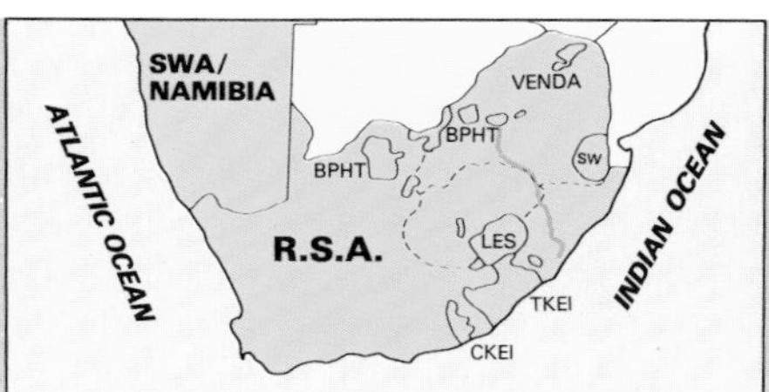

AA Office AA House, 395 Schoeman Street, Pretoria 0002 Tel. (012) 283829
AA Office AA House, 66 De Korte Street, Braamfontein, Johannesburg 2001 Tel. (011) 4035700
AA Office 10 Permanent Plaza, 58 Scott Street, Newcastle 2940 Tel. (0343) 21910
AA Office AA House, 537 Smith Street, Durban 4001 Tel. (031) 3010341

Durban - Greytown - Dundee - Newcastle - Volksrust - Standerton - **Johannesburg (620 km)** - **Pretoria (670 km)**

DRIVE NORTH OUT OF Durban, either on the N2, or on the old main road that follows the coast through La Lucia and Umhlanga Rocks. Note your kms as you pass the resort of Umdloti Beach, and roughly 10 km later turn left onto the R614 for Tongaat.

This road leads inland through huge fields of sugar cane. Lining the road are beautiful indigenous trees and colourful displays of bougainvillea. As you approach Tongaat you come to a T-junction with the R102 — turn right here onto the R102, for Stanger. Roughly 4 km later, turn left at the traffic lights onto the R614 for Fawn Leas — noting your kms.

After travelling on this road for some 67 km you pass the road to Fawn Leas on your right, and 3,2 km later you pass on your left a road to Wartburg and Pietermaritzburg. Continue straight ahead for Dalton. (On your right at this junction you will see a large sugar-processing plant — watch out for trucks stacked high with raw sugar cane.)

A further 5,3 km brings you to the town of Dalton, in the heart of the Natal Midlands. Pass through the town, but on the outskirts turn right for Sevenoaks. Just over 15 km later you reach a T-junction with the R33 — turn right here onto the R33 for Sevenoaks and Greytown. After 3,7 km you pass through the small town of Sevenoaks, and some 20 km later you reach Greytown (see below).

At the first stop street in Greytown, turn right for 'Dundee/Kranskop' — then almost as soon as you have left the town, turn left to stay on the R33 for Dundee. Roughly 30 km after leaving Greytown you pass through the tiny settlement of Keate's Drift, where the people of KwaZulu come to trade the produce they have grown and to buy provisions. The countryside has now become noticeably drier, and is covered with thousands of rounded rocks and boulders — looking like so many giant marbles.

Note your kms as you pass through Keate's Drift. Continuing north from here the road begins to climb and twist among hills, and after 7,5 km you reach the crest of a ridge with a magnificent view over the valley below. (Beware of goats and cattle straying onto the road in this area, and note that in wet weather there are often rockfalls onto the narrow road.)

15 km from Keate's Drift you reach Tugela Ferry. The ferry is long gone, and you now cross the Tugela (the one that startles) River on a single-lane steel bridge. The small settlement here has an open-air market place selling fresh produce grown in the area.

25 km after crossing the Tugela you pass through the small town of Pomeroy, and roughly 52 km later you reach Dundee, in the Natal coalfields (see opposite).

Dundee to Volksrust

You enter Dundee on Commercial Road, which leads into Wilson Street. At the traffic lights turn left into Victoria Street. You pass the town's civic centre on your right, then reach a traffic circle. Go half-right here into Karel Landman Street, which becomes the R68 for Ladysmith. Roughly 23 km later, turn right onto the

Sugar cane covers the hilly countryside near Greytown.

Late afternoon sun lights up winter grasslands near Newcastle.

Brightly coloured motifs decorate the entrances to Zulu huts.

TIMBER TOWN IN THE MIST BELT

Greytown was founded on the banks of the Mvoti River in the early 1850s and named after the popular Cape governor Sir George Grey. The town lies in Natal's 'mist belt', where moisture-laden winds from the Indian Ocean form blankets of cloud and drizzle, and serves as the centre of a busy and growing timber and wattle-bark industry.

The Boer statesman Louis Botha was born on a nearby farm, Honeyfontein, on 27 September 1862. He became Commandant-General of the Transvaal Republican forces (1900-1902), Prime Minister of the Transvaal (1906-1910), and first Prime Minister of the Union of South Africa in 1910.

R23 for Newcastle — which you reach after a further 42 km (see below).

Continue on the R23, and after a further 49 km you reach Charlestown, which was at one time the customs post between the British colony of Natal and the Transvaal Republic. Some 2 km later you cross the modern provincial border from Natal into the Transvaal and you enter the historic town of Volksrust. Just outside Volksrust are the remains of Convention Bridge, where President Paul Kruger and British High Commissioner Sir Henry Loch met to sign the Third Swaziland Convention in 1894. As both men refused to negotiate on foreign soil, a train carriage was drawn onto the centre of the bridge across the Grensspruit (border stream), and the meeting was held across a conference table with each man sitting in his own territory.

Volksrust to Johannesburg

You will have entered Volksrust on Laingsnek Street. Turn left into Joubert Street, then fourth right into Dan Pienaar Street — following the signs for Johannesburg and Standerton. Dan Pienaar Street becomes the R23 again, and leads through the south-eastern Transvaal for 82 km to the town of Standerton. Standerton lies on the banks of the Vaal River, and parts of the town have occasionally been flooded when the river has come down in spate. The area around the town was formerly the scene of great concentrations of game during dry seasons, when the animals collected here in search of water and grazing.

Continue on the R23 through Standerton. After a further 57 km you pass Greylingstad, and 19 km later you pass Balfour (originally called McHattiesburg). Roughly 24 km after passing Balfour you reach a junction with the N3 — turn right here onto the N3 for Heidelberg and Johannesburg. The N3 by-passes the town of Heidelberg a few kilometres later (see pages 132-3) on its way into Johannesburg and northwards to the N1 and Pretoria ●

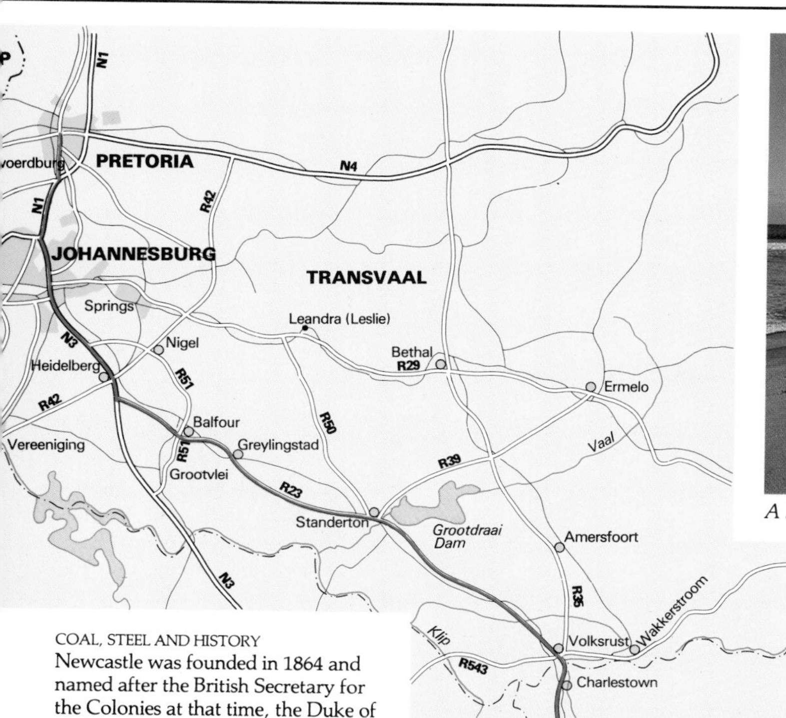

A lone angler waits for a bite at Umdloti Beach on Natal's north coast.

COAL, STEEL AND HISTORY

Newcastle was founded in 1864 and named after the British Secretary for the Colonies at that time, the Duke of Newcastle. The town lies in the Natal coalfields, and is the site of the third Iscor steel-producing plant. It also supports a considerable volume of heavy industry. The power station at the nearby Chelmsford Dam is the largest in Natal, producing roughly half a million kilowatts.

Newcastle is home to the prestigious St Dominic's Academy for Girls, founded in 1896. At the school stands the Pavilion, a 30 m wooden structure that was built in 1916 and is now a national monument. For tourists, Newcastle serves as the most convenient 'jumping off' point for many of the Drakensberg resorts.

During the First Anglo-Boer War, it was from Newcastle that General Sir Pomeroy Colley led his force to defeat at Majuba on 27 February 1881. During the Second Anglo-Boer War, Newcastle served as the principal stronghold from which the Boer forces controlled northern Natal, and besieged Ladysmith and Dundee. The town was named Viljoensdorp by the Boers, until it fell to the advancing British in 1900.

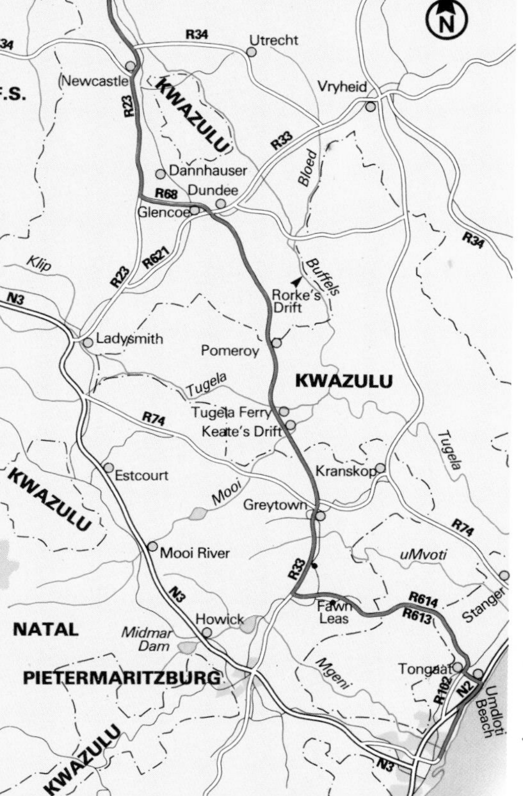

2 700 MILLION TONS OF COAL

Dundee, set amidst the slopes of the Biggarsberg range, was laid out on the farms Talana and Dundee by their owner Thomas Paterson Smith. The area had long been known for its surface deposits of coal; the Voortrekkers had collected pieces from the beds of streams such as the Steenkoolspruit (coal stream). In the 1860s Smith had begun selling wagonloads of coal in Pietermaritzburg, and eventually he formed the Dundee Coal and Estate Mining Company. The reserves of high-quality coal lying near the surface in northern Natal are now estimated at 2 700 million tons.

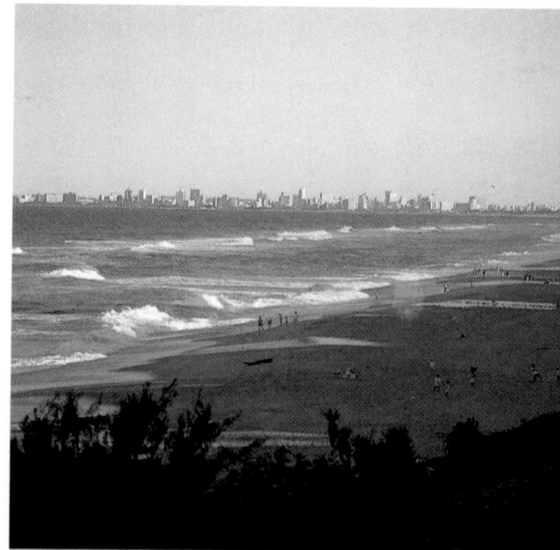
The Durban skyline from Umhlanga.

From Durban to the Kruger National Park through northern Natal and the Kingdom of the Swazis

Travellers from Durban and Natal's south coast will find this an attractive route to the Kruger National Park. The Jeppe's Reef border control post, through which you leave Swaziland and re-enter South Africa, closes at 16h00 — hence we recommend that you make this a two-day drive, staying at Mbabane or in the Ezulwini Valley.

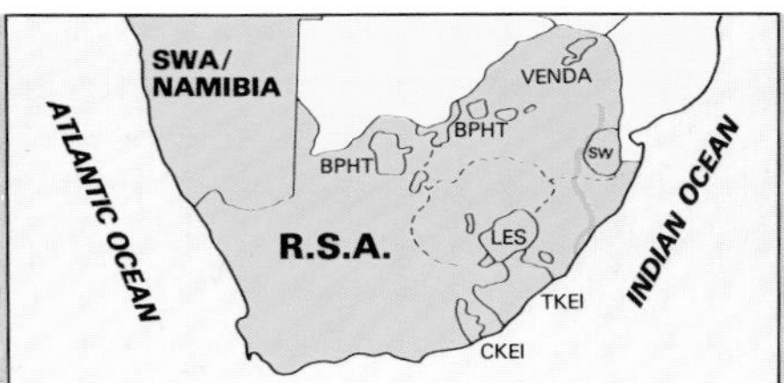

AA Office AA House, 537 Smith Street, Durban 4001 Tel. (031) 3010341
Vryheid Information Office Public Library, cnr Hoog and Mark Streets, Vryheid 3100 Tel. (0381) 2133
AA Office 56 Brown Street, Nelspruit 1200 Tel. (01311) 24631
AA Office Skukuza, Kruger National Park 1350 Tel. (0131252) 13

Durban - Eshowe - Vryheid - Amsterdam - Mbabane - Pigg's Peak - Malelane Gate - **Skukuza (880 — 900 km)**

DRIVE NORTH OUT OF Durban on the N2, which runs parallel to the coast and offers glimpses of the Indian Ocean on your right. You pass the sugar towns of Tongaat and Stanger, and roughly 27 km after passing Stanger you cross the Tugela (the one that startles) River. Some 24 km later, just before entering Gingindlovu, turn left onto the R68 for Eshowe and Melmoth — noting your kms.

The R68 passes through huge fields of sugar cane as it climbs the coastal hills, and stretches of the road are lined with sub-tropical flowering trees. After 20 km you pass a road on your left that leads into Eshowe — an attractive and historic town, once the capital of the Zulu Kingdom and now administrative capital of KwaZulu (see pages 26-7, and day-drive, pages 164-5). A further 47 km on the R68 brings you to the small town of Melmoth. Near here is the site of Dingane's Kraal, and also the grave of the Voortrekker leader Piet Retief — both of which are national monuments. In the vicinity of Melmoth the sugar cane gradually gives way to cool forests of wattle (see opposite). Shortly after passing through Melmoth, continue straight ahead on the main road, now the R34, where the R68 turns off left towards Dundee.

The R34 leads through the valley of the White Mfolozi River, and follows the river inland for part of its course. Roughly 130 km after leaving Melmoth you enter the historic town of Vryheid on West Street (see pages 26-7, and day-drive, pages 156-7). Turn left into Kerk (Church) Street, then right into Emmett Street, the R33 for Paulpietersburg.

The R33 now leads through an attractive stretch of countryside, and you reach the outskirts of Paulpietersburg (see opposite) some 48 km after leaving Vryheid. Turn left at the sign for 'Paulpietersburg/Piet Retief/R33' to stay on the R33. The road now traverses the Phongolo River valley, and roughly 17 km after Paulpietersburg you cross the Phongolo and enter the Transvaal. After a further 36 km, turn left onto the R29/R33, to enter the town of Piet Retief roughly 4 km later (see pages 26-7).

Drive north-east out of Piet Retief on the R29/R33, and after 10 km go right on the R33 for Amsterdam (where the R29 leads left for Ermelo). After a further 37 km you enter the town of Amsterdam on Voortrekker Street (see opposite). Turn right at the stop street onto the R65 for Nerston.

After a little over 14 km you reach another stop street, where the road left leads to Lothair and the road right leads to Nerston. Turn right here for Nerston. 200 m later you cross the border into Kangwane, and after a further 2 km you pass through the Nerston/Sandlane border post into Swaziland. (Passports are required, but South African citizens do not need visas. The border is open from 08h00 to 16h00. See pages 104-5.)

Nerston to Pigg's Peak

Once inside Swaziland, the tarred road twists and turns for some 34 km through the largest man-made forest in the world — eventually reaching the town of Bhunya and the huge wood-pulping works of the Usutu Pulp Company. Keep a watch here for logging trucks on the narrow road. After crossing a single-lane bridge you reach a T-junction near to the pulping plant. Turn right here, noting your kms. Pass a turn-off to 'Malkerns', and after roughly 32 km, turn left for Mbabane.

The road now leads through the Ezulwini (place of heaven) Valley to the Swaziland capital, Mbabane. Scattered throughout the valley are numerous hotels offering overnight accommodation, or you may prefer to drive on to Mbabane (see pages 22-3) and stay overnight there. As you drive through the valley you pass Lobamba, site of the Royal Residence and the nation's Parliament. There are often groups of traditionally dressed Swazis walking alongside the road here, but always ask permission before taking photographs.

Before leaving Mbabane, visit the craft market at the southern end of Allister Miller Street, where it is possible to obtain particularly fine curios and craftwork. After visiting the market, drive north out of Mbabane on the main road towards the Oshoek/Ngwenya border post and

Pine plantations cover the hills near Pigg's Peak.

Swazis in traditional costume perform the reed dance.

DREAMS OF A NEW SCOTLAND

In 1864 a newly arrived immigrant named Alexander McCorkindale conceived the idea of establishing a Scottish republic in the eastern Transvaal — it was to be called New Scotland, and its capital city would be called Roburnia after the Scottish poet Robbie Burns. The Transvaal government welcomed the idea of injecting new life into the ailing economy, and offered to sell McCorkindale a huge tract of land next to the Swaziland border for £8 000. McCorkindale sailed back to Britain to raise the capital, and there he formed the Glasgow and South Africa Company. He returned in 1866 and toured the area with President Pretorius, choosing sites for two other towns, to be called Londina and Industria.

McCorkindale planned to settle the new republic with 300 Scottish families, who would build the towns and cultivate farms — and develop a port on the coast, somewhere near the Mocambique border. The first 50 Scottish settlers arrived in 1867 and they established such well-known farms as Bonnie Braes, Lochiel and Waverley. But McCorkindale was unable to raise the full amount he needed, and he died of malaria in 1871. His dream-capital Roburnia did become a reality — but only for one year. The town was renamed Amsterdam in 1882.

Johannesburg. Roughly 11 km after leaving Mbabane, turn right onto the road for Pigg's Peak — noting your kms. This is a good tarred road that winds through one of the most scenic parts of the country (see pages 102-3).

After a little over 21 km you pass a general dealer's store on your left, and shortly after this you pass a turn-off to the old Forbes Reef mine workings, which date back to the last century. Soon after this you pass on your left a road leading into the Malolotja Game Reserve — note your kms again as you pass this turn-off. After travelling 4,9 km from here, park on the shoulder of the road for a good view over the Ngwenya and Silotwane hills. Continuing from this viewsite, the road winds down into a forested valley, but after a further 9,5 km there is another good viewsite on your left.

After meandering through forested hills you eventually find yourself driving along the tree-lined main street of Pigg's Peak — where beautiful hand-woven cloth may be bought.

Pigg's Peak to Skukuza

Continue straight through Pigg's Peak, and note your kms as you pass through the crossroads where the road left leads to 'Bulembu/Barberton' and the road right is signposted 'Police'. 1,1 km later, at the stop street, continue straight ahead for 'Matsamo/Kruger Park', where a road leads right to 'Balegane/Manzini'. After a further 3 km you pass the Rocklands sawmill on your right. The road now passes through forested mountains, and later a sprinkling of fragrant orange groves — watch for children and livestock on the road.

After travelling roughly 31 km from Pigg's Peak you pass another road on your right leading to 'Balegane/Manzini', and some 8 km later you pass through the Matsamo/Jeppe's Reef border post (open from 08h00 to 16h00). The road now leads through the bushveld of Kangwane, and a little over 40 km after leaving the border post you reach a T-junction with the N4. Turn left onto the N4, and after 100 m turn right for the Malelane Gate into the Kruger National Park (see pages 106-117). Skukuza, the administrative headquarters of the park, lies roughly 64 km from Malelane Gate, on a road (H3, then H1-1) with fine game-viewing ●

Skukuza, the Kruger Park's administrative centre.

A TOWN FOR PETER AND PAUL

The small town of Paulpietersburg was established in 1888, at the foot of a mountain known to the Zulu people as Dumbe, from the Zulu name for a wild fruit that grows on the mountain's slopes. The town was named after two of the most important leaders in the Transvaal's turbulent history — President Paul Kruger; and Commandant-General Piet Joubert, under whose direction the Transvaal forces won the battles of Laing's Nek and Majuba.

Today Paulpietersburg serves as the commercial centre for a large timber-producing region and a number of coalfields, and a resort, the Lurula Natal Spa, has been established around hot springs that lie roughly 15 km outside the town.

Vryheid's church spire dominates the town.

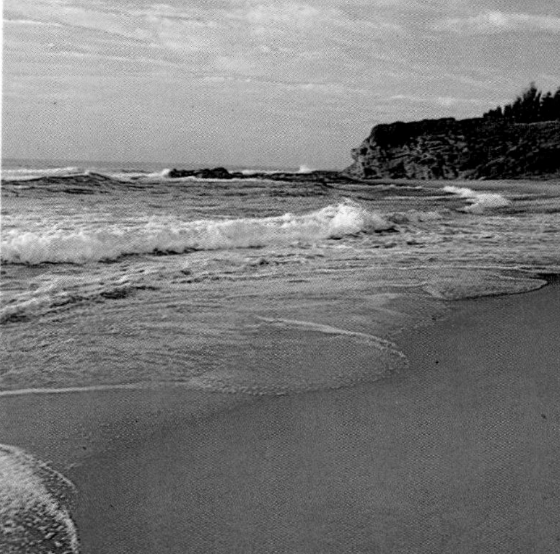

The Indian Ocean laps the north coast of Natal.

THE VALUABLE WATTLE

Much of Natal's high-lying mist belt is covered with cool plantations of wattle trees. The first wattles (*Acacia mearnsii*) were brought to this country from Australia in the 1860s and they flourished in the Natal midlands. In 1884 a farmer, George Sutton, noticed a liquid oozing from beneath the bark of the tree, and he sent a sample to London for chemical analysis. After a 12-year delay the sample was noticed in a storeroom, tested, and found to contain a high proportion of tannic acid, used in the leather-tanning industry. The tree became a valuable commodity, and its bark is now exported to all parts of the world.

'The Golden Way' from the Witwatersrand to Colesberg across bright fields of corn and sunflowers

This first half of the main route south from the Transvaal to Cape Town (N1) crosses the great plains of the Orange Free State — retracing the steps of early missionaries, explorers and Voortrekkers. The province's vast fields of maize, wheat and sunflowers, and its mineral wealth, have given this route its name: 'The Golden Way'.

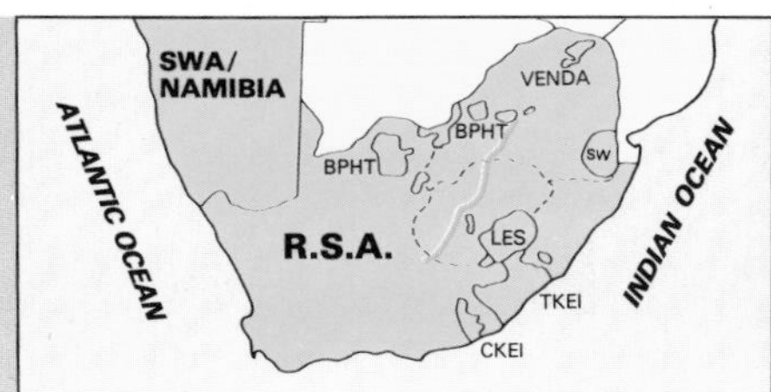

AA Office AA House, 395 Schoeman Street, Pretoria 0002 Tel. (012) 283829
AA Office AA House, 66 De Korte Street, Braamfontein, Johannesburg 2001 Tel. (011) 4035700
SA Tourism Board Suite 4611, Carlton Centre, Johannesburg 2001 Tel. (011) 3315241
AA Office AA House, 56 Church Street, Bloemfontein 9301 Tel. (051) 76191

Pretoria (680—700 km) - Johannesburg (625—645 km) - Parys - Kroonstad - Winburg - Bloemfontein - **Colesberg**

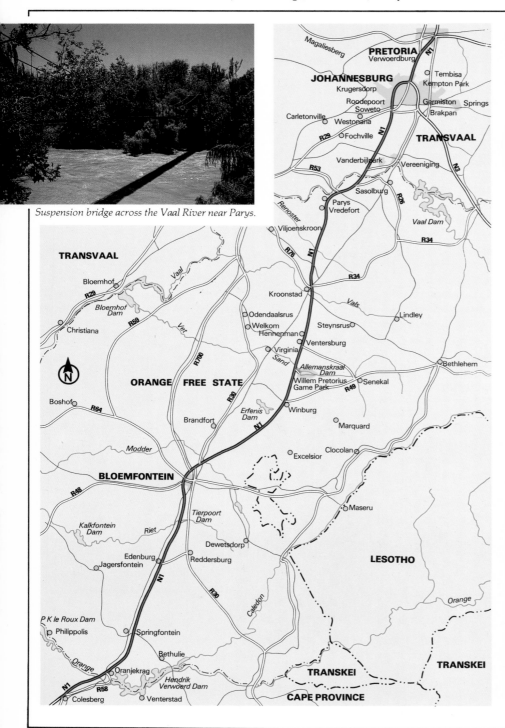

Suspension bridge across the Vaal River near Parys.

Statue of Voortrekker religious leader Sarel Cilliers

COLESBERG

In 1778 Governor van Plettenberg erected a stone beacon near modern Colesberg to mark the north-eastern boundary of the Cape Colony. The town was founded more than 50 years later, in 1830, and named after the Governor of the day, Sir Galbraith Lowry Cole. A number of national monuments and other interesting old buildings, including the Anglican church with its intricately carved lectern, stand in the town. Many of these edifices are over 150 years old. The Colesberg and Kemper Museum in Murray Street is housed in an imposing double-storeyed building which was originally a hotel and later the municipal offices.

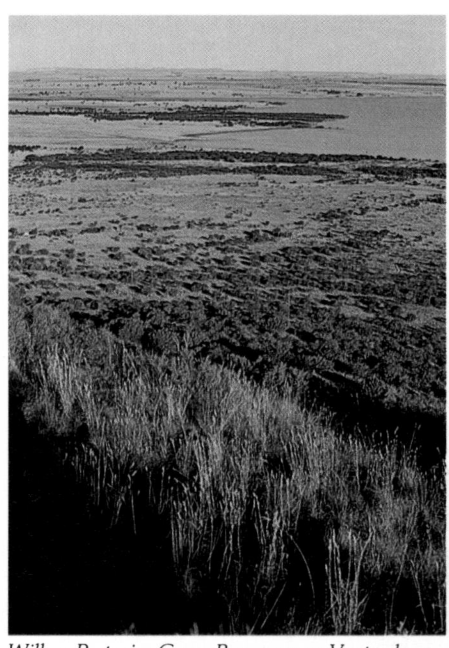

Willem Pretorius Game Reserve near Ventersburg.

IF YOU ARE STARTING your journey from Johannesburg, drive south on the N1, which remains a double carriageway until about 10 km beyond the Vaal River. If you are starting from Pretoria, drive south on the R28 and continue straight onto the N1 south at the Brakfontein interchange.

Roughly 28 km after crossing the Vaal River, the N1 enters Parys on Loop Street. You pass the town's Voortrekker centenary monument. (Two picturesque suspension bridges in the town lead to islands in the Vaal River.)

From Parys follow the signs for the N1 and Welkom. You soon cross the Skulpspruit, and roughly 13 km from Parys you enter Vredefort (peace fort), whose silos are visible for some distance. The road now crosses wide plains with grainfields, where names such as Renoster (rhinoceros) River are reminders of the game that roamed here in distant years. 72,2 km from Vredefort you pass a road on your right into Kroonstad. (The town, named after a Voortrekker leader's horse that drowned in the Vals River, has a resort and caravan park on the river banks.)

1,8 km after the Kroonstad turn-off, turn left. This road becomes a double carriageway, which reverts later to a single carriageway. 58 km beyond the Kroonstad turn-off you pass a crossroads with turn-offs to Senekal and Hennenman — note your kms here. You then pass Ventersburg on your right alongside the N1.

The road descends slightly towards the Sand River, and after 18,6 km you reach a turn-off on your left to the farm Sandrivierspoort. (This narrow gravel road leads after about 50 m to a small hillock with a cairn commemorating the Sand River Convention of 1852, which recognised the independence of the Transvaal Republic.) 300 m beyond the Sandrivierspoort turn-off you cross the Sand River bridge, and after a further 1,5 km you reach the turn-off to the Willem Pretorius Game Reserve on your left (swimming facilities, braai and picnic sites, restaurant and shop; small entry fee).

Note your kms at the game reserve turn-off, and 32,4 km later turn left for Winburg (see opposite). Turn left at the T-junction, then turn right at a stop street into Voortrekker Street. You pass the stone Magistrate's Court building on your right. Turn left into Brand Street after this. On your right, on the corner of Sibella Street, is a historic Voortrekker cemetery, and on your left further along Brand Street is the Town Hall, where tourist information is available.

Return to Voortrekker Street and turn left. Follow the tarred road where it turns left, and pass a gravel road on your left to Excelsior. Soon afterwards you reach the striking Voortrekker Monument and Museum.

THE FIRST FREE STATE CAPITAL

Winburg was established in 1842 after five local groups of Voortrekkers had elected Piet Retief as their 'governor', and the town claims to have been the first capital of the Orange Free State. The present dining room of Ford's Hotel (one of two hotels in the town) once served as the parliament's council chamber.

The town is the second-oldest in the Free State — Philippolis was founded more than 20 years earlier as a mission station. It was given its name, which was originally spelt Wenburg (victory town), to commemorate the victory of one faction over another about the siting of the town. The site favoured by the losers is known to this day as Mompeling (muttering) because of their dissatisfaction.

The striking Voortrekker Monument just outside Winburg was built in 1968 on a portion of the farm Rietfontein, birthplace of President M T Steyn. The adjacent Voortrekker Museum has many relics of the pioneers, and lifelike displays of everyday incidents in their lives.

Above: *Court of Appeal building in Bloemfontein.*
Above right: *Trekker monument — Winburg.*

BLOEMFONTEIN

This sunny capital city of the Orange Free State, with its spacious feeling, houses the gracious old Appeal Court — product of Bloemfontein's status as judicial capital of South Africa. The city's central position in the country has made it an important junction for road and rail traffic, and last century allowed it to benefit from the boom of both the diamond diggings around Kimberley and the goldfields in the Transvaal.

After the British annexed the area in 1848, Bloemfontein became the administrative centre, thus deposing Winburg. The town was laid out by the first British Resident of the Orange River territory, Major Henry Douglas Warden.

Overlooking the city is Naval Hill, site of the Franklin Game Reserve, and so named because the British placed an adapted naval gun on the summit during the Anglo-Boer War.

The elegant fourth raadzaal, completed in 1893, is now the seat of the OFS Provincial Council.

Winburg to Colesberg

Turn left as you leave the museum exit, then turn left onto the N1, noting your kms. The N1 crosses great plains for about 80 km, then winds among low koppies as you near Bloemfontein. The road becomes a double carriageway for about 36 km as it bypasses Bloemfontein. If you wish to stop in the town, exit left, following the signs (see opposite; and pages 146-7).

Note your kms at the end of the double carriageway. About 63 km later you pass a road on your left to Reddersburg and Edenburg (which can be seen on your right). Roughly 40 km later you pass a road on your left to Trompsburg (which is on your right) and to Philippolis — note your kms at this turn-off.

After a further 25 km you pass the small town of Springfontein on your right. Roughly 40 km later the town of Oranjekrag becomes visible on the slopes of a hill on your left. To view the Hendrik Verwoerd Dam and the dam wall — adding 15 km to your total journey — turn left 70 km after noting your kms, following the sign for 'Verwoerddam/Venterstad'. (See day drive, pages 214-5. After crossing the dam wall, turn right at the T-junction onto the R58 for Colesberg.)

If you continue on the N1 without making the detour to view the dam, you cross the Orange River 9,2 km after the turn-off. Almost immediately afterwards you enter hilly country. 23 km after crossing the river you can see the prominent Cole's Kop ahead of you, and slightly to the right of it the smaller Suffolk Hill — scene of the defeat and surrender of four companies of the Suffolk Regiment to the Boers in January 1900.

After a further 13 km, turn left for Colesberg, then turn right at the T-junction, entering the town on Kerk Street ●

Colesberg to Cape Town — across an arid land where lone windpumps stand against wide skies

South of the Orange River grainfields give way to the dry expanse of the Great Karoo. In a land dotted with rocky koppies and lone windpumps probing for precious water, each little town is an oasis of green, with strong reminders of a pioneering past. Eventually the scene changes again — to the well-watered lushness of the Boland.

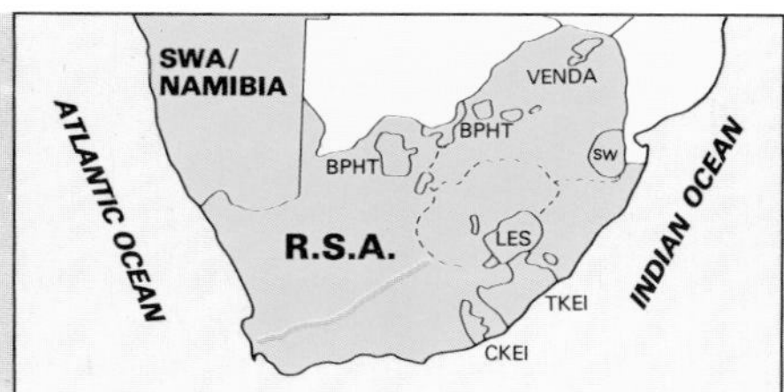

Colesberg Municipality Church Street, Colesberg 5980 Tel. (05852) 20
S A Tourism Board Level 3, Golden Acre, Adderley Street, Cape Town 8001 Tel. (021) 216274
AA Office AA House, 7 Martin Hammerschlag Way, Cape Town 8001 Tel. (021) 211550

Colesberg - Hanover - Richmond - Three Sisters - Beaufort West - Worcester - **Cape Town** (780—800km)

LEAVE COLESBERG BY turning left at the southern end of Kerk Street (in front of the Dutch Reformed Church) into Sarel Cilliers Street. Follow the road right into Ventershoek Street, and turn right into Sluiterweg. Turn left near the bypass road, then turn right at the fork onto the N1, noting your kms.

On your right is the prominent Cole's Kop, formerly known as Torenberg (tower mountain) and also Towerberg (magic mountain). Koppies soon fade into the distance as the road crosses the wide plains of the Karoo — a Khoikhoi word meaning arid or dry ground.

After roughly 58km you crest a hill and see ahead of you the trees of Hanover. After 75km on the N1 you reach a crossroads outside Hanover. Turn right here and enter the town on Queen Street (see opposite).

You pass the municipal offices on your left (where you may collect a key to the town's museum). At the head of Queen Street turn left in front of the police station of 1881, then take the first turn to your right. On your right at the second intersection, after about 100m, is 11 Grace Street, where the author Olive Schreiner lived during the Anglo-Boer War. To your left and behind you is the imposing Dutch Reformed Church of 1907, and in Viljoen Street, next to the church, is the museum.

Return to the N1 and turn right, noting your kms. After 20km there is a profusion of flat-topped koppies that show vertical erosion patterns near their tops. Roughly 20km later on your left there is a large, stone-built sheep-pen and on your right immediately afterwards there is a matching stone wall — relics from the days before wire fencing. 63,8, km from Hanover you reach a turn-off on your left to Richmond, lying amid small, jumbled koppies. Note your kms as you pass this road.

Richmond to Prince Albert Road

Beyond Richmond the koppies become larger, tending to form ridges. Some 95km later, as you round a bend, you see ahead of you three cone-topped koppies close together. This feature, known as the Three Sisters, is best viewed after you have passed it — from opposite the Three Sisters railway siding on your left just under 110km from Richmond.

Note your kms about 500m beyond the siding as you pass the R29 to Victoria West on your right (see pages 36-7). After 11,8km the road crosses a bridge with the railway line and a large stone blockhouse on your left. Like other blockhouses in this area, this was built during the Anglo-Boer War specifically to guard the rail bridge. After a further 800m a similar blockhouse can be glimpsed among the trees, guarding another rail bridge.

You pass two turn-offs on your left to Nelspoort, where there is a sanatorium for tuberculosis patients. (The dry Karoo air has for many years been said to be beneficial to those with chest ailments.) The Nuweveld Mountains rise on your right, and you pass a turn-off to Loxton and Carnarvon, just before entering Beaufort West about 75km from Three Sisters.

Go left around the square on which the jail stands, then turn left into Donkin Street (the main through-road to Cape Town). On your left at the corner of Devenish Street (the second street on your left) is the original stone Anglican Church of 1855, now converted into a dwelling known as Christ Church Lodge. In the next block on your left is number 25, a fine Victorian double-storeyed building with cast-iron balconies. On your left at the robot-controlled

Brilliantly coloured spring flowers bloom in Worcester's Karoo Garden.

The lattice-fringed Post Office in the Victorian village of Matjiesfontein.

HEX RIVER VALLEY

This beautiful region, intensively planted with vines, is tucked between the great Hex River and Kwadouw mountains that are covered with snow for several months each year. Many folk-tales and even poems celebrate the hex or heks (witch) of Hex River — the legend telling of a beautiful young woman, Eliza Meiring, who challenged a young man to prove his love by bringing her a disa which grew only at the top of a precipitous peak.

He made the attempt, but fell to his death, and Eliza became demented with grief. One night she cut her initials and the date — 1768 — into the window of the room in which she was confined, and then killed herself. The real origin of the name, however, is to be found in early maps and reports, which refer to the Ekse (criss-cross) River, which crossed and re-crossed the wagon route through this fine valley.

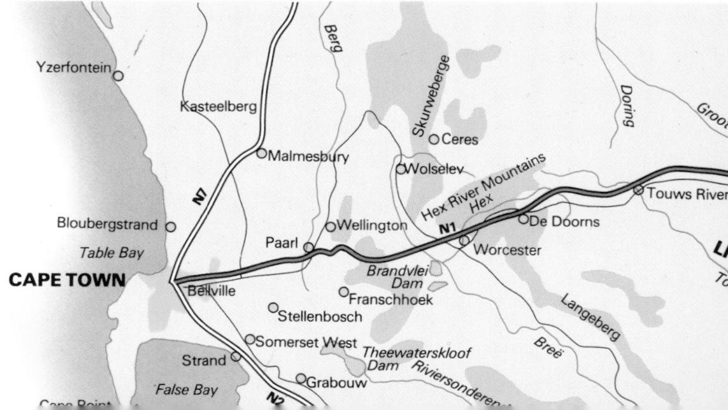

intersection with Kerk Street is the historic complex of Dutch Reformed Church, old town hall, and the rectory in which the noted cardiac surgeons Chris and Marius Barnard grew up.

About 4 km beyond Beaufort West you pass the R29 on your left to Meiringspoort and Oudtshoorn — note your kms here. You soon leave the mountains behind and cross a wide expanse of typical Karoo country. After 70 km the road crosses the Leeu River, with a railway bridge and another Anglo-Boer War blockhouse on your left. Soon afterwards you pass the little village of Leeu-Gamka on your left. (Leeu is Afrikaans for 'lion', while Gamka is a Khoikhoi word believed to mean 'lion' or 'deep'.)

112 km after noting your kms you pass Prince Albert Road, railhead for Prince Albert (see pages 258-9). Soon afterwards you can see the finger-like peak of Towerkop (see pages 262-3) in the distant Klein Swartberg range to the south-west.

You pass through a crossroads where the road on your left leads to Koup station and on your right to Merweville. As you ascend a slight incline roughly 10 km later (with a turn-off to Saaipad on your left) you can clearly see Towerkop on your left, far to the south.

Prince Albert Road to Cape Town

Just short of 19 km later a blockhouse guards a five-span rail bridge on your left, and 12 km later you enter Laingsburg, the small Karoo town that was laid waste by floods in 1981. (See day drive, pages 262-3.)

Soon after leaving Laingsburg you pass a turn-off on your right to the region known as the Moordenaarskaroo (murderer's Karoo). Roughly 27 km later the road on your left leads after 800 m into the restored Victorian village of Matjiesfontein (see below). Note your kms here.

Beyond the Matjiesfontein turn-off the N1 crosses the Baviaans River, and then the Monument River. After 10,6 km, as the road descends slightly, there is a gate in the fence on your left. If you pass through this gate you will reach an old cemetery after about 350 m. Buried here is the commander of the Highland Brigade, General A G Wauchope, who was killed at Magersfontein, whose body was reinterred at the site by James Logan (a fellow-Scot), so that his grave could be honoured more readily.

After a further 43 km you reach Touws River, an important railway centre, with its 'graveyard' of great old steam locomotives clearly visible on your left. 28 km after Touws River the road begins to wind down through the Hex River Pass into the wide and fertile Hex River Valley, famous for its vineyards that turn from a brilliant green in summer to a wonderful blend of browns and reds in autumn.

The road traverses the length of the valley for about 30 km, then swings to the left through forest plantations. Remain on the N1, and pass Worcester on your left. For 25 km after Worcester the road passes through more vineyards, before the Du Toits and Slanghoek ranges close in at the start of the Du Toit's Kloof Pass. The pass is scenically magnificent for the whole of its length, and it is well worth stopping at the large parking area on your right a few hundred metres beyond the summit — there is a splendid view from here over the Berg River Valley, with the towns of Paarl and Wellington at your feet. On a clear day you can see Table Mountain in the distance. (A new toll road and tunnel are planned for completion by 1988.)

You cross the Berg River on the outskirts of Paarl, then reach the double carriageway that leads into metropolitan Cape Town ●

A rocky outcrop on the Buffels River near Laingsburg.

MATJIESFONTEIN

Visiting Matjiesfontein is like stepping back to the turn of the century. The town — named after the 'matjiesgoed' rush *Cyperus textilis* — centres on the Lord Milner Hotel of 1900 and has been proclaimed a national monument in its entirety. It was founded in 1883 by James Logan, a Scot who established dining places and later hotels alongside the railway line in the days before dining saloons were attached to trains. Many famous people have stayed at Matjiesfontein, including Cecil John Rhodes, author Olive Schreiner and Lord Randolph Churchill.

HANOVER

This famous merino-breeding centre is overlooked by Trappieskoppie (little hill of steps), with its stone cairn commemorating the town's first magistrate, who supervised the street lay-out in 1876. The town had been founded 20 years earlier, on the farm of Gert Gouws, and named after Gouws's ancestral home in Germany.

The town's first Dutch Reformed clergyman, the Reverend Thomas Francois Burgers, was suspended by the church synod for his 'liberal' preachings, but was reinstated after winning an appeal to the Supreme Court. In 1872 he became President of the Transvaal Republic. After the British annexation of 1877 he left the Transvaal to farm near Hanover.

Samuel Cronwright-Schreiner, husband of author Olive Schreiner (whose surname he assumed), had a law practice in Hanover during the Anglo-Boer War.

Matjiesfontein's Lord Milner Hotel.

Rising from the flat Karoo landscape — the Three Sisters.

From gold to diamonds: a journey through the rich heartland of South Africa

Golden fields of maize cover the high plains between Johannesburg and Kimberley, hiding even greater riches below — real gold and glittering diamonds. This route (R29) from the southern Transvaal to the Cape, an alternative to the N1, crosses this golden landscape before joining the N1 at Three Sisters in the heart of the dry Karoo.

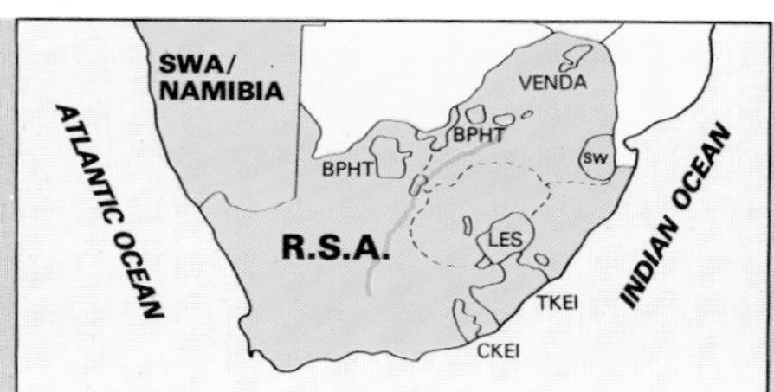

AA Office AA House, 395 Schoeman Street, Pretoria 0002 Tel. (012) 283829
AA Office AA House, 66 De Korte Street, Braamfontein, Johannesburg 2001 Tel. (011) 4035700
AA Office 3 Stockdale Street, Kimberley 8301 Tel. (0531) 25207
AA Office Limna Building, cnr Delvers and Emily Hobhouse Streets, Klerksdorp 2570 Tel. (018) 24781

Pretoria (960—990km) - Johannesburg (890—920km) - Potchefstroom - Klerksdorp - Kimberley - Victoria West - **Three Sisters**

If you are starting your journey from Johannesburg, drive south on the M1 through the city centre, join the N1, heading south, and shortly afterwards take the exit onto the R29 for Potchefstroom. If you are starting from Pretoria, drive through Johannesburg on the M1 and proceed as above, or drive around Johannesburg on the Western Bypass (N1) and take the R29 to Potchefstroom.

Roughly 10km after leaving the N1 you pass a turn-off onto the R559 and the R558, and later you pass a turn-off onto the R28. By now you are travelling through a great sea of maize fields, with chimneys and mine headgear visible here and there in the distance.

Shortly after crossing the R500 (stop street) look on your left for a gravel road signposted to the Danie Theron Monument (see opposite).

Return to the R29 and continue on it for 40km to Potchefstroom, entering the town on Holtzhausen Road. Continue straight ahead at the traffic lights, as Holtzhausen Road becomes Potgieter Street. Turn left into Kerkstraat to reach the picturesque old Town Hall on your left, opposite the Hervormde Kerk — the oldest congregation of the church in the Transvaal.

Potchefstroom to Kimberley

Return to Potgieter Street and turn left, noting your kms. As you pass Van Riebeeck Street, glance left for a view of the 'Landdrost Post en Telegraaf Kantoor' — the combined magistrate's and post offices dating from the days of the old Zuid Afrikaansche Republiek. Leave Potchefstroom on Potgieter Street, which becomes the R29 for Klerksdorp. On the outskirts of the town, after crossing the railway, you will see on your left the remains of the fort in which a British garrison withstood a siege by Transvaal burghers in 1880-81.

42km after leaving Potchefstroom you enter Klerksdorp. Note your kms at the first set of traffic lights, and proceed straight ahead, passing a road on your left that leads into central Klerksdorp and Ventersdorp. You cross a long bridge over the Skoonspruit (clear stream), then continue straight ahead along the double carriageway.

The road now leads through wide plains with large tracts of bush country, crossing the Jagspruit (hunt stream) after 12,3km, then the Renosterspruit (rhinoceros stream) after a further 16,7km. The countryside gradually becomes more hilly, and after travelling roughly 40km from Klerksdorp, and passing a road that leads off to Sendelingsfontein (missionary spring) and Harrisburg, the landscape becomes noticeably drier, with extensive maize fields stretching away to the horizon.

On the outskirts of Wolmaransstad, roughly 80km from Klerksdorp, you pass on your left the R504 to Leeudoringstad — the little town that made headlines in 1932 when a trainload of 1000 tons of dynamite exploded nearby.

After crossing the Makwassie Stream you enter Wolmaransstad on Broadbent Street. Look out for the old Town Hall with its distinctive dome. Proceed straight through Wolmaransstad, and 500m outside of the town, note your kms as you pass the junction with the R505. The road continues through wide plains and maize fields, and after 55km you pass the Bloemhof Dam Nature Reserve on your left. Roughly 3km later you can see the wall of the dam on your left, and another 1km brings you into Bloemhof — a town dominated by huge grain silos.

Drive through Bloemhof, staying on the R29. Note your kms on the outskirts of the town, as you pass a road on your left to Hertzogville. 36km later you pass on your left the Rob Ferreira Nature Reserve and mineral spa, and from the road you can often see large mammals, including white rhino. 46,6km from Bloemhof you pass the entrance to the resort on your left.

The road continues through flat veld, passing the town of Christiana, and crossing the Cape border (78km from Bloemhof) and the Vaal River (85km from Bloemhof). Shortly after crossing the river you pass a road on your right that leads into the town of Warrenton — a short detour into Warrenton will take you across a long and attractive old bridge over the Vaal. Continuing south on the R29, Kimberley comes into view after roughly 55km, as you top a slight rise, and you enter the town 15km later (see pages 316-7).

Kimberley to Three Sisters

Leave Kimberley on Memorial Road, passing the Honoured Dead Memorial. Note your kms as you pass on your left McDougall Road, leading to B J Vorster Airport. After 14,7km you pass the Spytfontein (spring of regretfulness) rail siding on your left, where Boer forces gathered in December 1899 before taking up positions further south at Magersfontein. To reach Magersfontein battlefield, turn left immediately after passing Modder River station (30,8km from Kimberley) towards 'Scholtzburg' and 'Magersfontein'. This side road, mainly good gravel, leads after 10km to the museum and observation post at the battle site.

Continue south on the R29, noting your kms at the Magersfontein turn-off. After 1,5km you cross the Riet (reed) River, and you can see on your left the rail bridge, still guarded by a stone blockhouse. Continue on the R29, passing a road on your left to Jacobsdal and Bloemfontein, and later a road to Heuningneskloofstasie and Enslin. Less than 1km after the Enslin turn-off you will see a granite tablet on a small rocky hill on your right. This commemorates men of the Royal Navy killed at the Battle of Enslin on 26 November 1899, and at the Battle of Graspan fought the day before.

35,7km from the Magersfontein turn-off you pass a road on your left leading to Graspan station, and at 48,5km from the Magersfontein turn-off there is another road on your left lead-

POTCHEFSTROOM

Voortrekker leader Andries Potgieter established this, the first white town in the Transvaal, and its former capital, in 1838. Situated on the banks of the Mooi (pretty) River, it was known by several names until 1840 when it was named partly after its founder, Potgieter, and the river, or 'stroom'.

The town's museum records human activity of the area, from the Stone Age to the present. Among the vehicles displayed is a wagon used at the Battle of Blood River. Of particular interest are 75 paintings by German-born Otto Landsberg (1803-1905).

Potchefstroom's Hervormde Kerk.

The town hall at Wolmaranstad

ing to Belmont station — used by the British as a hospital and casualty clearing station during their advance on Kimberley.

The road crosses the Orange River a short distance after this, then passes through the outskirts of Hopetown — where South Africa's first diamond was discovered in 1866. You pass roads leading to the P K le Roux Dam, into Hopetown, and to Boomplaas (tree farm). 55 km from Hopetown you pass a road that leads into Strydenburg — the name means 'town of strife', and derives from the quarrels that arose over the best site for the town.

25 km after Strydenburg the road begins to wind through a tangle of little hills strewn with dark, weathered boulders. After a further 30 km rows of ridges and flat-topped hills come into view, and soon after this you enter Britstown on Market Street. Continue through Britstown, staying on the R29. 18 km after leaving the town you come to a picnic site on your right, where water is available from a hand-operated pump.

As you continue south you cross a number of rivers, including the Rietpoort and the Brak, and 98 km after leaving Britstown you enter Victoria West. Continue straight ahead, through the town, staying on the R29. You can now see looming ahead of you the cone-shaped Kapokberg — so named because it is often covered with a blanket of snow during winter.

38 km after leaving Victoria West you reach a T-junction with the N1 at Three Sisters — the name given to three distinct dolerite-capped koppies nearby. Turn right onto the N1, and continue your journey to Cape Town, following the route described on pages 34-5

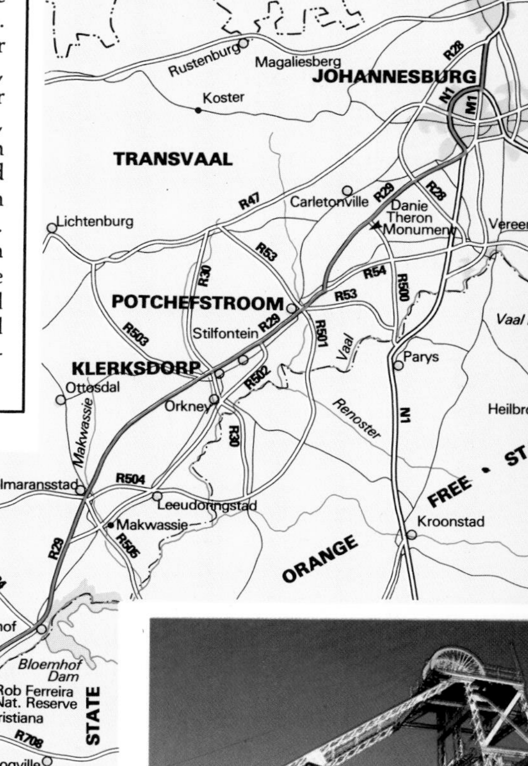

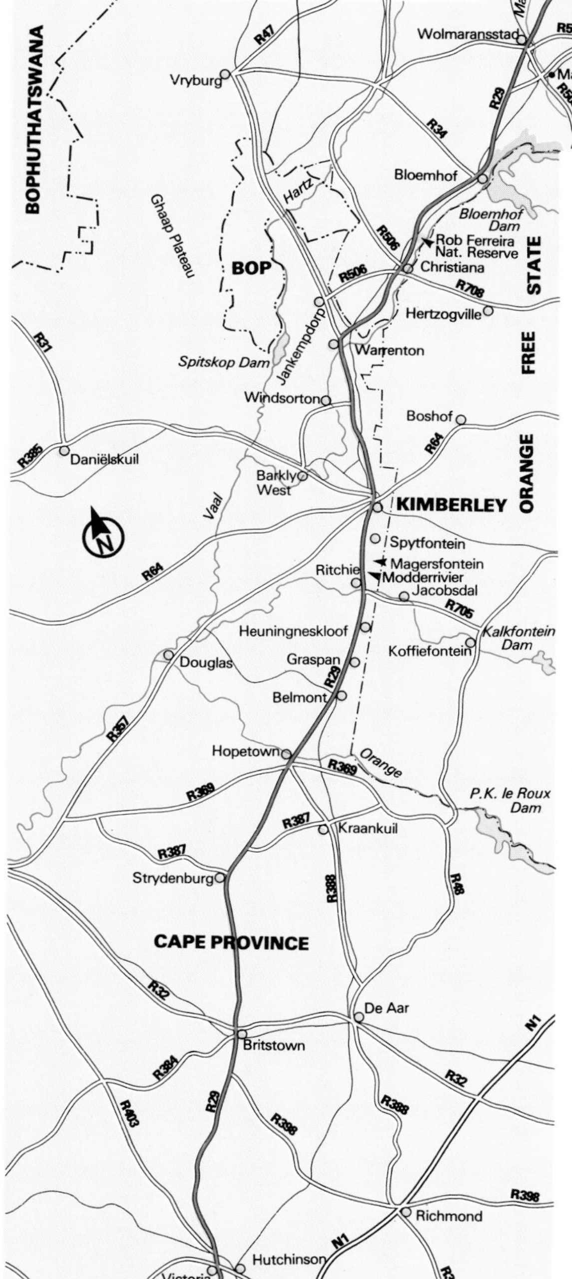

Honoured Dead Memorial, Kimberley.

WARRENTON

Situated on the great limestone plateau known as the Ghaap — from the Khoikhoi word for 'a large plain' — this little town was founded in 1884 on the farm Grasbult (grassy hump).

The town is named after Sir Charles Warren, who trained as a military surveyor and commanded the Diamond Fields Horse in 1877. He took part in campaigns in the northern Cape against the Koranna and the Griqua, proclaimed British rule in Bechuanaland (now Botswana); and was nominal commander of the British force disastrously defeated at Spioenkop during General Redvers Buller's attempts to break through the Boer lines in central Natal in 1900. For a while he was Commissioner of London's Metropolitan Police, receiving considerable criticism over his failure to solve the series of infamous 'Jack the Ripper' murders.

Today Warrenton is an agricultural centre, with a kaolin (china clay) mine nearby.

Dammed Zeekoegat River, Victoria West.

Old mine headgear, Kimberley.

DANIE THERON

The monument to Danie Theron, on the Gatsrand (ridge of holes) between Johannesburg and Potchefstroom, marks the spot where he fell in 1900.

At the outbreak of the Anglo-Boer War, Theron formed a corps of cyclists, and soon became known for his daring exploits as a scout. Later he formed 'Therons Verkenners Korps' (Theron's Scouting Corps). Following the death of his fiancée in 1898, it was said that he no longer cared whether he lived or died.

VICTORIA WEST

This attractive Karoo town, originally named Victoria, was laid out in 1844. It changed its name to Victoria West when the district of Victoria was created in the Eastern Cape in 1855. A museum attached to the library in Main Street includes a fine collection of old cameras and film projectors; and medals won by Group Captain P H Hugo, a Battle of Britain fighter-pilot who was born on the nearby farm Pampoenpoort and educated in the town. His nickname locally was 'Piet Khaki', although to his companions in the Royal Air Force he was 'Dutch' Hugo.

Range after range of mountains lead down to the vineyards of the south-western Cape

The scenic 'mountain' route from the southern Transvaal to Cape Town leads along the edge of Lesotho's Maluti Mountains, then through the Great and Little Karoos to the green valleys of the 'old Cape'. We have divided the route into two sections, but recommend that it be treated as a leisurely exploration taking three or four days.

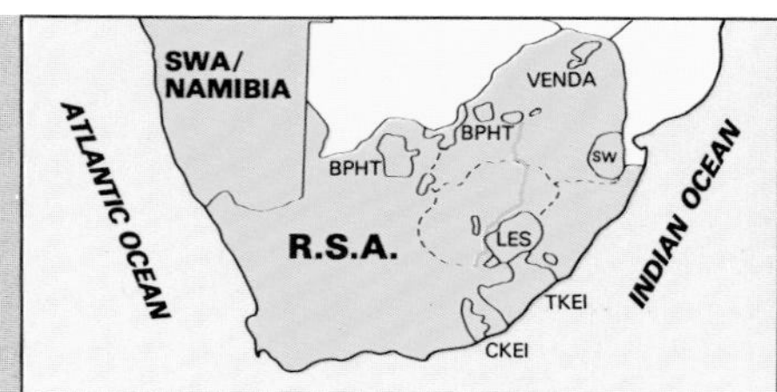

AA Office AA House, 395 Schoeman Street, Pretoria 0002 Tel. (012) 283829
AA Office AA House, 66 De Korte Street, Braamfontein, Johannesburg 2001 Tel. (011) 4035700
Aliwal North Municipality Barkly Street, Aliwal North 5530 Tel. (0551) 2441

Pretoria (720-740 km) - **Johannesburg** (670-690 km) - Frankfort - Bethlehem - Ficksburg - Ladybrand - **Aliwal North**

DRIVE SOUTH FROM Johannesburg on the R26 towards Vereeniging. (If you are starting from Pretoria, drive south towards Johannesburg on the R28 and then the N1, turn onto the N3 at the Buccleuch interchange, take the M13 at the Elands interchange, then turn onto the R26 south towards Vereeniging at the Reading interchange.)

After roughly 24 km on the R26 you pass the old Witkop blockhouse on your left, a three-storey sandstone building dating from the Anglo-Boer War. Note your kms as you pass the blockhouse, and 23 km later take the exit for Arcon Park and Three Rivers. Turn left at the T-junction, and at the second T-junction turn right into Van Riet Lowe Street. At a third T-junction 1 km later, turn left. 1,3 km after this, turn left for 'Vaaldam/Vosloopark', and stay on this road (R54) for 25,7 km. Turn right onto the R549 for Vaal Dam at the crossroads where the road left leads to Heidelberg.

You now have good views over the Vaal Dam on your left, and you cross the Vaal River after 10,8 km. 2 km later you pass Deneysville. 900 m later take the left fork to 'Oranjeville/R716', and 11,5 km after this, turn left on the R716 for Oranjeville.

As you enter Oranjeville, turn left into Hans Street, then right into Malan Street, then turn left at the T-junction into Van Niekerk Street. Cross the narrow Magrieta Prinsloo Bridge, and continue eastwards on the R716.

38 km from Oranjeville, turn right at the T-junction onto the R51. At the next T-junction, 16 km later, turn right again — staying on the R51. You now pass on your right the town of Frankfort, with its towering maize silos, typical of the towns of the 'maize triangle'. 6 km after Frankfort you cross the Wilge (willow) River on the Fred Wentzel Bridge, and 500 m after the bridge turn left — still on the R51.

The town of Tweeling (twins) comes into view after a further 32 km, framed between the two similar hills that gave it this name. Later the huge maize silos at Reitz can be seen (see opposite). After passing Reitz you soon see ahead of you the Rooiberg and Witteberg ranges, and 50 km from Reitz you reach Bethlehem.

Drive through Bethlehem, keeping straight ahead at both sets of traffic lights, and leave town on the R49 towards Kestell. Roughly 6 km after the second set of traffic lights, turn right onto the R711 for Clarens and Golden Gate — noting your kms at the turn.

From here the mountains begin to close in towards the road. There are sandstone cliffs on your left after some 25 km, and 2 km later you pass on your right the massive rock formation known as Titanic Rock. 1 km after this, park on the side of the road (opposite the hotel entrance) and look back at this rock to appreciate how it resembles an ocean liner steaming directly towards you.

A further 1 km brings you to a turn-off on your right into the picturesque village of Clarens (see opposite, and pages 142-3). Take this turn-off if you wish to make a detour through the village, as there is a road on the other side that will bring you back onto our route (the R711). If you do not turn into Clarens, then turn right shortly afterwards to remain on the R711.

Clarens to Aliwal North

Roughly 4 km after Clarens, park on the side of the road at the 'Boesmantekeninge' sign — to view the San rock art on the walls of the nearby overhang.

To your left the Maluti Mountains now present spectacular ridges. Keep straight at the crossroads 35 km after Clarens, where left leads to Caledonspoort and right leads to Fouriesburg. Immediately after this, turn left onto the R26, noting your kms.

The road soon passes close to a number of mountains and sandstone outcrops. One of the more prominent of the outcrops is known as Soutkop, which you pass on your left after about 30 km. 12 km later you pass the town of Ficksburg (see opposite) on your left, and 34,5 km later you pass Clocolan on your right.

Among the mountain features you now pass on your left are the prominent Wonderkop, and Tandjiesberg (little teeth mountain). You pass a road on your left that leads to Tandjiesberg, then 3 km later you pass the town of Ladybrand on your right. 4 km after Ladybrand you pass a road on your left (R64) that leads to Maseru, capital of Lesotho (see pages 148-151).

Roughly 15 km from Ladybrand, go left at the fork for Hobhouse, which you pass after some 40 km. The little town was named after the British suffragist Emily Hobhouse, who championed the cause of Boer women and children living in British concentration camps during the Anglo-Boer War. 30 km after passing Hobhouse, turn left at the T-junction for Wepener — scene of one of the lesser-known sieges of the Anglo-Boer War.

You pass Wepener some 8 km after the T-junction, and continue south on the R26 — with the plains of the eastern Free State sweeping away on your right to the Great Karoo, and the mountains of Lesotho still prominent on your left. Aasvoëlberg (vulture mountain) comes into view long before you reach the town of Zastron that nestles at its foot.

You pass Zastron 61,5 km after Wepener, and 30 km later reach Rouxville. Turn left at the T-junction in Rouxville. 34,4 km later you cross the Orange River — then the road divides. The left road, Barkly Street, leads into the centre of Aliwal North (see pages 212-5); the right road, Robinson Road, leads on to Burgersdorp. The route to Cape Town continues on the following pages ●

Brightly coloured sails decorate the Vaal Dam.

HOBHOUSE

Emily Hobhouse publicly condemned the British conduct of the war in South Africa from 1899 to 1902 — and was derided as a traitor by many of her countrymen. In particular she drew attention to the poor conditions prevailing in the concentration camps, and succeeded in arousing a 'national conscience'. She died in London in 1926, and her ashes were brought to South Africa to be interred at the National Women's Monument in Bloemfontein. The little town that bears her name stands on the banks of the Leeu (lion) River, at the centre of a rich agricultural region.

Below: *Magnificent Golden Gate scenery.*

Row upon row of mountains flank the road between Ladybrand and Hobhouse.

REITZ

Named after President Francis William Reitz of the Orange Free State, this town is dominated by its gigantic maize silos. During the Anglo-Boer War, on the night of 11 July 1901, a later president of the Orange Free State, M T Steyn, was resting here in the town with his staff and members of his 'government in the field' when a British raiding party galloped down the main street — capturing some 29 Boer officers and the country's treasury. President Steyn escaped, however, to remain in the field until the end of the war.

Near the town there is a cave, decorated with San paintings, in which General de Wet concealed supplies and ammunition during the long guerilla campaign he waged in the latter stages of the war.

'HOUSE OF BREAD' ON THE JORDAN

Bethlehem — from the biblical 'house of bread' — is an appropriate name for this town, set in the heart of a prosperous agricultural region. The town was founded in 1864 on a river that early settlers had named the Jordaan — after the biblical Jordan. The Jordaan has subsequently been dammed to form Loch Athlone — where a masonry replica of the ocean liner *Athlone Castle* serves as a restaurant.

Bethlehem's former mission church, a national monument, now houses a museum of local history, and a number of old vehicles are exhibited in the grounds. The Pretorius Kloof Bird Sanctuary is adjacent to the residential area of the town, and has a restaurant, braai sites, water and toilets.

Isolated koppies topped by fortress-like sandstone cliffs near Ficksburg.

TOWN OF THE CHERRY FESTIVAL

The Caledon River serves as the boundary between the Orange Free State and Lesotho, and the town of Ficksburg was founded on its banks in 1867 at the close of the Basuto War. It lies at the centre of an area noted especially for its extensive cherry orchards. Each year a cherry festival is held in the town.

The hall of Ficksburg's high school was decorated with a frieze by the artist J H Pierneef, and the school has since built up a considerable collection of works by various South African artists.

CLARENS

During the Basuto War of 1865-6 Paul Kruger led a punitive expedition into the north-eastern Orange Free State and took part in the decisive Battle of Naauwpoortnek. Half a century later, when local farmers founded a village on the farms of Leliehoek and Naauwpoort, they honoured Kruger by naming it Clarens — after the Swiss village where he had died in exile.

Clarens is close to the Golden Gate Highlands National Park, and there are many examples of San rock-art to be seen in the area.

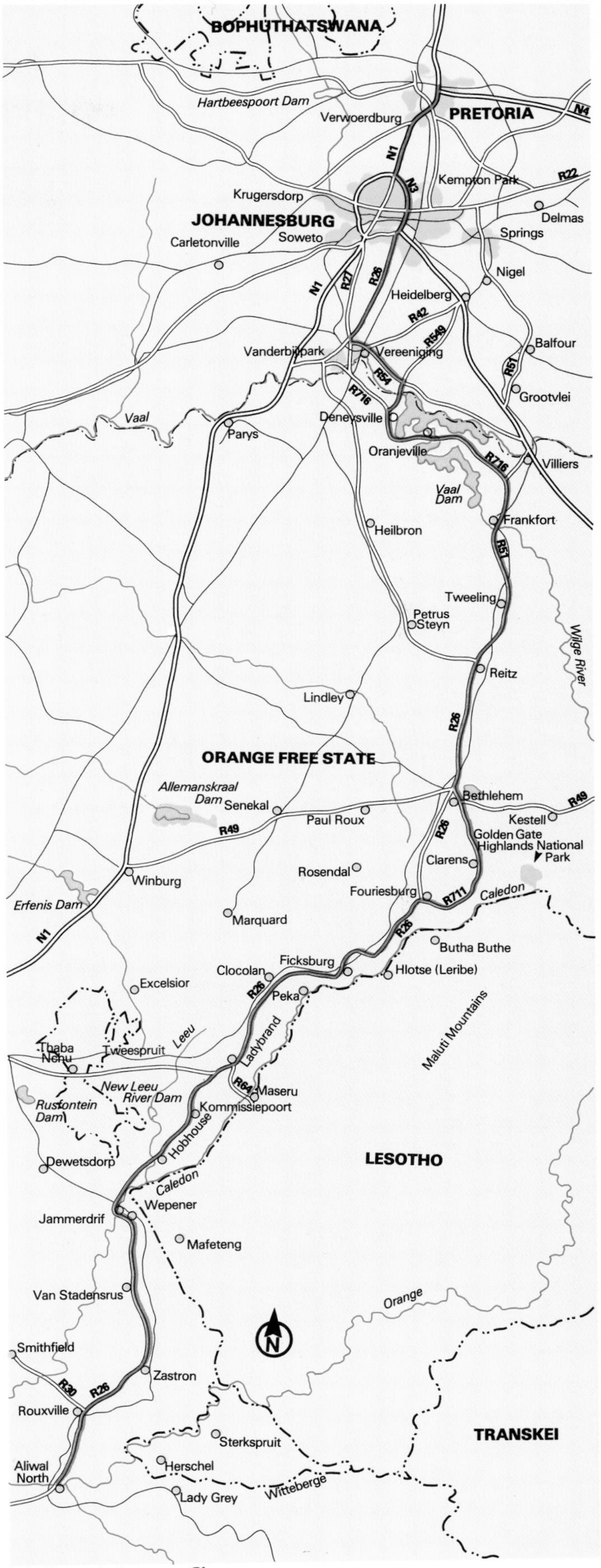

Left: *San paintings near Clarens.*

Meandering across the wide open spaces of the Karoo to the Breë River valley and the fairest Cape

South-west of Aliwal North we cross the Great Karoo — a seemingly inhospitable area, yet home to many plants, birds and antelope. Then we head through the fertile Langkloof valley to the Little Karoo, kingdom of the ostrich, and on to the rich Breë River valley. The road finally climbs over Du Toit's Kloof Pass to reach Cape Town.

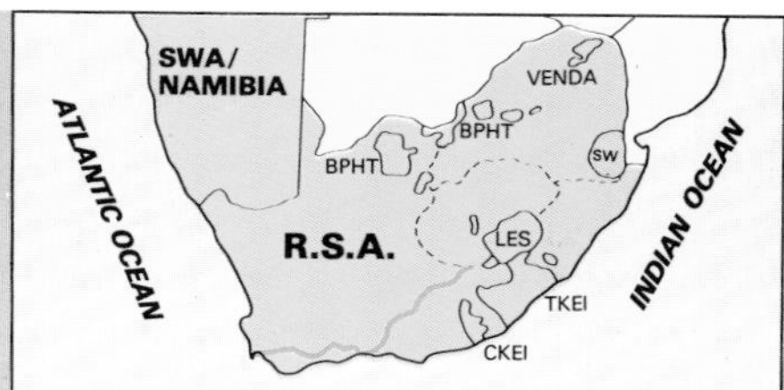

Aliwal North Municipality Barkly St, Aliwal North 5530 Tel. (0551) 2441
Graaff-Reinet Information Reinet Museum, Church St, Graaff-Reinet 6280 Tel. (0491) 23801
Oudtshoorn Publicity Office Civic Centre, Voortrekker Rd, Oudtshoorn 6620 Tel. (04431) 2228
AA Office AA House, 7 Martin Hammerschlag Way, Cape Town 8001 Tel. (021) 211550

Aliwal North - Graaff-Reinet - Uniondale - Oudtshoorn - Robertson - Worcester - **Cape Town** - **(1070—1090km)**

TURN WEST OUT OF Aliwal North's Somerset Street into Grey Street. This leads into Robinson Road, which becomes the R58 for Burgersdorp. The Stormberg range soon becomes visible, with an outlying spur on your left known as Dreunberg (roar mountain) because of the thunder that is sometimes a feature of the area.

You cross the Stormberg River 37km from Aliwal North, and 16,7km later you reach the historic town of Burgersdorp. You enter the town on Piet Retief Street, which takes you downhill and under the railway bridge. Immediately after the bridge on your right is a well-preserved blockhouse dating from the Anglo-Boer War and known locally as the Brandwag (sentinel). On your left 600m beyond the railway bridge you pass the garden of the civic centre, containing the town's historic Taal Monuments (see pages 214-5).

At the T-junction, turn left into Taylor Street, then take the second road to the right, and turn half-left for 'Steynsburg'. Note your kms as you pass under the railway bridge on the outskirts of the town.

After 36,5km turn right at the T-junction onto the R56 for Steynsburg. Roughly 31km later you enter Steynsburg, the centre of a rugged sheep-farming district noted for merino-breeding. Since the completion of the Orange-Fish River Tunnel, increasingly large tracts have been farmed under irrigation.

Steynsburg to Aberdeen

Continue through Steynsburg on the R56 for Middelburg. Almost 5km beyond Steynsburg, as you crest the first hill out of the town, there is a gravel road on your right that leads after 12,5km to the restored farmhouse of Bulhoek (see below).

17,5km beyond the turn-off to Bulhoek you pass between two prominent hills that flank the R56 — on your right is Koffiebus (coffee chest) and on your left is Teebus (tea chest). The small settlement of Teebus is at the outlet of the Orange-Fish River Tunnel (see pages 214-5).

Roughly 77km from Steynsburg, you reach Rosmead, and after another 10km you enter Middelburg. Keep driving into the centre of town, and then turn left into Meintjies Street. Follow this road out of town as it becomes the R57 for Graaff-Reinet.

Roughly 38km from Middelburg the road begins the climb up Lootsberg Pass, reaching the summit of 1785m after a further 4km. A parking area on your right just beyond the summit offers superb views over the Karoo plains, as does another site on your left within the next 1km. (During winter this pass may be closed by snowfalls.)

Continue on the R57, cross the Sundays River, and pass the R61 to Cradock on your left. 66km from Middelburg the road descends the Naudesberg Pass to the plain below.

You cross the Sundays River a second time, and 5,5km later you will see the Andries Pretorius monument on the hillside on your right. (A gravel road on your right after a further 1km leads to the monument, to the historic gunpowder store, to the Union Monument, and to a site with fine views over the historic town of Graaff-Reinet.)

Continue on the R57 into Graaff-Reinet (see pages 240-1). Remain on the R57 through the town, with its many interesting old buildings,

Towering Boland mountains close in around the road through Du Toit's Kloof.

DU TOIT'S KLOOF PASS

This mountain pass takes its name from Francois du Toit, a Huguenot settler who farmed near Dal Josafat in 1692. Du Toit, however, did not attempt to build a road — although a cattle path was mentioned fairly early (possibly one used by Khoikhoi of the Hawequa tribe).

Another farmer, Detlef Schönfeldt, later obtained funds and assistance from local farmers, and started a rough wagon road in the 1820s. A comment on this road was that 'one false step would plunge the traveller into eternity'. The first tar road was opened in 1949.

BREË RIVER VALLEY

Portuguese mariners who passed the mouth of this river around 1500 named it Rio de Nazaret. Dutch settlers later changed the name to Breede (broad), which became the Afrikaans Breë. The river rises in the Ceres basin and, over millenia, has cut a deep gorge through the barrier of mountains, along the route now followed by the attractive Michell's Pass road.

Joined by its major tributaries, the Hex, the Riviersonderend and the Kingna, the Breë supplies large town dams, as well as irrigation systems along its fertile valley. It flows into the Indian Ocean south-east of Swellendam at Witsand, where the forgotten harbour of Port Beaufort once stood. Upstream, at Malgas, the river is still crossed by a pont — the last one that operates regularly in South Africa.

The restored Trekker home, Bulhoek.

Cultivated fields near Oudtshoorn.

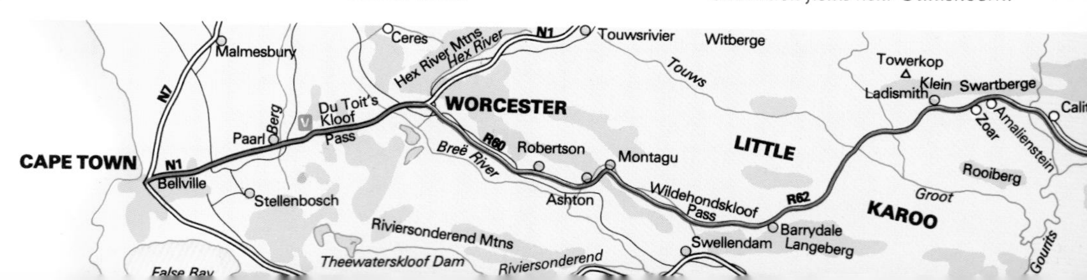

and note your kms on the south side as you pass the R63 on your left to Port Elizabeth.

42 km from Graaff-Reinet you cross the Camdeboo River, and 4 km later on your left is the low hill known as Gordon's Kop (see below).

Some distance before you reach Aberdeen, you can already see the spire of the town's Dutch Reformed Church, reputedly the tallest in the country. Go left at the fork that takes you into this picturesque old town (see pages 56-7).

Aberdeen to Ladismith

As you leave Aberdeen, note your kms where the bypass road joins in from your right. After 86 km through typical Great Karoo countryside, you cross the Groot River, with the wall of the Beervlei Dam on your right (there is a picnic site below the dam wall).

After a further 28 km you pass the R329 to Steytlerville on your left. You then pass two roads on your left into Willowmore — note your kms as you pass the second.

37 km later you pass a turn-off on your right that leads to Oudtshoorn via Barandas, and after a further 17 km you pass a second road similarly signposted. 2,4 km later you pass a road on your left into Uniondale. Note your kms as you pass a second turn-off to Uniondale roughly 3 km later. After 11,5 km you reach the top of the Potjiesberg (little pot mountain) Pass. Continue straight 2 km later past a turn-off to Joubertina and Port Elizabeth (the R62).

You now travel through the fertile Langkloof valley (see pages 56-7), and 25 km beyond Uniondale you cross the Keurbooms River. 500 m later you pass a road on your left signposted De Vlugt. (This picturesque drive leads to Knysna via Prince Alfred's Pass — but should be avoided in wet weather.)

Roughly 50 km later you pass a road on your left that leads past the village of Herold and over Montagu Pass to George. 8,7 km beyond this turn-off, go right at the fork to reach the 'ostrich capital' of Oudtshoorn after a further 31 km (see day drive, pages 254-7).

Leave Oudtshoorn by driving west on Voortrekker Street, which becomes the R62. Note your kms just outside the town opposite the R328 on your left (which leads to Mossel Bay via Robinson Pass). The road passes through typical Little Karoo landscape (see pages 56-7), and enters Calitzdorp after 46 km.

A road on your left in the town of Calitzdorp leads for some 25 km to a hot springs resort on the Olifants River.

Continue through Calitzdorp on the R62. 4 km beyond the town you enter the winding Huisrivier Pass, with its walls of intricately folded sandstone strata, and secluded valleys irrigated from the Huis and Gamka rivers.

26,7 km beyond Calitzdorp, you pass the mission village of Amalienstein on your left (see pages 262-3). The village lies opposite the road that leads to the spectacular Seweweekspoort Pass. After a further 3 km you pass another mission village, Zoar, also on your left.

8 km later you pass a turn-off on your right to Hoeko, birthplace of the poet C J Langenhoven, and after a further 10 km the road enters Ladismith. The great cleft peak of Towerkop can be seen half to your right.

Ladismith and the Breë River Valley

West of Ladismith you pass through irrigated fields. After 75 km you reach Barrydale, and a further 23 km brings you to the Wildehondskloof Pass, which offers good views over fields and the widening river valley.

After a further 37 km you reach the old-world town of Montagu (see pages 264-5). A few kms west of Montagu, you pass through Cogmanskloof Pass, and its tunnel.

You pass through the small town of Ashton, and shortly afterwards reach the 'muscadel capital', Robertson (see day drive, pages 270-1).

Continue through Robertson to Worcester. Turn left at the T-junction in the town, then right at the first robot-controlled intersection. At the T-junction just outside the town, turn left onto the N1.

About 25 km later you reach the start of Du Toit's Kloof Pass (see opposite). The road passes through a tunnel 11 km later. Just over 500 m beyond the summit there is a viewsite on your right with outstanding vistas of the Berg River valley. (A new toll road and tunnel are to be opened in 1988.)

After 15 km winding down the mountainside, you reach the start of the double carriageway outside Paarl. The road passes extensive vineyards and farmlands before reaching Cape Town ●

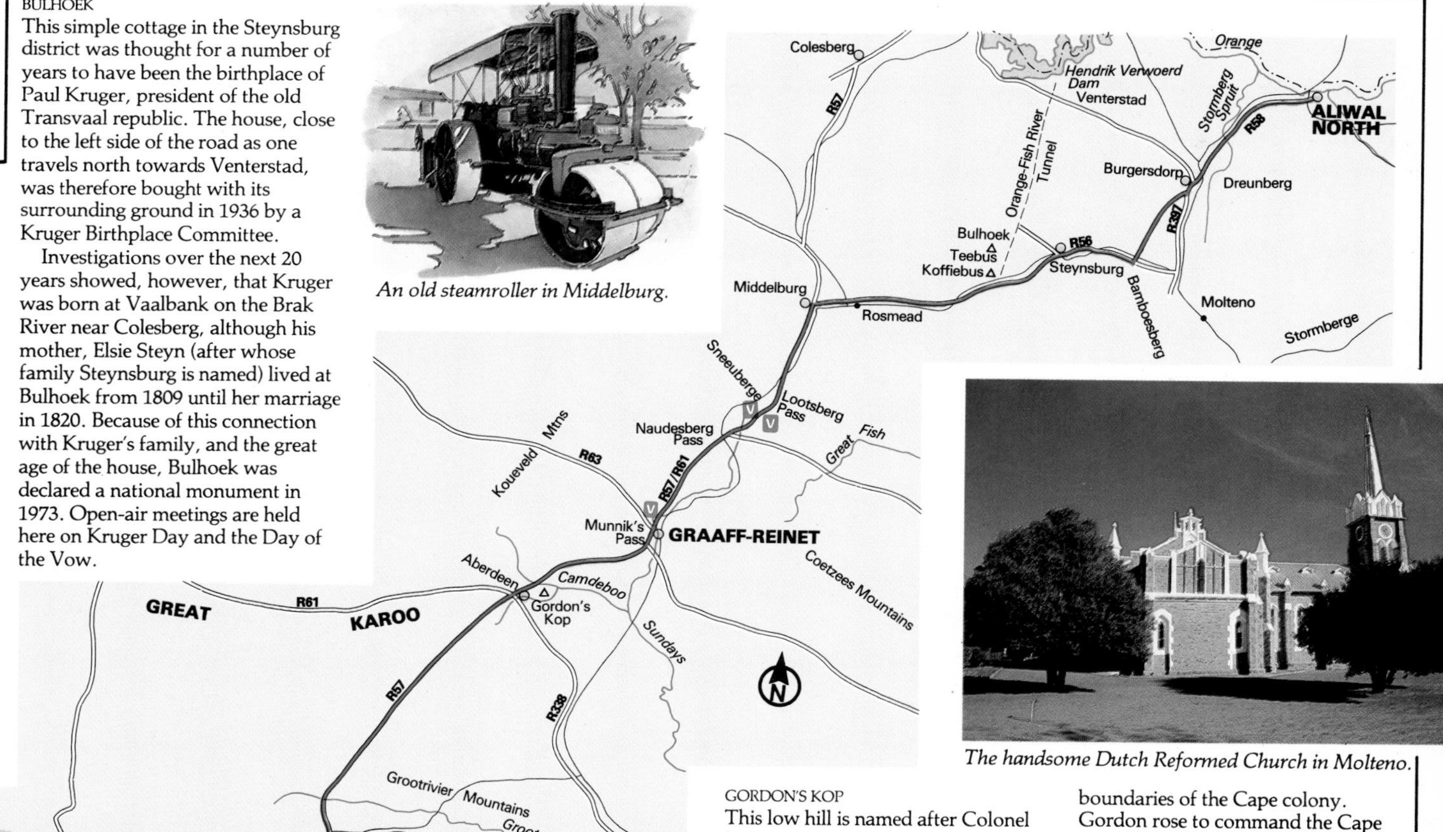

BULHOEK

This simple cottage in the Steynsburg district was thought for a number of years to have been the birthplace of Paul Kruger, president of the old Transvaal republic. The house, close to the left side of the road as one travels north towards Venterstad, was therefore bought with its surrounding ground in 1936 by a Kruger Birthplace Committee.

Investigations over the next 20 years showed, however, that Kruger was born at Vaalbank on the Brak River near Colesberg, although his mother, Elsie Steyn (after whose family Steynsburg is named) lived at Bulhoek from 1809 until her marriage in 1820. Because of this connection with Kruger's family, and the great age of the house, Bulhoek was declared a national monument in 1973. Open-air meetings are held here on Kruger Day and the Day of the Vow.

An old steamroller in Middelburg.

The handsome Dutch Reformed Church in Molteno.

GORDON'S KOP

This low hill is named after Colonel Robert Jacob Gordon, a soldier and explorer of Scots-Dutch descent who climbed it in 1778 while he was part of an expedition to determine the boundaries of the Cape colony. Gordon rose to command the Cape garrison but committed suicide in a fit of despair over the surrender of the Cape during the first British occupation.

South from the Orange Free State through the border country to East London

Motorists travelling from the Transvaal to East London should use this route for the second part of their journey. If driving south on the N1 (pages 32-33), you turn onto this route immediately after passing Bloemfontein. If driving south on the more scenic 'mountain route' via Ladybrand (pages 38-39), you join this route at Rouxville.

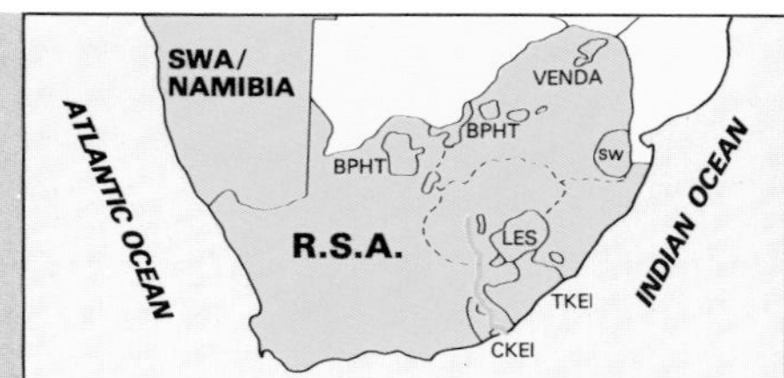

AA Office AA House, 56 Church Street, Bloemfontein 9301 Tel. (051) 76191
AA Office AA House, 3A Terminus Street, East London 5201 Tel. (0431) 21271

Bloemfontein (570 km) - Rouxville (400 km) - Aliwal North - Queenstown - King William's Town - **East London**

THE N1 BY-PASSES Bloemfontein by swinging to the west and curving around the city. As you travel south on this Western Bypass, take the last of the six exits to Bloemfontein, signposted 'Ferreira/R30/Reddersburg'. About 3 km later you reach a T-junction with the R30, which is a southern extension of Bloemfontein's Church Street. Turn right onto the R30, noting your kms.

The road runs through flat fields of maize and sunflowers to reach the small town of Reddersburg (town of the Saviour) after 49 km (see below). On your left, in the main street, you will see a white obelisk. This is known as the General de Wet or Klein Paardekraal Monument, and commemorates the last occasion on which the Boer general addressed a public gathering on the traditional 'feesdag' (festival day) of 16 December, in 1920. De Wet and each member of his audience placed a stone on a pile to symbolise the building of unity.

Continue through Reddersburg, noting your kms on the outskirts of the town as you pass the R717 to Edenburg on your right. The road sweeps on across enormous plains, with views to the left of the distant mountains of Lesotho. After 67 km you reach Smithfield, established in 1848 and named after the Cape governor Sir Harry Smith. The town was originally laid out on the farm Waterval, some 24 km to the west, but was moved to its present site because of a water shortage. Outside the magistrate's court you can see 'Ou Grietjie' (old Margaret), a muzzle-loading cannon used in the war against the Sotho in 1865.

Leave Smithfield by turning left as you enter the town into President Hoffman Street — which becomes the R30 to Rouxville. The road now undulates between large, rocky ridges, and you can see typical Karoo 'koppies' in the distance. Roughly 12 km after leaving Smithfield you cross the Caledon River, and 34,5 km from Smithfield, immediately before you enter Rouxville, you pass the R26 to Zastron on your left. (Motorists who have travelled south on the 'mountain route' via Bethlehem and Ladybrand (see pages 38-39) join our route at this point — after driving roughly 30 km from Zastron on the R26, turn left onto the R30.)

Rouxville to Queenstown

The R30 becomes Voortrekker Street as it passes through the outskirts of Rouxville (see below). Note your kms as you cross the railway line roughly 1 km south of the town. After driving 15,5 km from here you pass on your right a sign that reads 'Beestekraalnek'. On your left at this point, set back a few metres from the road, there is a stone monument erected by burghers of the Rouxville and Zastron com-

The De Wet Memorial in Reddersburg commemorates the great Boer General.

'TOWN OF THE SAVIOUR'

Much of the ground on which the present town of Reddersburg stands was once owned by the Dutch Reformed Church, which drew up a series of articles that residents were to abide by. This included an undertaking to live 'restfully and peacefully' and to abstain from the use of 'vexatious or reprehensible words'. Unrepentant wrong-doers had to leave town within eight days.

During the Sotho war of 1865 the inhabitants fortified their church with sandbags, but the expected attack did not occur. The occasion led to the building of a 'kruithuis' or powder magazine, which still stands. A monument to local burghers who fell in the Anglo-Boer War stands in the grounds of the church.

ROUXVILLE

In 1856 the Orange Free State Volksraad (parliament) authorised President Boshoff to establish a new town close to the Cape border in order to smooth out 'irregularities' in the post handled at Aliwal North. The town was named after the Reverend P Roux of Smithfield, in gratitude for his offer to conduct religious services for the fledgeling congregation. Rouxville lies at the heart of an area noted for cattle and wool farming. Horses are bred in the district and the Kalkoenkrans Dam offers good sport for the angler.

The Caledon River between Smithfield and Rouxville.

GERMAN SETTLERS

The many German place-names along this route — such as Stutterheim, Berlin and Breidbach — recall the King's German Legion, which fought as part of the British Army during the Napoleonic wars, and was raised again during the Crimean War of 1854-56. Under the command of General Baron von Stutterheim, a number of these legionnaires and their families were landed at East London in 1857 in order to farm the recently-pacified frontier and to establish fortified posts. Being professional soldiers, they experienced great difficulties in adapting to the life of agriculturalists, and the Governor, Sir George Grey, later arranged for the immigration of several hundred labourers from Germany to help them. There are monuments to the German Settlers in East London and King William's Town.

mandos as they set out to invade the Cape Colony at the outbreak of the Anglo-Boer War in October 1899.

31 km after leaving Rouxville you cross the General Hertzog Bridge over the Orange River and enter Aliwal North (see day-drives, pages 212-5). Turn left into Barkly Street, then turn right at the traffic lights into Somerset Street, and proceed straight through the town. Note your kms as you pass a road on your left signposted 'Warmbronne 1 km'.

After leaving Aliwal North the road enters fairly hilly country, with the Witteberg range visible on your left, and the foothills of the Stormberg range to your right. After driving 40 km from the 'Warmbronne' sign there is a granite monument set among trees on your right — the plaque records that this farm was formerly occupied by Commandant Lourens Wepener, who was killed in an unsuccessful assault on the Sotho stronghold of Thaba Bosiu in 1865 and after whom the town of Wepener is named.

Roughly 11 km after this monument you pass through the village of Jamestown, then the road traverses the scenic Penhoek Pass over the Stormberg range — and some 50 km later you enter Queenstown on Cathcart Road (see day-drive, pages 216-7).

Queenstown to East London

Drive around the Hexagon in the centre of Queenstown and continue on Cathcart Road, which becomes the R30 again for East London. Note your kms as you cross the bridge over the Komani River. South of Queenstown you pass through more hilly countryside, covered with acacia thorn trees. After 23,6 km you cross the Imvani River, and 4 km later you cross the Umlelo River. At 33 km you cross the Black Kei River, with the old bridge visible to your left, and at 39 km you cross the Waqu River. After passing the R351 to Whittlesea (mis-named after Sir Harry Smith's birthplace of Whittlesey, England) the road climbs Hobbshoogte, offering wide views of the surrounding hills, to reach the summit of Windvogelsnek — before reaching Cathcart (see day-drive, pages 218-9).

Drive straight through Cathcart, passing on your right the R345 to Hogsback and Fort Beaufort. The road now leads through rolling, grassy hills and the pine plantations of Fort Cunynghame State Forest, before winding downhill into Stutterheim. Continue straight through Stutterheim, and note your kms as you pass on your left the R348 to Kei Road.

After Stutterheim the road descends through maizefields to the Kubusie River, then it begins to climb again, with views on both sides of fields, forests, and hillsides dotted with traditional settlements. After twice crossing the Buffalo River, and then the Balazi River, the road enters the fascinating old frontier town of King William's Town on Alexandra Road (see pages 210-211).

Continue straight through the town, passing on your right the R347 to Zwelitsha and Kidd's Beach. After a short distance the road becomes a double-carriageway — you are now on the N2, which runs the whole length of the east coast. Roughly 43 km from King William's Town you reach the outskirts of East London. Follow the exit signs for East London if you wish to drive into the city ●

An attractive old building in Cathcart.

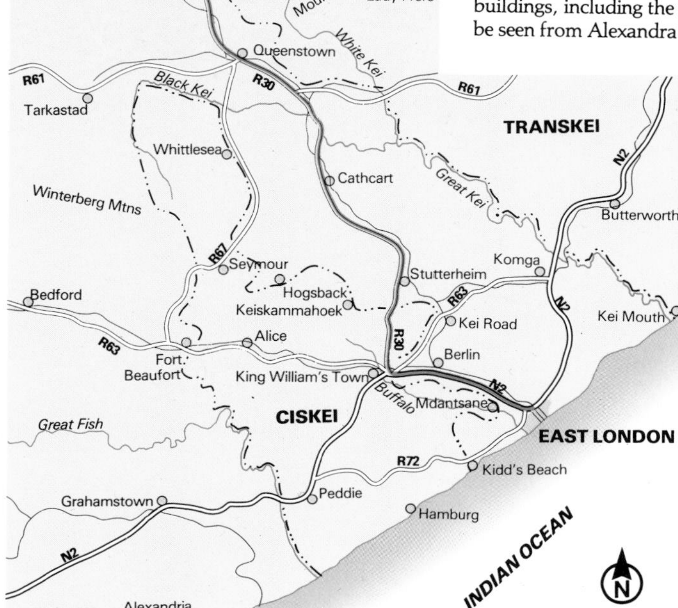

KING WILLIAM'S TOWN

Originally a mission station established by John Brownlee, King William's Town was created as the capital of the newly formed Province of Queen Adelaide after the frontier war of 1835. Brownlee, who had already been there for 10 years, was incensed to find that his home had been commandeered as the residence for the Province's governor, Colonel Harry Smith. However, official British policy led to the abandonment of the province and the withdrawal of the troops, and Brownlee's home was returned to him.

Shortly afterwards King William's Town became the capital of British Kaffraria, created in 1847 after yet another frontier war, and served as a garrison town for many years. Many attractive buildings, including the Kaffrarian Museum, can be seen from Alexandra Road (see pages 210-211).

The old mission building in King William's Town is now a museum.

To Port Elizabeth via Graaff-Reinet and the Sundays River Valley

Motorists travelling on the N1 from the Transvaal to Port Elizabeth should use this route to complete their journey. The first part of the trip, from the Transvaal to Colesberg, is described on pages 32-3. This second part leads south from Colesberg through the Karoo to Graaff-Reinet, then on through the Sundays River Valley to Port Elizabeth.

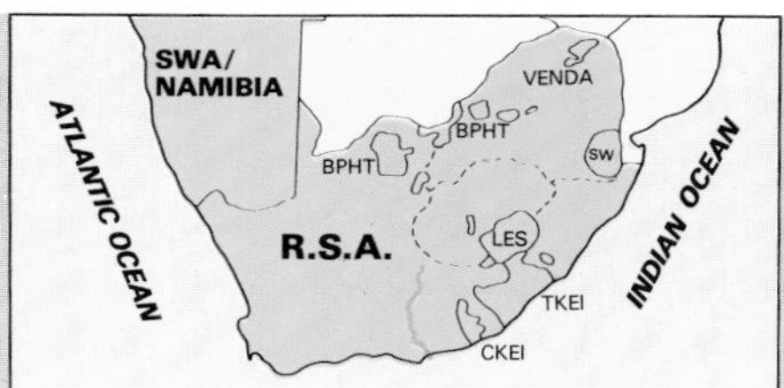

Colesberg Municipality Church Street, Colesberg 5980 Tel. (05852) 20
Graaff-Reinet Information Reinet Museum, Church St, Graaff-Reinet 6280 Tel. (0491) 23801
AA Office 2 Granville Road, Greenacres, Port Elizabeth 6001 Tel. (041) 341313

Colesberg — Middelburg — Graaff-Reinet — Jansenville — Uitenhage — **Port Elizabeth (460—470 km)**

As you travel south on the N1, you pass the town of Colesberg on your left. At the end of the by-pass around the town, turn left onto the R57, noting your kms. 3,4 km after turning onto the R57 you pass a gravel road on your left leading to Oorlogspoort (war gorge) — the name recalls an incident during the early days of colonial settlement when a band of stock farmers in the region clashed here with San hunters.

After 44 km on the R57 you cross the Noupoort (narrow gorge) Stream, in a region of low hills and flattish ridges. 5 km later you reach the important rail junction of Noupoort (see opposite). Note your kms again as you pass the road into town on your right.

3 km later you pass large railway sheds on your right, after which the road begins to descend, winding among hills and offering panoramic views over the Karoo plains. At 18,2 km you pass the R32 to Hanover and De Aar on your right, and shortly after this you can see ahead of you the Renosterberg (rhinoceros mountain), a spur of the Sneeuwberg (snow mountain) range.

Middelburg to Graaff-Reinet
37 km after Noupoort you pass on your left the entrance to the Grootfontein College of Agriculture. Immediately after this you pass the town of Middelburg (see opposite) on your right, and the R56 to Rosmead and Steynsburg on your left. You cross the Droë and Klein Brak rivers, and 5 km after passing Middelburg you reach a junction. Keep right here to stay on the R57. (The road leading left is the R32.)

30 km later the road begins the short ascent of the Lootsberg Pass, which in winter may be closed for short periods by snowfalls. The 1789 m summit of the pass is followed by viewsites on both sides of the road — looking down over the great plains towards Graaff-Reinet. As the road descends, you can see on your right the 2502 m Kompasberg (compass mountain), the highest peak in South Africa outside the Drakensberg range. It was named during a 1778 expedition into the interior led by Governor van Plettenberg.

After descending from the summit of the Lootsberg Pass you cross the Sundays River, and 2 km later you pass a gravel road on your right leading to Nieu Bethesda and Bethesda Road railway station. Immediately after this you pass the R61 to Cradock on your left, then the road descends the Naudesberg Pass. From the bottom of this pass the road runs fairly level, with wide views of plains and mountains. Ahead of you the double dome of Spandau Kop towers above Graaff-Reinet.

As you approach Graaff-Reinet you pass on your right the farm 'Wellwood', housing a world-renowned fossil collection, and later, on your left, the farm 'Pretoriuskloof' — once the home of Voortrekker leader Andries Pretorius. Pretorius is commemorated by a granite statue on the right of the road just before the last short descent into Graaff-Reinet (see pages 240-3), roughly 105 km after passing Middelburg.

Graaff-Reinet to Port Elizabeth
Drive through the historic town of Graaff-Reinet, following the signs for Jansenville. You leave the town on Church Street, which changes its name to College Road. On the outskirts of the town turn left onto the R63 for Port Elizabeth. Immediately after turning you cross the Sundays River again, and soon you will see ahead of you, slightly to your left, the Tandjiesberg (little teeth mountain).

Roughly 25 km after Graaff-Reinet the road divides — the R63 leads left to Pearston and Somerset East, and the R75 continues to Jansenville. Continue straight ahead here on the R75 for Jansenville.

Into the Noorsveld
You now cross wide, flat grasslands, dotted with thornbush and an increasing number of aloes. 65 km after leaving Graaff-Reinet you pass through Ravelskloof, and enter a corner of the Karoo known as the Noorsveld — the name comes from 'noorsdoring' (hedgehog), which is the local name for the spiky *Euphorbia caerulescens* that grows in the area.

Roughly 13 km after Ravelskloof you drive through the town of Jansenville. Note your kms as you cross the Sundays River once again on the outskirts of the town. Soon after crossing the river you pass on your right the R337 to Klipplaat and Steytlerville. You now pass through a stretch of flat, bushy country, but soon have attractive views of hills, fields and river gorges, as you pass through the Klein Winterhoek mountain range.

92 km after leaving Jansenville you pass on your left the R336 to Kirkwood and the Addo Elephant National Park. A little over 17 km after this you cross the Bezuidenhouts River, and roughly 13 km later you cross the Coega (shallow) River. You reach Uitenhage (see opposite) 131 km after leaving Jansenville, and from here a freeway leads into Port Elizabeth ●

Dutch Reformed Church in Jansenville.

A TOWN BUILT ON WHEELS
Uitenhage is renowned as a motor manufacturing centre, and also has extensive railway workshops. There is a steam-transport museum at the town's railway station, and two other interesting museums not far away — one in the old Drostdy, and an interesting cultural museum just outside the town in the Cuyler Manor (see pages 230-1).

It was the American-born Jacob Glen Cuyler who established Uitenhage in 1810, six years after the district was created in 1804. A plaque on a house at 34 Cuyler Street records that this was the birthplace, in 1826, of Joseph Petrus Crowe — who in 1857, during the Indian Mutiny, became the first South African to be awarded the Victoria Cross.

Shaded shopfront at Jansenville.

A train puffs its way towards Noupoort.

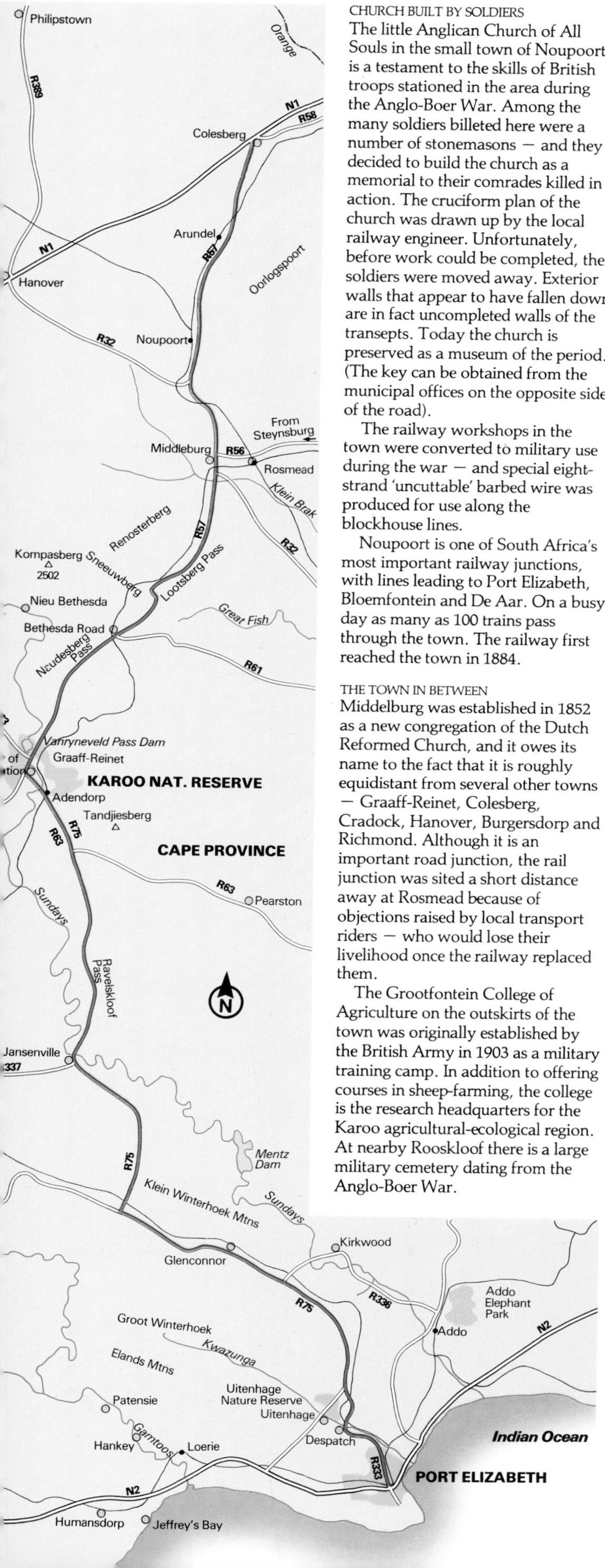

CHURCH BUILT BY SOLDIERS

The little Anglican Church of All Souls in the small town of Noupoort is a testament to the skills of British troops stationed in the area during the Anglo-Boer War. Among the many soldiers billeted here were a number of stonemasons — and they decided to build the church as a memorial to their comrades killed in action. The cruciform plan of the church was drawn up by the local railway engineer. Unfortunately, before work could be completed, the soldiers were moved away. Exterior walls that appear to have fallen down are in fact uncompleted walls of the transepts. Today the church is preserved as a museum of the period. (The key can be obtained from the municipal offices on the opposite side of the road).

The railway workshops in the town were converted to military use during the war — and special eight-strand 'uncuttable' barbed wire was produced for use along the blockhouse lines.

Noupoort is one of South Africa's most important railway junctions, with lines leading to Port Elizabeth, Bloemfontein and De Aar. On a busy day as many as 100 trains pass through the town. The railway first reached the town in 1884.

THE TOWN IN BETWEEN

Middelburg was established in 1852 as a new congregation of the Dutch Reformed Church, and it owes its name to the fact that it is roughly equidistant from several other towns — Graaff-Reinet, Colesberg, Cradock, Hanover, Burgersdorp and Richmond. Although it is an important road junction, the rail junction was sited a short distance away at Rosmead because of objections raised by local transport riders — who would lose their livelihood once the railway replaced them.

The Grootfontein College of Agriculture on the outskirts of the town was originally established by the British Army in 1903 as a military training camp. In addition to offering courses in sheep-farming, the college is the research headquarters for the Karoo agricultural-ecological region. At nearby Rooskloof there is a large military cemetery dating from the Anglo-Boer War.

Uncompleted transept wall of All Souls Church, Noupoort.

Van Ryneveld's Pass Dam in the Karoo Nature Reserve near Graaff-Reinet.

End of the road — King's Beach and pool on the coast of Port Elizabeth.

Across the dry plains of Bushmanland to the emerald banks of the Orange River

This first leg of the 'northern Cape' route from Cape Town to the Transvaal leads through the long-settled wheatlands of the south-western Cape, traverses the Olifants River valley and Vanrhyn's Pass, then heads north across the desolate plains of Bushmanland to the life-giving Orange River and the oasis-like town of Upington.

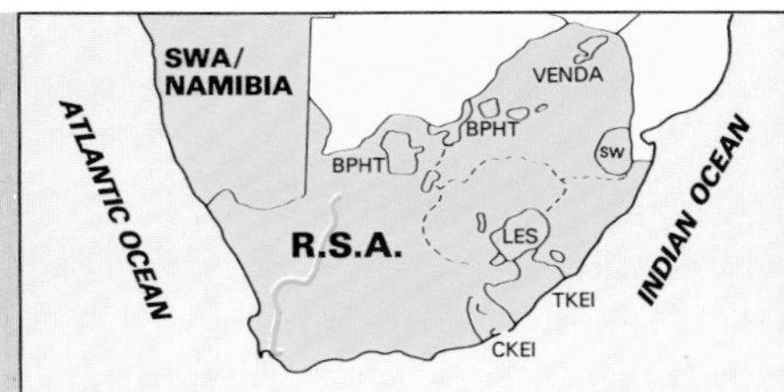

AA Office AA House, 7 Martin Hammerschlag Way, Cape Town 8001 Tel. (021) 211550
Calvinia Museum Kerkstraat 44, Calvinia 8190 Tel. (02772) 43
Keimoes Information Centre Keimoes Municipality, Hoofstraat, Keimoes 8860 Tel. (05492) 26
Upington Tourist Bureau Library Building, Market Square, Upington 8800 Tel. (0541) 6911 ext 2151

Cape Town - Citrusdal - Clanwilliam - Nieuwoudtville - Calvinia - Kenhardt - **Upington** (840 km)

LEAVE CAPE TOWN ON the N1, and 11 km after passing the harbour area take Exit 4 for the N7 to Malmesbury. The N7 quickly becomes a 'country road' through wheatfields and dairy farms, and roughly 19 km along it there are good views of the Atlantic on your left. Pass Malmesbury, and about 3 km later stop on the side of the road where it tops the long rise — for a fine view back over the wheatfields to Table Mountain.

You are now travelling through the Swartland (black land), so named by early explorers because of the dark renosterbos that originally blanketed the area. It is now one of the country's principal wheat-producing districts, and in Moorreesburg, which you pass roughly 34 km after Malmesbury, there is a Wheat Museum devoted to this valuable crop.

33 km after Moorreesburg, still on the N7, you pass the town of Piketberg, the site of a military outpost established in the 17th century. Note your kms as you pass on your left the R366 that leads into the town.

33 km after Piketberg the road begins to climb the Piekenierskloof Pass over the Olifants River Mountains (see pages 298-9). There is a fine viewsite 37 km from Piketberg, and another 3 km later — both offering vistas over seas of wheatfields stretching to the horizon.

You reach the summit of the pass at 519 m above sea level, and as you begin the descent the landscape changes dramatically. The Olifants River has cut a wide valley through the Kouebokkeveld and Cedarberg mountain ranges, and the dark green citrus plantations that cover the valley floor soon come into view.

Citrusdal to Vanrhynsdorp

You pass Citrusdal on your right some 6 km after the summit of the pass (see day drive, pages 298-9). As you continue towards Clanwilliam the surrounding mountains and rock formations become increasingly rugged. The road leads alongside the Olifants River, then along the western side of the Clanwilliam Dam. 500 m before you reach the dam wall there is a shaded picnic site on your right, with views of the mountains reflected in the calm water of the dam. Opposite the dam wall there is another shaded picnic site.

Note your kms as you pass on your right the R364 to Clanwilliam (see day drives, pages 300-1). 55 km later you pass the village of Klawer on your left. 6 km after this you cross the Wiedouw River, and 22 km from Klawer the Troe Troe River. Immediately after crossing the Troe Troe River turn right onto the R27, and a few hundred metres later turn left at the T-junction to enter Vanrhynsdorp. On your right you pass the town's museum, which is housed in the old jail of 1895.

Turn left at the T-junction with Troe Troe Street, then turn right into Kerkstraat. Note your kms as you then turn left into Residential Street — which leads out of town.

Vanrhyn's Pass and Nieuwoudtville

The vegetation now becomes extremely sparse and scrubby, with thin lines of thorn trees edging the river beds. 25 km after leaving Vanrhynsdorp you can see Vanrhyn's Pass ascending the Bokkeveld Mountains ahead of you, and you begin the ascent roughly 10,5 km later. You soon pass two viewsites on your left, but the most spectacular views are from a parking area on your right which you reach after climbing for 5,7 km, and from where you can look out over the vast and inhospitable plains known as the Knersvlakte. 'Kners' is an Afrikaans verb meaning 'to gnash', and one can imagine that there must have been much gnashing of teeth during the early exploration of this seemingly waterless and endless landscape. 1,5 km later you reach the summit of the pass (at 820 m) and after a further 1 km you come to a sheltered picnic site under pine trees.

After passing on your left the road to Loeriesfontein, you reach the outskirts of Nieuwoudtville (see below), set amid fertile irrigated fields. Except for these small patches of irrigated land

MOUNTAIN OF THE LITTLE RED ONION
The town of Calvinia, founded in 1848 and named after the religious reformer John Calvin, lies at the centre of an administrative district equal in size to the entire Orange Free State. A former synagogue in Kerkstraat (No 44) now houses the town's museum, which has as its theme 'life in the Hantam'. One curious exhibit is a sheep that was lost for several years and so went unclipped — the massive-looking creature must have given its eventual discoverers quite a fright.

The Hantam is an extensive high-lying plateau to the north of the town, renowned for its profusion of spring wildflowers. There is some doubt as to the origin of the name 'Hantam', but the most likely explanation is that this is a corruption of a compound Khoikhoi term meaning 'mountain of the little red onion'.

Donkey power on the national road north of Cape Town.

The Doring River waterfall, 5 km north of Nieuwoudtville.

NIEUWOUDTVILLE
Sometimes referred to as 'the boland of the Karoo', this charming little town of cool sandstone buildings offers a welcome haven to travellers who have journeyed across the hot and barren Knersvlakte. Gladioli and other bulb-plants flourish in this area, and rooibos (red bush) tea is an important local crop. Five kilometres north of the town, just off the road to Loeriesfontein, the Doring (thorn) River plunges over a dramatic 30 m waterfall — a memorable sight after particularly good rains have fallen in the region.

the countryside here appears desolate for much of the year, but the region is renowned for its springtime displays of wildflowers that paint the entire landscape in brilliant colours.

38 km after passing through Nieuwoudtville you will see on your right a stone memorial that commemorates the handing over of weapons by a Boer commando — several weeks after the formal ending of the Anglo-Boer War. Built into the memorial are a Mauser rifle and bandolier of the period.

Calvinia to Upington

The road crosses the Oorlogskloof (war ravine) River, and enters Calvinia 71 km after leaving Nieuwoudtville. Turn left into Kerkstraat, where the Calvinia Museum is housed in a former synagogue of 1920 (see opposite). There are hotels in Calvinia that provide lunch.

Turn right out of Kerkstraat into Hofmeyrstraat, then turn left at the T-junction into Stasieweg. Turn right almost immediately into Paul Kruger Street — which leads out of town.

Turn left after 22 km for Brandvlei and Upington. The road, still the R27, now runs straight across the stony flats of Bushmanland, passing through the village of Brandvlei roughly 125 km from the turn. (Brandvlei's neo-Gothic Dutch Reformed Church dates from 1905 and is a national monument.)

The next 140 km stretch from Brandvlei to Kenhardt crosses one of the driest districts in South Africa, including Grootvloer — a particularly extensive sand-flat or 'pan'. Roughly 30 km from Brandvlei you pass a road on your right leading to Verneuk Pan, another large sand-flat that was the scene, in 1929, of Sir Malcolm Campbell's unsuccessful attempt to break the world land speed record in 'Bluebird I'. The word 'verneuk' means to deceive, and refers to the mirages that shimmer above the sun-baked ground throughout the heat of the day.

An increasingly common feature of the landscape as you travel further north are the enormous communal nests of social weaver birds — attached in most instances to telegraph poles because so few substantial trees can tolerate the dryness of the region.

Eventually the road crosses the Hartbees River and passes through Kenhardt, after which the appearance of the countryside begins to change — you are now entering the area where it is possible to irrigate the land with water drawn from the Orange River.

Roughly 72 km after Kenhardt you pass through Neilersdrif, just south of the Orange, and shortly after this you cross four narrow bridges over channels of the river.

2 km later the road enters the farming town of Keimoes. Keep straight at the traffic lights in Keimoes, and continue on the R27/64 for a further 37 km as it leads along the north bank of the Orange River to Upington. (While you are in this part of the country, you might consider the day-drive to the Augrabies Falls — see day drive, pages 310-1) ●

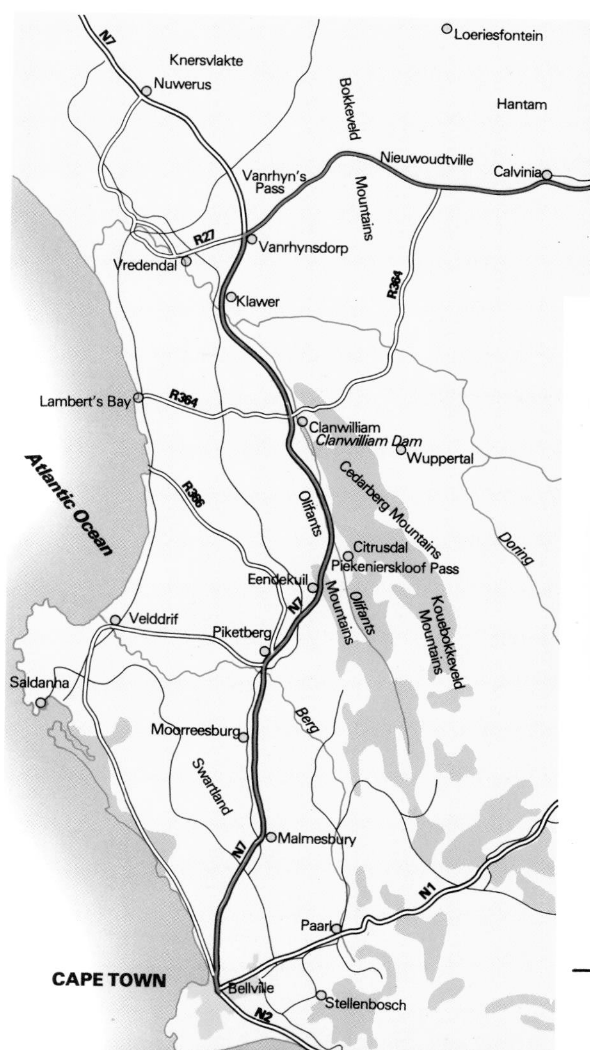

Social weaver nest on a telegraph pole.

THE KENHARDT 'MOUNTIES'

Early last century there were persistent clashes between stock farmers who had ventured north of the Orange River and the various peoples already settled there, especially the Korana. Eventually the stock farmers withdrew to the south bank of the river, and the Cape Government decided to protect its northern border by sending a magistrate and fifty mounted troopers into the region. The 'mounties' and the magistrate were based at what was then the extremely remote outpost of Kenhardt.

Clanwilliam Dam from Ramskop Nature Reserve.

BURNING HEART OF BUSHMANLAND

The small settlement of Brandvlei lies like an oasis in the heart of Bushmanland, roughly halfway between Calvinia and the Orange River. Its name, meaning 'fire marsh', is appropriate, suggesting days of unremitting heat. From salt pans just west of the town some 36 000 tons of salt are produced each year — the salty water is pumped 53 km to Sakrivier station to be processed.

Through the dune-country to Kuruman, Mafikeng and the Groot Marico district

The second part of this 'northern Cape' route from Cape Town to the southern Transvaal takes us across the sun-scorched plains of Gordonia to the oasis-town of Kuruman, then leads through the cattle-ranching country around Vryburg to the historic siege-town of Mafikeng and the dry but fertile farmlands of the south-western Transvaal.

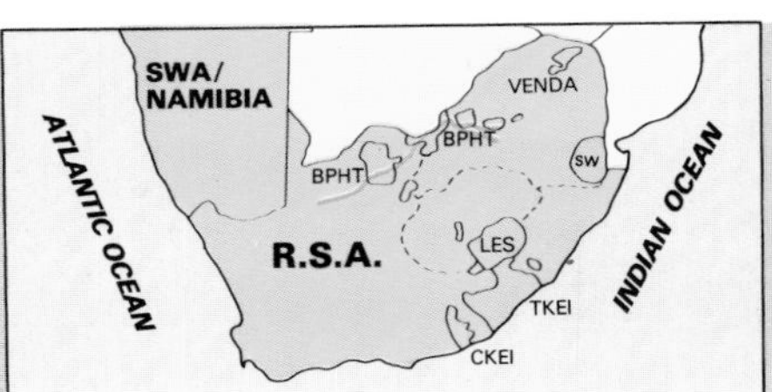

AA Office AA House, 13 New Main Street, Kimberley 8301 Tel. (0531) 25207
Kuruman Public Library Skoolstraat, Kuruman 8460 Tel. (01471) 21095
Mafikeng Museum Martin Street, Mafikeng 8670 Tel. (01401) 33051
AA Office AA House, 395 Schoeman Street, Pretoria 0002 Tel. (012) 283829
AA Office AA House, 66 De Korte Street, Braamfontein, Johannesburg 2001 Tel. (011) 4035700

Upington - Olifantshoek - Kuruman - Vryburg - Mafikeng - Zeerust - **Pretoria (910 km) Johannesburg (910 km)**

LEAVE UPINGTON BY driving north-east along Schröder Street, which becomes the R27. Note your kms as you pass under the railway bridge. The road stays fairly close to the Orange River for a little over 30 km, then veers away into the great plains of Gordonia — noted for the permanent calcreted sand dunes that undulate across the landscape, created by the prevailing winds in prehistoric times.

Minor roads lead off to places whose names reveal the character of the area — Grootdrink (big drink) commemorates the point at which thirsty travellers reached the Orange River; Pearson's Hunt records a hunting expedition at Gamateep Pan, some 80 km to the north. The inappropriate name 'England' was presumably bestowed by some homesick settler. 123 km after leaving Upington the road tops a hill, offering spacious views over the surrounding plains to distant mountain ranges.

Olifantshoek to Kuruman

Roughly 37 km after this you pass a road on your right to Beeshoek and Postmasburg, and ahead of you here you will see a mountain that is said to resemble the outline of an elephant's back, with the hindquarters to the right and the trunk stretched out to the left. 5 km beyond this junction the road enters Olifantshoek — said to be named, not after the mountain, but because elephant bones were found here long ago.

After passing through Olifantshoek, note your kms on the outskirts of the town as you pass a road on your left to Barton. After 22 km you reach a T-junction — turn left here, and pass a road on your left to Sishen 1 km later.

94 km after leaving Olifantshoek you enter Kuruman. To visit the Moffat Mission (see opposite) turn left into Voortrekker Street, and note your kms as you pass the town's information office on the corner of Voortrekker and Skoolstraat. After 4,2 km turn right into Moffat Avenue, and 100 m later turn left into Thompson Street. The entrance to the mission is on your right after 100 m.

After visiting the mission, turn left at the T-junction into Moffat Street, and turn right at the next T-junction 800 m later. On your right, between 3,2 km and 3,3 km from this last turn, you will see a large karee tree known as 'The Silent Witness' under which a pro-German rebel force on the way to German South West Africa accepted the town's surrender in 1914.

At the second robot-controlled intersection that you reach (a T-junction) turn left to continue on your journey. The powerful freshwater spring known as the Eye of Kuruman is on your right immediately after turning. (There is a restaurant here in the landscaped grounds.)

Kuruman to Mafikeng

From Kuruman the road (R27) leads through flat plains with occasional maize fields, and eventually enters the cattle-ranching country known as 'the Texas of South Africa'. 140 km after leaving Kuruman you reach Vryburg, the 'capital' of this vast area (see below).

You will have entered Vryburg on De la Rey Street. Turn right into Market Street, then left into Moffat Street — which becomes the R27 to Mafikeng. (Just after turning into Market Street you pass the entrance to Hayes Park on your left, opposite the municipal buildings. Hayes Park has toilets and water, and is a shady place for a picnic lunch — shaded roadside picnic places are rare in this region.)

44 km after leaving Vryburg you pass the small town of Stella on your left, and 56 km later you pass a road on your right that leads south for 15 km to Kraaipan, where the first shots of the Anglo-Boer War were fired. A further 50 km then brings you to the outskirts of Mafikeng (see opposite). Just before entering Mafikeng you pass Lucas Mangope Way on your left, leading to Mmabatho (capital of Bophuthatswana) and Montsiwa.

In Mafikeng you cross a bridge over the railway line, and shortly after this the road widens. Keep to the left here and turn left into Station Road, then take the first turn right into Martin Street. Local information may be obtained from the museum, which is housed in the former town hall in Martin Street.

Kokerboom in the Gordonia district.

BOSMAN'S TOWN

The town of Zeerust and the Groot Marico district that it serves, features in many of the famous short stories of Herman Charles Bosman, who spent some years in the district as a teacher. Bosman, who was condemned to death for murder but later reprieved, is renowned for his development of a wry, Afrikaans-flavoured style of English.

A TOWN OF FREE MEN

A star features prominently on the municipal crest of Vryburg, because this was once the capital of the independent Republic of Stellaland — Land of the Star. White volunteers who had supported Chief Massouw of the Koranna in a war against Chief Mankoroane of the Batlapin were each given a plot of land on the conclusion of hostilities in 1882. The new citizens proclaimed themselves independent and free of any other republic or territory, and so named their town Vryburg (free town). Less than three years later however, after incessant wrangles between the South African Republic and the British authorities, the young republic was annexed by Britain.

Vryburg today is a town of green gardens and the centre of an immense cattle-ranching region, with more than 200 000 head being auctioned annually in the town.

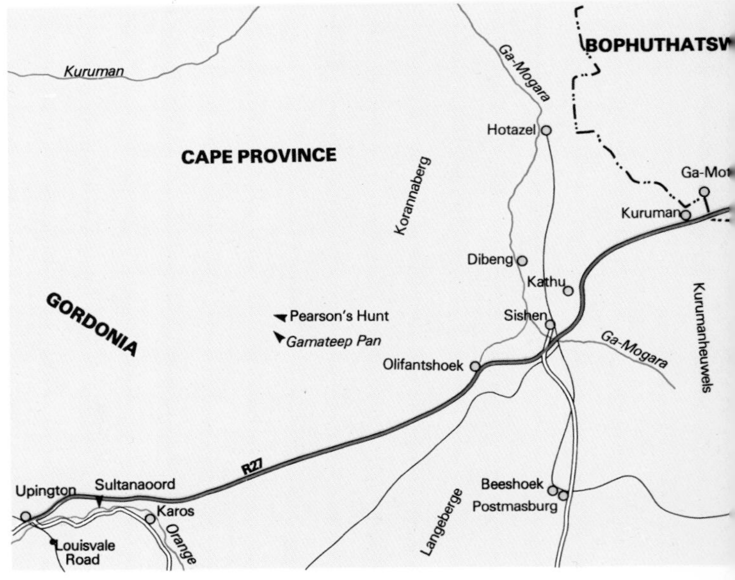

Mafikeng to Zeerust

From Martin Street turn right into Voortrekker Street, then turn left into Shippard Street, which becomes the R27 to Zeerust. Note your kms as you pass a road to Mmabatho and Lobatse — just after you pass under a road bridge. After 7 km you pass the railway siding of Cowan's Post on your left. This is the site of one of the outer fortifications during the siege of what was then Mafeking. Several kilometres after Cowan's Post you will see on your right the extensive cement works at Slurry.

47 km from Mafikeng you pass on your left a gravel road to the site of the battle of Mosega, fought in 1837. It was this battle that resulted in the Voortrekkers, under the command of Hendrik Potgieter, driving the Matabele warriors of Mzilikazi northwards into what is now Zimbabwe. (To reach the site of the battle, and a small memorial to the first Transvaal mission station, follow the gravel road and turn left just before reaching the railway level crossing. You reach the monuments — on your right — roughly 1,4 km after leaving the tar.)

12 km beyond this turn-off the R27 enters Zeerust, centre of the Groot Marico district immortalised by the writer Herman Charles Bosman. You enter the town on Church Street, and pass a memorial park on your right, on the corner of President Street. (In President Street, just in front of the war memorial, you can see a relic of more leisurely days — a hitching rail, to which the reins of horses were tied when their riders dismounted.)

Leave Zeerust on the R27 for Swartruggens and Rustenburg, noting your kms as you pass out of the built-up area. After roughly 30 km you will see on your right a roadside monument commemorating the fiercely fought battle of Kleinfontein — the last major clash in this area during the Anglo-Boer War. 6 km after this you pass Groot Marico on your right, and a further 31 km brings you to Swartruggens.

The R27 passes straight through Swartruggens, then crosses the Elands River and a railway level crossing. 1,4 km after the railway level crossing you reach a turn-off right onto the R509 for Koster. If you are travelling to Pretoria, ignore the R509 and continue straight on the R27, which proceeds directly to Pretoria via Rustenburg. If you are travelling to Johannesburg, turn right onto the R509. (After 32 km you enter Koster on Jameson Road. Turn left at the T-junction. After a further 68 km you reach Magaliesburg, where you turn right at the T-junction to join the R24 to Johannesburg. After 15 km turn left onto the R47 to reach the Western Bypass.) ●

Hartbeespoort Dam near Pretoria.

BIRTHPLACE OF THE BOY SCOUTS

Now renamed Mafikeng and a part of the capital city complex of Bophuthatswana, Mafeking gained world-wide publicity during the protracted siege of 1899-1900. The siege brought fame to the town's commander, Colonel Robert Baden-Powell, founder of the Boy Scout movement.

The town's museum in Martin Street contains many relics from the siege, including an ancient ship's gun that was nicknamed Nelson and another cannon captured from the Boer forces and dubbed Gentle Annie. (Nelson had been found serving as a gatepost, but it was dug up and used in the defences.) Fort Warren and Cannon Koppie are open to the public.

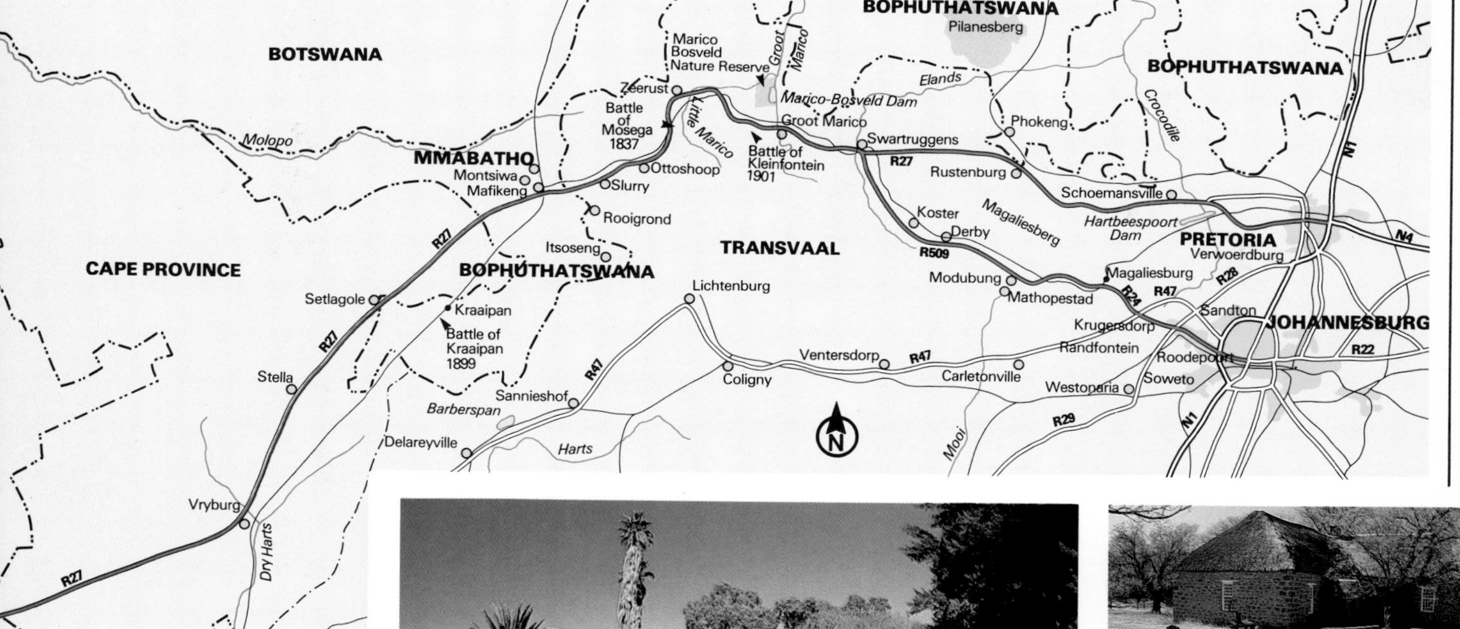

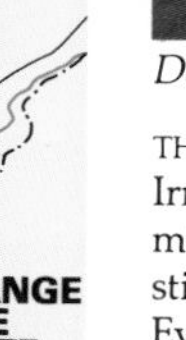

Thatched roof of Moffat's Mission.

Deep blue waters of the 'Eye of Kuruman', a powerful freshwater spring.

THE MOFFAT MISSION

Irrigation furrows built by the missionary Robert Moffat in 1827 still carry water for 4 km from the Eye of Kuruman to the mission gardens where he and his wife Mary toiled for 50 years.

Today the mission is a place of peace — the silence broken only by birdsong. In the Love Garden, where the missionary-explorer David Livingstone proposed to the Moffats' daughter (also Mary), you can still see the ancient stump of the almond tree under which the couple courted.

It was here at the mission that Moffat translated the Bible into Tswana, and printed it on a press that is now on display in the Kimberley Public Library. Letters posted in the postbox near the Moffat homestead receive a special franking.

The 'Strelitzia Coast' and the hauntingly beautiful hills of Transkei

This first third of the coastal N2 route from Durban to Cape Town sweeps down through Natal's south coast, then turns inland for Kokstad, passing the scenic Oribi Gorge. We then travel to East London through Transkei, a land of giant valleys and huge hut-covered hills. Travel documents are needed to enter Transkei.

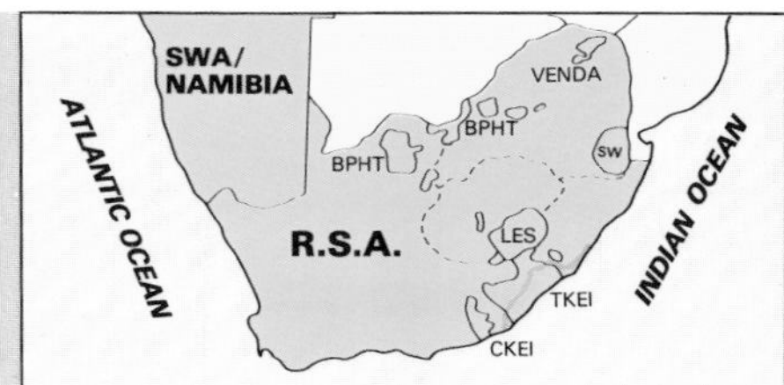

AA Office AA House, 537 Smith Street, Durban 4001 Tel. (031) 3010341
SA Tourism Board Suite 520, Southern Life Centre, 320 West Street, Durban 4001 Tel. (031) 3047144
Transkei Tourist Bureau York Road, Umtata, Transkei Tel. (0471) 25191
AA Office AA House, 3a Terminus Street, East London 5201 Tel. (0431) 21271

Durban - Port Shepstone - Kokstad - Umtata - Butterworth - **East London (680 — 700 km)**

DRIVE SOUTH FROM Durban on the N2 freeway, following signs to the 'South Coast Resorts'. The road runs fairly close to the sea and crosses numerous rivers, often giving attractive views to the left over the river estuaries. In the rainy season the sea around the river mouths is stained brown with mud, particularly the Mzimkulu River, which you cross just before entering Port Shepstone.

The freeway ends soon after crossing the Mgababa River, and resumes again after Scottburgh, with good views of the sea and canefields. It finally ends some 3 km past the Mfazazana River, near Hibberdene.

In Port Shepstone, turn right to stay on the N2, following signs for 'Harding and Marburg'. The road now rises through hilly country where quaint houses cling to the slopes, each house in the middle of its own cultivated garden. A road on your right some 10 km from Port Shepstone leads to a spectacular view of the Oribi Gorge (follow signs to 'viewsites', and see pages 192-3).

Note your kms as you pass through the little settlement of Paddock on the narrow-gauge railway line linking Port Shepstone and Harding. 6 km past the village, from the parking area at Wilson's cutting, there is a fine view over hilly countryside dotted with rural settlements.

75 km after leaving Port Shepstone you pass the town of Harding — founded in 1877 as a military outpost below Ngeli Mountain, and named after the first Chief Justice of Natal. 15 km beyond Harding turn left at the T-junction and continue on the N2 through the dense pine plantations of the Weza and Ngeli forests. Ngeli Mountain, on your left, was the scene of South Africa's first major air tragedy when, in October 1951, a Dakota flew into the slopes in thick mist, killing all 17 occupants.

Just before Kokstad, swing left to continue on the N2 towards Mt Ayliff and Umtata. (Kokstad, 4 km from this junction, is an attractive

Fishermen wait patiently for a bite at Umkomaas Beach.

A winter drought leaves the Transkei hills brown and lifeless.

PORT SHEPSTONE

Sugar, marble and tourism have made Port Shepstone the largest of the towns on Natal's south coast. A harbour was constructed here at the mouth of the great Mzimkulu River in 1880, and the growth of the town on the river's banks was boosted by the arrival of 200 Norwegian settlers six years later. Persistent silting of the river channel created problems, however, and the port was finally killed by the arrival of the railway line from Durban in 1901, although the river remains navigable by small craft for more than 20 km.

The town is named after Sir Theophilus Shepstone who, at the age of 20, began a long and distinguished career in public service in Natal. To the Zulus he was known as Somtseu (great hunter), although the Transvaal Boers, whose country he annexed in 1877, dubbed him 'Stoffel Slypsteen' (Christopher Whetstone). Near the town is the beautiful Oribi Gorge on the Mzimkulwana River.

A CITY OF TWO CATHEDRALS

Modern buildings line the bustling, colourful streets of Umtata, capital of Transkei. The city has two cathedrals — Anglican and Roman Catholic. The attractive Town Hall was completed in 1908, and there is a cannon in its gardens said to have come from the wreck of the fabled treasure-ship Grosvenor.

Umtata began in 1869 when the chiefs of the Pondos and Tembus allowed white settlers to farm a strip of land along the Umtata River to act as a buffer between their warring tribes. The town grew slowly, and 10 years later consisted of little more than a few huts near the river housing the Chief Magistrate of Tembuland, Major (later Sir) Henry Elliot. The post office, on the site of the present Elliot Hospital, was no more than a sod hut with a grass roof, and the most substantial building was the Grosvenor Hotel on the outskirts of the town. A newer Grosvenor Hotel now occupies the same site.

town with an imposing Roman Catholic Cathedral and other interesting buildings and memorials. These include the tomb of Adam Kok III, the last 'coloured king', in the main street next to the police station.)

Kokstad to Umtata

The N2 enters Transkei roughly 10 km after the Kokstad turn-off. (South African citizens need passports or identity documents to enter Transkei, others need passports and visas. A speed limit of 100 km/h is severely enforced throughout Transkei, and ask at the border if a curfew is in force.) From the border the road climbs steeply, with views over hut-studded hills and green slopes gashed with red where the soil has been exposed by erosion.

You pass Mount Ayliff on your left, and 5 km later you cross the Mzintlava River. From here the road winds through grassy hillsides, and roughly 28 km after passing Mount Ayliff there are views on your left over the Mzimvubu River. The road then sweeps down and crosses the river, and 10 km later you pass through Mount Frere.

Just over 1 km beyond Mount Frere there is a picnic site on your left, with attractive views over valleys and hills. 3 km after this there is a second picnic site — similar, but offering more shade. 21 km after this second picnic site you cross the Tina River.

5 km beyond the Tina River you pass a road on your right to Sulenkama, where the magistrate of Qumbu, Hamilton Hope, and two of his clerks were killed by Chief Mhlontlo in 1880, at the start of the Pondomise uprising — sparked off by disarmament laws passed by the Cape government. The road then passes through Qumbu, and 10 km after Qumbu you cross the Tsitsa River. At various points along this road you will see that aloes have been planted on the hillsides to form large enclosures. Most of these are no longer used, but they were originally planted to fence in cattle and goats.

Umtata to East London

60 km after Qumbu you enter Umtata, capital of Transkei (see opposite, and pages 196-201). Keep straight at the two sets of traffic lights, then turn right into Alexandra Road, which becomes the N2 for East London. Note your kms as you pass a sign to the University of Transkei.

After 15 km you pass a road on your left to Coffee Bay — a popular holiday and angling resort, named after coffee trees that sprang up after a barrel of coffee beans had been washed ashore from a wreck (see pages 200-1).

You will see the Mbashe River long before you reach it — 50 km from Umtata, and after a long and gentle descent into its valley. The Mbashe is known for its extraordinary meandering. At one point its meanders extend over 46 km and return to within 1 km of their commencement. This sequence of twists and turns is known as the 'collywobbles' — a play on the name of General George Colley, special magistrate of the Idutywa district, who was later killed at the Battle of Majuba in 1881. You reach the town of Idutywa roughly 30 km after the Mbashe.

26 km after Idutywa you pass a road on your left to Mazeppa Bay, named after a schooner that traded along the coast during the 1830s. 7 km past this turn-off you enter Butterworth, established as a mission station in 1827 and named after an official of the Wesleyan Missionary Society (see pages 202-3). 20 km after Butterworth the road begins a gradual descent to the border post on the Great Kei River (see opposite), with magnificent gorges on both sides of the road. Note your kms as you leave the South African border post on the southern side of the river.

The road climbs from the river through hills dotted with aloes, and after 9 km you pass the R63 on your right to Komga and King William's Town. Keep straight for East London, passing fields of pineapples. 67 km after leaving the South African border post, take Exit 23 'Beacon Bay/North East Expressway' off-ramp to reach East London's central area ●

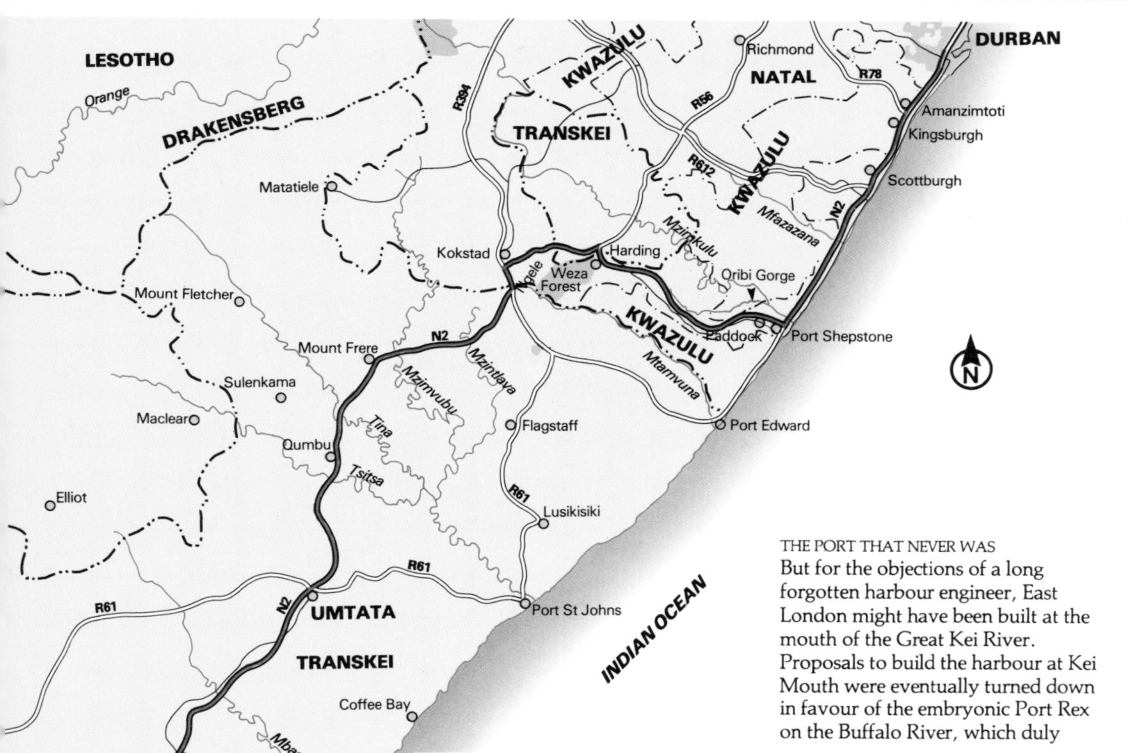

THE PORT THAT NEVER WAS

But for the objections of a long forgotten harbour engineer, East London might have been built at the mouth of the Great Kei River. Proposals to build the harbour at Kei Mouth were eventually turned down in favour of the embryonic Port Rex on the Buffalo River, which duly became the harbour and city of East London.

The word 'kei' is of Khoi origin, and is believed to mean 'sand', or possibly the 'shine' that is reflected from the sand and stones of the river's bed. Later, the Xhosa gave it the name Nciba.

The Great Kei, with its tributaries, the Indwe and the White Kei, forms the boundary between Ciskei ('on this side of the Kei') and Transkei ('beyond the Kei'). Another important tributary is the Black Kei, with its source in the Stormberg.

Left: *East London harbour.*

Traditional garb in Umtata.

From aloe-covered hills to the forests of the Tsitsikamma

Deep river gorges and aloe-covered hills mark a country once torn by conflict and fear — where battle-scarred towers still recall many a desperate fight between Xhosa and encroaching white settlers. From here our route takes us past Port Elizabeth and through the deep forests of the Tsitsikamma, to the beaches of the Garden Route.

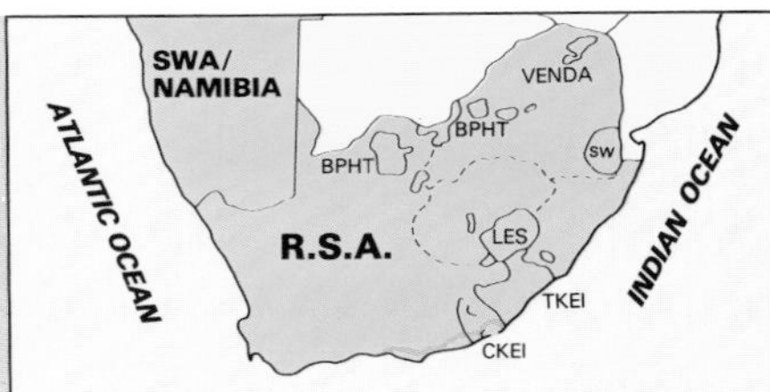

AA Office AA House, 3a Terminus Street, East London 5201 Tel. (0431) 21271
AA Office AA House, 2 Granville Road, Greenacres, Port Elizabeth 6001 Tel. (041) 341313
Plettenberg Bay Publicity Association Sewell Street, Plettenberg Bay 6600 Tel. (04457) 32050
Knysna Publicity Association 40 Main Street, Knysna 6570 Tel. (0445) 21610

East London - King William's Town - Grahamstown - Port Elizabeth - Plettenberg Bay - **Knysna (580 — 600 km)**

FROM EAST LONDON, drive inland on the N2 for King William's Town, passing grassy hills dotted with aloes. After 35 km you pass a road on your left to Berlin, and 13 km later you pass a road on your right to Breidbach. These settlements were named by former members of the British-raised King's German Legion — veterans of the Crimean War — who settled this area in 1857.

Just over 50 km from East London you enter King William's Town, former capital of the short-lived province of Queen Adelaide, and later British Kaffraria (see pages 210-11). Turn left opposite the town's museum into Cathcart Street, which becomes the N2 to Grahamstown. You cross the Buffalo River on the outskirts of the town, and the road then leads through low hills and grasslands, sparsely dotted with trees and scrub, before winding downhill through the 5 km Keiskamma Pass to the Keiskamma River.

You cross the river — the 'shining water' of the vanished Khoikhoi people — 33 km after leaving King William's Town. The riverine vegetation includes cactus-like euphorbias and thorny acacias. The Keiskamma, which enters the sea at Hamburg, was named by the early

Mouth of the Keurbooms River Lagoon at Plettenberg Bay.

A sea rescue launch enters the Knysna Lagoon.

PRESERVING THE TREES

The luxuriant forests that once covered the coastline of much of the southern Cape have been ruthlessly exploited — leaving only a few patches that are now protected in the Tsitsikamma Forest and Tsitsikamma Coastal National Parks. The best known species of tree in these forests is the Outeniqua Yellowwood *(Podocarpus falcatus)*, and a fine example can be seen just to the right of the N2, 3,5 km west of the Storms River Bridge.

HARKER OF HARKERVILLE

The small settlement of Harkerville, between Plettenberg Bay and Knysna, is named after Captain Robert Harker, who was appointed Government Resident at Plettenberg Bay in 1826. He and his wife, Maria, arrived with seven children, and soon began to add more to their family. Harker was praised for his great kindness to survivors of ships wrecked on this wild and dangerous coast. The gravestones of the family may be seen close to the concrete approach road at the eastern end of Plettenberg Bay.

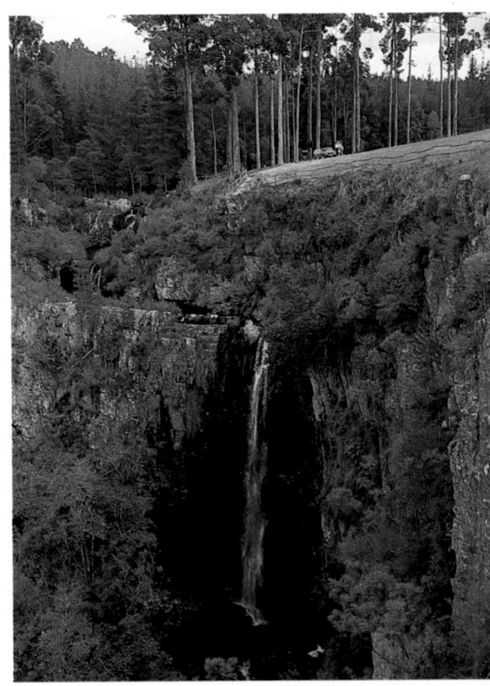

Bracken Hill Falls in the forest near Knysna.

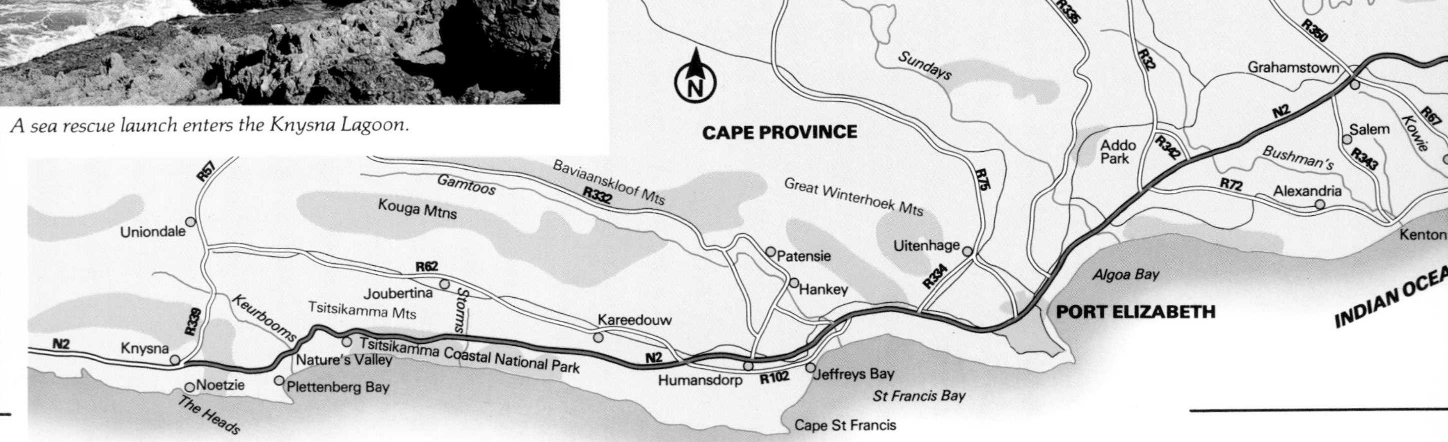

Portuguese explorers Rio de Sao Christovao (River of St Christopher).

The Gwanga River, some 10km beyond the Keiskamma, was the scene of bitter fighting in the frontier days, and at Peddie, 8km further, the tower still stands where settlers withstood a determined siege during the War of the Axe in 1846 (see below).

Peddie to Grahamstown

About 7km beyond Peddie you pass on your right the deep gorges and wooded slopes of the Paradise River, a tributary of the Gqora, which in turn flows into the Great Fish River — for many years the eastern boundary of the Cape Colony. The name of the Great Fish, which you cross 17km from Peddie, is a direct translation of its Khoikhoi name of 'oub' (see below). 4,5km after crossing the river you pass a road on your right to Committee's Drift and Trumpeter's Drift (properly Trompetter's), fortified outposts during the frontier wars. A gravel road on your left 10km from the river leads to the well-preserved tower of another 1820 Settler fort, Fraser's Camp.

22km past the Fraser's Camp road, on your right, another outpost is commemorated in the name of a farm, Governor's Kop. These outposts were built with towers tall enough to allow signals to be seen from one to the other. However, they were described by a wit of the time as 'signal failures' because frequent mists made signalling impossible.

After passing the R67 to Fort Beaufort on your right, the road descends into Grahamstown (see pages 222-7) 65km from Peddie.

Grahamstown to Port Elizabeth

Keep straight in Grahamstown on Beaufort Street (which becomes Grey Street), heading for Port Elizabeth. You pass on your right the 1820 Settlers Monument on Gunfire Hill. Shortly after passing through Grahamstown the road climbs, then descends through the wooded hills and crags of Howison's Poort, where archeological excavations have uncovered many interesting Stone Age tools.

12km from Grahamstown you pass on your left the R343 to Alexandria and Kenton on Sea, which also leads to the picturesque 1820 Settler village of Salem. 5km beyond this turning you cross the Kariega River — the Khoikhoi name refers to the steenbok that used to drink here. The road then passes through wide cultivated lands, before descending past great ridges and valleys to the Komgha ('rich in clay') River, 43km from Grahamstown.

6,5km later you cross the Boesmans (Bushmans) River, recalling the vanished San inhabitants of the area, then the road descends steeply and you pass on your left an exit for the Addo Elephant National Park. A few hundred metres after this, turn left where the road divides, heading for Port Elizabeth (see pages 230-9).

93km from Grahamstown you cross the Sundays River — its name probably derived from the Zondagh family — with salt pans on both sides of the road and occasional glimpses of the sea. The freeway into Port Elizabeth starts about 112km from Grahamstown, and there are a number of exits to the 'friendly city'. Unless you wish to stop in Port Elizaberth, stay on the N2 freeway for Humansdorp.

Port Elizabeth to Knysna

About 55km from Port Elizabeth the road crosses the Gamtoos River, believed to have been named after a Khoikhoi tribe living in the area. The Kabeljous River, which you cross 10,5km later, takes its name from the popular sea fish. After crossing the Kabeljous, look out for the start of the characteristic Cape fynbos, which appears in increasing profusion from here, clothing the foothills of the Tsitsikamma Mountains in colour.

25km after crossing the Gamtoos River you pass the town of Humansdorp on your left. 88km from the Gamtoos you cross the deep gorge of the Storms River, and there is an information centre for the Tsitsikamma Forest National Park on your right at the far end of the bridge. After crossing the Storms River you travel through dense indigenous forest, and 3,5km after the river there is a parking area on your right, from where a path leads to a 'Big Tree' (see pages 246-7).

Shortly after this the road crosses the Elandsbos River, where the R102 leads right. (The N2 becomes a toll-road from this point, with soaring, spectacular bridges over mighty gorges. The R102, formerly the National Road, offers an alternative route — slower but very picturesque.) Continue on the N2 through dense forest and the small settlement of The Crags, shortly after which the road offers a grand view over Plettenberg Bay and the Robberg Peninsula. There is a parking area and viewsite on your left.

The road crosses the Keurbooms and Bietou Rivers, then climbs the hill above the town of Plettenberg Bay — with glorious views back over the Keurbooms River Lagoon and the long, gentle curve of the bay itself.

Beyond Plettenberg Bay the forests crowd the roadside, with indigenous trees dotted among plantations of pine and eucalyptus. The road passes the small settlement of Harkerville (see opposite) and 8km later there is a short gravel road on your left leading to the scenic Bracken Hill Falls (see pages 248-9). A few kilometres later the road drops gently down into Knysna ●

THE GREAT FISH RIVER

In 1488 a Portuguese caravel bearing Bartholomew Dias, and piloted by Joao Infante, edged its way cautiously into the estuary of a large river on the coast of south-east Africa. It was here that Dias's men, homesick and apprehensive, forced their commander to abandon his quest for a sea route to the Indies, and to turn back.

They named the river Rio Infante, after their steersman, although, unknown to them, it already had a name. To the Khoikhoi it was the Oub — the river of fish — and their name, in translation, has survived to this day.

With two of its tributaries, the Tarka and the Baviaans rivers, the Great Fish became the eastern boundary of the Cape Colony, a 'border' repeatedly crossed by cattle-raiders from both sides.

Evening sun lights up the hills near the Great Fish River.

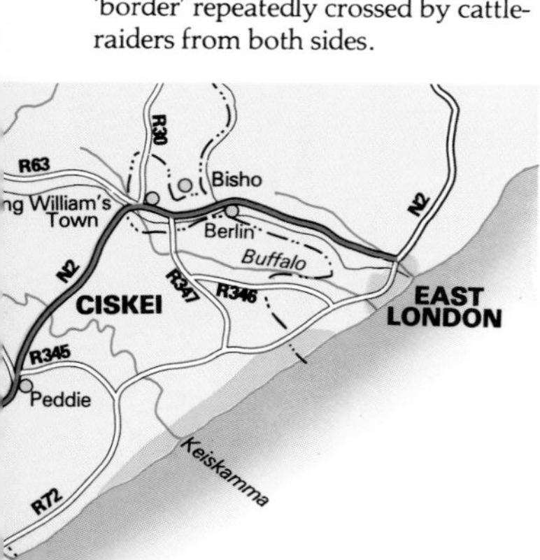

FRONTIER FORTS

Named after Colonel John Peddie of the Seaforth Highlanders, Fort Peddie was built in 1835, and still stands on the ridge overlooking the town that grew up nearby. This oldest of the eastern frontier forts stands midway between the Great Fish and the Keiskamma rivers — a stretch of country that was proclaimed 'neutral territory'. In order to create a buffer against the Xhosa, some 17 000 Mfengu (Fingo) were settled in this area, and several forts were built for their protection. The original fort at Peddie, which was little more than an earthwork, was replaced by the substantial tower in 1841. Other stone buildings in the town also date from this troubled period.

Right: *White water curls towards the shore at East London's beachfront.*

A scenic highway through the forests and farmlands of the southern Cape

This third section of the N2 from Durban to Cape Town winds through the forested hills of Knysna and passes the Lake District to Wilderness and George. We then cut across the southern tip of the continent, through the rolling farmlands of Swellendam and Caledon — to look down upon 'the Fairest Cape' from the heights of Sir Lowry's Pass.

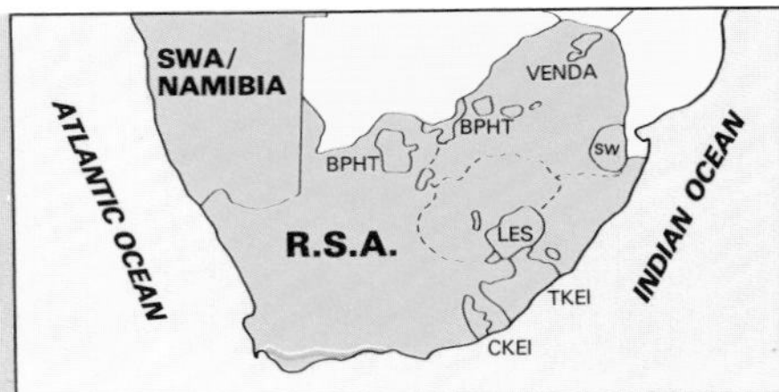

AA Office Millwood Building, Cnr York and Victoria Streets, George 6530 Tel. (0441) 742090/1
George Publicity Association 44 Courtenay Street, George 6530 Tel. (0441) 742271
SA Tourism Board 124 York Street, George 6530 Tel. (0441) 5228
AA Office AA House, 7 Martin Hammerschlag Way, Cape Town 8001 Tel. (021) 211550

Knysna - Wilderness - George - Mossel Bay - Swellendam - Caledon - **Cape Town** (450 — 480 km)

DRIVE WEST OUT OF Knysna on Main Street (N2), skirting the lagoon of the Knysna River. Note your kms at the far end of the long, low bridge that takes you across the lagoon. The road immediately climbs among forested hills, and after 5,6 km you cross the Goukamma River — the name is a corruption of the Khoikhoi word for a wild fig.

Your are now entering South Africa's Lake District, and you soon pass the first of the lakes, Groenvlei, on your left (see pages 250-3). Shortly after this you pass the holiday village of Sedgefield, then the road runs along the crest of a line of low coastal hills, with the Indian Ocean on your left and a string of lakes on your right — Swartvlei, Rondevlei, Upper Langvlei and Lower Langvlei. Lower Langvlei, also known as Island Lake, is joined to the Touw River by a narrow channel called the Serpentine, and you eventually reach the delightful holiday settlement of Wilderness on the banks of the Touw River's lagoon.

After passing Wilderness the road climbs briefly, offering views over the ocean and back along Wilderness's beach, then you descend into the picturesque gorge of the Kaaimans River. You cross the river on a curved bridge, then begin to climb again towards George, crossing the Swart River and passing a road on your left to the popular surfing spot of Victoria Bay. The road runs straight between tall trees as you approach the town of George.

You enter George on Knysna Road, which crosses a railway line and becomes Courtenay Street (see pages 254-5). In the centre of the town, turn left out of Courtenay Street into York Street following the sign for 'Cape Town/Mossel Bay'. Roughly 7 km out of town, turn left, following signs for the N2. The road leads around P W Botha Airport, and roughly 3 km later turn right onto the N2 freeway for Mossel Bay.

The N2 descends to sea level in a succession of grand sweeps, offering fine views over Mossel Bay to Cape St Blaize in the distance. Eventually the road crosses the Great Brak River, with the sea and an attractive lagoon on your left and the small town tucked away among hills on your right (see opposite).

Roughly 10 km after crossing the Great Brak River you cross the Little Brak River, and soon

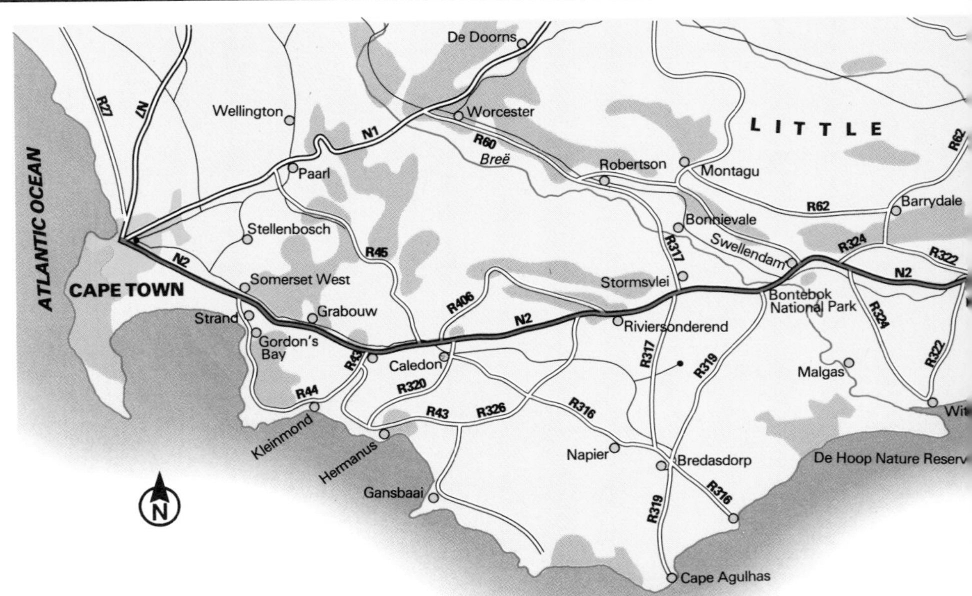

A TOWN WITH A DISTINCTIVE SCENT
The chances are that you will catch the scent of Riversdale well before you get there — the air around this attractive southern Cape town is saturated with the antiseptic-like odour of various species of *Agathosma* shrubs. The town was founded in 1838 and named after Harry Rivers, magistrate of nearby Swellendam. The Julius Gordon Africana Centre in Versveld House displays paintings by well-known South African artists, including the locally born J E A Volschenk.

North of Riversdale the tarred Garcia's Pass, named after a civil commissioner of the town, follows for some of its length the original road built by Thomas Bain, and offers fine views. The old toll house on the pass is a national monument.

Thatched cottage on a Cape wine farm.

Sheep dot a field near Riviersonderend.

after this you pass on your left the exit for the historic town of Mossel Bay (see below). As the road climbs the coastal hills you can see the town spread out on the hillsides to your left. The freeway ends roughly 8 km after passing the turn-off into the town.

Mossel Bay to Swellendam

About 36 km from Mossel Bay the road descends to cross the Gourits (rustling) River. There is a picnic site with toilets just before you reach the bridge, on the right side of the road, and a footpath leads from here to a viewsite overlooking the river gorge. (There are good views from the old road bridge on the right.) Some 15 km past the Gourits River you pass a road on your right into Albertinia, a centre for the mining of ochre and kaolin, and the extraction of aloe juice. After passing a road on your left to Still Bay, and crossing the Kafferkuils River, the N2 then enters Riversdale.

Beyond Riversdale the N2 moves closer to the Langeberg range on your right, passing through the outskirts of Heidelberg and the little settlement of Buffeljagsrivier, from where a gravel road leads to Malgas and Port Beaufort (see pages 266-7). A few kilometres later you pass a crossroads, where left leads to the Bontebok National Park, and right leads into Swellendam (see pages 264-9). Some 5 km past this crossroads you cross the Breë River, and shortly after this you have fine views of the river on your right.

Swellendam to Cape Town

37 km from Swellendam you pass a road on your left to Protem, which was given its name early this century when work on the railway line was suspended *'pro tempore'* (for the time being) — the line has never been extended. 2 km after this Protem road you pass the R317 on your left to Cape Agulhas, the most southerly point on the continent, and to the De Hoop Nature Reserve.

The road continues through Riviersonderend, after which you pass the R326 on your left to Gansbaai and Hermanus. 38 km later you pass the town of Caledon on your left — and on your right you pass a road to the Caledon Botanic Garden, renowned for its springtime displays of wild flowers (see pages 274-5).

Ahead of you now are the Houwhoek Mountains, and you pass a road on your left for Hermanus and Bot River. The village of Bot River can be seen on your right as you begin the ascent of the scenic Houwhoek Pass. Once over the pass, the road winds through fynbos and forest to reach the apple country of Elgin and Grabouw, just off the National Road.

You cross the Palmiet and Steenbras rivers, then begin to climb Sir Lowry's Pass. The pass is named after Sir Galbraith Lowry Cole, governor of the Cape from 1828 to 1833, who went ahead with an ambitious road-building programme despite opposition from his superiors in England. At the top of the pass, on your left, there is a large parking area with superb views over the valley of the Lourens River and across False Bay to Table Mountain. The road then winds down the mountainside and passes between Strand and Somerset West, before leading into Cape Town on Settlers Way ●

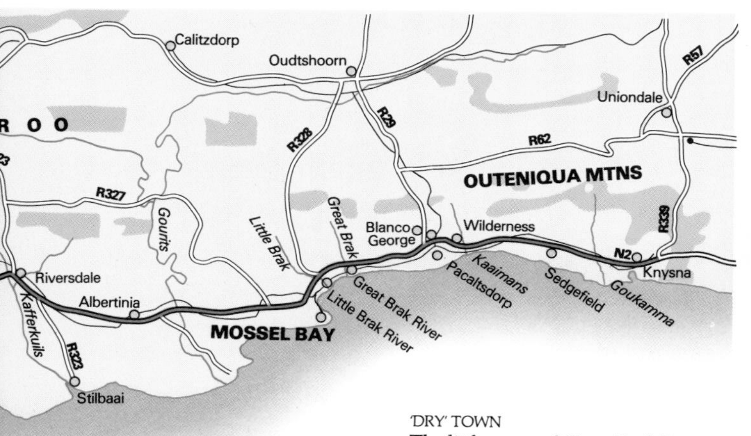

'DRY' TOWN

The little town of Great Brak River is one of the few municipalities in South Africa where the sale of liquor is prohibited (another is Fish Hoek in the Cape Peninsula). It was founded by the Searle family, which operated the toll at the causeway over the river from 1852. To while away the time, and to bring in extra income, Charles Searle began to make boots and shoes for sale to passers-by. From these beginnings grew the large footwear industry and village of Great Brak River. The processing of timber grown nearby is also carried out here on a large scale. There are attractive beaches on and near 'The Island', at the mouth of the river (see pages 254-5).

The evening sky glows golden over the waters of Knysna Lagoon.

LANDFALL AFTER ROUNDING THE CAPE

Mossel Bay is a town closely linked to the sea. Named after mussels found in the area by Dutch sailors in 1595, the town is now home to an extensive fishing fleet — although the harbour is too small for larger vessels. The maritime museum near the harbour recalls the town's seafaring past, while nearby the latest technology is being developed in order to exploit gas from newly discovered offshore wells.

Mossel Bay was the first landfall of Bartholomew Dias after he unknowingly rounded the Cape in 1488. It was later visited by Vasco da Gama, who named it Aguada de Sao Bras (the watering place of St Blaize). Early navigators on their way to the East used to place mail here in the trunk of a large milkwood tree, to be collected by ships returning from the East to Europe.

The Blackbacked Gull — common along the southern Cape coast.

A group of surfers wait for the perfect wave at Mossel Bay.

From Table Bay to Graaff-Reinet through a land of remarkable contrasts

Starting from the 'Mother City' and her green, long-settled surroundings, we travel to the arid plains of the Karoo, where the veld retains a pre-historic wildness. Side-roads invite exploration — of colourful mission villages, green valleys, or magnificent rock strata. This is the first part of a scenic three- to four-day inland route to Durban.

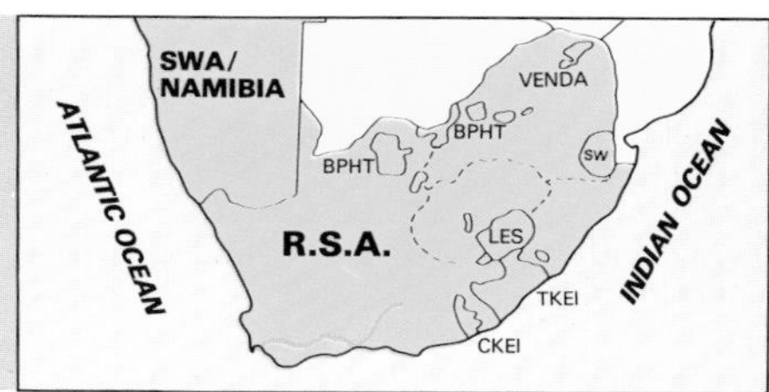

AA Office AA House, 7 Martin Hammerschlag Way, Cape Town 8001 Tel. (021) 211550
SA Tourism Board Level 3, Golden Acre, Adderley Street, Cape Town 8001 Tel. (021) 216274
Worcester Publicity Association Stofberg House, 23 Baring St, Worcester 6850 Tel. (0231) 4408
Oudtshoorn Publicity Office Civic Centre, Voortrekker Rd, Oudtshoorn 6620 Tel. (04431) 2228
Graaff-Reinet Information Reinet Museum, Church St, Graaff-Reinet 6280 Tel. (0491) 23801

Cape Town - Worcester - Montagu - Ladismith - Oudtshoorn - Uniondale - **Graaff-Reinet (750—780 km)**

LEAVE CAPE TOWN on the N1. The road crosses the Tygerberg hills — so named by early Dutch settlers not because the area was the haunt of tigers, but because the bush-dotted slopes reminded them of a leopard's skin.

The soaring Taal (language) Monument is visible ahead and to your left roughly 49 km from Cape Town. About 10 km later you pass the exit to Paarl, and the freeway ends 6 km later.

The road winds through the craggy Hawequa, Klein Drakenstein and Du Toit's mountains along Du Toit's Kloof Pass (see pages 40-1). 8 km beyond the end of the freeway there is a shady picnic site on your left with views towards the town of Paarl, overlooked by massive granite domes, and of Table Mountain in the distance. There is another viewsite after a further 1 km, and a third after an additional 1 km, each offering wider views (but no picnic facilities).

Beyond the summit of the pass (820 m above sea level), you enter a road tunnel through a spur of rock known as the Kleygat. (A new toll road and tunnel are being built, and are expected to be in use from 1988.)

21 km beyond the tunnel, you pass a turn-off on your right to Rawsonville and on your left to Goudini. You are now in the fertile Breë River valley (see pages 40-1), and you cross separate channels of the river over three bridges.

You pass the R43 to Wolseley and Ceres on your left, and 1 km later turn right off the N1 onto the R43 for Worcester and Villiersdorp, noting your kms.

After 1 km you enter Worcester on Trappes Street, and pass a number of historic, thatched houses (see below). 2,8 km from the N1 turn left into Hoogstraat (High Street), with the imposing 1824 Drostdy building at the head of

WORCESTER

This principal town of the Breë River valley was founded in 1820 and named after a brother of Governor Lord Charles Somerset, the Marquis of Worcester. The town grew rapidly after 1822 when the seat of the magistrate was moved here from Tulbagh, where the drostdy was reported to have been irreparably damaged (although it stands to this day). The town lies among high mountains, snow-capped in winter.

The interesting Worcester Museum is housed in three historic buildings on the corner of Baring and Church streets. The home of Hugo Naudé, the town's renowned landscape artist, at 113 Russell Street has been restored and contains a collection of his works. Another fascinating place to visit is the Boland Open-air Agricultural Museum, where 19th century farming methods are demonstrated — including the art of distilling 'witblits' (white lightning).

Vivid green farmlands blanket a valley amongst the mountains near Worcester.

LANGKLOOF

This broad, long and fertile valley stretches for about 160 km between the Outeniqua and Tsitsikamma mountains in the south and the Kammanassie and Kouga ranges in the north. The explorer Isaac Schryver named it Langkloof (long valley) in 1689, and it has been farmed and settled by whites since about 1760. The chief crops of the valley are apples and pears.

THE LITTLE KAROO

Just as it is impossible to define the boundaries of the Great Karoo — the 'dry' or 'arid land' — so do the borders of the Little Karoo tend to be blurred. Generally accepted limits place the area between Montagu in the west and Willowmore in the east, between the Swartberg ranges in the north and the Langeberg and Outeniqua mountain chains in the south. The rainfall is slightly higher than in the Great Karoo, and stronger-flowing rivers permit a greater degree of irrigation.

The Little Karoo is the land of the ostrich, and of spectacular rock formations and exposed, contorted rock strata. The Swartberg foothills are riddled with limestone caverns, of which the Kango caves are believed to be just a part. There are many scenic passes, and a number of green, hidden valleys, such as Gamkaskloof, formerly known as 'Die Hel', a peaceful farming community living deep in the mountains.

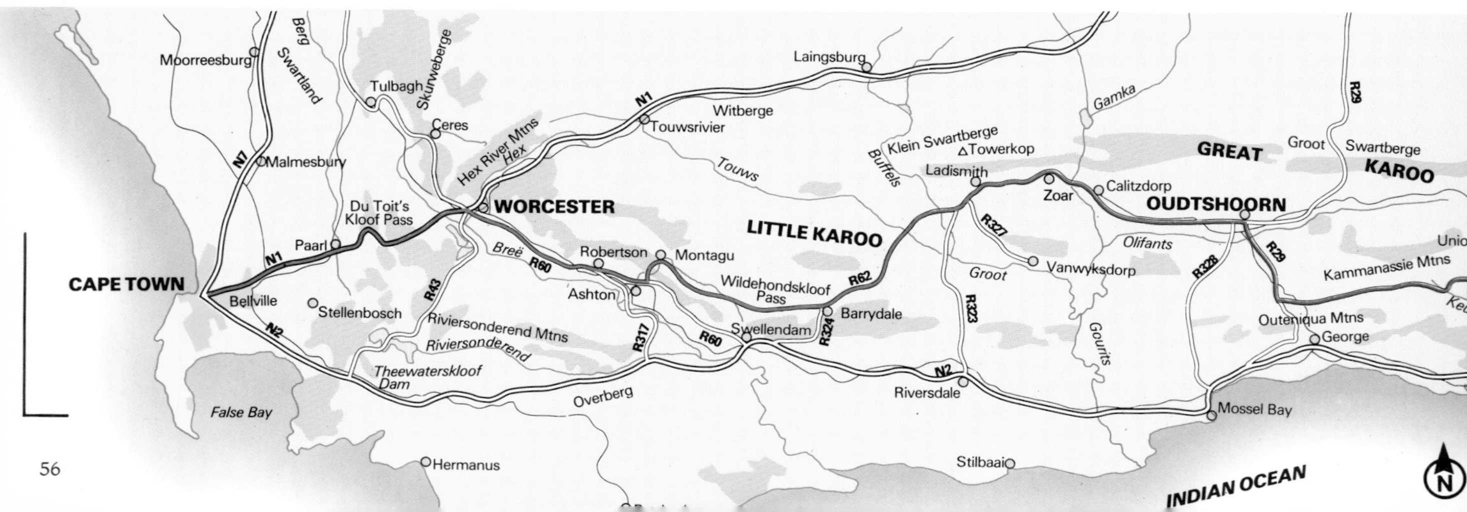

the main street on your right. On your left after the Adderley Street intersection is the Dutch Reformed Church with its unusual steeple. Turn right 4,5 km from the N1 onto the R60 for Robertson and Montagu, noting your kms.

The road traverses scrubby, hilly country before entering the vineyards of the Robertson wine district. After 45 km there is a turn-off on your right to the Berg River resort of Silver Strand, and 1 km later the R60 enters Robertson (see day drive, pages 270-1).

Robertson to Calitzdorp

Continue on the R60, and pass the R317 to Bonnievale on your right. Roughly 13 km later you enter Ashton. This straggling town, now the centre for a fruit-processing industry, was once the site of the workshops of the long-defunct Cape Central Railways. A retired steam locomotive rests at the left of the road, and on the same side there is an extraordinary building constructed to represent the outline of an aircraft, including a balcony that looks like a propeller boss.

Continue straight beyond Ashton where the R60 turns right for Swellendam. You now wind through the Cogmanskloof Pass (see pages 264-5) before you enter the town of Montagu on a street lined with many lovely buildings.

Note your kms as you cross the white bridge on the far side of Montagu. The road passes farmlands, mostly vineyards and orchards, and after 34 km begins to climb the Wildehondskloof Pass. Soon after the road descends, 4 km after the start of the pass, you cross a bridge — on your left here is an attractive oak-shaded picnic site.

24 km later, on the outskirts of Barrydale, you pass on your right the R324 to Swellendam via Tradouw Pass, then pass through the outskirts of Barrydale. The landscape becomes gradually more arid as you penetrate deeper into the Little Karoo (see opposite).

Roughly 62 km beyond Barrydale you pass the R323 to Riversdale on your right. After a further 4,5 km you pass the R327 to Van Wyksdorp on your right, and the chimney-like Towerkop (magic mountain), with its cleft peak, comes into view on your left (see pages 262-3). You enter Ladismith roughly 75 km from Barrydale. Turn right at the T-junction, noting your kms. (There are several shaded picnic sites along this road, within the town limits of Ladismith.)

After 11,2 km you pass a turn-off on your left to Hoeko, birthplace of the poet C J Langenhoven. On your right roughly 6 km later is the mission village of Zoar, and after a further 2 km you reach another mission village, Amalienstein, at the point where the Seweweekspoort Pass road leads in from the Klein Swartberg on your left.

Keep straight at this intersection, and enter the scenic Huisrivier Pass. Many people assume the name of the pass to be the Afrikaans for 'house river', but it is in fact derived from the Khoikhoi word for 'willow'. A stone monument on your right 37 km from Ladismith commemorates the fifth anniversary of the Republic of South Africa. The road crosses the Huis River, the Gamka (Khoikhoi for 'lion') River, and the Nel's River, then you enter Calitzdorp 48 km from Ladismith.

Calitzdorp to Willowmore

The countryside now changes to the scrubby flats and hills typical of the Little Karoo. 47 km beyond Calitzdorp you pass the R328 on your right (which leads to Mossel Bay via Robinson Pass), then enter the town of Oudtshoorn on Voortrekker Street (see pages 254-7).

Leave Oudtshoorn by turning right into Langenhoven Street at the second robot-controlled intersection on Voortrekker Street, noting your kms. This becomes the R29 out of Oudtshoorn. After 34 km keep straight on the R62 at the fork, noting your kms. (The R29 goes right to George.)

A road on your right after 8,7 km leads to the village of Herold, generally regarded as the western end of the Langkloof (see opposite). Continue on the R62 for a further 62 km through this broad, fertile valley, then keep straight where the R62 turns off to the right for Port Elizabeth and Joubertina.

A few kms later you reach the summit of Potjiesberg (little pot mountain) Pass, and the road then winds down to the village of Uniondale on your right. A further 61 km on the R57 takes you past Willowmore, also on your right.

Willowmore to Graaff-Reinet

32 km beyond Willowmore, you cross a bridge over the Groot (great) River, and you pass the Beervlei Dam wall, with a picnic site below the wall on your left.

The landscape now becomes that of the true — or Great — Karoo along the stretch of countryside that separates Willowmore and Aberdeen. About 86 km beyond Beervlei Dam, a road leads on your right into Aberdeen, a well-preserved Karoo town that grew around its church (see opposite). Note your kms at the crossroads where a second road leads into Aberdeen on your right (the road on your left leads to Beaufort West).

After 8 km you pass on your right the low hill known as Gordon's Kop after the 18th century explorer and garrison commander Colonel Robert Jacob Gordon. The Camdeboo Mountains appear to run parallel to the road, and after 26 km the rounded peak of Spandau Kop becomes clearly visible ahead.

After 54 km you enter the historic town of Graaff-Reinet on College Road. The road changes its name to Church Street, a thoroughfare lined by historic buildings, and dominated by the massive stone Dutch Reformed Church (see pages 242-3) ●

ABERDEEN

This is one of the best-preserved little Karoo towns, and many of its buildings date from the Victorian era. Formerly a part of the parish of Graaff-Reinet, the town was laid out in 1855 on the farm Brakkefontein and named after the birthplace of the Reverend Andrew Murray, minister of Graaff-Reinet. The town is dominated by the Dutch Reformed Church building, which is said to have the tallest spire in South Africa. The magistrate's court of 1898 has hideous gargoyles which must have intimidated many an 'accused'.

The sun's final rays touch the mountain tops near Montagu.

Erosion has created 'sculptures' of myriad bizarre shapes in the Valley of Desolation, which lies west of Graaff-Reinet.

Across the Great Karoo from Graaff-Reinet to the southern buttresses of the Drakensberg

Many millions of years ago the Karoo was a lush jungle in which nightmarish creatures roamed. Today the arid plains yield their fossils, frozen in rock. From this harsh, dry land our route takes us past the ominously named Stormberg to a gentler countryside of green hills, and streams and rivers that flow from the craggy southern Drakensberg.

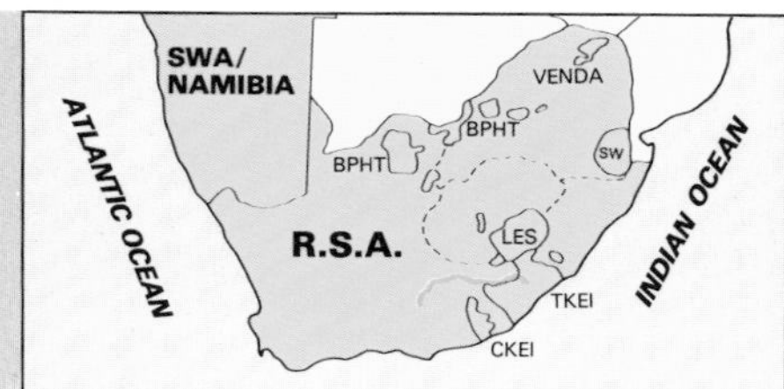

AA Office AA House, 3a Terminus Street, East London 5201 Tel. (0431) 21271
Molteno Municipality 35 Smith Street, Molteno 5500 Tel. (04572) 21
Dordrecht Museum Grey Street (Box 20), Dordrecht 5435 Tel. (045512) 17/18
Elliot Municipality 15 Maclear Road, Elliot 5460 Tel. (045312) 11

Graaff-Reinet - Middelburg - Steynsburg - Molteno - Dordrecht - Indwe - **Elliot (680 — 700 km)**

LEAVE GRAAFF-REINET ON THE Middelburg road (R57), and pass, on your left, Magazine Hill and the Andries Pretorius monument, which features a wagon wheel surmounted by a bust of the Voortrekker leader. About 6,5 km beyond the town you cross a bridge over the Sundays River.

The road climbs among the hills of the Goliatskraal Heights, where there was a tollhouse and a popular wayside inn during the 19th century. The road runs level for a while, and roughly 27 km from Graaff-Reinet you pass a turn-off on your left to New Bethesda and Wellwood Farm (see alongside).

10 km later you start the ascent of Naudesberg Pass, then you pass the R61 to Cradock on your right. You cross the Sundays River a second time, and soon begin the ascent of Lootsberg Pass, which offers outstanding views of the Karoo plains through which you have just been travelling. (During winter this pass is sometimes closed by snow.)

Middelburg to Dordrecht

Roughly 41 km from the summit of the Lootsberg Pass, as you approach Middelburg on your left, take the right fork for Colesburg (R32) and Rosemead (R57). 3,2 km later exit left on to the R56 for Rosemead and Steynsburg. After 10 km you pass the village of Rosmead on your right, and as you approach closer to the Stormberg range you can see for some distance the distinctive hills of Koffiebus (coffee chest) and Teebus (tea chest) ahead of you. The road eventually passes between the two, with Teebus on your right. The small settlement of the same name — at the end of the Orange-Fish River tunnel — is on your left soon afterwards.

Roughly 8 km later you pass the R390, and after a further 5,4 km there is a turn-off on your left that leads to Bulhoek, a modest farmhouse where Paul Kruger's mother once lived (see pages 40-1).

3,5 km beyond the Bulhoek turn-off you enter Steynsburg. Turn left into Van Riebeeck Street, which takes you out of town on a road lined with eucalypts and poplars.

You pass the substantial stone buildings of Lenton Grove railway siding on your left 4 km after leaving Steynsburg, and after a further 22 km there is a large grove of willows on your left, with a shaded picnic site.

Soon afterwards you pass the tarred R391 to Burgersdorp on your left as you approach closer to the foothills of the Stormberg. The road then passes a turn-off onto gravel to Hofmeyr, and roads to Vegkoppies and Stormberg Junction, before you enter Molteno (see opposite) 57 km from Steynsburg. There are two hotels in the town that serve lunch.

Leaving Molteno, follow the signs for Dordrecht and Queenstown, and note your kms as you cross the Stormberg Stream on the far side of town. After 3,3 km you pass the gravel R397 on your right to Sterkstroom. (Just over 4 km along this road is the rail siding and tiny ghost town of Syfergat. Coal was mined here for more than 60 years, and other industries included a brick-and-tile works which produced South Africa's first sewer pipes. All that remains of the works is a splendid brick chimney bearing the initials of a former manager of the works.)

The hills appear to recede, and the scenery becomes gentler, with cultivated fields and dark green trees around the farmhouses. 32 km from Molteno you pass a road on your right that leads to the R30 for Queenstown/Aliwal North, and a few hundred metres later you cross a bridge over the R30.

The view of plains and fields widens as the road descends slightly, and after a further 28 km you begin to see Dordrecht, with the town's name and the badge of the Voortrekker

The elegant lines of the restored Drostdy in Graaff-Reinet.

THE KAROO'S FOSSIL LEGACY

On the farm Wellwood, north of Graaff-Reinet, a private museum houses a collection of fossils that is known throughout the world. Farmer Sidney Rubidge took an interest in palaeontology after his 11-year-old daughter discovered a fossilised skull in 1934, and collected more than 800 skulls of animals that roamed these plains 180-240 million years ago. Among these fossils are 117 'type specimens' — those from which new species were first identified. Karoo fossils show a gradual change from reptilian to mammalian.

Tree-shaded picnic site near Rosmead.

Patches of green farmland and Karoo koppies typify the area between Graaff-Reinet and Middelburg.

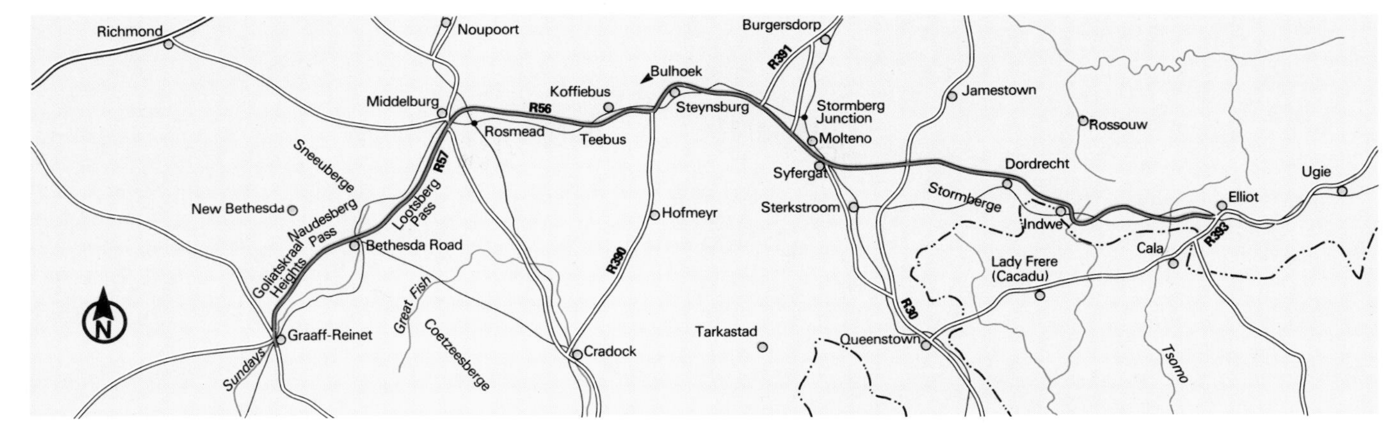

MOLTENO

With the gradual expansion of coal-mining in this area, George Vice, son of 1820 Settlers, decided to establish a town. He bought the farm Onverwacht (unexpected) for £70, and in 1874 started selling the first plots for £3 to £76. The town was later named after Sir John Molteno, first Prime Minister of the Cape under responsible government.

Molteno, and Stormberg Junction nearby, were heavily garrisoned during the Anglo-Boer War. Among the graves in Molteno's historic cemetery is that of the Honorable Raymond de Montmorency, a holder of the Victoria Cross and commander of the irregular unit known as Montmorency's Scouts who was killed in action in the Stormberg.

The museum, in the library building, has an excellent collection of firearms and turn-of-the-century photographs by pioneer photographer Ambrose Lomax.

TOWN IN THE MOUNTAINS

Spectacular buttresses of the southern Drakensberg tower above the town of Elliot, established in 1885 and named after Sir Henry Elliot, who led an adventurous life as a soldier, diamond-seeker, and later as Chief Magistrate of Tembuland.

There are outstanding views of the surrounding mountains from Thompson Dam, which lies 3 km from the town along the airfield road. The 80 m high Gilliecullem Falls on the Slang (snake) River are also well worth a visit. The falls lie 18 km out of the town along the road that leads past the railway station. (Inquire about the state of the road at Elliot's municipal office before setting out.)

War memorial to Dordrecht's burghers.

The distinctive Koffiebus rises abruptly from the surrounding Karoo plains.

DORDRECHT

During the Anglo-Boer War of 1899-1902 Dordrecht briefly became a part of the Orange Free State in terms of a proclamation read in public by the invading burghers. Sympathy in this border area was very much for the Boer side, and a monument in the grounds of the Dutch Reformed Church of 1882 commemorates those who died fighting the British.

The Methodist Church dates from 1879, and there are several good examples of Victorian architecture in the town. Dordrecht's museum houses a general collection of local interest, although one intriguing exhibit comes from St Helena. This is an old painted and varnished board, lettered in French and English: 'Road to the grave of the Emperor Napoleon'. Napoleon's body was interred on St Helena island from his death in 1821 until it was moved to France in 1840, and the signboard presumably dates from then. How it arrived in Dordrecht is no longer remembered.

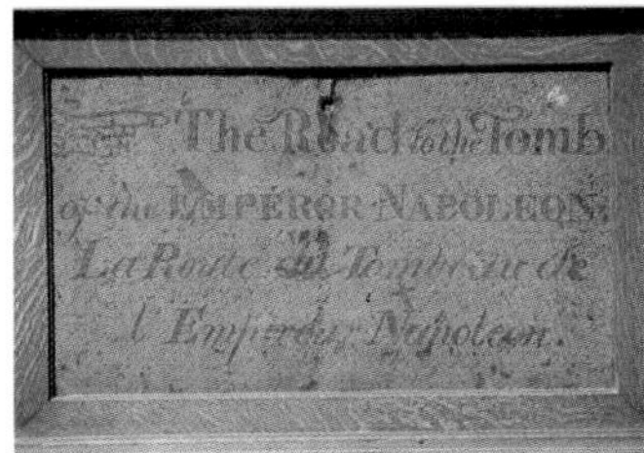

The mysterious St Helena sign that made its way to Dordrecht's museum.

youth movement picked out in white stones.

You enter Dordrecht, about 69 km from Molteno, on Church Street, facing the Anglican Church of St Augustine, built in 1883. At the T-junction in front of the church, turn left into Grey Street. Among the many old and picturesque buildings in this road is the stone building housing the Anderson Memorial Museum on your right. This was originally a general dealer's store, built in 1903. Another striking building is that of the Dutch Reformed Church (see above).

To leave the town, continue straight past the Dutch Reformed Church. The mountains ahead of you are the southern end of the Drakensberg, beneath which lies the small town of Indwe, 35 km from Dordrecht (see day drive, pages 216-7). As you drive through Indwe, you pass the stone building housing the magistrate's court and post office on your right.

Indwe to Elliot

About 1 km beyond the town you pass the R396 to Lady Frere/Cacadu on your right. The road winds steadily upwards through grassy hills, and you pass a number of minor roads on your left (some of which lead to scenic passes over the Drakensberg). You pass crossroads at the towns of Ida and Ulin, then 38 km from Indwe you cross the Tsomo River. The road passes under a rail bridge, and soon afterwards you pass the tarred R393 to Cala and Engcobo.

Roughly 54 km from Indwe the road begins to climb sharply, and mountains seem to fill the horizon on your left, until you top a rise to see Elliot ahead of you, overlooked by magnificent, craggy cliffs. Whitewashed stones pick out the name Elliot and the dates 1885-1985. You enter Elliot on Maclear Road 58 km from Indwe, with the municipal buildings on your left, and the town gardens on your right (see above; and day drive, pages 212-3) ●

From Elliot to Durban — through the giant hills of Transkei to a coastal world of golden beaches

Leaving the high ground of the Drakensberg, we soon enter Transkei, where picturesque huts cluster on the hillsides. We then descend gradually to the plains below — seen in tantalising glimpses, and sometimes in broad, stunning vistas. The road rolls on over Natal's hills through historic Pietermaritzburg to the coast.

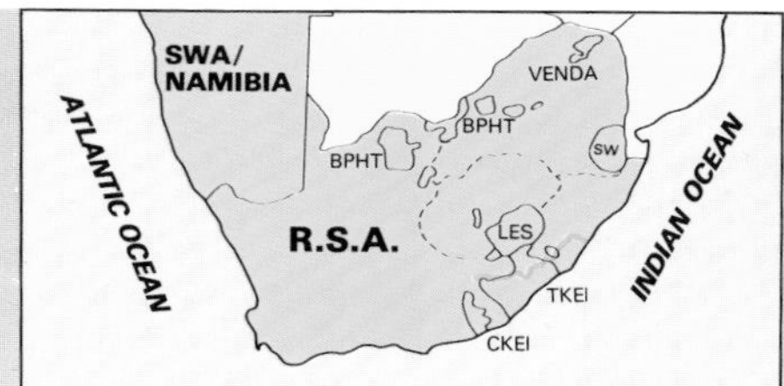

Elliot Municipality 15 Maclear Road, Elliot 5460 Tel. (045312) 11
Kokstad Municipality G F Heyns Building, Hope Street, Kokstad 4700 Tel. (0372) 3133
AA Office NAU Building, cnr Buchanan and Carbineer Streets, Pietermaritzburg 3201 Tel. (0331) 20571
AA Office AA House, 537 Smith Street, Durban 4001 Tel. (031) 3010341

Elliot - Maclear - Tsolo - Kokstad - Richmond - Pietermaritzburg - **Durban** (510—530 km)

LEAVE ELLIOT BY travelling east on Maclear Road (R56). The road climbs fairly steeply through wide, cultivated fields with soaring cliffs on your left. Among the peaks is the distinctive Gatberg (hole mountain), with a clearly visible hole through its top. You pass wooded hills and grand mountain scenery before you reach Ugie, 48 km beyond Elliot.

Continue straight through Ugie. On the far side of the town you cross a bridge with a beautifully built arched stone bridge alongside it on your left. The road rises, with vast plains on your right and majestic mountains on your left. You cross a bridge on the outskirts of Maclear, then enter the town a few hundred metres later, roughly 19 km from Ugie (see below; and day drive, pages 212-3).

If you intend to be on the road late at night, check before you leave Maclear that there are no curfews in force. Turn right at the T-junction, noting your kms. The road soon reaches rolling fields dotted with traditional painted huts, and after 14 km you begin to descend, with wide views over gently rolling countryside. 17 km from Maclear you cross the Transkei border. Roughly 8 km later you descend sharply, and you can see the road uncoiling far below into a broad, rugged valley.

You enter the town of Tsolo 56 km from Maclear. Keep straight through the town on the main road, and after a further 6,4 km turn left onto the N2, noting your kms. Soon afterwards you cross the Tsitsa River, and after 21 km on the N2 you pass through Qumbu. You pass a road on your left to Sulenkama, after which there are sweeping views across fields and valleys. As you cross the Tina River, you can see its old iron predecessor on your right.

After 55,6 km on the N2 there is a picnic site on your right with grand views over a huge valley dotted with huts and hills. From here the road winds downward, and the country seems to rotate about you as new segments come into view with each change of direction.

Mount Frere to Kokstad

You soon enter the town of Mount Frere, and 2 km later you pass a quaint, toy-like church on your left. After a further 10 km you cross the Mzimvubu River (river of the hippopotamus), and roughly 17 km later you pass the wooded gorges of Ntsizwa on your left. Soon afterwards you pass a turn-off to Tabankulu (big mountain), then you cross the Mzintlava River,

The Drakensberg looms behind a farmhouse near Elliot.

IXOPO

Set amongst forested hills, Ixopo is an agricultural and timber centre. It lies on a branch of the narrow-gauge railway line between Donnybrook and Esperanza. The town, laid out in 1878, was named Stuartstown in honour of the district magistrate, but soon reverted to its Zulu name, which refers to the sound of a foot being pulled from marshy ground.

The site of Cecil John Rhodes's first home in South Africa, a rondavel at Lion's Kloof, lies north-east of Ixopo, and is marked by a National Monuments Council plaque.

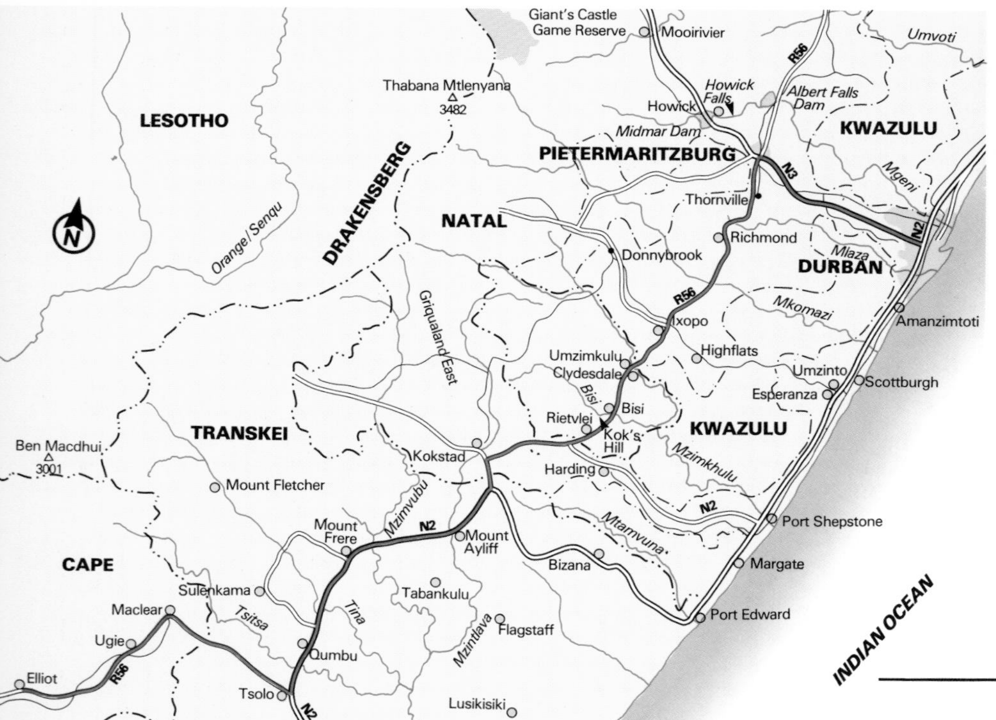

Stone arches of the Sivewright Bridge, Maclear.

MACLEAR

This centre for sheep and dairy farming is situated on the banks of the Mooi (pretty) River in the Drakensberg foothills. During the Pondomise uprising of 1880-1 the town was besieged and, on the night that the civilian garrison decided to slip through their enemy's lines, they heard the first distant shots fired by a relieving force from Dordrecht. The garrison made an orderly withdrawal, but the little town was burnt to the ground. When it was rebuilt, it was named after the Cape's Astronomer Royal, Sir Thomas Maclear.

before passing the village of Mount Ayliff on your right.

You cross the Inkweceni and Mvalweni rivers, and pass a turn-off on your right to Port Edward, Port St Johns and Bizana. The road climbs soon afterwards, offering views down over contoured, cultivated slopes.

After 140 km on the N2, the main route (N2) leads to the right to Harding and Umzimkulu — the road straight ahead leads after 2 km into Kokstad (see below). Note your kms as you pass the feeder road entering the N2 from Kokstad. 27 km later you pass through the Weza State Forest.

Kokstad to Ixopo

After 31 km you pass a motel and garage on your left. 18 km later go straight on the R56 for Ixopo and Richmond where the N2 leads right to Harding and Port Shepstone, and note your kms. The road snakes around soft, rolling hills, and passes through Rietvlei, with its mission buildings on both sides of the road. You then pass through Kok's Hill, and soon afterwards you cross the Bisi River.

As the road ascends, the scene of traditional huts scattered on green foothills widens to take in large, cultivated valleys, and beyond them densely wooded hills and slopes. 36,5 km after leaving the N2 you pass through Clydesdale, and 3 km later you pass through Umzimkulu.

Roughly 2 km later you reach the Transkei border post and passport control office. If you do not yet have a road-levy clearance-certificate, you will need to buy one at a small fee. You cross the Mzimkhulu River, then reach the South African border post.

Continue on the R56, through country that is much flatter, and intensively irrigated. You also pass large plantations of eucalyptus trees.

61 km after leaving the N2 you pass on your left the town of Ixopo, with its many jacaranda trees. The road descends, then crosses the narrow-gauge railway line. Note your kms soon afterwards at the crossroads where the road on your left leads to Ixopo and Donnybrook, and the road on your right leads to Highflats and Umzinto (see day drive, pages 190-1).

Ixopo to Richmond

The road passes forested hills with occasional windbreaks that form geometric patterns. 4,2 km after the crossroads you pass the attractive buildings of Mariathal Mission on your right amongst the trees. Cross the Mzimhlanga River, and about 18 km after last noting your kms you reach a narrow road-cutting with a picnic site immediately afterwards on your left offering magnificent views over hills and valleys that stretch away seemingly without end.

After a further 9 km you cross the Mkomazi (Umkomaas) River, then climb steeply for about 2 km before you wind downhill to cross the Mkobeni River. 46 km after last noting your kms, there is a turn-off on your left to the town of Richmond (see pages 172-3). Another road 500 m later on your right also leads into the town.

Richmond to Durban

Beyond Richmond the road passes through hilly country with citrus orchards. You cross the Mlaza (Umlaas) River, and soon afterwards there is a turn-off on your right to Umlaas Road. (If you wish to bypass Pietermaritzburg, turn right here, then turn right onto the N3 for Durban at Umlaas Road). Note your kms here.

After a further 6 km on the R56 a part of Pietermaritzburg comes into view after you crest a hill, and after another 6 km you reach a double-carriageway. You enter Pietermaritzburg on Richmond Road, which becomes Alexandra Road at a robot-controlled intersection 13 km after you last noted your kms. To continue to Durban, turn right at this intersection into Ritchie Road then follow the signs on to the N3 into the city ●

Rugged buttresses of the Drakensberg rear up near the town of Kokstad.

THE GRIQUA 'TREKKERS'

Kokstad (Kok's town) is named after Adam Kok III, the Griqua leader who took his people on an epic journey across the country after most of their land around Philippolis in the Cape had been lost through the repudiation of treaties by the British. About 2 000 people, with 300 wagons and 20 000 head of livestock, trekked for two years, eventually crossing the Drakensberg to settle in 1862 in an area between Transkei and Natal that was officially called No Man's Land. Ironically it was only after the Cape authorities annexed the Griqua state that it became known as Griqualand East. Kokstad was laid out in 1871, and today has broad, oak-shaded streets lined by water furrows. Adam Kok III, who died in 1875, lies buried next to the main street. The Mzintlava River, at the edge of the town, is stocked with trout.

A rich patchwork of farmlands covers Natal near Richmond.

TSOLO

The town of Tsolo (Xhosa for 'pointed') was given its name because of the pointed hills of the area. During the Pondomise uprising of 1880-1, at a time when the town was situated on the Inxu River, about 30 settlers were besieged in a small stone prison for a week before relief arrived from Umtata. The town was later moved to its present site on the Xokonxa River, where today it is the centre of a large agricultural district. A college for the sons of chiefs and an agricultural college have been established nearby.

A tranquil corner of the Botanical Gardens in Pietermaritzburg.

The inland route from Durban to Cape Town — shortest distance from port to port

The quickest route between Durban and Cape Town takes you on the N3 through the Natal Midlands and across the Drakensberg to Harrismith. From here you cross the eastern Orange Free State to link up with the N1 to Cape Town via Bloemfontein (see pages 32-5). No passports are necessary, as the entire drive is in South African territory.

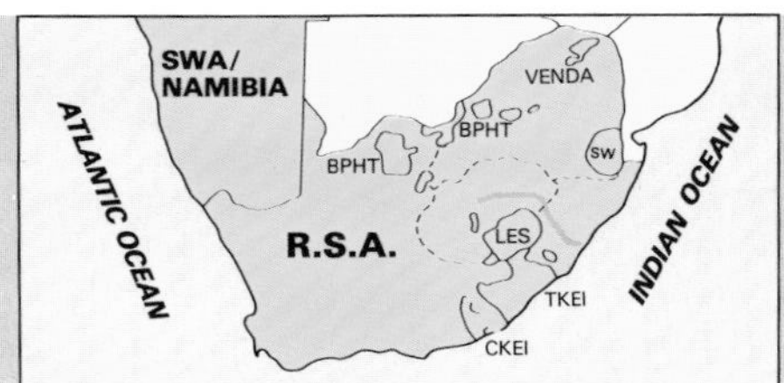

AA Office AA House, 537 Smith Street, Durban 4001 Tel. (031) 3010341
AA Office AA House, 56 Church Street, Bloemfontein 9301 Tel. (051) 76191
SA Tourism Board Third Floor, 320 West Street, Durban 4001 Tel. (031) 3047144
Harrismith Tourist Information Municipal Offices, Andries Pretorius Street, Harrismith 9880 Tel. (01436) 21061

Durban - Pietermaritzburg - Ladysmith - Harrismith - Bethlehem - Winburg - N1 to **Cape Town (1670—1690 km)**

LEAVE DURBAN BY TRAVELLING inland on the N3 (for Pietermaritzburg). Roughly 15 km from the city centre you have a choice of turning off left onto the R613 (the old Pietermaritzburg road that leads over the steep Fields Hill and offers an optional detour to the Valley of a Thousand Hills — see pages 178-9). Alternatively, you can remain on the N3, which for a small toll fee offers a faster route.

Inland of Durban you cross attractive, hilly countryside, which changes gradually from lush, sub-tropical vegetation to cultivated farmlands and canefields, then to sparser bushveld on the approach to Pietermaritzburg.

Roughly 50 km from Durban you pass on your right the distinctive, flat-topped Table Mountain, which dominates the head of the Valley of a Thousand Hills, and after a further 10 km you have views ahead over the city of Pietermaritzburg in the Msunduze River valley.

After a few more kilometres you pass an exit left for Mkondeni and Cleland — at the far side of the fly-over you can see on your left a stone church built by Italian prisoners of war. About 70 km from Durban you have a choice of taking the exit left for Pietermaritzburg (see pages 176-7, and day drives, pages 172-5) or of bypassing the city on the N3 for Mooi River.

Beyond Pietermaritzburg the N3 climbs the attractive, forested Town Hill, giving you good views down into Chase Valley on your right. The road levels out at the top of Town Hill and you pass an exit left to Hilton. 10,2 km later there is an exit left for Howick and Midmar Dam (a short detour to visit the grand 110 m Howick Falls is well worthwhile — see pages 174-5).

A few hundred metres beyond the Howick turn-off the N3 crosses the Mgeni River, and you can see the Midmar Dam wall on your left.

The stately facade of Pietermaritzburg's City Hall.

Colourful huts decorate the countryside near Harrismith.

SCENIC DRIVE AND A PETRIFIED TREE

A few kilometres north of Harrismith a mountain drive turns off the N3 and leads to the slopes below the spectacular heights of Platberg. From here there are magnificent views over Harrismith and the surrounding countryside, making it an ideal spot for a lunchtime picnic.

Among Harrismith's historic buildings is the red-brick City Hall on Warden Street. In the gardens lies a 33 m petrified tree-trunk dating back about 150 million years, and monuments honour the Scots Guards and Grenadier Guards who died during the Anglo-Boer War.

THE NIGHT OF THE 'GREAT MURDER'

A few months after the Voortrekkers had made their journey across the Drakensberg to the fertile land of Natal, their euphoria was shattered by a series of deaths at the hands of the Zulus. First came the slaying of their leader, Piet Retief, and his men at Dingane's kraal on 4 February, 1838. The Zulus then set out to attack the rest of the Voortrekkers, who had spread out across a wide area in spite of warnings to remain close together. On the night of 16-17 February, the Zulus surprised one laager after another in a night of gruesome killing that lived on in many memories as the 'Great Murder'. On 16 December, 1895, the remains of the men, women and children who died — as well as those of the revered leader, Gert Maritz — were re-interred at the scene of the worst Voortrekker suffering at Blaauwkrantz (or Bloukrans, as it is also known). The site has been declared a national monument.

A PIONEERS' PROMISED LAND

The Voortrekkers who founded Bethlehem in the 1860s named the river flowing through it the Jordaan (Jordan) in celebration of the promise it held in its fertile valley. Their optimism was well founded — today the town is the centre of a wealthy farming area (maize, wheat, fruit, vegetables, sheep, cattle and racehorses), as well as for industry.

Loch Athlone, a recreational and supply dam on the Jordaan, has been developed as a holiday resort, with a restaurant in the shape of the *Athlone Castle* mailship, a swimming pool, bungalows, and caravan and camping sites. The dam is stocked with fish, including bass and yellowfish. The nearby Saulspoort Dam also offers good fishing. Below Loch Athlone's dam wall lies the Pretorius Kloof Bird Sanctuary, a nature reserve offering fine bird-watching. The town's museum is housed in the old Nazareth Mission Church of 1906.

A magnificent winter scene in the north-eastern Orange Free State.

The road now begins a steady climb through the Natal Midlands towards the interior. The grass-covered hills of this area contrast attractively with patches of dark green forest.

Howick to Van Reenen's Pass

Roughly 40km from Howick you pass the town of Mooi (pretty) River on your left, and the road crosses the river after which the town was named. About 20km later there is a magnificent view ahead of you and to your right of Estcourt's surrounding hills, covered with acacia trees and aloes. The area through which you are now travelling has been the scene of many battles: amongst Nguni-speaking peoples during the Zulu war for supremacy, then between Boers and Zulus, then between British colonial forces and Zulus, and finally between Boers and Britons during the Anglo-Boer War. One of the remaining forts from the British colonial era — Fort Durnford — overlooks the farming and meat-processing centre of Estcourt.

100m beyond the Estcourt/Lowlands exit you pass the wall of Wagendrift Dam on your left. Note your kms as you pass the exit left to 'Estcourt/Loskop/Central Berg Resorts'. From here the road traverses rolling countryside towards the northern spur of the Drakensberg, and you also have glimpses of the high wall of the Natal/Lesotho section of the Drakensberg to the west.

After 18,9km you pass a turn-off right to Blaauwkrantz Monument, scene of great Boer losses during a battle with the Zulus (see opposite). 5,3km beyond this side road, there is another turn-off right to Chieveley Station and the Chieveley Military Cemetery (see pages 24-5), and 5km later you pass on your left the entrance to Clouston Military Cemetery and Garden of Remembrance.

4km later you pass the town of Colenso on the banks of the Tugela River on your right. Beyond the Tugela you have excellent views from the road of the Drakensberg and its foothills. Roughly 23km after crossing the Tugela you have an option of turning off onto the R23 for Ladysmith (see day drive, pages 168-9).

Ladysmith lies in a loop of the Klip River — note your kms as you cross the river on the far side of the town (if you have stayed on the N3, this will be the second time you cross it). Beyond the town the road rises steadily, and after 26,8km you reach the start of Van Reenen's Pass over the Drakensberg. 14,7km later — 41,5km after noting your kms — there is a turn-off left to the Windy Corner viewpoint, which offers magnificent views over the valleys and plains through which you have been travelling.

Van Reenen's Pass to Bethlehem

600m beyond the viewsite turn-off you reach the summit of the pass at 1680m, and soon afterwards you pass through the town of Van Reenen on the Natal/Orange Free State border. From here the road crosses high plains dotted with sandstone outcrops.

Roughly 30km from Van Reenen you reach the outskirts of Harrismith, lying at the foot of the imposing Platberg (flat mountain) — see opposite, and day drive, pages 142-3. You pass a turn-off right for the N3 to Warden and Johannesburg, and 400m later reach a crossroads where right leads into Harrismith town centre. Unless you plan to stop in Harrismith, continue straight here and follow the signs onto the R49 for Kestell.

The R49 leads through attractive farming country, where sandstone farm buildings nestle amongst tall trees, and there are views to your left of the Drakensberg and Maluti Mountains in the distance. You pass the attractive hillside town of Kestell (see pages 142-3), then, still on the R49, you meander across hilly country dotted with sandstone formations. Roughly 17km beyond Kestell the Langberg (long mountain) comes into view on your right.

Just short of 45km from Kestell you enter Bethlehem, an attractive farming and industrial centre on the banks of the Jordaan River (see opposite). Roughly 1,5km after entering the town turn left at the traffic circle (the road becomes Church Street). 200m later you pass a turn-off right to the town's museum. Drive straight through the town on Church Street, which has a number of historic buildings, and continue on the R49 for Senekal and Winburg.

Bethlehem to Winburg

Beyond Bethlehem lie farmlands dotted with clusters of colourful huts and interspersed with flat-topped koppies. 37km after leaving Bethlehem you pass the quaint little town of Paul Roux on your right. Notable for its tree-lined streets and backdrop of a sandstone koppie, Paul Roux was used by Voortrekkers and the old post coach as an outspan place.

After a further 32,5km you enter Senekal. At the first traffic lights turn left off the R49 into Charl Cilliers Street, for 'Kerkplein/Petrified Treetrunks'. 200m later you reach Church Square, where the magnificent sandstone church of 1895 is surrounded by a large collection of petrified trees of a fossil species dating back 250 million years.

Return to the R49, and turn left to continue your route. From here, the road enters the flat maize fields and grasslands that many people associate with the province. 64km beyond Senekal you pass an exit left to the old Voortrekker capital of Winburg, and 3,7km later you reach the turn-off onto the N1 for Bloemfontein. (For the continuation of the route from here to Cape Town, see pages 32-5) ●

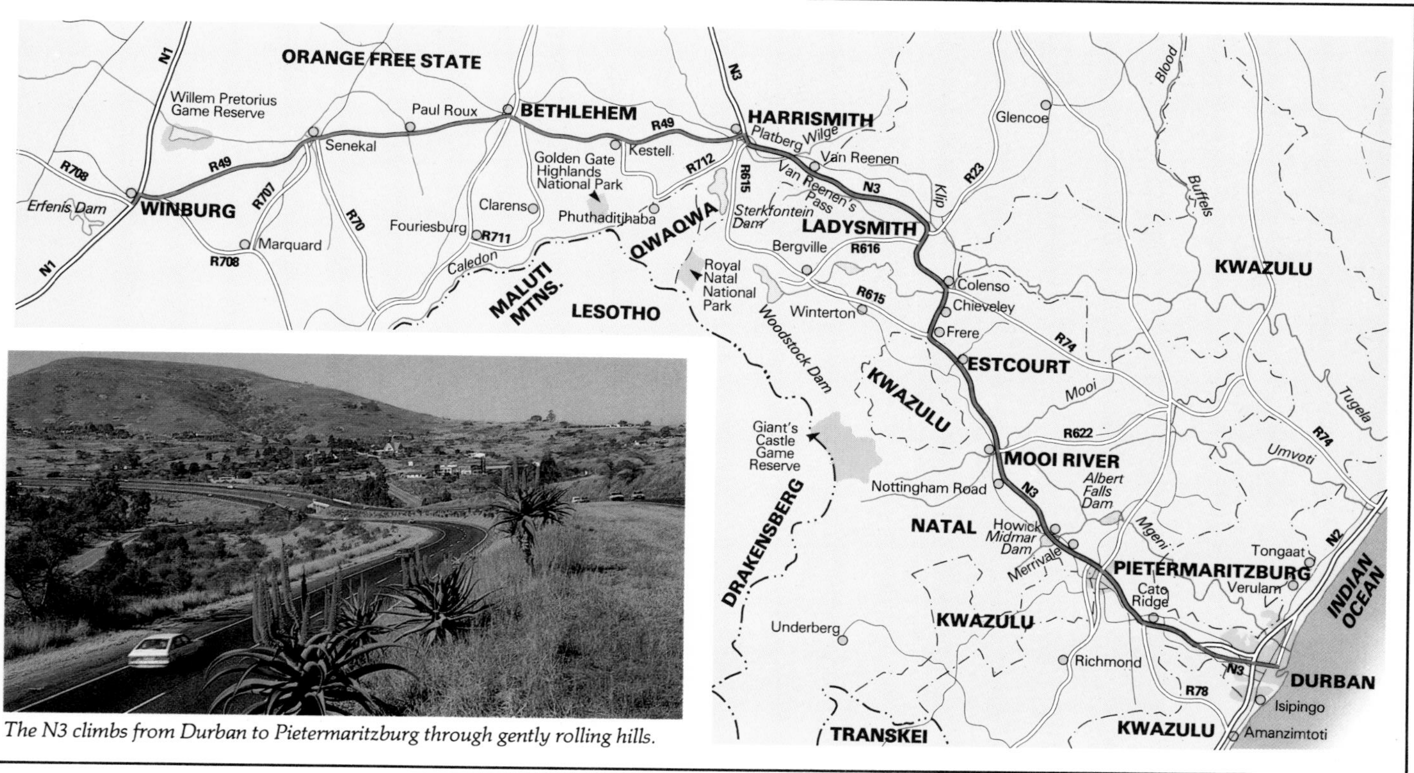

The N3 climbs from Durban to Pietermaritzburg through gently rolling hills.

Adventure into a sun-baked wilderness on the southern fringes of the Kalahari

In summer the arid plains of the northern Cape bake under a relentless sun, with temperatures regularly reaching up towards the 40°C mark. And yet this thirstland that our route passes through has a strange appeal — owing something to the silence and desolation of such a vast, empty landscape with views that stretch on forever.

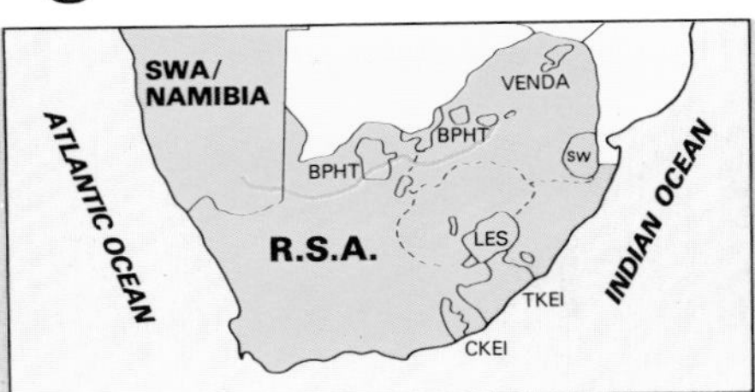

AA Office AA House, 395 Schoeman Street, Pretoria 0002 Tel. (012) 283829
AA Office AA House, 66 De Korte Street, Braamfontein, Johannesburg 2001 Tel. (011) 4035700
AA Office Johan Dreyer Building, cnr Kerk and Potgieter Streets, Potchefstroom 2520 Tel. (01481) 5434
AA Office Limna Building, cnr Delvers and Emily Hobhouse Streets, Klerksdorp 2570 Tel. (018) 24781

Pretoria (1170km)/Johannesburg (1100km) Klerksdorp - Vryburg - Kuruman - Upington - **Grünau**

IF YOU ARE STARTING YOUR journey from Johannesburg, drive south on the M1 through the centre of the city, join the N1, heading south, and shortly afterwards take the exit onto the R29 for Potchefstroom. If you are starting from Pretoria, either drive through Johannesburg on the M1 and proceed as above, or drive around Johannesburg on the Western Bypass (N1) and take the exit onto the R29 heading towards Potchefstroom.

The road traverses an area known as the Gatsrand (ridge of holes), named for the numerous sink-holes and caves that occur in its dolomite plateau. About 48kms after turning off the N1, a narrow gravel road on your left leads to the Danie Theron Monument, which is clearly visible from the road (see pages 36-7).

The R29 enters Potchefstroom on Holtzhausen Road, just over 90km from the N1. Proceed straight through the traffic lights, as the name of the road changes to Potgieter Street. On your left, in Kerk Street, is the oldest stone-built Herformde Kerk in the Transvaal (1859). Immediately after crossing the railway line, note on your left the whitewashed remains of the fort unsuccessfully besieged by Transvaal burghers during the 1880-81 war with Britain.

25km after leaving Potchefstroom you pass on your left the Stilfontein gold mine — one of the first of the mines on the Far West Rand. 10km later you pass a road leading off to the modern town of Stilfontein. A further 7km brings you to the town of Klerksdorp.

Klerksdorp to Kuruman

Keep straight at the traffic lights on the outskirts of Klerksdorp, passing a road on your left that leads into the town centre. After Klerksdorp the road leads through wide, bush-covered plains.

On the outskirts of Wolmaransstad, roughly 80km from Klerksdorp, you pass on your left the R504 to Leeudoringstad — the town that made world headlines in 1932 when a trainload of over 1000 tons of dynamite exploded nearby. (14,5km along this road, on the farm Witpoort, is the site of the first mission in the Transvaal — established in 1822 by the Wesleyan missionaries S Broadbent and T L Hodgson, who are believed to have been the first whites to cross the Vaal.)

After crossing the Makwassie Stream you enter Wolmaransstad on Broadbent Street. Turn right into Kruger Street for Schweizer-Reneke. The road crosses a railway line and

The railway station at Grünau — named after a suburb of Berlin.

THE KALAHARI

The R32 between Upington and Karasburg leads through the southern fringes of the Kalahari Desert. Stricty speaking a semi-desert rather than a desert, the Kalahari (or Kgalagadi) is a vast region of fine sand, ranging in colour from reddish to grey, and interrupted here and there by rocky hills.

There is some rain in winter, but little of it ever reaches the sea. Most collects in shallow pans — providing drinking water for the animals of the region. In the drier southern parts the sand has only a thin cover of grass, dotted with a few lonely camel-thorn trees *(Acacia giraffae)*.

Last century, the American explorer William Hunt — who earned his living as a tightrope walker — claimed to have discovered a lost city in the Kalahari, but no subsequent expedition has been able to confirm this find.

An early tar-spraying machine is preserved at Vryburg.

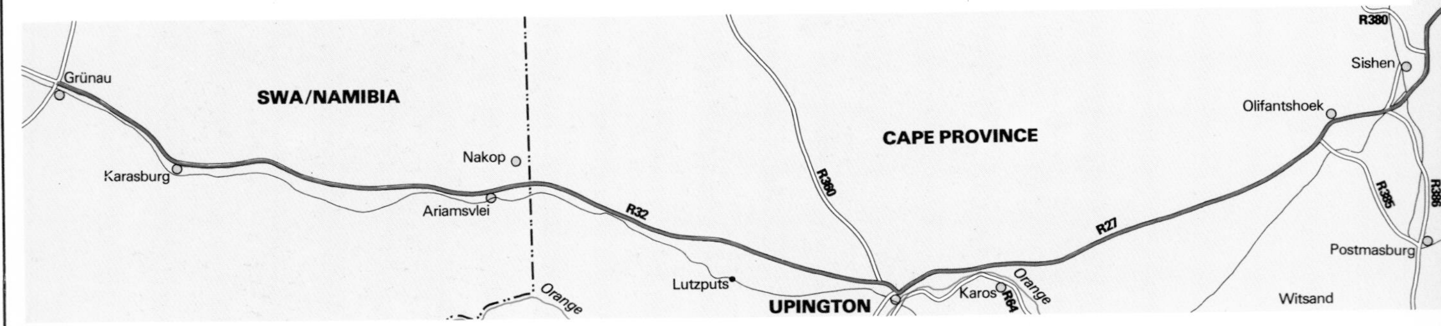

becomes the R504, running through a sea of maizefields. 70 km after leaving Wolmaransstad you enter Schweizer-Reneke on Schweizer Street (see below). After crossing several intersections, turn right into Olivier Street — which becomes the R34 to Vryburg.

You now pass large maize silos, and a peanut processing factory on your left. Roughly 30 km after leaving Schweizer-Reneke you cross the border of the Transvaal and enter the northern Cape, and some 30 km later you enter the town of Vryburg on Market Street (see pages 48-9). After passing the Civic Centre on your left, turn left into De la Rey Street, which becomes the R27 for Kuruman. About 1 km after turning into De la Rey Street, you will see on your right a section of the historic town jail.

As you travel towards Kuruman you pass several roads on your left that lead to Reivilo — the name of a former clergyman, the Rev A J Olivier, spelt backwards. 140 km after leaving Vryburg you enter Kuruman, once famous as the mission station of Robert Moffat. You enter the town on Main Street, and you pass on your left the 'Eye of Kuruman', an unfailing spring of fresh water that played a key role in the siting of the mission and the town. (If you wish to make a short detour to visit the historic mission buildings, see pages 48-9 for directions.)

Kuruman to Grünau

Leave Kuruman on Main Street, which becomes the R27 for Upington. The road leads west through hilly country dotted with low trees and thorn-bush. After roughly 45 km you will see ahead of you and to your right the iron ore dumps at Sishen. Keep straight when you come to the crossroads with the R380, where the road on your left leads to Postmasburg and the road right leads to Hotazel (named 'in honour' of the very high temperatures experienced here). Roughly 75 km after leaving Kuruman turn right to continue on the R27 to pass through the town of Olifantshoek on Van Riebeeck Street. Soon after this you pass a road on your left that leads to Witsand — where great tracts of white sand overlie abundant water in an otherwise inhospitable desert. (In this area are the 'roaring sands', high dunes that emit a roaring or grunting sound in certain weather conditions — believed to be caused by the sand particles rubbing together.)

130 km beyond Olifantshoek you reach what appears to be a great oasis in the midst of the desert — actually the irrigated banks of the Orange River. The sight of vineyards and bright green fields makes a dramatic contrast with the barren plains. The R27 runs close to the river for some 30 km before entering the town of Upington on Schröder Street (see pages 310-11). Note your kms as you pass beneath the railway bridge in the town.

Keep straight at the first set of traffic lights, and at the second set turn right into Keimoes Road for Keimoes and South West Africa/Namibia. Keep straight at two further sets of traffic lights, and cross the railway line at 4,2 km. Keep straight at the stop street you come to 1,3 km later. Turn left at the intersection at 7 km, and turn left again at 8,8 km onto the R32 towards 'South West Africa/Kalahari Gemsbok National Park'.

The road now passes through low hills that have been split into piles of boulders by millenia of alternating heat and cold, and roughly 140 km after leaving Upington you reach the border of South West Africa/Namibia, near the Nakop (mountain tortoise) River. 17 km after crossing the border you come to Ariamsvlei, a small town that caters to the needs of the surrounding farming community.

The next 130 km stretch of road leads from Ariamsvlei to Karasburg, and crosses several river beds — normally dry. Picnic sites are rare on this road, but the few that there are have thatched shelters that give a small amount of shade (see opposite). Look out for Karakul sheep in this region — the pelts of newly born lambs are highly prized in Europe where they are made into coats and hats.

Drive through Karasburg, following the tarred road as it bends to the right. Shortly after passing through the town, you pass on your right the Great Karasberg (rocky mountain) range. There are four shaded picnic sites along this part of the route — before you reach Grünau, some 50 km from Karasburg (see opposite). You pass Grünau's railway station, and 1 km later you reach a T-junction with the South West African N1. Turn right here for Keetmanshoop and Windhoek. (For the continuation to Windhoek, see pages 66-7.)

KARASBURG
Old Nama pastoralists watered their goats at a place they called Nomsoros — the chalky place with springs. Later, Europeans called it Kalkfontein (chalky or lime spring), but this was confused with another Kalkfontein to the north, so the name of the nearby mountain range, Karas, was adopted — and coupled with 'burg' (town).

Under the German colonial regime, a railway line was built from Lüdertzbucht, and following the South African invasion of German South West Africa during the World War I, this was linked to the South African railhead at Upington. Karasburg is now the rail and trading centre for a large rural community. There is a hotel in the town.

Left: *Town Hall at Schweizer-Reneke.*

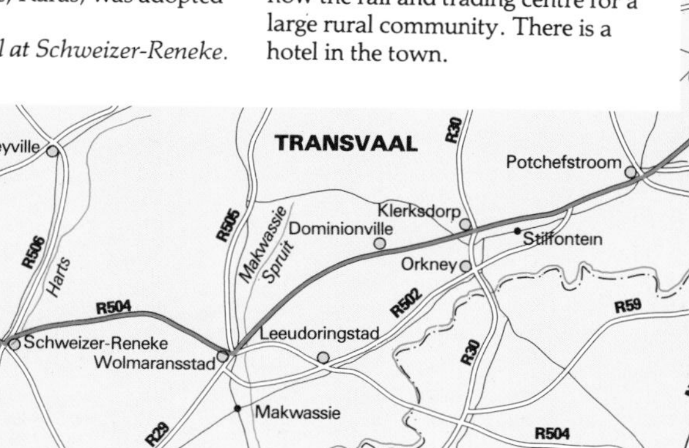

LAST STAND OF THE KORANNA
A few years after Britain's military humiliation in the Anglo-Transvaal War, the London Convention of 1884 granted to the Transvaal land that traditionally had belonged to the Koranna people. The Koranna, fortified the summit of the hill known as Mamusa and on 2 December 1885 a battle took place on the mountain's slopes between the Koranna defenders and a Transvaal commando. Ultimately the Transvaal forces drove the Koranna away, but they left ten of their own men dead.

Among the dead were Captain Constantin Schweizer and Field Cornet C N Reneke, and the town that later grew up below the hill, on the banks of the Harts River, was named after them. The ruins of the Koranna fort are still to be seen on the hilltop, from where there is a good view of the town.

Left: *A shady spot in Kuruman.*

North to Windhoek across the vast plains of South West Africa/Namibia

This route leads from the Orange River across the enormous southern plains of what was formerly German South West Africa — an extraordinary, moody land of sand and weathered rock, cut through with a network of dried-out river beds. We arrive eventually at Windhoek, a capital city that retains much of its German atmosphere.

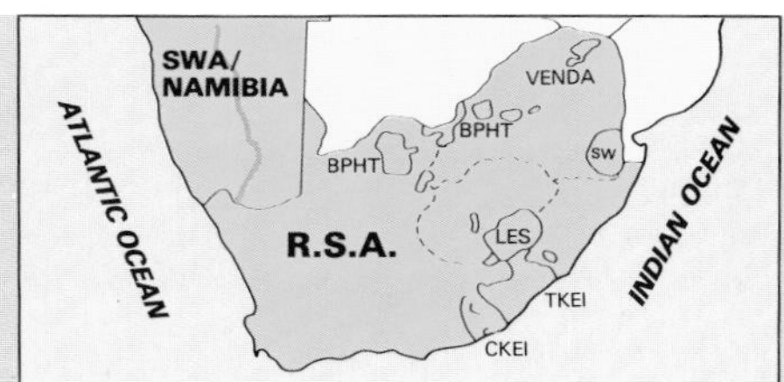

AA Office AA House, 7 Martin Hammerschlag Way, Cape Town 8001 Tel. (021) 211550
Keetmanshoop Municipality Kaiser Street, Keetmanshoop Tel. (0631) 3317
Tourist Office Hardap Dam Recreation Resort, Mariental Tel. (0661) 381
AA Office Carl List Haus, cnr Kaiser and Peter Muller Streets, Windhoek 9100 Tel. (061) 24201

Vioolsdrif (780—800km) - **Grünau** (640—660km) - Keetmanshoop - Mariental - Kalkrand - Rehoboth - **Windhoek**

THIS IS THE continuation of our routes to Windhoek from Cape Town (see pages 68-9) and from the southern Transvaal (see pages 64-5). Travellers coming from Cape Town will begin this second leg of their journey at Vioolsdrif. Travellers coming from the southern Transvaal, or from the northern Cape, join this route at Grünau.

If you are coming from Cape Town you cross the Orange River at Vioolsdrif on the D F Malan bridge. Note your kms at the northern end of the bridge. After 3,3km you pass a motel and the small settlement of Noordoewer, then the road climbs out of the valley of the Orange River into a harsh desert landscape.

After 41km you pass a road on your left leading to Ai-Ais, in the grand Fish River Canyon (see opposite). 8,8km later you pass the first of the many picnic spots situated along this road — each consists of thatched umbrellas, tables and seats. At 59,3km you pass a road on your right leading to Karasburg, and you enter a grassy stretch of countryside. At 107km you pass a second road to Karasburg, and at 113km you pass a second turn-off for Ai-Ais.

144kms after crossing the D F Malan bridge you pass the small settlement of Grünau on your right. Roughly 600m later you reach a junction, where the road from Karasburg and Upington leads in from the right. (Travellers coming from the southern Transvaal via Upington arrive on this road and join our route at this point — see pages 64-5). Continue north towards Keetmanshoop, noting your kms at this junction.

Grünau to Vingerklip

After driving some 35km from the Grünau junction you enter a landscape of rock-strewn koppies, large boulders and dry river beds. After 82km you pass a road on your right to Warmfontein and Aroab, and after roughly 150km you cross the Huns River, from where you can see the town of Keetmanshoop ahead of you. After roughly 10km you pass a road on your left leading to Luderitz, Goageb, Aus and Seeheim — and you enter Keetmanshoop.

Continue straight through Keetmanshoop, noting your kms as you leave the town. After some 3km you pass a turn-off right to Aroab and Koës — this road also leads to the farm Gariganus and its protected forest of quiver trees (kokerbome). You now pass through semi-arid karakul farming country. After roughly 20km you cross the Aub River, then pass a turn-off to Gariganus Station, where a high tower dominates the flat landscape.

As you continue north you cross several dry river beds, and after travelling roughly 81km from Keetmanshoop you pass a road on your left to Berseba. 1km after passing this turn-off you reach a petrol station at the small settlement of Tses. 26km after Tses, petrol is again available at Brukkaros.

Roughly 23km after passing through Brukkaros you reach a road leading right to Vingerklip (finger rock), also known as the 'Finger of God'. This side-trip is worth making (see opposite). If you choose not to visit the rock, note your kms as you pass this road. If you do visit it, note your kms as you return to the main road and turn right to continue your journey.

Vingerklip to Mariental

1,7km after this turn-off to Vingerklip you reach the small town of Asab, which offers petrol and accommodation. Continue through the town. North from here the road runs parallel to a flat-topped escarpment on your right. This is called the Weissrand (white ridge) and on its summit at various intervals stand communication towers.

The road climbs and after some 38km from the Vingerklip turn-off you pass a road on your left to Gibeon, a small town on the banks of the Fish River 8km from the main road (petrol available). Immediately after this you pass a turn-off right to Gochas. (Travellers wishing to visit the Kalahari Gemsbok National Park should turn onto this road.) Roughly 60km after passing this turn-off to Gochas, you pass a road on your right leading into the town of Mariental, lying in a spacious grassy plain. Note your kms as you pass this turn-off.

Mariental to Windhoek

As you travel north from Mariental you leave the dry plains and penetrate an increasingly wooded and more mountainous landscape. 9,4kms from Mariental you pass a road on your right to Stampriet, the main route to the Kalahari Gemsbok National Park. 4,5km later you pass a road on your left to Hardap Dam — the third-largest dam in southern Africa and a popular recreation resort. 600m later you cross the Dabib River, and enter the country's principal karakul sheep farming region.

Roughly 60km after passing Mariental you reach Kalkrand — a small village situated near 'Die Kalk' plateau, a vast sandstone escarpment after which the settlement was named. Here you pass a gravel road leading left to Maltahöhe. As you continue north from Kalkrand you again enter a fairly arid stretch of countryside. 147km after passing through the town of Mariental you cross the Tropic of Capricorn, and 14kms later you reach the small mission station of Rehoboth. The mission was established over a century ago and is now the main settlement of the Baster (half-breed) clan, whose ancestors were European trek farmers and local Khoikhoi girls.

6km after Rehoboth you pass a road leading left to Solitaire. 67km later you pass a sign on your left indicating a hotel, and shortly after this you cross a railway line. A further 22km brings you to the outskirts of Windhoek, the capital city of South West Africa/Namibia, set attractively against a mountain range roughly 2000m above sea level (see opposite) ●

The Fish River Canyon near Keetmanshoop.

There is a recreation resort at Hardap dam.

WINDHOEK

Windhoek (windy corner), the legislative and administrative capital of South West Africa/Namibia, was established by Germans in 1890. They chose a site previously settled by the Nama chief, Jonker Afrikaner, in the Swakops River valley. A fort was built on a hill above the town by Major Curt von Francois. Known as the Alte Feste (old fort), it became the headquarters of the German administration of the territory, and today houses a small museum.

Windhoek is a cosmopolitan city, where German colonial buildings still stand alongside modern office blocks. A distinctive feature of the city is the presence of the dignified Herero women who continue to wear the stately Victorian dresses introduced by missionary wives 100 years ago.

A distant view of the Vingerklip (finger rock), or 'Finger of God'.

KEETMANSHOOP

Named after a wealthy German merchant, John Keetman, who donated funds for a mission station to be built here, Keetmanshoop was established on the banks of the usually dry Swartmodder (black mud) River. A town grew up slowly around the mission station, and a fine stone church stands proudly above the buildings, many of which were built in the German colonial style. The town is surrounded by hot, dry semi-desert, and is now the centre of a large karakul sheep farming area. 14 km north-east of the town there is a protected forest of kokerbome (quiver trees) on the farm Gariganus.

Equestrian statue in Windhoek.

Aloe dichotoma — *the kokerboom.*

FISH RIVER CANYON

This magnificent natural phenomenon, dating back over 2 000 million years, stretches 161 km from its northern end to its junction with the Orange River. In the bed of the Fish River are a number of hot sulphur springs, believed to possess medicinal powers. Around one of these a holiday resort has been established, named Ai-Ais, a Nama word meaning 'scorching hot'. The resort attracts both those in search of cures for their ailments and also keen hikers who wish to explore the floor of the canyon. An 86 km hiking trail extends from the main lookout point over the canyon to Ai-Ais — an exciting four-day scramble. Kokerbome and aloes flourish along the river bed, and birdlife in the vicinity of the canyon includes the fish eagle, Egyptian geese, hamerkops and herons.

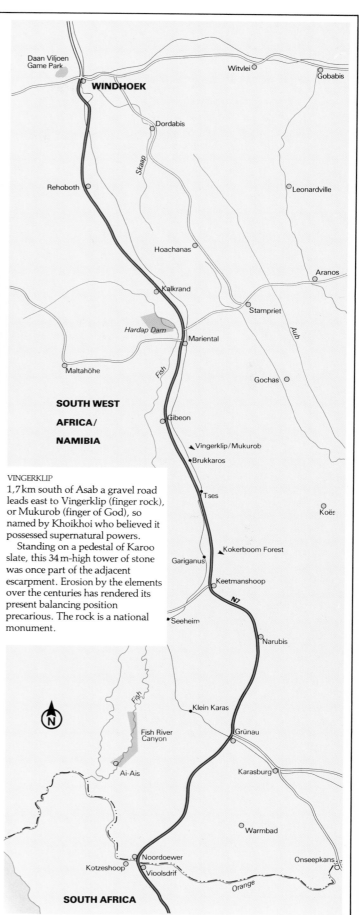

VINGERKLIP

1,7 km south of Asab a gravel road leads east to Vingerklip (finger rock), or Mukurob (finger of God), so named by Khoikhoi who believed it possessed supernatural powers.

Standing on a pedestal of Karoo slate, this 34 m-high tower of stone was once part of the adjacent escarpment. Erosion by the elements over the centuries has rendered its present balancing position precarious. The rock is a national monument.

Beyond the Copper Mountains to the land of the kokerboom

This is the main route linking Cape Town and South West Africa/Namibia. For nearly half the journey we cover the same ground as in the 'northern Cape' route from Cape Town to the Transvaal, but then we strike out northwards from Vanrhynsdorp to the 'copper mountains' of Namaqualand and the lower reaches of the Orange River.

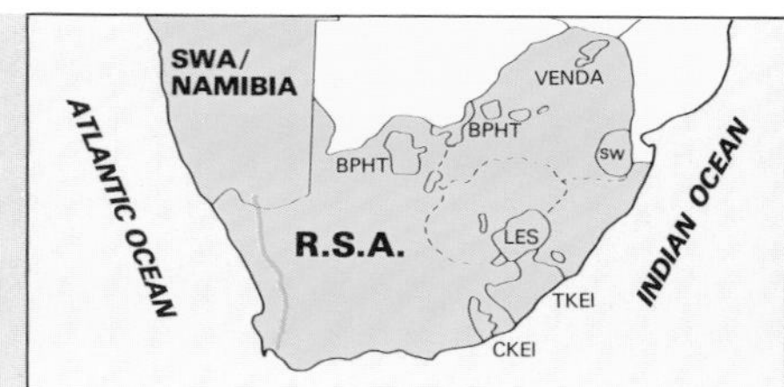

AA Office AA House, 7 Martin Hammerschlag Way, Cape Town 8001 Tel. (021) 211550
Clanwilliam Municipality and Divisional Council Main Street, Clanwilliam 8135 Tel. (02682) 28/215
Tourist Information Springbok Cafe, Voortrekker Street, Springbok 8240 Tel. (0251) 21321
SA Tourism Board Level 3, Golden Acre, Adderley Street, Cape Town 8001
Tel. (021) 216274

Cape Town - Citrusdal - Clanwilliam - Vanrhynsdorp - Garies - Springbok - **Vioolsdrif (670—690 km)**

THIS ROUTE FOLLOWS THE N7 for its entire length from Cape Town to the SWA/ Namibia border at Vioolsdrif, and the first section of the journey takes the same route as that from Cape Town to the Transvaal via Upington. Directions for this first part of the journey can be found on pages 46-7, detailing the route onto the N7, through the Swartland, and past Clanwilliam as far as Klawer.

Travelling north on the N7 you pass the village of Klawer on your left. 6 km later you cross the Wiedouw River, and 10 km after this the Troe Troe River. Immediately after crossing the Troe Troe River you pass the turn-off onto the R27 on your right, which leads directly into Vanrhynsdorp. Unless you wish to stop in Vanrhynsdorp, continue on the N7, noting your kms as you pass this junction.

Vanrhynsdorp to Garies

On your right you now have the vast and desolate plain known as the Knersvlakte ('kners' meaning to 'gnash', and 'vlakte' meaning 'plain'), with the Bokkeveld Mountains far away in the distance. On your left the dune country of the Hardeveld stretches westwards to the sea. For much of the way you can trace the route of an older road, marked by the line of telegraph poles on your right. The old road, built with pick and shovel, had to skirt around major obstacles such as hills, whereas the new road simply forges ahead through huge cuttings.

After 64 km you pass the gravel R363 on your left, which leads onto Nuwerus (new rest), a small village that lies 100 m from the highway. (During early spring there are often magnificent displays of wildflowers to be seen in the stretch of country through which the R363 passes.) 15 km after Nuwerus you reach Bitterfontein, the railhead for Namaqualand's copper mines. Granite is also quarried extensively in the district, and great blocks of granite are railed from here, for building and monumental work.

A further 60 km brings you to the town of Garies — this name being a Khoikhoi word for couch grass. A few hundred metres before you reach the entrance road into Garies you pass a broken monument on a low mound to your left. This marks the grave of an English officer killed here during the Anglo-Boer War.

Garies to Springbok

North of Garies the granite outcrops become more frequent, and the road passes tumbled hills with huge boulders perched precariously on their slopes. Roughly 27 km after Garies you pass the small settlement of Garagams (Karkams), and a further 27 km brings you to Kamieskroon. Kamieskroon lies near the foot of the Kamies Mountains, one of whose highest peaks is the 'kroon' (crown) topped by an enormous cleft boulder (see opposite). You can see this formation from the road you are travelling on, but the cleft in the great boulder is only partly visible from this angle. A lone, pointed peak nearby is known as 'Weeskind' (orphan).

After Kamieskroon the road winds among towering outcrops, and roughly 12 km from Kamieskroon you pass a gravel turn-off on your right to Bowesdorp (see opposite). 40 km from Kamieskroon you pass a road on your left that leads to Hondeklipbaai, once the harbour for the copper mines (see pages 306-7), and to Soebatsfontein. Literally translated, 'soebatsfontein' would mean 'spring of pleading', but the name is probably a corruption of Sievertsfontein — from a frontier farmer named Sievert who was killed here by the San people in the 18th century.

7,6 km after passing this road to Hondeklip-

Table Mountain from Bloubergstrand, with Devil's Peak on the left and Lion's Head on the right.

Blooms in the Biedouw Valley near Clanwilliam.

THE ORIGINS OF THE NAMA

The first recorded contact between European settlers and the Nama people living in the area now named after them, Namaqualand, occurred in 1661, when an expedition led by the surgeon Pieter van Meerhof encountered a group of these people somewhere in southern Namaqualand. The entry in the official journal kept by the expedition describes the Nama as 'gorgeously ornamented with copper beads'.

The Nama comprised several distinct tribes, each with its own recognised territory in Little Namaqualand (south of the Orange River) and great Namaqualand (now South West Africa/Namibia). They were pastoralists, and practised no agriculture, but at some time in the distant past they had evidently mastered the techniques of smelting mineral ores. Similarities in language between the Nama and the Sandawe people of Tanzania have led to speculation that the original home of the Nama was somewhere on the coast of east Africa.

baai you reach the turn-off to Springbok on your left. Springbok is the starting point for the day drive described on pages 306-7, and several establishments in the town provide lunch.

Springbok to the Orange River

If you choose to bypass Springbok and stay on the N7, you will see on your left, 6 km after the turn-off and on the outskirts of Springbok, the stone chimney of an old copper-smelting plant. This was built in 1866 and has now been proclaimed a national monument.

5 km beyond the chimney you pass a road on your left that leads to Okiep and Nababeep (sometimes spelt Nababiep). You will see to the right of the road the mine workings and part of the residential area of Okiep. After a further 15 km you can see on a ridge to your left a building shaped rather like an old-fashioned wagon tent. This was once an explosives store for one of the local mines. 500 m later, also on your left, you pass a round stone building reminiscent of a fortress. This was the foundation of a water tower used by the old Port Nolloth-Okiep railway. The railway no longer exists, but from several places along the road you can see traces of the old embankments and carefully built stone culverts.

50 km after Springbok you reach the small settlement of Steinkopf, on the edge of the notoriously barren Richtersveld. Among the more modern houses in the village you can see many traditional huts, known as matjieshuisies (little mat huts). Beyond Steinkopf the road is closely hemmed in by bare hills, then emerges onto a wide, flat plain, with range after range of hills shimmering in the heat ahead of you. 56 km after Steinkopf the hills close in again as you enter Vyfmylpoort (five mile gorge), following the course of a dry river bed that you can see on your left.

Roughly 6 km into the gorge you will see, down in the river bed, a cemetery of simple headstones and rock-covered graves. Soon after this the road begins to descend towards the Orange River and, in sudden contrast to the dry, rocky landscape you have been travelling through, you reach bright green fields — irrigated with water drawn from the Orange River. After passing the tiny settlement of Vioolsdrif, you reach the D F Malan bridge that carries the road across the Orange River into South West Africa/Namibia. Look to your left for a dramatic view of the riverside cliffs. (The continuation of this route, from the Orange River to Windhoek, is described on pages 66-7) ●

THE EXTRAORDINARY QUIVER TREE

A characteristic sight throughout Namaqualand, Bushmanland and the Northern Cape is the kokerboom (quiver tree), which owes its name to the fact that the San people used its bark to make quivers for their poisoned arrows. Although tree-like in appearance, the kokerboom is an aloe *(Aloe dichotoma)*, and in fact belongs to the lily family. The blooms appear in late winter — the yellow, candle-like flowers protruding from among the leaves. A mature specimen of this unusual plant can grow to a height of seven metres, its bark becoming gnarled and wrinkled with age.

The Kokerboom. Not a tree, but an unusual species of aloe.

Wild flowers dot the roadside in Namaqualand.

PLACE OF THE SPECIAL WOMAN

Steinkopf has grown around one of the oldest of Namaqualand's mission stations — founded by the London Mission Society at a place known to the Khoikhoi as Tarakhois (special woman).

The Nama huts in the village were originally known as 'matjieshuisies' (little mat houses) because they were made of reed mats tied to a wooden frame. With the coming of the mining companies, however, sacking has replaced the reeds.

From Steinkopf there is a 93 km road (R382) leading west over the Anenous Pass to Port Nolloth on the 'Diamond Coast'.

THE TOWN THAT MOVED

The little town of Kamieskroon lies on the plain at the foot of the Kamies (grass veld) Mountains. The town is overlooked by one of the range's highest peaks, topped by a huge boulder that has been split in two. The mountain is known as the 'kroon' (crown) and also as 'Kardouw' (narrow passage), both names referring to the cleft boulder, and the town takes its name from the first of these two names for the mountain.

The town was established as recently as 1924, after a remarkable Namaqualand character, Dr W P Steenkamp, decided that the town of Bowesdorp, a few kilometres to the north, was unhealthily situated in its narrow valley with no space for expansion. Bowesdorp, which had been settled for some 60 years, was accordingly abandoned, and Kamieskroon arose to take its place. It is situated in an area rich in wild flowers.

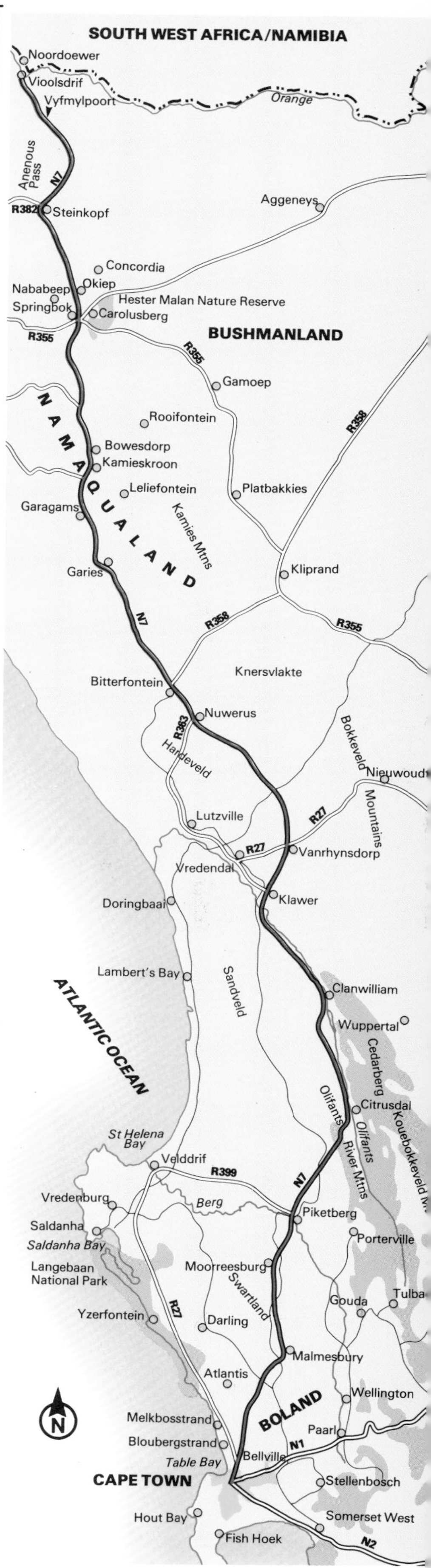

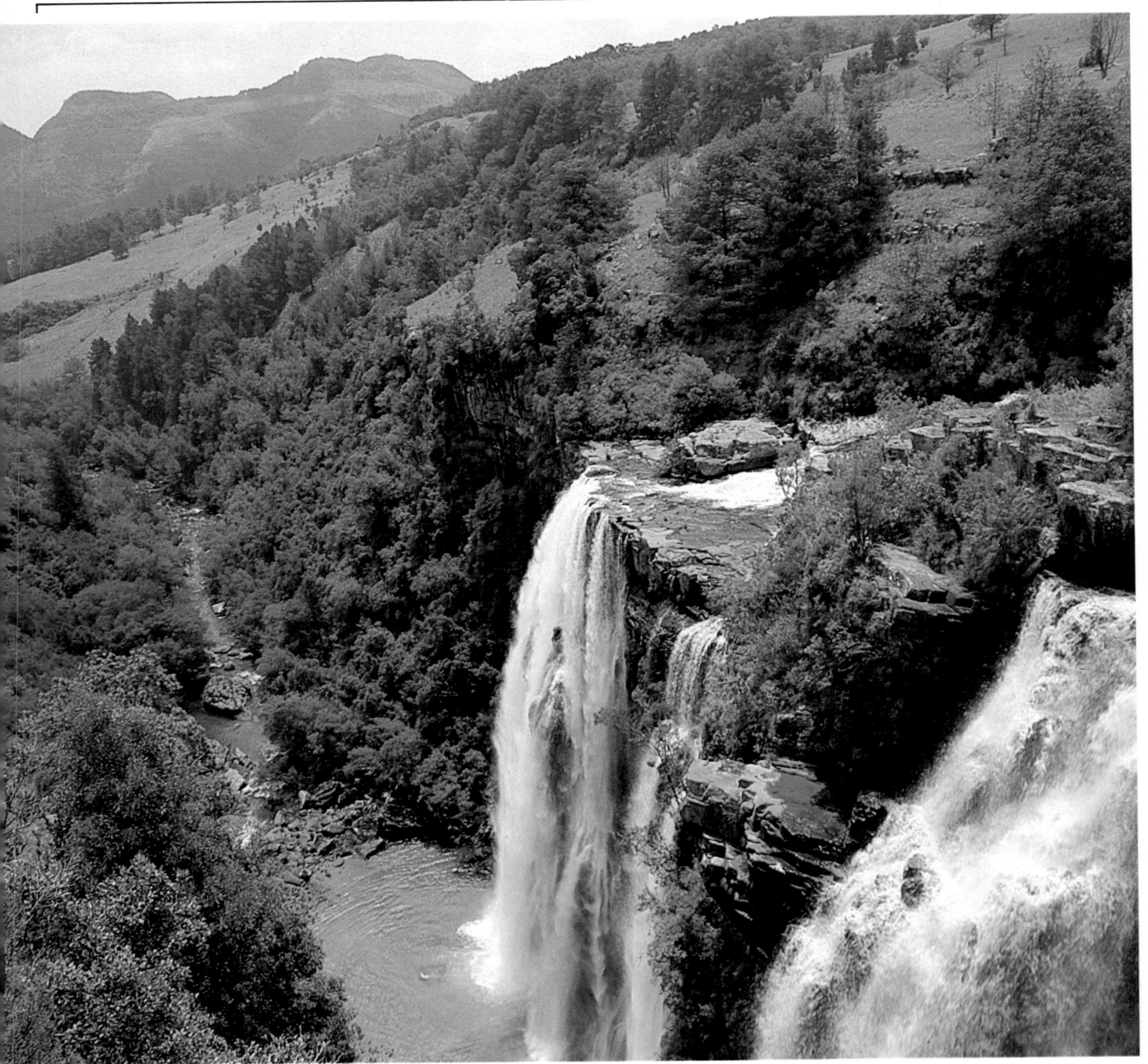

Summer rains have swept the Highveld, painting the landscape in rich shades of green and swelling the waters that tumble over the Lisbon Falls.

DAY DRIVES

FOLLOW A MEANDERING mountain track to meet *T'Numkwa*, the 'Mountain of the Clouds', wander barefoot along golden sands that curl languidly around a translucent coastal lagoon, quietly pay your respects at a sacred waterfall where ancient spirits are still propitiated with small gifts of food and drink, walk in a gentle mountain breeze across rocky slopes where hopeful prospectors dipped smoke-blackened pans into streams that ran with gold, sip fine old wines under graceful gables amid the vineyards of the Cape — each of the day drives described on the following pages is a carefully assembled composition of such magic moments.

Not only are these drives designed to show you the most beautiful and most interesting places in each region of the country, but the order of events that make up each day has been carefully arranged to provide contrast, to bring you to each place at the best time, and ultimately to create a wonderful adventure-in-one-day.

Before you set out on any of the day drives, it is important that you read the explanatory notes provided on pages six and seven under the heading 'How to use this book'. One point that bears repetition is that you should plan your day well in advance. Contact the regional AA office (shown in the information panel) to discover if there have been any alterations to the roads, prepare thoroughly the evening before you intend to set out, and when the day comes, make an early start. Each drive has been designed to fill a complete day.

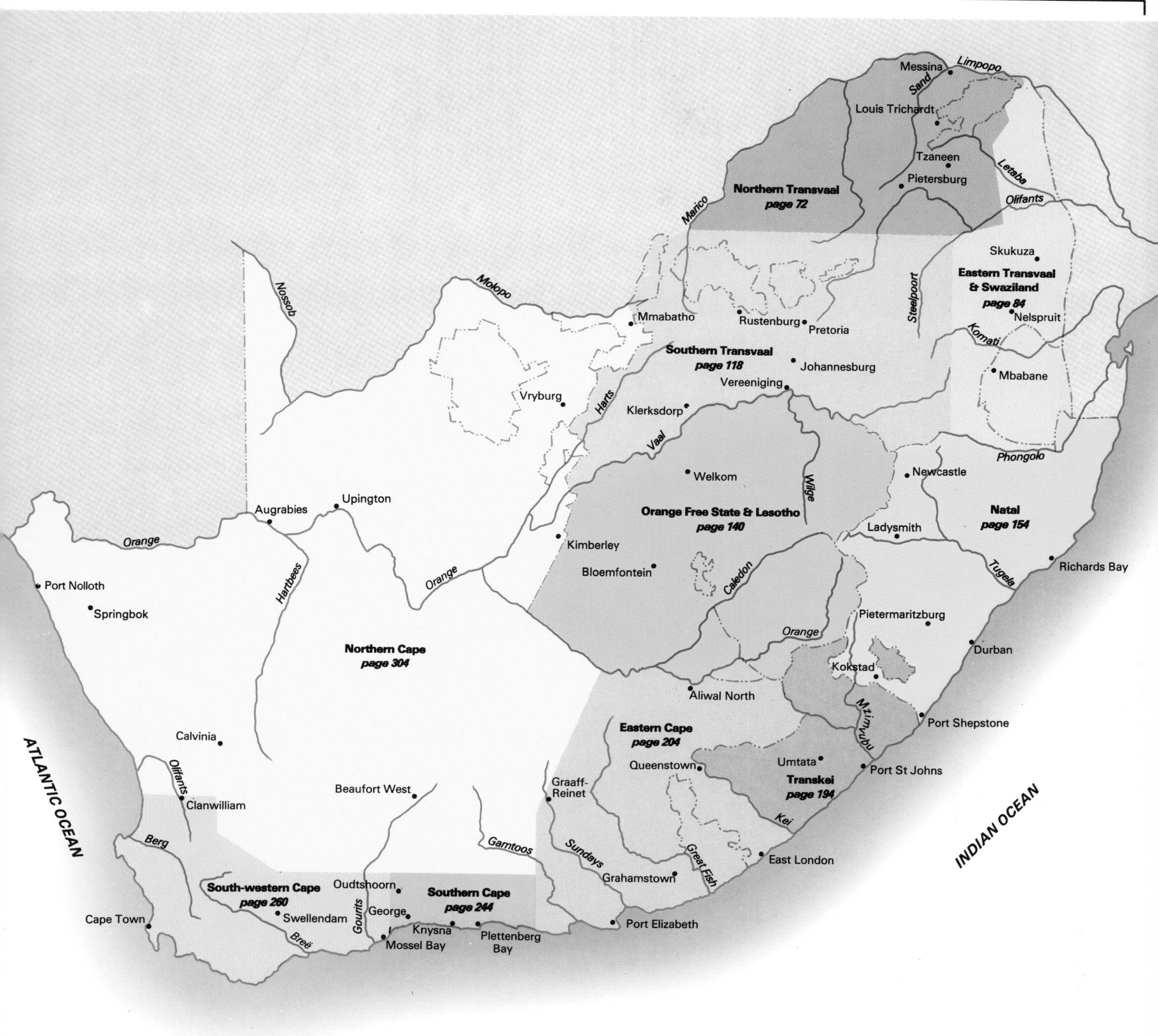

Northern Transvaal
page 72
Eastern Transvaal & Swaziland
page 84
Southern Transvaal
page 118
Orange Free State & Lesotho
page 140
Natal
page 154
Transkei
page 194
Eastern Cape
page 204
Southern Cape
page 244
South-western Cape
page 260
Northern Cape
page 304
ATLANTIC OCEAN
INDIAN OCEAN
Messina
Limpopo
Sand
Louis Trichardt
Tzaneen
Letaba
Pietersburg
Olifants
Marico
Skukuza
Nelspruit
Steelpoort
Komati
Mbabane
Molopo
Nossob
Mmabatho
Rustenburg
Pretoria
Johannesburg
Vereeniging
Klerksdorp
Vryburg
Harts
Vaal
Welkom
Wilge
Phongolo
Newcastle
Ladysmith
Tugela
Richards Bay
Kimberley
Bloemfontein
Caledon
Orange
Augrabies
Upington
Port Nolloth
Springbok
Hartbees
Pietermaritzburg
Durban
Kokstad
Mzimvubu
Port Shepstone
Aliwal North
Umtata
Port St Johns
Queenstown
Kei
Calvinia
Olifants
Clanwilliam
Beaufort West
Graaff-Reinet
Gamtoos
Sundays
Great Fish
East London
Grahamstown
Berg
Oudtshoorn
George
Gourits
Swellendam
Cape Town
Breë
Knysna
Mossel Bay
Plettenberg Bay
Port Elizabeth

NORTHERN TRANSVAAL

Above: *Tea-picking in Magoebaskloof.* **Left:** *Lush sub-tropical fruit orchards give way to the gentle forest-covered foothills of the Soutpansberg.*

A land of forests — where spirits dwell in lake and waterfall

This drive leads east from Louis Trichardt, passing through lush tropical plantations of fruit, nuts and tea, and climbing the cool forest-clad slopes of the Soutpansberg. Crossing into Venda, we visit the Phiphidi Falls, and drive deep into the Thathe Vondo Forest to view the sacred Lake Fundudzi. Roughly half of the route is on tar.

Louis Trichardt
Entabeni Forest
Levubu
Thohoyandou
Phiphidi Falls
Thathe Vondo Forest
170 — 190 km

Venda boys fishing in a tranquil stream.

Dutch Reformed Church, Louis Trichardt.

LOUIS TRICHARDT
The Voortrekker leader Louis Trichardt arrived at the foot of the Soutpansberg in 1836 and camped here for some months with his party before setting out on his epic trek to Delagoa Bay — which resulted in the death of Trichardt himself, his wife and many of his followers. The present town, named after this courageous leader, was founded in 1899. During the Anglo-Boer War it was evacuated and was totally destroyed by the local indigenous people, as nearby Schoemansdal had been several decades earlier (see pages 78-9). Large forestry plantations surround the town, and these provide attractive walks.

The Phiphidi Falls tumble into a sacred pool.

SPIRITS OF THE PHIPHIDI FALLS
Ancestors of the Tshivhase royal family are buried in a sacred grove near the top of these attractive falls, and they are periodically given offerings of beer, which are left on a rock above the falls. About 2 km above the falls there is a pool that is said to be the home of the spirits of the BaNgona, the original occupants of this country. People who cross the Mutshindudi River here must obtain the protection of the spirits by making an offering — whether it be food, beer, an article of clothing or even a strand of hair from one's head — and these tokens are placed in the hollow of a large boulder at the edge of the pool.

DRIVE EAST OUT of Louis Trichardt on Trichardt Street. Note your kms at the crossroads with the N1 and proceed straight across onto the R524. The road passes through tropical plantations, including citrus fruit, pecan nuts and mangoes, and gradually approaches the forested slopes of the Soutpansberg. 17 km from the N1 you cross the Levubu River, and 5,5 km beyond this point turn right onto a gravel road to visit the Albasini Dam. After 2,4 km on this gravel road turn right into the area of the dam wall. (Opposite this entrance, on the left, a track leads for some 300 metres to a grove of jacaranda trees surrounding the graves of the pioneering family after whom the dam is named.)

Return to the R524 and turn right, noting your kms. After 13,3 km turn left for a short excursion into the Entabeni Forest. This side-road changes to gravel after 100 m. Go right at the fork, noting your kms. Pass a road on your left leading to the Little Australia Hut, and after 3 kms you reach the gate to the forestry reserve. A permit is issued here and you may be required to pay a small fee. Turn left at the T-junction 700 m beyond the gate. After a further 3 km take a sharp left turn opposite the Timbadola sawmill on your right. This road winds up the hillside, offering wide views over plantations of pine and eucalyptus to the waters of the Albasini Dam.

Entabeni Forest to Phiphidi Falls

Return to the R524 and turn left, noting your kms. After 500 m turn right for Levubu. The road passes through fruitful orchards and a profusion of flowers and trees. Turn left at the first T-junction, pass a road leading right, and turn right at the second T-junction, passing through plantations of bananas. Turn left at the next two T-junctions to rejoin the R524 after a pleasant detour through this extremely fertile tract of country. Note your kms as you turn right onto the R524.

After 18 km you reach, on your left, the brightly painted, traditional-styled buildings of the Venda State Arts and Crafts Centre. It is worthwhile stopping here to view the work on display, and to obtain information on the area. (There is a detailed map here, showing the roads in the Thathe Vondo Forest).

Just under one kilometre past the Centre turn left off the R524 onto the road to Sibasa and Thohoyandou, noting your kms. Follow this road for 4,8 kms, passing a large shopping centre on your right, the university on your left, and then a hotel and government offices on your right. The road climbs until you reach a four-way stop street. Turn left here, noting your kms. The road surface soon changes to gravel and passes many villages with homes of both traditional and modern design, and there are wide views to your left over the lower-lying countryside and back over Thohoyandou. After 8,7 km, opposite the Phiphidi Centre, turn right at a signpost marked 'Mukumbani Tea Estates'. After 100 m turn right again to reach the gate to the Phiphidi Falls area.

The road descends some 400 m to reach a neat parking area, where there are braai sites, drinking water and toilets. A short footpath leads to a sheltered grove of indigenous trees, where the Phiphidi Falls tumble into a large, quiet pool, named Gubukhuvo. Do not disturb any jars or other objects in the area, and do not pick the flowers here (see pages 76-7). (In wet weather the road to the parking area, and the footpath, may be slippery.)

Phiphidi Falls to Louis Trichardt

Return to the main road and turn right, noting your kms at the turn. After a short distance you cross the Mutshindudi River. Carry on through large tea plantations to reach the start of the pretty Thathe Vondo Pass. After 6,7 km you reach a crossroads. Continue straight ahead here. The road now climbs through forestry plantations. At about 10,4 km you pass a gravel road on your left, and a sign reading 'Thathe Vondo Pass 1 077 m' comes into view on the left side of the road. Turn right just before reaching the sign, then turn right again, to reach the gate into the Thathe Vondo Forest.

An attendant will ask you to record details in

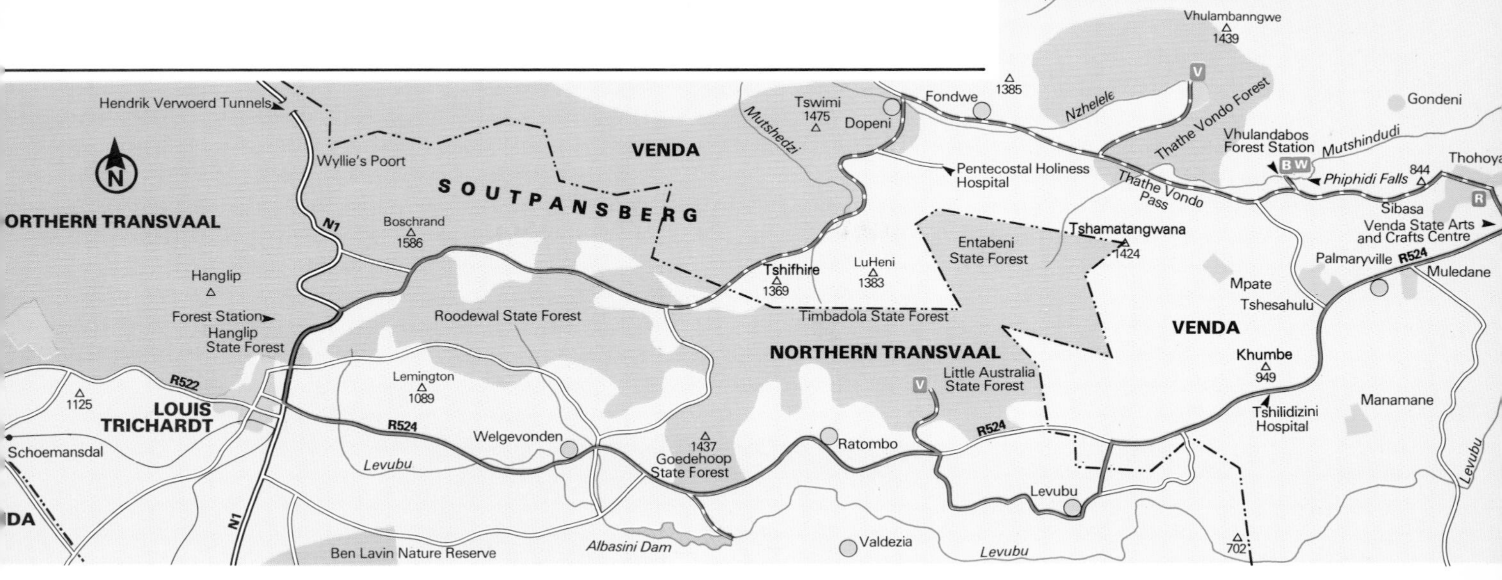

The lush Entabeni Forest covers the gently rolling slopes of the historic Soutpansberg range.

The mysterious Lake Fundudzi.

PIONEERING JOAO ALBASINI

The son of a sea captain, Joao Albasini was 18 years old when he landed at Delagoa Bay in 1831. Lured by the wildness of Africa he left his ship and became an elephant hunter. He later became a trader and also established a model farm at Schoemansdal. He lived there until his death, staying on after the town was put to the torch in 1867 by the Venda. His gravestone records that he was 'hoofd-kapitein de Knopneusen' (paramount chief of the Knob-noses). (See also pages 78-9).

Traditional thatch-roofed huts and kraals decorate the hills of Venda.

THE SACRED LAKE FUNDUDZI

This forbidding body of water, encircled by mountains, was created in ancient times, when a landslide blocked the course of the Mutale River. Many legends are connected with the lake, which is regarded with veneration by the Venda. It is the home of the great Python God, who is placated annually with gifts of beer poured onto the water. The public may visit the lake only with permission from the Venda government.

a book. Note your kms here.

The gravel forestry road climbs fairly steeply for the first few hundred metres. Keep straight ahead on the largest road. After driving 4,5 km from the entrance gate, park on the side of the road for a good view to your right over the Mukumbani dam lying among the hills below. 2,4 km later a road forks to your right and another road leads left; ignore these and drive straight ahead.

After a further 3,1 km you pass a small building and a side-road on your right. A little over 700 m later go right at the fork. 3,6 km after the fork, the road separates into three — keep straight on the middle road. Just over 1 km later you drive through a gate. 400 m beyond this the road forks — take the road leading right, passing a Zion Christian building on your left. A few metres later you reach a fence in front of a fire-watchers' tower. Go left here, following the fence, then stop. Ahead of you, and half to your left, you can see the mysterious Lake Fundudzi far below — within its ring of mountains (see above).

Return to the tar at the summit of the pass, and note your kms as you turn right. Descend slowly, as there may be some patches where the tar surface is in a poor condition. At 4 km you cross the Nzhelele River over a long bridge. 200 m beyond this the tar ends. At 9,6 km turn left, just after passing a garage on your left. The road surface changes back to tar a few metres beyond the turn, and after 600 m the road crosses the Nzhelele River again.

The tar changes to gravel again soon after crossing the river, and the road enters hilly country where villages clinging to the slopes look out over wide maizefields. 19 km after your second crossing of the Nzhelele River the road levels and you drive back onto tar — where you pass a road on your left to Welgevonden. 16,3 km later you reach a T-junction with the N1. Turn left onto the N1, noting your kms. After 6,4 km you reach a four-way stop street. Turn right into Trichardt Street, which leads back into Louis Trichardt ●

AA Office Talmot Building, 53 Schoeman Street, Pietersburg 0700 Tel. (01521) 71442
Venda Department of Tourism Thohoyandou Shopping Complex, Thohoyandou, Venda Tel. (01559) 21131
Venda State Arts and Crafts Centre Box 9, Sibasa, Venda Tel. (01559) 21980
Louis Trichardt Public Library Krogh Street, Louis Trichardt 0920 Tel. (01551) 2212

Young Venda girls weave sinuously in the traditional 'domba' or python dance, performed twice a day around a sacred fire by initiates preparing for marriage.

The sacred python dance and a haunted forest

MANY HUNDREDS OF years ago the beautiful mountain country of Venda — 'the world' or 'pleasant place' was settled by a mysterious and peaceful people known as the BaNgona, who allowed strangers from north of the Limpopo to live among them. These strangers were named the Vhatavhatsinde — the people of the yard of the stem — named from a tradition of erecting a stone or pole in the yard of their kraals. The Vhatavhatsinde were regarded as powerful medicine-men, and many of their descendants still live in their original mountain settlement at Mphephu.

Towards the end of the 17th century there was another migration from the north. The newcomers, named the MaKhwinde, were military-minded — and under their chief Dimbanyika they conquered the country. Where these MaKhwinde originated is uncertain, but it is known that they spent many years in present-day Zimbabwe.

Dimbanyika was succeeded by his eldest son, Popi, who assumed the name of Thoho ya ndou (the head of the elephant). Today the capital of Venda recalls the name of this almost legendary character.

A new mountain settlement

Because of raids by neighbouring groups, including the Sotho and the Swazi in the south and south-east, Thoho ya ndou led his people away from the place where his father had died and built a new mountain-stronghold capital in the Soutpansberg at Dzata, which is now looked upon as the ancestral home of the Venda. The name was taken from that of their earlier home in Zimbabwe, and they continued the tradition of building impressive walls of stone. Ruins of these structures still remain at Dzata.

Tradition holds that Thoho ya ndou ruled over an area larger than the Venda of today, including large parts of Zimbabwe. He was a powerful chief, but his death remains a mystery. He set out one day, with a few companions, to gather support against his three jealous brothers who were trying to overthrow him. He was last seen crossing the Nzhelele River and then he disappeared without a trace. Legend has it that Thoho ya ndou will one day return to lead his people to their former greatness.

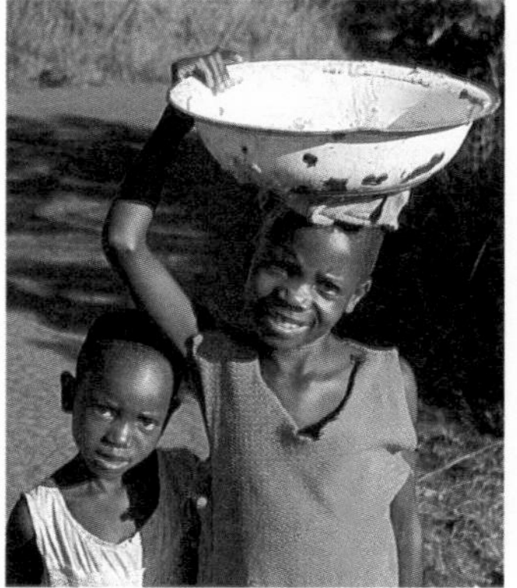

The friendly faces of Venda children.

Phiphidi Falls and their sacred pool.

Thoho ya ndou's grandson, Makhado, became known as 'the lion of the north' because of his firm opposition to white settlement in the area. During the reign of his father, Rampulana (the treacherous), use had been made of the Voortrekkers and their firearms to settle quarrels among minor chiefs. These early settlers formed the town of Soutpansbergdorp which later became known as Schoemansdal. By 1847, the town had become host to white ivory hunters

Ritual drums accompany the 'domba' dancers as they move around the fire.

Venda huts on a hillside near Sibasa.

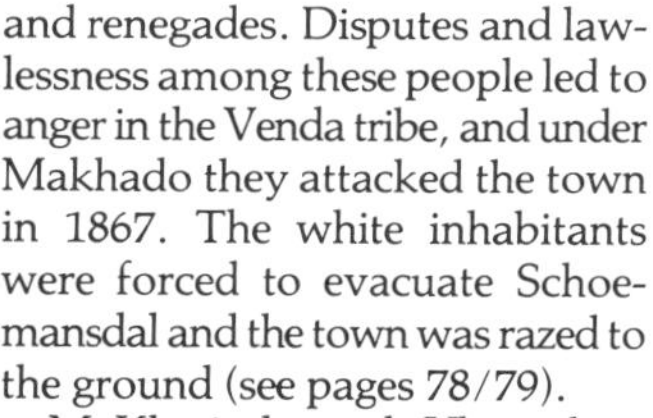

and renegades. Disputes and lawlessness among these people led to anger in the Venda tribe, and under Makhado they attacked the town in 1867. The white inhabitants were forced to evacuate Schoemansdal and the town was razed to the ground (see pages 78/79).

MaKhwinde and Vhatavhatsinde comprise by far the greater part of the present population of Venda — the BaNgona having been completely assimilated. However, there is also a small group called the Balemba whose origin is a mystery. According to one theory, they are descended from Arab slave traders, and are traditionally known as the metalworkers and traders among the Venda people.

The people of Venda (BaVenda) have never worn much ornamentation, but old beads, handed down through the generations, are highly-prized heirlooms. The most valuable are small blue beads known as *vhulungu ha madi* (beads of the sea). These are worn only by wives of important men and chiefs, and are believed to be very old. The long opaque white beads called *limanda* (powerful ones) are believed to possess a magical strength. Chiefs' wives used to wear the *malinga*, an ivory bracelet, and the *ndalama*, the flat operculum of a seashell. A waistband of ostrich eggshell beads, the *maphungo*, is often presented to a child at its naming ceremony. Apart from these items, ornamentation is confined mainly to wire bracelets and anklets.

The power of the crocodile

Throughout Venda the crocodile is a symbol of witchcraft, and is regarded with a mixture of fear and reverence. The brain of the crocodile is believed to contain a deadly poison, small portions of which can easily be slipped into the food or drink of an enemy. Because of this, Thoho ya ndou made it an offence punishable by death to touch these reptiles.

Traditional initiation rites form an important part of the attainment of adult life. In the case of young girls, these ceremonies last for three to nine months and take place in the *domba* school. Here the young girls must assume an attitude of submission and humility, and are not allowed to stand upright. They receive sex education in preparation for marriage, and dance instruction. The principal dance that they learn is the *domba*, or 'python' dance — one of the best-known of Venda customs. The rhythmic thudding of drums accompanies the dance, which is performed around a sacred fire every morning and evening.

The circumcision lodge for boys, the *murundu*, was introduced into Venda life only this century, and has largely replaced the original initiation school or *thondo*. The initiation hut is surrounded by a wall, and is built by the elderly men of the kraal on a site selected by a medicine man and approved by the chief. Formerly the *thondo* was exclusively to educate the sons of chiefs in tribal laws and customs, but today the school is attended by all Venda boys. The main feature of their stay at the school is the circumcision ceremony. After this ceremony the boys must squat in an icy river for six consecutive nights to wash away their boyhood (*vhutumba vhutuka*) and to relieve the pain. The ceremony ends with each boy climbing a traditionally symbolic pole and shouting out in triumph. After the ceremonies, the boys and girls are regarded as adults and are ready for marriage and parenthood.

The spirit world of the Venda

The traditional deity of the BaVenda is Raluvhimba, who was believed to show himself to their great chief in a cave on the mountain known as Tsha-wa-dinda — the place of the messengers. Many other places in Venda are associated with ancestral spirits.

Spirits of the BaNgona people, the earliest inhabitants of the land, live in the Phiphidi Falls and in Gubukhuvo, the pool into which they flow. Beer and food are left on a sacred stone near the top of the falls, close to the graves of the Tshivase, the BaNgona royal family.

Perhaps the best-known of the sacred places in Venda is the mysterious Lake Fundudzi. The area around the lake was settled by the Vhatavhatsinde people under the chief Netshiavho, and their spirits still inhabit this region. It is said that disaster will overtake any chief of the MaKhwinde people who should venture near the lake.

The Thathe Vondo forest is sacred to the MaKhwinde. A ferocious spirit in the form of a lion is said to haunt the forest and is believed to be the reincarnation of one of the MaKhwinde chiefs, who are buried in this sacred forest ●

Grinding mealies — a daily chore — while tobacco dries under the eaves.

Part of the Soutpansberg range near Schoemansdal — the original capital of the first independent Voortrekker community in the northern Transvaal.

Violence and courage on an untamed frontier

ALTHOUGH THIS AREA was called Venda by its earliest inhabitants (see pages 76-7), the mountainous region became known to the early white settlers as the Soutpansberg — mountain of the salt pan — from the large salt pan that lies at the western end of the range. The precise origin of the name is unknown, but it was probably bestowed by the first white man to settle here — the notorious Coenraad de Buys.

Coenraad de Buys was born near Cogmanskloof, in the Montagu district of the Cape, in about 1761. A giant of a man, he courted adventure on the frontiers of the Cape, and became a popular man with a large following of admirers. He married legally only once, to a black woman recorded only as Elizabeth, but had many unrecorded wives and children. In about 1819, after being declared an outlaw, and with a price on his head after some shady dealings, Buys trekked away with his families and followers and settled near the salt pan at the western end of the Soutpansberg, far beyond the reach of the Cape law.

In 1823, after the death of Elizabeth, Buys told his people to stay at the settlement, but announced that

Fort Hendrina at Louis Trichardt.

he himself was going away. They never saw him again, but the Buys families were eventually granted rights to the land they had occupied, and today their descendents still live at the old settlement near Mara.

Thirteen years after Buys's disappearance, in May 1836, a small party of Voortrekkers led by Hans van Rensburg arrived at the Soutpansberg and set up camp. For much of their journey from the Caledon River they had been accompanied by the trek of Louis Trichardt, but the two leaders had quarrelled over wastage of ammunition — a dispute from which Strydpoort (quarrel pass) derives its name — and the Van Rensburg trek had continued alone to the Soutpansberg. Early in July they trekked on towards Delagoa Bay, only to be slaughtered by a far-ranging Zulu impi.

The birth of Zoutpansbergdorp

It was the influential Andries Hendrik Potgieter who, desiring to live well outside the area falling under the jurisdiction of the British government and its representatives at the Cape, decided to establish a permanent settlement in the Soutpansberg. The independent Voortrekker community ('maatschappij') of Zoutpansbergdorp was established in 1848. The first buildings believed to have been erected are the church and the fort, the site of which is now marked by a plaque of the Historical Monuments Commission. The commercial life of the town was greatly stimulated by the arrival of the Portuguese trader Joao Albasini (see pages 74-5) who transported the ivory culled by the Boers to the coast at Delagoa Bay.

In 1852 Andries Hendrik Potgieter died and his place as leader of the community was taken by his son Piet. Piet died in a raid against the Ndebele chief Makapan and was succeeded by his brother Hermanus as joint Commandant-General with Marthinus Wessel Pretorius. However, the people of Zoutpansbergdorp wanted a free election, and they appointed Stephanus Schoeman as their new leader in 1855. He renamed the town — Schoemansdal (see map, pages 74-5) — and married the widow of Piet Potgieter.

Unfortunately Schoemansdal became host to bands of unsavoury renegades and fortune-seeking ivory hunters, and the town became an increasingly lawless place. This led to discontent among the neighbouring Venda people and in 1867, after many raids, the white people abandoned the town — which was then razed to the ground by the triumphant Venda.

Painstaking excavations on the site of Schoemansdal are revealing the layout of the original settlement and plans are being made to reconstruct the town as an outdoor museum.

A new Voortrekker capital

Some thirty years after the abandonment of Schoemansdal, in 1898, a Venda uprising under chief Mpefu was quelled in the Soutpansberg by Commandant-General Piet Joubert. The spot where the decisive battle was fought was selected as the site for a new capital in the Soutpansberg — to be named after the Voortrekker

The cool Hanglip Forestry Reserve.

leader Louis Trichardt, who had camped here in 1836 before leaving on his fateful journey to what was then Lourenco Marques.

The new town was proclaimed in February 1899, but had unhappy beginnings. The Anglo-Boer War broke out in October of the same year and the women and children were evacuated to Pietersburg while their menfolk went to battle. The new town, like Schoemansdal before it, was razed to the ground by the Venda. After the war Louis Trichardt was re-established and today it is a handsome town with wide streets and gardens filled with fragrant flowering trees.

Attractions within the town include the Dutch Reformed Church on Main Street, the Indigenous Tree Park at the municipal caravan park where 114 species of trees are preserved, and the historic steel structure of Fort Hendrina behind the municipal offices in Erasmus Street. Fort Hendrina was erected to offer some protection against raids by neighbouring tribes.

The baobab (Adansonia digitata) *has edible fruit rich in vitamin C.*

Voortrekker graves and Andries Potgieter memorial at Schoemansdal.

Soutpansberg attractions

Louis Trichardt serves as a convenient base from which to explore the Soutpansberg area. The mountain range is densely wooded with plantations of indigenous trees, including the tree fern, stinkwood and yellowwood, and government-owned plantations of exotics. From the northern end of the town's Krogh Street, Forestry Road leads to the Hanglip Forestry Reserve, named after a peak that overlooks the town. The 90 km Soutpansberg Hiking Trail starts at the forestry office just inside the reserve. The main attractions of this 5-day trail, which runs along the ridge of the Soutpansberg range to the Entabeni Forest Station, are the beautiful woods, the wide variety of birds and wild animals, and magical glimpses of Venda villages through the trees and the mists.

The Hanglip Forestry Reserve also contains a variety of shorter walks — several of which lead to points that offer magnificent panoramic views. Excellent views may also be had from the 15 km Bluegumspoort road, which leads west from the N1 north of Louis Trichardt just before the N1 enters the scenic Wyllie's Poort.

Along the length of the Soutpansberg, especially to the east of Louis Trichardt, are vast plantations of sub-tropical and tropical fruits. The Levubu Experimental Farm, 30 km east of Louis Trichardt on the main road to the Kruger National Park and Venda, is well worth a visit — prior arrangements should be made by telephoning Levubu (015552) 20 and asking for the tour officer. Here experiments are undertaken on sub-tropical and tropical fruits, such as guavas, bananas, avocado pears and macadamia nuts, and the visitor can see how these crops are grown. Many hectares of land along the Soutpansberg are also devoted to extensive tea and coffee plantations.

About 6,5 km south-east of the town lies the Ben Lavin Nature Reserve, established in 1976 and preserving wildlife such as giraffe, wildebeest, zebra and ostrich. There are several walking trails here, a few interesting archeological sites, and a game viewing hide. Accommodation may be reserved by telephoning the warden at (01551) 3834 ●

Trekker leader Andries Potgieter.

Rural dwellings shelter below the Soutpansberg.

Old and new roads through the scenic Wyllie's Poort.

Debengeni Falls and the land of the mysterious Rain Queen

This route begins with a journey through the Molototsi valley to the sacred cycad forest at Modjadji, hilltop capital of the secretive Rain Queen. Then it leads through Duiwelskloof and the Woodbush Forest — often shrouded in mist — to the smooth-flowing Debengeni Falls. Roughly two thirds of the route is on gravel, one third on tar.

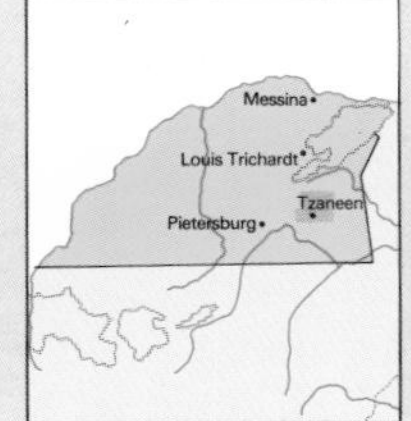

Tzaneen
Modjadji
Duiwelskloof
Koedoes Valley
Woodbush Forest
Debengeni Falls
200 — 220 km

DRIVE OUT OF TZANEEN on the R71 towards Gravelotte and Phalaborwa. Almost immediately you cross a bridge over the Great Letaba River. Several hundred metres after this, turn left onto the road for Deer Park. Turn left again 5 km later for Modjadji. The road leads through tall eucalyptus plantations to reach a T-junction after 2,5 km. Turn right at this T-junction and note your kms.

The road surface changes to gravel after 2 km, and shortly after this you pass on your left a road to Duiwelskloof. Eventually you emerge from the eucalyptus plantations. Roughly 13 km from the T-junction, turn right onto a road that leads along the floor of the Molototsi valley. Note your kms as you turn.

After 10,8 km turn right, and follow this side-road as it climbs the hills on the south-eastern side of the valley — offering spacious views over the surrounding countryside. 3,4 km along this side-road you reach a fork. Take the road on your right, and when the road forks again several hundred metres later, go left (uphill). After a further 700 m turn left into the Modjadji Nature Reserve (see opposite). There is a small entry fee to the reserve, which has a refreshment kiosk, plus toilets, water and braai places. There are also short walks here.

Modjadji to Duiwelskloof

Retrace your route towards Tzaneen, but 2 km after the road surface changes to tar, continue straight past the road on your left on which you came from Tzaneen. Stay on the tarred road, crossing two bridges over the Fanie Botha Dam, then turn right at the crossroads onto the R36 towards Duiwelskloof.

After 2,6 km on the R36 you pass a road on your left, then you pass the Hans Merensky Dam on your left. After roughly 9 km on the R36 you reach Duiwelskloof, where there is a hotel that serves lunch, and an attractive picnic site. (To reach this site, turn left at the first stop street in the town into Boltman Street, then after 400 m turn right into Mabel Street. A little over 1 km after this turn, turn left at the T-junction onto a gravel road. After 1 km this road swings sharply to the left, uphill. You pass a road on your left, and reach the picnic area after a further 800 m. There are braai sites here, toilets, taps that provide drinking water, and a shaded path that offers a pleasant 5 minute walk into the kloof to a small but pretty waterfall.)

Continue through Duiwelskloof on the main road (R36), passing on your right the municipal offices, which also house the town's library. In front of the municipal offices there are several monuments — one to 15 local men who died in the Anglo-Boer War, another commemorating the opening of the Voortrekker Monument in 1949, and another the Taalfees of 1975.

Stay on the R36 for roughly 15 km after leaving Duiwelskloof, then, 300 m after crossing the railway line, turn left onto a gravel road for Houtbosdorp — noting your kms. This road leads along the Koedoes River valley. 5 km along it you pass on your left the prominent hill known as Kranskop. Roughly 4 km after this, also on your left, the bare slopes of Vaalkrans come into view, rising above the forest. The road winds uphill. 26 km after turning onto the gravel, park in a parking area on your right for a fine view back over the Koedoes River valley.

Woodbush Forest and Debengeni Falls

36 km after turning onto the gravel, turn left for 'Magoebaskloof/Dap Naudé Dam', noting your kms. (This intersection is approximately the site of Houtbosdorp — see pages 82-3.) The road enters pine plantations, and after 3,6 km you pass a road on your right to Veekraal. Roughly 6 km later you pass another road on your right coming from Veekraal. A little over 14 km from the Houtbosdorp intersection, turn sharp left for the Woodbush State Forest.

After 100 m you pass through a gateway into the forest reserve — note your kms here. The road now leads through tall eucalypts and pines. Roughly 1 km from the gate you pass a

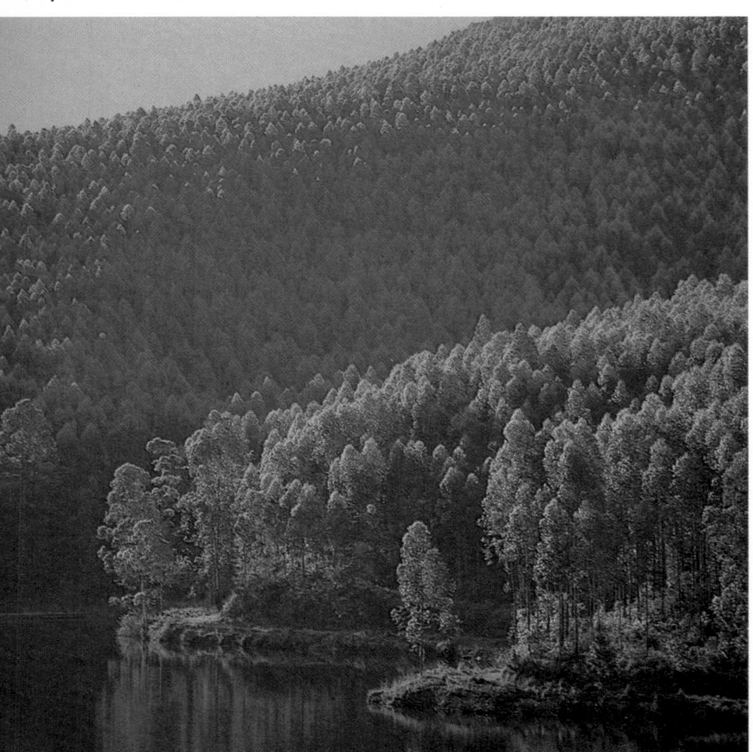

Forest-clad hills reach down to the still waters of the Magoebaskloof Dam.

'HAPPY LAND' OR 'LITTLE BASKET'

The origin of the name Tzaneen is uncertain. Tradition has it that the name comes from a Sotho word for a small round basket, *tsana*, and refers to the fact that the town lies in a basket-like circle of hills — hence the town's crest incorporates a basket. More recent research, however, has shown that one of the first European settlers in the valley was told by Chief Magoeba in 1892 that the region was called *tsaneng*, meaning 'the happy land' — Tzaneen being an obvious corruption.

DEVIL'S VALLEY

The name Duiwelskloof (devil's valley) was given to this valley by early travellers whose wagons frequently became stuck here in thick mud. The name was taken over by a farm in the valley, and then by the small village that grew up on the farm. Eventually the village was moved to a neighbouring farm called Skraalhans (scrawny Hans) to take advantage of a better water supply, but it kept its original name. Duiwelskloof is now an important centre of the timber industry, and it is renowned for the profusion of flowering plants that fill its gardens.

Mist drifts quietly through the trees.

small memorial on your right to the pioneer forester Alexander O'Connor. 2,4 km from the gate the road forks — go right here for 'Debengeni Falls & Forest Drive'.

The road now passes through large tracts of dense indigenous forest, and offers several fine views over the lower slopes of the escarpment to the bright green of distant tea estates. 1,5 km along this road (3,9 km from the gate) you enter De Hoek Forest. At 7,5 km from the gate go left at the fork. At 8,5 km from the gate turn right at the T-junction. At 9,6 km from the gate go left at the fork. At 10,8 km from the gate go right at the T-junction, note your kms, and continue downhill. 2,4 km later, just before a right-hand bend, stop to look back over the upper section of the Debengeni Falls.

300 m after this, turn sharp left (a small admission fee may be charged) and drive down to the falls. There are braai sites and toilets at the falls. Although the smooth stone gives these falls a friendly appearance, they are in fact dangerous and have claimed many lives. The smooth rocks are especially dangerous when dew or rain has made them wet and slippery.

Drive back up the hill to the forest drive and continue in the direction you were travelling. After 3 km you reach the tarred R71 through Magoebaskloof. Turn left here onto the R71 for a 17 km drive back to Tzaneen, passing through neat, fresh-green tea estates ●

AA Office Talmot Building, 53 Schoeman Street, Pietersburg 0700 Tel. (01521) 71442
Tzaneen Municipal Tourist Office Agatha Street, Tzaneen 0850 Tel. (015236) 20132
Duiwelskloof Public Library Municipal Building, Box 36, Duiwelskloof 0835 Tel. (015236) 3246
SA Tourism Board Cnr Vorster & Landdros Mare Streets, Pietersburg 0700 Tel. (01521) 3025

The mirror-like surface of the Hans Merensky Dam reflects the forested hills of the lower Mabitse valley.

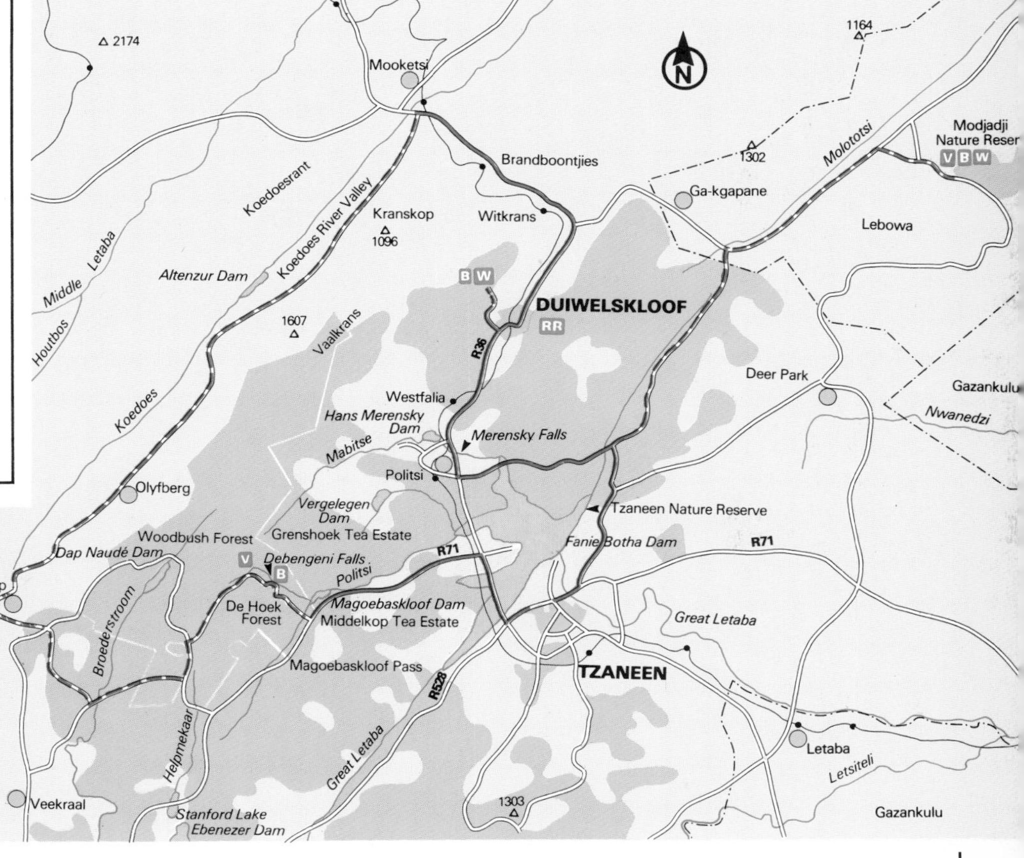

The seemingly gentle Debengeni Falls.

THE RAIN QUEEN

Tradition tells of a chief's daughter who, some 300 years ago, was seduced by her half brother and bore a son. To escape her angry father, who ruled in what is now Zimbabwe, she fled south, with her baby and a few followers, and settled where their descendents the Lovedu are to be found to this day. With them they brought secret rain charms.

The community flourished, but a tradition of male succession caused constant strife. Early last century a chief, Mugudo, decided to end this turmoil by instituting a rule of female succession. The chief committed incest with his daughter Modjadji, and when she bore a daughter, he took poison and Modjadji became the first Rain Queen.

Her fame as a rain-maker spread, and supplicants would come from great distances to seek her help. Tradition dictates that her successors must live secluded lives and all business is conducted through counsellors. Reverence for the Rain Queen became so great that her people escaped the terrible tribal wars that swept across the Transvaal, and her territory became a place of refuge. The Rain Queen provided the inspiration for Sir Henry Rider Haggard's novel *She*.

A few of Modjadji's sacred cycads.

SACRED CYCADS OF MODJADJI

Growing on the hilltop in the Modjadji Nature Reserve are the strange trees often referred to as Modjadji palms. In fact they are not even closely related to palms. They are cycads, remnants of a relatively primitive type of plant that flourished at about the time when dinosaurs trod the earth. The Modjadji cycads *(Encephalartos transvenosus)* are among the largest in the world and may reach a height of 13 m.

The seeds of the Modjadji cycads are believed to be poisonous, but the pith of the stem, which is rich in starch, has traditionally been used to make a type of bread — hence their common name 'bread trees'. The large number of mature specimens in the Modjadji reserve owe their existence to the fact that they have long been regarded as sacred to the Rain Queen — and hence untouchable.

Where zebra-drawn stage coaches carried gold through the kloofs

The forestry station at New Agatha has one of the Transvaal's finest views — over the Letsiteli Valley to the crest of the northern Drakensberg. Today's route climbs to this viewsite, then leads on via the Ebenezer Dam to the Woodbush Forest and Magoebaskloof — with an optional visit to the Debengeni Falls. All but 30 km is on tar.

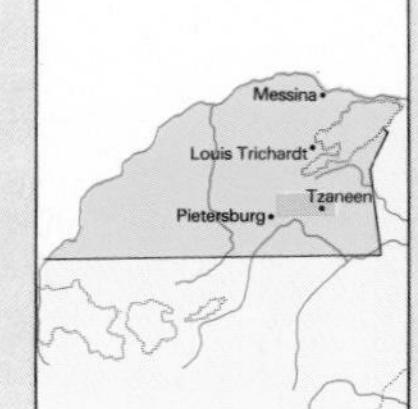

Tzaneen
Letsiteli Valley
New Agatha
Forest
Ebenezer Dam
Woodbush Forest
Magoebaskloof
200 — 220 km

LEAVE TZANEEN BY driving south on the R36 towards Lydenburg. After about 10 km you cross into Gazankulu. 4,2 km later, turn right for the Letsiteli Valley — noting your kms. From here the road leads through extensive orchards of tropical fruit — notably mangoes, pawpaws and papinos — and citrus plantations. After 9 km on this road, turn right onto a gravel road for New Agatha, noting your kms.

The road now climbs the foothills of the Drakensberg escarpment and soon enters cool plantations of eucalyptus. After 7 km you pass on your left a hotel that was formerly a coach house on the old road between Pietersburg and Leydsdorp — in the days when the 'wild west' stage coaches that travelled this route were sometimes drawn by zebras (see opposite).

2 km after passing the hotel, turn left into the New Agatha Forest. The avenue of tall eucalyptus trees that lines the left side of the road here is believed to date from the old coaching days. 2 km along this road you pass a side-road on your left, and a few hundred metres after this you reach the forestry station. From the forester's office you have outstanding views in several directions. (You do not need a permit if you are going no further into the reserve than this.)

New Agatha Forest to the Ebenezer Dam
Retrace your route past the avenue of eucalyptus trees and turn left as you leave the forest reserve, noting your kms at the turn. The road surface changes to tar, and you pass a road on your right to Tzaneen after a few hundred metres. Turn right onto a second road to Tzaneen 3,7 km from the turn. This road winds gently down into the Letaba Valley and offers sweeping views over fruit farms and forests.

After travelling on this road for 10,6 km turn left at the T-junction onto the R36 and note your kms. Just over 1 km later exit onto the R528 for George's Valley.

George's Valley is the upper valley of the

Two views from the New Agatha forestry station: south past a coral tree over the magnificent Letsiteli Valley, and west to the forested slopes of the Drakensberg.

The serenely beautiful Ebenezer Dam, viewed from the upper section of George's Valley Road.

HAENERTSBURG
Now a centre of the timber industry, the village of Haenertsburg was once the heart of the Woodbush Goldfields. Many prospectors struck gold in the surrounding hills, among them the two Haenert brothers, one of whom discovered the Ellen's Fortune Reef and the other a reef that he named Haenerton. Which of the two brothers founded the village is uncertain, but it is estimated that it had a population of over 400 by the late 1890s. The slopes above Haenertsburg are riddled with shallow workings, but few men became rich, because the reefs were generally of a poor quality.

THE GEORGE OF GEORGE'S VALLEY
This scenic drive along the course of the Great Letaba River, with its views towards the massive Wolkberg and the Iron Crown, takes its name from George Deneys, a relative of the Zeederberg family who operated the stage coaches through the area. After being captured and imprisoned by the British during the Anglo-Boer War, Deneys returned to the Transvaal and applied himself to the construction of roads. He spent many years supervising the building of this road through the valley, and planted many trees and flowering aloes along the route.

GOLD IN THE HILLS
Early settlers found yellowwood trees growing in the dense forest that filled the valleys between the Great Letaba and the Koedoes rivers. So they named the area De Houtbosch (wood forest). Woodcutters founded the settlement of Houtbosdorp, then prospectors found payable gold in the nearby hills and the hitherto quiet region experienced all the excitement of a goldrush. The Berlin Mission Society established a station nearby in 1878, and this later moved to where the Kratzenstein Mission still operates. In 1901 a running battle took place here between British and Boer forces.

Great Letaba River, and the road is fringed for much of the way by colourful poinsettias and bougainvillea. On both sides stretch wide plantations of citrus, mangoes and bananas. Higher up the landscape becomes wilder. Gorges and ravines come into view on your left, then the cliff-topped peak known as the Iron Crown.

Roughly 30km after last noting your kms, turn right onto a gravel road for the Ebenezer Dam — noting your kms again. After 2,2km turn right at the T-junction. A further 300m brings you to picnic sites on your left, with views over the dam and part of the dam wall. To reach picnic sites close to the water's edge, turn left after a further 300m.

The Ebenezer Dam to Houtbosdorp

Our route continues past this strip road turn-off, through shady forest, skirting the edge of the dam and offering many fine views across its waters. At all points where the road forks, stay on the larger road. At the T-junction with the tarred Magoebaskloof road (R71), turn right towards Tzaneen and note your kms.

After 2,5km you pass the Magoebaskloof Hotel on your right (which serves lunch, and commands a panoramic view over Magoebaskloof). 2,3km beyond the hotel, turn left onto a gravel road leading into the Woodbush Forest signposted 'Houtbosdorp', noting you kms at the turn.

This road leads through extensive pine plantations, crosses the small Helpmekaar (help each other) River, and reaches a fork after 2,4km. Go left at the fork, and 4,8km later you cross a small bridge over the Broederstroom (brother stream). 300m beyond the bridge, turn right for Houtbosdorp. Keep straight at the crossroads 5km later, after which the road begins to wind downhill, offering wide views towards the Lowveld over fields and forest.

16,5km after leaving the tarred Magoebaskloof road you reach a T-junction with the gravel Koedoes River Valley road. This is the site of Houtbosdorp (see opposite). Turn left at this T-junction, noting kms as you turn.

Magoebaskloof and Debengeni Falls

The road surface changes to tar after just over 1km, and 5km after this you cross the border into Lebowa — entering drier, higher-lying country, dotted with huts and koppies. 18km from the turn you pass the town of Turfloop and the University of the North. 18,6km from the Houtbosdorp turn, at the end of the university block, turn left into Sovenga Street. At the stop street turn right, then immediately left, to reach a T-junction with the Magoebaskloof Road.

Turn left onto the Magoebaskloof road (R71) and return to Tzaneen by driving down the full length of Magoebaskloof. (To visit the Debengeni Falls, note your kms as you pass the Magoebaskloof Hotel and turn left 11,7km beyond the hotel onto a gravel road. 3km along this road, turn off right and drive downhill to the falls — see pages 80-1.) ●

AA Office Talmot Building, 53 Schoeman Street, Pietersburg 0700 Tel. (01521) 71442
Tzaneen Municipal Tourist Office Agatha Street, Tzaneen 0850 Tel. (015236) 20132
SA Tourism Board Cnr Vorster & Landdros Mare Streets, Pietersburg 0700 Tel. (01521) 3025

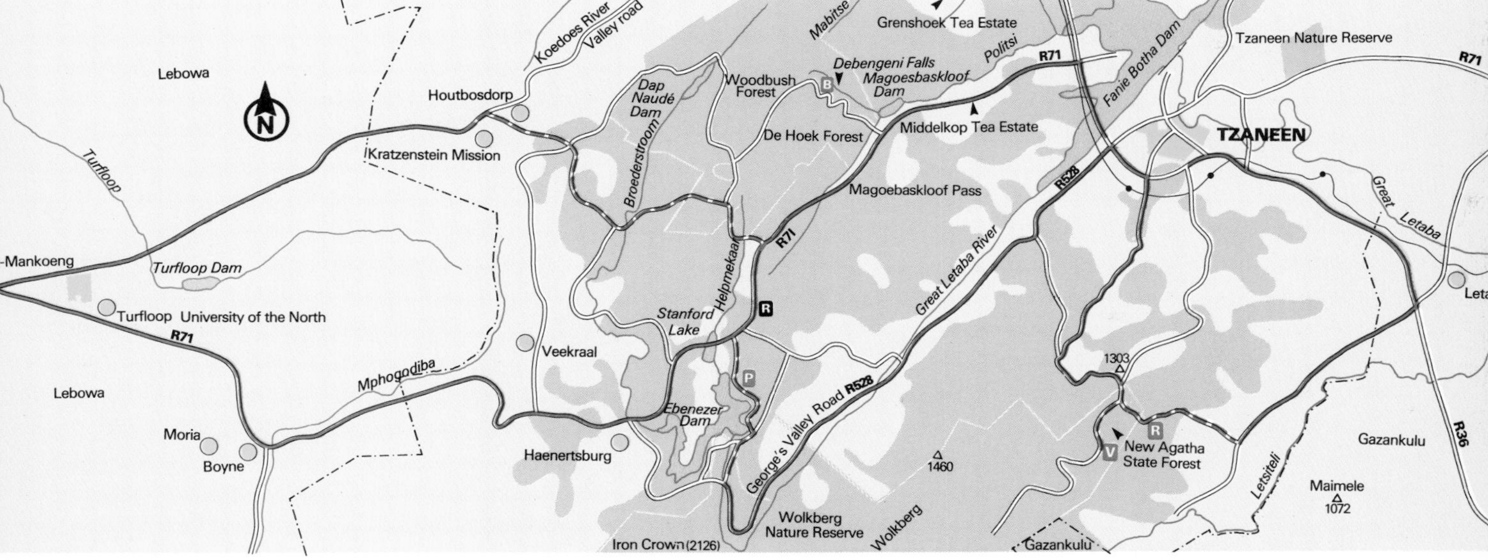

Holiday rondavels in Magoebaskloof.

AGATHA'S ZEBRA-DRAWN COACHES

Late last century a number of small mining companies flourished in the Lowveld at the foot of the northern Drakensberg — in an area that was christened Agatha after Agatha Joubert, wife of the South African Republic's mining commissioner. Eventually malaria and bilharzia — and sheer heat — drove the settlers up the slopes to a site that became known as New Agatha. The present hotel at New Agatha was originally a staging post for the Zeederberg Coach Company, which ran a service between Pietersburg and the gold-mining town of Leydsdorp.

The coachmen had to contend with highwaymen, wet weather that left the roads impassable for days on end, and most worrisome of all: a high death rate among their horses, caused by the tsetse fly. To solve this last problem the Zeederbergs trained a team of zebras to pull the coaches. The zebras lacked the horses' stamina, but they had a natural immunity to the tsetse-borne horse sickness.

Malaria continued to plague the region until well into the 20th century. In 1930 the Dutch specialist Professor N Swellengrebel was consulted on the problem. He identified the principal mosquito carriers of the disease and devised a method of combating it. A vigorous spraying of the breeding grounds was undertaken and a research station was established at Tzaneen. It was here that the South African Dr D S Annecke worked for 24 years studying the problems of both malaria and bilharzia.

A zebra-drawn stagecoach operated between Pietersburg and Leydsdorp.

EASTERN TRANSVAAL & SWAZILAND

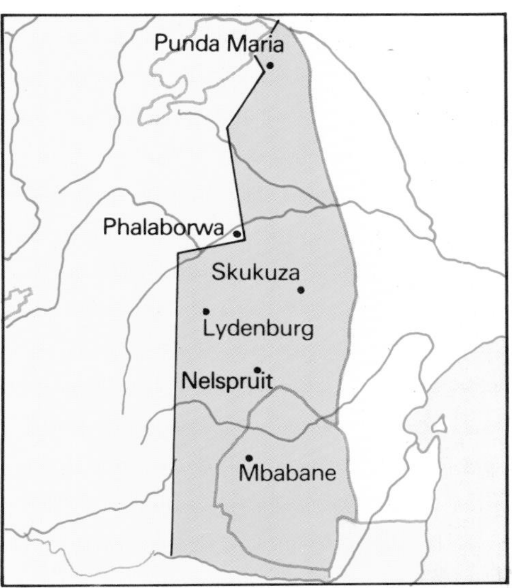

Above: *Sunlight catches the spray of the Lisbon Falls.* **Left:** *The steep cliffs of the Drakensberg escarpment tower over the waters of the Blydepoort Dam.*

A bewitching world of soaring cliffs and tumbling crystal waters

Our route leads from the forests of Sabie and the grassy slopes of Graskop down over the scenic Kowyn's Pass. We cross a stretch of Lowveld savanna to reach the Blyde River Canyon, climb the Abel Erasmus Pass, and return to Graskop and Sabie by following the spectacular edge of the escarpment. All but 4 km of the route is tarred.

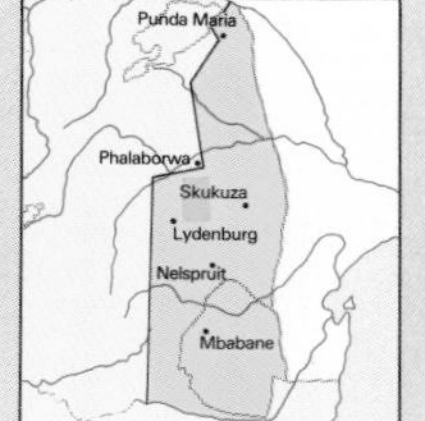

Sabie
Mac-Mac Falls
Graskop
Blydepoort Dam
Abel Erasmus Pass
Bourke's Luck
330 – 350 km

LEAVE SABIE ON THE R532 for Graskop and note your kms as you cross over the Sabie River. The road climbs for 5 km through plantations of eucalyptus and pine, then begins a gradual descent. Roughly 10 km from the Sabie River, turn right onto a 1,1 km gravel road for the pretty Mac-Mac Pools.

Return to the R532 and turn right, noting your kms. Less than 2 km later the gorge of the Mac-Mac Falls becomes visible on your right (see opposite). Park in the signposted parking area on your right. From here a path leads to several platforms giving clear views of the falls.

Continue on the R532, noting your kms. After 2,5 km you cross a railway line. Immediately after this there is a picnic area under pine trees on your right (braai sites, water). On your left, opposite the picnic area and a short distance away from the road, is the small but attractive Maria Shires waterfall. Roughly 10 km later you reach a Y-junction below the rocky hillock known as The Bonnet. Turn right here for Graskop. After some 3,5 km you enter Graskop on Pilgrim's Road.

Graskop to Blyde River Canyon

Turn right into Main Street (R533), noting your kms. After 1,5 km you pass a gravel road on your left leading to the Panorama Gorge and Falls (see pages 90-1). Shortly after this you begin the scenic descent of Kowyn's Pass, and at 5,2 km you reach a cairn in a parking area on your right recording the opening of this road over the pass. Park here for a fine panoramic view northwards over the steep escarpment.

Driving on from here you pass under a shelter constructed as a protection against rock-slides. At 11,2 km from Graskop you pass the R535 to Hazyview on your right. Continue straight until, at 35,2 km, you cross the Nwaritsana River. Slow down for the built-up area just beyond the river, and at the T-junction 4,2 km after the river, turn left onto the R40 for Acornhoek. Note your kms here.

10,8 km along the R40 you pass on your left a picnic site sheltered by an enormous tree that overhangs the road. After 35,7 km on the R40 you pass a road on your right to Acornhoek, and after a further 7,2 km you cross the Klaserie River. 500 m later the R40 turns right. Keep straight here and note your kms — you are now travelling on the R531.

Immediately you pass on your left a road leading to Klaserie. Within 200 m you pass beneath a railway bridge, then cross the Mbezi River, passing through dense indigenous vegetation. After 4,5 km on the R531 you cross the eQunduhlu River (Undothlospruit) and 11,5 km later you pass a turn-off left to Mariepskopskool. 3 km after this, turn left for the Sybrand van Niekerk Public Resort (Swadini).

The road leads towards a jumble of mountains with the towering Swadini Buttress to the right, and after 7,7 km you reach the entrance to the Blyde River Canyon Nature Reserve. 3,5 km later you pass the entrance to the Sybrand van Niekerk Resort on your right. The resort has a restaurant, braai facilities and other amenities, including a swimming pool. (If you propose to eat at the restaurant, inform the gate attendant, and provided you leave within 2 hours and produce the restaurant receipt, no admission fee will be charged.)

Roughly 2,1 km after passing the resort, where the road ahead is closed, turn right — and note your kms. Stop at the barrier just after the turn, where the gate attendant will give you an information brochure. The road now crosses the Blyde River and you pass the Nature Reserve Office on your left. 1,8 km from the turn-off you reach a small parking area on your left. Stop here for a fine view of the Blydepoort Dam wall. 1,4 km beyond this parking area the road ends at a second parking site from which a path leads left to a visitor's information centre, a viewing balcony (see pages 88-9) and toilets.

Return to the T-junction with the R531, and turn left onto the R531 — noting your kms. Amidst the typical Lowveld thornbush that you now pass through there are great plantations of citrus, bananas, mangoes and pawpaws. After 8,4 km you pass a tarred road on your right to Hoedspruit and Phalaborwa, and 3,5 km later you reach a T-junction. Turn left here to stay on the R531, noting your kms.

You cross the well-shaded Blyde River after 2,3 km, and at 17,7 km you pass a road on your right to Tzaneen. Roughly 5 km later you can see the Abel Erasmus Pass ahead, ascending from left to right, and some 3 km after this you reach the start of the pass. After climbing for 1,3 km you reach a small parking area on the right offering views over the Olifants River. 1,5 km later you reach another small parking area at the entrance to the J G Strijdom Tunnel.

At the far end of the tunnel there is a parking area offering completely different views. A striking waterfall can be seen, cascading over a tufa-formation that it has created in the course of many centuries (see page 89 column 2). Note your kms as you leave this parking area.

Over the Abel Erasmus Pass

You now pass several picnic sites as the road gradually climbs over the Abel Erasmus Pass. At around 15 km you reach a shady picnic site on your left, from where there are fine views over cultivated valleys ringed by mountains. After 22 km, turn left onto the R532, noting your kms at the turn. (If you continue straight here, you will reach the gravel turn-off to the Echo Caves after 1,1 km.)

After 1,4 km you cross the Ohrigstad River, passing tobacco fields and drying sheds on your left. The road winds upward with the Ohrigstad River gorge visible on your left, through rolling country with the Drakensberg always in view ahead and to your left. You pass the F H Odendaal Public Resort on your left.

Cross the Kadishi (Kadisi) River after 22 km — it is very small at this point — and 1,8 km later turn left onto a 3 km side-road to the Three Rondavels viewsite. Return to the R532, driving slowly to appreciate the views on your left over the gorge. The T-junction with the R532 appears suddenly at the top of a small rise. Turn left onto the R532, noting your kms.

Turn left after 4,7 km and follow another side-road for 400 m to reach the Lowveld

Waterfall and tufa in the Abel Erasmus Pass.

Dawn tinges the Lowveld sky above Wonderview.

Water tumbles through the Bourke's Luck 'Potholes'.

Lichen colours the Drakensberg's rock-faces.

BOURKE'S LUCK

Where the Blyde (joyful) River is joined by the Treur (sorrow) River, there is a remarkable record of an erosion process that started thousands of years ago. Minor imperfections in the dolomite rock have been worn away by the swirling water with its load of grit and pebbles, causing 'potholes' to appear. Thomas Bourke, an early owner of the farm on which this feature is situated, discovered gold at the bottom of the holes. His farm became known as Bourke's Luck.

ABEL ERASMUS PASS

This magnificent road across the Drakensberg was opened in 1959. For much of its route it follows a wagon track pioneered in the 1840s. Travelling south-west from the Lowveld, the road rises 610 m above the Olifants River, then drops 335 m to the level of the Ohrigstad River. The pass is named after Abel Erasmus, who owned the farm Graskop in the 1870s, and who was responsible for keeping peace with the various indigenous communities of the Eastern Transvaal.

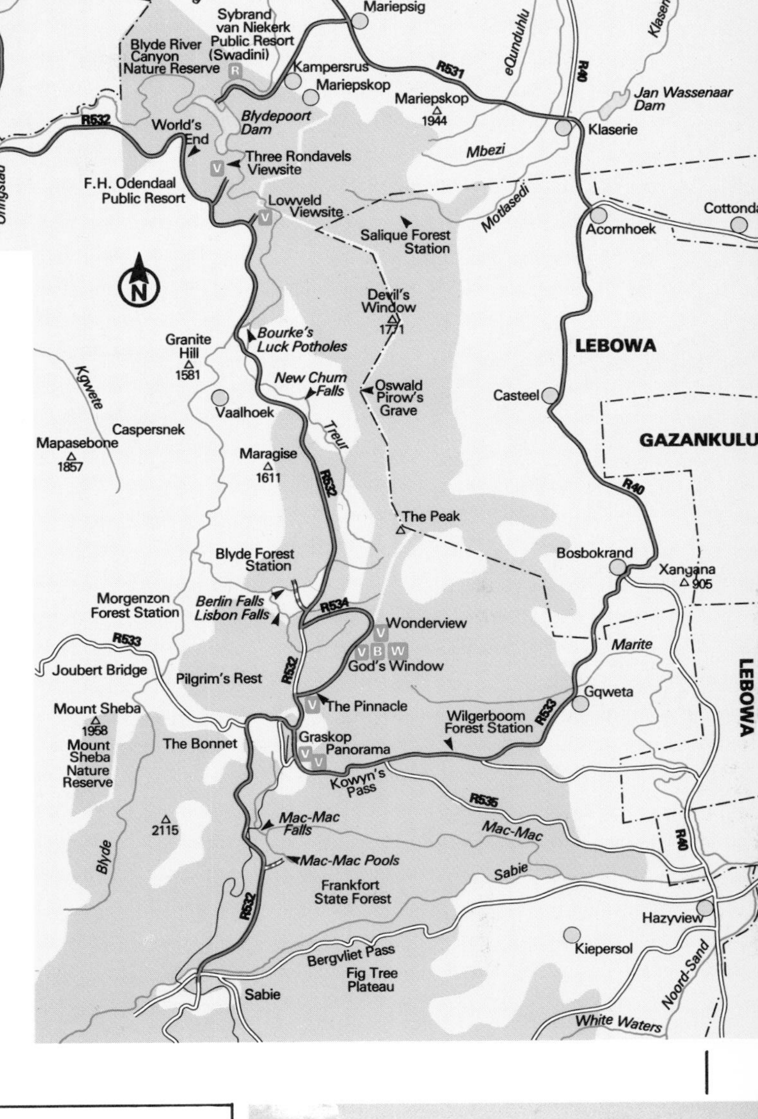

Morning sun on the Mac-Mac Falls.

MAC-MAC FALLS

Although President Burgers is said to have named the area after the many Scotsmen among the early diggers, another source claims that the name of the falls can be traced to the MacClaughton brothers, who led the rush to this area. The search for gold spread to this scenic waterfall on the Watervalspruit, and particularly to the pool below its 56 m drop. In an attempt to divert the flow, which was hampering their operations, the miners planted a large charge of gunpowder at the top of the falls. The resultant explosion failed to achieve the desired effect, but it did result in the single stream being split into twin falls.

viewsite. Return to the R532 and turn left, noting your kms as you turn. After 9 km turn left into the Bourke's Luck picnic site (entry fee, braai sites, refreshment kiosk, toilets). A short path leads to the remarkable Bourke's Luck 'potholes'. Take either route where the path forks. None of the fencing in the area is entirely 'child-proof', and small children must be managed with care. (See above.)

Allow about an hour at Bourke's Luck, then return to the R532 and turn left, noting your kms. After 500 m you cross the Blyde River, and at 2,3 km and 5 km you cross and re-cross the Treur River (see pages 88-9). At just over 9 km you pass a cairn on your left commemorating the Voortrekkers. Cross the Watervalspruit at roughly 22 km, and after a further 4,8 km turn right onto a gravel road for the Berlin Falls. Pass a road on your left after 1,1 km on the gravel, and turn left 800 m later. 300 m beyond this, you reach a parking area. A path (sometimes slippery) leads from the car park to a viewsite at the edge of the gorge.

Return to the R532 and turn right, noting your kms. After 1,2 km turn left onto the R534 for God's Window. Along the R534 there are several clearly marked viewsites on your left, looking out over the Lowveld. The first is Wonderview, 7 km from the turn, followed by God's Window and The Pinnacle (see pages 90-1).

After 16 km on the R534 you rejoin the R532 at a T-junction. Turn left here onto the R532, to enter Graskop on Hugenotestraat. Turn right into Louis Trichardt Street, and 500 m later turn left into Main Street. Turn right at the four-way stop street into Pilgrim's Road, and retrace your outward route back to Sabie ●

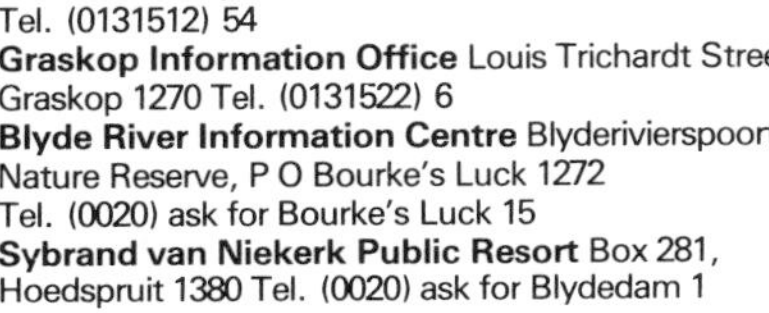
Sabie Forestry Museum Ford Street, Sabie 1260 Tel. (0131512) 54
Graskop Information Office Louis Trichardt Street, Graskop 1270 Tel. (0131522) 6
Blyde River Information Centre Blyderivierspoort Nature Reserve, P O Bourke's Luck 1272 Tel. (0020) ask for Bourke's Luck 15
Sybrand van Niekerk Public Resort Box 281, Hoedspruit 1380 Tel. (0020) ask for Blydedam 1

Amid rolling hills — the unexpected Berlin Falls.

The Blyde River swirls between brightly coloured cliffs at the start of its magnificent canyon.

Ancient, soaring buttresses and a mighty canyon echo the cries of war

As they trekked further into the interior to escape British domination, the 'emigrant Boers' — the Voortrekkers — became increasingly conscious of their need to find access to a seaport which was not under British control. In 1838 Louis Trichardt had succeeded in reaching the Portuguese town of Lourenco Marques (now Maputo) at Delagoa Bay, but the journey was costly: many of Trichardt's party died of fever. In 1844 Andries Hendrik Potgieter, accompanied only by a few men on horseback, set out on another trek to the coast, and left his party's cumbersome wagons behind at the top of the Drakensberg escarpment — with the women and children, and a few armed men.

The base-party outspanned the wagons at a river, and awaited the return of their leader. The time agreed upon for the return passed, but the group stayed on until, eventually, they abandoned hope of ever seeing Potgieter and his companions again. Sadly, they loaded the wagons for the long haul back to Potchefstroom. Before they left, the disconsolate trekkers named the river by which they had camped the *Treurrivier* — the river of sorrow. Later, while they were fording another river some kilometres to the west, they heard distant shots. Looking around, they saw Potgieter and his comrades ride into view, the successful journey having taken much longer than anticipated. There was great rejoicing at the reunion, and the river they were in the process of fording was named the *Blyderivier* — the river of joy.

Blyderivierspoort Reserve

Today the Blyde River, and the magnificent canyon through which it flows, are part of the Blyderivierspoort Nature Reserve. The reserve includes all the land surrounding the Blydepoort Dam, and extends upstream almost to Graskop.

The Blyde River has its source in the Drakensberg, close to Pilgrim's

Rest, and flows north, being joined by the Treur at the remarkable Bourke's Luck Potholes, before entering the great canyon that it has helped to create in the course of millions of years. The Blyde River flows strongly throughout the year and has by far the highest run-off of any South African river — some 40 per cent compared to a national average of only nine per cent. This means that 40 per cent of the total rainfall actually appears as stream flow, the remainder being lost to evaporation. The high run-off is due in part to the steep terrain of the catchment area, and also because the underground rock 'stores' water, releasing it into the flow as the water-table drops.

A great tilting of the land surface, following a massive volcanic disturbance in the central Transvaal millions of years ago, produced the mighty Transvaal Drakensberg escarpment. Layers of sand and mud, deposited by vanished inland lakes, have become compressed to form quartzite and shale. On its long journey to the sea, the Blyde River carried suspended particles ranging from grains of sand to great boulders, and their erosive effect created the formations we see today. At the great Swadini buttress, the harder quartzite forms the vertical cliffs, while softer shales have eroded to form the talus, or sloping sections which are now covered with vegetation.

The Three Rondavels and the higher Mapjaneng dominate the gorge.

Capping the escarpment is a layer of hard, Black Reef quartzite.

Opposite the buttress, on the road that enters the Swadini resort area, is the peak of Mariepskop, which reaches a height of 1 944 m. Mariepskop is named after Maripi Mashile, a chief of the Mapulana tribe who helped the Pedi defeat a force of Swazi invaders here in 1864, in a battle known as *Moholoholo* — the great, great battle. Swadini means 'the place of the Swazi', although it was actually the home of the Pedi, who lived here throughout the year, except for the very hottest months, when they moved to the top of the cooler escarpment. Swazi raiders would then move in, wreck their settlements, and reap their crops. Maripi's strategy was to scale the mountain with his warriors, and taunt the Swazi into attacking them there. As the Swazi climbed after them, they were demolished by an avalanche of boulders hurled down the slopes by the wily Pedi tribesmen.

Maripi and his wives

The hills to the right of Mariepskop are known as Rodille, or 'the bundles', because they resemble a file of women carrying bundles on their heads. The striking Three Rondavels, which can be seen best from the top of the escarpment (see pages 86-7) are named after three of Maripi's wives. From lowest to highest, they are Magabolle, Mogoladikwe and Maseroto. The peak at the end of the row, and highest of all, is Mapjaneng — the chief — also named in honour of Maripi.

As you look across the water of the Blydepoort Dam from the balcony of the Visitors' Centre at Swadini, you see the 1 087 m peak of Thabaneng at a bend in the dam. Its name means 'the mountain with a shadow that moves' and it is known also as The Sundial. To the right, and beyond a further stretch of water, are the unique Kadishi Falls, the largest active tufa formation in the world.

To the left of the waterfall is a cave which, many years ago, was a part of the river's course — now blocked by the formation of tufa. (Tufa is a porous deposit of calcium carbonate formed — when the temperature changes — from calcium bicarbonate carried in solution by a river.)

The dam is at the confluence of the Blyde and Ohrigstad rivers, the latter entering from the west — your right as you face the Kadishi Falls. The pools that formed here before the construction of the dam were inhabited by large numbers of hippo and crocodiles, but raising the water level has destroyed much of their suitable environment. A small group of hippo can be seen sometimes on the shoreline to the left of Thabaneng. Few crocodiles remain, and they generally confine themselves to the muddy islands.

Brooding Blydepoort Dam — heart of the Blyderivierspoort Nature Reserve.

Blyderivierspoort Hiking Trail

The bird life in the reserve includes white-breasted cormorants, black eagles and crowned eagles. Buck species include steenbok, klipspringer and kudu, while baboons and samango monkeys — and leopards — inhabit the forests and kloofs.

Traversing the reserve from south to north is the Blyderivierspoort Hiking Trail, starting at the magnificent viewsite known as God's Window near Graskop, and ending at the Swadini resort. The 65 km trail takes five days to complete. The trail passes the scenically beautiful New Chum Falls, Bourke's Luck Potholes and the Kadishi Falls, and ends with a suspension bridge. There are spectacular views along the entire trail, as well as glimpses of the old coach-road, but the most scenic areas are traversed on the last day, where the route is dominated by the Three Rondavels.

There are four short walks within the reserve, ranging from half an hour to three hours. Obtain permits first at the control point just before crossing the Blyde River on the way to the Visitors' Centre.

Boat trips may be undertaken from a jetty near the Visitors' Centre, where bookings should be made. Swimming pools and other amenities are provided at the Swadini and F H Odendaal resorts. The headquarters of the Nature Conservation team is at Bourke's Luck, where there is also an interesting Information Centre and a variety of further walks ●

Without any warning the Highveld gives way to a chasm 700 metres deep.

Between Highveld and Lowveld, a land of gold mines and waterfalls

This route leads from the forest-and-waterfall country of Sabie down to the tropical fruit plantations of the Lowveld, then up over the Drakensberg by means of Kowyn's Pass. We pass through Graskop, visit God's Window and the Lisbon Falls, then climb still higher over Bonnet Pass to Pilgrim's Rest. All but 8 km of the route is tarred.

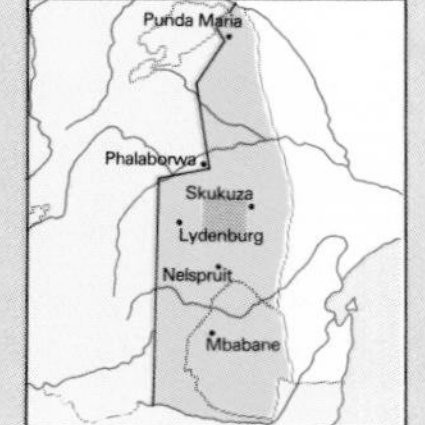

Sabie
Lone Creek waterfall
Hazyview
Graskop
Lisbon Falls
Pilgrim's Rest
200 – 220 km

DRIVE DOWN Sabie's Main Street towards Graskop, and turn left into Lydenburg Road. After 2 km you cross the railway, then pass a gravel road leading right to the Bridal Veil Falls. You cross the railway a second time, then pass a gravel road leading left to the Horseshoe Falls. 100 m later you cross the Sabie River.

Keep left where the road divides. Roughly 2,5 km from the river you will see the Lone Creek Waterfall ahead — tumbling over a rock face above the trees. You reach a parking area 300 m later (braai sites, water, toilets). A short circular walk leads to the foot of the 68 m fall.

Sabie to Hazyview

Retrace your route to Main Street in Sabie, and turn right (uphill). Continue straight through town for Hazyview and White River. A few hundred metres after leaving the town, turn right onto the R537 for White River, noting your kms. The road now winds through extensive forests, and after roughly 8 km you will see the prominent Spitskop on your right (see opposite).

16 km from Sabie the road descends sharply, and 4,6 km later it crosses the Blinkwaterspruit (sparkling water stream). 26 km from Sabie you pass a gravel road on your left to Hebron, and 2,7 km later you pass a gravel road leading left into the Swartfontein (black spring) Forest. After a further 1,5 km turn left onto a second gravel road for Swartfontein — noting your kms. (Drive slowly in wet weather.) This road skirts the wood-fringed Danie Joubert Dam. After roughly 8 km on gravel, turn left at the T-junction onto the R40 for Hazyview — noting your kms.

The R40 leads through forest and citrus groves. After 4,8 km you cross the White Waters River, and 600 m later there is a good view back over the Da Gama Dam. After this you pass through extensive banana plantations. After roughly 26 km on the R40 you reach a junction with the R538 — take the exit-road to your left and note your kms as you turn onto the R538.

Hazyview to Graskop

Drive through the settlement of Hazyview, passing the R536 to Skukuza on your right after 2,5 km. 1 km later you pass the R536 leading left towards Sabie, and you then cross the Sabie River. After crossing the river, turn left onto the R535 for Graskop — noting your kms.

The road begins to climb, offering views over forested hills. After 21,5 km you pass through a crossroads, then plunge again into dense forests. After 26,5 km on the R535, turn left at the T-junction onto the R533 for Graskop.

The road now climbs steeply up the Drakensberg escarpment by means of Kowyn's Pass. At first trees block your view, but later you have fine views of the escarpment to your right. The road passes under a shelter built to guard against rockfalls, and soon after this there is a small parking area on your left, with a cairn commemorating the opening of the pass.

After 9,7 km on the R533 you pass the Panorama Gorge and the Panorama Falls on your right. If there has been rain recently, it is worth parking off the road on your right to view the falls — but note that the cliff-top is unfenced and children should be held.

1 km after passing Panorama Gorge you enter Graskop on Main Street (Hoofstraat). Keep straight at the intersection with Pilgrim's

The Pinnacle near Graskop.

Sabie — extensive forestry plantations.

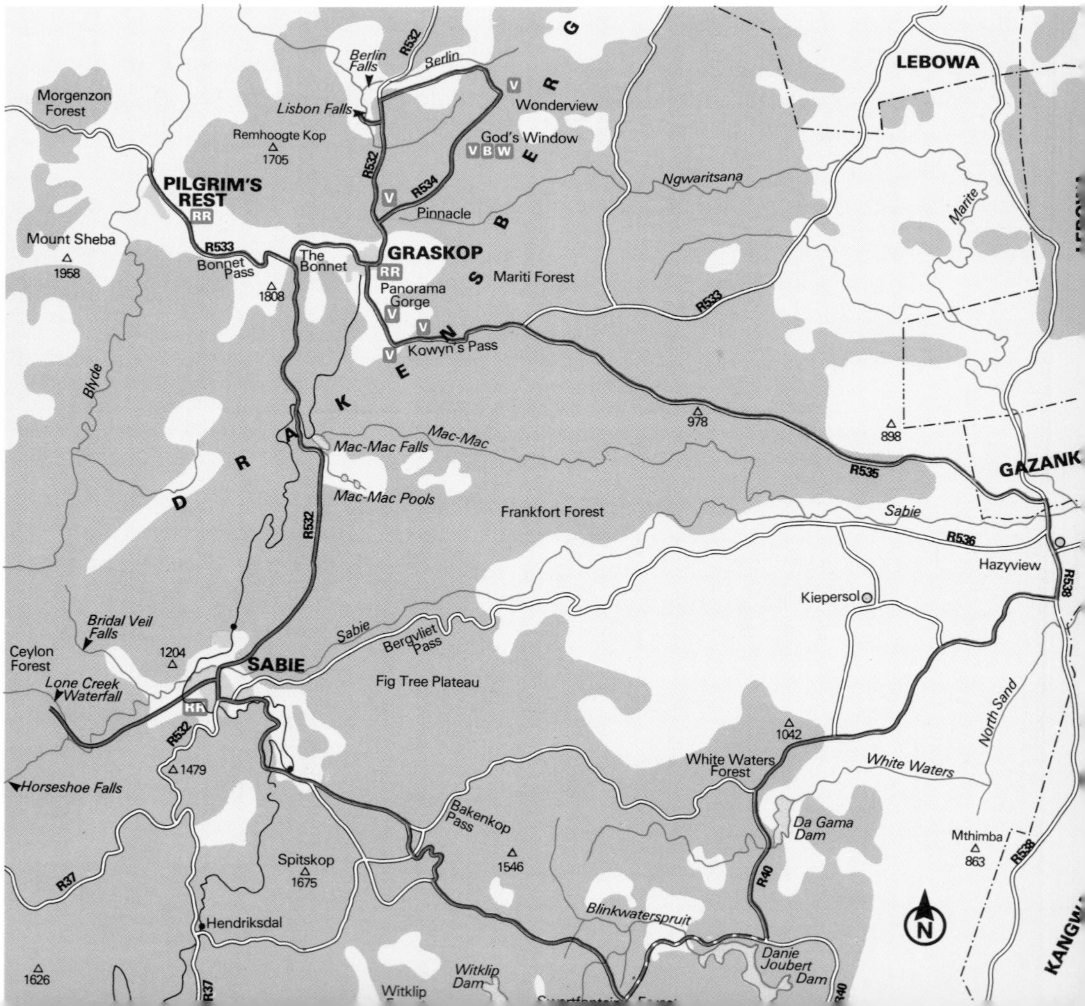

Way and Richardson Avenue, and turn right into Louis Trichardt Avenue. You now pass the Tourist Information Office on your left. Turn left into Hugenote Street — which becomes the R532 for the Blyde River Canyon — noting your kms as you turn.

Graskop to the Lisbon Falls

After 1,9 km turn right onto the R534, and after a further 1,4 km turn right into the parking area for the Pinnacle viewsite. There is a good view from here over the Pinnacle and the distant Lowveld, but again the cliff edge is unfenced and young children should be held.

Drive back onto the tar and turn right. You now pass several parking areas and viewsites on your right, and roughly 5 km later you reach the parking area for God's Window, also on your right. There are braai places here, water and toilets, and a short footpath leads to the God's Window viewsite (fenced). The 'window' is the head of a narrow gorge.

Continue along the R534, and after a further 1,3 km you reach the Wonderview viewsite (fenced, but not entirely safe). You cannot see the escarpment from here because you are standing on the crest of it, but on a clear day you can look far out over the Lowveld.

The R534 now swings to the west, away from the escarpment, and joins the R532 in a T-junction. Turn left here towards Graskop, then turn right onto a gravel road after just 800 m. This 2,2 km gravel road leads to a parking area alongside the 82,5 m Lisbon Falls. A 100 m footpath leads to a fine viewsite.

Return to the R532 and turn right, noting your kms. You pass through dense pine plantations and cross the Lisbon River, to reach Graskop again after 6 km.

Graskop to Pilgrim's Rest

Turn right into Louis Trichardt Avenue, then left into Main Street. At the stop street, turn right into Pilgrim's Road. The road begins to wind through hilly country, and roughly 1 km out of town there is a parking area on your left next to a small natural rock bridge — a national monument. Roughly 3 km later you reach a Y-junction at the base of the rocky outcrop known as The Bonnet. Go right here on the R533 towards Pilgrim's Rest. (The road left, R532, leads to Mac-Mac Falls and Sabie).

The R533 climbs over Bonnet Pass, and as you descend on the western side of the pass, you can catch glimpses of Pilgrim's Rest in the valley below. Within a few kilometres you enter the outskirts of the village, which straggles for a short distance on both sides of the main road (see pages 92-3). The Royal Hotel serves lunch, and there is a picnic site at the caravan park at the bottom end of the town — follow the concrete road that leads left just before the tarred R533 crosses the historic Joubert Bridge over the Blyde River. There are braai sites here, firewood for sale, water and toilets — also a restaurant and a swimming pool.

From Pilgrim's Rest, retrace your route to The Bonnet, and go right on the R532 for Sabie. As you drive through patches of forest you will see, scattered among the trees, white-painted cairns surmounted by tin notices — these are prospectors' claims. The drive back to Sabie is very short, and you pass on your left, first the Mac-Mac Falls, then a gravel road leading to the Mac-Mac Pools (see pages 86-7) ●

Sabie Forestry Museum Ford Street, Sabie 1260 Tel. (0131512) 54
Graskop Information Office Louis Trichardt Ave, Graskop 1270 Tel. (0131522) 6
Pilgrim's Rest Information Office Main Street, Pilgrim's Rest 1290 Tel. (0020) ask for Pilgrim's Rest 28 or 50

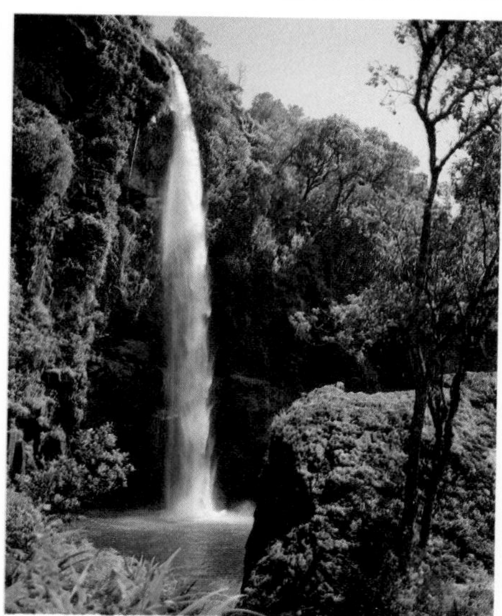

Lone Creek waterfall near Sabie.

THE FORESTRY MUSEUM, SABIE

Sabie's Forestry Museum is the only museum of its kind in South Africa. Its exhibits cover the natural marvels of trees and their wood, and illustrate the ingenious ways in which people have put this wood to use — from violins and matches to the heat-absorbing nose-cones of modern inter-continental rockets. Also illustrated is the growth of the South African timber industry, from the earliest days to the highly complex enterprise it is today.

SPITSKOP GOLD

The first alluvial gold to be discovered in the eastern Transvaal — occurring in payable quantities — was found on the slopes of Spitskop ('pointed hill') early in 1871.

Among the discoverers was Edward Button, who promptly sent a letter to the landdrost at Lydenburg claiming a reward that had been offered by the Volksraad. No reward was in fact paid, but Button was rewarded in the sense that he was appointed Gold Commissioner of the Transvaal — and he went on to initiate gold mining at Eersteling, near Pietersburg.

Little now remains of the venture at Spitskop, except for a few shallow workings that have been largely obliterated by extensive pine plantations.

A LUCKY STRIKE THAT CREATED SABIE

The little town of Sabie grew up on a farm called Grootfontein — which had been bought by the hunter Henry Glynn in 1880. An earlier owner had paid a mere £7 10s for the same farm, but Glynn had to pay £600 — now that gold had been discovered in the area. Glynn's purchase turned out to be highly profitable, however. One day he was taking part in a little target practice, when a bullet chipped off a piece of rock to reveal traces of a gold reef. The mine that resulted produced gold for the next 70 years. Mining operations required timber for props — and this need gave birth to the extensive forest plantations that now surround the town.

The historic Joubert Bridge across the Blyde River.

Undulating hills and cool forests surround the holiday resort of Graskop.

GRASKOP

The town of Graskop awaits the traveller at the summit of the scenic Kowyn's Pass, at a height of 1 488 m. The name can be translated as 'grassy hill', but nobody knows which of the many surrounding hills and mountains this name originally referred to. The town began as a mining camp late in the 19th century, established on a farm that had been owned by Abel Erasmus — a prominent figure in the history of the eastern Transvaal. Graskop now serves as a centre for the timber industry, and makes a convenient base for holiday-makers.

Early morning mist curls around the red roofs of Pilgrim's Rest — the Leadley's building stands in the foreground.

'Wheelbarrow' Patterson, and furniture made from dynamite boxes

A WALK DOWN THE historic main street of Pilgrim's Rest is a walk back in time — to the days when dreamers and desperadoes from around the world converged on this little-known valley in the Drakensberg in a hectic scramble for the riches that lay beneath its grassy hillsides.

Pilgrim's Rest owes its name to a group of men who had dug for gold at nearby Mac-Mac. They called themselves 'The Pilgrims'. The group included one crusty old loner named Alec Patterson, also known as 'Wheelbarrow' Patterson from his habit of carrying his meagre worldly goods in a wheelbarrow — it was cheaper than a horse, he said, and it could not die of horse-sickness. In 1873 Patterson found Mac-Mac too crowded, so he loaded up his wheelbarrow and wandered away, following a game-trail over the mountains, until he looked down into a valley through which flowed a clear stream on its way to join the Blyde River. Down he went and, even before pitching camp, he panned some of the river gravel. The golden tail in the pan showed a richness beyond his wildest expectations.

Shortly after setting up camp, Patterson was joined by another digger, William Trafford, who had wandered into 'his' valley. Stunned by the wealth in his pan, Trafford is said to have called out in delight: 'The pilgrim is at rest'. The hills echoed 'pilgrim... rest...' and so the first thoroughly profitable goldfield in South Africa received its name.

From Mac-Mac, from Kimberley, from around the world, diggers poured into this rich valley, setting up the main diggings where the river — soon named Pilgrim's Creek — flowed through the former farm of Ponieskranz. Within a year there were more than 14 bars selling liquor to the diggers, with names such as 'Our House' and 'Stent's Cathedral'.

Corrugated iron

As men dug away at the slopes above Pilgrim's Creek, the tent town that had sprung up almost overnight was gradually replaced by more substantial structures, built mainly of corrugated iron on wooden frames. These were easy to bring in by wagon, quick to erect — and nobody expected the field to last long enough to justify brick and mortar. The diggers also feared that one day, and possibly without warning, they would be ordered out by the Transvaal Government: a brick house that had to be left behind would represent a considerable loss.

The Old Print House now serves as tourist's gift shop.

Probably the oldest surviving brick structure is the little *Anglican Church of St Mary* **(1)**, which is on your left as you enter the long main street from Sabie. It was built in 1884, by which time mining operations had recovered from the setbacks caused by the British annexation of 1877, and the Anglo-Transvaal War of a few years later.

In those days church functions were held in the corrugated iron *Town Hall* **(2)**, two doors down from St Mary's. On the right side of the road here a plaque records the town's history. (Excavations made by the alluvial-diggers can be seen on the opposite bank of the river, forming shallow depressions in the slope.)

The well-restored *Leadley's building* **(3)**, on your left as you travel downhill, is now a hotel annex. Next on your left are the *Old Print Shop* **(4)** and the *Pilgrim's and Sabie News* **(5)**. The *European Hotel* **(6)**, on your left, with its attractive verandah typical of Pilgrim's Rest, now houses a restaurant furnished in a turn-of-the-century style. A little further down on your right is the wide verandah of *Chaitow* **(7)**, formerly the home of Mr C H Chaitow, one-time hairdresser, tobacconist and stationer in the town. An untarred loop road on your right leads to the *Informa-*

tion Centre **(8)**, where you should obtain admission tickets to the town's museums before proceeding.

Opposite the Information Centre is the *Royal Hotel* **(9)**, the bar of which once served as a chapel in Lourenco Marques (now Maputo) until it was purchased by an enterprising transport-rider heading for Pilgrim's Rest in the 1890s. It now houses fascinating relics of Pilgrim's Rest's more riotous days, including prospecting pans, helmets, lamps, and numerous liquor bottles drained and discarded by thirsty diggers.

The ox-cart was the main form of transport until early this century.

Robber's grave in the old cemetery.

Home-made furniture

Just past the hotel on your right is the *Miner's House Museum* **(10)** depicting the home life of a miner during the period 1910-20. Furniture and equipment is robust and simple, and often home-made, as in the case of the paraffin-box converted to a chair, the cupboards made from dynamite boxes, and the paraffin-tin baking pans.

Across the road from the Miner's House Museum is the *Post Office* **(11)**. The town's first postmaster (and also public prosecutor) Mr J E Glinister, was appointed in 1877. The building now houses a museum. After you pass the Victorian Cottage on your right, which serves as an annex to the hotel, there are public toilets.

Opposite the Victorian Cottage a gravel road leads left to the Methodist Church, and climbs steeply to the historic *cemetery* **(12)**, which can also be reached by car along a different road. As you walk to the cemetery, it is easy to appreciate why it was necessary to have relays of bearers at funerals. In the early days of the diggings, although life was robust and rowdy, there was little serious crime. Stealing from the tent of a chum was unforgivable, and a digger, whose name has been forgotten, was once caught in this act, thrashed, and told never again to show his face in the camp. Unwisely, he did return, was seen and recognised in the dusk, and promptly shot. He was buried where he fell, lying along a north-south axis to mark him as unmourned. A day or so later there were two more deaths in the camp, more graves were dug nearby, and so the cemetery — unplanned — grew.

Return to the main road and turn left. The first building you pass on your left is the turn-of-the-century *Dredzen & Company general store* **(13)**. Most of the building is original, including the shelves and counter, and the shop, as was the custom, is divided into two major sections: a business section in front, with living quarters in the rear.

Continuing down the hill, you pass several buildings and an open section before reaching the lower half of the town. Look out on your right for a six-arched cement stage, or ore-bin, where ore was loaded.

The charmingly restored Royal Hotel houses many relics from the past.

War memorial

The first building in the lower half of the town is the *Roman Catholic Church of the Sacred Heart* **(14)**, followed by a number of shops and the Highwayman's Garage (see page 21). Turn left after passing the Dutch Reformed Church to visit the *Central Reduction Works*, built in 1896 **(15)**. There are a number of attractive old iron buildings on your left. Once inside the works area, note the little stone memorial, almost entirely hidden by bushes, on the left where the road leads up to the offices. It was erected in memory of residents who died during World War I.

The works themselves are a forlorn collection of buildings that echo the frenzied activity that once drove their dark and decaying machinery. The buildings include huge stables that once housed the mules that dragged countless tons of ore from the various mines, with the adjacent farrier's and wheelwright's shops still displaying all the tools of these trades. The large carpenter's shop is being used for restoration work, but others — like the fitter's shop and the smithy — are deserted except for old tools and machines. Among the old vehicles preserved in the works is an ox-wagon once used to transport goods from Lydenburg.

Return to the main road and turn left, to pass a cluster of old buildings — mostly shops — before a road on your left leads to the caravan park (see pages 90-1). At this point the Blyde River is crossed by the stone *Joubert Bridge* **(16)**, built in 1896 and named after the republic's mining commissioner. The Joubert Bridge can be taken as marking the end of the old town, but after returning to your car, you may if you wish visit Alanglade. Now maintained as a museum, this is a period house of the Art Nouveau and Art Deco era, dating from 1915 to 1930. To reach Alanglade, drive across the Joubert Bridge, keep straight where the road left leads to Lydenburg, then turn left shortly afterwards ●

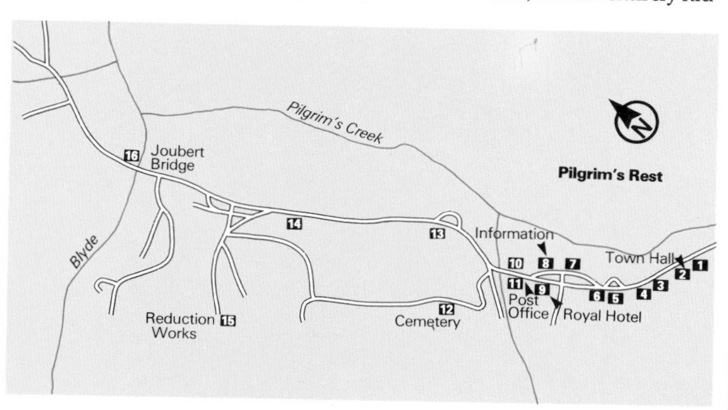

The Chaitow family outside their store.

Mysterious caves, and misty memories of Long Tom's thunder

From Nelspruit we drive through forests to visit the ancient Sudwala Caves. We then cross the Crocodile River, view the Montrose Falls, and wind through the attractive Schoemanskloof and Skaapwagters Pass to Lydenburg. From here we drive over Mauchsberg, then down the full length of the magnificent Long Tom Pass. The entire route is tarred.

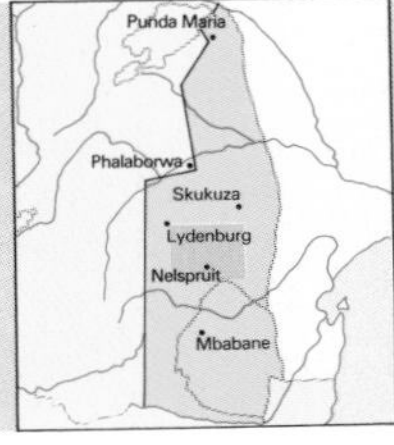

Nelspruit
Sudwala Caves
Montrose Falls
Schoemanskloof
Lydenburg
Long Tom Pass
Sabie
250 — 270 km

DRIVE NORTH FROM Nelspruit on the R40 towards White River and cross the Crocodile River on the outskirts of the town. 500 m later turn left onto the R37 and note your kms.

Part of the road is lined with African Flame trees *(Spathodea campanulata)* which form an avenue of bright scarlet blossoms in summer. There are wide views to your right over rolling hills and citrus plantations. You then enter an area of pine and eucalyptus forests, beneath the tree-lined ridges of Bossieskop and Roodewal. After 28 km, turn left onto the R539 for Sudwala — and note your kms.

The road soon enters dense forests that stretch away to the green hills in the distance. After about 11 km, from where the road begins to descend, there are particularly fine views over the forested hills. After 15,4 km you cross the Houtbosloop (wood forest stream) and reach a T-junction, where the road on the left leads to Nelspruit. Turn right here for Sudwala, noting your kms.

After 1,1 km turn right for the Sudwala Caves and the Dinosaur Park. 400 m later the road forks. (On your left is a hotel with a restaurant and swimming pool. Picnic sites are available at a small fee.) Go right at the fork, passing on your right a large orchard of pecan trees. Trailers and caravans are not permitted on this steep cement road which leads to the caves. After just under 1 km you reach another fork. Go left here, and park where the road ends in a shaded parking area. From here a flight of steps leads to the entrance of the cave system.

The caves are open from 08h30 to 16h30 and tours are conducted irregularly. The standard tours last approximately one hour, but they can be extended on request. From the entrance to the caves, a path leads to the right to the Dinosaur Park. Among the stones used for lining and paving the paths are some that show fossilized ripple marks and mud cracks. The Dinosaur Park, also known as the Owen Museum, is open during the same hours as the caves. (There are entrance fees to both the caves and the park.)

Sudwala to Montrose Falls

Retrace your route to the tarred road and turn left, noting your kms. After 6,5 km you reach a T-junction with the N4. Turn right onto the N4, noting your kms. After 4,5 kms you cross

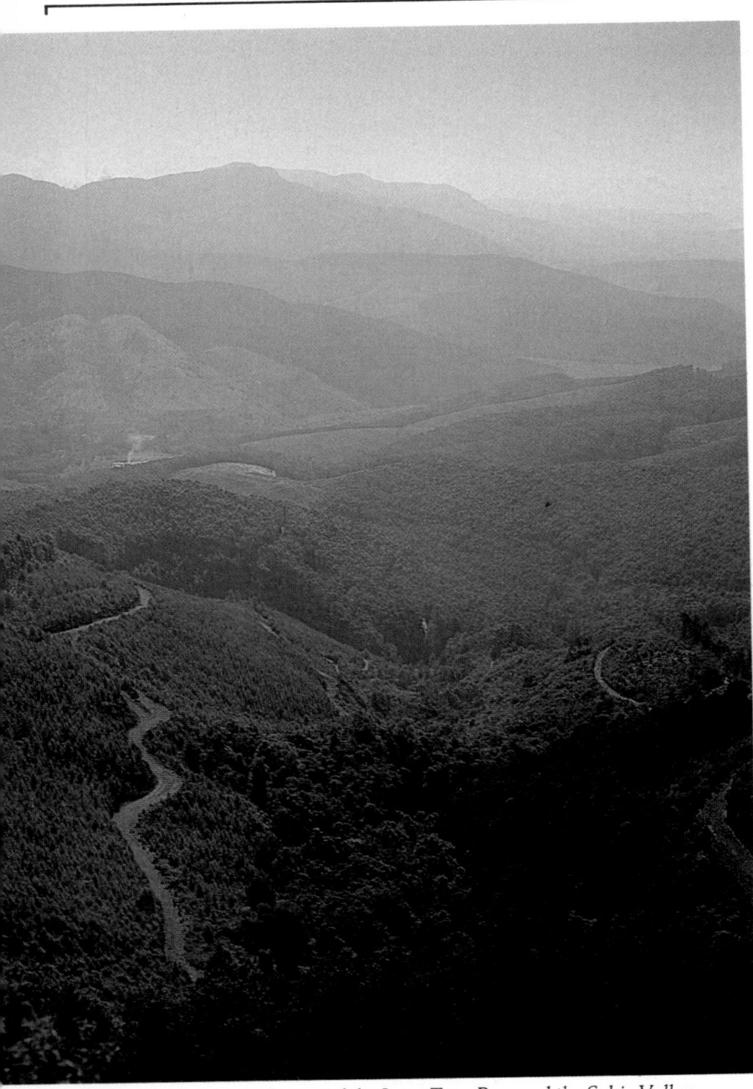

Looking out over the forests of the Long Tom Pass and the Sabie Valley.

SUDWALA CAVES

Unmeasured expanses of tunnel and cavern lie undiscovered beneath the bush-clad hill known as Mankelekele (crag upon crag). Man lived close to the cave entrance in prehistoric times, but the depths preserve a record of life that dates back over 2 000 million years — in the form of fossilized colonies (known as stromatolites) of the algae Collenia, a primitive single-celled plant.

The dolomite rock in which the caves have formed was laid down by water at the time when the Collenia were living. Water flowing into cracks in the dolomite eroded weak regions in the rock, creating a cave system decorated with stalagmites and stalactites. The best-known of these dripstone formations is the 'Screaming Monster', and the largest is the 14 m 'Rocket Silo'.

Early last century a Swazi king sheltered here from pursuing Zulu impis, who attempted to smoke him out by building a huge fire at the entrance — where scorch marks may still be seen. The caves are named after a Swazi officer who took refuge here after a bloody battle in the valley. Many tales of lost treasure surround the caves, including the legend of the 'Kruger millions'.

Rock formations — Sudwala Caves.

Dinosaur Park's Tyrannosaurus Rex.

LYDENBURG — TOWN OF SUFFERING

This town on the eastern escarpment of the Drakensberg was founded in 1849 by the survivors of the fever-smitten settlement of Ohrigstad, some 50 km to the north-east. In memory of their recent hardships and heartache they named their new town Lydenburg (town of suffering). In 1857 Lydenburg was made the capital of the new Republic of Lydenburg, which was later absorbed into the South African Republic (the modern Transvaal).

The Voortrekker School in Church Street, built in 1851, is the oldest building in the town. The Dutch Reformed Church alongside it was built in 1894 and is still in use. The old powder magazine in Viljoen Street was constructed in part from stones taken from nearby Fort Mary, which endured a 84-day siege during the Anglo-Transvaal War of 1880-81.

the Crocodile River. Turn left at the crossroads immediately afterwards, where the road on the right (R539) leads to 'Bambi'.

Pass the hotel and the parking area for shoppers on your right, and then pass the petrol station, also on your right. Immediately after this, turn right, following the gravel road. Park on the loop road — 400 m from the N4 — to view the Montrose Falls. A path with cement steps leads down to several viewsites from which the two main falls can be seen tumbling into the gorge. The first site can be reached in under five minutes, but it is worth walking further down for a closer view.

Return to the N4, note your kms, and proceed straight across onto the R539 for Bambi. The road climbs for some 3 km, then descends amid forested hills and below rocky cliffs. After about 16,5 km you may see a sparkling waterfall to your right, if there have been good rains recently. The road leads through Schoemanskloof and the scenic Skaapwagters (shepherd's) Pass. After 44,3 km turn right onto the R36 for Lydenburg, noting your kms as you turn.

After 2,7 km you reach the start of the Chomse se Hoogte (Chomse's Height) Pass. Soon after this the road rounds a right-hand bend to reveal a fine vista of valleys and mountains. After 9,8 km you pass a road on your right leading to the Braam Raubenheimer Dam, and 2 km later you cross the Crocodile River. For the next few kms you have the dam on your right. After 45,3 km you pass the R540 on your left, cross the Doornbergspruit (thorn mountain stream), and enter Lydenburg on Viljoen Street. At the caravan park in Viljoen Street there are braai facilities, toilets and drinking water. There is also a hotel in the town.

Over the Long Tom Pass

Turn right out of Viljoen Street into Voortrekker Street, following signs for 'Kruger National Park and Sabie'. Note your kms as you pass beneath the railway bridge on the outskirts of the town. The road climbs towards the summit of the Long Tom Pass, offering good views to both sides over deep, rugged gorges. Eventually you round Mauchsberg and begin the grand descent of the Long Tom Pass (see pages 96-7). 20,5 km after leaving Lydenburg you reach a fine viewsite on your left. There are a number of shady picnic sites along the route.

After 31,4 km you pass on your right the Long Tom Memorial with its full-scale replica of one of the Boer Creusot siege guns. A few hundred metres beyond the memorial there is a viewsite on your left, from which you can look down on the road as it loops its way smoothly towards Sabie. After 43,5 km you pass the R37 to Nelspruit on your right. 8 km beyond this you enter Sabie (see pages 90-1).

At the T-junction in the middle of Sabie, turn right (onto the R537) and note your kms. (On your right is the stone church of St Peter, designed by Sir Herbert Baker in 1912). Some 500 m later, turn right to stay on the R537 for White River. After 8,5 km you will see on your right the forested hill known as Spitskop (pointed hill) — it was here that the first payable alluvial gold deposits in the Transvaal were discovered in 1871. After about 13 km there are superb views over a sea of forested hills. 42,1 km from Sabie you reach a T-junction with the R40. Turn right here for Nelspruit ●

AA Office 56 Brown Street, Nelspruit 1200
Tel. (01311) 24631
Lydenburg Museum cnr Viljoen and Voortrekker Streets, Lydenburg 1120 Tel. (01323) 2121
Sabie Forestry Museum Ford Street, Sabie 1260
Tel. (0131512) 54
Sudwala Caves P O Box 30, Schagen 1207
Tel. (0131232) 3913

The Crocodile River tumbles over the impressive Montrose Falls.

KARL MAUCH AND MAUCHSBERG

Karl Mauch was a German geologist and geographer who arrived in Natal in 1865. During his travels in southern Africa he discovered gold on the Witwatersrand, near Lydenburg, and in what is now Zimbabwe. He recorded cartographically the region stretching south as far as Kimberley, north to the Soutpansberg, west to Marico and east as far as Delagoa Bay. He also drew the first accurate geological map of the Transvaal. He died in his native Germany in 1875. His name was given to Mauchsberg, the grass-topped peak near Lydenburg.

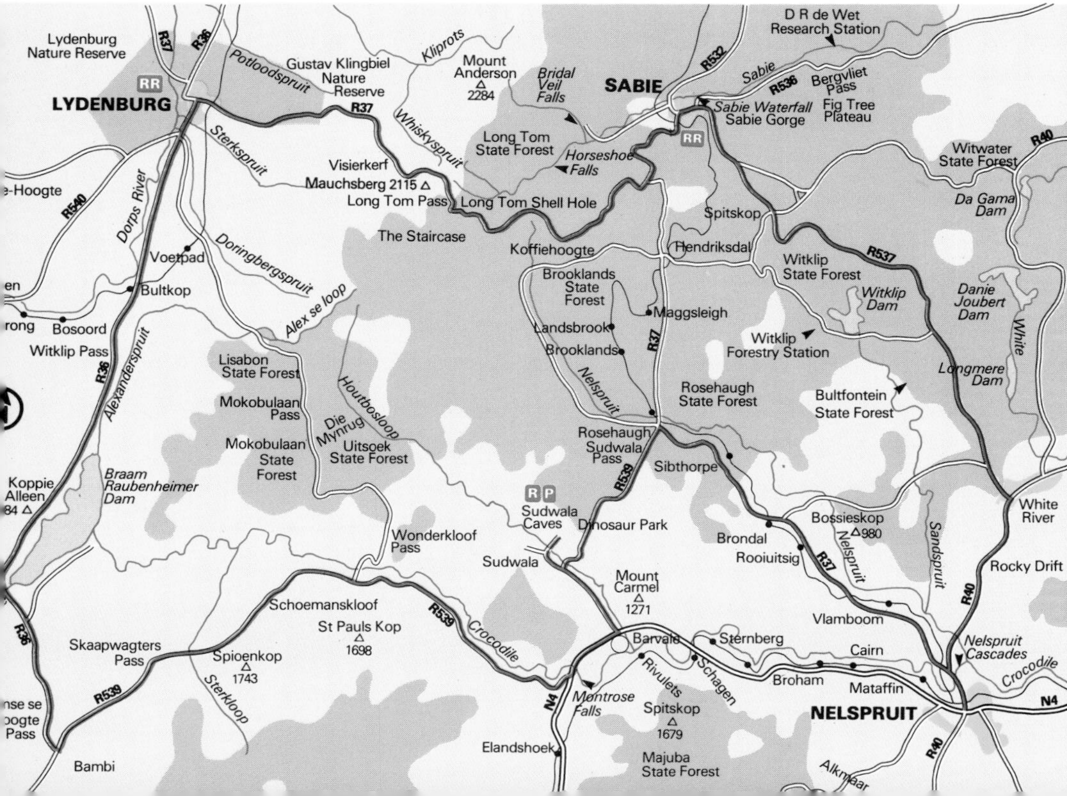

The attractive Cascades at Nelspruit.

NELSPRUIT

Unlike many Lowveld towns, which came into being with a flourish on the discovery of gold, Nelspruit began modestly as a railway station on the Pretoria/Delagoa Bay line — constructed in 1892. The town was named after the stream at which the three Nel brothers used to water their flocks and herds during the winter months.

Today Nelspruit is the centre of a vast citrus-growing region and is the rapidly-growing commercial capital of the Lowveld. Its attractions include an art gallery (housing some 70 works by South African artists), the Town Hall with its unusual sundial, and the Lowveld Botanic Garden, which preserves more than 500 species indigenous to the Crocodile River Valley. The Nelspruit Cascades, also known as the Crocodile Falls, are situated alongside the garden. Picnicking is allowed but no fires may be lit.

Man-made forests cover the Drakensberg foothills along the Long Tom Pass.

The present road over the Long Tom Pass was opened in July 1953.

A fighting retreat over the high road to the sea

THE SPECTACULAR tarred road that winds down over the eastern Transvaal's Drakensberg range from Lydenburg follows a route rich in history.

In the 1840s the Voortrekkers had set up a republic in the Transvaal, with Potchefstroom as its emerging capital. But when the British government extended its authority northwards to include Potchefstroom, many of the Voortrekkers, under the leadership of Andries Potgieter, moved away and established a new 'capital' in a fertile valley just west of the Drakensberg — naming the new settlement Andries-Ohrigstad. Unfortunately this proved a tragic choice. Within a year the damage caused by floods and the death-rate from malaria were so severe that the site had to be abandoned. So the 'capital' moved to Lydenburg.

All the while, the Voortrekkers had been interested in establishing a route to the east coast — a route that would give them an outlet to a port that was not under the control of the British. Now that the effective centre of the young republic was established on the eastern edge of the highveld, with the Indian Ocean just 210km away, the advantages of such a route became indisputable — and the obvious point to aim for was Lourenco Marques (Maputo) on the shores of Delagoa Bay.

Replica of the original Long Tom.

Looking down from the pass.

Several earlier expeditions had reached Lourenco Marques, but the terrain that had to be crossed was extremely difficult. The principal obstacle was the Drakensberg range, running south to north like a giant wall and reaching a height of over 2000 metres.

It was President Thomas Francois Burgers, a much-maligned man of good intent, who took the decisive steps. He recognised that an easy and reliable route to Lourenco Marques could prove extremely valuable to the young republic, and he managed to wring the equivalent of R3000 from his Volksraad (parliament) to finance its construction.

With this modest sum in hand, work was begun. The contractor was Abraham Espag, and most of the road building was done with pick and shovel — with occasional help from charges of gunpowder. In mid-1874 the first wagons to use the new road arrived in Lydenburg from Delagoa Bay, but the trip had proved so arduous that the drivers were grateful to have survived. A report of a crossing in 1877 mentioned 'the most dreaded part of the road, called the Devil's Knuckles... when on top of one of these points the wagon looked as if it were stuck on the point of a sugarloaf, and that any attempt at a descent must result in a headlong roll down many hundred feet.'

Ruins at the 'Devil's Knuckles'.

Highest pass in the Transvaal.

The arrival of the 'Long Toms'

During those early days this hair-raising pass over the Drakensberg was known simply as Die Hawepad (the harbour road). It was only after this route to the sea had played a part in the Anglo-Boer War that the pass took on a new significance — and acquired a new name.

With war clouds gathering, the two Boer republics of Transvaal and Orange Free State decided in 1896 to up-date their armaments, and this included the purchase of four 155mm guns from the firm of Schneider et Cie of Le Creusot in France.

The Boers at first nicknamed the guns 'die Fransmanne' (the Frenchmen), but the British at the siege of Ladysmith called the gun that fired on them 'Long Tom', and this was the name that stuck. Even the Boers eventually adopted the name, despite President Kruger's disapproval.

At the start of the war, the Long Toms outranged any gun the British

Army had in South Africa. Large-calibre (4,7 inch) guns were dismounted from British warships and fitted to improvised carriages, and a single, massive 9,2 inch harbour defence gun was removed from the fortifications at Cape Town and sent north mounted on a railway carriage. It reached Belfast, but was too late to participate in the battle of Bergendal on 27 August 1900. It was at this battle that all four Long Toms were brought together for the only time, although it is not certain that all were used in the action.

After the battle, the Boer forces split up, and General Louis Botha accompanied the larger group northward to Lydenburg. With them they took two of the Long Toms.

The Boers had proclaimed long before that their last stand would be made at Lydenburg, so it was a nervous British advance guard that entered the town — and found to their great relief that the Boers had gone. But as the Union Jack was being hoisted, Boer gunners up on Mauchsberg opened up with both Long Toms, dropping shells among the British transport column.

The British 4,7 inch guns replied, but were unable to silence the long Toms. So, on 8 September, infantry advanced under cover of artillery and machine-gun fire. The engagement ended inconclusively as a thick mist swept over the mountain, and the Boer gunners withdrew to a new position. Casualties for the day were 19 men of the Gordon Highlanders — victims of Long Tom.

The Long Tom Pass was tarred in 1964 making the old pass even easier.

A 'magnificent coup' by the Boers

The British advance resumed the next day, and from the summit of Mauchsberg the Boer wagon train could be seen crossing the Devil's Knuckles. On 10 September, cavalry — Strathcona's Horse and the South African Light Horse — galloped forward, sure that they were about to capture the prized guns. An eyewitness later reported:

'When the cavalry were half a mile behind the rear gun, and we regarded its capture as certain, the *leading* Long Tom deliberately turned and opened fire with case shot (shrapnel) at the pursuers, streaming down the hill in single file, over the head of his brother gun. It was a magnificent coup, and perfectly successful. The cavalry had to retire, leaving a few men wounded, and by the time our heavy guns had arrived both Long Toms had got clean away.'

The site from which this Long Tom fought off imminent capture is marked today by the memorial. The rearmost gun continued down the slope past its comrade and, at the position signposted as the 'last covering position' of the Long Tom, it was unlimbered and prepared for firing to cover the removal of the gun that had been in action.

Naming the road over the pass

The present road over the pass, following the old harbour road in places, was officially opened on 22 July 1953. Suggested names included 'Skyline Road', Trichardtpad', 'Oukoetspad' (old coach road) and 'Long Tom Pass' — the last being the name formally given to the road at its opening. The road was tarred in 1964.

Little remains of the original road over the pass, but stretches of it are signposted in several places. Here and there wheel ruts can be seen in the rock, ground into the stone by locked wheels as wagons were slid down the terrifying slopes, and travellers who take this high road over the mountains from Lydenburg will pass many other reminders of the old days:

Whiskyspruit (whisky stream) commemorates a theory that the water in the local stream, when mixed with even inferior whisky, produces an excellent drink.

Die Geut (the gutter), also known as 'The Staircase', was a particularly steep section of the old road.

Blyfstaanhoogte (stay-standing height) was the name given to another very difficult stretch where one had to proceed so slowly that one seemed to be standing still.

Old Trading Post — there was a trading post here in the mid-19th century; a site now occupied by a modern motel.

The Devil's Knuckles, a series of hillocks mid-way along the downhill stretch, were considered the most alarming part of the journey. It is not known precisely how or when they received their name.

Brooklands State Forest was once a farm named Onverwacht (unexpected), the starting point for afforestation in the area. At the time of the battle on the pass, the farm was occupied by the Shires family, and Florence Shires recorded in her diary on 8 September 1900 that 'we have heard cannon ever since daylight'.

Koffiehoogte (coffee height), some distance south of the present road, was probably where the old transport-riders rested their animals and enjoyed a coffee-break after the first really steep section on the way up the pass.

Olifantsgeraamte was once the name of a farm on which the skeleton (geraamte) of a long-dead elephant was found ●

To a Valley of Gold through the Crocodile River Gorge

East of Nelspruit the Crocodile River winds through a rugged gorge. We follow the river's course, then head south into the De Kaap Valley — last century's Valley of Gold. Our route leads past the old Sheba Mine, Jock of the Bushveld's Tree, and up the Saddleback Pass for a beaufitul view back over the valley. All but 44 km of the route is tarred.

Nelspruit
Krokodilpoort
De Kaap Valley
Saddleback Pass
Barberton
The Cascades
Hilltop Pass
220 — 240 km

The boulder-strewn Crocodile River Gorge.

VALLEY OF DEATH

The valley known as De Kaap — the Cape — after the imposing spur of the Drakensberg that dominates it, was originally known to early transport-riders as the Valley of Death. This came about because of the diseases of malaria and sleeping-sickness that claimed many lives before the causes were isolated and brought under control. Further misery was caused after Bray's discovery of gold in Sheba Reef, when fraudulent companies sold shares in fruitless mines in the valley, and many men were ruined financially.

However, the 'Valley of Death' has provided some compensation for its hazards by giving garden-lovers throughout the world the handsome Barberton daisy (*Gerbera jamesonii*) and the colourful 'Pride of De Kaap' (*Bauhinia galpinii*).

Prospectors' graves in the old Sheba cemetery.

View over the De Kaap Valley from Saddleback Pass. Many men were lured here by the promise of gold.

DRIVE EAST FROM Nelspruit on Louis Trichardt Street, which becomes the N4 towards Komatipoort. Note your kms as you pass Valencia Road on your left, near the outskirts of the town. The N4 is lined for some 8 km with palms, planted in the 1920s, and orange groves extend on both sides of the road. After 19,4 km the road crosses Gould's Salvation Spruit, named after the Resurrection Hotel which a certain Edward Gould ran on its banks in the early gold-prospecting days. Cross the Crocodile River 200 m beyond this to enter Krokodilpoort (Crocodile gorge) — where the road winds through stony hills, with the river flowing below you on your right.

After 24,8 km you pass a rock on the right bearing a plaque commemorating the construction of the road and its re-opening in 1967. Pass a parking area after a further kilometre and stop at the next one, at 27 km. This site is marked by a jacaranda tree and a large rock close to the road. From here there are good views down to the river. After 33,5 km the road crosses the Crocodile River again and you enter more open country. At 35,5 km turn right opposite the Kaapmuiden railway junction on your left, onto the R38 for Barberton. Note your kms.

After 8,3 km you cross Revolver Creek (see pages 100-1) and at 19,2 km you pass Honeybird Creek. The countryside becomes more mountainous, with successive ridges visible ahead. After 26,6 km you reach a gravel road on your left leading to 'Sheba'. Turn here if you wish to visit the old Sheba cemetery or the ghost town of Eureka City. The pioneer cemetery lies some 3,4 km along this gravel road. Park 50 m past the cemetery on the left.

Continue past the old cemetery along the main gravel road and turn right after 1 km at the T-junction. The road reaches the Sheba Mine — the oldest working gold mine in the world — 3 km later. If you wish to explore the remains of Eureka City, ask here for directions and permission to use the private road — see pages 100-1.

Retrace your route to the tarred R38 and turn left, noting your kms as you turn. You pass Noordkaap railway station on your right after 10 km, and 3,6 km later, just after a right-hand bend, there is an old thorn tree on your left. This is known as Jock's Tree, after the famous canine hero of *Jock of the Bushveld*, and a plaque here commemorates the trek made in 1885 by Jock and his master, Sir Percy Fitzpatrick.

Into nostalgic Barberton

After a further 7 km you enter the outskirts of Barberton on Sheba Road. Turn left at the crossroads onto the R40 for 'Havelock'. Follow this good tarred road as it climbs to the top of the Saddleback Pass. From the heights there are panoramic views over the De Kaap Valley.

Retrace your route down the pass to the junction with the R38 and turn left, to enter Barberton on Sheba Road. Sheba Road eventually swings right and becomes Crown Street. Stop at the Publicity Bureau in the Market Square to obtain a map of the town, showing places of interest. A visit to Belhaven — a late Victorian gentleman's residence overlooking Rimer's Creek, where the first gold was found — is worthwhile.

Leave Barberton by driving along Crown Street, passing beneath the Havelock mine's aerial cableway, and turning second right into Kruger Street. Note your kms at the turn. The road changes to good gravel after 6,8 km and leads through forests and plantations of tobacco and citrus. After about 14,7 km, in an area of indigenous bush and trees, there is a sign on the left of the road indicating a narrow bridge. Stop in the parking area on your right, and walk through the gateway to reach the scenic Tegwaans Pools on the Queen's River — a one minute walk — and picnic site (no facilities).

Note your kms as you leave the parking site opposite the pools, and continue on the main gravel road, which climbs alongside the impressive river gorge. After 3,5 km you cross a narrow causeway and the road passes through tangled, bushy hills. After 7 km the road enters the Nelshoogte Forest and you pass a sawmill on your right. 300 m later, just beyond the sawmill, go right at the fork, and cross a further causeway after a further 300 m.

The road passes through attractively wooded country, and after 11,5 km you cross another narrow causeway and enter a dense pine plantation. Stop about 1,3 km beyond the causeway, just before reaching a fork on an uphill section of the road. Below you, on your left, a fine waterfall — known as 'the Cascades' — tumbles into a rocky gorge.

When you drive on from the waterfall, go right at the fork. The road climbs until, after passing a shop on your right, you reach a T-junction. Turn left here, and left again after 100 m, and follow this main gravel road for 5 km to reach a T-junction with the tarred R38. Turn right onto the R38 and note your kms. The road winds downhill, unveiling grand views over the De Kaap Valley. After 25,6 km you reach a T-junction with the R40. Turn left

Anchor of the Dorothea *wrecked at Cape Vidal in 1898 — now in Nelspruit.*

THE CHRISTENING OF BARBERTON

After Graham Barber discovered gold in Rimers Creek in 1884, there was the inevitable rush of fortune-seekers to this corner of the De Kaap Valley. The Mining Commissioner, David Wilson, named the new settlement Barberton, and 'christened' it by breaking a bottle of gin on a rock — no bottle of champagne being available at the time. Within a year the town had shot up with amazing speed. In 1885, with the discovery of the Sheba Reef by Yorkshireman Edwin Bray, the nearby town of Eureka City was founded. Two stock exchanges were established in Barberton, and today the facade of the 'Kaap Gold Fields Stock Exchange Limited' still stands in Pilgrim Street, next to the library and museum. Nearby is the former Globe Bar, a typical corrugated iron building of the gold rush times. Extreme contrasts in styles of this period may be seen in the small blockhouse at the end of Judge Street, and in the stately Belhaven in Lee Street.

Nature's palette — graceful jacarandas enhance historic Barberton.

Orange groves flourish in Nelspruit's rich soil.

Jock of the Bushveld — the famous canine hero.

JOCK AND HIS MASTER

Outside the Town Hall of Barberton stands the statue of a dog. This is Jock, famed in literature as Jock of the Bushveld. As the 'runt' of the litter, and known as 'the rat', the puppy was given to a young transport-rider named Percy Fitzpatrick. Fitzpatrick, who was born in King William's Town, travelled to the Eastern Transvaal as a young man in 1884 and worked at a variety of jobs, including a spell as an editor of Barberton's Gold Field News. He later moved to the Witwatersrand, where he was active in the fields of gold mining and public affairs, and he was knighted in 1902. He then moved to the Sundays River Valley and developed citrus farming in the area. His classic book, telling of his adventures with Jock during the early days of the Transvaal gold discoveries has been reprinted many times since it first appeared in 1907.

here and note your kms. You now pass through an avenue of acacia trees that meet overhead and after 900 m you cross the Suidkaap River. After 8 km you pass a gravel road on your left leading to Kaapsehoop, and after a further 6,5 km you pass a gravel road on your right to Noordkaap. Cross the Noordkaap River and continue on the R40 over the Hilltop Pass — which offers wide views to your left towards Kaapsehoop. From the top of the pass the road descends gently into Nelspruit ●

AA Office 56 Brown Street, Nelspruit 1200
Tel. (01311) 24631
SA Tourism Board Joshua Doore Building, cnr Paul Kruger and Louis Trichardt Streets, Nelspruit 1200
Tel. (01311) 23443
Barberton Publicity Association Market Square, Barberton 1300 Tel. (01314) 3373

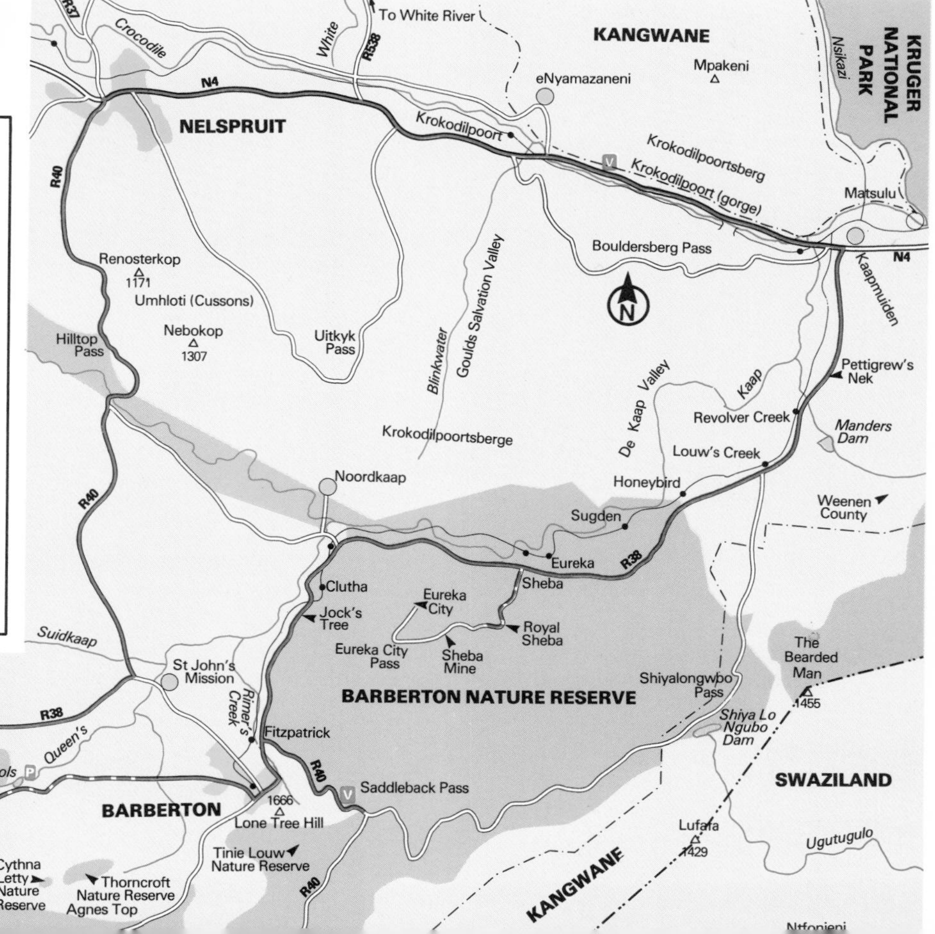

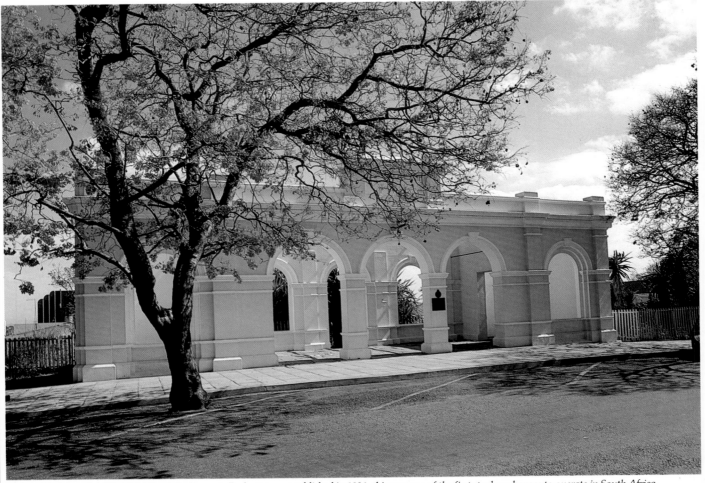

The nostalgic facade of the Gold Stock Exchange in Barberton — established in 1886, this was one of the first stock exchanges to operate in South Africa.

A wealth of gold in the fabled De Kaap Valley

SOME OF THE ROCKS of the mineral-rich De Kaap valley are among the oldest in the world — the granites having been dated at around 3000 million years. Scattered throughout the strata and rock systems are deposits not only of reef and alluvial gold, but also of iron, talc, asbestos and nickel. Early prospectors in the valley searched for gold in its alluvial form — gold that is washed from a reef, carried downstream by rivers and deposited along river beds and banks as nuggets or gold dust.

Their basic tools were a shovel and a prospector's pan, the inside of which had been blackened with smoke in order to make the minute specks of gold more visible. The hopeful prospector scooped gravel into his pan, added water, and carefully removed the larger stones by hand. He then swirled the water around gently, washing the small particles of gravel over the side of the pan. The gold, having a much greater mass, sank to the bottom, to be revealed as a glistening 'tail' when the last of the water was tipped out.

In 1874 Tom McLachlan, who had found the first gold on Spitskop near Sabie, was the first modern prospector to discover gold in the De Kaap Valley — but he decided that the deposits were not payable and moved on. Charles Anderson, known as Charlie the Reefer, was among the next prospectors on the scene, and he found workable gold deposits on the farm Berlyn.

A series of 'richest ever' finds

Other reefs were found and the inevitable 'rush' took place. A tent-town arose almost overnight on the edge of the valley, on a plateau named Duiwelskantoor (Devil's Office) because of the enormous granite boulders and gloomy shadows that dominated it. The town however was christened Kaapsehoop (hope of the Cape), and it quickly became a magnet for hopeful prospectors.

In 1883 the Transvaal republican government sold the farm Berlyn to private owners who then began to charge exorbitant fees for the

A 20-kilometre aerial cableway links Barberton with the Havelock Mine.

A prospector in search of a 'tail' of gold.

right to work on their property. Disgruntled, many diggers left and fanned out across the valley. Auguste Robert, known as French Bob, was the leader of a party that found a good deposit along the Noordkaap River. News of the find leaked out and another rush took place, leading to the establishment of yet another mining-camp, named Jamestown after Ingram James who had originally made the discovery.

George Pigot Moodie, the Transvaal Surveyor General, owned several farms in the De Kaap Valley, and it was on one of these that French Bob found the Pioneer Reef — the richest gold ore yet. News of the find spread, not only in South Africa but throughout the world. Dazzled by the prospect of wealth, Moodie resigned his government post and raised the capital to establish the Moodie Gold Mining and Exploration Company. The company began to demand high fees from the diggers and, as before, many of them moved off to prospect on cheaper government-owned land.

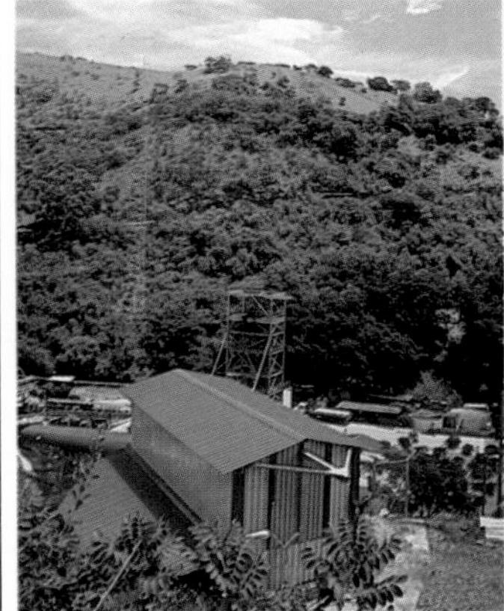

Sheba Mine — oldest in the world.

From all over the world they came, fortune hunters in pursuit of a dream.

Barmaids of Barberton

In 1884 a group of prospectors including Graham Barber from Natal and his two cousins Fred and Harry detected gold in a white quartz reef along the wall of a narrow gully in the valley. Crushed and washed, this proved the richest find to date. As obliged by law, Barber reported his find to the gold commissioner at Kaapsehoop, and the news was out. The commissioner named the site Barberton and christened it by breaking a bottle of gin on the reef — as no champagne was available.

The town mushroomed as prospectors arrived from all over the world to seek their fortunes. These tough characters gambled and brawled, and Barberton became the scene of much violent crime. Even murder was a relatively common occurrence. Revolver Creek recalls the murder of a lone prospector on the banks of a previously unnamed stream.

It is said that by 1885 the town had one bar or canteen for every fifteen residents — most of whom spent their spare time drinking, fighting and carousing. To keep their customers from moving on, the bar-owners brought in barmaids. At least one of these, known as Cockney Liz, achieved notoriety by each evening parading on a billiard table, coquettishly snapping her garters at the noisy band of drinkers, and auctioning herself to the highest bidder.

A side verandah of Belhaven House.

Prospecting in the valley was haphazard, but it is estimated that payable gold was found on more than 4 000 claims. Many reefs were exposed quite by chance. Honeybird Creek was named by a digger who, following a honeybird, was led to a snake. In killing the snake, he exposed a gold reef.

Sheba Reef and Eureka City

The richest find of all was discovered in May 1885 by Edwin Bray, while following his daily route along a narrow trail between tall walls of rock. He knocked his shin on a projecting spur of rock and swung at it angrily with his hammer. In so doing he uncovered the famous Sheba Reef, in what came to be called Bray's Golden Quarry. The Sheba Mine today is the world's oldest working gold mine.

A former prospector named Sherwood opened a hotel on Sheba Hill overlooking the mine. This was the start of Eureka City, which expanded within a year to include two more hotels, several canteens, a music hall and even a race course. As a mining town, Eureka City was even more violent than Barberton. In 1887 a gang known as the Irish Brigade rampaged through the town, wrecking hotels and beating up bystanders. It took the local police and reinforcements from Barberton more than a week to restore order.

In 1899, with the outbreak of the Anglo-Boer War, the mines closed and the people of Eureka City moved to Barberton. Some returned after the war, but the town never flourished again. The buildings were removed and only a few foundations and decayed walls now remain.

The De Kaap gold mines were so productive that President Paul Kruger came on a special tour of inspection and addressed a crowd of diggers at Barberton. But only six months after his visit the boom collapsed. A number of mines were very profitable, but immense sums of money had been invested in schemes that were unlikely to pay dividends. Overnight Barberton became a shadow of its former brawling, noisy self, as many of the prospectors moved on to the Witwatersrand to try their luck all over again. A few years later a disastrous fire razed much of Barberton to the ground, but the town re-established itself and today is one of the major attractions of the eastern Transvaal ●

Pride of De Kaap (Bauhinia galpinii).

Cockney Liz, a reigning beauty.

The magic of the old mining town — jacarandas in bloom and a cool stoep.

A remote highland world of granite peaks and silent forests

Our route leads north from Mbabane, climbing through forests to the village of Piggs Peak and the wild mountain scenery of north-western Swaziland. We then sweep down over the Saddleback Pass to visit Barberton and the scenic Queen's River region, before returning to Mbabane via Badplaas, Lochiel and the Oshoek/Ngwenya border.

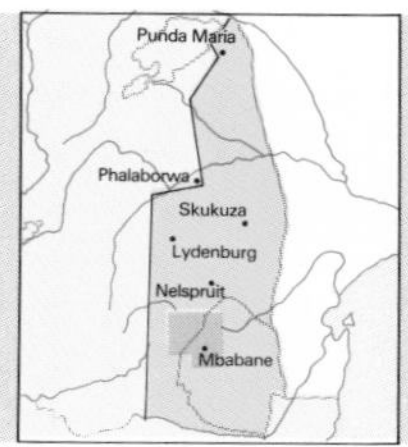

Mbabane
Forbes Reef
Piggs Peak
Havelock Mine
Barberton
Cascades
Badplaas
220 — 240 km

Barberton daisy in bloom.

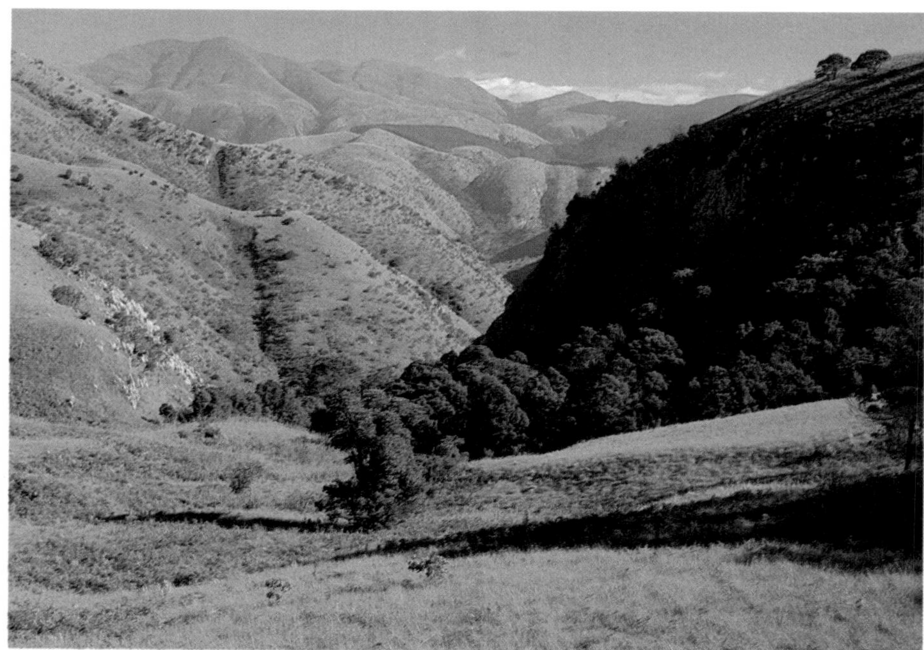

Forests spread across the Drakensberg hills above the historic town of Barberton.

LEAVE MBABANE BY driving north-west along Gilfillan Street towards the Oshoek/Ngwenya border post. Note your kms at the T-junction where Gilfillan Street joins the main road from Manzini, and turn right onto the main road. After 11 kms turn right at the turn-off for Piggs Peak. This tarred road climbs through hills scattered with wattle plantations, outcrops of ancient granite, and small farms and dams.

After 21,3 kms you pass a general-dealer store on your left. Shortly after this a road leads on the left to Forbes Reef, the remains of mine workings started in 1884 by Alex Forbes, and worked sporadically until 1965. (The mine is now inside the Malolotja Nature Reserve — entrance fee.)

Continuing along the tarred road towards Piggs Peak, you pass several roadside stalls selling wood and stone carvings. Note your kms as you pass on your left the road leading to the new Malolotja Game Reserve. 4,9 kms later, park on the shoulder of the road for a panoramic view of the Ngwenya and Silotwane hills. The road now begins a winding descent into a green, forested valley. At 14,4 kms you reach another good viewsite on your left.

When you enter the village of Piggs Peak, set in the midst of pine and eucalyptus forests (see opposite), follow the tree-lined main street until you reach the sign for 'Barberton/Havelock'. Turn left here onto a gravel road, noting your kms as you turn. Relatively good in dry conditions, this road can be treacherous in wet weather, and there are hairpin bends that require caution as logging trucks frequently use this route. 6,5 km after turning onto this road, stop at a cleared area on your left for a fine view over the forested Drakensberg escarpment.

Piggs Peak to Queen's River

After about 15 kms from Piggs Peak, the road surface changes to tar again at the Havelock Asbestos Mine at Bulembu (place of the spider). When you first catch sight of the mining valley, park in the small area on your left for a view of the multi-coloured miners' houses and headgear. 500 m beyond this point, look up to see the beginning of the 20 km cableway that carries asbestos ore over the mountains to Barberton. After a further 2,8 km, around several sharp switchback corners, you reach the Bulembu/Josefsdal border post between Swaziland and the Transvaal (open from 08h00 to 16h00; travel documents needed).

Note your kms as you leave the border post, and follow the main gravel road (now the R40) as it begins its magnificent winding descent over the Saddleback Pass into the De Kaap Valley (see pages 98-9). Numerous wrecks along the route testify to the steepness and danger of this road when wet. 3 kms after driving back onto the tar, stop on your left and cross the road for a splendid view across the De Kaap Valley.

At the foot of the Saddleback Pass you reach a junction with the R38. Turn left here and enter Barberton on Sheba Road, which eventually swings right and becomes Crown Street. Stop at the Publicity Bureau in Market Square for a map of the town, showing places of interest. There are several hotels and restaurants in the town that offer lunch.

To leave Barberton, drive along Crown Street (which passes under the cableway) and turn right into Kruger Street (second street after passing under the cableway), noting your kms as you turn. After 6,8 kms the road surface changes to gravel. You drive through farmlands and forests, and pass the Barberton airport on your right. After about 11 kms you cross two narrow causeways, and after 14,7 kms you reach a narrow-bridge sign on your left and a parking area on your right. Park here and walk through the gateway — a short walk brings you to the lovely Tegwaans Pools on the Queen's River. (Picnic area, no facilities, water unsuitable for swimming or drinking.)

Continue along the main road, noting your kms. The road climbs through attractive scenery with the impressive Queen's River gorge on your right. After 1,2 kms bear left at the fork and after 3,5 kms you cross another causeway. After approximately 7 kms you enter the Nelshoogte State Forest. Pass the sawmill on your right here, and 300 m later go right at the fork. After a further 300 m you cross a narrow causeway. After 12,8 kms you reach a fork in the road. Stop here and look below you to the left to see the impressive 'Cascades' waterfall tumbling into its rocky gorge. Look up to the right and slightly behind you to see the hills known as the 'Duiwelskneukels' (Devil's knuckles).

Queen's River to Mbabane

Bear left at the fork, noting your kms as you turn. After about 1,5 kms you pass the Queen's River Forest Station. Continue for 9,8 km until you reach the T-junction with the tarred R38 and turn left here for Badplaas, noting your kms as you turn. After about 23,3 kms you pass the R541 for Machadodorp on your right, and after 24 kms you enter Badplaas on the R38. Follow the signs to the mineral springs on the right side of the road. There are spacious lawns here, bungalows, a caravan park, and four magnifi-

HAVELOCK ASBESTOS MINE AND CABLEWAY

The 20 km cableway carrying asbestos from the Havelock Mine in Swaziland to Barberton in the Transvaal, and bringing in supplies and equipment on the return journey, is a marvel of engineering. 52 pylons support the cables and carriers — which convey their cargo at a steady 9,5 kms per hour. The mine itself originated in 1923 when the Canadian asbestos company of Turner and Newall began working here at the recommendation of two prospectors. The cableway was finally completed in 1939. The mine provides employment for hundreds of people who are housed nearby in an attractive town surrounded by magnificent mountains.

Swazi wood carver at work.

THE OLDEST MINE IN THE WORLD

The Ngwenya iron-ore mine lies below the Ngwenya (crocodile) Mountain, 4,5 km from the Oshoek border post on the road to Mbabane. Near the modern mine are the remains of ancient workings, in what is known as Lion's Cavern. Radiocarbon dating techniques have shown that red oxides and haematite were being mined here between 41 000 and 36 000 BC — making this the oldest known mine in the world. It is thought that the ores extracted were not smelted, but were probably used as body paints.

Permission to visit the site, and the nearby remains of ancient Sotho huts, may be obtained from the Swaziland Iron Ore Development Company in Mbabane.

This area of Swaziland is still rich in minerals — as modern-day mining operations show.

PIGGS PEAK

The small village of Piggs Peak is named after the prospector William Pigg, who discovered gold near here in 1884. The village has become an important forestry centre, with plantations of eucalyptus and pine covering the slopes of its magnificent mountain setting.

In the village there is a fascinating handcraft market, and a famous weaving school — the finely coloured fabrics created here are exported throughout the world.

cent medicinal baths set in a valley surrounded by the mountain range known to the Swazi as Ndlumudlumu (the place of thunder).

At the T-junction in Badplaas, turn left onto the R541, noting your kms as you turn. You now drive through the Komati River valley and over the scenic Naudeshoogte. After 20 km turn right to 'Lochiel/Oshoek', and a further 17 km brings you to a junction with the R39. Turn left to the small town of Lochiel. A further 26 kms brings you to the Oshoek/Ngwenya border post (open from 07h00 to 22h00; travel documents needed). Note your kms again as you leave the border post.

After about 4,5 kms you pass on your left the Ngwenya iron-ore mine, site of the oldest mine in the world — the Lion Cavern (see above). Permits to visit the site must be obtained from the Swaziland Iron Ore Development Company in Mbabane. Continue on the main road, passing the turn-off that you took to Piggs Peak, and reaching Mbabane 23 km after leaving the Oshoek/Ngwenya border post ●

Barberton Publicity Association Market Square, Barberton 1300 Tel. (01314) 3373
Swaziland Tourist Office Swazi Plaza, Allister Miller Street, Mbabane Tel. (0194) 42531

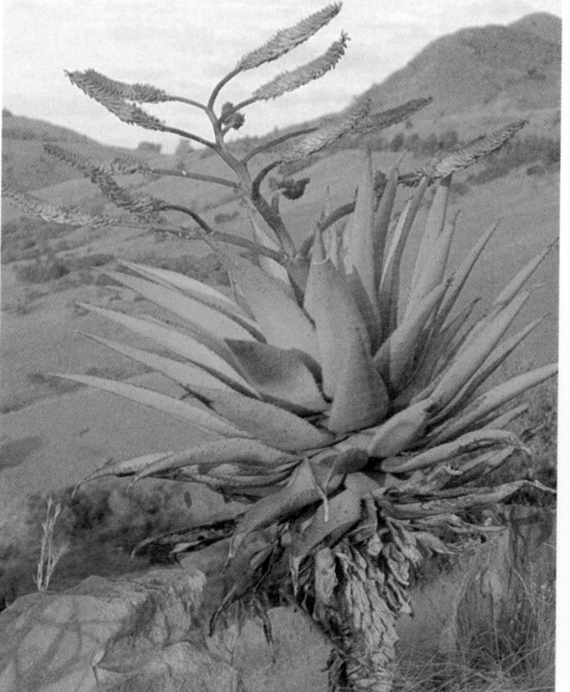

Aloe Marlothii *photographed near Barberton.*

Nelshoogte State Forest.

The *Incwala* — sacred rites herald the New Year

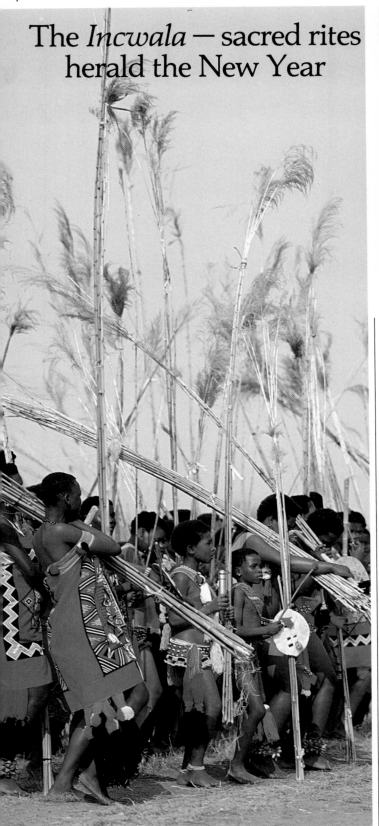

Swazi girls in bright costumes prepare for the 'reed dance' at Lobamba.

THE KINGDOM OF Swaziland, one of the smallest in the world, has a population composed mainly of Nguni and Sotho groups who joined to form the Swazi nation. Their traditions and sacred

Resplendent in their traditional dress, warriors dance during festivities.

ceremonies have changed little in spite of the influence of western civilisation. Royal succession is still decided according to age-old tradition — and the most recent ceremony was attended by royalty from all over the world. This richness of tradition, combined with the country's scenic attractions and its flora and fauna, has made the small kingdom a popular tourist destination.

A colourful history

Ancestors of the Swazi came to this area from the north during the mid-eighteenth century. The main stream of migrators, under chief Dlamini, moved on south to the region known today as Kwazulu, but the Ngwane, named after their leader, settled in the fertile uSutu (dark brown) valley in Swaziland. Ngwane conquered small neighbouring clans, thus enlarging his area of control.

His grandson, Sobhuza I, wished to extend the Ngwane area of authority, but came to blows with a neighbouring Ndwandwe chief over land along the Pongola River, and was forced to flee northwards. He settled near the present-day site of the royal kraal at Lobamba, at the entrance to the Ezulwini valley. Sobhuza developed his kingdom, incorporating the Sotho people who already lived there, and maintained a tenuous peace with the Zulus to the south by sending two of his daughters to their warring chief Chaka.

Sobhuza's son, Mswati or Mswazi, after whom the Swazi are named, succeeded him in 1840. Mswazi moved his capital to Hhohho (a name derived from the barking noise made by baboons) from where he could closely monitor attacks on the Sotho in the north, while at the same time strengthening his army in order to repel the growing number of attacks by the powerful Zulu army.

It was during Mswazi's reign that the first white settlers, missionaries and traders came to Swaziland. Gold was discovered in the hills and the inevitable rush took place, bringing with it the attendant swindlers, bandits and riff-raff. Mswazi's son, Mbandzeni, granted over 500 land concessions to these newcomers for the building of railways, prospecting, and countless other activities, in the belief that these concessions expired on the death of their owners. The situation became intolerable when it was realised that almost the entire country was owned by concession-owners whose descendants had merely to continue to pay their dues to ensure ownership of the property.

Mbandezi's son, Sobhuza II, succeeded to the throne in 1921, and led many delegations to London in attempts to restore the country of his ancestors to national ownership. By the time Swaziland was granted full independence by the British government in 1968, over 60 per cent of the land had been regained. Sobhuza ruled his beloved country with a fair and understanding hand for 62 years, and Swaziland flourished. In 1986 a new king, Mswati III, was appointed.

In spite of western influences, traditional customs have survived. The king, also known as Ngwenyama (the lion), is regarded with adulation and reverence. His fertility and health are taken as a direct reflection of the fertility and prosperity of his country. One of the most sacred of

The warm welcoming smile of a Swazi maiden.

In Incwala *attire, a warrior stands outside a typical beehive-shaped hut.*

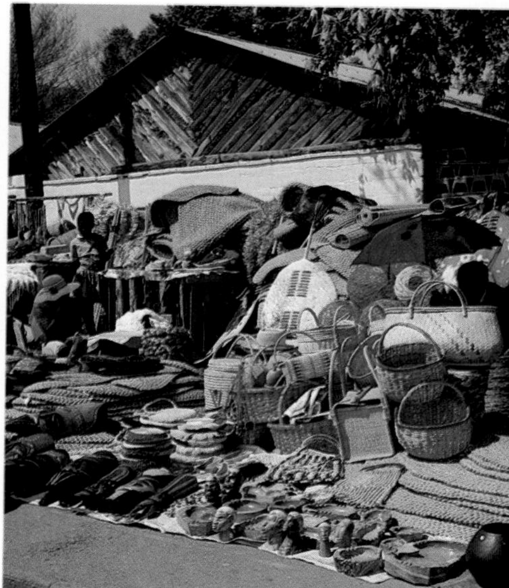
Local handcrafts at the open-air market, Mbabane.

his kingly rituals is the *Incwala*, a lengthy ceremony held during the first new moon every year.

The complex *Incwala*

Strictly speaking, the *Incwala* is divided into two parts — the Little Incwala and the Big Incwala. During the Little Incwala (held during the preceding new moon) special envoys are sent to certain rivers and to the sea to collect water and sacred herbs, which are then returned to the royal kraal at Lobamba. On the following morning the king samples the first fruits of the season in a ritual ceremony which is accompanied by singing and dancing.

The Big Incwala ceremony lasts for six days and reflects the maturity of the king — the more mature he is, the merrier the festivities. On the first day Swazi youths gather at the king's residence to sing songs of praise and then march 40km to Egundwini to collect branches of the *lusekwane* tree. These are returned to the royal kraal on the second day. On the third day a shelter is constructed from these branches, and the king joins his warriors, resplendent in their skins and feathers, to sing sacred songs. A black ox is driven before the king and slaughtered by the youths, who then dismember the corpse. On the fourth day, the king joins the warriors in a great festive dance, with the women of the royal family taking part. No work is done on the fifth day, which is reserved for meditation and peace. The *Incwala* then ends on the sixth day with a ritual cleansing — a bonfire is lit and all the king's clothes, bedding and the remains of the slaughtered bull are burnt — and the new year is welcomed. (Visitors may watch the proceedings, but must obey the instructions of officials. No photographs may be taken.)

At the end of August, a colourful ceremony takes place at the royal kraal of the Queen Mother at Lobamba. During this ritual, known as the 'reed dance' (uMhlango), Swazi maidens bring reeds from all over the kingdom and construct a screen around the Queen Mother's residence. The highlight of this colourful ceremony is the beautiful dance performed by the maidens in bright costumes of beads, anklets, bracelets and necklaces. On the final day of the celebrations the girls dance before the Queen Mother, and feast and sing well into the night.

The Swazi people are very particular about their appearance, and their clothes are colourfully ornamented with feathers, skins, cloths, and significant beadwork — similar though not identical to that of the Zulus (see pages 180-1). Combinations of beads in different colours are used to placate ancestral spirits, to bring good luck, or to encourage a loved one. At four months old, babies receive their first strings of white beads — symbolising goodness and purity — which they wear around their wrists, ankles and waists until they are weaned.

Intricately-woven huts

The traditional domed huts in which the Swazi live have been associated with people of Nguni origin throughout the country. These huts, largely replaced by wattle-and-daub or stone-walled huts in other areas, are now built almost exclusively by the Swazi and the Zulu in northern Natal. Saplings are woven together into a semi-circular framework using plaited grass ropes, eventually forming a beehive-shaped hut that is strong and weather-resistant.

Swaziland is a predominantly agricultural country, and most of the population live on small farms. The principal crops are maize, sugar, cotton, tobacco, vegetables and subtropical fruit. Cattle provide beef and milk, and pigs and poultry are also kept. Forests cover much of the mountainous western side of the country — where visitors can enjoy many peaceful walks and magnificent scenery ●

Left *In their finery for the 'reed dance'.*
Right *The Little Usutu River meanders through the lovely Ezulwini Valley.*

Dawn breaks over the Kruger as a party of tourists prepare for a day's trailing through the park.

Kruger Park: Journey through the primeval heart of wild Africa

World-famous for its diverse and abundant wildlife, the Kruger National Park is more than just a place to see lions, elephants and an array of other animals. Its magnificent scenery and unique wildness straddling the Tropic of Capricorn make it one of the few remaining areas of South Africa where the old, primeval heart of Africa still throbs.

COVERING MORE THAN 19 000 km² in the north-eastern corner of the Transvaal, the Kruger National Park is one of the largest national parks in the world; with the greatest diversity of wildlife species: 149 mammals and 480 birds. It is rightly one of the major tourist attractions in South Africa with more than 300 000 visitors a year. Although mainly flat with vast grass-filled plains, it also has undulating and mountainous regions, and the southern half of the park especially is richly covered in a daunting array of plant-forms, including an abundance of gigantic trees. The park is roughly 350 km from north to south and about 60 km wide.

Inevitably, the southern half of the park, being closer to the Witwatersrand and Pretoria, is more popular with visitors. Fortunately it also has a greater diversity and abundance of wildlife, a more extensive network of tarred and gravel roads, and most tourist camps.

However the north also has many attractions: a greater abundance of elephant and buffalo, roan antelope, tsessebe, eland and nyala and magnificent baobab trees. Perhaps the greatest attraction of the north is the tremendous atmosphere it generates, a sense of primitive wilderness and isolation; of plains reaching into the distant, hazy horizon, with no sign of human presence.

In the far north, craggy sandstone hills with multi-coloured, lichen-covered boulders rear up amid baobabs and other tropical vegetation.

The first steps

It was President Paul Kruger who, in 1884, first suggested that a wildlife conservation area be established in this region. But only in 1898 was the Sabie Game Reserve finally officially proclaimed, encompassing the area between the Sabie and Crocodile Rivers. In 1903 the addition of the Shingwedzi Game Reserve greatly increased the conservation area.

The first warden of the new reserve was Major — later Colonel — James Stevenson-Hamilton, who assumed duty in 1902 and was to play a decisive role in the consolidation of land and the ultimate proclamation of the giant Kruger National Park. There were ceaseless battles with landowning associations who wanted the land for agriculture; and innumerable discussions with politicians to convince them of the need for a national park. In the end persistence paid off, and the Kruger National Park was proclaimed on May 31, 1926.

When to visit

Winter, between May and October, is the best time to visit the park. The days are usually cloudless and warm, with an average maximum temperature of 23°C. It cools down rapidly in the late afternoon and the nights are cold, generally about 8°C during the early hours before sunrise.

In summer, daytime temperatures frequently go above 40°C, with an average of about 30°C. The nights are warm, with minimum temperatures hovering around 18°C.

The hottest months are December and January, and the coolest June and July.

Mid-winter is the better time to view game, particularly around June, July and August when all the smaller pools and streams have dried up and animals concentrate around the larger dams and rivers. Most of these are close to tourist roads and, as many trees have dropped their leaves and the vegetation cover as a whole is reduced, it is much easier to locate and observe animals.

A winter visit does have certain disadvantages: you miss the tremendous scenery of summer, especially in a season with good rain. Luxuriant groves of trees in full bloom complement the rich green fields of revitalised grasses. Many of the larger mammals bear their young during this time when environmental conditions are most favourable.

Where to stay

Scattered throughout the Kruger are 17 camps, varying in size from small private camps, which accommodate up to eight people and have to be reserved in their entirety, to giant camps such as Skukuza, which has nearly 200 huts, plus guest cottages and dormitories for school tours. Most camps also have well-tended camping areas for caravans and tents, together with fuel-stations, shops, restaurants and other facilities.

Several types of huts or housing units are available in the park, the most popular being a thatched hut with one room with two or three beds, air-conditioner or fan, refrigerator, shower, toilet, handbasin and an adjoining verandah, table and chairs. Some camps also have family cottages with two rooms with two or three beds, air-conditioner, shower or bath, toilet and handbasin, and a small kitchen with gas stove, refrigerator, washing-up bay, cooking and eating utensils.

Reservations should be made well in advance by writing to The Chief Director, Reservations, National Parks Board, P.O. Box 787, Pretoria, 0001, stating the number of adults and children in the proposed group, and your choice of camps, the intended duration of stay in each camp, and the type of accommodation you require. Do not send money with the initial application; this will be requested once accommodation has been reserved.

The reservations office will send you a voucher which must be presented when entering the park and at camps where you have reserved accommodation. At the entrance gate you will have to pay a small fee for the car and all occupants above the age of six.

Reservations need not be adhered to strictly. The reception office in each camp will gladly enquire from other camps if suitable accommodation is available, and reservations may then be transferred to whichever camp you prefer ●

Good gravel and tarred tourist roads cover most areas of the park.

APPROXIMATE NUMBERS OF THE LARGER ANIMALS IN THE KRUGER PARK

Lion	1 500
Leopard	+ 900
Cheetah	± 250
Wilddog	250-300
Elephant	7 000
Buffalo	26 000
White rhino	936
Impala	139 434
Waterbuck	5 068
Zebra	29 964
Blue wildebeest	12 227
Kudu	11 041
Giraffe	5 354
Sable antelope	2 275

There are 900 leopard in the park.

TRAVELLING HOURS

Visitors to the park are allowed out of the camps only during daylight hours. All the camps are fenced and the gates locked at the times listed.

	Opening	Closing
January	05h00	18h30
February	05h00	18h30
March	05h30	18h00
April	06h00	17h30
May	06h30	17h30
June	06h30	17h30
July	06h30	17h30
August	06h30	17h30
September	06h00	18h00
October	05h30	18h00
November	04h30	18h30
December	04h30	18h30

The main entrance gates have the same opening and closing times as rest-camps, except in November, December and January when they open at 05h30. Main entrance gates close between 13h00 and 13h30.

GENERAL REGULATIONS

1 No pets are allowed: they may transmit diseases to the animals.
2 Fire-arms have to be declared on arrival at the park. The firearm will be sealed and the seal removed when you leave.
3 Heed speed limits indicated (generally 50 km/h). Wild animals are unpredictable and may jump in your path when speeding. Speed traps operate in the park.
4 Do not leave your car or let your head, shoulders or arms protrude from the window: visitors have been bitten by animals which appear tame.
5 Do not feed animals, especially baboons and monkeys. This misguided kindness makes them aggressive towards visitors who do not feed them, and they may be shot.
6 Don't litter: tins and other refuse are not only unsightly but they could kill animals which eat refuse.
7 Keep to the designated tourist roads. If you break down along a fire-break or other no-entry road it may be days before park officials locate you.
8 Consider other visitors by not playing a musical instrument, radio or tape deck at a disturbing volume.
9 Never throw a burning match or cigarette-end out of the window.

Tranquil waters of the Sabie River.

SEEING THE PARK IN FIVE DAYS OR LESS

The next 10 pages contain a five-day tour of the Kruger Park, each double-page spread featuring a day's drive of about 200 km. The routes have been chosen for scenery and game-spotting.

The tour begins in the south at Skukuza and ends in the far north at Punda Maria. Visitors with less time should begin their route in the south, exiting at Orpen Gate (two days), Phalaborwa Gate (three days) or Punda Maria Gate (four days without visiting Pafuri). Each day's drive is covered in detail on the pages indicated. The area between the Sabie and Olifants Rivers is the richest in game, so make sure this features prominently in your allocated time. If you plan to follow the entire route you will need to book these camps well in advance (see Where to stay, opposite): 1 Skukuza; 2 Lower Sabie; 3 Satara; 4 Letaba; 5 Punda Maria; 6 Punda Maria.

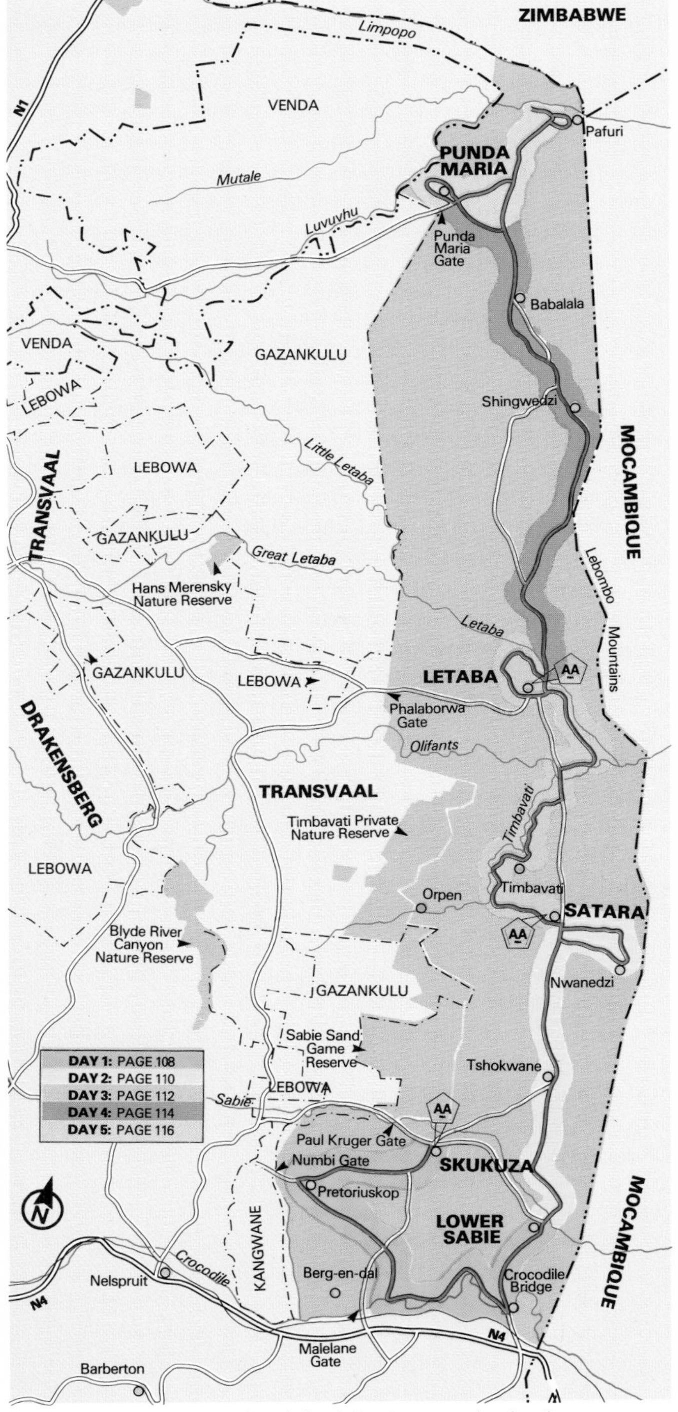

Parts of this route are unsurfaced. See following pages for details.

Follow Jock of the Bushveld through the lush south

Our first day takes us through the densely vegetated southern area of the park, dotted with bouldered hills — home of the rare klipspringer antelope and favourite stamping ground of the rhinoceros. Part of the route parallels the path followed by the old transport riders to Delagoa Bay, and used by the dog of legend, Jock of the Bushveld.

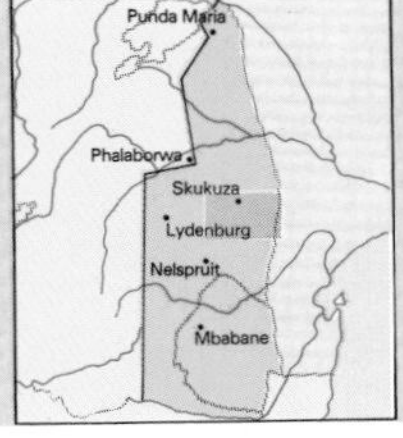

Skukuza
Pretoriuskop
Afsaal
Crocodile
Bridge
Lower Sabie
200—210 km

LEAVE SKUKUZA EARLY in the morning before breakfast, as soon as possible after the camp gates open, and follow the H1-1 tarred road to Pretoriuskop, ignoring several other roads which branch off within the first 2 km. The road gently winds and dips through fairly dense vegetation much favoured by lions in the early morning. Look out also for nomadic packs of wild dogs.

6 km after leaving the camp, you pass a gravel road on the left to Malelane and Crocodile Bridge. Continue on the tar, turning left 5 km later on a short gravel road to Granokop, a granite extrusion which provides a magnificent view of the surrounding countryside in all directions. Spend no more than 5 minutes on this hill, then return towards Pretoriuskop.

Roughly 14 km from Skukuza the road passes between rocky outcrops where, with a little luck, a rare klipspringer may be seen silhouetted atop the granite boulders. At this point a tarred road branches off to Berg-en-Dal, but you should continue straight on.

Ignore the next turn-off, but at 21 km from Skukuza take a gravel road on the left to the Transport Dam, which is about 2 km from the main road. You should spot some animals gathering for their first drink of the day; but don't stay too long as a heavy day's driving and several dams and watering points still lie ahead.

Return to the H1-1 tarred road towards Pretoriuskop for a further 21 km and turn left on a short (1 km) gravel road to Shitlhave Dam. This is another good spot from which to look out for early morning game. Return to the H1-1 for a further 7 km until you reach a T-junction. Turn left along the tarred road until Pretoriuskop is reached 2 km further. Time now for breakfast and, very important, to refuel your car if it is less than half full.

Pretoriuskop to Afsaal

Try to leave Pretoriuskop by 09h30 at the latest. Less than 0,5 km beyond the gates turn right onto a gravel road (H2-2) known as the Jock of the Bushveld Road. This scenic drive parallels the route followed by the old transport riders to Delagoa Bay, the same route along which Sir Percy Fitzpatrick and his famous dog Jock shared so many experiences. Keep a lookout for rhinoceros on this road.

13 km out of Pretoriuskop you pass a large mass of boulders on the right known as Ship Mountain, so named because it resembles the inverted hull of a ship.

35 km from Pretoriuskop you reach a T-junction with the H3 tarred road and the Afsaal Picnic Site (cooldrinks and other light refreshments available). The road between Pretoriuskop and Afsaal should take no more than 2 hours.

Afsaal to Crocodile Bridge

From Afsaal, head south on the tarred road over a bridge before turning left after a few hundred metres onto the gravel H2-2 again. Continue for 8 km until you reach the T-junction with the S114. Turn right and continue south for 9 km, crossing the Mlambane River, until you reach the S25 gravel road on the left. Follow this for 38 km through undulating country dotted with occasional low hills and fairly dense vegetation. Keep your eyes peeled for game — this stretch of road is usually well stocked with animals.

42 km from Afsaal there is a well-signposted gravel road to the right heading for 3 km to Hippo Pool in a bend in the Crocodile River. Hippo are usually seen sunning themselves on a sandbank — and an occasional elephant

Lights twinkle in the warm African night as darkness falls at Skukuza.

SKUKUZA

Meaning 'he who turned everything upside down' or 'he who sweeps clean', Skukuza was the name his African staff gave Colonel James Stevenson-Hamilton, the first warden of the Sabie Game Reserve. By far the largest camp, Skukuza is also the operational and administrative headquarters of the park.

Situated on the banks of the Sabie River, the camp has lost much of the intimacy that allows visitors to identify with the surrounding wilderness. Nevertheless, Skukuza is popular because of its accessibility.

It is the only camp with a bank (Volkskas, although other cheques may be cashed here), plus a large modern post-office and public telephones. The Stevenson-Hamilton Memorial Library is worth a visit, with a wide range of displays on wildlife. The Selati Train Restaurant, a converted dining and lounge carriage, serves à la carte meals.

The AA office is opposite the bank, and the workshop/garage is alongside the petrol station.

The main entrance gate at Skukuza.

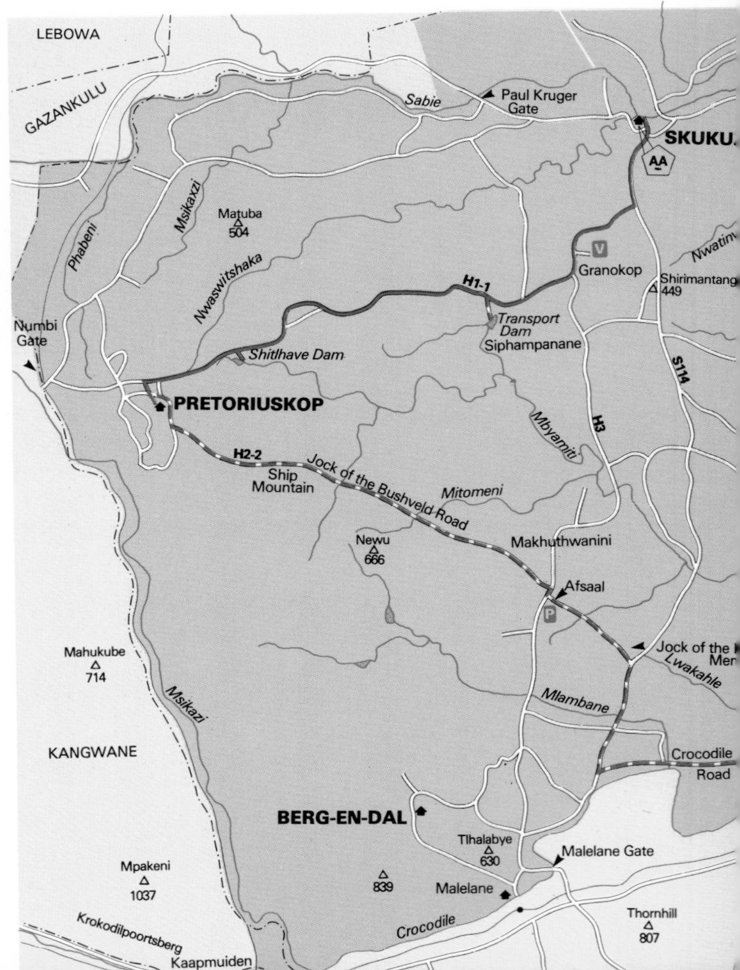

sometimes wanders down for a drink. San paintings adorn the cliff overlooking the pool.

Return to the S25 for the short drive into Crocodile Bridge (cool drinks on sale).

Crocodile Bridge to Lower Sabie

From Crocodile Bridge head north on the H4-2 in the direction of Lower Sabie, which is reached after 35 km. This road is very good for spotting buffalo and a wide range of different antelope species ●

AA Emergency Service Centre Skukuza Rest Camp.

Always watch for elephants in or near dams and rivers.

WILD DOG

Sometimes called hunting dogs, wild dogs are generally found in packs of between 5 and 20. They have long slender legs and a lean body — advantages to any predator which depends on its running ability to catch its prey. Their large, rounded ears are very distinctive, as is their blotched or mottled colour, generally a mixture of black, orange-brown and white.

Nomadic for much of the year, wild dogs roam over enormous areas, constantly searching for prey to satisfy their almost continuous hunger. Once the pack has chosen its next meal — usually an impala, zebra, kudu or other antelope — it hunts down the victim with dogged persistence and stamina. The dogs may rip and snap chunks of flesh from the fleeing animal as it gradually tires and slows. Once down, the unfortunate prey is reduced to a mass of skin and bones within minutes by the milling throng of ravenous dogs — a fearsome and memorable sight for those lucky enough to see it.

When pups are born the pack will cease its nomadic pattern and remain in the same general vicinity. The pups are left in burrows, and adults return after a hunt to regurgitate meat for the youngsters to eat.

The 300 to 350 wild dogs in the park tend to favour flat country, but there is no particular area of great abundance.

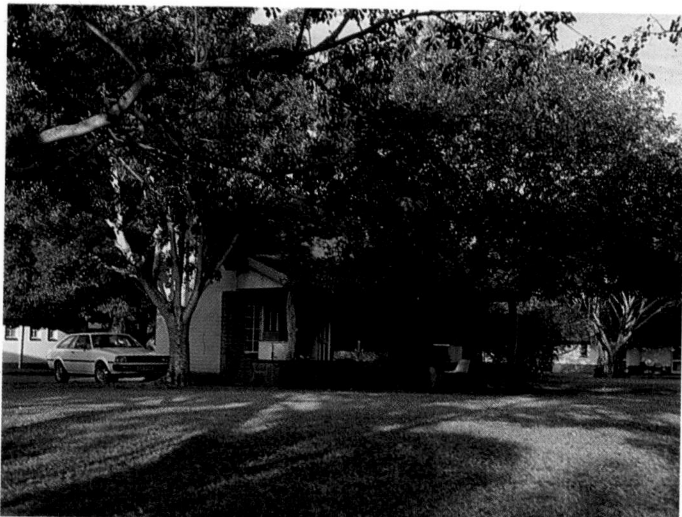

Early morning sunlight casts long shadows at Lower Sabie Rest Camp.

LOWER SABIE

A lovely setting, ideal size and great natural beauty makes this camp highly popular with visitors at any time of year. The camp lies on a slight elevation with excellent views of the Sabie River. In the evening animals can be seen coming to drink, while buffalo and elephant often feed on the reed-fringed banks of the river. Green, well-tended lawns grace the areas between huts and tall, shady broad-leaved trees help make the camp an oasis of relaxation and enjoyment.

Lower Sabie is located in a prime game-viewing area. The greater part of the surrounding country is made up of flat plains covered with acacia, marula, leadwood, bush-willow and several other species of trees, with thick grass-cover, particularly during summer rains, between.

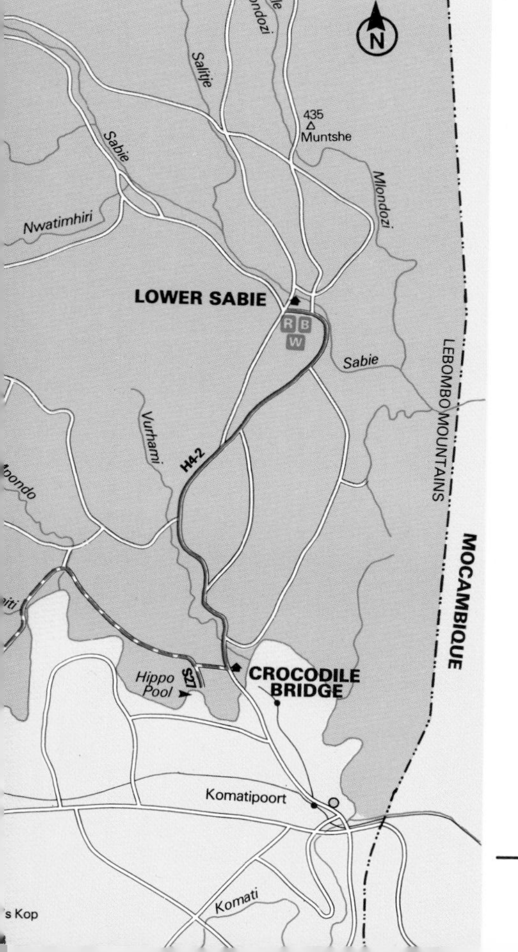

JOCK OF THE BUSHVELD

Written by Sir Percy Fitzpatrick and published in 1907, this story of a man and his dog in the early Transvaal gold-rush days is a classic.

Disillusioned by his job in a Cape Town bank, the young Fitzpatrick opted for a job as transport rider, carting by ox-wagon supplies for the mining camps from Delagoa Bay to the gold-fields in the Highveld.

A good dog was an invaluable ally in this harsh environment, and Fitzpatrick was given a bull-terrier pup, the smallest, weakest and ugliest of the litter. But as the dog grew it showed great intelligence, toughness and braveness. Jock, as Fitzpatrick named him, became an inseparable companion.

RHINOCEROS

Once plentiful in the area now covered by the Kruger Park, both black and white rhino were hunted to extinction and had to be reintroduced from Natal.

There is no real colour difference between the two species. White rhino are generally larger, with a flattened or square mouth, feeding on grass. Black rhino have a pointed mouth which they use to strip leaves and break twigs. They have a mass of about 1 500 kg. Young black rhino run behind the cow, whereas juvenile white rhino run ahead.

The distinctive shape of Ship Mountain in southern Kruger.

The 'horn' of the rhino is formed from normal hair that has fused.

A good route for game spotting in the great plains

Our second day takes us through the richest area in the park for animal life. Lions are abundant, together with numerous herds of zebra, wildebeest and giraffe. The road snakes lazily northwards through the enormous plains of the central district stretching from horizon to horizon and providing a home for the occasional cheetah.

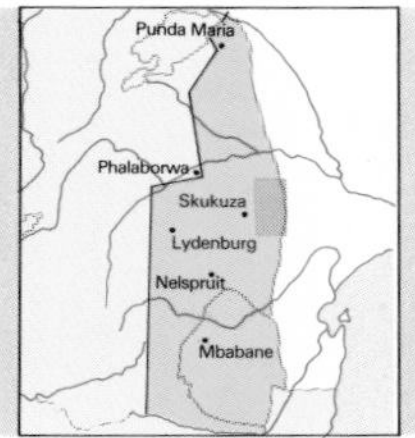

Lower Sabie
Tshokwane
Satara
Nwanedzi
Satara
150 — 170 km

After an early breakfast at Lower Sabie (trying to leave by 07h30), cross the Sabie River bridge by turning right onto the gravel road immediately outside the camp gates (a new bridge is under construction). Less than 1 km after crossing the bridge turn right onto another gravel road (S29). Keep straight on over the crossroads with the tarred road and stay on the gravel, passing the S122 until, about 14 km from Lower Sabie, a turn-off to the right (S68) takes you to a hill-top observation area with a magnificent view over the Mlondozi dam and surrounding area.

Hippo and crocodile share the dam with a large number of birds, such as ducks, herons, kingfishers and storks; while kudu, waterbuck, impala and occasionally elephant approach the bank for water or to feed on the nearby vegetation. There are toilets at this lookout point and cooldrinks are on sale. Spend no more than a half-hour here.

Return to the S29 and turn right. After 3 km turn right at the crossroads with the H10 tarred road. Stay on this road, travelling north and passing gravel roads on the left, right and left, until you reach the S32 gravel road on the right signposted to Orpen dam 3 km away. From your hill-top position at the dam crocodiles are frequently seen lazing on the banks, and elephant occasionally arrive to quench their thirst. Toilets are next to the parking area.

Retrace your steps to the H10 and turn right. After 1 km you reach a T-junction with the main H1-2 tarred road; turn right for the short drive into Tshokwane, where snacks, tea and other refreshments can be obtained and enjoyed on the quaint verandah built around the base of a huge sausage tree. Braai facilities are also available.

Tshokwane to Satara

From Tshokwane drive northwards again on the tarred road (H1-3) which for several kilometres hugs the normally dry Nwaswitsontso stream before shearing away to continue through the grassy plains so characteristic of the central area of the park. Along the way Mazithi and Kumana dams are passed, and this whole area between Tshokwane and Satara is filled with numerous herds of zebra, wildebeest, impala, kudu, waterbuck and giraffe. Lion are also frequently seen.

Watch out, too, for ground hornbills strutting in small groups on tourist's roads in their never-ending search for food: insects, reptiles, small mammals and even tortoises. These are the largest of the six species of hornbills in the park, and can be easily identified from their characteristic large curved and pointed bills, stark black body and, in the males, brilliant red bare skin on the head.

The distance from Tshokwane to Satara along the tarred H1-3 is 50 km, and you should budget your time so that Satara is reached for an early lunch. Before eating, check in at the reception office to find out where your hut is. The office is closed between 13h00 and 14h00. For lunch you can choose between a self-help restaurant or a cafeteria offering light meals. The reception office, restaurant and cafeteria all conveniently adjoin each other.

Satara to Nwanedzi

After lunch, and possibly a short rest or stroll around camp, you can look forward to a particularly pleasant drive. Take the tarred road (H1-3) out of camp again towards Tshokwane, but take the second left after about 3 km on the tarred road (H6) to Nwanedzi.

Do not be disappointed if you don't see much game on the way to Nwanedzi — it is the return drive that will make the afternoon's trip worthwhile. Even so, the short 20 km trip to Nwanedzi should result in sightings of several herds of zebra, wildebeest, impala and perhaps some ostriches. Nwanedzi camp is out of bounds except to visitors actually staying there, so go straight to the Nwanedzi lookout point. Here you will find a setting so beautiful it will probably be remembered as one of the most pleasant sights of your visit. The thatch-roofed lookout point, with ample seating, stands on the very edge of a sheer cliff which drops to the calm, clear waters of the Sweni River. To the west flat plains stretch all the way to the horizon, whilst eastwards loom the rock-littered craggy heights of the Lebombo mountains.

Animals can be seen coming in for an afternoon drink and waterbirds are plentiful.

Nwanedzi to Satara

From the Nwanedzi lookout point take the gravel road (S41) northwards for 12 km, then turn left into the gravel S100 which travels along the Nwanedzi River back towards Satara. This very pleasant drive provides great scenic views and many animals. Look out for storks, herons and ducks on the tranquil waters of the river; while waterbuck, zebra, wildebeest, impala and kudu are common. After 16 km the tarred road (H1-3) is joined again immediately south of Satara. Turn right onto the tarred road to get back to camp to relax for the evening ●

AA Patrol Station Satara Rest Camp.

Giraffe are common in the central park.

GIRAFFE

The tallest animals in the world are also the most unusual of all Africa's mammals. Their extraordinary long legs and necks allow them to feed on leaves and seed-pods of trees at a level where they have no competitors amongst the other major herbivores.

Several giraffe are killed each year by lions. The great cats jump onto the back of a fleeing giraffe, grab a firm hold and bite into the neck. However a kick from a distraught giraffe can kill or severely injure a careless predator.

Fighting occasionally takes place between males, the contestants arranging themselves side by side and exchanging vicious sweeping blows with their necks and heads.

Giraffe are generally seen in small groups of between 3 and 10 animals, and are common in the acacia savannahs of the central and southern park.

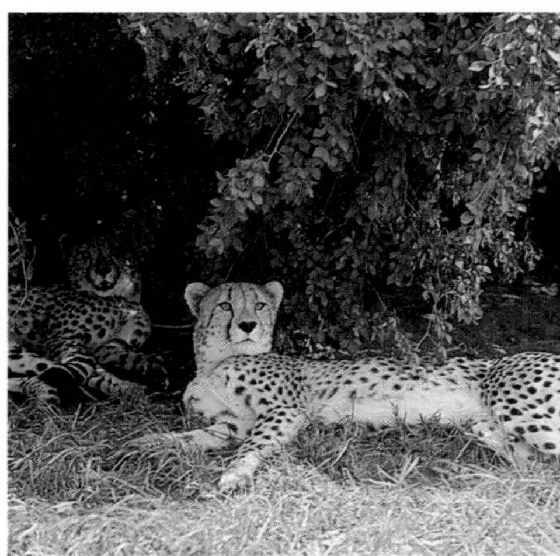

The cheetah: a daytime hunter.

Kudu are largely nocturnal, feeding between evening and early morning.

WOLHUTER'S LION

A tall, quiet man of few words, Harry Wolhuter was an exceptionally able hunter, respected by all who knew him. Late one evening in 1903, he was on horseback patrol with three assistants about 50 km north of Lower Sabie when he was attacked by two lions. One lion jumped on the horse, and Wolhuter fell onto the other lion, which sank its teeth into his right shoulder.

Feigning death and hanging limply between the lion's legs as he was being dragged off to be eaten, Wolhuter carefully unsheathed his knife and, in quick succession, plunged it twice into the lion's chest and once in the throat. The lion let go and ran off, to die a short distance away.

In extreme agony Wolhuter dragged himself up a tree and used his belt to secure himself to a branch in case he lost consciousness. There the second lion found him, walking back and forth below the tree, with Wolhuter's dog barking and worrying nearby.

Several hours later Wolhuter was found by his assistants, and without dressings and water for the initial part of the trip, they took him to Barberton for medical attention, arriving four days later.

SATARA

Second in size only to Skukuza, this camp lies near the centre of the vast plains between the Sabie and Olifants rivers. The camp is surrounded by flat, grass-filled country dominated by tall knobthorn, acacia and marula trees. Despite its size, Satara retains a tranquil and intimate atmosphere with little of the impersonal detachment so often associated with a large camp.

Bird-life is profuse and large numbers of starlings, buffalo weavers and sparrows fly about between the huts in search of crumbs. Hornbills peer from their tree-top perches, occasionally venting their mocking staccato calls.

A small waterhole has been created just off the restaurant side of camp, where you can watch animals coming in to drink.

A large self-service restaurant is situated in the same building, which also houses a self-help snack bar, the reception office, shop and rest-rooms. An AA Patrol Station is located at the entrance gate.

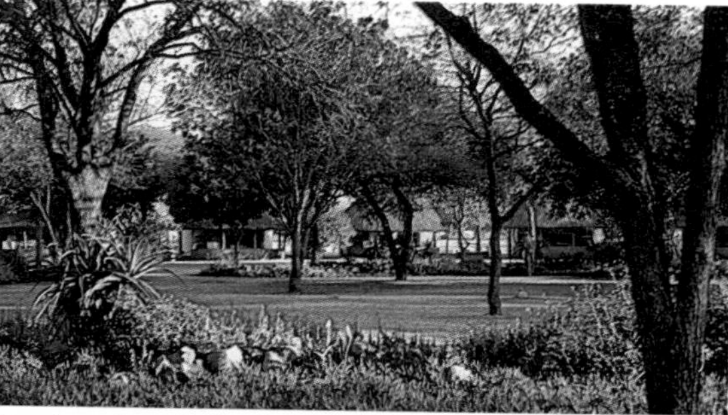
Marula and acacia dot the grounds of Satara.

A sausage tree dominates the tea room at Tshokwane.

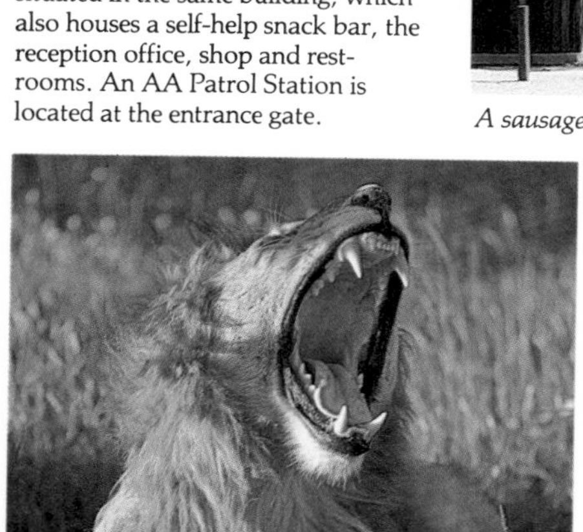
Essentially lazy, lions leave the females to hunt.

LION

With their magnificent, dignified stature, undeniable power, and a less definable aura of wild prowess, these animals still remain the greatest attraction in the park. Although they occasionally make daylight kills, lions are mainly nocturnal hunters.

Lions are normally found in prides of two to six individuals, each pride having a fairly defined area in which it will hunt and live. When ready for mating, a male and female withdraw from the pride for several days, neither hunting nor searching for food. The males especially become irritable and aggressive during this 'honeymoon' stage and need little provocation to attack any intruders. Females give birth to between two and five cubs.

About 1 500 lions are scattered throughout the park, mostly in the central district and around Lower Sabie, the area most abounding in zebra and wildebeest, their favoured prey.

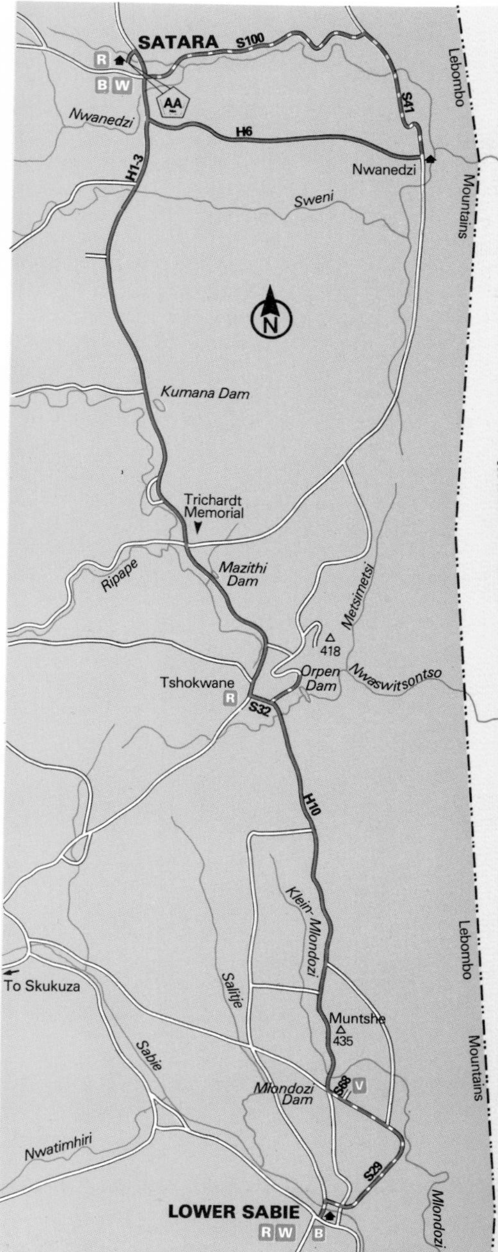

Elephant, giraffe and lion on the winding road north to Letaba

The third day's drive meanders past a series of water-courses, the first half passing through scenic acacia-savannah with an abundance of giraffe, waterbuck and lions. The flat plains eventually give way to rugged hills stubbled with mopane trees and increasing numbers of elephants. Hippopotami can occasionally be seen in the rivers.

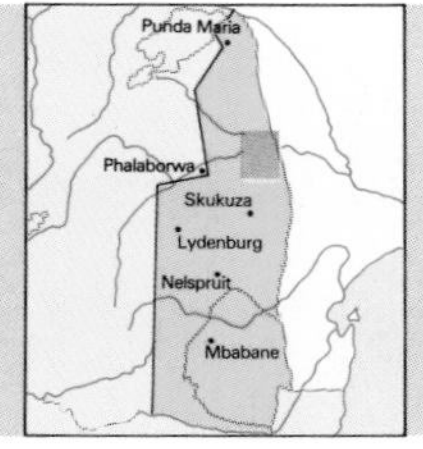

Satara
Timbavati
Olifants
Letaba
170 – 190 km

AFTER AN EARLY breakfast at Satara (try to leave camp by 07h45) take the H7 tarred road towards Orpen Camp. After 7 km a gravel road leads north. Stay on the tar — immediately beyond this junction lies Nsemani dam, a watering point for many animals and interesting bird species.

Spend a few pleasant minutes at this scenic spot before continuing along the H7, ignoring a gravel road veering north 5 km further.

13 km after Nsemani dam turn right onto the gravel S39 which parallels the Timbavati River, wending its way through very interesting bush with much atmosphere and an abundance of animals. Zebra, wildebeest, impala and kudu are common; and giraffe, elephant, buffalo and lion are often seen.

After about 31 km a well-marked short detour leads to the Timbavati picnic site (cooldrinks and toilets available). Try not to stay more than half an hour here to stretch your legs. Return to the S39, looking out for a large solitary baobab tree, one of the very few in the central part of the park.

Timbavati to Olifants

Turn left back on the S39, which continues its winding path beside the Timbavati River. Along the way you will pass some exquisitely shaped umbrella thorns.

30 km from the Timbavati picnic site you reach the H1-4 tarred road. Turn left, and after heading in a northerly direction for 5 km, cross the Olifants River. The high-water bridge affords an excellent view of the river where elephant or buffalo are frequently seen.

Continue along the tarred road (now the H1-5) for another 5 km, then turn right to join the H8 — also a tarred road — which leads directly to Olifants Camp 9 km further. Ignore the gravel roads which turn off first to the right and later to the left near the Olifants Camp.

You should reach camp in time for lunch in the restaurant, otherwise refreshments are

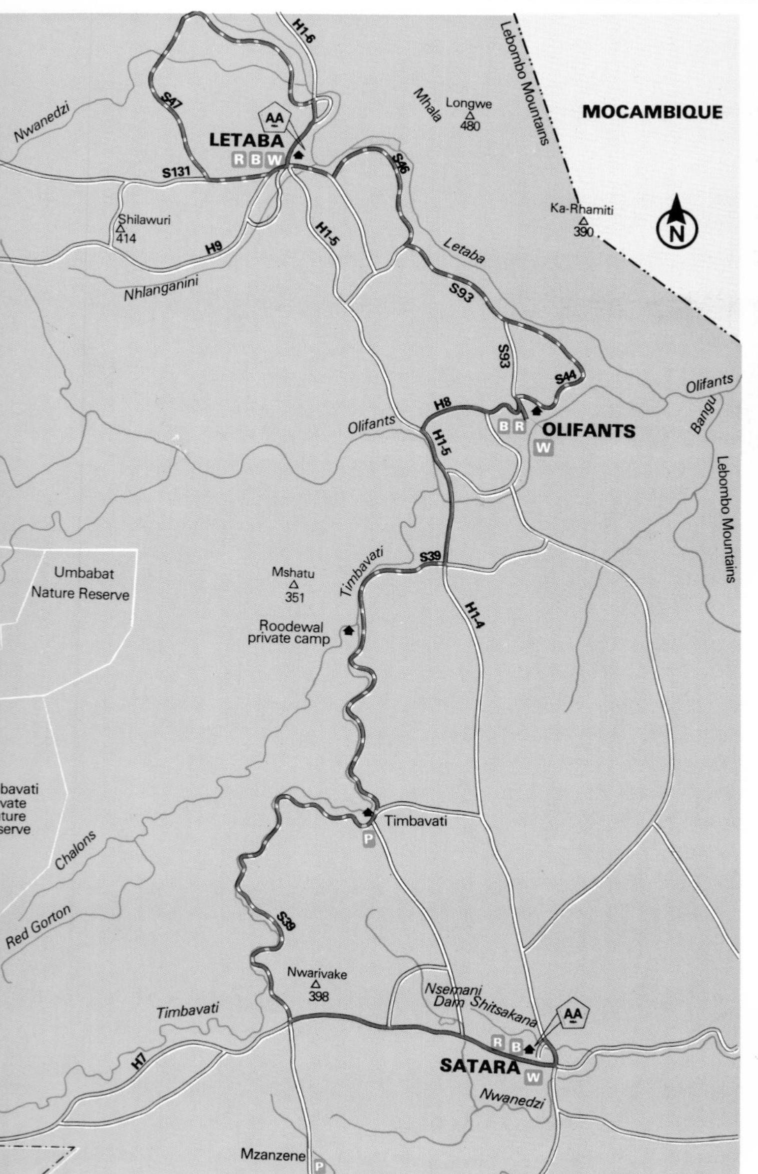

Elephants drink up to 200 litres of water every day.

AFRICAN ELEPHANT

With an adult mass of between 6 000 and 7 000 kg, these animals are the largest terrestrial animals living today. They feed mainly on grass, roots, bark and leaves, each animal consuming vast quantities each year.

Both males and females have tusks (some have none), although the females' tend to be thinner and smaller. The trunk, really an elongated nose, is useful for feeding, and water is sucked up into the trunk and then squirted either into the mouth for drinking, or over the body for cooling and cleaning. They sometimes raise their trunks to sniff the air if danger or any other source of disturbance is suspected.

The African elephant differs most obviously from its Indian counterpart by having larger ears: rounded, flat and thin-skinned, with many blood-vessels close to the surface. By gently flapping their ears they create a breeze that allows heat exchange to take place through the surface blood vessels as excess body heat diffuses out through the thin skin.

Elephants generally occur in herds averaging about 14 individuals, but numerous solitary bulls are also found. Most elephant are concentrated in the area north of the Olifants River.

Olifants Rest Camp.

served on the verandah. In front of the restaurant/reception office/shop complex is an observation area which offers a magnificent view of the Olifants River and surrounding bush.

Olifants to Letaba

From Olifants Camp take the gravel road (S44) which turns off the S93 about 1 km from the camp. This scenic drive with excellent views parallels the Olifants River, giving you plenty of opportunities to spot the many bird species associated with water.

After bearing eastwards for several kilometres the road veers sharply in a northerly direction eventually to parallel the Letaba River. As you progress along the S44, the vegetation changes rapidly to mixed mopane veld until, about halfway to Letaba, mopane trees vastly outnumber all other species. The rare Sharpe's grysbok is sometimes seen along this drive. Near the junction of the S44 with the S93 the road passes close to a hill covered with large boulders; klipspringer antelope are often seen standing atop these rocks.

15 km from the Olifants Camp, the road links up with the gravel S93, which after 9 km joins the S46. Keep right at both junctions. The S93 and S46 closely follow the Letaba River, allowing you to spot animals drinking or feeding along the edges. Lion are also often found in this area. After some 13 km on the S46 the road links up with the S94 (turn right), which ends at Letaba Camp 3 km further.

Letaba to Mingerhout Dam

After an early afternoon tea at Letaba take the H9 tarred road out of camp towards Phalaborwa. After 2 km turn onto the gravel S47 and follow it for 18 km to the Mingerhout Dam, where hippopotami and crocodiles can be seen. Return on the gravel S47, which twists along the Letaba River, with good sightings of elephant, zebra, waterbuck and several other species. You join the tarred H1-6 after 15 km, where you turn right for the 5 km drive back to Letaba ●

AA Patrol Station Satara Rest Camp.
AA Workshop and Petrol Station Letaba Rest Camp.

Letaba River from Letaba Rest Camp.

MALARIA

Malaria, caused by microscopic blood parasites transmitted by *Anopheles* mosquitos, occurs sporadically during summer throughout the park. Symptoms include vomiting, general body ache and severe fever. Although few visitors contract the disease, it is advisable to take preventative tablets, which are obtainable at most pharmacies. Although on sale in the park, doctors recommend that tablets be started prior to arrival.

Sunset over the Olifants River.

LETABA

One of the larger camps in the park, Letaba is spread along the southern bank of the river from which it takes its name. Many people regard this as their favourite camp because of its relaxed atmosphere.

Tall mlala palms — from which local tribesmen derive an intoxicating liquor by allowing the extracted juices of the tree to ferment — add a tropical touch and share the camp grounds with gnarled apple-leaf trees, Natal mahogany and thorny acacias. Short-cropped lawns cover the area between huts, and aloes grace several rock gardens.

Letaba has one of the most beautiful restaurants in the park: a large building with dining area, bar counter, lounge (where refreshments are served) and a long verandah with a beautiful view of the river where you can watch elephants.

Zebras live in small family groups, led by a stallion.

CHEETAHS

Cheetahs love the open plains, shunning densely wooded or mountainous regions. They run their prey down in a short burst of very high speed, knocking the animal over and biting into its throat.

Generally encountered in groups of two or three, cheetahs roam over large areas throughout the park. Unlike leopards, they are more active by day and can be distinguished by solid black spots all over the body instead of the leopard's rosette patterns. Also look for the characteristic black 'tear-mark' running from the inside of each eye down to the outside of the mouth. Lanky, streamlined animals, they are built for speed, with long thin legs, a relatively elongated thin chest and abdomen, and a head which is less bulky than that of a leopard.

ROLLERS

These exquisitely coloured birds are a constant source of delight, their delicate hues blending to produce a beautiful effect. Five species of rollers have been recorded in the park.

They can be seen perching singly on prominent dead trees or projecting branches of living trees, waiting until an insect moves into view. With graceful acrobatic movements they then swoop down to snatch the prey, and return to the perch to stun the insect by flicking it against a branch before swallowing it. So intent on their task are these dedicated hunters that little will distract them, often flying straight into the path of oncoming traffic in their darting flights after some morsel.

All the rollers have a rough, raucous call. They nest in holes in trees, laying up to three white eggs.

CHACMA BABOON

Baboons live in troops of 10 to 30 individuals, with a definite 'pecking order' determining the status of each member in the social hierarchy. Generally a dominant male, known as the alpha male, is the leader and has the best choice of females and food. Immediately below him follow a number of large aggressive males, who serve as the protectors of the troop. They feed and roam on the outskirts of the community, always ready to warn or defend the others against danger.

Highly intelligent animals, baboons have a very strong protective instinct towards their young. If an infant has been injured the members of a troop will rally around and carry it, never leaving it behind. When an infant is threatened or held by a predator, the large males will fearlessly charge and make desperate attempts to save it. Mother baboons are regularly seen carrying babies which have been dead for several days.

Baboons are common along the major rivers of the park, where they spend much of their active time looking for insects and other titbits.

Baby baboon and family.

Driving north through an endless sea of mopane trees

Our fourth day takes us through a vast expanse of flat plains with only a rare hill breaking through the endless sea of mopane trees. This area is home to numerous herds of buffalo and elephant, and antelope species such as tsessebe, roan, sable and eland. Multicoloured lilac-breasted rollers display their brilliant plumage from tree-top perches.

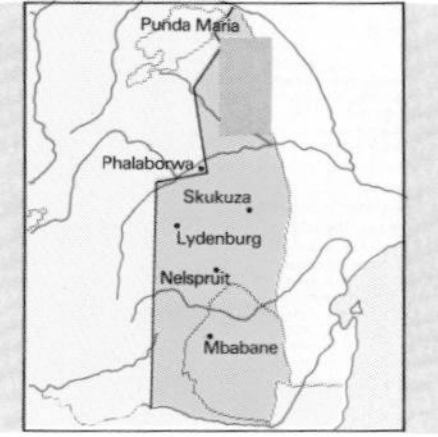

Letaba
Shingwedzi
Babalala
Punda Maria
170 – 190 km

After an early breakfast at Letaba, follow the tarred road (H1-6) north towards Shingwedzi. 6 km after leaving camp you cross the Letaba River, where buffalo and elephant are frequently seen in the reed-dotted riverbed.

The scenery is strikingly different from the southern half of the park. Vast stretches of seemingly endless mopane scrub-land roll from horizon to horizon, broken only by herds of zebra, wildebeest, impala, tsessebe and elephant. Stop for a while at Malopanyana and Middelvlei windmills, 20 and 25 km from Letaba, and look out for antelope such as tsessebe. Lion are also regularly seen in the vicinity.

About 33 km from Letaba, turn right onto a gravel road (S50) heading for the Lebombo Mountains. This road will take you past several dams and streams where zebra, impala, tsessebe, elephant and waterbuck are common. You may also see a rare reedbuck.

Tropic of Capricorn

In years with good rainfall Shawu Dam, about 45 km from Letaba, presents a wonderful sight when an abundance of waterbirds perch on the dead trees rearing up from the dam. Shortly after the dam, the road crosses the Tropic of Capricorn, and you enter the tropics.

As you approach the slopes of the Lebombo Mountains the road veers north to parallel the line of rock-strewn hills. These hills, together with the apparently endless mopane plains flowing from them, evoke a quiet sense of desolate timelessness. If you want to feel far removed from city life, this is the place to be.

Some 88 km after leaving Letaba, the S50 reaches the Shingwedzi River and veers northwesterly to follow the river, with many sightings of waterbuck, storks and other animals.

The Kanniedood dam, nearly 100 km from Letaba, is a magnificent expanse of water with many waterbirds and animals in the vicinity. Darters are abundant, posing breathtakingly on the logs and rocks rising from the water. You are also likely to see buffalo and elephant.

After a further 20 km you reach Shingwedzi Camp for a much-needed break after the long drive from Letaba. A leisurely lunch and stroll around camp should stretch the legs and any aching backs. A large swimming pool is also available in the southwestern corner.

Shingwedzi to Punda Maria

The distance from Shingwedzi to Punda Maria is about 77 km and you should allow about 2 hours 30 minutes for this drive.

After leaving Shingwedzi, turn right, cross the river using the high-water bridge on the tarred H1-6. At the bridge the H1-6 changes its designation and becomes the H1-7; continue along this road for 5 km before turning left onto the gravel S56. This road travels beside the Mphongolo River through beautiful groves of tall nyala, jackal berry and appleleaf trees, which provide a welcome relief from the mopane plains dominating most of the northern half of the park.

There are two points along this 29 km gravel road where you can turn off to the right to rejoin the tarred road, but this is not advised as more animals can be seen along this riverside road, and it is also more scenic. You rejoin the tarred H1-7 at Babalala picnic site, where you may want to get out for a walk and short rest.

Continue northwards along the H1-7 for another 18 km until just past a lone rounded hill known as Dzundwini. Here turn left on a gravel road (S58) for a short 4 km scenic drive near the base of Dzundwini where Sharpe's grysbok are frequently seen.

Turn left at the T-junction with the tarred H13-1 towards the Punda Maria border gate. Follow this road westwards for 11 km, before turning right onto the tarred H13-2. Ignore the gravel roads leading off this road at several points, and continue to Punda Maria camp. As the camp comes into view slow down and look out for bushbuck and nyala which regularly feed along the road at this point ●

AA Workshop and Petrol Station Letaba Rest Camp.

Impala dot the Shingwedzi River bank in the northern Kruger.

The buffalo: even lion are wary.

Martial eagle.

Vervet monkey.

ANTHRAX, A KILLER DISEASE

One of the scourges of the Kruger is anthrax, a bacterial disease probably introduced into southern Africa when the first cattle entered the area several hundred years ago.

The disease is now endemic in the northern areas of the park and occasional epidemics occur, especially during very dry seasons, killing more than a thousand large animals in only a few months. Unfortunately some of the rare animal species, such as roan antelope, are very susceptible to anthrax and there is a very real risk that a single outbreak could wipe out the entire population of this and other rare species.

During the early 1970s park researchers started an immunisation programme to ensure that a significant proportion of roan antelope would survive such an outbreak, and each year more than a hundred are darted from a helicopter with an immunising dart. On impact, the dart squirts a dye on to the animal's coat so that it can be easily recognised as having been treated against anthrax.

AFRICAN BUFFALO

About 25 000 buffalo are spread throughout the park, mostly in the northern half, with herds numbering between 10 and 600. Deceptively docile, these animals are powerful and aggressive – particularly older bulls ejected from the main herd who form small bachelor herds, generally wandering not far from a river or waterhole. These displaced bulls can be irate and vengeful, and if wounded in a fight will readily charge any animal that disturbs them. Nevertheless, in spite of their temper, they are regularly preyed upon by lions.

Both males and females have massive curved horns which serve as formidable weapons, although the males' tend to be heavier and wider. Mainly nocturnal, buffalo usually take their daily drink of water at night, and graze mainly on coarser tufts of grass.

A rinderpest outbreak in the late 19th century reduced the number of buffalo in the park to less than 100, but concerted conservation efforts resulted in a gradual resurgence of these powerful creatures.

Elephants cross the Letaba River. Natural migration routes are now cut off.

WHY CULL?

The need for culling — the shooting of certain animals to protect the species and its environment — still remains a controversial subject among conservationists and wildlife enthusiasts.

The root of the problem is simply that, in spite of its size, the park is essentially an artificial, controlled environment.

Fencing began in 1959, and resulted in the Kruger Park becoming an artificial ecosystem with the animals fenced in, unable to migrate along traditional seasonal routes. In 1948 the number of elephant in the park was estimated at between 400 and 500. In 1959 the population had doubled to 986, and by 1964 exploded to 2376. The buffalo population showed a similar increasing trend.

Because of the increasing damage that especially elephants were inflicting on trees and other vegetation, the National Parks Board in 1965 decided that where a species became a threat to itself, other animals and the vegetation, the population should be reduced to a level which could be adequately supported by the environment. From 1966 controlled culling was instituted, and the elephant population is still being maintained at between 7000 and 7500, and buffalo at about 25000.

Male leopard are essentially loners.

LEOPARD

Leopards generally rest during the day and are active in the evening and night. They prefer riverine areas and craggy hills, although occasionally they may be seen in open bush.

They tend to be solitary, and are often seen resting on a comfortable branch or in a clump of thick bush. In spite of their size, they are very good climbers often dragging their prey high into a tree, out of reach of hyaenas and other scavengers.

Leopards are occasionally confused with cheetah, but have several distinguishing characteristics. They do not have the black 'tear-marks' linking the eyes and sides of the mouth; and have rosettes or circular spots along the side and back of the body. Leopards are also more like domestic cats in build, with compact bodies and large head.

There are more than 900 leopards in the park, but are seldom seen because of their nocturnal activities and secretive habits.

A healthy hippo can live 40-50 years.

An oasis of water at Shingwedzi Rest Camp.

HIPPOPOTAMUS

In spite of their bulk — hippo reach an adult mass of 2000 to 3000 kg — these animals are amazingly graceful, especially in their aquatic environment. They prefer to remain in or near water by day, and if disturbed will submerge for several minutes, finally breaking surface with a spray of vaporised water.

During the day the males bellow loudly, which may cause several others to respond with similar deep-throated, staccato grunts. They feed at night, leaving the water to forage on grass and shrubs along the river.

Male hippos occasionally become very aggressive and domineering, fighting over territory and females. The loser of such a fight is usually forced to leave the herd. Watch when a hippo yawns — those teeth can inflict severe wounds.

Hippos generally occur in groups of 5 to 10, but may congregate in herds of more than 50.

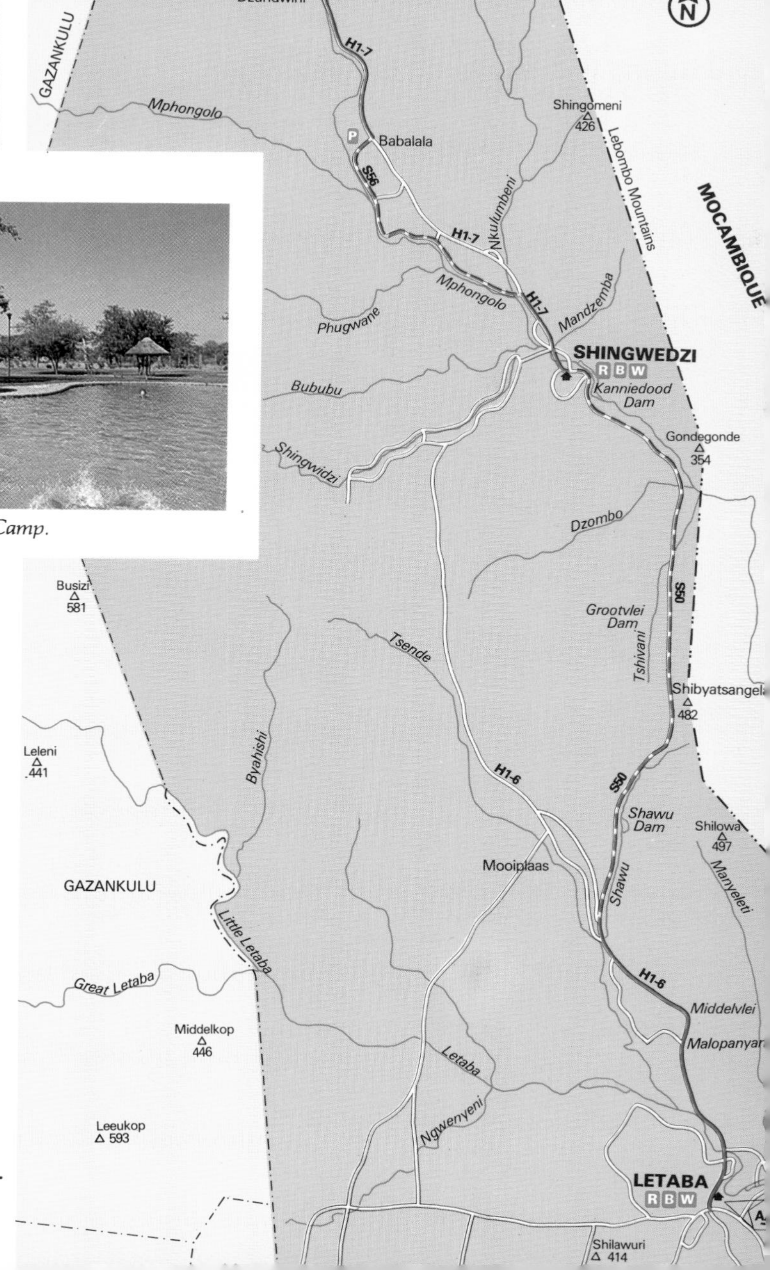

A mysterious forest-fringed river where crocodiles lie in wait

Our last day in the Kruger takes us to the far north of the park through sandstone hills covered in brightly coloured lichens. As you approach Pafuri, magnificent baobabs dot the landscape, and lush riverine forest fringe the Luvuvhu River, sheltering a large number of nyala and masses of birds. Crocodiles are commonly seen in the river.

Punda Maria
Mahonie Drive
Luvuvhu River
Pafuri
Punda Maria
150 – 170 km

OUR DRIVE STARTS before breakfast on the Mahonie circular drive around Punda Maria Camp, which should take only about 45 minutes to one hour to complete, with the various stops. Try to leave camp by 06h30, following the tarred H13-2 for about 300 m before turning left onto the gravel S99. Within the first 3 km you pass a waterhole on the left where animals may already be present.

Continuing, you enter the highly diverse mixed vegetation so characteristic of the sandveld north of Punda Maria, with an occasional pod mahogany majestically towering upwards. Halfway along the 20 km drive you reach the Matukwala Dam at the base of a hill, with a convenient off-road clearing under a tree where you can stop for a few minutes. Large numbers of buffalo often congregate around this dam.

The final stretch of the S99 takes you through fairly dense bush populated with herds of buffalo before you reach the H13-2 tarred road. Turn left to return to Punda Maria Camp.

Punda Maria to Pafuri

After a leisurely breakfast at Punda Maria, pack a picnic lunch and take the H13-2 out of camp. About 4 km from the camp take the S60 gravel road to the left, passing after a few kilometres the elongated and heavily overgrown Gumbandebvu hill on your left. Ignore a gravel turn-off to the right some 12 km along the S60, continuing on the S60 for a further 4 km before

A lioness surveys her territory.

PUNDA MARIA

Perhaps because of its small size and relative isolation, Punda Maria is one of the gems among camps in the Kruger. Far from civilization, here you can 'feel' the wildness of the remote bushveld.

The camp began as a ranger's station, established in 1919 by Captain J J Coetser. His wife apparently had a liking for striped dresses, and he named the station Punda Maria, the Swahili term for 'striped donkey' or zebra.

The camp is built in tiers on the slopes of a large hill, looking down on mopane-filled plains dotted with hills. The huts are built on terraces, with an appealing rustic appearance. A large, spacious camping area is spread along the base of the hill, complete with ablution blocks and kitchen units.

A small shop at the reception office sells curios, film and food, with a small restaurant next door.

NYALA

Occasionally mistaken for kudu or bushbuck — especially the females — there are definite differences in both habit and colour between the species. Bushbuck are almost invariably seen individually or in pairs, whereas nyala and kudu generally occur in small herds. The legs of male nyala are characteristically orange below the knees. When full grown the lyre-shaped horns of the male are only about half the length of those of a kudu. Females of both species lack horns.

Nyala are rare and localised in the park. A small population survives along the Sabie River, while other small, scattered herds live along the eastern half of the Olifants, Letaba, Shingwedzi and Mphongolo rivers and in the tall mopane woodland around Punda Maria. Only in the luxuriant riverine forest adjoining the Luvuvhu and Limpopo rivers in the far north of the park are nyala abundant.

Nyala are usually seen in small groups, although they have been known to gather in herds of up to 30 individuals. They are predominantly browsers, eating leaves, twigs, flowers and fruit of a wide variety of plants.

Bushbuck, nyala and kudu all have an unusual barking sound, like a sharply voiced deep grunt, that they often emit at night.

Nyala in the northern riverine forests.

Terraced huts at Punda Maria.

Impala with her new-born calf.

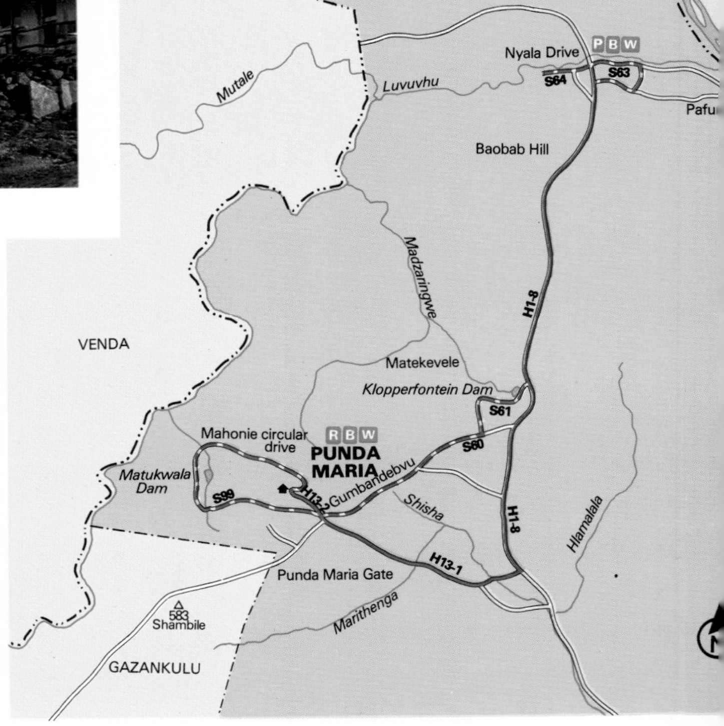

turning left onto the gravel S61. The tall mopane trees now give way to the more familiar mopane-scrub, with baobab trees and low hills making an appearance. Kudu, zebra, impala, buffalo and elephant are regularly seen.

After about 7 km on the S61 you reach the Klopperfontein dam, which is viewed from a short detour off the main road. Spend a few minutes here to enjoy the tranquil setting with its numerous water lilies and plentiful water-birds gaily trotting along the floating leaves. Jacanas and ducks are common, and a hippo occasionally makes this dam its home.

A few hundred metres beyond Klopperfontein Dam the S61 joins the tarred H1-8. Turn left and follow this road for 28 km until you reach the Luvuvhu River. Stop briefly on the high-water bridge and scan the riverbanks for any crocodiles basking in the sun. With a little luck a fish-eagle may be resting on one of the trees.

Turn around and back-track for about 100 m before turning right into the gravel S64. This 4 km drive, known as the Nyala Drive, parallels the Luvuvhu River offering some magnificent scenery. Look out for the tall nyala, jackal berry, Natal mahogany and fig trees, and you are almost certain to see several groups of nyala shyly appear among the lush riverine vegetation. Bird life is very abundant in this area, and you are likely to hear the eerie, plaintive sound of the trumpeter hornbill. Crested guinea fowl are frequently seen along this road.

Having completed the Nyala Drive, back-track along the S64 and cross the tarred road onto the S63, which also follows the Luvuvhu.

After 4 km a short turn-off to the left takes you to the Pafuri picnic site which overlooks the Luvuvhu River. This is an ideal spot to enjoy your picnic lunch (toilets, braai facilities and boiling water available).

Pafuri to Punda Maria

After lunch continue along the S63, which after about another 6 km veers south. The road passes through a dense grove of fever trees, with characteristic yellow-green bark. The road turns westward to pass through more typical mopane country until it rejoins the tarred H1-8 about 9 km further on.

Travel back towards Punda Maria along the H1-8, but do not turn right until you reach the main H13-1 tarred road near Dzundwini Hill. Depending on your accommodation arrangements, drive on to Punda Maria camp or Punda Maria border gate. If you exit through the border gate, the road continues through the Republic of Venda to Louis Trichardt, Pietersburg, Pretoria and Johannesburg ●

AA Workshop and Petrol Station Letaba Rest Camp.

BAOBAB TREE

This giant of African trees is easily recognised by its extreme girth and dominating appearance. Common only in the extreme northern regions of the park, many gigantic specimens dot the mopane landscape and rugged hills in the Pafuri area. Scattered individuals occur as far south as near Tshokwane.

The trees average about 25 m when fully grown, with stem diameters of up to 10 m. The characteristically thickened stem ends rather abruptly in a series of twisted branches with rapidly tapering ends. The bark has a fascinating gnarled and flabby appearance, much like the texture of molten wax.

Covered in summer with large, glossy leaves, the foliage falls with the approach of winter, giving the tree a stark and forlorn appearance, like a survivor from a previous age. Some trees are believed to be up to 4 000 years old.

Baobabs have very soft wood which rapidly disintegrates when the tree dies. Even in life the central part of the stem is very often hollow with an entrance at the top, providing natural and protective nesting and roosting sites for a range of birds, bats, and smaller animals such as centipedes and scorpions.

Baobabs have large white flowers, which are usually borne in November. The fruit is large, vaguely similar to that of the sausage tree, but is light green in colour and covered with a dense layer of fine velvety fur. Baboons eat the fruit for the pulp and seeds inside.

Tribal legend has it that at the beginning of life, the gods provided all animals with seeds and plants to cultivate. Last of all came the hyaena, and it received the baobab. In keeping with its supposedly stupid nature, the hyaena planted the tree upside down. During winter, when the branches are bare, the baobab certainly does look as though it has been upended.

Inquisitive hamerkop at Punda Maria.

Fever trees dot the Luvuvhu River near the Mocambique border.

SCOTCH AND DOGS

Among the memorable characters who pioneered the northern Kruger was a Scotsman with 25 years of military service in India, Major Affleck Frazer. Appointed a ranger in 1903, he had an unequalled ability to consume vast quantities of Scotch whisky without any visible effect.

On one occasion Harry Wolhuter had to spend a night at Frazer's house. Being winter he ventured through in the early morning hours to ask Frazer if he had a spare blanket, only to find Frazer snoring on the floor with his pack of 25 dogs.

The root-like branches of the baobab give it the nickname 'upside-down tree'.

LEGENDARY POACHER

One of a regular band of cross-border ivory hunters in the northern Kruger, Cecil Barnard was an outlaw for 20 years, defying all attempts by police of three countries to catch him. With a supply base in Crooks' Corner — the infamous junction of South Africa, Mocambique and the old Rhodesia — Barnard roamed a vast area of this truly wild and harsh region in the adventurous days around the turn of the century. He was christened 'Bvekenya' by the local natives, meaning 'he who swaggers when he walks'.

Of average height, he was powerfully built, with extraordinary reserves of toughness and stamina, attributes sorely needed in rugged bush conditions.

The borders of the three countries met at a beacon on an island in the Limpopo River where outlaws would occasionally pitch camp. Depending on which police were patrolling in the vicinity, they would shift the beacon so their camp would be in another country and thus legally out of reach of the police.

The adventures of Bvekenya and other colourful personalities are related in 'The Ivory Trail' by South African author T V Bulpin.

SOUTHERN TRANSVAAL

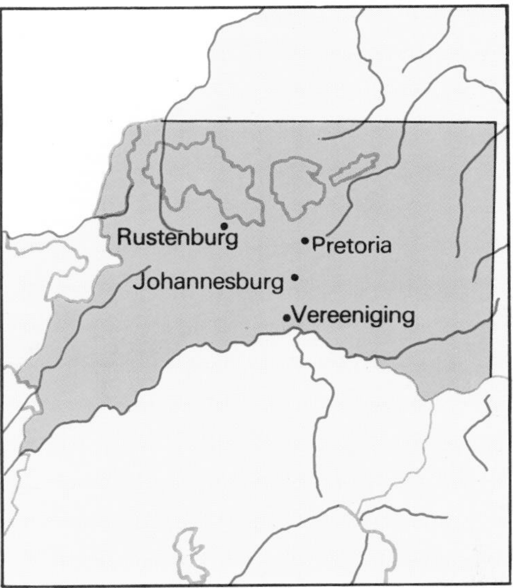

Above: *The vividly coloured Ndebele village at Botshabelo.* **Left:** *Glittering Johannesburg — bustling modern city with a history steeped in gold.*

Against Sekukuni's warriors — a German fort on the African veld

This one-day outing is not so much a tour as a visit to two interesting places — first the Willem Prinsloo Agricultural Museum at Rayton, then the rest of the day spent at the old Botshabelo Mission, visiting the colourful Ndebele village nearby, and last century's stone-walled Fort Merensky. Except for the two access roads, the entire route is tarred.

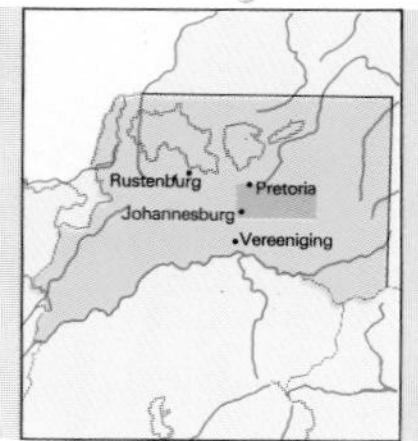

Pretoria (260—280 km)
Johannesburg (340—360 km)
Rayton
Middelburg
Botshabelo
Fort Merensky

LEAVE PRETORIA BY driving east along Schoeman Street, which becomes the N4 to Witbank. Stay on the N4 and note your kms as you pass through the N1 intersection. (If you are starting from Johannesburg, drive north on the M1 and N1 towards Pretoria and Pietersburg for roughly 60 km from the city centre, then exit left, following the signs onto the N4 for Witbank. Note your kms as you join the N4.)

After roughly 25 km on the N4 (from the N1 intersection) exit left for the R515 to Rayton. At the end of the off-ramp turn left onto the R515, and at the four-way stop street turn right onto the R104 for Valtaki. The R104 runs almost due east, parallel to the N4, and after travelling roughly 4 km along it, turn left onto the short gravel access road into the Willem Prinsloo Agricultural Museum (small entrance fee).

The farm on which the museum has been established was the home of the Prinsloo family during the last century, and a portion of it was donated to the National Cultural History and Open Air Museum in 1976. It has been developed as a living exhibition of farm life in the Transvaal during the last century (see below). There are also shaded braai sites here, a cafeteria and toilets.

Return to the tar (R104) and turn left. After roughly 16 km you reach the town of Bronkhorstspruit, near the site of the 1880 Battle of Bronkhorstspruit that marked the start of the First Anglo-Boer War. Drive through the town and at the stop street on the far side, turn right. Turn left shortly after this to re-join the N4 towards Witbank and Middelburg, noting your kms as you re-join the N4.

Bronkhorstspruit to Botshabelo

Continue on the N4 past Witbank. 65,3 km after re-joining the N4, exit left for Middelburg

One of several carriages at the Willem Prinsloo Museum.

FARM BREAD AND PEACH BRANDY

The aim of the Willem Prinsloo Agricultural Museum is to bring the past back to life. The original farm homestead has been fully restored and re-furnished as it must have appeared a century ago, and the effect of stepping back through time to a living moment is enhanced by the presence of farm animals and clucking poultry. Several new buildings have been erected nearby to house a collection of horse-drawn vehicles, and a fascinating variety of early farm equipment.

The emphasis has been on making this a 'living' museum. It remains a functioning farm, and often the old equipment is used for the farm chores. At weekends visitors can see the smithy and the leatherworks in action, watch sheep being dipped or bread being baked — or see the fiery 'mampoer' peach brandy being distilled in the traditional manner. (Most demonstrations are held on Saturdays.)

NAZARETH ON THE HIGHVELD

Roughly 120 years ago the Dutch Reformed Church established a tiny settlement on the south bank of the Klein Olifants River, and named it Nazareth. There were objections to this name — for reasons unknown — and a few years later the settlement was renamed Middelburg. Still standing in the town is the so-called 'white church', dating from 1890. In the early days, when farmers flocked into the town to celebrate *Nagmaal* (Communion) once every three months, the grassy fields around the church became a bustling 'city' of tents and oxwagons. The church can still be visited, as can the old Meijers Bridge across the river — which also dates back to 1890.

NDEBELE VILLAGE

Some of the descendants of the refugees who sheltered at the Botshabelo mission now live in the brightly painted Ndebele village on the south bank of the Klein Olifants River — just a few hundred metres from the old mission buildings.

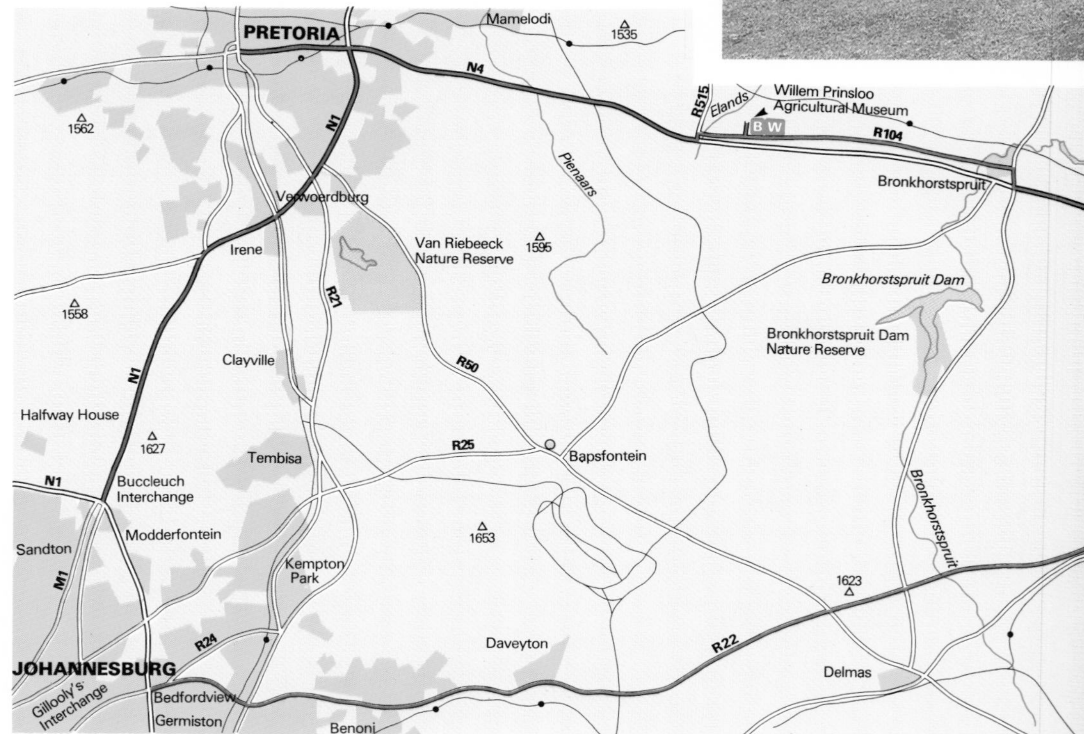

(presently at the end of the double carriageway). Follow the signs for Middelburg — a further 8,4 km. The town owes its name to the fact that in pioneer days it served as the halfway house between Pretoria and Lydenburg (see opposite).

You will have entered Middelburg on Kerkstraat. Continue on Kerkstraat, and note your kms as you pass Jan Van Riebeeck Street (the N4 for Belfast and Nelspruit) on your right. Kerkstraat becomes the R35 for Groblersdal. After 400 m you pass a turn-off left to the town's old cemetery, where there are a number of Anglo-Boer War graves, including those of local concentration camp victims. 200 m after this turn-off you pass the 'white church' on your right. 8,4 km after noting your kms, turn left into the Botshabelo Game Reserve (entrance fee). A gravel road leads through the reserve for 4 km to the entrance to the old mission station — turn right just before driving down to the mission, in order to first visit the romantic ruins of the stone-walled Fort Merensky that overlook the mission (see below).

From the fort, return to the access road, which leads after a few hundred metres to a parking area opposite a shop (where brochures are available). The mission, on the north bank of the Klein Olifants River, is now the centre of a variety of attractions. The original buildings are today a museum, and along the grassy banks of the river there are tree-shaded braai sites, with water and toilets. On the bank opposite the mission there is a picturesque Ndebele village notable for its brightly and imaginatively painted houses. The whole complex lies in the centre of the Botshabelo Game Reserve, and there are walks through the reserve ranging from four to six hours.

On your return from Botshabelo, retrace your route through Middelburg onto the N4 towards Witbank. If you are returning to Pretoria, stay on the N4 for the entire journey. If you are returning to Johannesburg, turn off onto the R22 shortly before Witbank — the exit is well signposted ●

AA Office AA House, 395 Schoeman Street, Pretoria 0002 Tel. (012) 283829
AA Office AA House, 66 De Korte Street, Braamfontein, Johannesburg 2001 Tel. (011) 4035700
Willem Prinsloo Agricultural Museum Box 3300, Pretoria 0001 Tel. (01213) 4273/4/5
Botshabelo Museum and Nature Reserve Box 14, Middelburg 1050 Tel. (01321) 23897

A FORT TO FRIGHTEN SEKUKUNI

The name Botshabelo means 'place of refuge', and the mission of this name was established in 1865 by Alexander Merensky of the Berlin Mission Society to serve as a refuge for Christian converts persecuted by the warriors of Chief Sekukuni.

To protect the mission and its inhabitants from further attacks, Merensky built a fort on the hill above the mission. The fort, originally Fort Wilhelm, was a mixture of Sotho stonework and German castle, and it now makes a romantic memorial to the days when the African veld was a frontier land of mystery and adventure.

From the fort you can look down over the tree tops to the spire of the little church (which you may visit through a side door).

A colourfully dressed Ndebele woman outside her home at Botshabelo.

Fort Merensky retains a romantic flavour of exciting African-frontier days.

BOTSHABELO GAME RESERVE

The reserve surrounds the old mission and is home to eland, blesbok, springbok, wildebeest, hartebeest and many other smaller animals. There are no dangerous predators, and visitors can choose from three walks through the area — two of these take approximately four hours each, and the third is a more substantial hike lasting six hours. There are also short stretches of road through the reserve, allowing visitors to view the game from their cars.

Below *The old Botshabelo Mission building.*

Manicured lawns surround the stately sandstone Union Buildings — the administrative seat of South Africa's national government.

A mingling of old and new in the Jacaranda City

PRETORIA TODAY is a mix of ultra-modern architecture and stately old buildings dating from its days as the capital of the Transvaal republic. It is a pretty city — its gardens and trees flourish in the fertile, well-watered soil of the Apies River valley, and springtime brings the spectacle of tens of thousands of flowering jacaranda trees.

This mix of modern and historic is also found in the many places of interest in the city. The visitor will find a variety of museums that preserve relics of days gone by, and also fascinating glimpses of up-to-the-minute scientific and industrial developments. Over weekends, residents have easy access to the surrounding countryside, where highveld meets lowveld along the ridge of the Magaliesberg, and rivers and lakes offer lovely settings in which to relax.

Nguni-speaking settlers, who became known as the Ndebele (derived from their Sotho nickname of 'refugees'), are thought to have been the first people to recognise the suitability of the Apies River valley as a place to put down roots. They named the river after one of their chiefs, Tshwane (little ape), which was later translated into the Afrikaans 'Apies'. During the migratory wars in Natal, another band of refugees arrived here under the leadership of Mzilikazi, but they were forced to abandon their villages in their flight from a regiment of Zulu raiders in 1832.

Voortrekkers were the next people to settle in this lovely valley, with its protection provided by the surrounding rocky ridges. The site was eventually chosen in the 1850s as a central seat of government for the bands of Voortrekkers scattered across the Transvaal. They named their capital Pretoria after Andries Pretorius, the Boer hero at the Battle of Blood River against the Zulus (see pages 156-7).

As you approach Pretoria from the south, you see the monolithic granite *Voortrekker Monument* on Voortrekkerhoogte. Built in 1949, it has four large granite statues of Voortrekkers on its corners, and the surrounding wall has been sculpted with 56 wagons representing the laager at Blood River. Inside the monument, marble friezes depict the Great Trek, which started in 1834. A museum in the grounds contains furniture, clothing, household goods and other Voortrekker relics, and also has a restaurant. Picnic tables near an adjacent amphitheatre offer fine views over the city. (Museum and monument open daily except Good Friday and Christmas; small entry fee for museum; strict dress code; restaurant closed Tuesday; tel. 323 0682.)

The high-rise skyline of central Pretoria is softened by trees and gardens.

Hill-top forts

Nearby are two hill-top forts that formed part of the Boer defence of the city: *Fort Schanskop,* which is reached on the Voortrekker Monument access road; and *Fort Klapperkop,* situated on the scenic Johann Rissik Drive. Both have been restored by the South African Defence Force as military museums — Fort Schanskop (tel. 715560) concentrates on the period from before the Voortrekkers' arrival to the Second Anglo-Boer War of 1899-1901; while Fort Klapperkop (tel. 427127) contains military equipment from World War I to the present. (Both open daily except Good Friday and Christmas.)

Johann Rissik Drive winds through part of the Fountains Valley Nature Reserve, and offers excellent views of Pretoria, particularly during jacaranda time in October/November, when the city is amass with the white and purple blooms. From here you also have fine views of the *Union Buildings* across the valley — the magnificent sandstone administrative centre for the national government — designed by Sir Herbert Baker at the time of Union in 1910. Built on the slopes of Meintjies Kop, the curved main building, collonaded and flanked by two 55 m domed towers, faces beautiful terraced gardens. Another scenic drive leads between the Union Buildings and the gardens, offering fine city views, and a walk up Meintjieskop will reward you with panoramic vistas.

'Old lion' remembered

The focal point of the city centre is *Church Square*, at the intersection of Church and Paul Kruger streets. In the central garden stands an imposing statue of President Paul Kruger, sculpted by Anton van Wouw to honour the 'old lion' of the Transvaal, who achieved world fame when his small *Zuid-Afrikansche Republiek* took on the might of the British Empire in 1899. Several impressive old buildings face onto the square, including the old republican *Raadsaal* (council chamber), and the *Palace of Justice*, which was used as a military hospital during the Anglo-Boer War and now houses the Transvaal Supreme Court.

Next to the Raadsaal stands the *Transvaal Provincial Building* (entrance on Bosman Street), its modern lines contrasting with those of its stately predecessor. Tours of the Provincial Building, which houses many South African art treasures, can be arranged (tel. 201 3449).

On Church Street, west of the square, you can visit the *Kruger House Museum*, the simple home where President Kruger lived from 1884 until his exile in 1900. Apart from the original furnishings, there are also many of the president's personal possessions, the wagon in which his family trekked to the Transvaal, his state coach and railway carriage, and a collection of mementoes of the ZAR. (Open daily except Good Friday and Christmas; small entry fee; tel. 269172.)

Across the street is the *Gereformeerde (Kruger) Church*, where the president sometimes delivered the Sunday sermon, and a few blocks further west lies the cemetery known as Heroes' Acre, where Kruger is buried alongside other famous South Africans such as Andries Pretorius and Prime Ministers HF Verwoerd and JG Strijdom.

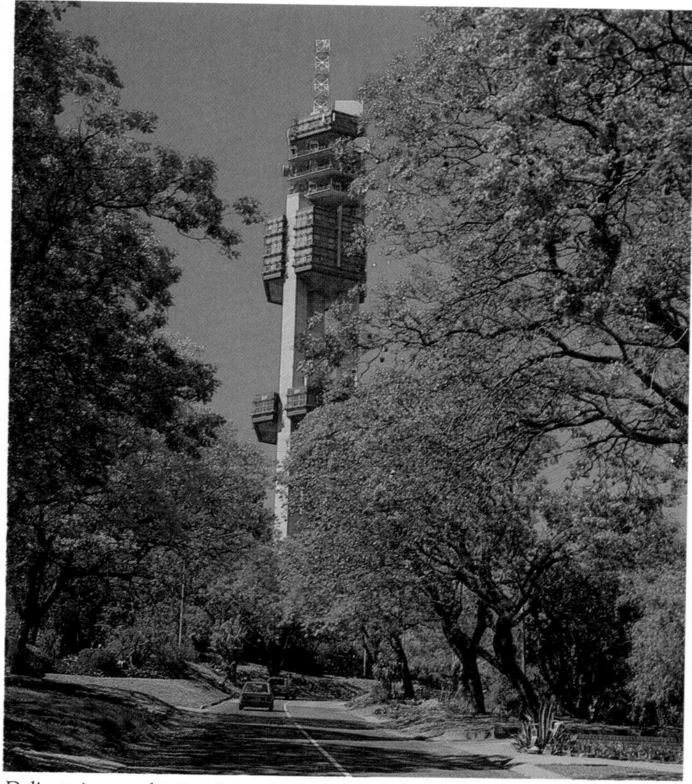

Delicate jacarandas tint the spring air a hazy mauve.

Another interesting collection of items from the ZAR days is housed in the *National Cultural History and Open-Air Museum* on Boom Street. This museum also contains an ethnological section, collections of furniture, costumes, porcelain, ceramics, firearms, Bibles, Anglo-Boer War relics, medals and coins, as well as an archeological section where a 2 000-year-old mummy is the central exhibit. (Open daily except public holidays; small entry fee; tel. 323 3128.)

The awesome Voortrekker Monument.

Mammals and birds

The *Transvaal Museum of Natural History* on Paul Kruger Street houses an excellent display on life's genesis, as well as exhibits of mammals, reptiles, amphibians and insects. It also incorporates the Austin Roberts Bird Hall and the Museum of Geological Survey, which has fascinating rock and mineral specimens. (Open daily except New Year, Good Friday and Christmas; small entry fee; coffee shop; tel. 287387.)

Pretoria's historic *City Hall* is across the street from the museum. It has an imposing clock tower with a carillon of 32 bells, and the grounds feature a collonade of fountains, and statues of Andries Pretorius and his son, Marthinus Wessel Pretorius, who became the first ZAR president. Further south along Paul Kruger Street is the *Pretoria Railway Station*, designed by Sir Herbert Baker, where an 1889 locomotive can be seen.

At the close of the Anglo-Boer War, the Peace Treaty of Vereeniging was signed in a beautiful old Victorian house of 1886 on Jacob Maré Street. Known as *Melrose House*, it has been well preserved as a period house museum, containing antique furniture, stained-glass windows, mosaic floors, ceiling mouldings, and a fine doll collection. (Open Tuesday to Sunday except public holidays; small entry fee; tel. 267893.)

The house faces onto *Burgers Park*, laid out in 1882 and named after President Thomas Francois Burgers, of whom there is a statue in the park. The area was used by early visitors to Pretoria to outspan their wagons. It contains a kiosk (closed Monday) next to the bandstand, and a 'florarium' housing indigenous and exotic plants.

The *Post Office Museum* in the GPO headquarters (entrance on Proes Street) offers a fascinating insight into the world of communications. The exhibits include a replica of an old post office — crammed with antique equipment — and displays explaining every aspect of communications from mail to telegraphy, telephony, radio, microwave and space communications. You can try your hand at morse code, or watch the intricate switchings as you dial a telephone. More than 750 000 stamps may be viewed on request. (Open Monday to Friday except

A view of Church Square, with the old Raadsaal building in the background.

public holidays; tel 293 1066.)

Another museum dealing with modern technology is the *South African Museum of Science and Technology* on the second floor, Didacta Building, Skinner Street. It has a resources centre for school children, and exhibitions on such subjects as atoms and nuclear energy, space travel, anatomy, and water. (Open Monday to Friday except public holidays; tel. 260035.)

Crime and criminals are the subjects of the *South African Police Museum,* Compol Building, corner Pretorius Street and Volkstem Avenue. (Open Monday to Saturday except public holidays; identity document required; no bags or coats; tel. 211678.) The *South African Mint* at 103 Visagie Street has a collection of coins and medals from around the world. (By appointment only; open weekdays; tel. 265611.)

The simple life

Slightly further afield, at the *Pioneer Open-air Museum* on Pretoria Road, Silverton, you can see an old thatched farmhouse that brings home the simplicity of the lifestyle of the early settlers. Braai and picnic sites overlook the restored old farmyard on the banks of the Moreleta Spruit. On Saturdays museum staff bake bread in an outdoor oven and offer it for sale, while during school terms various skills are demonstrated in the mornings, such as soap-making, coffee-roasting, and corn-stamping. (Open daily; entry fee; kiosk; tel. 832171.) The *Willem Prinsloo Agricultural Museum* on the old Bronkhorstspruit road offers similar attractions in a rural setting (see pages 120-1).

Another old farm that will interest visitors from both Johannesburg and Pretoria is the old Doornkloof Farm and *Smuts House Museum* at Irene. This unpretentious wood-and-iron farmhouse has been restored to its original state when South African Prime Minister Jan Smuts lived here with his wife, Isie, in sparsely furnished simplicity. There is a tearoom here, and braai and picnic sites on the lovely, wooded hillside. A short walk takes you up Smuts Koppie, where there is a family memorial. (Open daily except religious holidays; small entry fee; tel. 65476.)

Delville Wood Memorial — a tribute to soldiers killed during World War I.

One of the best collections of South African art is housed at the *Pretoria Art Museum* in Arcadia Park. The museum has large holdings of works by Pierneef, Oerder, Van Wouw and Wenning, as well as modern South African artists. The Association of Friends of the Pretoria Art Museum has a full programme of lectures, films and concerts. (Open Tuesday to Sunday except religious holidays; tel. 444271.)

The *SA Association of Arts* concentrates on South African artists — both established and unknown — at their gallery on the 37th floor, Volkskas Building, on the impressive JG Strijdom Square. (Open Monday to Saturday; tel. 218741.)

A 1920s cigarette factory at 218 Vermeulen Street (across the road from the old Reserve Bank Building) has been converted into the *Pierneef Museum.* Furnished in the style of the Twenties, the double-storey building houses a fine collection of Pierneef's paintings, drawings and sketches. (Open weekdays except public holidays; tearoom, entry fee; tel. 323 1419.)

The Performing Arts Council Transvaal presents a full programme of theatre, opera and ballet at the ultra-modern *State Theatre* at the corner of Church and Prinsloo streets. Twice a week there are guided tours for the public, lasting about 90 minutes. Tours include visits to the various auditoriums, and the wardrobes and decor studio. The theatre has a restaurant and coffee bar. (Tel. 219440 for information; watch local press for programme schedules.) Bargain-hunters can visit the regular flea market held outside the theatre on Saturday mornings (except long weekends).

Animal kingdom

A favourite with visitors to Pretoria is the famous *National Zoological Garden* on Boom Street. This beautifully landscaped zoo covers 40 ha of hillside, and offers a scenic cablecar ride to the top of the koppie. From here you can stroll down past large enclosures containing big cats, antelope, hippo, camels and rhino. There are enclosures with owls, eagles and other birds, monkeys and apes — a total of 140 mammal species and 240 bird species. The grounds offer picnic and braai sites on the banks of the Apies River, a restaurant, an information kiosk, and lectures and tours for groups on request. (Open daily; entry fee; carnivores and seals fed daily; tel. 283265.) Outside the zoo colourful items of craftwork are for sale.

Next to the zoo on Boom Street is the *Aquarium and Reptile Park,* which houses an impressive collection of freshwater and sea fish, snakes, crocodiles, tortoises and lizards. (Open daily; small entry fee; tel. 283265.) Further out of town there is another aquarium near Hartbeespoort Dam, as well as a snake and animal park in Schoemansville (see pages 128-9).

Also near the dam is the *De Wildt Cheetah Research Station,* which is reached off the R513. The station experiments with breeding endangered species in captivity in an attempt to ensure their survival. On the two tours by vehicle offered on Saturdays, you can see cheetah — including the striped king cheetah — wild dog, brown hyena and Cape vulture. (Advance booking essential; no children under six; tour fee; duration two hours; tel. 01204-917 or 921.) Also at De Wildt, off the R513, is *Croco Farm,* which breeds Nile crocodiles in captivity. (Open weekends only; entry fee; souvenirs and refreshments for sale; tel. 01204-704.)

Central Pretoria is well-endowed with parks and nature areas. On the southern edge of the city is the 500 ha *Fountains Valley Nature Reserve* — proclaimed as a game park in 1895. About 60 ha have been set aside as a regional park, with braai and picnic facilities amidst lawns and trees, tennis courts, a children's playground, a swimming pool, and a tearoom. The park is reached from Fountains Circle, along the Johannesburg/Verwoerdburg road.

Indigenous trees and shrubs

The *National Botanical Gardens* (entrance on Cussonia Avenue near the CSIR) grows more than half the South African tree species in its 77 ha of ground. It offers a lovely area for walking amidst the climatically grouped plants. Tours for groups can be arranged. (Tel. 861165.)

Faerie Glen Nature Reserve, which forms part of the *Moreleta Spruit Trail,* is one of the most attractive open areas in Pretoria. Many indigenous Transvaal trees, shrubs and aloes have been planted here, and it has a rich variety of birds. The trail also takes you through the *Meyers Park Nature Reserve,* as the paths wind along the banks of the Moreleta

The Transvaal Museum on Paul Kruger Street houses a fine collection of natural history exhibits.

A statue of Andries Pretorius in front of the imposing City Hall.

Spruit from Menlyn Drive, Garsfontein, to the Pioneer Open-air Museum in Silverton. (Further information available from the Pretoria Parks and Recreation Department, Munitoria Building, corner Van der Walt and Vermeulen streets, tel. 213411.)

Also under the authority of the parks department is the *Wonderboom Nature Reserve* (reached off the R55/M1). The focal point of the reserve is the 'wonderboom' (wonder tree) — a wild fig more than 1000 years old which, with its subsidiary trunks, spreads its branches over 55 m. There is a children's playground here, braai and picnic sites, and a hiking trail to an Anglo-Boer War fort on top of a nearby koppie. Monkeys, dassies (hyrax) and a wide variety of birds make their home here.

The *Austin Roberts Bird Sanctuary* on Boshoff Street, New Muckleneuk, is named after the South African naturalist whose 1940 book of birds is still regarded as a standard work. The fenced sanctuary has a hide overlooking a dam that attracts a fascinating assortment of waterbirds, and you can also see a large number of other species here. (A small museum displays local birds.)

Nearby, at *Magnolia Dell* on Queen Wilhelmina Avenue, a charming park with beautifully laid-out gardens offers a family venue popular over weekends. The park has statues of Peter Pan and Wendy, a children's playground, a small pond for miniature boats, and a refreshment kiosk. Once a month it features Art in the Park — an open-air market for paintings and crafts.

A short distance out of the city, *Derdepoort Regional Park* (on the N7 near the R513 intersection) offers a bushveld-farm atmosphere for picnics and braais. There is a miniature farmyard with farm animals, playgrounds for children, and a hiking trail along the Moreleta and Hartebeest spruits. (Open daily; small entry fee.)

Highveld habitat

The *Silkaatsnek Game Park* near Brits on the R511 offers a variety of buck, giraffe and smaller mammals in their natural highveld habitat. There are picnic and braai sites, a swimming pool, and hiking trails. (Open Tuesday to Sunday; entry fee; tel. 01211-31408 and ask for Silkaatsnek.)

The Hennops River valley, Magaliesberg, Hartbeespoort Dam and Buffelspoort Dam are all popular retreats, where various pleasure resorts and braai and picnic areas attract many visitors over weekends. Apart from those mentioned elsewhere (see pages 128-131), there is also the *Magalieskloof Pleasure Resort* on the northern slopes of the Magaliesberg (reached off the R513), which offers braai and picnic spots in a beautiful bushveld setting, walking trails, a playground, swimming pool, beer garden, restaurant, chalets, and caravan and campsites. (Entry fee; tel. 01204-707.)

On the Breedt's Nek road, south of Buffelspoort Dam, a turn-off leads to the 960 ha *Mountain Sanctuary Park*. This private nature reserve offers many kilometres of walking along streams and through rocky mountain scenery overlooking the beautiful Sterkstroom valley and Buffelspoort Dam. There are a number of antelope, small mammals and birds, and you can swim in the rivers or in a pool near the braai and picnic sites. There are chalets, caravan and camping sites. (Entry fee; tel. 0142222-1430.)

Waltzing waters

Two other dams that attract water-sport enthusiasts and nature-lovers are the *Roodeplaat Dam*, north of Pretoria on the extension of the N7, and *Rietvlei Dam*, east of Verwoerdburg. Roodeplaat Dam and its surrounding nature reserve offers fishing, canoeing, yachting, power-boating, a bird sanctuary, walking trails, a swimming pool, braai and picnic sites, chalets, camping and caravanning, as well as game-viewing. (Entry fee; tel. 821547.) Rietvlei Dam and the surrounding Van Riebeeck Nature Reserve is less developed, and is popular for picnics, braais, fishing and walking. (Open daily; permit required from parks and recreation department, tel. 213411.)

At *Verwoerdburg Dam* you can watch canoeists and boardsailors from a number of restaurant terraces at the Verwoerdburgstad shopping centre. Every evening there are several 'Waltzing Waters' shows — with illuminated fountains synchronised to music (tel. Verwoerdburg Parks and Recreation Department 622123.)

Paul Kruger's Dutch Reformed Church.

Those with an interest in science and technology may wish to visit the *Council for Scientific and Industrial Research*, with its headquarters at Scientia near the N4. The CSIR, which conducts research into almost every aspect of life, offers tours by arrangement (tel. 869211 and ask for the visitors' office). The *South African Bureau of Standards* in Groenkloof also offers tours of its premises, where it performs a quality-control role for household and industrial goods (tel. 341 1311).

Iscor, the iron and steel plant at Wespark, conducts guided tours of its mills, blast furnaces and smelting and coke ovens once a week. (No children under 12; closed shoes essential; tel. 794421).

At Cullinan, where the magnificent 3106-carat Cullinan Diamond was discovered in 1905, you can visit the *Premier Diamond Mine*. A tour lasting about two hours takes you to the big hole and shaft, as well as the grease tables and sorting area. (Sturdy shoes essential; no children under ten; tel. 01213-30050.) While you are in the area, it is worth visiting the mine museum on the road to the mine entrance, and the town of Cullinan, where many of the wood-and-iron buildings date from the early days of the century.

There are also a number of places of interest in and around Johannesburg and the greater Witwatersrand area, all of which are within easy reach of Pretoria — see pages 126-139. For further information on Pretoria and its surroundings, contact the Pretoria Publicity Association, Munitoria Building, corner Van der Walt and Vermeulen Streets, Pretoria 0002. Tel. 212461 ●

Memorial to J G Strijdom, Prime Minister from 1954 to 1958.

Dutch Reformed Church, Bosman St.

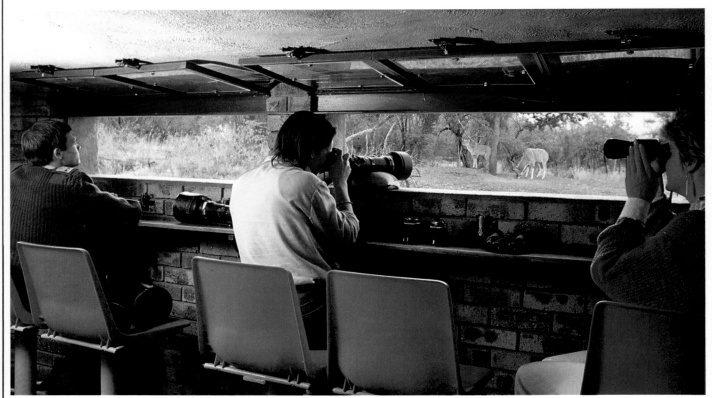

The submerged hide at the Kwa-Maritane lodge overlooks a waterhole and offers excellent game-viewing, especially during the dry winter months.

The volcano that gave birth to a game reserve

As you drive through the peaceful grasslands and granite outcrops of the Pilanesberg National Park, it is hard to imagine the cataclysmic violence that created the area and gave birth to its unique geology some twelve hundred million years ago.

For the hills of Pilanesberg, a 50 000 ha game sanctuary lying about 200 km northwest of the Witwatersrand in Bophuthatswana, are actually the crumbling foundations of an ancient volcanic crater — its centre now serving as the beautiful setting for a man-made lake known as Mankwe, the 'place of the leopard'.

In the last century, Pilanesberg served as a sanctuary of a different kind — Mzilikazi's rebel Zulu warriors passed through the area as they fled the wrath of Chaka. Not long after this, during the Anglo-Boer War, General Christiaan de Wet's commandos hid from the British amongst these same hills — perhaps prompting the later purchase of a farm in the area by South African Prime Minister Jan Smuts.

During the late 1970s, President Lucas Mangope of Bophuthatswana decided to re-introduce wildlife and turn the Pilanesberg area into a game reserve. The cattle farmers who then occupied the area were moved to new homes elsewhere, and work began on *Operation Genesis,* which involved the game-fencing of the entire reserve and the re-introduction of long-vanished species.

The creation of the Pilanesberg National Park was one of the most ambitious programmes of its kind undertaken anywhere in the world. Although initially it suffered perhaps in the public eye by being considered 'just another attraction' of nearby Sun City, Pilanesberg is a major game reserve in its own right, administered by the National Parks Board of Bophuthatswana, and not merely an adjunct to this holiday complex on its southern border.

At 500 square kilometres, Pilanesberg is the third largest game reserve south of the Limpopo. Since its official opening in 1979, 8 000 large animals of over 20 species have been re-introduced, so that today the park accommodates virtually every mammal of southern Africa with the exception of lion. (Lions will also be introduced as soon as the antelope herds have established themselves.)

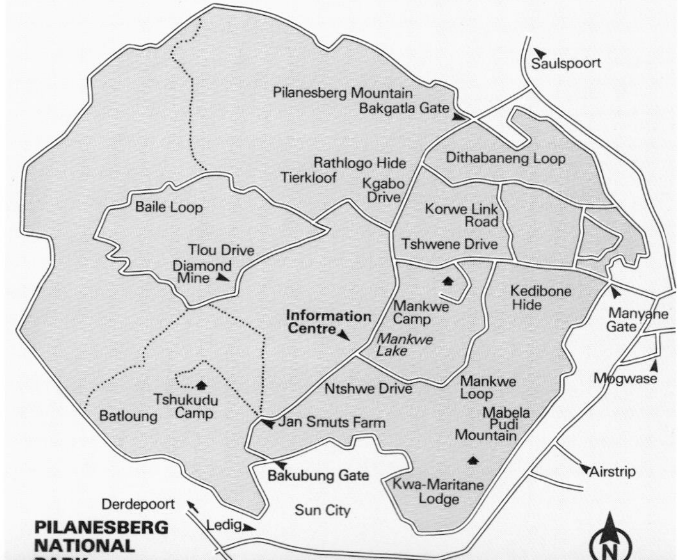

Where impala and springbok co-exist

Although some animals, including kudu, duiker, leopard and hyaena, have been in the Pilanesberg area for centuries, others have been brought in from various parts of the subcontinent: eland and giraffe have been brought from South West Africa/Namibia, Burchell's zebra and waterbuck from the Transvaal, black and white rhino and hippo from Natal, and elephant and buffalo from the Addo Park in the Eastern Cape.

Because Pilanesberg lies in a faunal transition zone, a climatic overlap area where animals and plants from both drier and wetter regions can survive equally comfortably, it is also one of the very few places where one can see both impala and springbok living in the wild.

Apart from its animal population, Pilanesberg has an extremely wide range of bird life — over 300 species have been recorded — and also a range of plants, shrubs and trees that is unique. (It has several hundred specimens of the rare Transvaal Red Balloon Tree — there are only a handful of others in the rest of the country.)

The animals, birds and plants of Pilanesberg are not the only attrac-

The park's vegetation makes it ideal for black rhino and giraffe, and provides a beautiful setting for the communal eating 'boma' at the Mankwe tented camp.

tions. The very topography makes the area a feast for the eyes. There are granite koppies, thickly forested ravines, natural lakes, typical northern Transvaal bushveld — and also rolling grasslands and gently wooded areas more reminiscent of central than southern Africa.

To reach Pilanesberg from Johannesburg, travel to Rustenberg either via Hartbeespoort Dam and the R27, or else via the town of Magaliesburg and the R24. (From Pretoria, take the R27 west to Rustenberg.)

From Rustenberg, drive 6,2 km on the Swartruggens road (R27), then turn right onto the Boshoek/Sun City road (R565). After a further 32,5 km, turn right again onto the Heystekrand/Sun City road. From here you have a choice: either turn left after 500 m to enter Pilanesberg through the Bakubung Gate, or else continue for some 15 km past Sun City, then turn left to enter through the main gate at Manyane. (There is an entrance fee.)

Times for entry and game-viewing

The park is open between 05h30 and 19h00 from April to August, and between 05h00 and 20h00 during the rest of the year. Within the park there are about 100 km of good, all-weather gravel roads, comprising a number of loops and scenic drives.

Two cool, dark hides overlooking waterholes are worth lengthy stops — the Kedibone Hide and the Ratlhogo Hide. (Park in the parking areas that have been set aside nearby, then walk in, so that you do not disturb the wildlife.)

Although animals can be seen at all times throughout the park, plan your game-viewing for the cooler hours of early morning and late afternoon. During winter, when animals tend to stay close to dwindling water supplies, the viewing is generally better than in the hot summer season.

While most traces of the earlier human presence within the park have been eradicated, some historical areas have been preserved — such as the site of Jan Smut's farm, and old diamond and fluorite mines.

The beautiful old building that was formerly used as the Pilanesberg Magistrates' Court has also been preserved and has now been put to use as an information centre.

The information centre's shop, and the larger supermarket at Manyane on the eastern side of the park, do supply basic requirements, but be sure to take your own food and refreshments if you wish to stop at any of the many picnic and braai sites within the park.

Arranging accommodation

The Bophuthatswana Government firmly believes that the Pilanesberg National Park should be seen as a national asset, and not merely as a playground for foreign tourists. Accordingly, the park's first director, Jeremy Anderson, says that emphasis has been placed on the education of the local population. Controlled professional hunting will eventually be allowed in the park, and the meat from culled excess animals will be sold cheaply to the nearby population. Part of the proceeds from hunting will also be used to assist small local businesses in the area.

Daily tours of the park are run from nearby Sun City, but it is also possible to stay overnight within the park itself. Accommodation includes the luxury Kwa-Maritane timeshare lodge, and the Tshukudu camp in the south-west of the park. The camp consists of four double bungalows which must be rented as a single entity. Other camps are the tented Mankwe and Kololo camps, the dormitory-type Bosele camp for large groups, and the Manyane caravan park at the main gate. For bookings and further information, write to The Reservations Officer, Pilanesberg National Park, Box 1201, Mogwase 0302, Republic of Bophuthatswana; or telephone 014652 then 2405, 2408/9 or 2426/7 ●

A trio of white rhino lumber leisurely away from the shores of Lake Mankwe.

Springbok Antidorcas marsupialis.

Into the rugged Magaliesberg — to Hartbeespoort and Breedt's Nek

Our route leads first to the Magaliesberg and the Hartbeespoort Dam, then we follow the northern slopes of the Magaliesberg, cut by rugged gorges, and pass through typical northern Transvaal bushveld to reach the Buffelspoort Dam. Here we turn south and cross the Magaliesberg over the scenic Breedt's Nek. All but 13 km of the route is tarred.

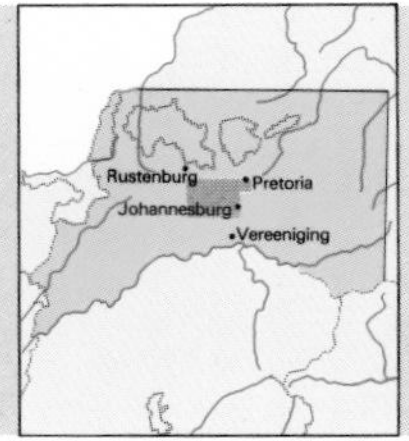

Johannesburg (260 — 280 km)/ Pretoria (240 — 260 km)
Magaliesberg
Hartbeespoort Dam
Breedt's Nek

IF YOU ARE STARTING FROM Johannesburg, drive first to Fourways in Sandton — this is a four-way intersection with the R564 running east/west and the R511 running north/south. Drive onto the R511, heading north, and note your kms. (If you are starting from Pretoria, leave the city by driving west on the R27 for Pelindaba, and join the route at the R27/R511 intersection — see below.)

After driving 15,2 km from Fourways on the R511, turn left to stay on the R511 for Hartbeespoort/Pelindaba. After a further 7,8 km you cross the Hennops River, and you pass on your left the Hennops Pride Pleasure Resort. (This resort has picnic and braai facilities, swimming, water-slides, trampolines, horse-riding and go-karts. There is an entrance fee.)

The road now winds through a series of kloofs, and roughly 2,5 km from the Hennops resort you pass on your right a hill covered with aloes. You cross the Hennops River twice more, and pass other resorts on both sides of the river. 9,1 km from Hennops Pride you reach a four-way junction with the R27 from Pretoria. (Travellers from Pretoria join our route at this junction, roughly 15 km from Pretoria's outskirts.) Note your kms at this junction and drive north-west for Schoemansville on what is now the R27/R511.

3,8 km later you crest a hill and you can see ahead of you the Hartbeespoort Dam and the long summit of the Magaliesberg. 1,1 km after this you pass on your right a stone cross set on top of a small koppie — this commemorates the Anglo-Boer War hero General Hendrik Schoeman, who farmed nearby. (The town of Schoemansville was named after him.)

8,6 km after noting your kms, turn right if you would like to visit what is claimed to be the largest fresh-water aquarium in Africa. It houses almost all species of South African fresh-water fish, and also crocodiles, seals and penguins. An entrance fee is charged.

Note your kms at this turn-off to the aquarium, and continue on the R27 towards Schoemansville. After 3 km turn right onto the R514, which leads towards Pretoria. 900 m later, turn left into the parking area for the Hartbeespoort Cableway. The ride to the summit makes a memorable introduction to the Magaliesberg. From the top there are panoramic views. (There is a refreshment kiosk alongside the upper cableway station, also shaded picnic and braai places, water and toilets.)

After descending from the mountain, retrace your route to the R27 and turn right — noting your kms. After 2,3 km, in the centre of Schoemansville, you reach on your left the entrance to the large Hartbeespoort Snake and Animal Park (entrance fee, see opposite). Picnicking is allowed in the grounds on terraced lawns overlooking the lake, and short boat trips around the lake are sometimes available. Across the road from the park there is a hotel that serves lunches and snacks, and a number of other establishments in the town also offer meals.

Kosmos and Breedt's Nek

Continue on the R27 towards Rustenburg. 1,1 km from the Snake and Animal Park you pass through a short tunnel, then you drive along the top of the Hartbeespoort Dam wall. 1,8 km later you reach a crossroads where the R513 leads right, the R512 leads left, and the R27 continues straight ahead. Here a decision is needed: If you have already lunched, turn left onto the R512 — noting your kms. If you wish to stop now for a picnic lunch, turn right onto the R513. (There are two picnic areas along this road. On your right after 1,6 km is Fiestaland, with merry-go-rounds, country-and-western music, shaded braai places, water, toilets and a kiosk. 300 m further, also on your right, there is the less developed Crocodile River Picnic Site on the Johan Rissik Estate, with shaded braai places, water and toilets. Both areas have entrance fees.)

If you choose to picnic at one of these places along the R513, then return to the R27/R512/R513 crossroads after lunch, and drive straight across onto the R512 — noting your kms. (If you chose not to turn onto the R513, then you will have turned left at the crossroads onto the R512.) The R512 climbs over Commando Nek, then sweeps down into the Magalies River valley, with the Hartbeespoort Dam becoming visible again on your left.

After 1,7 km on the R512, turn left onto the access road into Kosmos — a 4,8 km drive that skirts the shore of the dam. The little settlement of Kosmos is noted for its flower-filled gardens and attractive views over the water.

Retrace your route out of Kosmos and back to the R27/R512/R513 crossroads, and now turn left onto the R27 towards Rustenburg — noting your kms. You pass a number of flower nurseries and vegetable stalls on both sides of the road. After 5,3 km continue straight ahead where the R27 turns off right to Rustenburg.

You now pass through citrus groves, then typical northern Transvaal bushveld. On your left are the northern slopes of the Magaliesberg, gashed by river gorges to expose cliffs of red rock. After 31,6 km turn left for Maanhaarrand (immediately after passing the Buffelspoort Holiday Resort) and note your kms again at the turn. 3,1 km later you pass a turn-off left to the Buffelspoort Dam.

6,8 km after this turn-off to the Buffelspoort Dam, turn left onto the Maanhaarrand road, noting your kms again. The tarred surface gives way to gravel almost immediately, and the road begins to wind up the northern slopes of the Magaliesberg towards Breedt's Nek. After 5,1 km, shortly before reaching the summit of Breedt's Nek Pass, park on the shoulder of the road for a panoramic view.

Buffelspoort Dam provides 'seaside' excitements.

TIGERS AND CHIMPS ON THE HIGHVELD

The Hartbeespoort Snake and Animal Park occupies a long stretch of the narrow strip of land lying between the main road and the north-eastern shore of the dam.

The park contains an excellent reptile collection, and also lions, tigers, leopards, cheetahs and chimpanzees. Snake and seal demonstrations are held regularly at the park.

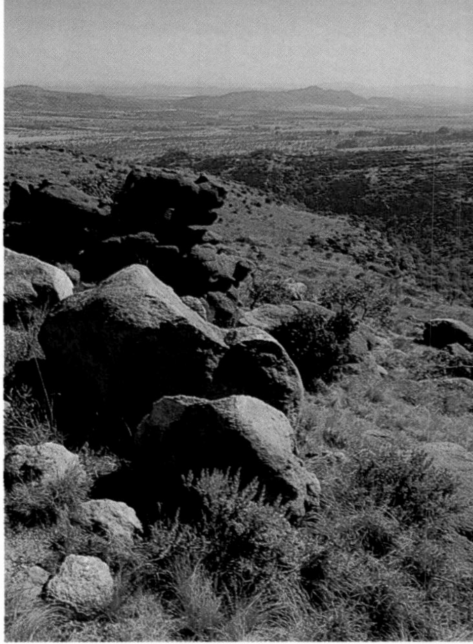

Looking north from Breedt's Nek to Buffelspoort.

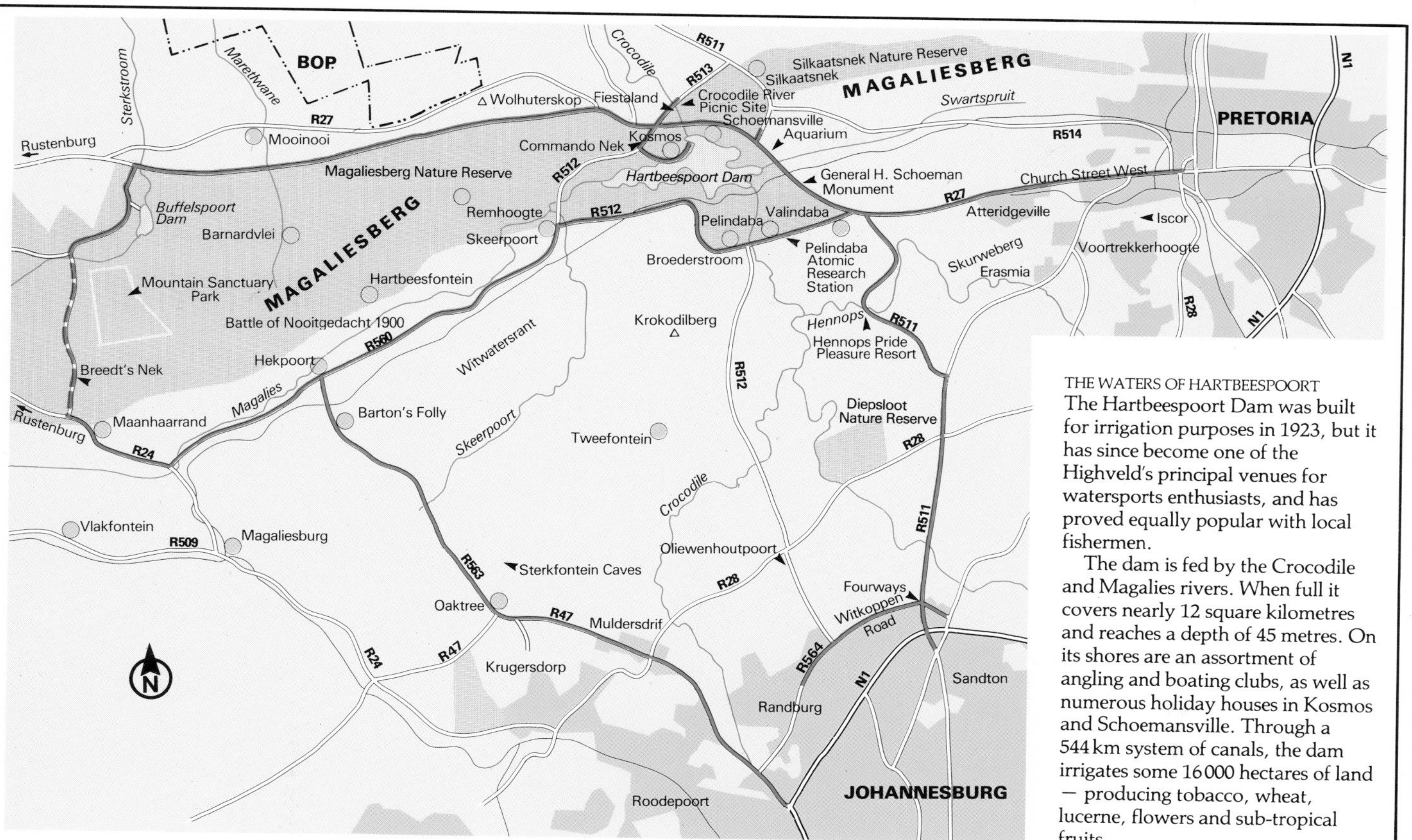

THE WATERS OF HARTBEESPOORT

The Hartbeespoort Dam was built for irrigation purposes in 1923, but it has since become one of the Highveld's principal venues for watersports enthusiasts, and has proved equally popular with local fishermen.

The dam is fed by the Crocodile and Magalies rivers. When full it covers nearly 12 square kilometres and reaches a depth of 45 metres. On its shores are an assortment of angling and boating clubs, as well as numerous holiday houses in Kosmos and Schoemansville. Through a 544 km system of canals, the dam irrigates some 16 000 hectares of land — producing tobacco, wheat, lucerne, flowers and sub-tropical fruits.

Flowers bloom near Hekpoort in the warm and fertile Magalies Valley.

Weekends see Hartbeespoort Dam transformed into a watersports playground.

SOARING TO THE MOUNTAIN TOPS

The 1,2 km Hartbeespoort Cableway soars upwards from the lower slopes of the Magaliesberg to a station at the summit. The journey lasts for a thrilling five minutes, and from the top of the mountain there are magnificent views over the surrounding countryside — the Magaliesberg range itself marking the division between southern and northern Transvaal. The cablecar runs every day of the week from 08h00 to 16h00 (except Friday afternoons). It is advisable, however, to check on the wind conditions before setting out — Tel. (01211) 30706.

PREHISTORIC MAANHAARRAND

The village of Maanhaarrand (mane ridge) between Breedt's Nek and Hekpoort is named for the steep rocky ridges of the Magaliesberg, which here resemble the maanhaar (mane) of a lion. The village lies in the centre of an area rich in prehistoric rock engravings — the precise origins of which are unknown. According to one theory they date back to the Late Stone Age, but no certain dates have been attached to them. Also found in the area are the remains of hundreds of Iron Age villages — in which fragments of pottery, bone, and human skeletons have been found.

Continue over Breedt's Nek Pass, to reach a T-junction with the tarred R24. Turn left onto the R24 towards Krugersdorp, noting your kms. You now pass through Maanhaarrand (see above). After 8 km on the R24, turn left onto the R560 for Hekpoort, noting your kms again. The road winds through a picturesque farming area with the craggy spine of the Magaliesberg towering on your left. After 12,6 km you reach a junction with the R563 — leading south on your right. Again a decision is needed:

If you are returning to Pretoria, continue straight ahead here on the R560 — after 21,5 km turn right onto the R512 for Pretoria, which will bring you to the R27/R511 junction at which you joined the route in the morning.

If you are returning to Johannesburg, turn right onto the R563 and note your kms. After 3,5 km you pass Barton's Folly on your left — a small fort built during the Anglo-Boer War by Major-General G Barton. Continue on the R563 through hilly, sunburned country. The R563 merges with the R47. 23 km after noting your kms, turn left to remain on the R47, which leads into the north-western suburbs of Johannesburg and links up with the N1 ●

AA Office AA House, 66 De Korte Street, Braamfontein 2001 Tel. (011) 4035700
AA Office AA House, 395 Schoeman Street, Pretoria 0002 Tel. (012) 283829
SA Tourism Board Carlton Centre, Commissioner Street, Johannesburg 2001 Tel. (011) 3315241

The weathered rocks of the Magaliesberg glow golden under a summer sky. This is the principal recreation area for the Highveld.

Ancient cliffs — where battles raged and vultures soar

IN GEOLOGICAL TERMS the Magaliesberg is no more than a ripple in the earth's crust, but the range has a formidable presence and its own distinctive atmosphere — a huge wall of sunburned rock reaching steeply up into the clear skies of the Highveld, rich in memories of human drama.

The name Magaliesberg means 'Magali's Mountain'. Magali (or Mohale) was a chief of the Po people who were living in the area when the Voortrekkers arrived during the 19th century. The range stretches in an almost unbroken line for roughly 125 km, from east of Pretoria to west of Rustenburg. The peaks reach to over 1 800 m above sea level, but this is seldom more than 300 m above the surrounding Highveld.

The Magaliesberg region is particularly rich in rock engravings, which palaeontologists have as yet been unable to date. According to one theory they were completed during the Late Stone Age, but there is still no idea as to who executed them. Maanhaarrand, a tiny settlement at the foot of the mountains, lies at the centre of an area that is famous for these engravings, and the remains of many small Iron Age villages have also been found in the vicinity.

Early last century the rebel Zulu general Mzilikazi settled in the Magaliesberg area after fleeing the wrath of the Zulu king Chaka. For some years he and his followers enjoyed the area's plentiful water supplies and hunted the game, which ranged from the larger antelope to herds of elephant, but clashes with neighbouring clans and early white settlers eventually drove Mzilikazi further north — where he founded the Matabele (or Ndebele) nation in what is now southern Zimbabwe. By the time the Voortrekkers settled in the Magaliesberg area, the central Transvaal was occupied by the Po people under Chief Magali.

Blockhouses

During the Anglo-Boer War the British built stone blockhouses in the area to watch for approaching Boer commandos, and many of these old blockhouses can still be seen. One of the best preserved examples is Barton's Folly — a few kilometres south of Hekpoort (see pages 128-9). It is clearly visible from the road, but is unfortunately on private property.

Many clashes between Boer and British took place in the Magaliesberg. Probably the most famous of these was the Battle of Nooitgedacht on 13 December 1900, in which a large British force under General Clements was defeated by the Boers under Generals Beyers, Kemp, De la Rey and Smuts. The battle site lies about 10 km north-west of Hek-

Left: *Lush green of a mountain kloof.*

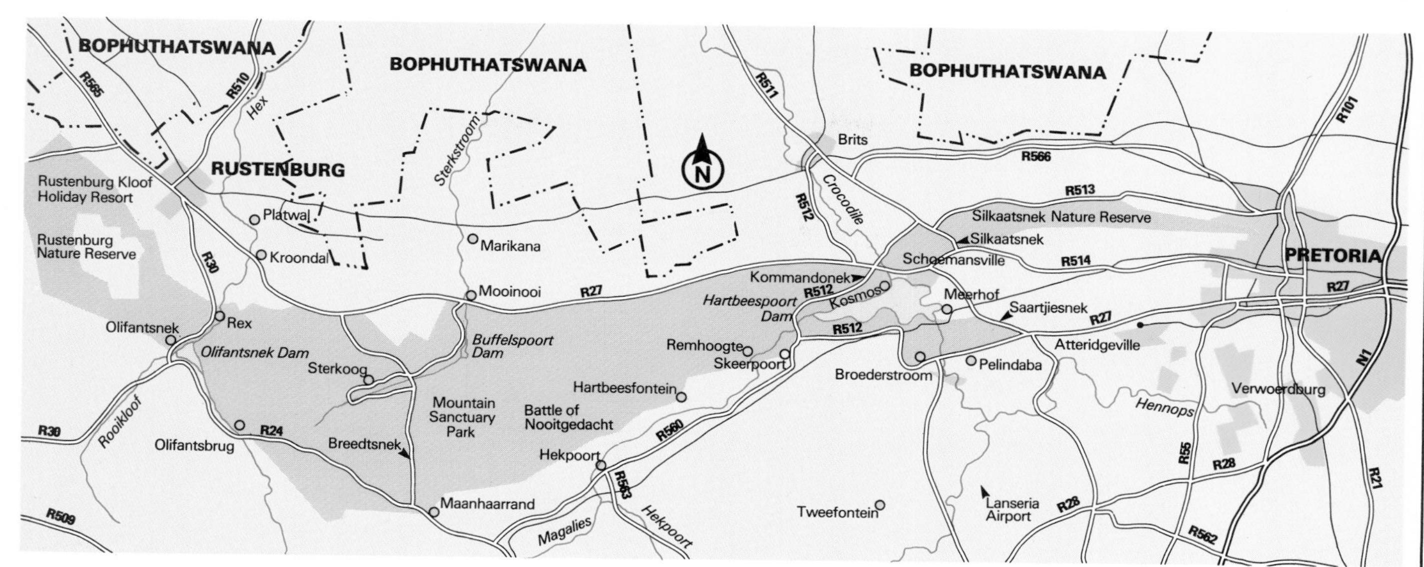

Mountain home of the Cape vulture.

poort, almost directly beneath the modern communications tower that stands like a sentinel on top of the range. Apart from a memorial to the dead, who have since been moved to the old cemetery in Krugersdorp, little evidence remains of the fierce encounter. The Boers surprised the British by climbing Breedt's Nek and moving east along the mountain crest under cover of darkness.

Wild character

Today the Magaliesberg is at peace with its memories. It has also managed to retain a great deal of its original wild character, even though encircled by major highways.

Although the large herds of elephant and antelope that once grazed on the mountain's well-watered slopes are now gone, a surprising number of smaller animals still live in inaccessible wooded ravines — duiker, steenbok, oribi, jackal, monkey, baboon and the rare brown hyena.

Cape vultures breed on many of the sheer south-facing cliffs, particularly those to the west of Olifantsnek. Their breeding sites are easily identifiable by their white droppings on the cliff faces. Until recently the vultures were in danger of extinction, many dying from a calcium deficiency caused by the lack of big predators to crush the bones of dead animals on the veld. Such bone fragments, rich in calcium, are a vital part of the vulture diet. Today feeding stations have been established where crushed bone is provided.

With the influx of white settlers on the Highveld, several dams were built in the Magaliesberg. Although these are primarily for irrigation purposes, they have also become popular recreation areas. By far the largest is the Hartbeespoort Dam (see pages 128-9) where a deep, narrow wall erected some sixty years ago impounds the Crocodile River. Some 30 km away to the west lies Buffelspoort Dam on the Sterkstroom, and a further 30 km west the Hex River has been dammed at Olifantsnek.

The best way to absorb the atmosphere of the Magaliesberg is to walk along its slopes. As yet there are no public walking trails, but control of some areas has been handed over to the Mountain Club of South Africa. Permission to visit these areas may be obtained from the Southern Transvaal Mountain Club Section, P O Box 4066, Johannesburg 2000, or from the Northern Transvaal Mountain Club Section, P O Box 1418, Pretoria 0001. There are also several private resorts in the area that include short walking trails.

The 2 898 ha Rustenberg Nature Reserve incorporates a farm that once belonged to President Paul Kruger, and is where the first sable antelope was recorded in 1836. Long since hunted to extinction in the region, sable and a wide variety of other antelope have now been reintroduced. The reserve offers two-day walking trails as well as the 4,6 km Peglerae Trail, which takes two to three hours. Adjoining the Rustenburg Nature Reserve is the Rustenburg Kloof Holiday Resort — a popular recreational area incorporating a well-wooded kloof with a variety of spectacular walks into the mountains ●

An unspoilt wilderness only a couple of hours drive from Johannesburg.

Right: *Farmland near Hekpoort.*

The Highveld as it used to be before the arrival of the Voortrekkers

Today's drive begins with a tour of the Suikerbosrand Nature Reserve, which enables the visitor to see what the Highveld looked like prior to the arrival of the Voortrekkers and the gold-seekers. We then visit the Vaal Dam, and the fine collection of old vehicles housed in Heidelberg's Transport Museum. All but 12 km of the route is tarred.

Pretoria (280 – 300 km)
Johannesburg (230 – 250 km)
Suikerbosrand
Vaal Dam
Heidelberg
Museum

FROM CENTRAL JOHANNESBURG, drive south along Eloff Street. On the outskirts of the central city area, take the entry ramp left for the M2. Follow the 'M2 East' signs, and note your kms as you turn onto the M2. After 9 km on the M2, at the Geldenhuis interchange, exit onto the N3 towards Heidelberg, noting your kms. (If you are starting from Pretoria, drive south on the Ben Schoeman Highway – R28 – and continue straight onto the N1 at the Brakfontein interchange. At the Buccleugh interchange, exit left onto the N3 – the Eastern Bypass around Johannesburg – and note your kms as you cross the M2 at the Geldenhuis interchange.)

After 3 km bear left to stay on the N3, and after travelling 29 km from the Geldenhuis interchange, exit left for the R550. Turn right onto the R550, crossing over the N3, and drive a fraction over 6 km along the R550 before turning left at the sign for 'Suikerbosrand Nature Reserve'. A further 4 km brings you to the gates of the reserve (entry fee; see opposite). Shortly after entering the reserve you reach the administrative centre at Diepkloof. Close to the modern building you will see one of the first farmhouses built in the Transvaal – dating back to 1850.

Suikerbosrand Nature Reserve

Suikerbosrand is famous for its 80 km of hiking trails, which offer walks of up to six days duration. But of more interest to the day visitor is the Cheetah Trail – an easy 4 km walk that starts and ends at the Diepkloof centre. (Report at the centre if you intend walking this 60-80 min trail.) A feature of the walk is that it passes the site of a kraal dating back to the late stone age.

From Diepkloof, drive through the reserve on the tarred tourist route – turning left at the T-junction 2,4 km after the start. The road winds amongst rocky ridges and grasslands studded with grazing antelope, and it is easy to imagine oneself back on the Highveld of two centuries ago. Roughly 27 km along the route there are picnic sites on your left.

After a further 9,5 km turn left at the crossroads on the western edge of the reserve. (The road right leads into the Kareekloof Public Resort, which is surrounded by the Suikerbosrand Nature Reserve but is a separate entity.)

Suikerbosrand to the Vaal Dam

Drive out of the reserve through the gate on the western boundary, and after roughly 300 m turn left onto the R557. After a further 3,9 km you reach a junction with the R551, and a decision is needed: if you have lunched and it is now mid-afternoon, turn left onto the R551 for Heidelberg and miss out the Vaal Dam section of the route. (You will enter Heidelberg on the R42, which becomes H F Verwoerd Street. Turn right into Voortrekker Street, then go left into Voortrekker Street Extension where the road forks on the far side of the town. The Transport Museum is on your right after 300 m.) If you toured Suikerbosrand more quickly, drive across the R551 and continue on the R557.

3,6 km further along the R557 you reach the R42, which runs between Vereeniging and Heidelberg. Drive straight across the R42 and continue on the R557, and note your kms where the road surface changes to gravel. After 1,3 km go left at the fork for 'Platkoppie'. 7 km later you cross the Suikerbosrand River, and after 12 km on gravel turn right onto the tarred R549 – noting your kms.

After 18,7 km on the R549 you cross the R54, and after a further 6,4 km you pass a picnic area on your left on the banks of the Vaal Dam. 1,3 km later, turn left into another picnic area (entry fee, braai sites, toilets, water, boat-launching areas).

Vaal Dam to Heidelberg

When you leave the picnic area, first turn left onto the R549 and park on your left after 3,2 km for a view of the dam wall and the Vaal River – then note your kms and return along the R549 towards Heidelberg. After some 51 km, as you enter Heidelberg, turn left onto the R23/R103. 400 m later turn right, and after a further 1,3 km turn right into Voortrekker Street Extension, to reach the Transport Museum on your right 300 m later (see opposite).

When you leave the museum, drive north-west along Voortrekker Street. This takes you past a number of buildings that date back to pioneer days.

Voortrekker Street leads you to the R103. Turn right onto the R103, then follow the signs onto the N3 to return to Johannesburg or Pretoria. (If you turn left onto the R103, 500 m will then bring you to the Heidelberg Kloof Resort on your right. There are several attractive walks here, and other resort facilities.) ●

AA Office AA House, 66 De Korte Street, Braamfontein, Johannesburg 2001 Tel. (011) 4035700
AA Office AA House, 395 Schoeman Street, Pretoria 0002 Tel. (012) 283829
The Officer-in-Charge Suikerbosrand Nature Reserve, Private Bag H616, Heidelberg 2400 Tel. (0151) 2181/2/3
Heidelberg Transport Museum Old Railway Station Building, 126 Voortrekker Street Extension, Heidelberg 2400 Tel. (0151) 6303

Rolling grasslands of the Suikerbosrand Reserve.

SUIKERBOSRAND NATURE RESERVE

Suikerbosrand (sugar bush ridge) Nature Reserve has been made up out of portions of 65 farms and now comprises 13 337 hectares of grasslands, rocky ridges and steep, tree-filled kloofs. Cheetah and smaller members of the cat family roam free, as do many antelope species – including eland, kudu, wildebeest, hartebeest and blesbok. Also to be found here are hyenas, jackals and baboons. There are 200 species of birds in the reserve, and a plant to look out for is the *Aloe davyana.* This is one of the smallest members of the aloe family, barely reaching 50 cm in height, whose salmon-pink flowers brighten the dry veld in the late winter months.

Kareekloof – a popular family holiday resort.

Hypoxis rigidula *brightens the Transvaal Highveld.*

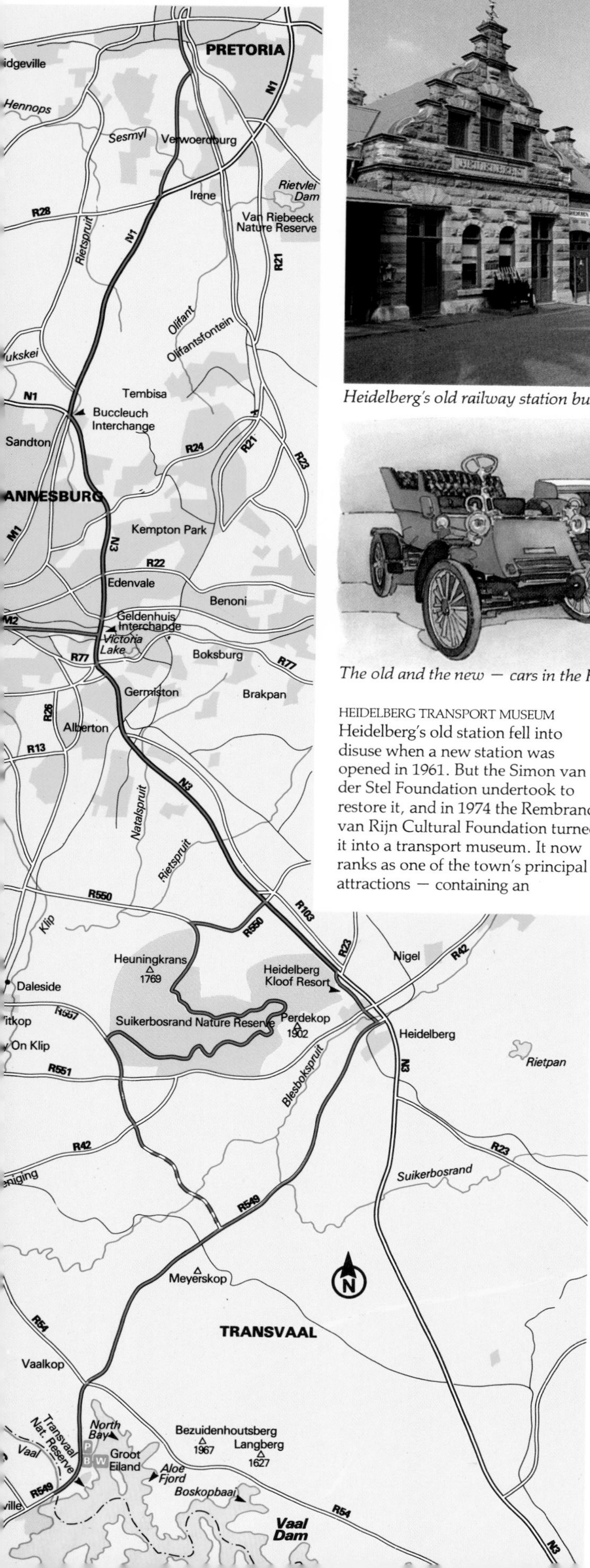

Heidelberg's old railway station building — home of the Transport Museum.

The old and the new — cars in the Heidelberg Transport Museum.

HEIDELBERG TRANSPORT MUSEUM

Heidelberg's old station fell into disuse when a new station was opened in 1961. But the Simon van der Stel Foundation undertook to restore it, and in 1974 the Rembrandt van Rijn Cultural Foundation turned it into a transport museum. It now ranks as one of the town's principal attractions — containing an impressive assembly of early means of transport. The museum includes South Africa's largest collection of bicycles, tricycles and motorcycles, and more than 30 veteran motor cars dating from as far back as the turn of the century. Other interesting exhibits include a sedan chair from the time of Louis XV, and a field ambulance from the Anglo-Boer War.

HEIDELBERG

The historic little town of Heidelberg was born around a crossroads — where the old wagon trails to and from Pretoria, Potchefstroom, Bloemfontein and Durban all intersected. A German trader named Heinrich Ueckermann established a trading store here in 1860, and he named the area after his old university town in Germany. A town was officially proclaimed here several years later, and this soon became the focal point of the region.

During the Witwatersrand gold rush the burgeoning town was able to boast as many as 18 hotels, and for a brief spell of three months during the Anglo-Transvaal War of 1880-81 it was the seat of the Transvaal government. The boom days are now past, but the town remains an attractive place and retains much of its original settler character.

THE HIGHVELD'S INLAND SEA

The large and impressive Vaal Dam, built in 1936, serves as Johannesburg's principal source of water. It is also a popular sailing and watersport venue, and has numerous resorts dotted along its several hundred kilometres of shoreline. Though it seems geographically impossible, much of the Vaal Dam's water comes from the Natal midlands. The water is pumped over the Drakensberg and released into the Sterkfontein Dam. From here it flows into the Wilge River, which eventually runs into the Vaal Dam. Along the dam's northern shores lies the Vaal Dam Nature Reserve, which has typical Highveld vegetation. The reserve is popular with watersport enthusiasts and holidaymakers — in spite of the dam's low water level during the last few years.

Weekends see the Vaal Dam transformed into a moving mosaic of bright sails.

The heights of Hillbrow and Berea overlook the busy streets of a part of the city that reputedly never sleeps. In the centre is the Strijdom Tower.

A tent town that grew into a 'Golden City'

JOHANNESBURG, South Africa's largest city, is barely recognisable as the rough mining town that sprung up in the 1880s after the discovery of the rich vein of gold that runs beneath the Witwatersrand (white water ridge). It still bustles with the energy of those early days, but the ragged rows of fortune-seekers' tents have been transformed into a mighty commercial and industrial centre — known locally as the 'Golden City'.

The city centre is dominated by mine dumps and skyscrapers, and yet its concrete heart is girded by a 'green belt' of parks, nature reserves, walking trails and game parks that provide a welcome breather for the millions who live and work here.

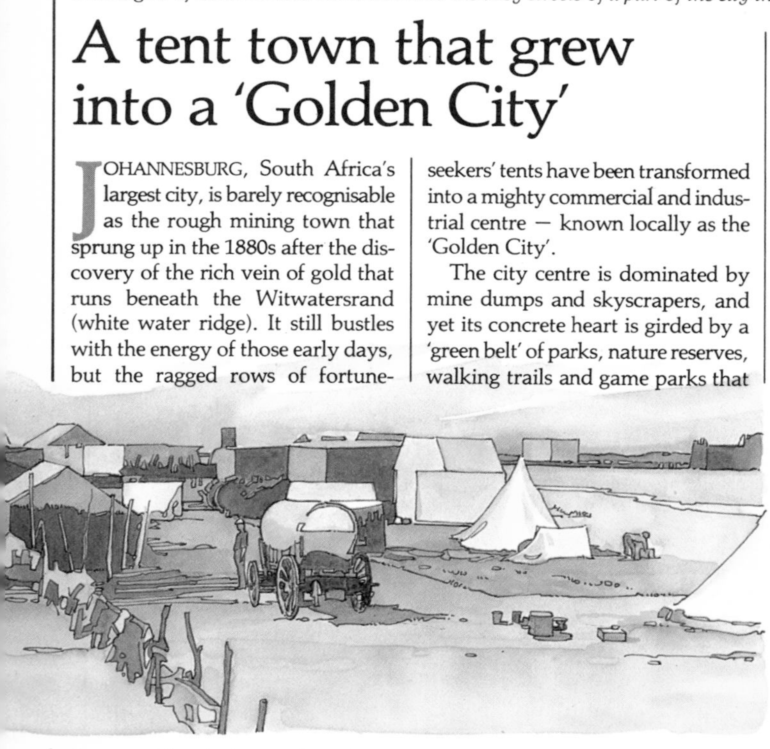

From small beginnings... diggers' camp in 1887.

Heading for the hills

Within sight of the ridge on which the thronging high-rise suburb of Hillbrow is situated lies *The Wilds*, a beautiful 17 ha park straddling two hills that flank Houghton Drive. The park has a tea garden, and several plant houses, and is criss-crossed by paths that offer excellent views northwards from an environment of indigenous plants, streams and ponds.

There are still finer views from nearby Linksfield Ridge, where the 6 ha *Harvey Nature Reserve* has been established. From here you can see as far as the Magaliesberg in the north, the Hillbrow skyline in the west, and an assortment of colourful mine dumps in the south. There is a fairly easy walk through the nature reserve from the entrance on Linksfield Drive, or the more energetic may prefer walking up the koppie from *Gillooly's Farm* on the eastern side. The 44 ha Gillooly's Farm on Boeing Avenue, Bedfordview, is a popular site for weekend rambles, picnics and braais. It offers wide open spaces, shade trees, a dam, pretty streams and a children's playground.

Another nature reserve that incorporates the rocky ridges so typical of this part of the country is *Melville*

Autumn colours in Emmarentia Park.

Koppies on Judith Road, Emmarentia. The reserve is administered by Johannesburg's Parks and Recreation Department (tel. 7771111), and is a sanctuary for wildlife and birds, as well as containing many plants indigenous to the highveld. It also contains a number of archeological sites. The reserve is open only from September to April on the third Sunday afternoon of each month, but special tours can be arranged through the Johannesburg Council for Natural History (tel. 6463612).

Further west, at *Kloofendal Nature Reserve* on Galena Avenue, Roodepoort, visitors can walk amidst indigenous flora on the slopes of an attractive koppie. There are several old gold-mining shafts that can be inspected. The reserve is run by the Roodepoort Parks and Recreation Department (tel. 4721439), and is open from sunrise to sunset from September to April.

Also in Roodepoort is the *Witwatersrand National Botanic Garden*, situated on Totius Road, Poortview, at the foot of the Roodepoort Falls (or Witpoortjie Falls, as they are also known). The garden offers short walks in attractive surroundings, and is open on Sunday afternoons (tel. 6621741 weekdays). It specialises in indigenous Transvaal plants, and houses two rare inhabitants — a breeding pair of endangered black eagles.

An extensive hilly area south of Johannesburg is enclosed in the *Klipriviersberg Nature Reserve*, which has an entrance on Fairway Drive, Kibler Park. This reserve offers many hours of walking on grassy hills, where aloes flourish and visitors can expect rewarding birdwatching. Slightly further from the city, in a south-easterly direction, the *Suikerbosrand Nature Reserve* is an attractive area for both drives and walks (see pages 132-3), while a number of recreational areas near Pretoria are also within easy reach of Johannesburg (see pages 120-131).

Parks and lakes

Many of the urban parks in Johannesburg are linked by the *Braamfontein Spruit Trail*, a hiking route that roughly follows the course of the spruit, and its tributary, the Sandspruit. The first section of the trail takes you through the historically interesting area of Parktown, with its many buildings designed by architect Sir Herbert Baker around the turn of the century. Brochures on the trail are available from the Johannesburg Publicity Association, or from the Sandton Civic Foundation in the old fire station alongside Sandton Civic Centre (tel. 8841317).

The largest park along the Braamfontein Spruit Trail is *Delta Park*, on Road No 3, Victory Park. This comprises 104 ha of grassland, with tall shade trees, a number of braai sites, and a children's playground. The highlight of the park is the *Florence Bloom Bird Sanctuary*, which has a number of viewing points along its fenced perimeter where visitors can watch a wide variety of water birds on the small lake. Near the sanctuary there is a charming conservation museum in the headquarters of the SA Nature Conservation Centre and the Wildlife Society of Southern Africa (open Tuesdays to Sundays; tel. 7821531; small entry fee).

Another favoured spot for birdwatching is the *Melrose Bird Sanctuary*, where more than 120 species have been recorded. Situated on Melrose Street, this forms part of the larger James and Ethel Gray Park close to the M1, and features part of the Sandspruit Trail.

The Oppenheimer Fountain — bronze impala leap gracefully over jets of water.

In front of the city library.

The Braamfontein Spruit has been dammed on the border of *Jan van Riebeeck Park*, creating Emmarentia Dam — venue for sailing, boardsailing and rowing, and haven for many species of ducks and geese. On the dam's western shore lies the *Johannesburg Botanic Garden* (on Olifants Road, Emmarentia), famed for its rose garden, herbs, hedges and trees. The garden has a tea kiosk, and is popular for picnics.

The whole of the Witwatersrand is dotted with lakes that provide attractive settings for walks and picnics. *Florida Lake* in Florida, Roodepoort, has braai facilities, a restaurant, miniature golf, an Olympic-sized swimming pool, and a caravan park on its shores, and offers good birdwatching. Germiston's *Victoria Lake*, home of several watersport clubs, is surrounded by attractive lawns and tall trees, with braai sites, a refreshment kiosk, a restaurant, plus a playground for children. For those who miss the sea, *Wild Waters* in Boksburg offers a pool with artificially created waves, water chutes and several other water attractions (open summer only; tel. 8266736).

Closer to the city, *Rhodes Park* in Kensington has a restaurant and tea garden overlooking its beautifully landscaped parkland and lake. *Zoo Lake* and its surrounding *Hermann Eckstein Park* in Parkview bustle over weekends. There are rowing boats for hire here, children's playgrounds, rolling lawns for picnicking or strolling on, a restaurant and tea garden, and the small islands in the lake are rich in birdlife. Over weekends artists display their works here in the open air.

Across Jan Smuts Avenue, also in Hermann Eckstein Park, are the *Johannesburg Zoological Gardens* (tel. 6462000; entry fee; open daily; parking on Upper Park Drive). The zoo is home to thousands of birds, reptiles and mammals, many of them in enclosures without bars, and the

Mists soften the outline of headgear at a gold mine outside Johannesburg.

Making electricity for the city.

big cats and primates are particularly popular with visitors. Other attractions include farmyard animals, donkey rides for children on Sundays and public holidays, refreshment stalls, a restaurant, and a small, open-air museum containing South African rock art.

On the eastern side of the park, on Erlswold Way, Saxonwold, is the *Museum of Military History* (tel. 6465513; open daily except Good Friday and Christmas; small entry fee on Sundays and public holidays). The museum contains relics from World Wars I and II, and the Anglo-Boer War, as well as a reference library, and gives audio-visual presentations on Sundays. Light refreshments are sold in the grounds.

Pioneer's Park on the banks of Wemmer Pan, La Rochelle, offers a variety of family entertainments. *Santarama Miniland* on the northern bank contains scale models of many of the country's best-known buildings, and there are working models of trains, a ferry in the mini-harbour, and a cable car. There is a souvenir shop and a restaurant, and at busy times there are rides on a miniature train or river boat. (Open daily; entry fee; tel. 268800.) Also on the banks of the pan is the *James Hall Museum of Transport*, a fascinating collection of horse-drawn, steam-powered and motor-driven vehicles. (Open daily except Good Friday and Christmas; miniature train rides on Sundays.) The *Illuminated Musical Fountains* on the south bank of the pan offer an unusual performance — the fountains play to the rhythm of popular tunes (Tuesday to Sunday evenings from September to June; tel. 7771111). The area surrounding the fountains is popular for pre-performance sunset picnics.

Viewed from the air, swimming pools dot the gardens of homes in Johannesburg's wealthy northern suburbs.

The *Rynfield Children's Park and Bunny Park* in Pretoria Road, Rynfield, Benoni, teems with rabbits and farmyard animals, including ducks, geese, cows, pigs, goats, sheep and chickens (open daily). Along the same lines, but on a smaller scale, is *Bokkie Park* in Southvale Road, Boksburg (closed Thursdays, Good Friday and Christmas).

In a more elegant vein are the displays given on Sunday mornings by the national Lippizaner team, trained in the manner of Vienna's Spanish Riding School. The beautiful white horses perform their graceful high-stepping at the National Equestrian Centre in Dahlia Road, Kyalami (tel. 7257911 or 7022103; entry fee; booking advisable).

Animals in the wild

If you prefer to view animals in their natural habitat, the *Johannesburg Lion Park* on the old Pretoria-Krugersdorp road offers a 10 km drive in the course of which you will see many species indigenous to this part of Africa — including the scores of lions that give the park its name, black wildebeest, gemsbok, impala, blesbok, zebra and ostrich. You can have your photograph taken with a lion cub (when they are small enough), and there are braai and picnic areas, a restaurant, curio shop, swimming pool, and an old Ndebele village. (Open daily; entry fee per car; tel. 7081814.)

West of Krugersdorp on the R24 lies the 1 400 ha *Krugersdorp Game Reserve*, which also offers a lion camp, as well as an unspoilt area of veld inhabited by 21 game species (including giraffe, white rhino, eland, blue wildebeest, kudu, impala, buffalo and blesbok). The reserve has a restaurant, picnic and braai sites, chalets and caravan sites. (Open daily; entry fee per car; tel. 6601076.)

A fine display of modern art is housed in the Johannesburg Art Gallery.

The stately Johannesburg Public Library — home of the Africana Museum.

A group of miners relax outside their tent at Rietfontein in 1887. The Rietfontein mine lies just north of the main Witwatersrand Reef near the present airport road.

The *Transvaal Snake Park* on the R101 at Halfway House has an excellent selection of reptiles, and specialises in African snakes. Crocodiles, alligators and terrapins are kept in custom-made pools, while some of the exotic species are kept in a terraquarium in which the climate is specially controlled. Snake-handling demonstrations are held daily. (Open daily except Christmas; entry fee; curio shop; tel. 8053116.)

The lure of gold

There are many reminders around Johannesburg that the city owes its existence to the gold-mining industry. There is even a monument to mineworkers near the Civic Centre. For an excellent glimpse of what the mining town looked like in the 1880s, you can visit the reconstruction at *Gold Reef City*, near the Xavier Street exit from the M1 (general entry fee, plus additional fees for some of the attractions; tel. 4944100; open daily). Gold Reef City stands on the site of the old Crown Mine, and visitors can descend the mine's 14 Shaft for an underground tour — or browse through a number of fascinating historic exhibits; shop for curios; take a ride in a vintage steam train or a horse-drawn carriage; see the Great Johannesburg Experience audio-visual presentation; or visit one of the many restaurants and old-time pubs in the grounds. The centre also has a theatre, and mine-dancing displays are held daily.

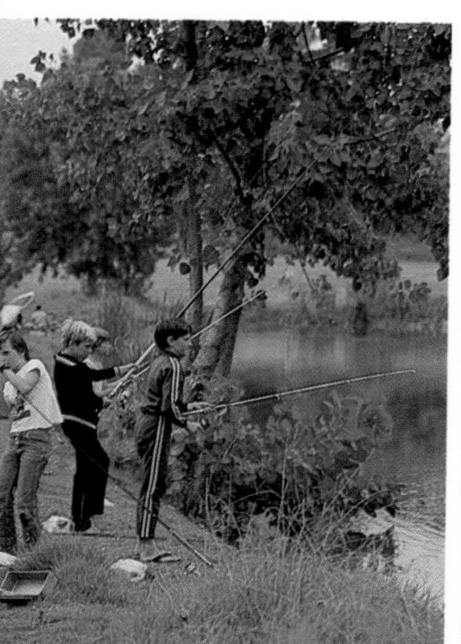

Waiting for a bite at Delta Park.

The Chamber of Mines arranges tours to active gold mines, but note that advance booking is essential (tour fee; tel 8388211). *Premier Diamond Mine* at Cullinan, east of Pretoria, offers tours of the mine and diamond sorting house on weekdays (tel. 01213-30050). The tours last 90 minutes to two hours, and again booking is essential. The mine entrance is on Oak Avenue, Cullinan, and you drive past the company's open-air mining museum on your way to the gate.

Two diamond cutting companies in Johannesburg offer tours of their works: *Krochmal and Cohen Diamond Cutting Works* at 240 Commissioner Street (booking a few days in advance is essential; tel. 3378803); and *Binyan Diamond and Gem Cutting Works*, Paulshof Building, on the corner of Twist and Plein streets (entry fee; tel. 230721).

The gold industry led to the establishment of the *Johannesburg Stock Exchange* as companies were formed to tackle the more expensive process of digging deep underground when the easily worked gold ran out. The stock exchange is now housed in an ultra-modern building on the corner of Pritchard and Diagonal streets, and conducted tours and audio-visual presentations are offered twice a day on weekdays (tel. 8336580).

Historic treasures

Johannesburg's past is beautifully captured by displays at the *Africana Museum* in the Johannesburg Public Library, Market Square (open daily; tel. 8363787). Of special local interest is the Johannesburg Room, but the museum also has an excellent collection of old South African photographs, prints and original paintings, as well as other historic memorabilia. The museum's ethnology section, and its collections of art, toys, dolls, costume and lace are housed in the *Africana Museum in Progress* in the Old Market Building, Bree Street, Newtown (open daily; tel. 8368482).

Also in the historic old Public Library building is the *Geology Museum*, which contains a vast collection of interesting rock samples, displays on the history of the earth, replicas of famous diamonds, and a special section with fluorescent rock samples (open daily; tel. 8363787).

Around the corner at 90 Market Street is the *Barclays Bank Museum*, housed in a historic bank building, and containing fascinating displays relating to banking in South Africa, money through the ages, and photographs of old Johannesburg (open Monday to Saturday; tel. 8365887).

The *South African Railways Museum* in the Station Concourse,

The M1 motorway north of the city.

De Villiers Street, collects diverse exhibits relating to railways, harbours and airways, and its prize items include the first locomotive to be used in the old Transvaal republic in 1890 (open weekdays; tel. 7739114). A gallery, which is opened on request, contains an excellent collection of commissioned landscapes by South African artist Pierneef.

The *Bensusan Museum of Photography* on the corner of Empire and Hillside roads, Parktown, is famous for its collection of old cameras, magic lanterns, photographs and plates — of interest to the enthusiast and layman alike (open daily except Good Friday and Christmas; tel. 6428727). The photographic section of the Johannesburg Public Library is also housed here.

Costumes and cars

A charming display of historic clothing is the focus of the *Bernberg Museum of Costume*, on the corner of Jan Smuts Avenue and Duncombe Road, Forest Town. Models are placed in period rooms, and there are fine collections of fans, buttons, parasols, fobs, pipes and handbags (open daily except Good Friday and Christmas; tel. 6460716). A private collection of old Cape furniture and Africana — said to be one of the finest in the country — may be viewed on Saturdays at *Die Ou Kaaphuis Museum*, 120 Main Street, Sandton (closed Christmas; tel. 8841054; small entry fee).

The *Kleinjukskei Motor Museum* on the corner of Witkoppen and Selborne roads, Randburg, has an extraordinary collection of old cars, motorcycles, photographs and toy cars. There is also a swimming pool here, braai and picnic areas alongside the river, a restaurant and tea garden (open Tuesday to Sunday; entry fee; tel. 7041514).

Roodepoort Museum, housed in the modern Civic Centre on Theatre Street, Roodepoort, is a fine local history museum focusing on the discovery of gold, and the changing lifestyles of the people who came to settle in the area — from the Voortrekkers' ox wagons to the art deco furniture of the 1930s (open Tuesday to Sunday except public holidays; small entry fee; tel. 6722147).

The history of Jewry in South Africa is traced through exhibits at the *Harry and Friedel Abt Museum*, in the premises it shares with the SA Jewish Board of Deputies Library in Sheffield House, on the corner of Kruis and Main streets (open Monday to Friday except Jewish and public holidays; tel. 3310331). Also on display here are superb examples of Jewish ceremonial art.

One of South Africa's most comprehensive collections of art is housed in the *Johannesburg Art Gallery and Sculpture Garden* on Klein Street, Joubert Park (open Tuesday to Sunday except Good Friday, Christmas and any Monday after a public holiday; tel. 7253180). The gallery has excellent 19th and early 20th century English and French paintings, a 17th century Dutch collection, more than 2500 prints dating from the 15th century to the present, and a contemporary international collection. The sculpture is exhibited in courtyards, as well as in the gardens in the surrounding *Joubert Park*. The park itself is well frequented. It has an open-air theatre, a conservatory with tropical plants, large hot-houses, restaurant, and a giant open-air chessboard.

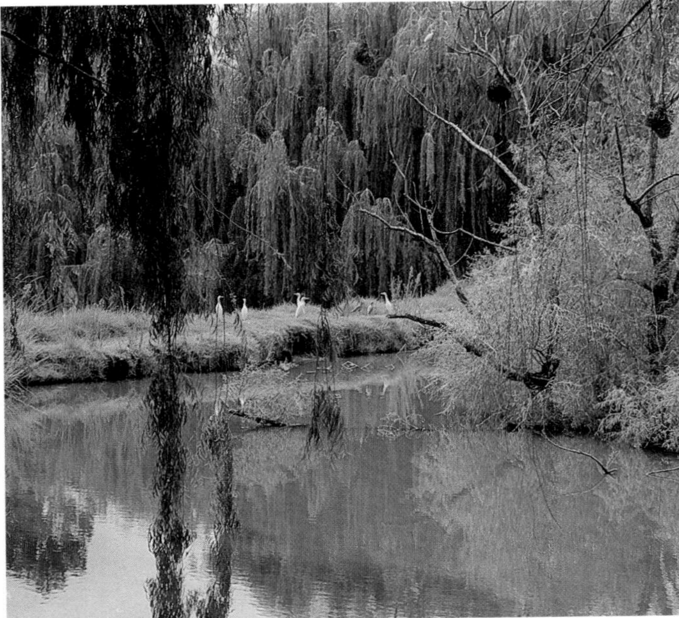

Tranquil waters of the Florence Bloom Bird Sanctuary in Delta Park.

The *Gertrude Posel Art Gallery* on the University of the Witwatersrand campus features a wide variety of temporary exhibitions, and also a permanent exhibition of African art in its Studio Gallery (tel. 7163632).

Campus tours and museums

The university offers tours of the campus on the first Wednesday of the month from February to November (tel. 7163162). Tours include a visit to the reconstructed library of South African Prime Minister Jan Smuts, containing his vast collection of books; and to the Africana collection in the William Cullen Library. Special tours can be arranged to take in any of the other fascinating collections on the campus, which include the Bernard Price Institute of Palaeontological Research (valuable fossil remains); the Hunterian Museum (an extensive collection of anatomical specimens, skeletons and masks made by African peoples); the Museum of the Zoology Department (collections of butterflies, insects, marine life and other animals); the Moss Herbarium's collection of tens of thousands of pressed flowers; the Social Anthropology Museum (specialising in items relating to African peoples); the Bleloch Museum of geology; and the Archeology Museum (primitive artefacts, rock engravings and beads, mostly from Africa). To visit any of these, telephone 7163162. The university's *Planetarium* in Yale Road offers shows from Thursday to Sunday (tel. 7163199).

Lily-filled pond in The Wilds, a 17 ha park within sight of Hillbrow.

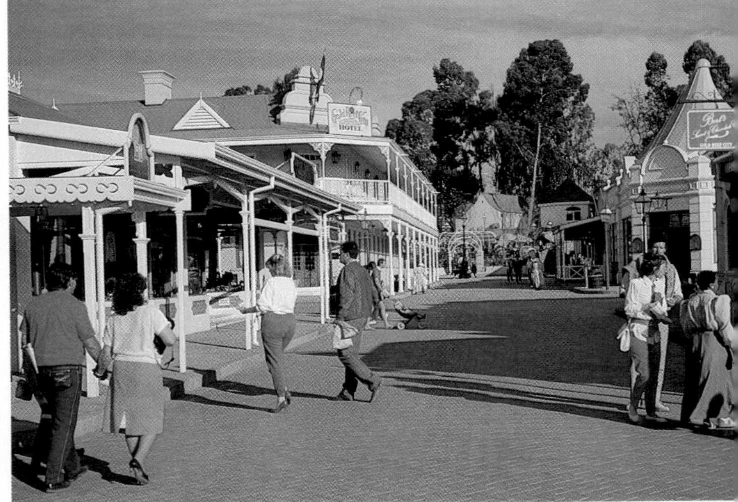

The reconstruction of Johannesburg as a mining town of the 1880s.

Another museum administered by the university is the *Adler Museum of the History of Medicine*, SA Institute of Medical Research, Hospital Street, Hillbrow. The well-displayed exhibits include the history of medical and surgical practices, an African herb shop, a traditional-doctor's room, an old pharmacy, and a turn-of-the-century operating theatre (open Monday to Friday; tel. 7253436 or 7252846).

Those interested in aviation may visit the *South African Air Force Museum* at Lanseria Airport (open weekdays; tel. 6591041). The museum is housed in a hangar, and contains memorabilia of the air force, as well as several carefully restored old aircraft. The airport has a cafeteria, from where you can watch light aircraft taking off and landing.

On the outskirts of Krugersdorp are the *Sterkfontein Caves*, where remains of the prehistoric 'apeman' *Australopithecus africanus* were found in 1896. Walking tours through the caves, with their spectacular lime deposits and underground lake, leave every half hour and last about an hour (take warm clothing; open Thursday to Sunday and public holidays; tel. 6696611).

Glittering interior of Sandton City.

Seeing the sights

The vast *Carlton Centre* in the centre of the city offers not only many hectares of shops, but also a grand panorama of the city from the 50th floor at the Carlton Panorama (entry fee; tel. 3311010). The Johannesburg Municipality runs bus tours on Sunday afternoons, alternating between a trip to the south of the city and one to the northern suburbs. The bus leaves from the corner of Main and Rissik streets (tel. 8362061; tour fee).

The *South African Broadcasting Corporation* in Auckland Park conducts public tours of their television and radio studios twice a day from Monday to Friday. The tour of the centre, which is one of the largest in the world, also includes visits to the wardrobe and scenery workshops. Booking should be done well in advance, as the tours are popular (tel. 7143744). Tickets may also be obtained for attendance at live radio and television shows (tel. 7143744).

For those who enjoy shopping, Johannesburg has much to offer. Hillbrow streets are packed with interesting shops and a flea market; while there is a strong African flavour to the shops at the northern end of *Diagonal Street*, where many herbalists practise their craft. The *Oriental Plaza*, built in an Eastern style, is crowded with shops selling everything from carpets to clothing and curios, and has a number of curry restaurants. A popular flea market is held every Saturday outside the historic *Market Theatre building* on Percy Fitzgerald Square.

One of several restaurants open to the public in Gold Reef City.

The performing arts

Johannesburg has a wealth of theatres and informal venues for the performing arts. The *Civic Theatre* in the Civic Centre complex is the venue for theatre, ballet and opera, often produced by the Performing Arts Council Transvaal (Pact). The *Market Theatre*, which comprises three venues in the old market building, also houses a photographic gallery where temporary exhibitions are held. Other theatres include the *Andre Huguenet* in Kaptein Street, Hillbrow, and the *Alhambra Theatre* on the corner of Beit Street and Sivewright Avenue. (The city in fact contains a great many theatres, see the local press for listings of current performances.)

Johannesburg's historic *City Hall* on Rissik Street is the venue for performances by the National Symphony Orchestra. The beautiful stone building is a national monument, noted for its sumptuous interior, and it occupies the old Market Square site. (The *Rissik Street Post Office* across the road was built in 1897, and is one of the few remaining buildings dating from the days of the old Zuid-Afrikansche Republiek.)

Further information about places of interest in and around Johannesburg and current events can be obtained from the Johannesburg Publicity Association, 84 President Street, Johannesburg, tel. 294961 ●

Old mining headgear looms over Gold Reef City south of Johannesburg.

A winter dawn breaks over the highrise flats of Hillbrow and Berea.

ORANGE FREE STATE & LESOTHO

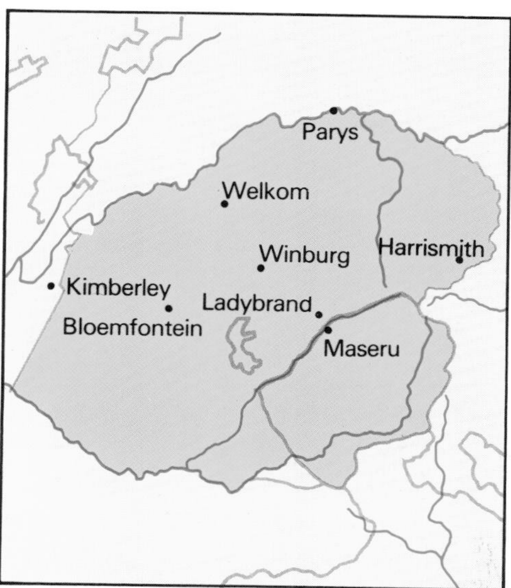

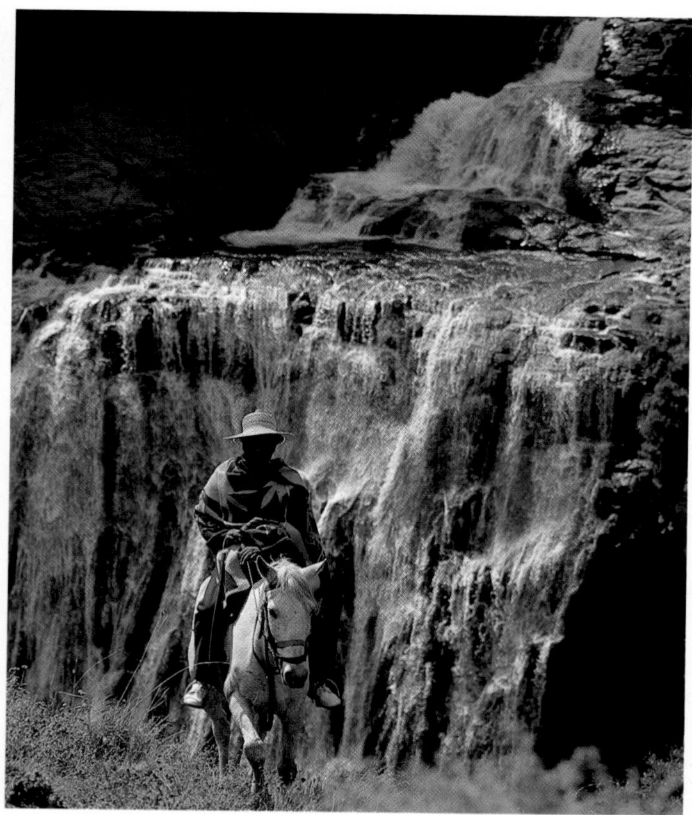

Left: *A lone rock outcrop stands sentinel over the plains of the Orange Free State.* **Above:** *Lesotho's Qiloane Falls — accessible only on horseback.*

Golden Gate's splendour and an eagle's view of the Drakensberg

The eastern Orange Free State is renowned for its magnificent sandstone mountains, and our route winds amongst the most spectacular of these in the Golden Gate Highlands National Park. On our way there we stop off at Sterkfontein Dam, then drive high into the Drakensberg for a view of imposing cliffs — towering over the valleys of Natal.

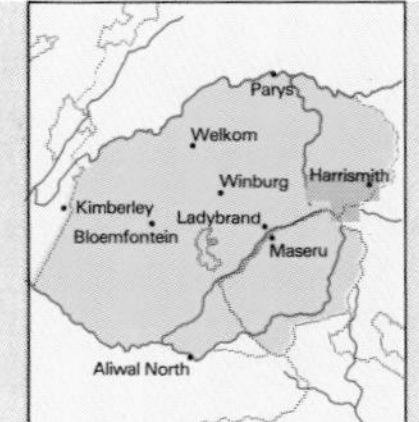

Harrismith
Sterkfontein Dam
Phuthaditjhaba
The Sentinel
Golden Gate
Clarens
270–290 km

LEAVE HARRISMITH by travelling south on Warden Street, noting your kms at the town's historic City Hall. After 200 m turn right at the T-junction, and 500 m later turn left at another T-junction. 2,2 km from the City Hall turn right for Kestell at the fork, then turn right immediately at the T-junction.

You cross the Wilge (willow) River, and 3 km later you cross the Nuwejaarspruit (New Year stream). Immediately afterwards — 6,6 km from the City Hall — turn left for the R712 to Qwaqwa and the R615 to Bergville, noting your kms. You now cross attractive farming country, dotted with farmhouses set amidst tall trees. After 8,7 km turn left at the foot of Baker's Kop onto the R615 for 'Bergville via Oliviershoek Pass', noting your kms.

From this road you can soon see the great escarpment of the Natal Drakensberg ahead of you. After 7,8 km you pass an entrance on your right to a camping area on the banks of Sterkfontein Dam. Beyond the turn-off, to your left and ahead of you, lies the imposing sandstone Kerkenberg, site of Retief Rock (see opposite). 12,5 km after noting your kms, turn right onto gravel for a viewsite overlooking the dam.

Sterkfontein Dam to Witsieshoek

Return along the R615 to the T-junction at the foot of Baker's Kop, and turn left onto the R712 for Qwaqwa, noting your kms. Just over 3 km later you pass the 3 km dam wall on your left. Beyond it you pass an attractive farm on your left with sandstone buildings typical of this area.

Roughly 25 km after rejoining the R712 you can see Qwaqwa mountain ahead of you, with its sheer sandstone cliffs (see opposite). The basalt heights of the Drakensberg are also visible on your left. After 29,4 km on the R712 turn left for Qwaqwa where the road straight ahead goes to Kestell and Golden Gate (your route later). Note your kms at this turn.

You now travel alongside Qwaqwa mountain on your right, towards the homeland of the same name. After 5 km you pass a turn-off into the town of Phuthaditjhaba (Sotho for 'meeting place of the nations'), and the road continues through straggling settlements towards the Drakensberg. Follow the signs for 'Bergoord' and 'Mountain Resort', which will take you southeast onto a gravel road. Roughly 30 km from the R712 you reach a toll gate where you can buy the permit needed for being in Qwaqwa.

2,1 km later pull off the road under a rock overhang on your right for a view into the attractive valley on your left. Continue from here up the pass — after a few hundred metres a view opens up on your right over Lesotho's spectacular Maluti mountains stretching away seemingly without end, and you can see the massive basalt buttress of The Sentinel looming to the west of the Amphitheatre.

4,7 km from the toll gate go right at the fork (left leads to the Witsieshoek Mountain Resort, which serves teas and lunches). Park after a further 1 km, below the Sentinel — a 300 m walk from here brings you to a point from which you have magnificent views over the Royal Natal National Park (see pages 166-7), and across to the Eastern Buttress and the Devil's Tooth at the far end of the Amphitheatre. (Allow 30-40 minutes. The path continues from here to chain ladders that lead to the mountain top, but time does not allow for the full walk on this outing.)

Witsieshoek to Golden Gate

Return through Phuthaditjhaba towards the R712 and exit left for Golden Gate and Harrismith. At the end of the off-ramp turn right for Golden Gate, noting your kms. After 800 m the road surface changes to gravel, and from here you travel through countryside characterised by colourful sandstone formations, and quaint old farm buildings made from the local stone.

After 8,4 km from the off-ramp you pass Silasberg on your left — an excellent example of why Clarens sandstone was formerly known as 'cave sandstone', because of its inclination to erode from below. Roughly 5 km later you can see Rondawelkop on your right alongside a wedge-shaped sandstone formation that juts from the side of the Rooiberge (red mountains).

15,5 km after noting your kms turn left at the T-junction for Golden Gate and Clarens (right leads to Kestell). You cross more farmlands, and after a few kilometres you begin to climb amidst beautiful mountain scenery through the first of several short passes. Soon afterwards the road is tarred for a short distance on the steepest section of the road — at the end of the tarred section pull onto the shoulder of the road for a fine view back over the countryside through which you have been travelling.

Roughly 25 km after noting your kms you enter Golden Gate Highlands National Park (see pages 144-5) — note your kms at the gate. Soon afterwards you enter the colourful valley carved through the sandstone Rooiberge by the Little Caledon River. After 1,8 km you can see ahead of you the distinctive cliffs known as Mushroom Rocks, and 800 m later the road surface changes to tar again. After a further 200 m there is a turn-off on your left to a gravel game-viewing road — a 7 km circular drive across grassy mountain slopes.

Soon afterwards — 3,6 km from the gate — stop on your right at the Glen Reenen reception to pay the entry fee for the park. Cross the road to the parking area at the Glen Reenen campsites (which have braai and picnic places on the banks of the river) for a walk to Mushroom Rocks — a trail that offers an excellent introduction to the geology, flora and birdlife of the park. (The walk starts at the footbridge across the river — allow 40-60 minutes.)

Golden Gate to Clarens

From Glen Reenen continue west, noting your kms as you rejoin the tarred road. After 500 m you pass on your right the sandstone formation known as Brandwag (sentinel), and 600 m later you pass on your left the luxury rest camp also known as Brandwag (there is a dining room and

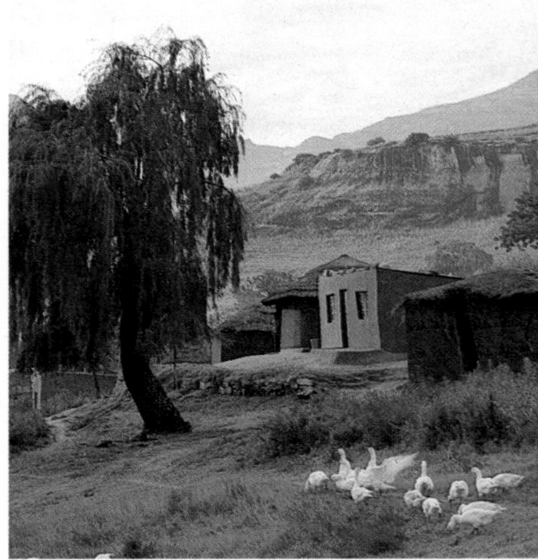

Farm cottages against a typical highland backdrop.

CLARENS

Much of the eastern Orange Free State owes its magnificent scenery to Clarens sandstone — weathered over millenia into fantastic shapes. The rock is named after the picturesque little village of Clarens, which in turn was named after the town in Switzerland where Transvaal President Paul Kruger died in exile in 1904. Kruger's connection with the area dates back to the Boer-Basotho War of 1886, when five men of his Transvaal Commando were killed at the Battle of Naauwpoort. A memorial in the town square commemorates their deaths. The village, founded in 1912, nestles at the foot of sandstone hills, and offers grand views of the Maluti Mountains. Nearby, the Highland Route takes a scenic meander among the foothills of the Malutis to Fouriesburg.

Winter farmland north of the Amphitheatre.

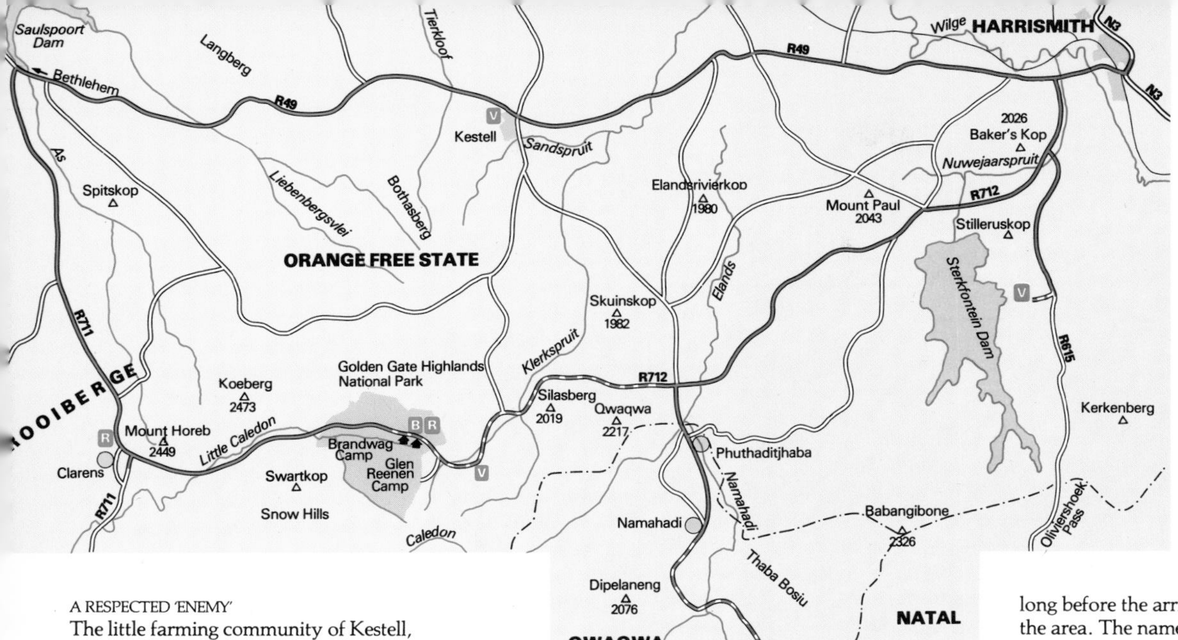

The sheer basalt cliffs of the eastern Amphitheatre.

A RESPECTED 'ENEMY'

The little farming community of Kestell, attractively laid out on a hillside, is named after the Reverend John Daniel Kestell, a respected minister who, among other exploits travelled with the Harrismith Commando during the Anglo-Boer War. His bravery during the Battle of Wagon Hill outside Ladysmith (see pages 168-9) on 6 January 1900, when he ministered to both sides under heavy fire, earned him the admiration of many British soldiers. At their request a small memorial plaque was erected on the hillside where he 'brought succour to friend and foe alike'.

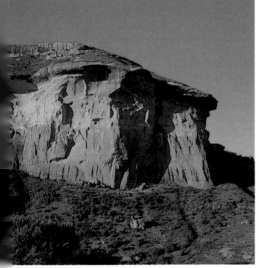

Sunlight washes over Mushroom Rocks.

KERKENBERG AND RETIEF ROCK

On 11 November 1837 a group of Voortrekkers who had outspanned at Kerkenberg near the edge of the Drakensberg escarpment received the glad news for which they had been waiting; their leader, Pieter Retief, had been assured that the Zulus and British traders in Natal would welcome them as new settlers. During the celebrations and thanksgiving the next day — which was also Retief's 57th birthday — the leader's daughter, Deborah, painted her father's name and the date in green on a rock face now known as the Retief Rock. Two days later the party of Voortrekkers, their wagons crammed with their possessions, began their extraordinary journey down the 1 000 m escarpment into the area Retief had described as 'this beautiful land, the most beautiful I've seen in Africa'.

THE 'WHITER THAN WHITE' MOUNTAIN

Qwaqwa, meaning 'whiter than white', was the name the San people gave to the massive sandstone mountain north of the Amphitheatre — long before the arrival of black or white settlers in the area. The name possibly derives from the weathering action on the Molteno sandstone that makes up much of its bulk — the rock is white when freshly exposed, although it later turns a greyish colour.

The name Qwaqwa has now also been given to the area previously known to white settlers as Witsieshoek — based on a corruption of Whêtse, the name of a cattle rustler who was defeated near here when he and his men were trapped in one of the many caves by a commando of Free State farmers in 1856.

The Sentinel trail — pathway to an eagle's world.

coffee shop here).

1,9 km later you pass the small graveyard of the Van Reenen family, on your right alongside Golden Gate Dam, and after a further 200 m you pass between the two sandstone buttresses known as the Golden Gate.

After driving out of the park through its western gate, you enter attractive farmlands nestling at the feet of sandstone mountains. 19 km beyond Glen Reenen you crest a hill and see the town of Clarens straggling across the hillside ahead of you. 2,1 km later you pass a turn-off left for Fouriesburg (the Highland Route) — continue straight on the R711 towards Bethlehem. 300 m beyond the turn-off, turn left for Clarens, and after a further 500 m go left around the town's central square. The quaint old post office and library face the square, and are among a number of the town's early buildings that still grace its streets.

Clarens to Harrismith

Retrace your route out of Clarens, and turn left onto the R711 for Bethlehem, noting your kms. After 1,3 km you pass a turn-off on your left to a hotel (the road also leads to Cinderella Castle — a structure built out of 55 000 beer bottles).

You cross a patchwork of farmlands lined with tall trees, and after 27,6 km on the R711 turn right at the T-junction onto the R49 for Kestell, noting your kms again. After roughly 13,5 km on the R49 the aptly named Langberg (long mountain) comes into view on your left. The road crosses several valleys.

After 45,9 km on the R49 exit left for Kestell, and at the end of the off-ramp turn right at the T-junction. 500 m later turn right into Kestell, and stop after a further 500 m at the imposing church that commands excellent views over the surrounding countryside. It is worth driving through the streets of the little town, with its many old sandstone homes and shops, before returning to the R49 for Harrismith ●

AA Office AA House, 56 Church Street, Bloemfontein 9301 Tel. (051) 76191
Harrismith Tourist Information Municipal Offices, Andries Pretorius Street, Harrismith 9880 Tel. (01436) 21061
Golden Gate Highlands National Park The Chief Director, National Parks Board, Box 787, Pretoria 0001 Tel. (012) 441191 or (014326) 711

Gateway to a mountain paradise — the sandstone cliffs of Golden Gate stand watch over a tranquil park scene.

Where sandstone cliffs tower in blazing gold and burnished copper

BETWEEN THE ROOIBERGE and the Maluti Mountains magnificent sandstone formations have been carved over eons by wind and water to create a brilliant display of gold and copper cliffs. Here, in the peaceful seclusion of the Little Caledon River valley, the Golden Gate Highlands National Park provides a spectacular world for walking, horse-riding, bird-watching and game-viewing.

The 6300ha park, which will double in size when expansion plans are implemented, encloses some of the country's finest highland scenery, where many species of game have been re-introduced to their natural habitat, and where roughly 160 bird species await the bird-watcher.

But it is the geology of the Golden Gate area more than anything else that has established its reputation as a popular holiday resort. Changing light and shadows play on the colourful rock surfaces, creating ever-changing moods, and myriad birds and small mammals make their homes amongst the rocks.

Magnificently coloured rock strata form a backdrop to the Brandwag camp.

Fossil remains

Geologists divide the park's rock formations into the Drakensberg lava (the layer of basaltic rock that forms the cliff-tops of the highest peaks); the Clarens sandstone (known first as Cave Sandstone' because of the many hollows in its cliffs); the red and purple Elliot formation; and the coarse-grained Molteno formation, with its cream colour streaked with blue and grey shale and mudstone.

Many millions of years before recorded history began, Golden Gate was inhabited by mammal-like reptiles, whose fossils have been left behind in the mudstone and siltstone beds. Prehistoric men left their stone implements as evidence of their sojourn here, and a rich legacy of magnificent rock art and stone and bone artefacts points to the existence of the San people in the area.

The San were lured to the region by its abundant game, which was never threatened by the conservative hunting of these little men. But the early years of the 19th century brought devastation to the wildlife of the area. Trekboer parties, armed with rifles, all but wiped out the vast herds of antelope, and soon after this the period of drought, war and deprivation that followed in the wake of the Zulu battle for supremacy in Natal rang the death knell for the larger animals of the south-eastern Orange Free State. Tribes scattered in all directions, placing extra burdens on limited food supplies.

It was during this period that the Sotho nation was established under the leadership of Moshoeshoe, who gathered the remnants of tribes fleeing from Natal and formed Masada-like settlements on the area's flat-topped mountains to resist attacks from outsiders.

A strife-torn past

In the early history of the nation, their land — known to them as Lesotho (place of the Sotho people) and to white colonists as Basutoland — extended through the Golden Gate area to the summit of the Rooiberg (red mountain) range on the northern side of the present park. However, the Sotho people soon clashed with the Voortrekkers over land and cattle, and during the resulting 'Basuto Wars' of 1858-68 the OFS/Lesotho border was moved to its present position along the Caledon River.

Strife again tore through the Golden Gate area during the Anglo-Boer War. A large force of Boers was cornered here by several British brigades who sealed off the passes. The Boer General Christiaan de Wet talked a small band of men into escaping, and their success persuaded a larger group to attempt a break-out through Golden Gate. At the steep corner just east of the present Glen Reenen camp — known as Kanondraai (canon corner) — the Boers lost a Krupp field gun down a cliff. About 1500 Boers later surrendered to the British at Klerksvley, a farm east of the park. The British blew up Boer ammunition wagons, scattering bullets and cartridge cases in the veld. Hikers often still find remnants of these today.

By the time this war broke out, the area had already been occupied by farmers for a number of years. Many of the Boer women were taken to concentration camps, and farms were burnt in the 'Scorched Earth' campaign. But one doughty woman, 'Ouma' (granny) Cilliers, hid out in a cave just north of the historic

Cilliers homestead that still stands near the park's stables.

Exploring the riches of Golden Gate park can be done either by car or on foot. Two gravel game-viewing drives — which are to be tarred — wind through the mountains. They offer the best viewing early in the mornings and in the evenings. From a car you are likely to spot any of about 100 species of birds, including the rare bearded vulture (lammergeyer), black eagle, Cape vulture and a variety of other raptors. The mammals you are likely to see include oribi, mountain reedbuck, grey rhebuck, springbok, blesbok, black wildebeest, Burchell's zebra and eland. The roads also offer panoramic views of the highlands, the Malutis and the Drakensberg.

Hiking trails

On foot there is even more to be seen. Apart from the larger game, you are also likely to spot smaller mammals such as dassies, mongooses and otters, and a wider variety of birds — up to 160 species. Langtoon and Golden Gate dams offer particularly good bird-watching.

The camp offices provide maps and information on the many trails in the park. There is a two-day, 30 km hiking trail known as the Rhebok Trail, on which hikers stay overnight in a hut that sleeps 18 people. This trail forms part of the National Hiking Way. It includes a climb of Generaalskop and takes you through lovely mountain scenery, crossed by streams and waterfalls.

Parts of the Rhebok Trail can also be used for day hikes, and a number of other shorter walks radiate from the camps at Glen Reenen and Brandwag. Starting from Glen Reenen are the following walks:

Mushroom Rocks This 40-60 minute walk takes you under magnificent overhangs of Clarens Sandstone formations (see pages 142-3).

Echo Ravine You walk up a mini-canyon and through a steep-walled ravine onto the top of the sandstone, from where there are fine mountain views. (Allow 60-90 minutes.) There is an optional link with the Brandwag Route.

Brandwag Route This steep path takes you through indigenous forest to the top of the Brandwag Buttress, one of the most spectacular formations in the park. (Allow 30-45 minutes.) From here there is an optional but strenuous route to the top of Wodehouse Kop.

Langtoon Dam Heading south from Glen Reenen, you walk through a secluded valley to the dam. This 30-40 minute walk through valley grassveld is good for bird-watching. There is an optional extension to Buffalo Cave — an overhang inhabited for many centuries by successive waves of people.

From Brandwag camp, there are the following paths:

Brandwag Buttress A steep path leads to the top of this magnificent formation. (Allow 30-40 minutes.)

Holkrans Route Another good bird-watching walk, this 60-90 minute trail leads south along the base of attractive cliffs, then up a series of ladders to the Holkrans caves, famed for their honeycombed sandstone formations.

From the Gladstone Information Centre, where the administrative offices are housed, walks lead to:

Bushman Paintings This short (1,5 km) walk leads north to a collection of San rock art. (Allow 20-30 minutes.)

The highlands setting offers hiking, bird-watching and game-viewing.

Cathedral Cave This elaborate rock formation is reached along a path leading south. (Allow about 2 hours for the 6 km round-trip.)

Close to the tarred park road you can take a short walk to Golden Gate Dam, and visit the family graveyard of the Van Reenens, who were among the earliest farmers in the area. One of the family members, Mrs S J L van Reenen, named the pair of imposing buttresses that flank the valley 'Golden Gate' when she and her husband first moved here in the 1870s — hence the name of the park.

During peak season the park offers a programme of guided walks for visitors, and throughout the year horse-riding trails leave from Gladstone. There are a minimum of three rides each morning lasting an hour each (with more rides laid on during holidays), as well as short pony rides for children. Or you may choose a two-hour afternoon ride along the Rhebuck Spruit, which includes a visit to the historic Noord Brabant homestead, a sandstone building typical of the early architecture of the area. Two-day horse trails, on which you camp overnight in Buffalo Cave, can be arranged on request.

Park officers warn visitors to steer clear of the upland portions of the park in thunderstorms, and to take warm clothing when walking above the sandstone, as sudden blizzards are a hazard at any time of year. On valley walks it is wise to avoid solitary eland bulls — their peaceful appearance is deceptive, as they are wild and dangerous.

Accommodation in the park is provided at Brandwag, in luxury chalets or in the main building, which also has a restaurant, ladies' bar, coffee shop and sports facilities. Glen Reenen has more rustic accommodation in huts, as well as a campsite, shop, braai and picnic facilities for day visitors, and a swimming dam.

Enquiries and reservations for accommodation should be made through the National Parks Board offices in Pretoria (012-441191), Cape Town (021-4195119) or George (0441-746924) ●

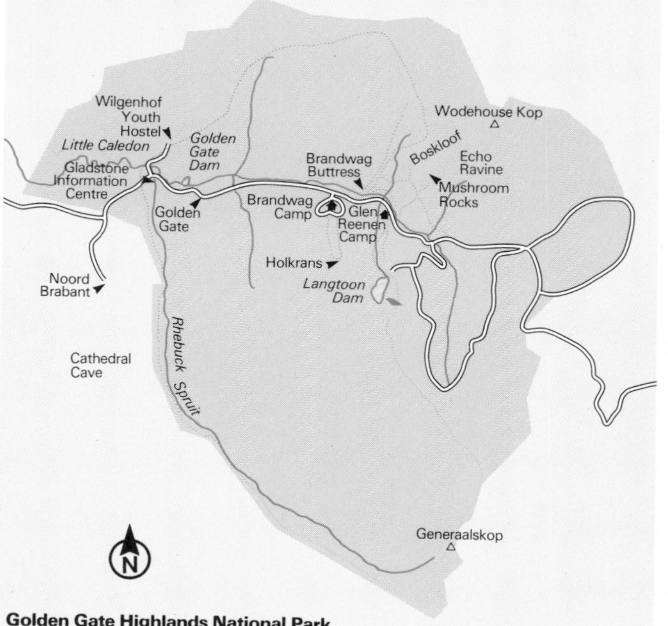

Golden Gate Highlands National Park

Glen Reenen — on the Little Caledon.

The spectacular Brandwag Buttress.

The Appellate Division of the Supreme Court — South Africa's final court of appeal.

A Voortrekker capital built around a 'spring of flowers'

IT WAS PROLONGED drought that led farmers, in the early years of the 19th century, to seek new grazing far from the settled areas of the Cape. One of these farmers was Rudolph Martinus Brits of Swellendam. In about 1820 Brits crossed the Gariep or Groot (great) River — officially known as the Orange River — to settle in the territory referred to as Transorangia.

He found a favourable site next to a clear, perennial spring, and was joined here by his nephew, Johan Nicolaas Brits. The older Brits, moved by the *trekgees* (wanderlust), later wandered away to the south-east to settle on the banks of the Koringspruit (corn stream). But his nephew stayed on at the spring with his family, and built a house of 'poles and spars, roofed with reed and plastered inside and out'. He dug a furrow from the spring, and planted a fruit orchard — of which two pear trees in the grounds of the Presidency **(1)** are said to be survivors. His wife laid out a flower garden, and this in time gave its name to the spring that had brought them here — *bloemfontein* (spring of flowers) **(2)**.

As more and more Voortrekkers settled in the territory, which at that time had its 'capital' at Winburg, a British resident or political agent was appointed: Major Henry Douglas Warden, a veteran of the frontier wars, and reputedly an illegitimate descendant of Prince Charles Edward Stewart, the Young Pretender.

Warden settled himself at Brits's Bloemfontein farm, and paid Johan Brits £37.10s for the improvements he had made — Brits being considered merely the occupier and not the owner of the land. Warden and his family moved into Brits's house, and clay huts were built for his troops in the vicinity of the present Queen's Fort **(3)**. This small settlement, when the territory between the Orange and Vaal rivers was annexed as the Orange River Sovereignty in 1848, became the new 'capital'. Major Warden laid out the town himself, naming several streets after members of his family — including Charles, Henry, Douglas and Elizabeth.

A 'prettily situated' village

Within a year or so of its founding as a 'town', Bloemfontein was described as 'a small village consisting of some half-dozen houses and some huts, prettily situated on the banks of a stream having as its source a bubbling fountain . . .'

When the Republic of the Orange Free State was declared in 1854, the town expanded across the Bloemspruit (flower stream) towards Bloemfonteinberg — which is now known as Naval Hill **(4)**. This new name was given during the Anglo-Boer War, when a Naval Brigade was formed to man heavy artillery — some of it removed from the turrets of warships — to oppose Boer gunners. Naval Hill is now the site of the Franklin Nature Reserve **(5)**, crossed by a network of roads from which a variety of game can be seen.

Within the reserve is an old astronomical observatory, built by the University of Michigan in the United States, and now used as a theatre **(6)**.

Statue of General Christiaan de Wet in front of the Raadsaal.

On the slopes of Naval Hill, and visible from Andries Pretorius Street, is the shape of a horse, picked out in white-washed stones. This was built by men of the Wiltshire Regiment during the Anglo-Boer War, and is a replica of a similar white horse on a hillside in the regiment's home county of Wiltshire.

The site of the original 'Bloemfontein' **(2)** is in the caravan park off Selborne Street, and is marked by a column bearing the city's crest. Although the oldest legible gravestone in the old cemetery dates from September 1846, the oldest existing building is probably the First Raadsaal (council chamber) **(7)** in St George's Street. This was completed in May 1849, and described as 'a large, fine building . . . nothing very handsome, but good, strong, plain work.' Originally it served as church and school, as well as the meeting-place of the Legislative Assembly and the municipal officials.

Although the Queen's Fort **(3)** — which is also known as Bloemfontein Fort — was built some months before the First Raadsaal, it subsequently collapsed in heavy rains, and was entirely rebuilt in 1879. It is now a military museum, and houses particularly fine collections of firearms and regimental badges.

Rebuilding a 'disgrace'

Just around the corner from the First Raadsaal, in the continuation of President Brand Street known as Eunice Street, is the imposing old Presidency **(1)**. Warden's old house, based as it was on the humble dwelling of Johan Brits, was continually extended to serve as the official residence of Orange Free State presidents, but was eventually described as 'a disgrace to the country'. A new building was erected in 1860, but this too was soon judged unsuitable. In

The First Raadsaal in St George's Street.

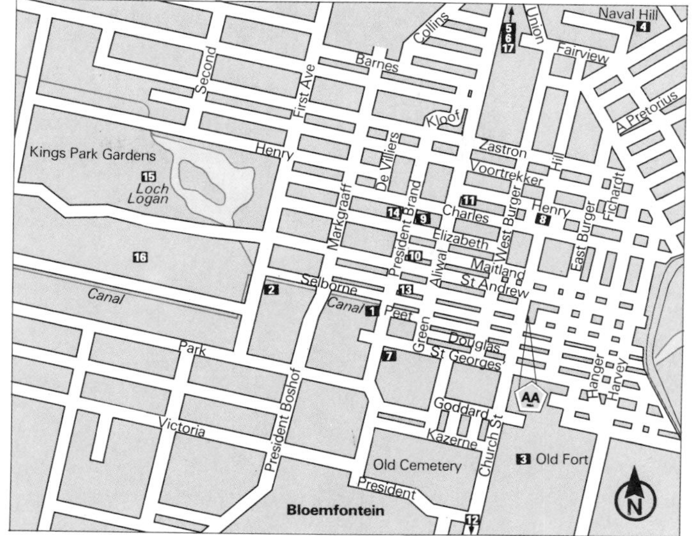

The Presidency in Eunice Street was finally completed in 1887.

1884 some 27 plans were submitted in a competition to design a new Presidency, the prize of £200 going to a firm of architects in Queenstown. The corner-stone was laid the following year, and within 16 months the building was completed. The Presidency has now been restored, and houses the Cultural History Museum of the Orange Free State.

One of the South Africa's most distinctive churches is Bloemfontein's 'Tweetoringkerk' (church with two spires), which stands at the head of Church Street.

The church was completed in May 1880, but 55 years later, in April 1935, the western spire collapsed. Fears about the security of the other spire led to its being demolished — down as far as the height of the main roof. A fund was later established for the restoration of the spires in their entirety, accomplished in 1943.

From a thatched schoolroom in St George's Street, successive governments of the Orange Free State moved to two other buildings, since demolished, before meeting for the first time in the Fourth Raadsaal **(9)** in President Brand Street, in 1893. Designed by Lennox Canning, architect of the Presidency, the Fourth Raadsaal is regarded as an outstanding example of late-Victorian architecture and as 'the architectural gem of the Orange Free State'. The Old Government Buildings **(10)** in Maitland Street, begun in 1875, were used as a military hospital during the Anglo-Boer War and today house the National Afrikaans Literary Museum and Research Centre.

The National Museum **(11)** in Aliwal Street houses natural history displays, especially of archaeological interest. Here one can see the fossilized skull and a reconstruction of 'Florisbad man' — thought by some scientists to have been an ancestor of the San peoples.

Bloemfontein's best-known monument is probably the Vrouemonument **(12)** — the National Women's Memorial. This commemorates the roughly 26 000 Boer women and children who died during the Anglo-Boer War, most of them in concentration camps. The cause of these 'refugees' was championed by an Englishwoman, Emily Hobhouse, whose ashes are buried at the monument — and by other distinguished people, including the guerilla leader General Christiaan de Wet, of whom there is an equestrian statue in the grounds of the Fourth Raadsaal.

The 'whispering wall'

The tall obelisk of the Women's Memorial is surrounded by a circular 'whispering wall'. The slightest sound made close to the interior of the wall can be heard clearly anywhere along its circumference.

The War Museum of the Boer Republics is in the grounds of the Women's Memorial, and houses many relics of the Anglo-Transvaal War of 1880-1881 and the Anglo-Boer War of 1899-1902. Within the grounds there is an interesting series of statues. One represents a typical Boer fighting man at the start of the war, while another shows him as a hardened and 'bittereinder' remaining in the field to the very end.

Bloemfontein is the judicial capital of South Africa. In addition to having a Provincial Supreme Court **(13)** in President Street, it is the home of the highest court in the land — the Appellate Division of the Supreme Court **(14)**. Both are richly furnished and panelled in stinkwood.

Apart from all the important official buildings, the city has a number of attractive parks, including the Franklin Nature Reserve **(5)** on Naval Hill and King's Park **(15)**, which contains Loch Logan and the Zoo. Also worth a visit is President Swart Park **(16)**, and Hamilton Park **(17)** on the western slope of Naval Hill. In Hamilton Park there is an orchid house containing over 3 000 plants ●

Twin spires of the 'Tweetoringkerk'.

Following the Mountain Road deep into the magic Maluti

We start this route at Maseru and penetrate deep into the heart of Lesotho by driving east on the 'Mountain Road'. We cross four magnificent passes that soar over the majestic Maluti mountains, and visit the well-preserved San paintings at Ha Khotso. Roughly half the route is on gravel. Take food, refreshments and fuel with you.

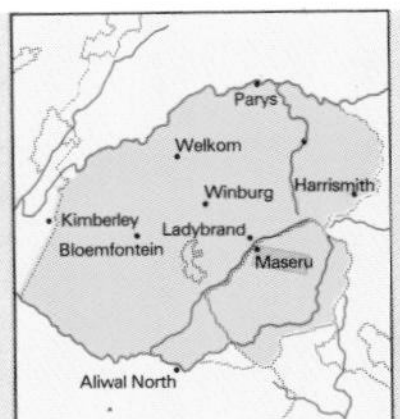

Maseru
Roma
Bushman's Pass
Blue Mountain Pass
Likalaneng Pass
Ha Khotso
250 — 270 kms

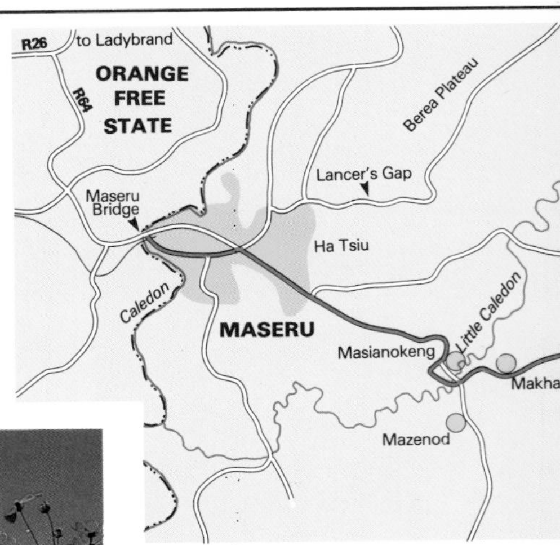

WE BEGIN OUR DAY WITH A visit to the Basotho Hat and the Basotho Shield gift shops. If you are entering Lesotho from the Maseru Bridge Border Post, note your kms as you leave the post and travel straight along the main road for 2,5 km to reach Maseru. Turn right at the traffic lights and immediately turn right again into the Basotho Shield parking area. These shops serve as an introduction to the many fascinating works of local craftsmanship that can be found in Lesotho.

Return to your car and turn left as you leave the parking area, then turn right onto Kingsway. Travel to the traffic circle at the end of Kingsway, overlooked by the twin-towered Catholic cathedral, and take the third exit from the traffic circle onto the road to Mafeteng. After travelling about 14 kms from the traffic circle, turn left onto the road for Roma and Thaba Tseka. Note your kms as you turn. (There is a petrol station on this corner.)

As you drive along this road you can see the mountains looming mistily in the distance, and the surrounding landscape becomes typical of the lowland farming areas. After 7,9 kms you reach the summit of a small hill that offers a magnificent view of the mountains ahead of you. After 12,3 kms you pass a turn-off for Thaba Tseka on your left — note your kms as you pass this road. At this point you can see directly ahead of you a large triangular rock formation and a small church. Continue straight towards Roma, passing steep cliffs on your left.

After 6,6 kms you enter Roma (see opposite) with the entrance to the university on your left and the Roma Business Centre on your right. Continue on the tarred road through this picturesque village, which has many buildings of honey-coloured sandstone. Continue through the village, and return to the entrance. Retrace your route back to the turn-off marked Thaba Tseka and turn right here, noting your kms as you turn.

First of the passes

You now begin the ascent of the first of the four passes we follow across the Maluti Mountains. After 6,1 kms park at the side of the road for a fine view back over Roma. From this spot you can also see the impressive Machache Mountain ahead of you. Continue straight and after 10,1 kms you reach the small settlement of Ha Ntsi where local beer is produced. Shortly afterwards you reach the settlement of Nazareth, and after 15 kms you pass 'Old Toll House', which has a small caravan site and a building from which refreshments are served. Note your kms as you pass the caravan park. You now begin the long winding ascent of Bushman's Pass, and after 4,9 kms you reach a corner protected by a crash barrier. Stop behind this barrier on the right side of the road for a magnificent view over the Lesotho lowlands.

Continue up the pass, taking particular care on these winding roads and negotiating blind corners slowly. At the top of the pass there is a sign showing the altitude (2 268 m) and you then begin the long descent into the valley. On the valley floor you cross the willow-lined Makhaleng River, and after a further 2,3 kms you reach the Molimo Nthuse Mountain Lodge — a convenient place to stop for refreshments.

Continuing on the same road, you now begin the steep ascent of the Molimo Nthuse (God help me) Pass, reaching the summit 2,9 kms after leaving the lodge. Note your kms here. The road changes to gravel at this point, and after a further 100 m you pass the Pony Trekking Station (see above) on your left.

A scenic drive of 2,4 kms brings you down onto the valley floor, where you pass the remains of an old trading store. You also pass a stream lined with willow trees that makes a convenient picnic spot. After 4,4 kms the road surface changes back to tar and you begin the ascent of the next scenic mountain drive — the Blue Mountain Pass.

As you penetrate deeper into the Maluti Mountains the scenery becomes more and more

Wild flowers dot the road in the spring.

ROMA

Roma, the home of the National University of Lesotho, lies 35 km from Maseru. It had its origins in 1862 when a Catholic mission was established here by Bishop J Allard and Father Joseph Gerard on ground granted to them by the Basotho chief Moshoeshoe. The mission became known as the place of the 'Ba-Roma' or Roman Catholics — hence its modern name. In 1945 the university started here as a Catholic college with 5 students and 4 teaching clergy. Today it has over 1 000 students. The university campus and the town lie in a beautiful valley surrounded by high mountains that are often snow-capped in winter.

Sweeping views greet motorists at every turn on Lesotho's mountain roads.

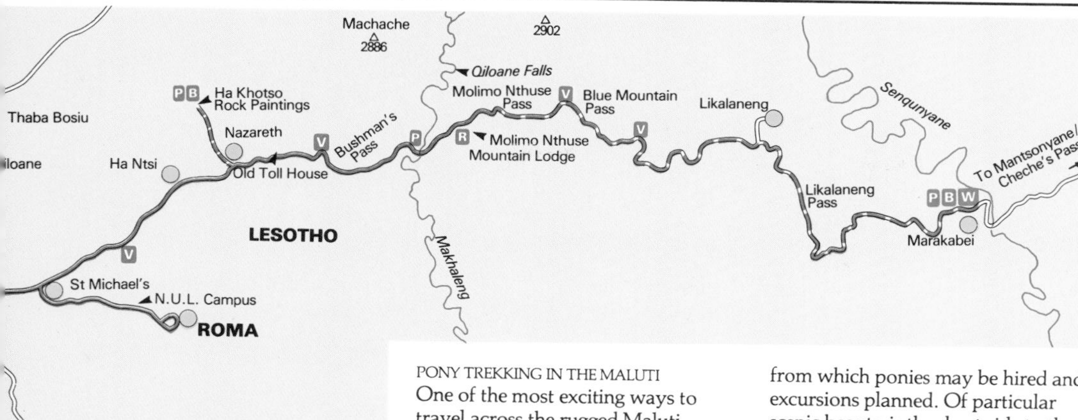

HA KHOTSO ROCK PAINTINGS

The colourful San rock paintings on an ancient overhanging rock shelter at Ha Khotso are among the best-preserved examples of rock art in southern Africa. A poorly defined footpath leads to the shelter, and the visitor is well rewarded by the quality and quantity of the paintings – representing animals, groups of human figures and hunting scenes. The curator at the shelter charges a small fee to open the gate, and you may picnic on the banks of the small stream that runs alongside the site. The surrounding area is a nature reserve and remains almost unchanged since the time when the San artists lived and worked in this part of Africa.

PONY TREKKING IN THE MALUTI

One of the most exciting ways to travel across the rugged Maluti mountain range is on the back of a sweet-tempered, sure-footed Basotho pony. The Basotho people are a nation of horsemen, and their ponies, descended from Javanese horses imported into the Cape, are well-trained and reliable. After extensive buying during and after the Anglo-Boer war the breeding stock deteriorated seriously, but the ponies were 'saved' by Irish experts.

At the top of the Molimo Nthuse Pass there is a pony trekking centre from which ponies may be hired and excursions planned. Of particular scenic beauty is the short ride to the Qiloane Falls where there is a large natural swimming pool and facilities for picnicking.

For the more adventurous, pony treks of several days are available. This form of travel will take the rider across mountains and through spectacular valleys – an exhilarating experience, offering an opportunity to see parts of Lesotho that cannot be reached by car. For further information contact the Basotho Pony Project, P O Box 1027, Maseru.

Ha Khotso; site of San paintings.

Winter scene in Bushman's Pass.

The white, tumbling waters of the Qiloane Falls.

San paintings at Ha Khotso.

dramatic, with weathered rocks and soaring peaks that are capped with snow in winter. At the top of the Blue Mountain Pass (2634m), where the tarred road ends, park at the side of the road and walk a few metres to your left for a panoramic view over rugged valleys stretching endlessly into the distance. Continue along the road, which for the next 5kms offers breathtaking views.

Marakabei and the Senqunyane River

You now begin the descent of the pass, and 10,5km after noting your kms at the summit of the Molimo Nthuse Pass, the road surface changes back to tar. At this point there is another fine viewsite on your left. The road surface changes to gravel again after 1,8km of tar, and several kilometres later you pass the small settlement of Likalaneng nestling against a steep hillside. After the village you cross a bridge that marks the start of the long Likalaneng Pass. As on many of these mountain passes, the road surface alternates between tar and gravel, but the wonderful views and pure bracing air at this high altitude are worth the inconvenience caused by the poor quality roads.

40kms after the summit of the Molimo Nthuse Pass, stop on the left side of the road to look out over the valley far below you. After 47,2kms you enter the settlement of Marakabei, and after a further 2,8kms you cross the scenic Senqunyane River. Turn around at this point to start the return journey.

Note your kms as you reach the tar at the summit of the Molimo Nthuse Pass. Roughly 19km later, 200m after passing a Caltex garage in the small mission settlement of Nazareth, turn right onto an unmarked gravel road to view a group of San paintings. After 4kms you reach a crossroads. Keep straight on for 1km and stop at the village of Ha Khotso to ask for a guide to take you to the paintings – allow 90 minutes for this excursion. After viewing the paintings, retrace your route to the tarred road and turn right for Maseru ●

Lesotho National Tourist Board 209 Kingsway, Maseru, Lesotho Tel. (050) 322896

Centuries-old crafts and a majestic mountain-top retreat

This route explores the area north and south of Maseru. The two formidable plateaus of Berea and Qeme are almost constant landmarks in this part of the lowlands, and the visitor to this 'mountain kingdom' is introduced to local handcrafts and history. Over two-thirds of the route is tarred. Take food and refreshments with you.

Maseru
Teyateyaneng
Kolonyama
Thaba Bosiu
Morija
220 – 280 kms

LEAVE MASERU BY DRIVING east along Kingsway. At the traffic circle, before the large twin-towered Cathedral of Our Lady of Victories, take the second exit left. Note your kms as you pass beneath the metal arch opposite the cathedral. You are now on the Leabua Highway, which leads through the outskirts of the town, and after 1 km you pass the Sebaboleng Dam on your right. After 2,7 km turn right off the main road onto a tarred road that winds up between two large rock formations to Lancer's Gap — where the Radio Lesotho transmitter masts are situated. From the summit there is a fine view looking back over Maseru. Return to the main road and turn right, noting your kms as you turn.

You now pass through farmlands typical of Lesotho's lowlands, with the Berea Plateau a constant presence on your right. After 15,3 kms you can see the Tlapaneng Mountain on your right, and often the early morning light will catch the smoke from wood-burning fires as it drifts against the backdrop of the plateau. After 29,1 km you pass the settlement of Lekokoaneng, and after 34,5 kms you cross the Teyateyaneng River. At 38,3 kms from the Lancer's Gap turn-off you reach the hilltop town of Teyateyaneng. Continue for a further 12 km, then turn left, following signs to the Kolonyama Pottery (see opposite). Allow 30-40 minutes for an interesting conducted tour of the pottery, where you may also buy produce.

Teyateyaneng to Morija

Retrace your route to Teyateyaneng (known locally as TY) and follow the second sign to the Setsoto Design craft centre — where rugs, tapestries and wall-hangings are made by hand from wool spun on the premises. Visitors may tour the workshops and purchase rugs.

Leave the Setsoto Design centre and head for the main road. Turn right as if you are returning to Maseru, then immediately left onto a gravel road signposted 'Mateka', noting your kms as the road surface changes to gravel (watch for potholes). After 4,4 kms turn sharp right onto a side-road (slightly uphill and not very visible from this direction). Continue along this road, which takes you into the heart of Lesotho.

After 16,2 km you reach a junction — turn left here onto a better gravel road. After 18,4 km you pass the small village of Sefikeng, with the mountain of the same name on your left. Continue straight on this road, which offers fine panoramic views all along its length. After 38 km the hilltop fortress of Thaba Bosiu comes into view on your left and you pass a modern church on your right. The road skirts the base of Thaba Bosiu, and after a short distance you reach the Thaba Bosiu Post Office sign on your right. Stop here for a magnificent view of the historic mountain — Moshoeshoe's natural fortress (see below).

Continue on this road, and 48 kms after leaving TY, turn right at the T-junction onto a tarred road — noting your kms at the turn. 6,3 kms later you reach another T-junction. Turn left here for Morija (not signposted). After a further 2,3 kms you pass a turn-off leading to the airport.

As you travel south, the large Qeme Plateau looms on your right. 24,2 kms after turning onto the tar you pass the turn-off to Matsieng, and after approximately 32 kms you can see the large Masite Mountain that overlooks Morija. Shortly afterwards you cross the Lerato River — note your kms as you cross. Pass a turn-off to Morija on your left, and 1 km after crossing the river, turn left to visit the Thabelang

Hairpin bend on the steep winding ascent to Lancer's Gap.

Moshoeshoe I statue in Maseru.

MOUNTAIN OF THE NIGHT

Thaba Bosiu (mountain of the night) is a remarkable natural fortress with steep cliff sides rising to over 1 500 m. The mountain stands in the valley of the Phuthiatsana River, and the founder of the Basotho nation, Moshoeshoe, established a stronghold here in 1824. From this impregnable position he repulsed attacks by many of the local clans. The ruins of his residence and his grave may still be visited on top of the mountain. One emotional feature on the mountain is a footprint carved on a ledge above a steep cliff. This is said to have been carved by one of Moshoeshoe's sons, who leapt to his death from this ledge after being refused permission to marry the girl of his heart.

View from the rural post office at Thaba Bosiu.

KOLONYAMA POTTERY

The people of Lesotho are masters at the crafts of weaving, jewellery-making and pottery. Visitors to craft centres in the tiny mountain kingdom are welcome to observe the skill of the craftsmen — and buy the finished articles. One such centre is the Kolonyama Pottery, 50 km from Maseru on the scenic Leabua Highway.

Visitors are invited to tour the workshops to watch craftsmen creating exquisite articles, and these are available for sale in a showroom above the working area. Rated as one of the finest potteries in southern Africa, Kolonyama is open to the public on weekdays and Saturdays.

Whitewashed walls of the Kolonyama Pottery.

Handcrafts Institute, which displays attractively printed cloth and garments.

After a short visit, retrace your route to the main road and turn right. 250 m later turn right again towards Morija (see below). After 1 km the road surface changes to gravel.

Continue for a short distance until you reach the stone Post Office building. Turn right here and stop at the side of the road to view the striking red church in the centre of the village. Approximately 100 m further along this road is the Lesotho Book Centre, behind which is a small museum (enquire at the Book Centre if you wish to visit the museum).

Morija to Maseru

Turn your car around and leave Morija with the Post Office on your right. Immediately after passing the Post Office building, take the right-hand road at the fork. Pass the Morija Cash Store on your right — the road surface now changes to poor quality gravel.

The road winds past large sandstone mountains which rise steeply on your right. After just a few kilometres you pass through the Royal village of Matsieng, and roughly 600 m later you reach a T-junction with a good tarred road. Turn left here for Maseru, noting your kms as you turn.

After 1 km you pass an attractive stone church set back from the road on your left. The Qeme Plateau is now directly in front of you. 5 kms after turning onto the tarred road you enter the small settlement of Mahloenyeng with attractive views of the Tlouoe Mountains to your right. After 10,5 kms you reach a T-junction with the road on which you travelled south. Turn right here and follow this road back to Maseru.

To end the day you might like to visit the statue of Moshoeshoe I in the heart of the capital. When you reach the traffic circle in front of the cathedral, take the first exit left onto Kingsway. Pass the Queen Elizabeth II Hospital, take the third turning to your left with the post office on the corner, and park a short distance down this road near a pair of gates. Walk through the gates down to steep steps that lead up to the statue ●

AA Office AA House, 56 Church Street, Bloemfontein 9301 Tel. (051) 76191
Lesotho National Tourist Office 209 Kingsway, Maseru Tel. (050) 322896

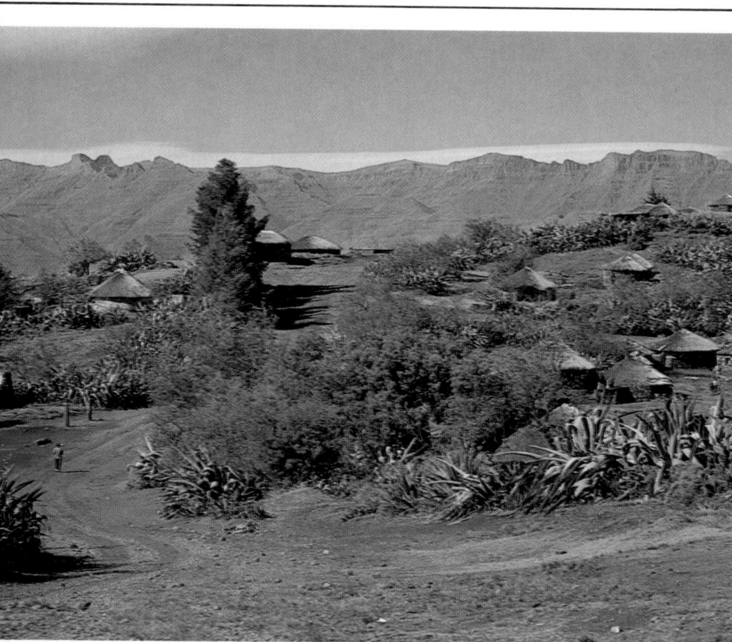

Lesotho village against a backdrop of the Maluti Mountains.

MORIJA

Founded in 1833 by pioneer French Protestant missionaries, Morija is still the headquarters of the Lesotho Evangelical Church, and is well known for its excellent mission press and book depot. Behind the depot is a small museum. In the centre of the village is a church with an eye-catching red roof. The roof is supported by octagonal teak columns made from ships' masts, brought by ox-wagon from Port Elizabeth in the 1860s. The Thabelang Handcraft Centre just outside Morija produces colourful, locally-designed garments.

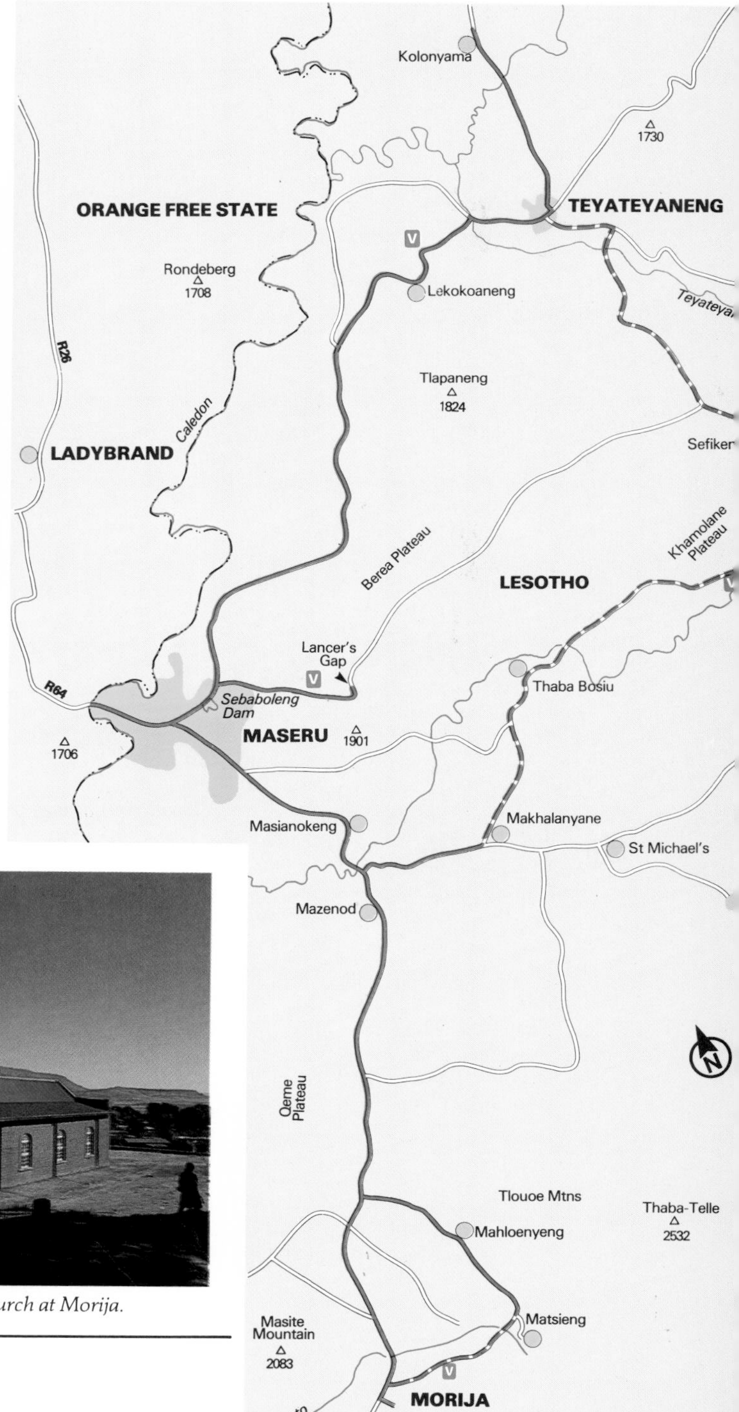

Left: *A tapestry takes shape.* **Above:** *Church at Morija.*

Most of Lesotho consists of rugged mountains, and the sturdy 'Basuto pony' is often the only reliable means of transport.

One of the richest stores of Africa's ancient traditions

SOME OF THE brooding mystery of this lovely mountain-land is expressed in the name of its famous stronghold, Thaba-Bosiu — Mountain of the Night. It is said that Zulu warriors eyed this flat-topped and apparently insignificant outcrop with scorn, and promised its defenders a swift and painful death. In a night attack, though, the Zulus found the way steep, and the mountain itself seemed to have grown larger, and higher. There were few paths to the summit, and these the defenders made impassable by rolling great boulders down on the attackers, smashing and demoralizing them. The Zulus withdrew, and the legend of the Mountain of the Night was carefully fostered to discourage future assaults.

Thaba-Bosiu is just one of many natural fortresses along the western fringes of Lesotho, all formed by the erosion of sandstone that overlies more resistant ironstone. In weathering, the sandstone has formed precipitous edges, and the saucer-like summits often can be reached only by a narrow pass, known as a *khoro*. The summits are grassy and usually well-watered from springs, and history has shown time and again that a few determined warriors established on such a summit, armed only with primitive weapons, can hold off vastly superior forces.

The earliest inhabitants of this region are known only through stone implements found in caves and along river banks, but later prehistoric people decorated the cave walls with paintings depicting battles, dances and hunting scenes. These were probably San hunters, joined some 400 years ago by the founding tribes of the present Basotho people, including the Bafokeng and Baphuthi. The Basotho — or South Sotho — are part of a larger group which alone managed to remain intact and unconquered during the tremendous upheavals unleashed by Zulu armies.

The distinctive design of a Basotho hat — symbol of a proud nation.

In addition to the chaos wrought by the Zulu nation, there was further upheaval when MmaNthatisi, fierce queen regent of the Tlokwa people, invaded the region occupied by the Basotho. The latter, however, sought sanctuary on their mountain fortress of Butha-Buthe, and escaped. Their leader was the young chief Moshoeshoe — 'the shaver' — a name he earned for a daring cattle raid on the powerful chief Ramonaheng. Moshoeshoe is an onomatopoeic word, signifying the sound made by a razor as it removes a beard. Moshoeshoe's cattle raid was seen figuratively as removing the beard of his rival.

It was in 1924 that Moshoeshoe led his people to Thaba-Bosiu, a fortress far more impregnable than Butha-

Colourful blankets are an effective protection against mountain winds.

The unaffected smile of a Basotho girl.

The traditional huts of Lesotho are noted for their simplicity and neatness.

Buthe. And here he repelled attacks by burghers of the Orange Free State, various other black tribes, and even the British regular and colonial forces. Lancers' Gap on Berea Mountain recalls the fate of some 20 British lancers who entered the wrong gully during an unsuccessful assault and were surrounded and killed by Moshoeshoe's warriors. Finally, threatened by encroachment from the Orange Free State, Moshoeshoe asked Britain to annex his country, so that his people might be as 'the lice in the blanket of the great Queen' — a reference to Queen Victoria. As a British protectorate, the country became known as Basutoland. This was changed to Lesotho when the country became independent in 1966.

The well-known and sturdy 'Basuto pony' is according to one theory the result of 'shaving' a British settler named Cawood in 1840. Cawood was a Grahamstown butcher who had imported a number of Shetland ponies from Scotland, and the sure-footed pony of Lesotho is said to be descended from these.

Of their own origins, ancient Basotho tradition tells of man emerging from the reeds of a river in a far distant country or, in another version, at Ntsuanatsatsi (near Vrede in the Orange Free State).

Traditions survive

Christian missionaries have been at work in Lesotho since the 1830s, but traditional religious practices, based on ancestor worship, survive in various forms — often combined with Christian teachings. Molimo is traditionally recognised as a Supreme Being and Creator, and he may be approached only through the intercession of the spirits of the ancestors, who in turn care for their living descendants. Beer and food are provided for the spirits' sustenance, particularly after good harvests.

Winter mornings are dry and cold.

Although death is traditionally regarded as birth into the world of the ancestors, it is also the time to perform rituals associated with an old belief that no person merely dies — he has been 'murdered'. If the death has occurred inside a hut, the body might be removed through a hole made in the back of the hut, rather than through the doorway. The body is buried in a crouching, or foetal position, symbolising re-birth, and the face is turned towards the rising sun, symbol of the new life. After death, the spirit is safe from the schemings of Moremo — the evil one — and finds happiness in Mosimo — the beautiful place.

In the realm of magic and divination the Basotho traditionally recognised a variety of specialist practitioners. Most unusual of these was the *ngaka ea balwetse*, a ventriloquist who would visit his clients with his doll, so that the doll could tell them the source of their trouble. The *dilaoli* was skilled at throwing the bones to foretell the future, while the *senohe*, another seer, could see the future in a bowl of clear water. The *moupelli* specialised in protecting houses against lightning, and the *monnesapula* was consulted to bring rain during times of drought.

The traditional Basotho hut is built of stone because, in many areas, there is a shortage of timber and reed. The huts may be round or rectangular, and are usually coated with a mud plaster on the inside and around the entrance. Finger-patterns and paint are applied by the women, and bright commercial paints are now replacing the traditional black and ochre. To protect the hut and its inhabitants, a number of pegs, treated with a magic potion by a diviner, may be hammered into the ground at the entrance.

Domestic centre

The floor of the hut is made of hard, smooth dung, which is also used as a fuel. Attached to the hut may be a semi-circular screen of reeds enclosing an open space. This is known as the *lelapa*, and is the centre for domestic activities such as cooking. A birth in the family may be announced by raising one of the reeds of the *lelapa* high above the others. This custom may be related to the belief that man first emerged from a bed or reeds.

A feature of the small rural village is the *lekhotla*, a sheltered enclosure usually attached to a small hut, where elders gather to discuss village affairs and to hear evidence in cases of alleged contraventions of the community code. Women are excluded from the *lekhotla*, except when they are required to give evidence. Traditionally the Basotho show great hospitality to strangers, and a newcomer will receive a hearty welcome and advice at the *lekhotla*.

Both the boys and girls of the Basotho have traditionally undergone initiation, although decreasing importance is now attached to these rites. Schools for boys may accommodate up to 60 initiates from a fairly wide area, and are usually organised by a chief, who appoints elders — or *babineli* — to instruct the boys. The initiation hut is built just before the time of circumcision, which takes place early in the initiation period. The operation marks the end of childhood, and the start of life as a man, and is followed by intensive lessons on the laws and customs the initiate will be expected to follow. Initiates are also taught the traditions of their tribe. They are confined to the hut for about a month after circumcision, during which time food is brought to them. Then follows a period when they may wander about to find their own food — by asking for it, foraging or even stealing. Those caught stealing are severely thrashed — not because of the theft, but for being caught at it.

The girls' initiation schools usually have only about 10 *bale* — as the girls are called — and begin at the time of the new moon, when the girls run to a river where they symbolically wash away their girlhood. Initiates cover themselves with dark ash, and later with white clay. During the initiation period the girls hide their identity behind a veil of grass and beads, and wear the traditional costume of a sheepskin apron with plaited grass cords around the waist ●

Colourful handmade wares on display at one of the many open-air markets.

NATAL

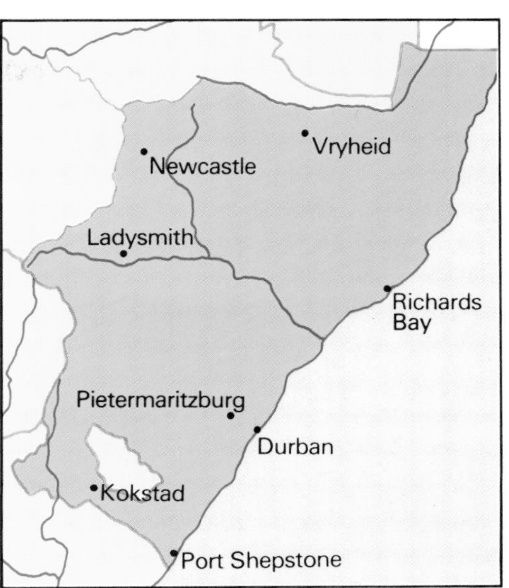

Above: *Durban — Natal's sparkling holiday playground.* **Left:** *Rugged buttresses of the Drakensberg rise serenely over the Royal Natal National Park.*

Assegais and laagers — exploring Natal's historic battlefields

This drive leads from Vryheid on a journey into the past. We visit the Prince Imperial's memorial, then Isandhlwana, Rorke's Drift, Talana and Blood River — scenes of epic battles that shaped South Africa's history. Over two-thirds of the route is on gravel, which can become slippery after rains. Take food and drink with you.

Vryheid
Prince Imperial's Memorial
Isandhlwana
Rorke's Drift
Talana
Blood River
350—370 km

LEAVE VRYHEID by driving west along Kerkstraat (Church Street) and note your kms as you pass the stone Dutch Reformed Church on your right. Four blocks later, turn left into West Street. At 1,8 km this becomes a gravel road. You pass a road to the airfield on your left, and after 4,4 km you cross a rickety steel bridge over the White Mfolozi River. After about 16 km you reach an intersection where a tarred road on your right leads to eMondlo. Continue on the gravel road, following the sign to Babanango. At about 30,2 km the road forks — take the road on the right even though the surface deteriorates slightly. After 43,8 km you cross the Mvunyane River.

After 46 km you pass the Mhlungwane Store on your right. About 100 m later turn right at the sign to the Prince Imperial's Memorial, noting your kms. The area is heavily eroded — at 2,5 km there is a shallow gully and rivulet across the road, and there are two more at 3,8 km and 5,1 km. They are easily passed, but approach them with caution. After 6,8 km you reach the Jojosi River. Park on the near bank, remove your shoes and walk across — the water is usually quite shallow. It is possible to drive across the river, but thick sand and the likelihood of high water after rains make it advisable to proceed on foot.

At the fork on the far side of the river, take the lesser used road to the left. This leads after 200 m to the spot where the last of the Napoleons fell (see opposite).

Prince Imperial's Memorial to Isandhlwana

Retrace your route to the main gravel road, turn right, and drive 39 km to meet the tarred R68. Turn right onto the R68, noting your kms. After 13,7 km turn left onto the gravel road to Isandhlwana, noting your kms.

After 8,6 km you come to a fork — take the road on the left. To your right is the hill whose shape gave it the name Isandhlwana (Zulu for 'second stomach of a cow'). On the slope of the hill is a monument, where you can buy from the watchman a brochure describing the Battle of Isandhlwana and can study a model of the area (see opposite).

When you drive back, cross the access road and drive through the gateway to see the gravestones of British soldiers and a memorial to the Zulu warriors who fell in the battle. White-painted cairns mark the graves of the dead.

Isandhlwana to Rorke's Drift

Retrace your route to the R68, and turn left onto the R68, noting your kms. After driving 12 km through a landscape of eroded dongas and scattered Zulu huts you pass through the dusty little settlement of Nqutu, and at 30,5 km you cross a bridge over the Buffelsrivier (Buffalo River) at Vant's Drift. After 31,3 km turn left onto a gravel road to Rorke's Drift, noting your kms.

After 12,2 km you pass a road leading to Helpmekaar, and at about 15 km the buildings of Rorke's Drift are visible on a hill ahead. At 17,2 km turn left into Rorke's Drift, park, and start your tour of the area by walking up to the church. At the time of the battle, Rorke's Drift was a Swedish mission station called Oscarberg, and the buildings had been taken over to serve as a military hospital.

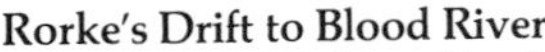

Rorke's Drift to Blood River

Follow the gravel road back to the R68, and turn left onto the R68, noting your kms. At 4,3 km there is a picnic spot. After 24,9 km you come to a T-junction — turn left onto the R33. About 3 km later, on your right, you come to the Anglo-Boer War battlefield of Talana — with a museum at the site.

If you wish to drive into the town of Dundee, continue on the R33. Otherwise, turn around here, and drive back along the R33 towards Vryheid — noting your kms as you leave the Talana battlefield.

After about 24 km turn right onto a gravel road leading to the Blood River monument — noting your kms. At about 1,2 km you cross a steel bridge over the Buffelsrivier, and shortly afterwards you come to a junction with the road from Vryheid entering on your left (your return route). Bear right at this junction, and at 21 km the stone ox-wagon monument marking the battle is visible on your right.

Enter the gates, and park outside the first building on the left. Obtain a pamphlet from the caretaker and examine the diorama on the right. Drive past the office and after about 100 m stop at the 1938 Centenary monument and the Blood River monument, before driving on to the impressive reconstruction of Andries Pretorius's laager. After visiting the laager, walk about 200 m east to Blood River, then 200 m south to see the old hippo pool and the historic donga behind the laager (see opposite).

Retrace your route towards the R33, but note your kms as you leave the Blood River monument, and take the road leading right at the fork — for Vryheid. At 16,9 km you pass over a stone bridge, and at 19,1 km you reach the tarred R33. Turn right onto the R33, which will take you back to Vryheid ●

Information Office Public Library, cnr Hoog and Mark Streets, Vryheid 3100 Tel. (0381) 2133

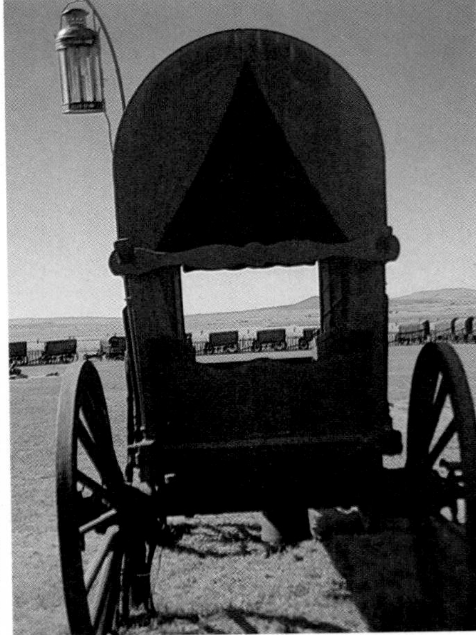

Reconstructed wagons at Blood River.

The calm waters of Blood River today.

SURPRISE ATTACK AT ISANDHLWANA

On 20 January 1879 a column under Lord Chelmsford, British commander-in-chief, crossed the Buffalo River at Rorke's Drift and set up camp below the hill known as Isandhlwana. One of three columns marching on Zulu chief Cetshwayo, they were unaware that a powerful Zulu force of about 20 000 men was hidden in the Nqutu hills just 8 km to the north.

On 22 January, the Zulu army attacked in classic ox-head formation. The British were totally unprepared, and the column was annihilated in half an hour. Afterwards, amongst the dead — 858 soldiers, 470 black allies of the British and about 1 000 Zulus — most of the British ammunition was found still packed in boxes.

Memorial to the Prince Imperial.

LAST OF THE NAPOLEONS

After the Franco-Prussian War of 1870 forced Napoleon III and his family to flee from France, the young Prince Imperial, Eugène Louis Joseph Napoleon Bonaparte, received a military education in England. In search of a successful military career to prove his worth to the French people, he begged the British commander-in-chief to allow him to go to the war in Zululand. As a lieutenant he was posted to Colonel Harrison's scouts in Dundee.

On 1 June 1879 the prince was part of a six-man advance party searching for a camp site for the main group near the banks of the Vumankala River. They had off-saddled for coffee at an apparently deserted kraal when they were attacked by about 50 Zulu warriors. The prince's horse panicked and bolted before he could mount, and he could only hang on to a saddlebag strap, which broke. He and two soldiers were stabbed to death with assegais.

THE DEFENDERS OF RORKE'S DRIFT

Shortly after news of the slaughter at Isandhlwana reached the military hospital at Rorke's Drift some 16 km to the west, scouts reported that a Zulu impi of about 4 000 men was heading for the drift.

Fewer than 100 men fought off the Zulu warriors from behind makeshift fortifications, retreating room by room as burning assegais were flung onto the hospital roof. The battle continued throughout the night, the defenders being scorched by their red-hot rifle barrels. At dawn, the Zulus finally fell back, and British reinforcements arrived. The British lost 17 men with 8 wounded, and the Zulus had about 500 dead. 11 Victoria Crosses were awarded to the British defenders.

British redcoats kept up a withering fire against attacking Zulus at Rorke's Drift.

BLOOD RIVER – THE DAY OF THE VOW

After the murders of Boer leader Piet Retief and his followers, Boer commander Andries Pretorius set out with a 465-strong commando in a punitive expedition against Dingane, the Zulu chief. Hearing reports that a large Zulu force was nearby, Pretorius established a tightly defended laager of ox wagons, with the Ncome Spruit ahead and a deep donga on the right serving as natural barriers. A vow had been made and repeated every night that if they were granted victory, the day would in future be held sacred.

When about 12 000 warriors, led by Ndlela, attacked on the morning of 16 December 1838, the concentrated Boer firepower was directed onto a narrow front. 3 000 Zulu warriors died. Only four Boers, including Pretorius, were wounded. The Day of the Vow as it is now known (16 December) is still one of the most sacred days in the calendar of the Afrikaner people.

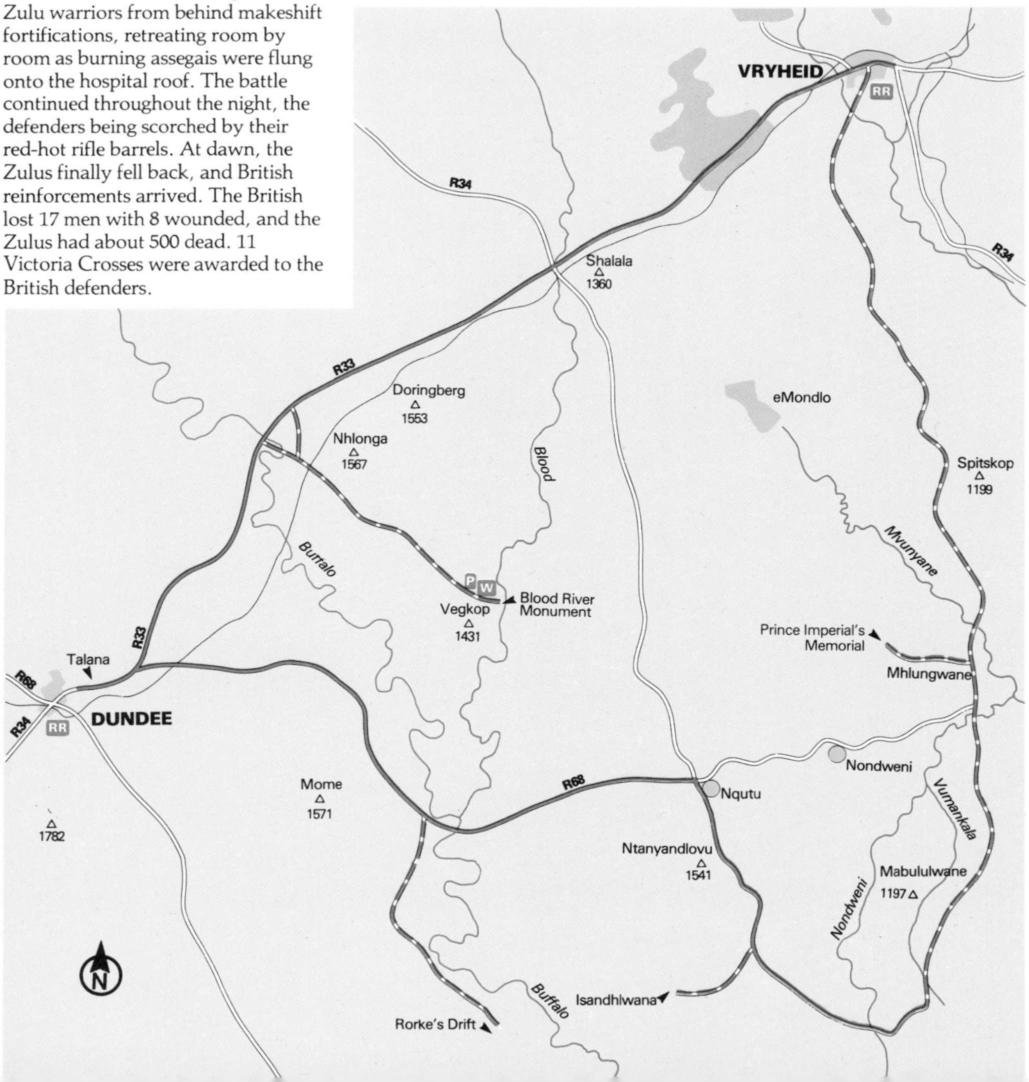

Uniforms of the Anglo-Zulu War: Warrior of the third Undi Regiment; and trooper of the 1st Dragoon Guards.

VRYHEID
RR
R34
Shalala 1360
R33
Doringberg 1553
Nhlonga 1567
eMondlo
Blood
Spitskop 1199
Buffalo
Mvunyane
P W
Blood River Monument
Vegkop 1431
Prince Imperial's Memorial
Mhlungwane
Talana
R68
R34
RR
DUNDEE
Nondweni
R68
Nqutu
Mome 1571
1782
Vumankala
Ntanyandlovu 1541
Mabululwane 1197
Nondweni
N
Buffalo
Isandhlwana
Rorke's Drift

The sky turns to pink as dawn edges over the hills in Hluhluwe Game Reserve.

Big game roams fearless where Zulu kings hunted

AT NIGHT LIONS have been known to wander through Hilltop, the aptly named hutted camp set high on the brow of a hill in the centre of Hluhluwe — one of the best-known game reserves in the world. Once the hunting preserve of Zulu kings, Hluhluwe is now a haven for wildlife that offers visitors unforgettable viewing of many species of animals and birds.

The game reserve — 23 000 ha of indigenous forest and Zululand thornveld — nestles amongst foothills rising from the coastal plain in the east. Centred on the Hluhluwe River valley, the partnership of hill and plain in the area offers an unusual combination of forest, woodland, savanna and grassland found only rarely in Africa.

Mbhombe forest

While the wide variety of animal life in the reserve is the obvious drawcard for visitors, game rangers are always at pains to point out that the Mbhombe semi-deciduous forest is also a distinctive feature of the area. Hluhluwe is one of the few places in Natal where a large forest of this type still survives.

One of Africa's oldest reserves, Hluhluwe was established in 1895 along with its sister reserves in the same area: Umfolozi (see pages 160-1) and St Lucia (see pages 162-3). The reserve, the nearby village and the river are all named after the thorny monkey rope, umHluhluwe, used by the Zulus to muzzle their calves during weaning.

While St Lucia to the east is a separate geographic entity, Hluhluwe and Umfolozi are joined by a broad strip of state-owned land known as 'the corridor', and are administered as one reserve.

It took 12 years to erect the 2,8 m high gameproof fence around the entire area, which comprises 96 400 ha in total — a task completed in 1979. (The fence includes two strands of old mine cable: the only fencing strong enough to contain the rhino.) The fenced area, although still less than six per cent of the size of the Kruger National Park, boasts 68 per cent of the total number of plant species found in Kruger.

At Hluhluwe the visitor is likely to see both black and white rhino (there is in fact no difference in colour), giraffe, buffalo, zebra, monkey, leopard, cheetah, wildebeest, nyala, the almost comically ugly warthog, baboon, kudu, impala, bushbuck, crocodile and lion — as recently as 1985 a game guard was killed and eaten by a lion in the reserve.

Elephants were reintroduced from the Kruger National Park to Hluhluwe in 1981 — they had been shot out of the area in the 19th century — and lucky visitors may spot hippo that occasionally wander into the Maphumulo picnic site from the Hluhluwe Dam.

Of all these animals, however, only the nyala, probably the most decorative and spectacular antelope in Africa, is specifically identified with Zululand.

Hluhluwe, 280 km north of Durban, is traversed by more than 80 km of good, all-weather gravel roads, allowing easy access to most of the reserve. There are two entrances, one at Gunjaneni Gate 35 km from Mtubatuba, and the other at Memorial Gate 17 km from Hluhluwe village. The camp at Hilltop is 16 km from Gunjaneni and 12 km from the Memorial Gate. All the roads in the reserve are clearly signposted, and every intersection is numbered on a triangular stone marker that corresponds with the map handed out at the gates.

A lesser masked weaver and his nest.

Crocodiles and superb views

From Gunjaneni the road dips to cross the Hluhluwe River, a good place to stop and look for crocodile. From here the road climbs steadily to Hilltop, giving spectacular views of the surrounding hills and valleys, one succeeding the other to the horizon. At the brow of the hill, about 14 km from the gate, watch out for a large cairn of stones to your right. The origin of the cairn, known as an isivivane, is hidden in the mists of Zulu folklore, but prudent Zulus still believe it is wise to add to the pile to ensure a safe journey.

Entering from the Memorial Gate you encounter even more breath-

A square-lipped (white) rhino and her calf venture into the open to graze.

Zebra and nyala around a waterhole.

taking views by driving to Hilltop over Magangeni Hill. At the summit you may get out of your car, and there are places to sit and admire the surrounding bushveld that stretches for many kilometres in every direction. During the afternoon and early morning you may see game on nearby slopes. (At all viewsites and picnic areas in the reserve you leave your vehicle at your own risk.)

No matter your entrance point, and even if you intend spending only a day in the reserve, a short visit to the information centre at Hilltop is worthwhile. The centre has a file of maps of the reserve, updated daily, that shows the latest game sightings — ideal for use as a guide to your own viewing. In addition there are two 'auto trail' pamphlets available at the centre. These describe two easy-to-follow self-guided tours of the reserve, each taking about three hours. The pamphlets are fascinating tutors, introducing the visitor to everything from the rhino's social habits to rubbing posts and middens.

Indigenous trees

The centre also provides a booklet on the Mbhombe forest trail, which begins immediately behind the huts. A 30-minute stroll through this indigenous forest will introduce you to such trees as the strangler fig *(Ficus natalensis)*, which strangles its host, the Natal milk plum *(Bequaertiodendron natalense)*, the ruikpeul *(Acacia nilotica)* and the Camdeboo stinkwood *(Celtis africana)*, a tree believed by the Zulus to protect one against witchcraft. Even if you do not have time for the complete trail, a 100 m stroll along it will bring you across a fine example of the umHluhluwe climber *(Dalbergia armata)*.

During the dry season, the Munywaneni hide can provide excellent viewing of animals and birds around a watering hole fed by a small stream.

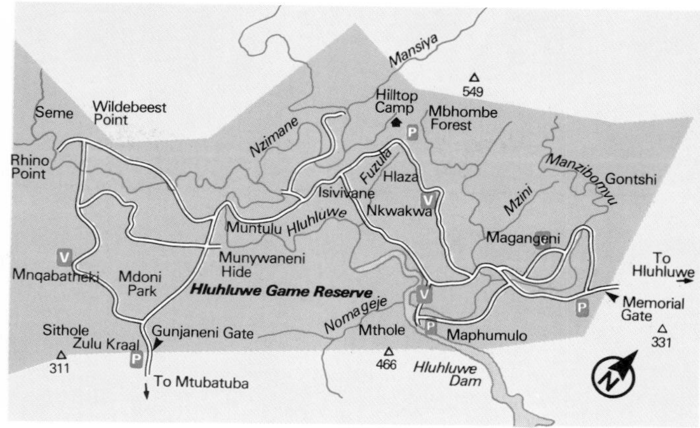

Hluhluwe's bushveld stretches across a succession of hills into the distance.

The hide is 5,7 km from the Gunjaneni Gate, just off the Hilltop road at intersection 15.

A few hundred metres to the west of the Gunjaneni Gate is the open-air site museum, an accurate reconstruction of a traditional Zulu homestead around the early 1800s. There is a self-guided, tape-recorded tour of the kraal, with its umThombothi-fenced huts, cattle enclosure and smelting 'workshop', and visitors may rest a while in the main hut.

'Rhino point' is a good place from which to spot both the black rhino and the white, or square-lipped, rhino. Because it is a grazer, the white rhino prefers short grass and is more likely to be seen. The black rhino is a browser, living off shrubs and bush, but does come into open spaces in search of young seedlings.

At 'wildebeest point' you may find both wildebeest and zebra, since the animals tend to stay together for mutual protection, and share a liking for open areas with short grass.

The reserve has three delightful picnic sites — at Gunjaneni, at Hilltop, and at the junction of the Hluhluwe and Manzibomvu rivers, known as Maphumulo. The site at Maphumulo overlooks a backwater created by the construction of the Hluhluwe Dam, and has trestle tables in a shady, grassed area from which you may see crocodiles basking on nearby banks.

Hilltop has fully serviced accommodation in single-roomed thatched rondavels or six-bedded cottages, with all bedding and utensils. Visitors must take their food and drink, however, since these are not sold in the reserve. Accommodation may be reserved through the Reservations Office, Box 662, Pietermaritzburg 3200, or by telephoning (0331) 51514.

Visitors should take precautions against malaria, and it is wise to take insect repellant with you. Petrol, film, postcards and mementos are sold in the reserve, but the nearest places from which to buy food, liquor and stamps are Hluhluwe village and Mtubatuba.

It is advisable to check the opening and closing times of the gates before you set off ●

The winsome warthog in profile.

Palm trees cluster on a stream bank.

This lion cub's spotted legs show his youth — the spots fade with age.

Nyala are often to be found amongst trees, where they hide from predators. The reddish ewes are markedly different from the rams — in size and colour.

Where the battle to save the white rhino was won

ALTHOUGH UMFOLOZI Game Reserve is now well-known for the wide variety of game viewing it offers the visitor, there was a time when it was customary for rangers to doff their hats to any animal they saw in the area.

The rangers' salute was a response to a sad episode in the reserve's history — the slaughter of more than 70 000 head of game during the 1940s in a futile attempt to control the blood-sucking tsetse fly. The fly, responsible for the spread of sleeping sickness, was eventually eradicated by aerial spraying.

Umfolozi (sometimes spelt Mfolozi) has recovered well, and today teems with wildlife. No fewer than 48 species of larger mammals, 37 species of reptiles, nine species of amphibians, more than 400 species of birds, and even 136 different butterflies await the keen-eyed visitor.

Set in the heart of Natal's bush country, the 47 700 ha Umfolozi Game Reserve was established in 1897, and more than any other reserve it has retained its wildness. About 24 000 ha of the reserve is a wilderness area accessible only on foot, as there are no artificial structures — not even roads.

The reserve is named after the White and Black Mfolozi rivers (Mfolozi being Zulu for zigzag), which meander through the area before reaching a confluence on the eastern border. It was in the narrow strip of land contained by the meeting of the two rivers that Chaka, king of the Zulus (1816-1828), organised vast game drives using his disciplined and well-drilled warriors to chase the animals into large, disguised pits.

Today the reserve is best known for the successful fight to save the white, or square-lipped, rhino from extinction, and it has the only naturally occurring population of these prehistoric-looking creatures. In 1929 only 150 of the white rhino could be found, and extinction seemed certain. But a determined campaign by the Natal Parks Board has seen the reserve's square-lipped rhino population rise to about 900. In fact, the fight has been so successful that more than 3 000 of the animals have been exported around the world.

The white rhino (whose colour is in fact no different from that of the black rhino) shares the reserve with buffalo, blue wildebeest, zebra, giraffe, impala, waterbuck, common and mountain reedbuck, nyala, kudu, bushbuck, steenbuck, duiker, warthog, leopard, cheetah, hyena and jackal, and elephants were reintroduced to Umfolozi from the Kruger National Park in 1985.

The lion came to stay

The lion, now widespread in the Umfolozi-Hluhluwe reserves, did not wait for Parks Board officials to reintroduce them to the area. Shot out of Zululand before World War II, the magnificent beast was considered another casualty of progress. Then a solitary male walked into Umfolozi in 1958 after an epic journey from Mocambique. Greeted by herds of well-fed antelope and zebra, he stayed, and was joined after years of celibacy by a female. Today the two reserves boast about 100 lion.

Warthog are among the more common animals in the area, and it is not unusual to find them wandering through the two hutted camps at Mpila and Masinda.

Perhaps the most easily observed birds in the reserve are the fish eagle, pied and malachite kingfishers, greenbacked heron and hamerkop, all of which are associated with water. Among the larger birds of prey that you may see are the tawny eagle, jackal buzzard, black-shouldered kite and secretary bird.

The best tip for aspirant game-watchers is to call in at the office at Mpila camp to consult their latest

Assured of survival by rangers' efforts, a white rhino grazes on short grass.

The lazy course of the Black Mfolozi.

map, which, as at Hluhluwe, is updated with the latest game sightings. The office will also provide on request an 'auto trail' pamphlet describing a five-hour self-guided tour through the reserve. For a nominal fee one can book a three-hour walk in the company of an armed guard (bookings must be made a day in advance). While at Mpila, it is worth making a short study of the various shapes and spirals of the horn collection mounted at the entrance to the picnic site, as these will help you later to identify game.

Umfolozi, which is traversed by 80 km of good gravel roads, has two entrances: Cengeni Gate in the west, which is reached by travelling south from Vryheid and through Ulundi; and Mambeni Gate in the east, 32 km from Mtubatuba — the reserve's nearest commercial centre.

A kudu with its distinctive stripes.

Visitors may get out of their cars only in the rest camps, or at one of the following places: a viewsite just west of the Sontuli Loop; the rustic hide at the Mphafa water hole; the Bekapanzi Hide; and a second viewsite west of Mpila.

The Mphafa water hole, which lies 10 km from the Cengeni Gate on the main road through the reserve, is well signposted. There is a hide 100 m from the car park, built simply of reeds and poles with a few benches. It overlooks a pool set below a small waterfall in the Mphafa Stream. Apart from the animals that you may see drinking here, many Cape terrapins sun themselves on the rocks.

The Bekapanzi Hide, with its protected walkway and narrow viewing slits, epitomises the game reserve for many visitors. The large, square room allows the viewer to move around unseen to watch animals and birds come down to the pan. This is a good spot for game viewing during the hotter months (although for part of the year in winter the pan is dry). Animals may visit the pan at any time, but the most common species, and particularly the wallowing animals such as warthog, buffalo and rhino, are most likely to be seen between 9 a.m. and 3 p.m. (The hide is reached by turning north from the main through-road at the intersection numbered 5, towards 'Sontuli Loop'.)

Crocodile haunt

From the Sontuli Loop viewsite, near the intersection marked 8, you overlook the Black Mfolozi River, which came down in flood during Cyclone Demoina in 1984 and washed away magnificent groves of figs that used to grow along the river banks. This viewsite is good for seeing white rhino, buffalo and zebra on the river banks.

The viewsite 2,6 km west of Mpila, marked by a rhino footprint painted in white on a rock, is on the northern boundary of the wilderness area, and gives a superb view of the White Mfolozi River.

About 10 km from the Cengeni Gate, driving north on the Sokhwezele road, you will notice a range of rolling hills on your left known as the Zintunzini Hills (frequented by a number of game species, particularly the common and mountain reedbuck). This entire area, now open acacia savanna, was cleared of bush in the 1930s in an attempt to form a buffer zone against tsetse fly. Stumps from the 3 km wide strip can still be seen, and some of them are used today as rubbing posts by the rhino to rid themselves of ticks.

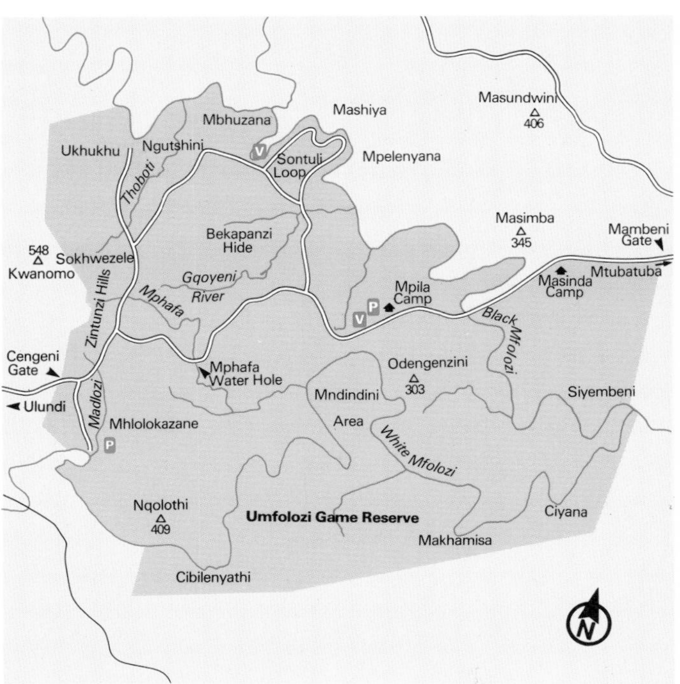

Umfolozi offers shady picnic sites at Mhlolokazane, 4 km from the Cengeni Gate, and at Mpila camp, 18 km from Mambeni Gate. Hutted accommodation is available at Masinda and Mpila (both named after the hills nearest to the camps). While Mpila has spectacular views of the Black Mfolozi River snaking through the wilderness area, Masinda — 7 km from the Mambeni Gate — is perhaps the more tranquil, and boasts a rich birdlife.

Bedding and utensils are provided, but visitors must bring all food and drink, as these are not sold in the reserve. Petrol is sold at Mpila only, as are postcards, curios and film.

Umfolozi also offers accommodation in two bush camps, each with an eight-bedded hut built on stilts. An armed guard and cook are in attendance, and walks in the reserve are available on request. Each bush camp must be reserved by an entire party.

There is a tented camp, Mdindini, which is open to the general public in December, January and February, while for the rest of the year it serves as the wilderness trail base. The wilderness hiking trails offer three days on foot with two nights under canvas in the bush. A 'primitive trail' is available on which hikers carry all their requirements with them and sleep in the open.

Anti-malaria precautions are advisable, as is insect repellant. Bookings for all accommodation as well as the various overnight trails should be made through the Reservations Office, Natal Parks Board, Box 662, Pietermaritzburg 3200, or telephone (0331) 51514 ●

Zebras are highly sociable animals, and are often to be seen with wildebeest.

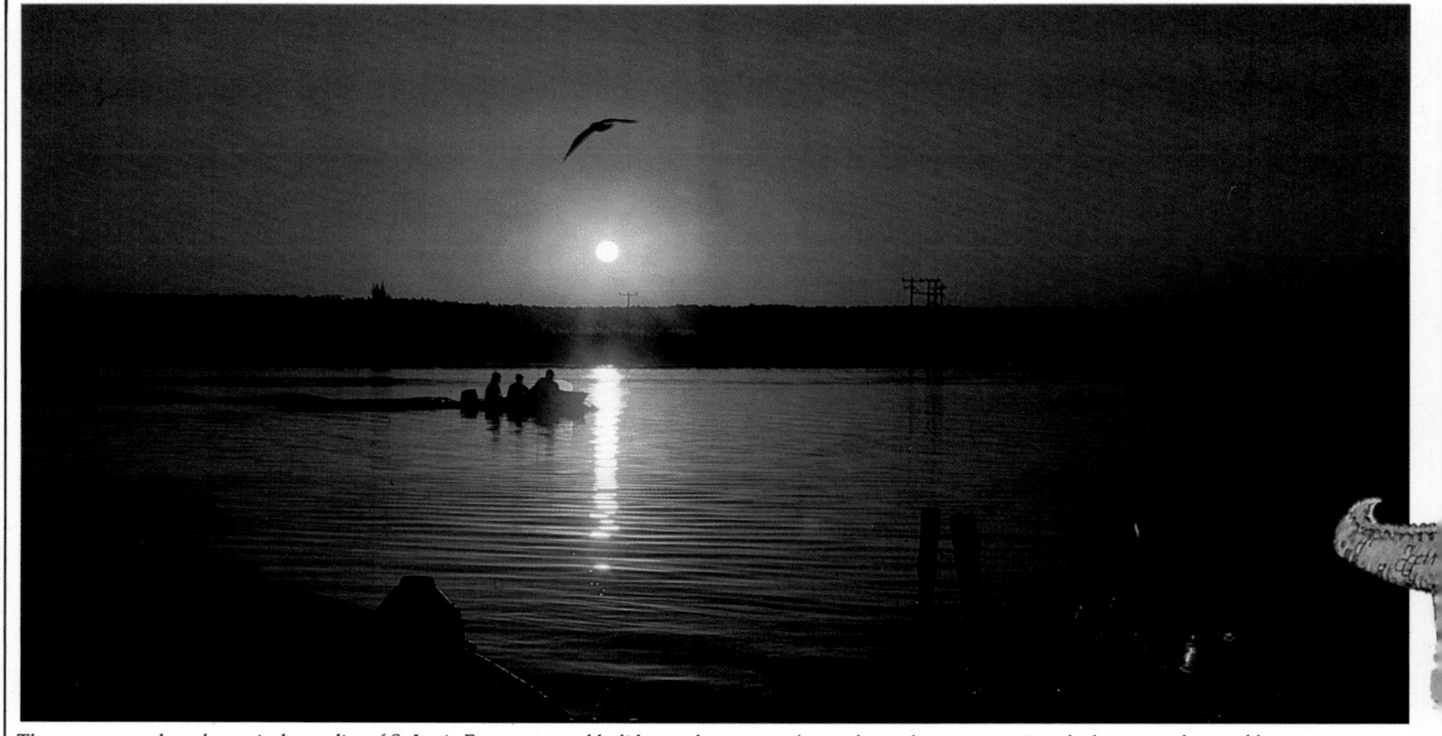

The sun sets on the sub-tropical paradise of St Lucia Estuary — and holiday-makers return from a leisurely outing to view the hippos and crocodiles.

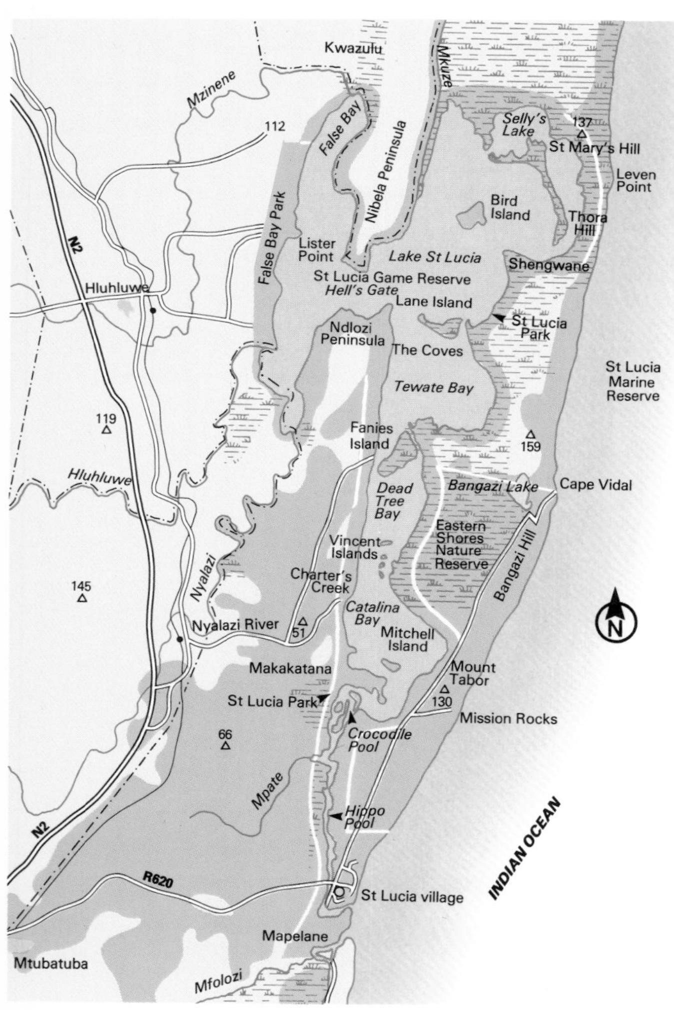

A lush waterworld lures anglers and birdwatchers

THE 19TH CENTURY hunter John Dunn once boasted of a morning's sport shooting 23 hippos in Lake St Lucia before 10 a.m. — a bag that helped his season's tally to 203. Many years later, during World War II, Catalina flying boats using the southern end of the lake as a base for anti-submarine patrols used to 'clear their guns' by shooting up crocodiles basking on sand banks near the Mkuze River mouth.

Today — gunfire a sound of the past — Lake St Lucia is a quiet haven for the nature lover, bird-watcher, angler and hiker.

The variety of birds at Lake St Lucia is astounding, and the complex is justifiably world-famous as an area to see spectacular birdlife. To date more than 360 species of birds have been recorded — one third of them inhabiting the mudflats, reeds and swamp around the water. Almost half of all the birds recorded in South Africa have been seen at St Lucia, and for at least 15 species the lake is their southernmost distribution.

The magnificent pink-backed pelican is not known to breed regularly anywhere else in the country, and in 1972 a flamingo breeding colony of 6000 was recorded.

Comprising more than half the estuarine habitat in South Africa, St Lucia is extremely important to fish life, and a great variety of freshwater, estuarine and marine species breed here. The lake is also the most important prawn habitat in the country.

Excellent fishing

St Lucia's fishing is deservedly praised, and in the holiday periods four-wheel-drive vehicles towing ski-boats outnumber more conventional vehicles. The lake is shallow, with an average depth of one metre, and is home to an estimated 2000 crocodiles and 700 hippo. The crocodiles, whose primary diet is fish, are nevertheless good reason for the Natal Parks Board to ban all paddling and swimming in the lake.

The St Lucia complex consists of four separate reserves. The lake itself with its islands — some 36000ha in extent, about 60km long, and shaped roughly like an 'H' (or perhaps a battle axe) — was proclaimed St Lucia Game Reserve in 1895.

In 1939 an 800m wide strip of land around the lake was proclaimed St Lucia Park. It stretches from the Mkuze River in the north to the Nyalazi River on the western shore, encompasses the village of St Lucia at the mouth of the estuary in the south,

A flock of flamingoes in flight over an isolated stretch of the lake.

The Nile crocodile (Crocodylus niloticus).

and must rate as the strangest shaped park in the world.

False Bay Park, proclaimed in 1944, protects 2247 ha of northern shoreline on False Bay, between the Hluhluwe and Mzinene rivers. Bird-watchers use the park as a base from which to get close to the colony of pink-backed pelicans.

The last of the four parks was proclaimed in 1978, after the Natal Parks Board and Department of Forestry had agreed jointly to administer the area between St Lucia Park and the coast. Known as the Eastern Shores Nature Reserve, the coastal strip boasts some of the highest forested dunes in the world, reaching a height of 150 m.

Game viewing

The habitat of the lake shore varies from the steep, wooded western shoreline to the marshy and reed-covered eastern bank. The marshes eventually give way to the grasslands of the Eastern Shores reserve — an ideal environment for the area's 4 500 reedbuck and grazing ground for the hippo. The grasslands are specifically managed for these two animals, and are so rich and prolific that the reedbuck breed all year.

Visitors to the complex may also see monkey, jackal, hyaena, cheetah, zebra, warthog, buffalo, red duiker, grey duiker, suni, waterbuck, impala, nyala and kudu. The best way to view game in the area is on foot — on one of the number of trails offered by the Parks Board — or by boat, as the roads in St Lucia complex are not designed for game-watching from your car.

The Natal Parks Board operates 10 overnight camps at St Lucia. There are hutted camps at Charter's Creek, Fanies Island, Mapelane and Cape Vidal; two campgrounds at St Lucia Estuary; as well as campgrounds at Cape Vidal, False Bay, Fanies Island and Mapelane. There are hotels and holiday flats in St Lucia village, which is well placed to serve as a base for the St Lucia area, and also Hluhluwe and Umfolozi game reserves.

Petrol is available at Fanies Island, Charter's Creek, Cape Vidal and the village, while food and drink is available only at the village ●

White pelicans are among the 360 bird species recorded around Lake St Lucia.

Places to visit at Lake St Lucia

FALSE BAY PARK

Rustic huts with minimal facilities at the Dugandlovu trail make an ideal base from which to organise a trip to the pink-backed pelican colony during their December to April breeding time. There is also a pleasant three-hour family walk through the northern reaches of the park, called the Mpophomeni trail, on which you may see zebra, reedbuck, nyala, duiker and suni.

The park has many delightful picnic sites along the shoreline, and there are 40 camping and caravan stands facing the dawn over the lake.

CHARTER'S CREEK

This camp, set on a rise next to the lake, has excellent views of the water. You may reserve a two-hour boat tour from here to see hippo at close quarters. (Booking is essential — at Mtubatuba 03552-1413.)

Two trails are offered: the Isikhova walk, which starts in the campground near the jetty, takes the walker through typical western shore coastal forest for three hours, during which you may see vervet monkey, bushbuck, nyala, duiker, warthog and banded mongoose. The shorter Umkhumbe walk starts just outside the camp gate.

FANIES ISLAND

'Fanies', as it is known locally, earned its popularity as a fishing spot. The camp is, in fact, not on an island, but on the west bank of the lake.

Within a small radius of the camp you can explore open parkland, coastal bush and the remnants of a dune forest by taking the 5 km Umkhiwane trail, on which there is a possibility of coming face to face with a hippo.

CAPE VIDAL

At the southern end of the St Lucia Marine Reserve, Cape Vidal offers underwater and surf fishing, while sunbathers can watch the yellow-billed kites, ospreys and fish eagles glide the thermals between sand and sea. The Mvubu three-hour self-guided trail takes the walker through the dune forest, and follows hippo paths in a number of places.

The 30 km gravel road from St Lucia village to Cape Vidal cuts through the Eastern Shores reserve, but is unlikely to offer game viewing. The road is badly corrugated and potholed in places.

On the way to or from Cape Vidal, it is worth turning off to Mission Rocks for a walk along the fascinating marine shelf that reveals itself at low tide. (Tide times are available from all Natal Parks Board offices.)

Just north of the Mission Rocks turn-off there is a beautiful, distant view of Catalina Bay on the lake.

Waterside camp at Charter's Creek.

The lake yields rewarding catches.

ST LUCIA VILLAGE

The crocodile centre, which has the local Nile crocodile as well as exotic dwarf and long-snouted West African crocodiles in its pool, is well worth a visit. The centre's gift store will also provide information on the many short walks available in the nearby game park, where impala, reedbuck, waterbuck, blue wildebeest and zebra can be seen. Boats may be hired from the Parks Board's office in the village.

MAPELANE

Although close to St Lucia as the crow flies, Mapelane is reached from the Empangeni-Mtubatuba road, and has remained an isolated place with excellent fishing, an abundant birdlife and safe swimming at low tide. There are Swiss-style log cabins and 40 camp and caravan sites. The old road was washed away by Cyclone Demoina, and the new route through the dunes can be very sandy and difficult at times. Consult the Parks Board about the condition of the road before you set out on the trip.

● All hutted accommodation should be reserved through the reservations officer, Natal Parks Board, Box 662, Pietermaritzburg 3200, or telephone (0331) 51514. Camping and caravan sites should be reserved through the various camp superintendents.

An unspoilt sub-tropical coast and the heart of Chaka's country

In the wild bushveld beyond Zululand's coastal mountains lies the Mhlatuze valley — an area rich in Zulu history. We follow in the footsteps of the great king Chaka through a landscape dotted with beehive huts, then visit the pretty town of Eshowe, before heading for the golden beaches that fringe the coast. More than half the route is on tarred roads.

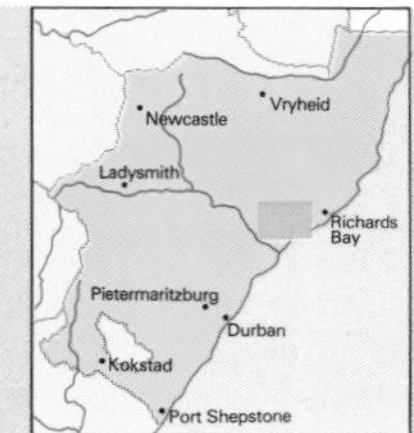

Empangeni
Enseleni Nature Reserve
Coward's Bush
Stewart's Farm
Eshowe
Mtunzini
140—160km

WE BEGIN THE DAY WITH a visit to Enseleni Nature Reserve. Leave Empangeni on the north-bound N2, noting your kms at the intersection with the R34 (the Melmoth/Richard's Bay road). 13,3km later you pass an entrance to the nature reserve on your left. 900m after this turn right onto gravel, following a sign for a picnic site. Roughly 150m along this side-road you reach the parking area at the head of the Umdoni trail, a delightful 2,4km walk through dense swamp forest on the banks of the Nseleni River. (After a few metres the path forks — go left here. Allow 40-60 minutes for the circular walk.)

Enseleni to Stewart's Farm

Retrace your route along the N2 to the R34, and turn right for Melmoth, noting your kms. The R34 takes you through Empangeni to the hilly country beyond the town.

After 13,7km on the R34 turn left onto the P230, noting your kms again. After about 1km the road gains height, and you can see along the broad valley of the Mhlatuze River that runs parallel to the coastal mountains. You gradually leave behind the more cultivated countryside, and indigenous bush becomes a feature of the landscape — including acacias, euphorbia trees and aloes.

After 5,6km you cross an attractive stretch of the Mhlatuze River on a single-lane bridge. 1km later go right where the road forks. The tar surface ends after 100m, and from here the countryside becomes even wilder. Goats and cattle graze on the hillsides, and soon you begin to see beehive huts amongst the more common mud-and-wattle structures.

17,7km after turning onto the P230 pull onto the side of the road for the magnificent view — on your left over sprawling settlements and across the Mhlatuzana valley towards the Ngoye mountains; and on your right over the hilly Mhlatuze valley.

Continue west, and after 18,6km on the P230 stop on your left at the Coward's Bush cairn (see opposite). After a further 800-900m on your right is another cairn, commemorating Chaka's kwaBulawayo kraal.

1,7km beyond the second cairn turn right at the fork onto the D132 for 'Zoeloekraal', noting your kms. The road begins to drop through dense bush as it winds towards the cultivated valley floor. After about 1,3km you can see directly ahead of you the distant Mandawe hill with its church tower and cross on the summit. After 4,1km on the D132 turn right and go through a cattle gate. Just over 1,5km later turn right onto the road to Stewart's Farm.

This side-road leads after 1,8km to the parking area at Stewart's Farm, where there is a traditional Zulu kraal. (There is a minimum entry fee covering admission for three people. Lunch can be obtained by prior arrangement — telephone 03546-748.)

Stewart's Farm to Mandawe

Return along the farm road, noting your kms as you go through the gate nearest the parking area. After 1,6km go right at the fork, and 100m later turn right onto the D132. You pass through canefields and citrus groves, and cross the Mhlatuze River on a single-lane bridge. 3,5km after rejoining the D132 you cross the railway line, and 100m later at the T-junction turn left onto the tarred R34, noting your kms.

After just over 3,8km you can see on your right a lovely gorge carved through the moun-

A shady drive through Dlinza Forest.

TOWN OF TALL TREES

Eshowe, with its well-established gardens and tall trees, is the centre for an extensive sugar-farming district. Established as a town only in 1893, it had a long history before that — as headquarters for the Zulu king Cetshwayo; as a Norwegian mission station; as a battle site during the Anglo-Zulu War. British soldiers stationed in the town after the war created the paths through the Dlinza Forest — now a nature reserve with bushbuck, blue and red duikers, bushpigs and vervet monkeys.

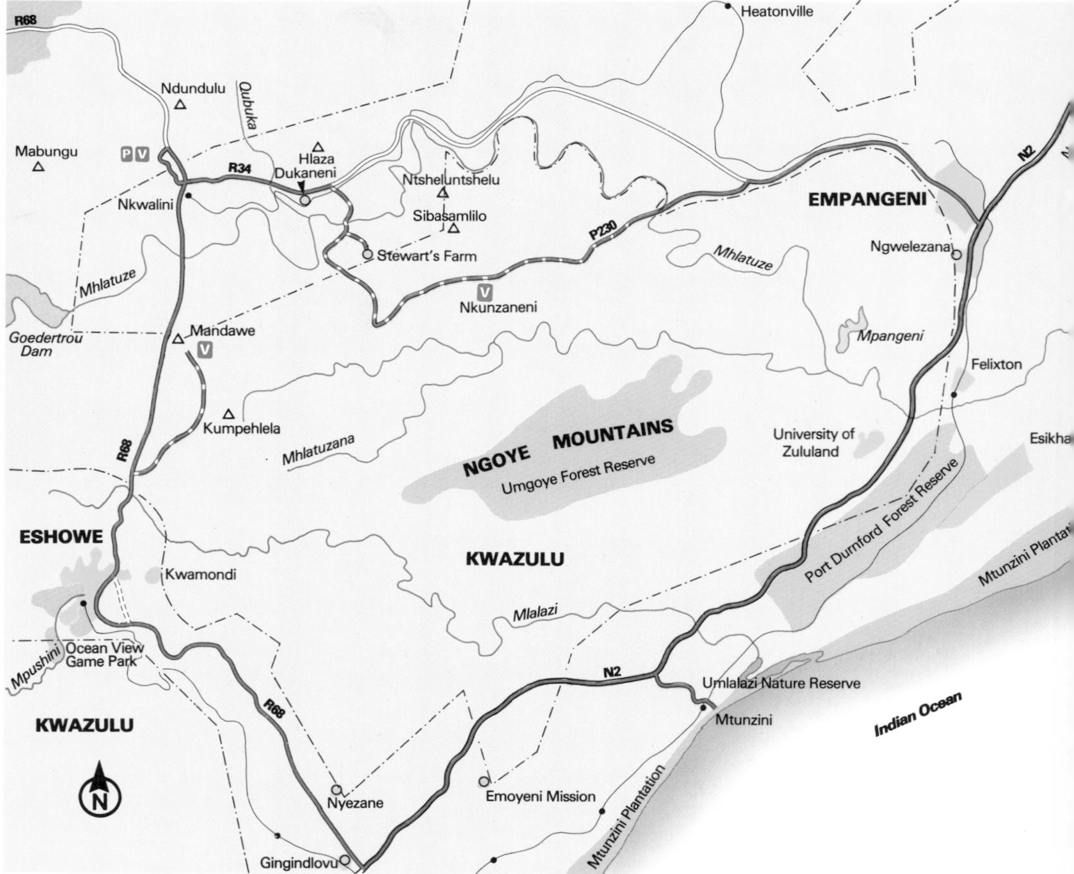

tain by the Qubuka River. 3,5 km later turn right at the T-junction for Melmoth (where the R34 joins the R68), noting your kms.

The road begins to ascend a pass. After 2 km pull into a viewsite on your left (with picnic tables) for the view of a softer aspect of the Mhlatuze valley. You can also see the old pass lower down the mountainside. Note your kms as you leave the viewsite, and continue uphill. Just after 2,1 km turn left onto the old pass.

As the road winds downhill, you have excellent views into deep, green valleys, with huts and mealie patches clinging to the steep slopes. The views open up as you approach the wide valley floor. At the bottom of the pass, at the T-junction in Nkwalini village, turn right onto the R68 towards Eshowe, noting your kms.

You cross the Mhlatuze River again after 3,4 km and pass a turn-off right to Goedetrou Dam. After 14,4 km on the R68 there is a turn-off left onto the P230 — a decision is needed here. To visit the Mandawe church, drive along the gravel P230 for 7,4 km then turn left onto a rough track. This leads after 2,2 km to the church, perched on the top of the hill. This track may be impassable after rain, but when visibility is good, and if you do not mind the bumpy ride, the excursion to the little church with its panoramic view is well worth while.

Whether or not you visit the church, note your kms at the intersection of the P230 and R68 before continuing towards Eshowe.

Mandawe to Mtunzini

After 6,5 km turn right for Eshowe and Nkandla, noting your kms again. After 3,3 km turn left onto a gravel road that takes you through part of Dlinza Forest. At the fork after 500-600 m go left, and 300-400 m later there is space to park alongside the Bishop's Seat picnic area on your left. After a further 400 m the road emerges from the forest and the surface changes to tar — note your kms here.

500 m later turn right at the stop street, and after a further 300 m (immediately after the police station) turn right into Windham Street for Zululand Historical Museum. Just after 800 m later turn left into Nongqai Road, and follow the tar road where it curves right into the parking area at the museum at Fort Nongqai.

After your visit to the museum, turn left out of the fort grounds into Nongqai Road. After 200 m turn right into Windham Street, and 800-900 m later at the stop street next to the police station turn left — noting your kms. This road curves to your right, and immediately afterwards (700 m after noting your kms) turn left into the parking area at Vukani — a Zulu handcraft centre.

Turn left out of the Vukani parking area, and cross the railway line after 100 m. After a further 200-300 m turn right for Durban onto John Ross Highway. 1,2 km later turn left into the viewsite at the gate of Ocean View Game Park. Near here the Zulu king Cetshwayo had his last kraal, backed by the mountain and facing the sea across the coastal plateau.

Continue down the mountainside, and at the T-junction after a few kms turn right onto the R68 by-pass road for Gingindlovu, noting your kms. After just over 9,6 km you pass on your right the site of the Battle of Inyezane (see below). 8,2 km later you pass, also on your right, a memorial to the British men who fell during the Battle of Gingindlovu. Roughly 19 km after rejoining the R68 turn left at the T-junction onto the N2 for Empangeni and Richard's Bay, noting your kms.

After 19 km on the N2 turn right for Mtunzini, noting your kms again. 3,3 km later turn right for Umlalazi Nature Reserve, and after a further 1,1 km you reach the reserve office on your left, which has a large outdoor map of the area. The reserve offers a choice of walks to end the day — along the beach, through the mangroves that fringe the river, or through the dune forest. From Mtunzini return to Empangeni on the N2 ●

Natal Parks Board Box 662, Pietermaritzburg 3200 Tel. (0331) 51514
SA Tourism Board Suite 520, Southern Life Centre, 320 West Street, Durban 4001 Tel. (031) 3047144

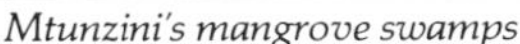
Mtunzini's mangrove swamps.

At Stewart's Farm spear-making is demonstrated with ancient implements.

COWARD'S BUSH AND CHAKA'S KRAAL

Chaka, the king who consolidated the great Zulu nation, built his second kraal on a hillside commanding a grand view over the Mhlatuze River valley. As with his first kraal on the White Mfolozi, he named his new military headquarters kwaBulawayo (place of the persecuted one), presumably because of his ostracism as an illegitimate child. The kraal, with its 5 km circumference, is thought to have housed 12 000 soldiers.

The Kei apple tree known as Coward's Bush was the scene of many executions at Chaka's behest. The name was derived from an incident when Chaka put to death the families, cattle and men of a defeated impi accused of cowardice.

MEMORIES OF THE ANGLO-ZULU WAR

At the start of the Anglo-Zulu War in 1879, 4 400 British men invaded Zululand from Fort Pearson on the Tugela River. They were engaged in battle near the Inyezane River by a force of 5 000 Zulus, but defeated their opponents and pressed on for Eshowe. No sooner had they formed a laager at the Kwamondi mission station at Eshowe, than they were besieged by Zulus under Dabulamanzi, who kept up the siege so vigilantly that the British dead had to be buried inside the fort. The force under Lord Chelmsford who set out to relieve the men at Eshowe won a battle along the way near Gingindlovu (which the victors nicknamed 'Gin, gin, I love you'), and eventually ended the siege after ten bitter weeks.

Intricately woven weaver-bird nests.

The quaint Fort Nongqai, built in 1883, now the Zululand Historical Museum.

MTUNZINI — THE SHADY PLACE

Mtunzini — meaning 'shady place' in Zulu — lies at the mouth of the Mlalazi (grinding stone) River. The town's 908 ha Umlalazi Nature Reserve incorporates a long stretch of golden beach, the sparkling lagoon at the river mouth, a mangrove swamp, and the Siyayi dune forest. Crocodiles and sharks may be found in the lagoon, and a number of buck can be spotted in the reserve. Birdwatching is excellent, and visitors may see fish eagles, or the rare palmnut vultures that breed here.

The church with the view at Mandawe.

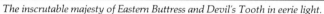

The inscrutable majesty of Eastern Buttress and Devil's Tooth in eerie light.

Fresh streams provide safe swimming.

A view over the lip of Tugela Falls.

Jagged cliffs and cascading waters at the 'mountain of beginnings'

IN THE NORTH-WESTERN corner of Natal a rugged wall of rock drops for more than a kilometre from a plateau as old as Africa. Over a sheer, 4 km-wide, basalt cliff-face — known as the Amphitheatre — the waters of several rivers plunge into a landscape exposed by erosion over millions of years.

The Amphitheatre, flanked by the distinctive Sentinel on the right and the Eastern Buttress on the left, forms a backdrop to the 8800 ha Royal Natal National Park, renowned around the world for its magnificent Drakensberg scenery. Here visitors flock every year to explore the park on foot or horseback, watch the game and great variety of birds, study the vegetation, fish for trout, or simply relax in the exhilarating environment.

The cliffs of the Drakensberg are part of a crust of volcanic rock that formed the surface of the Gondwanaland super-continent at the time that Africa broke away from it roughly 120-million years ago. Since then, Natal's rivers have steadily pushed back the cliff edge from the coast to where it is now — a dynamic process which still continues.

Above Royal Natal National Park is the Lesotho plateau, a remnant of the old Gondwanaland surface that now forms the watershed of southern Africa, and where five rivers have their source, including the Tugela and the Elands. It is the rising of these rivers that in 1836 inspired the French missionary-explorers Arbousset and Daumas to name the park's highest point (at 3 282 m) Mont-aux-Sources — 'mountain of beginnings'.

Although San hunters followed game here in summer, the area below Mont-aux-Sources was not permanently inhabited until early last century, when the San people sought refuge in its rocky shelters from nguni-speaking and white settlers. A pair of holiday makers on honeymoon in the area of the park in 1878 saw a few of these diminutive San — probably the last of them to live here.

Throughout the Drakensberg there are excellent examples of San rock art in the sandstone overhangs below the basalt cliffs. Most of the paintings occur further south (see pages 170-1), but a small number can be found in the Royal Natal National Park. The most easily accessible are those in the Sigubudu valley, which can be viewed from a walk that takes less than an hour.

Cannibals and woodcutters

The San were not the only people to hide out in these remote mountains. During the Mfecane — the migration caused by Chaka's 1818-28 territorial wars — food became so scarce that a number of tribes resorted to cannibalism. It is said that some of these desperate men lived in a shelter known as Cannibal Cave. The shelter, which also contains San paintings, can be reached on a hike via Surprise Ridge, which offers excellent views of the Drakensberg.

The magnificent yellowwood forests that are still a feature of the park's shady gorges brought more men into the area towards the end of the last century — woodcutters who were given concessions to chop tons of the beautiful wood. One promi-

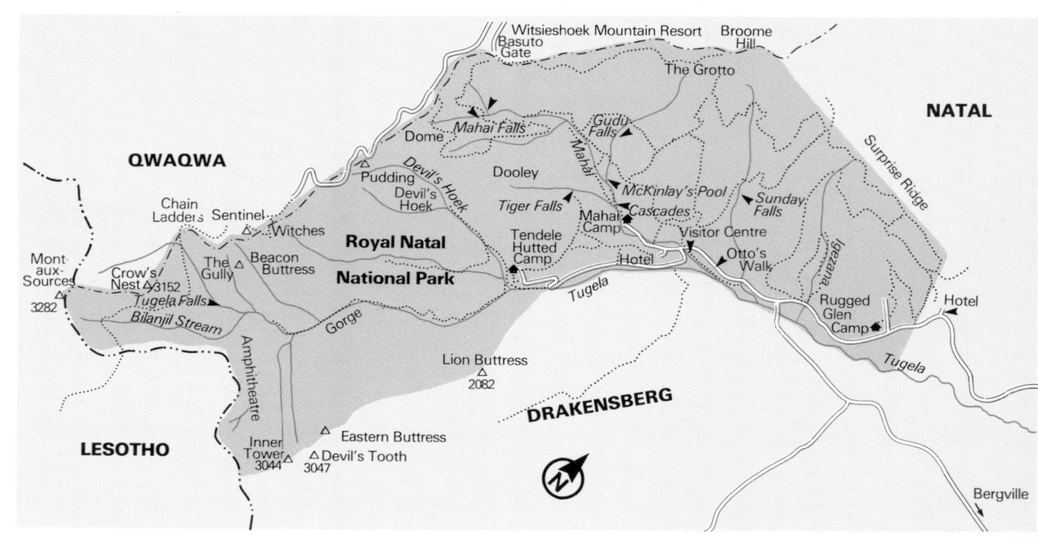

Sandstone cliffs, proteas and forested gorges typify Drakensberg trails.

The rugged Sentinel — aloof in a blue sky as clouds roll in over the park.

nent sandstone mountain bears the name of one of them, an Irishman called Dooley.

The 'Natal National Park' was proclaimed in 1916 — the 'Royal' being added to the name after the 1947 visit by members of the British royal family. Today the park offers a choice of 25 walks and hikes along a total 130 km of well-maintained paths. Described in an excellent guidebook sold in the park, they traverse areas with greatly varying altitude, and therefore a wide variety of plant, animal and bird life. Many follow river valleys, where you may swim or paddle in the clear mountain water (except in demarcated water catchment areas).

The Tugela Falls

One of the most breathtaking features of the park is the Tugela Falls. Within a few kilometres of its source on the 3 000 m plateau known as Phofung ('place of the eland') to the Sotho, the Tugela drops for almost 2 km over a series of falls and cascades, and through a dramatic gorge, to the valley floor. One sheer fall of 614 m is the highest in South Africa, while the combined drop of the Tugela Falls of 948 m makes it the second highest in the world after Angel Falls in Venezuela.

The Tugela has also created one of the most popular walks in the park: a six-hour hike up The Gorge to a feature known as The Tunnel, where the river has carved an impressive path through the white sandstone. You then have a choice of boulder-hopping through The Tunnel (when the water is low enough) or of climbing a chain ladder through a steep gorge into the Amphitheatre.

A popular shorter outing is the Cascades walk, which takes you past the trout hatchery to the Queen's Causeway and Cascades on the Mahai River. (Allow 30 minutes — or an hour if you continue to McKinlay's Pool higher up the river.) The trout hatchery may be visited for a nominal fee. An exhibit shows the life-cycle of the trout, while guided tours are offered on Mondays and Fridays at 10 a.m. The hatchery keeps the rivers and dams in the park stocked, making trout-fishing a popular activity. (A provincial licence and daily rod permit are required, both of which can be obtained from the Natal Parks Board office in the Visitor Centre.)

Mountaineering

The area has long offered challenging climbing to experienced mountaineers, and in 1927 the first guidebook was published. Those who wish to climb in the area must be members of a mountain club, or satisfy the Natal Parks Board that they are experienced enough and properly equipped. A mountain register is kept at the Visitor Centre, and must be signed by anyone venturing above certain altitudes or intending to overnight in the open.

For those who prefer to explore the area on horseback, the Natal Parks Board operates stables at the Rugged Glen camp, from where parties are led by grooms along a number of bridle paths. During peak seasons booking is advisable.

Bird-watching in the park can be very rewarding. Almost 200 species have been spotted here, including the rare Cape vulture, the bearded vulture (lammergeyer) and the black eagle. A number of antelope make their home in the park, and the visitor is likely to see mountain reedbuck on the grassy slopes. On the rocky heights you may see the klipspringer, the agile little buck that has been reintroduced after having been hunted out of the area because its hair was so popular for stuffing saddles. More prevalent amongst the park's mammals are the baboon and the rock hyrax (dassie).

Unique protea

Vegetation varies enormously with altitude. In the lowest reaches (the montane belt) you find yellowwood forests and protea savanna; in the subalpine belt there is scrub, fynbos and grassland; while the alpine belt on the plateau contains the sparser erica-helichrysum heath. A rare treasure is the little pink *Protea nubigena*, which is found in only one spot in the world — on the steep slopes of the Sentinel.

A valuable aid to the visitor is at the viewsite on your left 1,7 km after entering the park gate. Here you can match the spectacular view of the Amphitheatre with a sketch that names the prominent landmarks.

The magnificent Amphitheatre — scenery that draws visitors all year round.

Otto's Walk

The Visitor Centre, which lies 2,4 km from the entrance, is another worthwhile stopping point. It has exhibits on the area, including a model of the mountains, identifying the walks, roads, rivers and other landmarks. A self-guided trail called Otto's Walk starts at the far side of the parking area here — a booklet is available at the start.

The roads to the park, and the main internal road to the hotel, are tarred. Turn-offs to the camps are on gravel roads. Visitors (except those eating at the hotel) must bring all their own food and drink, but petrol is sold in the park. There are picnic sites around the trout dam along the Tendele turn-off, and along the Mahai River on the Cascades walk. Braai fires are permitted only in the fireplaces around the dam.

Hikers should enquire locally about the weather, as sudden thunderstorms, mist or snow make conditions extremely hazardous.

Reservations for accommodation are essential. For the hotel, book by telephoning Bergville (03642) and asking for Mont-aux-Sources 1. For campsites, telephone Bergville and ask for Mont-aux-Sources 3. Bookings for the hutted camp can be made through the Reservations Office, Natal Parks Board, Box 662, Pietermaritzburg 3200, tel. (0331) 51514 ●

A sortie into the Drakensberg across historic Anglo-Boer battlefields

West of Ladysmith lie peaceful hills that once rang with the sound of gunfire as Boer and Briton fought to possess the land. We visit Spioenkop, site of one such bitter battle, and drive into the area below Cathkin Peak and Champagne Castle for a walk to a waterfall in a lovely Drakensberg setting. Roughly two-thirds of the route is tarred.

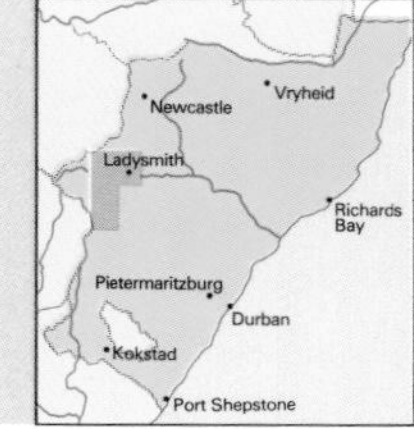

Ladysmith
Spioenkop Dam
Winterton
Monk's Cowl
Forestry Station
Bergville
Spioenkop
150 – 170 km

DRIVE SOUTH on Ladysmith's Murchison Street (the main road), and turn left into Buckingham Street. After 400 m turn right into Forbes Street. The road curves right into Short Street – park here at the footbridge for a visit to the Soofie Mosque.

Continue from the mosque along Short Street, and at the stop street turn left. Pass Murchison Street on your right, and note your kms soon afterwards as you cross the Klip River.

After 2,2 km (just before the N3) turn left towards the airfield, and after a further 250 m turn left onto gravel for the Burger Monument. 250 m later go left at the fork. The road surface changes to tar again roughly 2 km later, and after a further 300 m you pass the Wagon Hill military cemetery on your left.

100 m beyond the cemetery you reach the control gate at the entrance to the historic Platrand/Wagon Hill site controlled by the National Monuments Council. Turn left at the T-junction beyond the gate. (The gravel track on your right here leads after 1 km to a number of British memorials and to the grave of the Reverend J D Kestell, who travelled with the Free State Boers but ministered to both sides.) 600 m beyond the T-junction turn left into the parking area at the Burger Monument. From here you have an excellent view over Ladysmith and the surrounding hills, where many a battle was fought (see below).

Wagon Hill to Spioenkop Dam

Retrace your route to the intersection near the N3, and turn onto the south-bound N3 for Colenso. Roughly 2,5 km later turn right onto the R616 for 'Bergville/Berg Resorts', noting your kms. After 8 km turn left for Spioenkop Dam, Winterton and Central Berg Resorts, noting your kms again.

The prominent Twin Peaks and Spioenkop

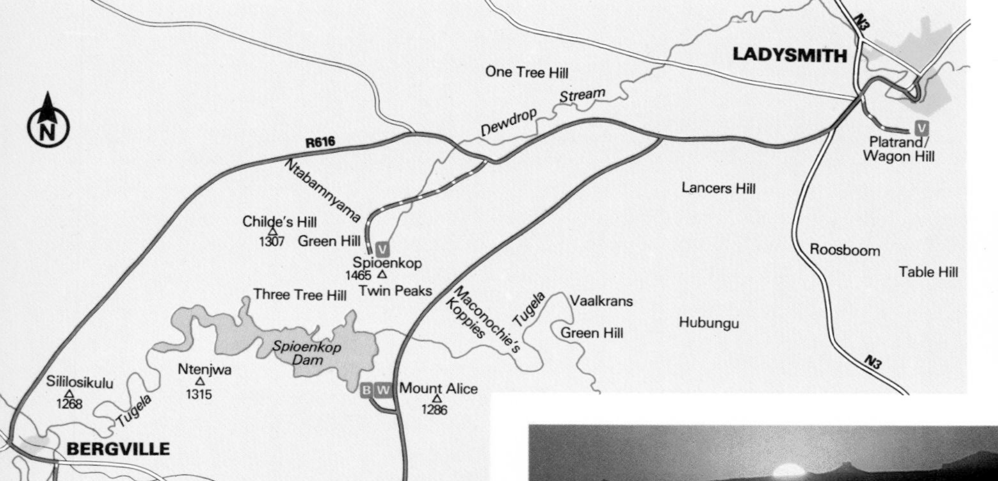

Drakensberg panorama from the Bergville road.

Spioenkop Dam's surrounding hills against the setting sun.

THE SPANISH BEAUTY

Ladysmith, an attractive town set on the Klip (stone) River and surrounded by a ring of hills, is an important agricultural centre, an industrial growth point, and one of the largest railway marshalling points in South Africa. Many of its interesting historic buildings date from the Siege of Ladysmith during the Anglo-Boer War, including the old Town Hall in Murchison Street which was shelled during the Siege. Next door is the Siege Museum, which has many fascinating relics from that time. The town's settler past dates back to 1847 when a group of Voortrekkers under Andries Spies formed the Klip River Republic here – but three years later the British annexed the area, naming it after Juana de los Dolores de Leon, the beautiful Spanish wife of Cape Governor Sir Harry Smith.

SIEGE THAT TOOK THE WORLD BY STORM

On 2 November 1899 Boer commandos besieged the British and colonial garrison at Ladysmith – a siege that was to last 118 days and capture newspaper headlines around the world. Several attempts were made by the British to relieve the town, leading to heavy losses – most of them British – at places such as Colenso, Spioenkop, Vaalkrans, Hlangwane and Pietershoogte (Pieter's Hill). There were also a number of deaths on Wagon Hill (or Platrand, as it was known to the Boers) during an attempt to breach the town's defences.

Disease and wounds took their toll of the defenders, and daily rations were eventually down to 230 g of bread and about 600 ml of horse extract (chevril), but the besieged community tried to keep morale high with a calendar of Shakespeare readings, open-air concerts, picnics and a Christmas party for the 250 children amongst them.

After several failed attempts, Sir Redvers Buller eventually relieved the town on 28 February 1900 – an event celebrated jubilantly in the streets of far-away London.

soon come into view on your right, and after 9,5 km you see Spioenkop Dam shortly before you pass Twin Peaks. You pass a loop of the Tugela River on your left, and pass a turn-off to your right to the dam wall about 2 km later.

Just over 22,6 km after turning off the R616 turn right for Spioenkop Resort. Soon afterwards you pass through the control gate (where a small entry fee is charged). After a further 300 m turn right at the office for a visit to the Interpretive Centre (the gravel road ahead of you leads to picnic sites at the water's edge). The centre has many fascinating photographs from the Anglo-Boer War, and several models showing positions during major battles.

Spioenkop Dam to Monk's Cowl

Leaving Spioenkop Resort, turn right for Winterton, noting your kms. On a clear day you can see the distant wall of the Drakensberg from this road as it winds through the farmlands of the Little Tugela valley. After 11,6 km turn left at the T-junction onto the R615 for Winterton and Central Berg Resorts, noting your kms. Soon afterwards you pass through the town of Winterton on the banks of the Little Tugela River (a hotel in the town serves lunch).

After 1,1 km on the R615 turn right for Cathedral Peak, The Nest, El Mirador, Cathkin Park, Dragon Peaks and Champagne Castle — and note your kms again.

The road on which you are travelling soon begins to wind closer and closer to the Drakensberg. After 13,2 km go straight at the crossroads where right leads to Bergville (your return route later in the day). After a further 7 km, in which you travel through attractive valleys dotted with farmhouses and huts, you have a panoramic view of the Drakensberg.

24,5 km after turning off the R615, turn left into the El Mirador Hotel for a visit to its attractive little thatched chapel — the large altar window provides an impressive view of Cathkin Peak, Champagne Castle, and the Mount Memory range. (The hotel serves lunch — booking advisable.)

You can also walk from the chapel to the MOTH National Shrine, which offers equally splendid views. The shrine, set in the Mount Memory Sanctuary, was built by the ex-servicemen's organisation, the Memorable Order of Tin Hats, to honour the dead of World War I and II. It is reached along a gravel track that turns off the main road just below the chapel — after 150 m on the side-road turn right to reach the sanctuary after a further 150 m.

Continue on the main road towards the mountains, noting your kms at the turn-off to the MOTH National Shrine. At the fork after 900 m turn left for Dragon Peaks and Champagne Castle. The tar ends soon afterwards, and the road winds through attractive farmlands with tall stands of trees, overlooked by the sandstone heights of the Little Berg and the more distant basalt cliffs of the Drakensberg.

You pass a turn-off right to the Drakensberg Boys' Choir school, and Dragon Peaks (a resort with a shop and picnic facilities). Soon afterwards the road is tarred for 1,3 km as it climbs steeply into the mountains.

8,4 km from the MOTH shrine go right (where a road branches off left for Champagne Castle Hotel). Roughly 1,7 km later you reach Monk's Cowl Forestry Station (small entry fee). Enquire at the gate or office for directions to Sterkspruit Falls — a 60-90 minute walk amidst magnificent mountain scenery. The stretch of river above the falls makes a lovely spot for a picnic, although there are no facilities.

Monk's Cowl to Spioenkop

Retrace your route for the roughly 22 km from Monk's Cowl to the Bergville/Kelvin Grove turn-off. Turn left, noting your kms. After 100 m the road surface changes to gravel. You wind through mealie fields, sorghum and cattle country, with the wall of the high Drakensberg running almost parallel to the road on your left. Pull onto the shoulder of the road after 16,3 km for a view of the mountains.

After 28,6 km on gravel turn left onto the tarred R615 for Bergville/Oliviershoek Pass, noting your kms. You cross the Tugela River, then enter the town of Bergville. After 2,2 km turn right onto the R616 for Ladysmith, noting your kms again.

You now travel parallel to another section of the Drakensberg — the northern extension, noted for its sculpted sandstone formations. After a few kms you enter hilly acacia bushveld again. After 30,8 km on the R616 turn right for Spioenkop Monument. This gravel road takes you after roughly 10 km to the top of Spioenkop, from where you can look out over the former battlefield to a magnificent scene — Spioenkop Dam, the Tugela valley and hills stretching towards the Drakensberg.

Retrace your route to the R616, and turn right for Ladysmith ●

CATHKIN PEAK AND CHAMPAGNE CASTLE

From afar you notice the distinctive shape of the 3 149 m Cathkin Peak with its flat top and sheer cliffs. Because it is detached from the main Drakensberg wall, it seems to tower above Champagne Castle to its south — at 3 377 m one of the highest points on the escarpment. David Gray, a Scot who moved here in 1858, named the peak after Cathkin Braes near his home town, but for many years it was also called Champagne Castle because of the mysterious disappearance of half of a bottle of champagne from the baggage of two explorers. The name Champagne Castle was eventually transferred to the then unnamed height on the main wall.

Above: *A hiker dwarfed by the Sterkspruit Falls.* **Below:** *The exotic Soofie Mosque in Ladysmith.* **Below left:** *Summer clouds over Cathkin Peak.*

Ladysmith Publicity Association Siege Museum, Murchison Street, Ladysmith 3370 Tel. (0361) 22992
Monk's Cowl Forestry Station P O Winterton 3340 Tel. (03682) 2204
Natal Parks Board Box 662, Pietermaritzburg 3200 Tel. (0331) 51221

The Bushman's River winds its way through the rocky hills below Giant's Castle, as the game reserve takes on its golden winter colours.

The mountain kingdom of the 'people of the eland'

ON A RECENT summer's day rangers counted a herd of 250 eland on the grassy slopes of Giant's Castle Game Reserve — a living tribute to the reserve's efforts to save the largest of all antelope from extinction.

When Giant's Castle was established in 1903 to save these handsome beasts from the hunters' guns, there were estimated to be only 27 of them left. Now 1 200 eland roam freely through the southern Drakensberg, and Giant's Castle has a population of 600-800.

The 34 000 ha reserve, overlooked by South Africa's highest peak on the massive basalt wall of the Drakensberg, offers visitors a number of special attractions apart from game and the popular Drakensberg activities of hiking, mountaineering, bird-watching, trout-fishing, swimming and horse-riding. Here you can explore the mountains on overnight horse-riding trails run by the Natal Parks Board; watch from a cliff-top hide as vultures feed close by; or discover one of the richest legacies of San (Bushman) rock art.

Unlike the eland, the San people did not survive the arrival of the white man in Natal early in the 19th century. The diminutive hunter-gatherers — known as the 'people of the eland' because they followed the herds as they migrated — had lived in perfect ecological harmony with their environment for thousands of years. When they saw the vast herds of game decimated by the white men's guns, they launched fierce retaliatory raids. But the San bows and arrows were no match for guns, and they were eventually hunted from the area like vermin. All that remains as a reminder of their occupation of the Drakensberg is a number of artefacts and a collection of paintings in the rock overhangs in which they lived.

Giant's Castle is one of the richest areas for San rock art, with more than 5 000 paintings, most of which have been recorded and catalogued. The reserve and the Ndedema area combined contain more than 40 per cent of all known rock art in South Africa.

Summer thunderstorms contribute to the rich legends of the Drakensberg.

Main Caves Museum

A popular walk in the reserve is through the spectacular mountain scenery to the Main Caves, where there are more than 500 paintings in a single, large shelter. A second shelter houses a site museum with life-sized models depicting the traditional San way of life. The caves are reached along a sign-posted path behind the Giant's Castle hutted camp. The area is fenced to prevent vandalism, and a game guard opens the gate on the hour every hour from 9 a.m. to 3 p.m. (There is a small entry fee. Allow two hours for the walk there and back along a gradual-to-steep path, and one hour for the guided tour of the caves.)

Before you set out for the caves, it is worth buying from the Natal Parks Board (for a nominal fee) a brochure on the Bushman's River Trail. The brochure takes visitors on a 'self-guided nature trail', and provides interesting information on the geology, vegetation and some of the history of the area.

The Parks Board also sells an excellent guide book that describes twenty walks that begin from the main camp, and another ten that start from the Injasuti hutted camp.

Injasuti is set in the beautiful valley of the eNjesuthi (well-fed dog) River, from which it takes its name.

The eland — largest of all antelope.

The area is renowned for its ancient indigenous forests with towering yellowwoods, and its magnificent setting below Cathkin Peak, Monk's Cowl and the highest point in South Africa — the eNjesuthi Dome (3410 m). In the valley lies Battle Cave, a shelter containing superb San paintings that depict a fierce battle between rival armies. The caves may be visited in the company of a game guard, who escorts visitors from the camp.

The main camp and the reserve are named after the 3314 m Giant's Castle — the peak known in Zulu as Bhulihawu (place of the shield-thrashers) because it is believed that all thunder (called 'thrashing of shields') is born here.

The Langalibalele Rebellion

Several other peaks take their names from a sad episode in the history of the area — the Langalibalele Rebellion of the 1870s. Langalibalele, powerful chief of the Hlubi people and a rain-maker and isangoma (diviner) of some repute, had come into conflict with the British colonial government in Natal over his refusal to levy taxes on his clansmen, to provide labour gangs for government projects, and to hand over the tribe's guns for registration.

Annoyed by Langalibalele's insubordination, and hearing that he planned to flee over the Bushman's River Pass into Lesotho, the government sent out a force to arrest him. But, after a series of disasters aggravated by foul weather and inaccurate maps, the men under Major (later Colonel) A W Durnford who were to head off Langalibalele at the pass arrived too late.

The men who died in the ensuing clash — Robert Henry Erskine, Katana, Edwin Bond, Charles Davie Potterill and Elijah Kambule — and the man who led them have all had peaks named after them.

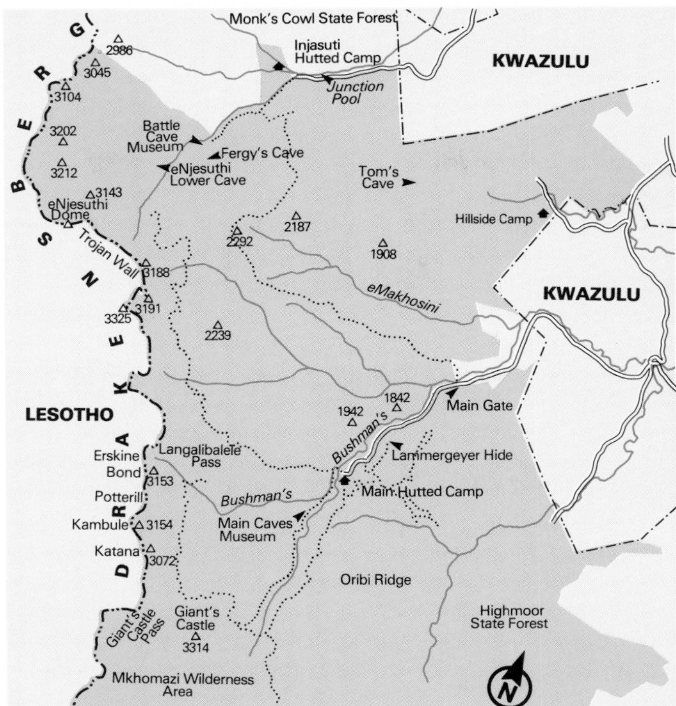

The pass, where the five fallen men are buried in a common grave, has been renamed after Langalibalele (who was later delivered to the British for trial and imprisoned on Robben Island). The pass provides a popular eight-hour hike along the Bushman's River valley into Lesotho. (For hikes above 2100 m, or overnight trips into the mountains, it is necessary to fill in a mountain rescue register at a Natal Parks Board or Department of Forestry office.)

Fauna and flora

While hiking in the reserve, you may see eland, common reedbuck, blesbok, bushbuck, mountain reedbuck, grey rhebuck, the rare oribi, grey duiker, red hartebeest or, in a few rocky areas, the klipspringer. The baboon and rock hyrax (dassie) are often seen, and the jackal is heard at night, though it is seldom visible.

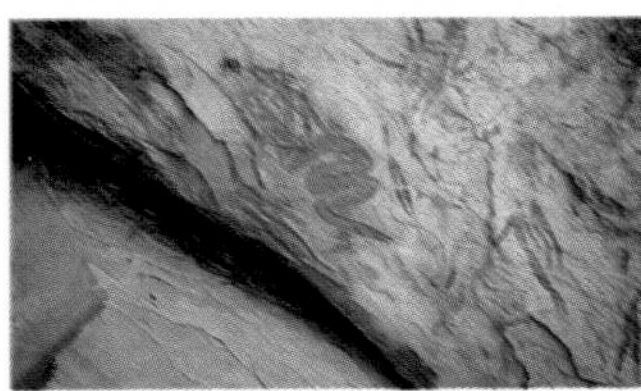

A rare San rock painting of a snake.

Giant's Castle, and the Drakensberg in general, is known for its wildflowers. Among the many hundreds of plant species in the region there are more than 60 species of ground orchids, and several plants that occur only in the Natal Drakensberg — such as the *Protea dracomontana*, which produces a creamish pink flower on the ground, a heath known as *Erica drakensbergiensis*, and the cycad *Encephalartos ghellinckii*.

For the amateur bird-watcher as well as the ornithologist there are many delights in the reserve, which

The sheer western eNjesuthi Triplet.

has a bird list of 140 species. During winter weekends there is the unique opportunity to watch the endangered bearded vulture (lammergeyer) through the one-way glass of a hide set high on the edge of a cliff. Here the Parks Board leaves bones for the vultures, to protect them against accidental death from poisoned carcases left out to kill jackals. The ossuary attracts a number of other birds, including the rare Cape vulture, the black eagle, jackal buzzard and Lanner falcon. (The hide must be booked in advance by telephoning the officer-in-charge at 03631-24616.)

Accommodation in the main hutted camp and the huts at Injasuti should be reserved through the Reservations Office, Natal Parks Board, Box 662, Pietermaritzburg 3200, or tel. (0331) 51514. There is also a campsite at Injasuti, where sites should be reserved through the camp superintendent (tel. 0020 and ask for Loskop 1311). Reservations for Hillside campsite should be made through its camp superintendent — tel. (03631) 24435. There are also three overnight huts in the park.

Visitors must bring all their food and drink, as these are not available at any of the camps. Petrol is sold at the main gate.

Snow in winter and thunderstorms or mist in summer can be hazardous to hikers. It is wise to enquire locally about the weather before you set out.

The road from the reserve gate to the main camp is tarred, but the gravel roads to the reserve are sometimes in poor condition after rains. The road to Injasuti should not be tackled in summer without chains, as it becomes very muddy ●

The skilfully camouflaged vulture hide atop its cliff.

An eagle's view at dawn towards the northern peaks.

The red cliffs of Hella-Hella and the foothills of the Sani Pass

This long drive takes you through richly varied landscapes — the settler country around Richmond, the red cliffs of Hella-Hella, and the towering peaks and sparkling trout waters of the Drakensberg. We venture to the foot of the forbidding Sani Pass, then head back through grand valleys and forests. More than two-thirds of the route is tarred.

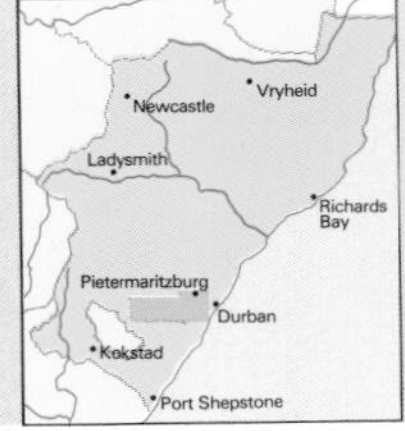

Pietermaritzburg
Richmond
Hella-Hella Pass
Underberg
Himeville
Sani Pass
Reichenau
350—370 km

TURN FROM Pietermaritzburg's Commercial Road into Alexandra Road (R56) for Richmond, noting your kms. The R56 takes you out of the city along a scenic road — after 11,2 km pull onto the shoulder (where a farm road leads left) for a pleasant view back over the hilly countryside towards Table Mountain in the distance.

5 km later you pass a turn-off left for the R623 to Umlaas Road and Durban — note your kms here. The road winds through the lush, cultivated valleys of the Mlazi (Umlaas) and Lovu (Illovo) rivers. 20,8 km from the R623 turn left for Richmond, and at the T-junction 200-300 m later turn right, noting your kms.

You soon enter Richmond on Shepstone Street, which is lined with a number of attractive old buildings (see below). After just over 1,5 km turn left, then turn right at the second intersection — the Richmond, Byrne and District Museum is on the corner here in a house that served as the Presbyterian manse from 1882 to 1982. (Worth a visit; nominal entry fee, opening times vary.)

Richmond to Hella-Hella

Return to Shepstone Street, and turn left. 1,5 km later turn left onto gravel for Eastwolds and Hella-Hella, noting your kms. After 600 m you pass a turn-off left to Indaleni Mission. The road begins to rise immediately after this, giving you ever-changing views over the surrounding hills, with the Byrne Valley on your right.

After 13 km on gravel keep right where a road leads left to a farm. Immediately afterwards you begin a gradual descent into the valley of the Mkomazi (Umkomaas) River and its tributaries, and after a further 6,3 km the towering red cliffs of the Helehele (buttresses) mountain come into view ahead of you. After 21,5 km on gravel you cross the wide Mkomazi River over the Hella-Hella Bridge. At the far side park on your right, and walk back to the bridge for a view of the impressive river gorge.

Note your kms as you leave the parking area and begin the steep ascent of Hella-Hella Pass (not suitable for towing). As you climb, you get ever-wider views of the gorge, the twisting river and the locked-in orchards on the valley floor. After 4,7 km turn left into the viewsite and picnic area close to the summit for the grand view.

The Mzimkulu River sparkles beneath the Drakensberg foothills.

The Sani Pass begins gently — then becomes a gruelling track over the mountains.

RICHMOND AND THE BYRNE VALLEY

The Byrne Settlers of 1850 occupied the banks of the Lovu (Illovo) River, and established a town they named Beaulieu after their home town in England — the seat of the Duke of Buccleuch in Hampshire. The name proved difficult to pronounce, and the town eventually became known as Richmond.

The area is also the main centre for the amaBhaca (people who hide), who slowly returned to the area after fleeing south during the Zulu territorial wars early last century. Bhaca women in their colourful traditional dress are often seen in the district.

THE HIGH ROAD OVER THE BERG

The little San hunters were the first people to cross the Drakensberg by the route now known as Sani Pass — today the only road access to Lesotho from the east. Herdsmen followed in their footsteps, and the path was eventually upgraded, first to a mule trail and then a jeep track to carry trade goods between eastern Lesotho and Natal. The pass follows the course of the upper Mkhomazana (little Mkomazi) River through exceptional mountain scenery to the edge of the escarpment, and the road then continues to the remote settlement of Mokhotlong in Lesotho. Spectacular walks and hikes abound in the area — including the Giant's Cup trail (named after the basin between the prominent twins, Hodgson's Peaks), and a number of excursions to San paintings. Most of the walks and hikes are on land owned by the Department of Forestry, and permits are required before setting out.

Left: *Thatched huts near Donnybrook.*

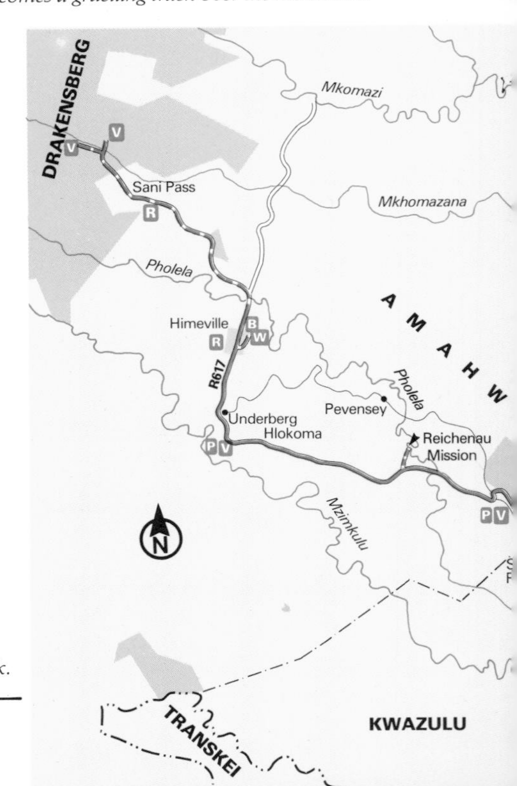

Hella-Hella to Underberg

Note your kms as you turn left out of the viewsite. After 12,1 km go right at the fork for Eastwolds and Donnybrook. 9,2 km later you cross a narrow-gauge railway, and after a further 100 m turn right at Eastwolds trading centre onto the tarred R612 for Donnybrook and Bulwer — noting your kms.

You travel along the crest of a hill for a while, with views into valleys on both sides — tribal lands interspersed with forests. You pass a turn-off on your left to Donnybrook after 8,4 km and another after a further 1 km. Roughly 2 km later you can see the spire of the red-brick church of Kevelaer Mission on your right.

After about 24 km on the R612 the road begins to wind amongst the foothills of the Drakensberg, and you can see the southern end of the distinctive Amahwaqa mountain ahead of you. After 26,8 km on the R612 turn left at the T-junction onto the R617 for Underberg and Himeville (where right leads to Bulwer — your return route). Note your kms here.

Roughly 7 km later you can see a sweep of the Drakensberg stretching to the west. After 9 km on the R617 turn left into a tree-shaded picnic site that offers a good view across farmlands towards the distant mountains.

Note your kms as you rejoin the R617. After 5,9 km you cross the Pholela River, and 2 km later on your right you have a glimpse of Reichenau Mission on its banks. 22,3 km after noting your kms turn left into another shady picnic area that offers a magnificent view over Underberg, the Drakensberg and the fairy-tale shapes of its foothills. 2 km later you enter Underberg. Pass the small traffic circle on your right, and 200 m later turn right for Himeville and Sani Pass, noting your kms.

Underberg to Sani Pass

Only a few kms separate Underberg and Himeville. After 5,3 km turn right in Himeville (with the town's museum on the corner) onto a gravel road leading to the nature reserve. 400 m later you enter Himeville Nature Reserve, and after a further 500 m you reach the office (where a nominal fee is payable). 800 m beyond the office you reach an attractive, shady picnic site alongside a trout dam — an ideal lunch stop (braai sites, water, toilets).

Retrace your route to the tarred main road, and turn right. After 200 m you pass the Himeville Arms on your left (which serves lunch). 3,4 km later turn left onto gravel for Sani Pass, noting your kms.

The road winds into the Mkhomazana River valley past a number of vleis. After 8,5 km you can see Khanti Ridge directly ahead of you, with balancing rock formations on its summit. 3,1 km later turn right into the Sani Pass Hotel. The hotel serves lunch, and there is also a delightful walk to a waterfall on the Mkhomazana River. (Walk towards the tennis courts, but 60 m before reaching them, branch off right through a gate and follow the occasional yellow stone markers through an avenue of poplars. Allow 40-60 minutes.)

Leaving the hotel, turn right, noting your kms. After 4,3 km turn right at the fork, and park near the bridge for a view up the valley towards the Twelve Apostles. Return to the fork and turn right onto the road that becomes Sani Pass. A further 1,1 km brings you to a good turning point — the road beyond here is steeper and narrower, and is not recommended without four-wheel drive.

Sani Pass to Lundy's Hill

Retrace your route through Himeville to the T-junction in Underberg, and turn left onto the R617 for Bulwer, noting your kms. After just over 15 km turn left onto a gravel track for Reichenau Mission, which you reach after 2 km.

Leaving the mission station, turn left onto the R617, noting your kms. After 17,7 km you pass the R612 to Donnybrook and Ixopo on your right, and 2,9 km later you enter Bulwer, nestling below the south-eastern end of the Amahwaqa. After a further 1 km turn right onto a gravel road that leads after a short distance to an unpretentious little chapel built a century ago entirely out of yellowwood.

Return to the tarred main road, and turn right, noting your kms. You travel through Bulwer, and after roughly 4 km the view opens out over a wide section of the Mkomazi valley. You begin the descent into the valley, and 16,7 km after noting your kms turn left into a parking area overlooking a horseshoe bend in the river.

Rejoin the R617, and cross the river soon afterwards. You then start the ascent of Lundy's Hill (from 920 m to 1 390 m), which gives excellent views of the valley. From the summit of the pass the road winds through hilly countryside towards Pietermaritzburg, eventually passing Midmar Dam on your left. Roughly 60 km from the Mkomazi River viewsite turn right onto the N3 for Pietermaritzburg. About 5,4 km later exit left for Hilton, and at the end of the off-ramp turn right. 2,7 km later turn left onto the R103 (Old Howick Road) for Pietermaritzburg, and after a further 2 km turn right for World's View/Boesmansrand for the splendid late-afternoon view (see pages 178-9) ●

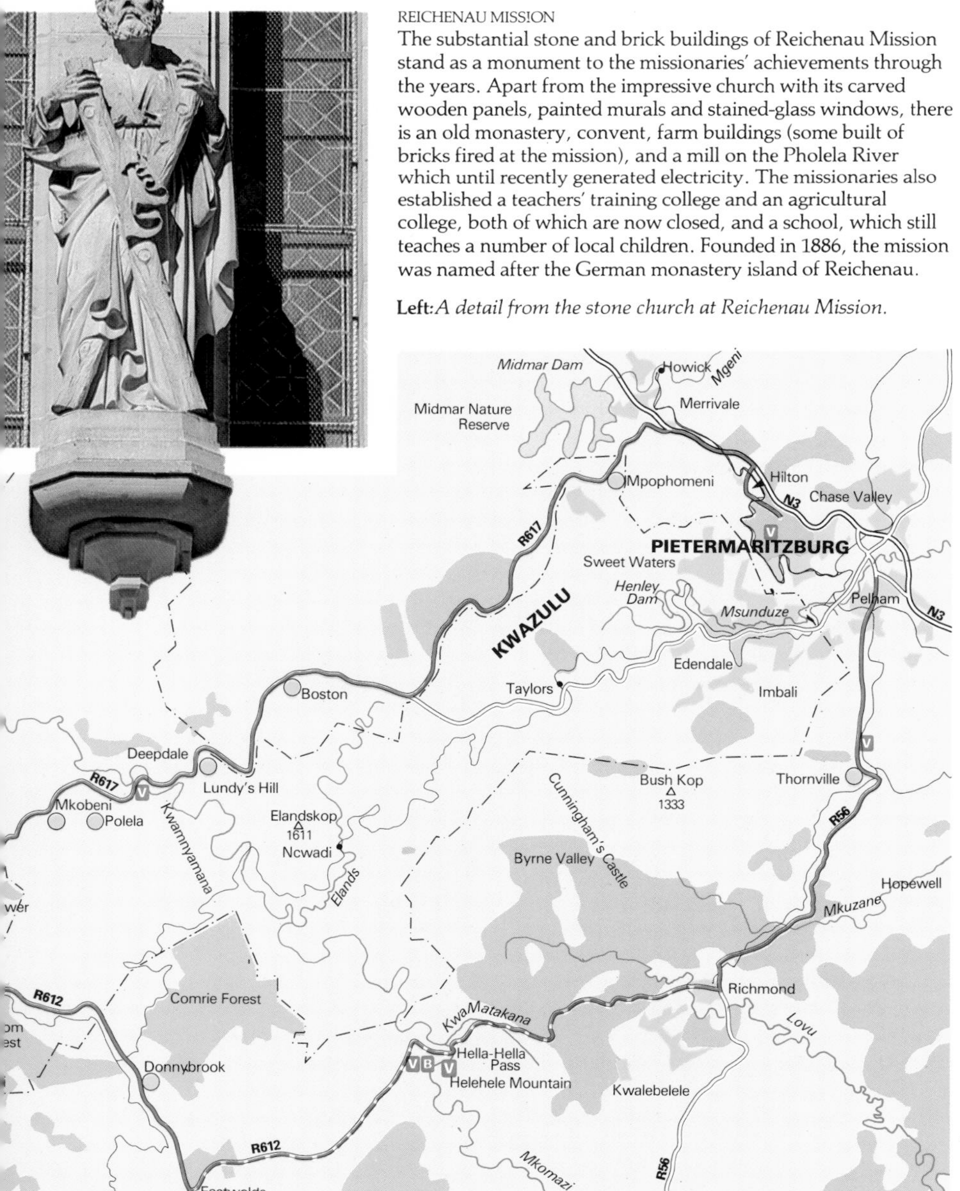

REICHENAU MISSION

The substantial stone and brick buildings of Reichenau Mission stand as a monument to the missionaries' achievements through the years. Apart from the impressive church with its carved wooden panels, painted murals and stained-glass windows, there is an old monastery, convent, farm buildings (some built of bricks fired at the mission), and a mill on the Pholela River which until recently generated electricity. The missionaries also established a teachers' training college and an agricultural college, both of which are now closed, and a school, which still teaches a number of local children. Founded in 1886, the mission was named after the German monastery island of Reichenau.

Left: *A detail from the stone church at Reichenau Mission.*

AA Office NAU Building, cor Buchanan and Carbineer Streets, Pietermaritzburg 3201 Tel. (0331) 20571
Pietermaritzburg Publicity Association cor Commercial Road and Longmarket Street, Pietermaritzburg 3201 Tel. (0331) 51348
Richmond, Byrne and District Museum cor Chilley and Victoria Streets, Richmond 3780 Tel. (03322) 3038

Meander through the Midlands to the grandeur of the Little Berg

Our route through the hilly country of the Natal Midlands begins with a visit to the imposing Howick Falls, then meanders through well-watered farmlands to the grassy plains below the Little Berg — with sweeping Drakensberg views. We return through forests to the lovely Mgeni River gorge below Howick. Roughly half the route is on tar.

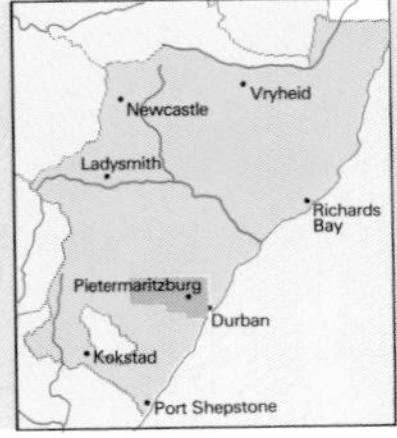

Pietermaritzburg
Howick Falls
Caversham Mill
Kamberg Nature Reserve
Umgeni Valley Nature Reserve
280—290 km

LEAVE PIETERMARITZBURG on the northbound N3 for Mooi River, and after roughly 25 km exit left for Howick and Midmar Dam. At the end of the off-ramp turn right for Howick. After 2 km turn left at the T-junction for Howick. 1,3 km later you cross the Mgeni River — immediately afterwards turn right into Morling Street, to reach a parking area at the Howick Falls observation point after a further 400 m (see opposite).

Return along Morling Street, and turn right into Howick's Main Street, noting your kms. After 300 m go left where the road curves, following the Mooi River sign. (The quaint old library building is on your right here.)

At the T-junction after roughly 6,5 km turn right onto the R103 for Lions River, Balgowan and Nottingham Road, noting your kms again. The R103 winds through attractive farming country with patches of forest, and follows the course of the railway line. After 3,5 km you enter the sprawling old settlement of Lions River, and 700 m later you cross the river from which it takes its name. (Both were named for the last lion to be shot in the area in 1856).

After 6,8 km on the R103 turn right onto gravel for Caversham, noting your kms. This pretty country lane winds its way to Caversham Mill — after 5,6 km turn right into a small parking area alongside the 1855 wood-and-iron mill. Set in beautiful surroundings on the Lions River (which drove the wooden mill wheel until the 1940s), the mill now houses a potter's workshop and craft studio.

Caversham to Rosetta

Continue northwards from Caversham Mill, noting your kms as you cross the single-lane bridge just beyond it. After 1,8 km turn right at the inclined T-junction, and 2,8 km later turn left for Balgowan. After a further 6 km turn right onto the tarred R103, noting your kms.

After 300 m you pass the school grounds of Michaelhouse on your left, alongside Balgowan railway station. 8,3 km later you pass, also on your left, Rawdon's Hotel (which serves lunch — booking advisable). A further 2 km brings you into the town of Nottingham Road (which has a hotel that also serves lunch).

10,4 km after rejoining the tarred road, turn left to remain on the R103 for the town centre, Rosetta and Sani Pass — and note your kms. The road takes you under the railway, and after 300 m you pass a turn-off on your left to Fort Nottingham. After a further 300 m you pass the attractive red-brick railway station on your right. 600 m later you pass on your left the road on which you will return later.

The R103 winds through rich farmland, then enters the town of Rosetta on the banks of the Mooi (pretty) River. After 7 km turn left in the town for Kamberg, noting your kms.

Rosetta to Kamberg

After 1,6 km you cross the Mooi River on a single-lane bridge, and soon afterwards the road surface changes to gravel. The main feature of this road is the magnificent panorama it soon offers of the high Drakensberg ahead of you. Just after 9,6 km turn right into a parking area for a view over farmlands towards the mountains — from the distinctive Giant's Castle on your left to the buttress of Cathkin Peak in the distance on your right.

11,7 km later you pass the small stone church of St Peter's, Kamberg, on your left. A turn-off 100 m later leads to an entrance to the church grounds — note your kms opposite this side-road. After roughly 3,5 km the scenery becomes dominated by the sandstone heights of the Little Berg, and you can see the round-topped Kamberg on your left. 5,1 km later (8,6 km from the church turn-off) turn left at the foot of Mount Lebanon for 'Kamberg Natuurtuin', noting your kms.

You cross the Mooi River after 5,1 km and almost immediately afterwards you pass a turn-off to your left to Loteni and Nottingham Road (your return route). Just over 1 km later you can see on your right the mushroom rock known as Thwalelinye jutting out from the side of Mount Erskine, and roughly 2 km later you enter Kamberg Nature Reserve.

9,3 km after noting your kms you pass a picnic site at the start of the Mooi River Trail on your right — an ideal lunch spot, with braai facilities, toilets and water. (Walking part of the trail makes a superb introduction to the area, but first continue to the office to obtain a booklet on the trail. The road to the camp and office branches off to your left 500 m later.)

Kamberg to Karkloof

Retrace your route from Kamberg, and 3,3 km beyond the gate turn right for Nottingham Road and Loteni, noting your kms. This road winds below the Little Berg, and after 2,3 km you pass through the Stillerus section of Kamberg Nature Reserve, with the mountain known as Gladstone's Nose on your right. 8,1 km after noting your kms pull over to the side of the road for a view back towards the profile of Gladstone's Nose.

After a further 5,2 km turn left at the T-junction at the foot of Spioenkop for Nottingham Road. (The road surface changes to tar.)

Roaring white waters plunge over Howick Falls.

HOWICK AND THE MGENI RIVER

The Mgeni River plunges roughly 110 m over the Howick Falls into a spectacular gorge below. One may view the falls from the easily accessible observation point in the town of Howick, or from the Mgeni Valley Nature Reserve — on a scenic drive along the edge of the gorge, or from one of the footpaths that criss-cross the reserve.

Owned by the Wildlife Society of Southern Africa, the Mgeni Valley Nature Reserve has an education centre, and offers accommodation, game-viewing, excellent bird-watching, and swimming in the Mgeni River.

The town of Howick, named after Viscount Howick (later Earl Grey), the British Colonial Secretary, grew up around the old river crossing above the falls. The Howick Museum, in its turn-of-the-century, red-brick house on Morley Street, preserves mementos of the town's past.

Caversham Mill and its lovingly restored wheel.

16,5 km along this road pull onto the shoulder for a view back towards the Drakensberg and the area through which you have been driving.

12 km later turn right at the T-junction in Nottingham Road for the R103, following the Balgowan sign. After a further 1,1 km turn left at the T-junction onto the road for Mooi River and Pietermaritzburg. Just over 200 m later you pass a turn-off on your left to the hotel and station, and after a further 500 m stop on your left for a visit to the little wood-and-iron building of St John's Gowrie Church, built in 1885 on the farm Gowrie.

Continue on the Mooi River road from the church, and 7,3 km later turn onto the N3 for

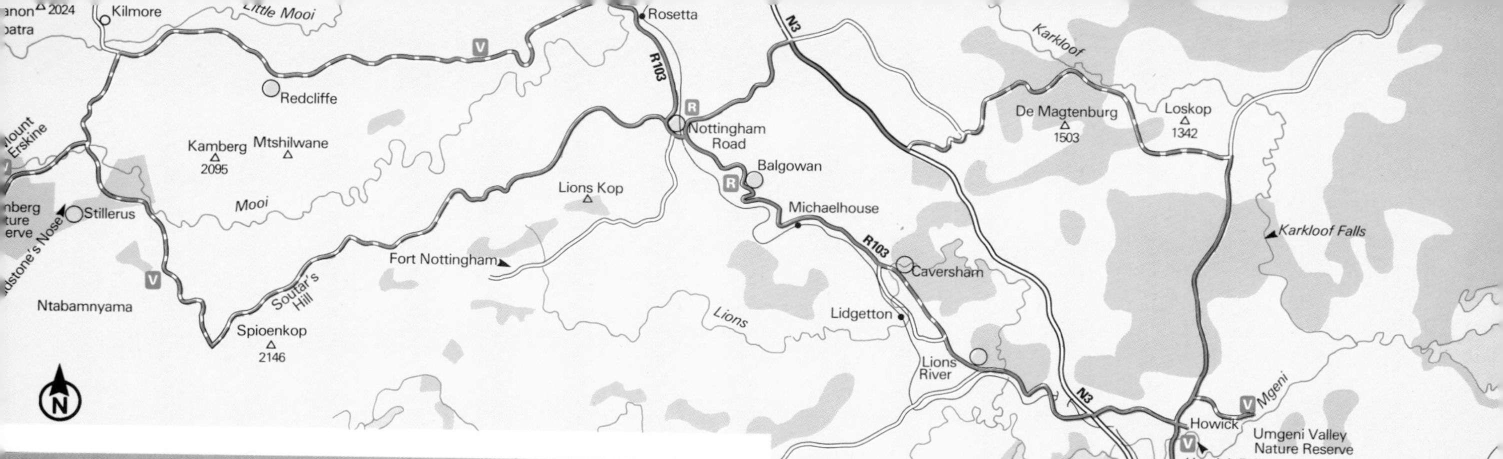

Kamberg Reserve — peaceful trout waters in a magnificent mountain setting.

THE KARKLOOF VALLEY

The beautiful Karkloof valley was once on the main wagon road between Natal and the Transvaal. Amongst its scenic attractions are the Karkloof Falls, where the river plunges for 88 m before it continues on its course to join the Mgeni River above the Albert Falls Dam. The road to the falls is closed during the week because of logging in the SAPPI forests, and during the dry winter months because of the fire risk.

The Karkloof district has a renowned polo club, dominated during its early years by a family of Shaw cousins who proved their skills with sticks and balls that they carved from indigenous wood. One member of the family — Campbell Shaw — developed such an excellent rapport with his pony that he could ride and play without a bridle.

A FEW PRECIOUS BARRELS

In 1890 a few barrels of brown trout spawn made a long, hazardous journey from Scotland to Natal. The eggs were hatched at Balgowan, from where the fingerlings were introduced to the Mooi River. Today trout-fishing is one of the attractions of the province, and Kamberg Nature Reserve — which now has its own hatchery on the banks of the Mooi — is renowned for the size of its trout. Parks Board hatcheries ensure excellent fishing throughout the Drakensberg, as well as providing stock for farm dams.

View from the edge of the Mgeni River gorge towards the distant plains.

The farmlands of the Kamberg region stretch towards the faraway Drakensberg.

Pietermaritzburg. 6,7 km later exit left for Balgowan and Currys Post, and at the end of the off-ramp 500 m later turn left for Currys Post, noting your kms.

The road surface changes to gravel after 50 m. Just short of 4,8 km later turn right at the T-junction for Currys Post and Howick. After 300 m turn left onto the D293, noting your kms. Soon you enter some of the forests that typify this section of the drive. After 6,4 km you round a bend in the road at the summit of a delightful pass that overlooks the densely wooded Karkloof valley, below the attractive Karkloof mountains. At the foot of the pass you skirt Loskop (loose hill), and cross the valley floor.

Continue straight through the crossroads where right leads to 'Currys Post/Howick', and after 17,3 km on the D293 turn right at the T-junction onto tar for Howick, noting your kms.

After 4,9 km you pass a turn-off left to the magnificent Karkloof Falls (open to the public between November and May, but only on weekends). 2,2 km beyond the falls turn-off you glimpse Albert Falls Dam on your left. After just over 12,6 km on tar, turn left into the Umgeni Valley Nature Reserve, and follow the gravel road that leads past Cascade Falls and Shelter Falls, then along the edge of the cliff of the Mgeni River gorge, giving you magnificent late-afternoon views of Howick Falls, dense indigenous vegetation, and the opening of the valley with Albert Falls Dam in the distance. (Although the scenic road continues for some 6,5 km from the entrance, you may turn around after 4,7 km if the road is in poor condition.)

Return to the tarred road, and turn left for Howick. Once in Howick, follow signs onto the N3 to Pietermaritzburg ●

AA Office NAU Building, cor Buchanan and Carbineer Streets, Pietermaritzburg 3201 Tel. (0331) 20571
Pietermaritzburg Publicity Association cor Commercial Road and Longmarket Street, Pietermaritzburg 3201 Tel. (0331) 51348
Natal Parks Board Box 662, Pietermaritzburg 3200 Tel. (0331) 51221

Memories of the 1890s live on at the old Pavilion and bandstand alongside the Oval at Alexandra Park.

Red-brick splendour and a Voortrekker past

PIETERMARITZBURG, set amidst forested hills and the rolling countryside of the Natal Midlands, is one of the best preserved Victorian cities in the world. Started as a well-laid-out Voortrekker town early last century, then expanded during British colonial rule into a grand seat for the new government, Pietermaritzburg retains an old-world flavour alongside its modern development.

The Voortrekkers had made their arduous crossing of the Drakensberg escarpment by ox-wagon in 1837 to establish a new republic. They encountered opposition from the Nguni-speaking inhabitants of this lush land, who a decade earlier had been consolidated into the Zulu nation by the warrior-king Chaka. After bitter fighting, the Boers defeated the Zulus in the Battle of Blood River in 1838, and settled down to establishing their Republic of Natalia. They named their new capital on the banks of the Msunduze River after their leaders Pieter Retief and Gert Maritz.

A few years later, in 1843, the British garrisoned the town, establishing their headquarters at *Fort Napier*, which still stands today in the grounds of a hospital. The town became the seat of government for the Colony of Natal, and after Union in 1910 it remained a capital — now of Natal Province.

Links with the settler past

The historic heart of Pietermaritzburg is dominated by the elaborately decorated, red-brick *City Hall* **(1)** with its tall clock tower, on the corner of Commercial Road and Church Street. The original building was built in 1895 on the site of the old Voortrekker Raadsaal (parliament), then rebuilt in 1901 after being destroyed by fire. It is the home of the *Tatham Art Gallery*, which has fine 19th and early 20th century French and English paintings, as well as china, glassware, and clocks.

Next door to the City Hall is the Pietermaritzburg Publicity Association, in the 1884 station built for the Borough Police. Excellent brochures on the city are available from here, including a number featuring self-guided trails through the historic centre of the city — notable for its magnificent old commercial buildings, charming lanes, stock exchanges, hitching rails, and other memories of the last century.

Across Commercial Road stands the historic *Old Supreme Court* **(2)** (completed in 1871), and around the corner on Longmarket Street are the twin edifices of the *Legislative Assembly Building* **(3)** (inaugurated in 1889) and the *Legislative Council Building* **(4)** (opened in 1900 after government was passed to a two-house parliament). The interiors of the Assembly and Council buildings may be visited by arrangement.

The *Carbineer Gardens* alongside the City Hall and the gardens of the Old Supreme Court contain a number of interesting statues and memorials commemorating aspects of the city's past.

An interesting collection of Voortrekker relics is to be found in the *Voortrekker Museum* **(5)** in Church Street, not far from the City Hall. The museum is housed in the original Church of the Vow — built by the Voortrekkers in 1841 in accordance with their vow to God to build a place of worship if He granted them victory at Blood River. Welverdient, the historic home of the commander at Blood River, Andries Pretorius, is also part of the museum. Statues of Pieter Retief and Gert Maritz stand in front of the new Church of the Vow, built alongside the old.

Another Voortrekker home, that of Petrus Gerhardus Pretorius on Boom Street, has been converted into a museum, known as the *Oldest House in Town* **(6)**. Built in 1846 of local shale, it is the only surviving double-storey Voortrekker house in the city, and still has its original yellowwood floors and ceilings beneath thatch.

The resting place of many of the early inhabitants of the town can be visited at the *Voortrekker Cemetery* **(7)** on Commercial Road, and parts of the old *Voortrekker Wagon Road* to the coast still survive on the outskirts of the city.

The *Natal Museum* **(8)** on Loop

The Oldest House in Town dated 1846. **Above:** *Plaque at World's View.* **Right:** *The Old Provincial Council Building.*

The City Hall's red-brick splendour.

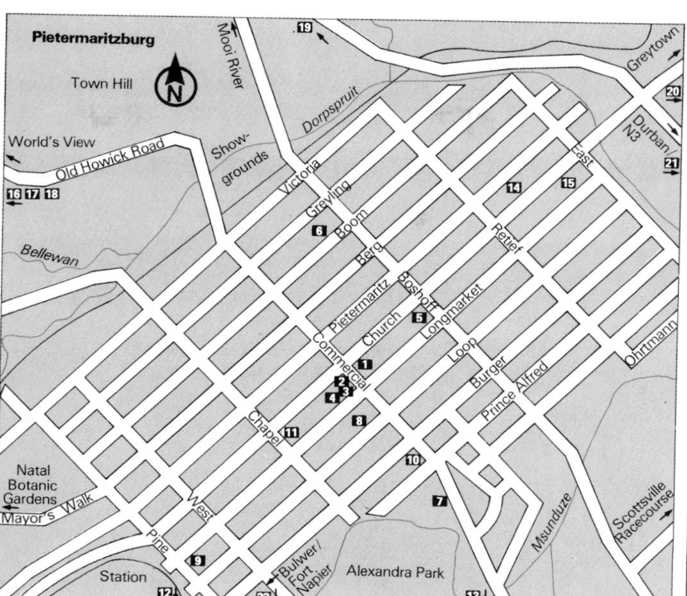

Street, one of five national museums in the country, offers an introduction to the history of the province in its Hall of Natal History, and also contains superb exhibits on mammals, birds, reptiles, fish, insects, geology, palaeontology and ethnology.

A fascinating glimpse into an elegant Victorian lifestyle is offered by the *Macrorie House Museum* **(9)** on the corner of Loop and Pine streets. Built in 1862, it was the home of Bishop William Macrorie, who was sent to Pietermaritzburg after Bishop John Colenso fell out with the church over ecclesiastical issues (and with the colonial government over politics). The charming house museum contains amongst its exhibits Bishop Macrorie's private chapel.

The city has a number of fine old churches, including *St Mary's* **(10)** on the corner of Commercial Road and Burger Street, which is a replica of Bishop Colenso's original church for Africans; *St Peter's* **(11)** in Church Street (Colenso's new 'cathedral' after his rift with the church); *St George's Garrison Church* **(12)** of 1897, near the historic railway station and Fort Napier; and the little *Italian Church* **(13)** in Golf Road, Mkondeni, built by Italian prisoners during World War II.

The arrival of Indians in Natal from 1860 introduced an Eastern influence on religious life in the province, and in Pietermaritzburg the two main creeds, Islam and Hinduism, are well-represented. Visitors are permitted at the largest of the Muslim mosques in the city, the *Islamia Mosque* **(14)** in Church Street. The main Hindu temple, the *Sri Siva Soobramoniar and Marriamen Temple* **(15)** in Longmarket Street, scene of the annual fire-walking ceremony on Good Friday, is also open to the public.

Parks and nature trails

Pietermaritzburg's moist climate and rich soil have seen to it that the city maintains a lush, garden quality, and beautiful parks abound. On the banks of the Msunduze River, start of the annual Duzi Canoe Marathon to Durban, is the 65,6ha *Alexandra Park*. The park has lovely gardens, including a rockery known as the Mayor's Garden, sportsfields, a swimming pool, and a tearoom alongside an ornate bandstand (built in 1892) and the onion-domed *Pavilion* (dating from 1897).

The tearoom in the *Botanic Gardens*, in its pretty setting alongside a lake, is another favoured retreat from the city bustle. Founded in 1870, the gardens are famed for their lovely avenue of plane trees, and the beautiful, tall trees in the Exotic Garden. In 1970 the Indigenous Garden was started to propagate the many varieties of Natal plants, and a fine collection of cycads, aloes and trees has already been established.

Wylie Park **(16)** on Taunton Road, Wembley, also specialises in indigenous plants, and is particularly attractive when the azaleas (the floral emblem of Pietermaritzburg) are in bloom in spring.

Queen Elizabeth Nature Reserve **(17)** on the city outskirts (see pages 178-9) is headquarters of the Natal Parks Board, and here visitors can see zebra, blesbuck, impala, duikers, bushbuck and rhino amidst dense vegetation (see pages 178-9). Bird-watching is also rewarding in the reserve, and there are several nature walks and picnic sites in the grounds. The Parks Board shows wildlife films from time to time in its theatre.

For those interested in walking or hiking, there are a number of Green Belt Trails through the *World's View* area (see pages 178-9), and the Department of Forestry offers a forest trail, as well as a shorter trail for the handicapped, at *Cedara State Forest* **(18)** (a permit from the forester is needed). There is a picnic site alongside a small dam in the forest.

Watersport and fishing

Inland watersport enthusiasts have a number of nearby venues to choose from. The Parks Board administers popular boating, fishing and recreational resorts at *Midmar Dam* **(19)**

Pretty facade of Macrorie House.

(see pages 178-9), which also has a fascinating historical village; and at *Albert Falls Dam* **(20)** on the Greytown road. Another attractive fishing and boating venue is *Nagle Dam* **(21)** at the head of the Valley of A Thousand Hills (see pages 178-9); and *Henley Dam* **(22)** off the Bulwer road offers fishing and picnicking.

Venturing further afield

Other out-of-town venues popular with people setting out from Pietermaritzburg include the magnificent *Howick Falls* and *Karkloof Falls* (see pages 174-5); the drive to *Otto's Bluff* in July/August when the aloes are in bloom; the *Natal Lion and Game Park* and adjacent *Zoological Gardens*; and *Natal Table Mountain* at the head of the Valley of A Thousand Hills (see pages 178-9).

A number of potters, weavers and other craftspeople in the Midlands also open their studios and workshops to visitors, providing an excuse for lovely drives into the country ●

Pietermaritzburg Publicity Assoc.
cor Commercial Road and Longmarket Street, Pietermaritzburg 3201
Tel (0331) 51348
Regional Directorate of Forestry
Brayleys Building, 242 Longmarket Street
Pietermaritzburg 3201 Tel. (0331) 28101
Natal Parks Board Box 662,
Pietermaritzburg 3200 Tel. (0331) 51514

Pietermaritzburg's railway station — a period piece in red brick and cast iron.

Valley of a Thousand Hills and the old Voortrekker wagon road

The breathtaking Kloof Falls set the tone for this drive, which then follows the high road along the edge of the spectacular Valley of a Thousand Hills. We visit the historic village on the shores of Midmar Dam, then meander back through the area traversed by the old Voortrekker route to the coast. All but 20 km of the drive is on tar.

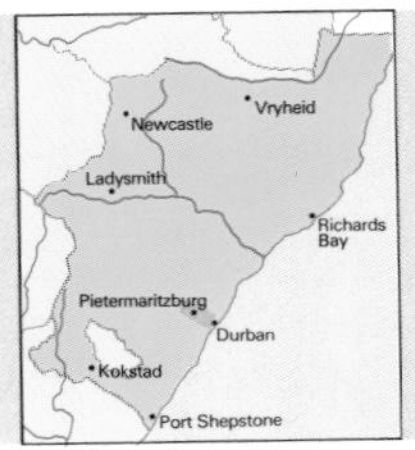

Durban
Krantzkloof
Valley of a Thousand Hills
Midmar
Pietermaritzburg
Nshongweni Dam
260 – 280 km

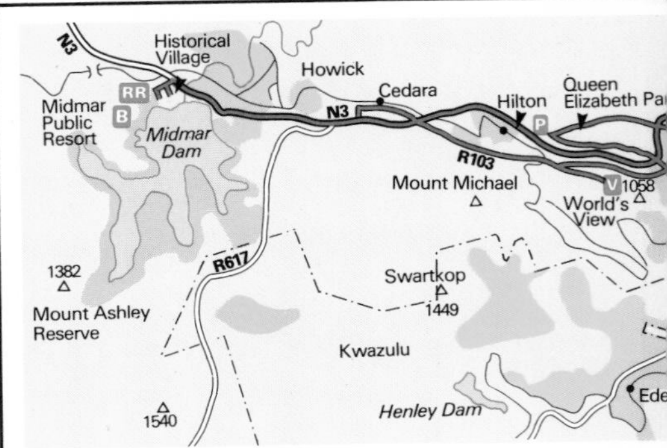

LEAVE DURBAN ON the N3 for Pietermaritzburg. Where the toll road leads right near Mariannhill, go left on the R613 for Pinetown and Pietermaritzburg. Roughly 25 km from Durban, exit left for 'Kloof Sta/Old Main Rd'. At the end of the off-ramp, turn right, noting your kms.

After 400 m turn right at the T-junction, and pass Kloof Station on your left. 600 m after noting your kms, turn left to cross a bridge over the railway line. Immediately afterwards turn left, and pass the station building again on your left. At the stop street 1,1 km from the R613, turn left, then immediately right into Kloof Falls Road.

This attractive, tree-lined road (which becomes Bridle Road) winds down into the valley, and after roughly 3 km you enter Krantzkloof Nature Reserve. Note your kms soon afterwards as you pass a gravel road on your right that leads into a picnic area alongside the river.

You cross the river, then begin to climb steeply. After 750 m turn right onto a gravel road that leads for 100 m to a parking area. A walk of a further 100 m brings you close to the edge of the cliff, with magnificent views of Kloof Falls and the rugged clifftop across the deep, forested gorge. (There is no barrier at the edge.)

Return to Bridle Road and turn right. After 100-200 m turn right onto another gravel road. At the end of it, a short walk to the left gives you an excellent view over the gorge where it opens up towards a broad sweep of the Mgeni River. (Again there is no barrier.)

Krantzkloof to Monteseel

2,1 km beyond the second viewsite turn left out of Bridle Road at the T-junction into Link Road, noting your kms. After 1,5 km turn left for Hillcrest, and after a further 6,8 km turn right onto the Old Main Road (R103) for Botha's Hill and Drummond, noting your kms again.

You enter Botha's Hill, and soon afterwards a view into the Valley of a Thousand Hills opens up on your right (see opposite). After 5,1 km turn right for the Rob Roy Hotel (which serves teas, and offers excellent views over the Valley of a Thousand Hills). If you continue along this side-road for 700 m beyond the hotel, there is a place to stop on your left for an equally attractive view into the valley.

Return to the Old Main Road and turn right. After 1 km turn right into Phezulu (meaning 'high up' in Zulu) — an African craft centre and traditional kraal perched on the edge of the valley. There is a small entry fee for the kraal, which covers a demonstration of Zulu dancing and a guided tour.

As you leave Phezulu, turn right onto the Old Main Road, and note your kms. The road winds along a line of hills, wandering first to one side of the crest, then to the other side, giving superb views into the valleys on both sides. After 4,8 km there is a large viewsite parking area on your right next to another Zulu kraal and a curio shop. Note your kms here.

3,5 km later turn right for Monteseel. At the T-junction after 100 m turn left into Albert Street, then turn right immediately onto gravel (Magdalene Avenue). Where the road forks after 150 m go left. Park after another 700 m, and walk to the edge of this spur of land for a magnificent view. In the wild kloof on your right there are three of four known cycads of the *Encephalartos natalensis* species. The oldest of the three is believed to have rootstock older than 1 000 years and has been declared a scientific monument.

Monteseel to Midmar

Retrace your route to the Old Main Road, noting your kms as you turn right. After 5,2 km turn right for Cato Ridge, and 6,4 km later turn right for the N3 to Pietermaritzburg.

After 11 km on the N3 there is a good view to your right of Natal Table Mountain, dominating the head of the Valley of a Thousand Hills. The countryside changes slowly as you venture further inland, with acacia trees becoming a feature of the landscape. Roughly 21 km after joining the N3, you crest a hill and look down on Pietermaritzburg and its surrounding hills.

Note your kms as you pass the exit on your left for Pietermaritzburg, and bypass the city. After 3,5 km you cross the Msunduze River, venue for the annual Duzi Canoe Marathon. 28,2 km after the city turn-off, exit left for Howick and Midmar Dam.

At the end of the off-ramp turn left for Midmar Dam, noting your kms, then curve right for the R103 to Midmar. There is an excellent view of the dam on your left, before the road dips behind the dam wall and crosses a bridge over the Mgeni River. After 2,7 km you pass a turn-off on your left to Midmar Historical Village, and after a further 400 m turn left into Midmar Resort. 100 m later you reach the control gate, where a small entry fee is charged. (See above. The resort has a restaurant and cafeteria, and there are lovely picnic and braai sites along the water's edge.)

Over weekends you can enter the fascinating Midmar Historical Village through a pedestrian gate from the resort. Otherwise return along the R103 and turn right into the village. (An additional small entry fee is charged.)

Midmar Dam — a popular venue for watersports.

MIDMAR DAM AND VILLAGE

The 2 831 ha Midmar Public Resort, set in the Mgeni valley amongst the Inhluzana hills, offers sports (particularly watersports), camping, caravanning, game viewing — from vehicle or boat tours — and a rich variety of birds. The historical village on the banks of the dam contains several original and reconstructed old buildings, and collections of old animal-drawn and motorised vehicles.

A fine vista over the Valley of a Thousand Hills.

Midmar to Nshongweni Dam

Return to the N3 for Pietermaritzburg. After roughly 7 km on the N3, exit left for Mount Michael and Cedara. At the end of the off-ramp, turn right for Mount Michael onto the Old Howick Road (R103). After roughly 5,5 km on the Old Howick Road you cross a railway line, and 600 m later turn right for Boesmansrand and World's View. A further 2 km brings you to the parking area at the viewsite and picnic spot overlooking the old Voortrekker wagon road and the magnificent countryside surrounding Pietermaritzburg (see above and pages 176-7).

Rejoin the R103, noting your kms as you turn

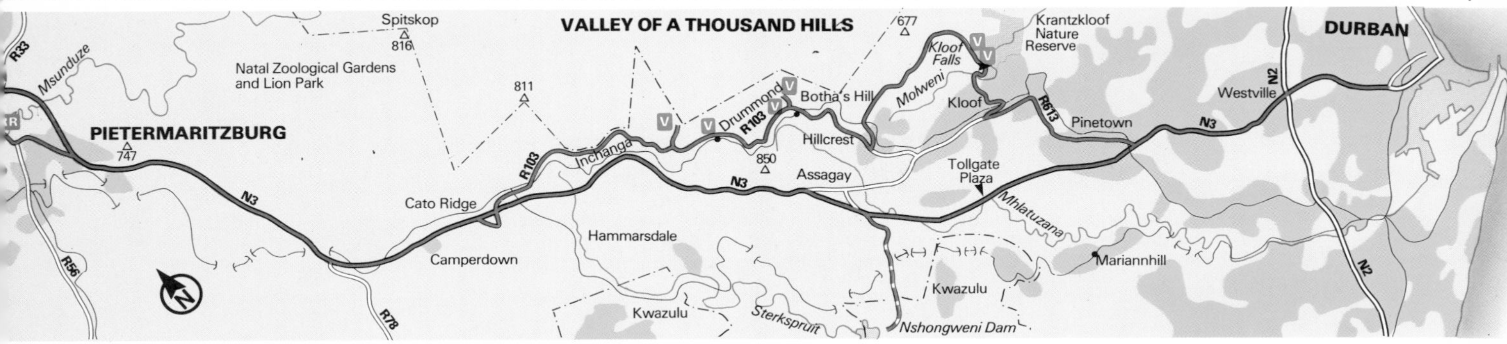

VALLEY OF A THOUSAND HILLS

For the last 64 km of its course, the Mgeni River (river of the acacia trees) winds its way through the spectacular, deeply eroded Valley of a Thousand Hills. The scenery in the valley varies from dense bush to farmland and tribal areas where huts cling to the steep slopes.

The 959 m Natal Table Mountain towers above the scenic Nagle Dam at the head of the valley. The mountain can be climbed along a relatively easy path from the western side. The dam, with its nature reserve, tearoom and picnic sites, is reached from the east. Both are popular venues for weekend outings from Pietermaritzburg.

Young girls offer a display of Zulu beadwork to passing travellers in the Valley of a Thousand Hills.

Krantzkloof, with its sheer cliff-sides and lush bush, is home to many birds.

The rugged, flat-topped Nshongweni hill rises above the dam of the same name.

THE OLD VOORTREKKER WAGON ROAD

North-west of Pietermaritzburg a spur of the Boesmansberg (Bushman mountain) forms a plateau that well deserves its name World's View. From here you can see the city nestling below in the Msunduze valley, and the extensive surrounding hills. Below the viewsite lies an old wagon road. The Voortrekkers, who crossed the Drakensberg by ox wagon in 1837, used this road to reach the coast at Port Natal (later Durban). The wagon road has been declared a national monument, and is part of Pietermaritzburg's system of Green Belt Trails.

THE SEEDS OF A THRIVING INDUSTRY

An Englishman of Dutch descent, John Vanderplank, arrived in Natal early last century with seeds of the Tasmanian black wattle shrub amongst his belongings. On one of his farms — named Camperdown after a battle in which the British defeated the Dutch — he planted these shrubs as a low windbreak, but to his surprise the seeds grew into large trees. Vanderplank did not live to benefit from the industry that grew from his accidental discovery — it was only after his death that wattle bark was found to contain commercially valuable tannic acid.

right. After 2,3 km turn left for Montrose/ Queen Elizabeth Park, and after a further 600 m turn left at the T-junction into Duncan McKenzie Drive. 800 m later you enter the park — note your kms here.

You pass the Natal Parks Board head office, then wind through luxuriant vegetation where you are likely to spot zebra, impala, blesbok, duikers or bushbuck along the roadside. At the fork 1,1 km beyond the park entrance, go left, and at another fork 500 m later go right.

Note your kms again as you leave the park, and 1,2 km later turn right at the stop street. After a further 6,5 km turn right into Church Street, and 500 m later, with the impressive red-brick City Hall on your left, turn left into Commercial Road, noting your kms.

After 900 m you pass the entrance to the historic Voortrekker cemetery on your right. Commercial Road becomes Durban Road, and eventually merges with the N3 on your left.

After roughly 45 km on the N3, exit left for 'Shongweni/Assegay'. At the end of the off-ramp turn right, noting your kms. Just after 1,3 km later turn left, then roughly 600 m later turn right onto gravel, and after a further 1,5 km go right where a road leads left. Within the next 3 km you can see the dam, set in a richly wooded gorge on your right, with the hill known as Nshongweni rising from it. After 5,9 km on gravel you reach the control gate, and the road becomes tarred.

This scenic tarred road leads for 2,7 km to the dam wall and picnic area, giving you good views over the dam. After your visit to the dam, return to the N3 for Durban ●

AA Office AA House, 537 Smith Street, Durban 4001 Tel. (031) 3010341
AA Office NAU Building, cor Buchanan and Carbineer Streets, Pietermaritzburg 3201 Tel. (0331) 20571
Natal Parks Board Box 662, Pietermaritzburg 3200 Tel. (0331) 51221
Pietermaritzburg Publicity Association cor Commercial Road and Longmarket Street, Pietermaritzburg 3201 Tel. (0331) 51348

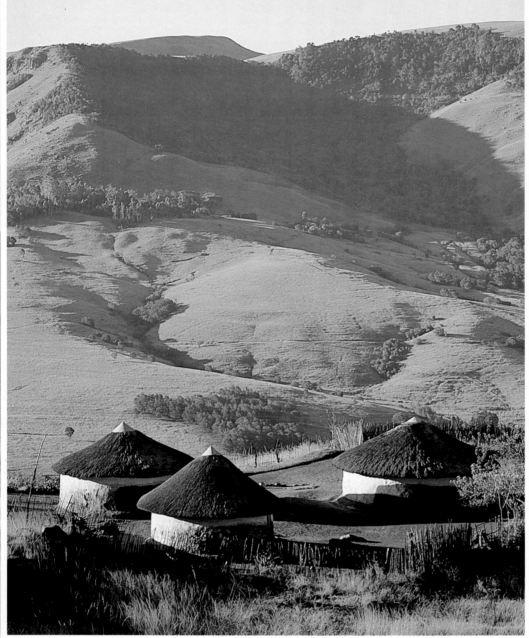

A cluster of rondavels with painted mud walls and thatched roofs grace the slopes of the serene rolling hills of Kwazulu.

The Zulu: a proud people whose name was once synonymous with war

THE RICH LANDSCAPES of Natal, a region blessed with some of the world's most splendid scenery, have been given an additional, distinctive character by the colourful traditions of the Zulu people. Almost every hillside is dotted with their beehive huts, the valleys are hazy with the scented smoke from their fires, and throughout the region the traveller can see elaborate, traditional costumes being worn by a people who take pride in their cultural heritage.

The Zulu are thought to be descended from several successive waves of settlers who, centuries ago, migrated southwards from central East Africa. The area these settlers penetrated was lush and fertile, with rolling hills as far as the eye could see, and there were few other groups to challenge their occupation of this land. For countless generations their descendants have hunted the wild game that thrived here, cultivated an assortment of traditional crops, reared the cattle that they brought with them from the north — and have gradually evolved a rich store of customs and cultural traditions.

The Zulu owe their national identity very largely to two of their

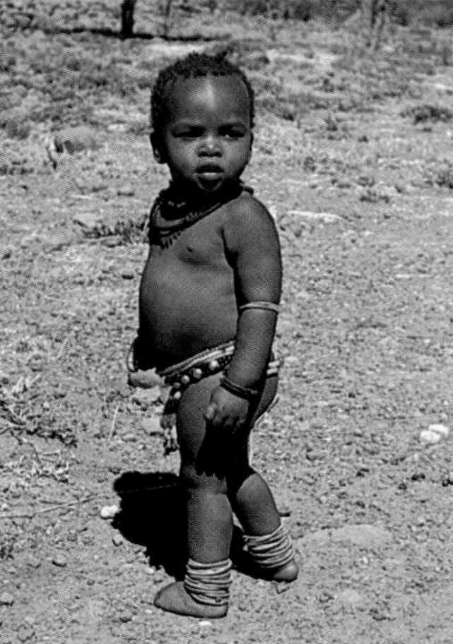

Brightly-coloured beadwork is the only dress worn by this little girl.

historic chiefs. The early settlers did not call themselves Zulu, but their descendants derived the name, which means 'heaven', from the first of these two leaders. Little else is known about this chief who gave his name to his people, but he is thought to have established his capital in the valley of the Mkhumbane River. The second of these two particularly influential chiefs was Chaka — the warrior leader who came to power early in the 19th century and who introduced a number of successful new military techniques that turned the Zulu into an all but invincible military force. Initially there had probably been little to distinguish this community from the many other tribal groups that were closely related, but Chaka's military victories gave the Zulu a strong and lasting identity.

Traditional roles in a rural economy

It has often been claimed that women comprise the economic backbone of the Zulu community. The women have traditionally been responsible for all cultivation of the soil, have fetched the water, prepared the food and cared for the children. The men meanwhile have been hunters and warriors, and the boys have traditionally been charged with looking after the cattle.

Cattle have always played an extremely important part in the Zulu way of life. Cow's milk, most often in a curdled form, makes up a large part of the Zulu diet, and hides have been used for making clothes and all-purpose thongs. Cattle are wealth, and the measure of a man's social worth. They are traditionally used for the payment of *lobola* (the compensation paid by a bridegroom to his father-in-law for his acquisition of his bride) and cattle have also been

A Zulu woman decorates her upswept hair with elaborate bands of beadwork.

used as sacrificial gifts to the spirits. The cattle enclosure has traditionally been regarded as a sacred place, and no women other than daughters of the house are permitted to enter it.

The everyday clothes worn by the Zulu in the early days were extremely simple, consisting mostly of skins and feathers, but the warriors adorned themselves more elaborately. Vestiges of the awe-inspiring dress and ornamentation worn by the warriors can still be seen on ceremonial occasions. In the 18th and 19th centuries the world of the Zulu was a violent one, characterised by almost constant warfare — against neighbouring tribes, against Afrikaner Voortrekkers, and against the regiments of the British Empire. The hide shields that the men now carry on ceremonial occasions are derived from that era — when each Zulu regiment was identified by the colour and design of its shield.

A colourful addition to Zulu dress, and to Zulu customs generally, came with the advent of imported beads. These first made their appearance when the communities living along the coast began to trade with European sailors journeying to and from the East — bartering gold and ivory for brightly coloured beads and other European goods. Like other indigenous peoples, the Zulu used these beads as personal ornaments, and an elaborate beadlore has evolved in the course of many generations.

The meaning of beads

Every stage in the life of the individual is marked by certain traditional styles of dress — including many kinds of ornate beadwork. Beads are also used to send messages. Zulu women are expert in weaving the beads into intricate patterns that spell out love letters *(iincwadi)* for their menfolk. Each colour of bead has a different significance. A red bead represents blood, and denotes tears and longing. A white bead represents bone and signifies love and purity. A blue bead, called *ijuba* (dove), symbolises faithfulness. Other colours indicate such things as jealousy, wealth, or doubt.

The beads are sewn together in necklaces in such a way that the recipient knows exactly what the message is, whether it is loving ('My heart is full of love and I want to wear the leather skirt of marriage') or admonishing ('You are telling lies about your possessions'). The recipient may then wear the message for all to see, or, as in the latter case, might prefer to hide it in shame.

This poetry in the language of beads is matched by a notably poetic way of speaking. The Zulu have a musical language, rich in metaphor and full of subtle meaning — the substance of remarks being very often implied rather than stated explicitly.

Echoes of an animated universe

As with many indigenous African peoples, a primitive life-style is a relatively recent memory for the Zulu — a fact that has resulted in a wealth of spiritual folklore. Many Zulu beliefs date back to an early period when there were few religious rites. The people who first migrated into this region saw themselves as presided over by *Nkulunkulu* (great, great one), but they were infinitely more aware of the supernatural world around them. Every pool, rocky outcrop, thunderstorm or change in the weather was attributed to a supernatural being or ancestral ghost.

Examples of local Zulu handicrafts.

Women are responsible for cooking, farming crops and child-rearing.

The early beliefs of the Zulu gave rise to two classes of what Europeans have misleadingly called witch-doctors. In fact the Zulu have the *Nyanga* (doctor) and the *Ngoma* (diviner). The *Nyanga* treats the sick while the *Ngoma* copes with such problems as unrequited love and protection from ill-willed spirits.

The Zulu traditionally believe that a man possesses, besides his own physical being, the spiritual qualities of breath or air, and a shadow or reflection. The prestige of a man is thought of as being intimately linked to the strength and length of his shadow. A chief has a very strong shadow, and much of his personal power is believed to lie in this. The shadow and the breath, together constituting what we might call the spirit, leave a person when they die. The socially significant dead, however, become ancestral spirits, and they continue to govern the lives of the living from their graves ●

A traditional beehive-shaped hut with its distinctive thatched roof.

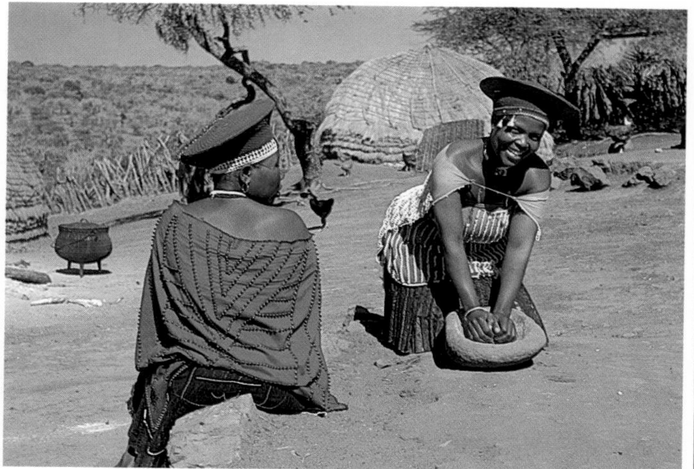
Colourfully dressed, a Zulu woman grinds maize on a well-worn stone.

Sub-tropical beaches lead north to 'the one that startles'

Natal's sugar country north of Durban presents an ocean of green edged with a golden sub-tropical coast. On our way to the mighty Tugela we stop off at some of the romantic coves that dot the shore — then make a sortie past rugged hills into the isolated Mvoti valley. All but about 20 km of the route is on tar.

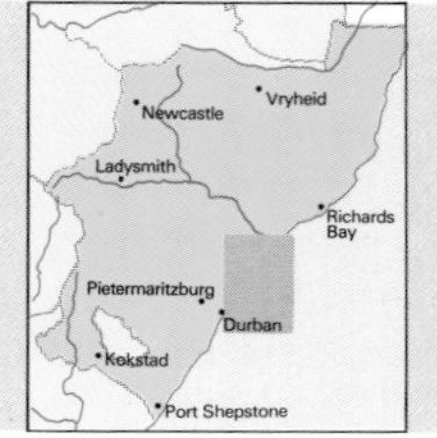

Durban
Umdloti Beach
Chaka's Rock
Harold Johnson Nature Reserve
Stanger
Umhlanga
310—330 km

LEAVE DURBAN ON THE M4 for the North Coast. You pass the Blue Lagoon on your right, then you cross a long bridge over the Mgeni River. At the end of the bridge exit left for Prospect Hall and Riverside. Go left 100 m later at the fork for the M21. After a further 200 m at the T-junction turn left into Riverside Road for the Umgeni River Bird Park, which is on your right 2 km later (entry fee).

Bird Park to Sheffield Beach
Retrace your route to the northbound M4, noting your kms as you rejoin the M4. Just short of 5,5 km later you merge with the R627, and after a further 3,7 km the road becomes a dual carriageway. Soon afterwards you pass the luxury resort of Umhlanga on your right, and beyond Umhlanga the road is flanked by dense coastal forest. 12,6 km after noting your kms you can see Umhlanga Lagoon on your right.

The lush green of rolling sugarcane soon becomes a feature of the landscape. 17,1 km after noting your kms (near the temporary link with the new N2), turn right for Umdloti, noting your kms again. The road winds through sugarcane down to the beach. After just over 1,7 km turn left onto North Beach Road, and after a further 600 m park anywhere on your right for a walk on the beach — with its interesting rocks and natural tidal pool.

Retrace your route inland and turn right onto the northbound coast road for Stanger (presently the N2, but soon to be 'renumbered' when the new N2 further inland is opened). Note your kms as you cross the Mdloti River on the outskirts of La Mercy. The road then hugs the coast for a number of kms, giving you glimpses of stretches of unspoilt beach. Near Port Zimbali the road veers inland, and soon afterwards you pass turn-offs to Ballito and Compensation Station.

After roughly 19 km exit left off the N2 for Chaka's Rock. At the end of the off-ramp turn right for Chaka's Rock, and 2,8 km later turn right at the T-junction into Ocean Drive. 700 m later turn left into Rock Lane, and turn left again immediately into a parking area. A short walk down Rock Lane brings you to a rocky outcrop believed by some to have been a lookout of the Zulu king Chaka and by others to have been a place where he executed miscreants by having them flung into the sea. There is a good view to your left over Chaka's Rock and Salt Rock beaches, while Thompson's Bay on your right offers a lovely short walk to the Hole in the Wall on its far side beyond the tidal pool. (Allow 30-40 minutes).

Turn right from Rock Lane into Ocean Drive, noting your kms. The road takes you through the resorts of Chaka's Rock and Salt Rock (where a number of places provide teas and lunches). After 3,1 km turn right into Hugh Dent Drive, noting your kms again. This road merges with Sheffield Drive, which winds through the resort of Sheffield Beach. The road attains some height, giving you good views over the sea and beach. After 2,1 km turn left into Colwyn Drive. 2,2 km later go left where a road joins from your right, and 500 m after this turn right for Umhlali. After a further 600 m turn right for the N2 to Stanger. Note your kms as you join the N2.

Sheffield Beach to the Tugela
From here the N2 passes through Natal's first canefields, which stretch across the coastal hills. After roughly 14 km you can see Stanger on the hillside to your left — an important centre for the sugar industry (see opposite).

Roughly 36 km after noting your kms turn right onto gravel for Fort Pearson, noting your kms again. After 700 m you pass a turn-off on your left to the Harold Johnson Nature Reserve (to which we return later). Soon afterwards there are good views over the mouth of the Tugela River, with the resort of Tugela Mouth on its north bank. 2,6 km from the tarred N2 you pass a turn-off on your right to a number of war graves from the Anglo-Zulu War of 1879. Immediately afterwards turn left for Fort Pearson and 'Naval and military graves'. Park 800 m later at the end of this side-road for a visit to the site of Fort Pearson, with its magnificent river view (see opposite).

Retrace your route for the 800 m along this side-road and turn left. After a further 1 km turn left onto a track that leads after 100 m to the Ultimatum Tree. From here retrace your route for the roughly 3 km to the nature reserve turn-off, and turn right. After passing through the gate, you reach a number of shaded braai and picnic sites overlooking the Tugela — an ideal lunch spot (water, toilets).

Tugela to Mvoti valley
Retrace your route to the tarred N2 and turn left. 7,4 km later turn left for Zinkwazi Beach, noting your kms. Just short of 7 km later there is an attractive view of a long, unspoilt, golden beach stretching northwards. Continue on this road (Nkwazi Drive), then after 8,1 km from the N2 turn left onto gravel for the public parking area alongside the beach and lagoon.

Return to the N2 and turn left towards Stanger and Durban, noting your kms. 9,6 km later exit left for the R74 for Stanger and Greytown, and at the end of the off-ramp turn right onto the R74, noting your kms. The R74 climbs as you pass Stanger on your left. You can see a domed mosque and impressive white-and-gold Hindu temple next to the road.

After 17,4 km on the R74 turn left for Glendale, noting your kms. The road you are on winds down through ever-changing scenery into the beautiful Mvoti valley, its rocky-crested hills contrasting with the cultivated fields. The tar gives way to gravel after 9,9 km.

800 m later you pass a road to your left that leads over Glendale Heights. (This gravel road eventually turns to tar, and links up with our return route near Chakaskraal — making it an attractive alternative route. However, after heavy rains a number of low causeways may be under water. 2,3 km later go left at the fork, then continue for a further 3,3 km as far as a single-lane bridge over a tributary of the Mvoti — for views over the less manicured valley landscape with its rows of hills stretching into the interior. On the far side of the bridge a road

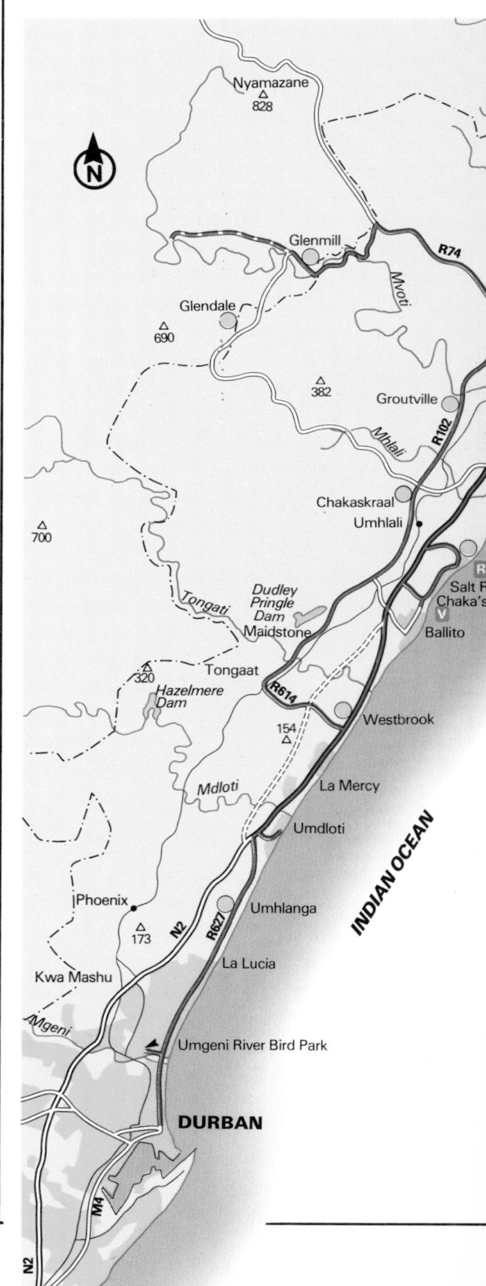

on your right offers a good turning point.

Mvoti valley to Umhlanga

Return from the valley to the R74, and note your kms as you turn right onto the R74, which offers sea views as you descend past Stanger. After 15,1 km turn right onto the R102 for Chakaskraal, noting your kms. The R102 winds through sugar country, and passes through the settlements of Groutville (where Albert Luthuli, president of the African National Congress and 1961 winner of the Nobel Peace Prize, was elected chief in 1935) and through Chakaskraal. After 24,7 km you pass a turn-off on your right to Esenembi and a road left to Compensation Station — the first sugar mill in South Africa operated near here.

A few kms later you enter Tongaat, with its picturesque 'Cape Dutch' labourers' cottages. The town is headquarters of a large sugar corporation. After 35,2 km on the R102 turn left onto the R614 for Tongaat Beach and Durban and 6,3 km later turn right onto the coast road on which you travelled in the morning — noting your kms as you turn.

Remain on the coast road for Umhlanga, and after 17,5 km exit left for Mount Edgecombe and Umhlanga. At the end of the off-ramp turn left, and 200 m later follow the road as it swings left. 500 m later turn left at the stop street into Lagoon Drive. At the end of Lagoon Drive you enter the Umhlanga Lagoon Nature Reserve (open sunrise to sunset) — park here for a late-afternoon walk through the coastal bush on the spur of land between the beach and lagoon to a lookout tower. If the reserve is closed, there is an equally pleasant walk along the beach promenade — park on Lagoon Drive near one of the lanes leading to the beach ●

AA Office AA House, 537 Smith Street, Durban 4001 Tel. (031) 3010341
Durban Publicity Association Church House, Church Street, Durban 4001 Tel. (031) 326946
SA Tourism Board Suite 520, Southern Life Centre, 320 West Street, Durban 4001 Tel. (031) 3047144

The Mvoti River takes a lazy course to the sea.

N2
Tugela
Harold Johnson Nature Reserve
Ultimatum Tree
Tugela Mouth
139
Nkwazi
Darnall
Zinkwazi Beach
lythedale Beach

Aloes bloom high above the Tugela River at the site of the historic Fort Pearson.

THE ULTIMATUM TREE

On 11 December 1878 representatives of the British Governor, Sir Bartle Frere, and the Zulu king, Cetshwayo, met under a large fig tree on the banks of the Tugela River alongside a ferry crossing. The British presented their ultimatum to the Zulu delegation — a list of demands that left no option other than war.

When Cetshwayo failed to meet the ultimatum date, the British marched into Zululand on 12 January 1879 from Fort Pearson — the start of the Anglo-Zulu War. Six months and many thousands of deaths later the British defeated Cetshwayo's army at Ulundi.

NAMES THAT TELL A TALE

Many of the names of towns along our route are corruptions of the original, picturesque Zulu names for the rivers of the area. We cross, among others, the Tongati and Mhlali rivers, both named after local varieties of the monkey orange tree. The Mdloti is named after a type of wild tobacco that grows on its banks. Mhlanga means 'reedy river', and Nkwazi is the Zulu name for the white-headed fish eagle. Our turning point — the Tugela (Thukela) — is named 'the one that startles', possibly because of the awe the river inspires when it is in spate.

KEEPING NATAL SWEET

Edmund Morewood built a crude sugar mill on his farm Conmpensation in 1851. This was the start of a lucrative industry that has shaped the landscape, population and fortunes of Natal. Vast seas of green canefields cover the coastal area north of Durban, and during the cutting season one will often see the bright orange of cane fires — deliberate burning to facilitate the milling process. The cane provides not only sugar, but a number of by-products such as fuel, paper, wallboard, chemicals and yeast.

In the 1860s large numbers of Indian contract labourers were brought to Natal to harvest the sweet crops, and many of their descendants still live in the predominantly Indian communities of Stanger and Tongaat. Mahatma Gandhi, the Indian lawyer and pacifist whose name became synonymous with passive resistance, worked for 21 years amongst the early Indian immigrants, and founded a communal farm at Phoenix settlement.

Left: *Palms near La Mercy beach.* **Above:** *Sugarcane reaches to the horizon.* **Right** *Umdloti's beachfront.*

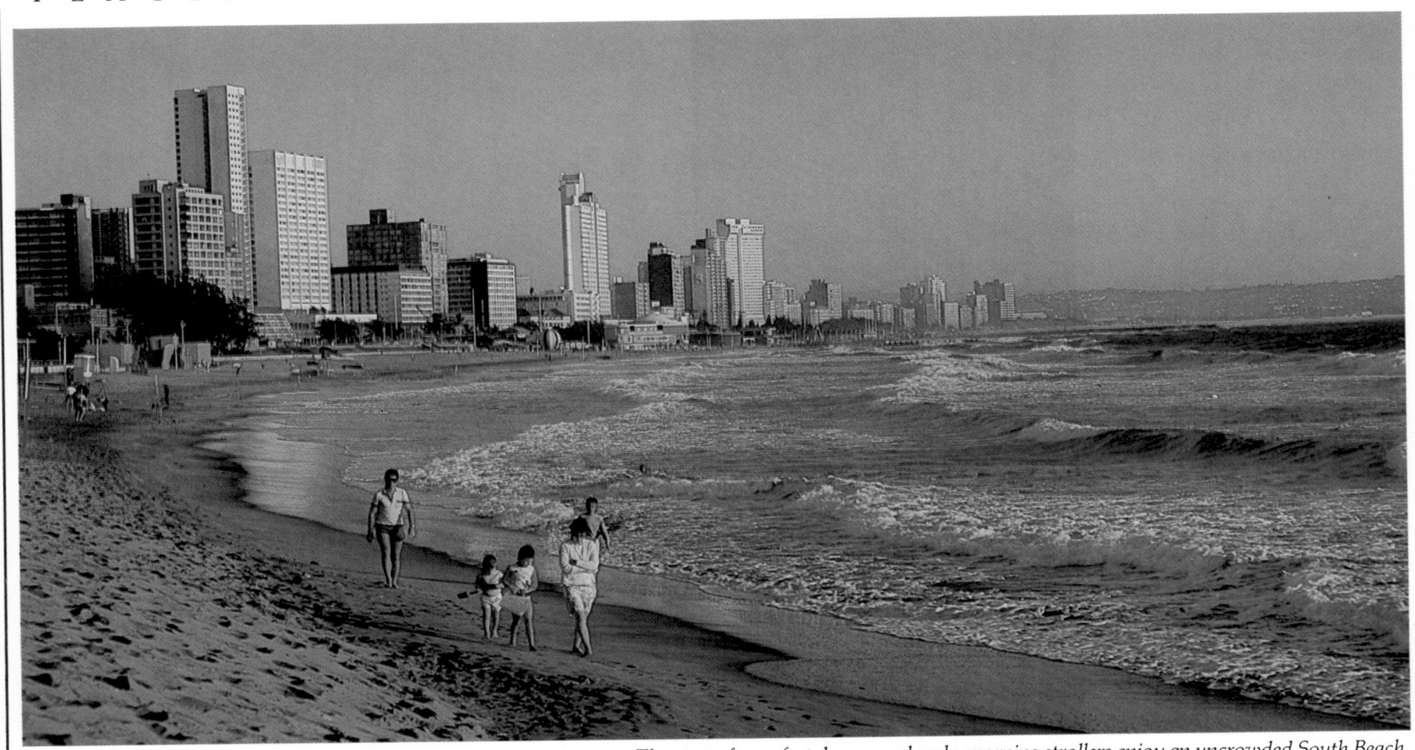

The start of a perfect day — and early-morning strollers enjoy an uncrowded South Beach.

East meets West in a sub-tropical holiday city

DURBAN — A NATURAL port that served in centuries past as a temporary refuge to successive bands of war refugees, adventurers and traders — has grown into one of South Africa's best-known and most popular coastal resorts. Stretches of safe, sandy beach, an abundance of holiday accommodation and all-year sunshine attract an estimated one million visitors to the city every year.

Most of these visitors content themselves with a lazy lifestyle — encouraged by the sub-tropical climate — cultivating an east-coast suntan and sampling the nightlife. But beyond the facade of carefree tourism, Durban has a great deal more to offer. It is one of the busiest harbours in Africa, and a bustling industrial centre, while the blend of African, Asian and European lifestyles makes it an interesting, cosmopolitan city.

Fun at the waterfront

Most holiday-makers head directly for Durban's beachfront, where bathing beaches stretch for some 4 km from Addington in the south to Country Club and Blue Lagoon in the north. (North from here to Umhlanga the coast is ideal for walks, but unprotected by shark nets.) The sea temperature is welcoming in summer, and bracing but not too cold in winter. The Rachel Finlayson saltwater pool alongside North Beach, and the nearby children's paddling pools provide even safer swimming.

For those tired of the beach, the *Marine Parade* area offers a number of other attractions. There are trampolines, a miniature golf course, and a mini pleasure park for children, with fun rides and an aerial cableway. During the holiday season, the brightly striped *Little Top* (tel. 326421) on South Beach runs open-air shows. *Sea World* (tel. 373536) combines aquarium displays, a fascinating shark tank, and lively dolphin and seal performances. (Check feeding and show times.)

One of the most memorable experiences is a ride along the beachfront in an extravagantly decorated ricksha, powered by an even more vividly garbed ricksha puller. The ricksha tradition started less ornamentally in the 1890s, as conveyance for cargo as well as passengers. The present-day ricksha pullers are based opposite the Malibu Hotel, and rates are set by time and distance. Not far from the rickshas, a group of Zulu women sell traditional handcrafts on the corner of West Street and Marine Parade, and another group can be found opposite the Maharani Hotel.

Also opposite the Maharani is *Minitown* (tel. 377892), a charming city scaled down to children's eye level. It has replicas of some of Durban's buildings and the harbour, models of aircraft and trains, and even a drive-in cinema. A minute's walk away is *Fitzsimons Snake Park* (tel. 376456), with cages and pits filled with snakes, lizards and tortoises. Informative demonstrations are held several times a day, and there is also a well-stocked curio shop.

Inland of Country Club Beach lies *Water Wonderland* (tel. 376336), where one entry fee admits you to several rides, water slides and jumps. (Further afield at Amanzimtoti beach a water shute is open daily during the holiday season, and a range of pleasure craft can be hired on the banks of the lagoon — see pages 188-9.)

The Bluff, the wooded headland that so effectively protects the bay, has inviting beaches and tidal pools at Anstey's and Brighton beaches. For those

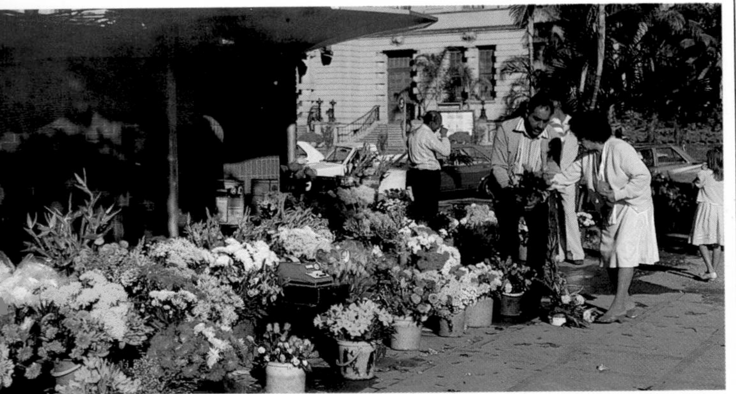

Flower-sellers add a splash of colour to the historic Church Street Plaza.

Golden domes of the Juma Mosque.

willing to drive a short distance out of the city, attractive beaches can also be found at Umhlanga and Umdloti (see pages 182-3).

Watersport and fishing

Ocean swimmers sometimes have to compete for water space. Durban is a famous surfing centre, with the Bay of Plenty a premier venue for the international contest circuit. Vetch's Pier, the expanse of beach stretching from North Pier to Addington, is a gathering place for boardsailers, paddle-skiers and skindivers. A popular inland watersport venue is *Hazelmere Dam*, near the sugar-producing centre of Verulam.

The coastal waters are a paradise for anglers, particularly during the famous annual marine phenomenon of the sardine run, which occurs in June/July (see pages 190-1). Catches along this coast include kob, shad, spotted grunter and Natal stumpnose. For rock and surf fishing, there are the groynes (breakwaters) and the beachfront, North and South piers flanking the harbour mouth, and Blue Lagoon. Deep-sea fishing cruises depart from the *Maydon Wharf Fishing Jetty* (tels. 377751 or 464300).

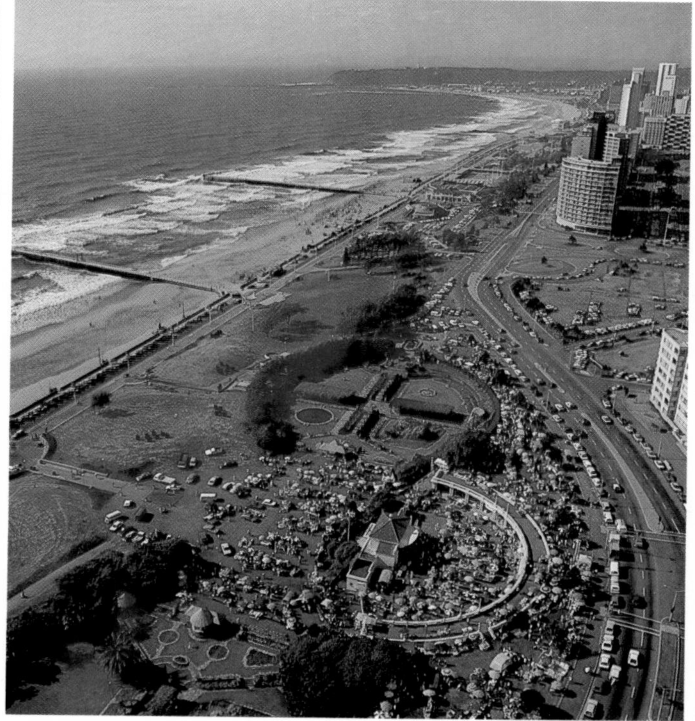

Golden beaches and the Indian Ocean make up Durban's 'Golden Mile'.

The harbour and Embankment

Durban's harbour is a constant source of interest, and bay cruises offer a sortie into the romantic world of the sea. Sarie Marais pleasure launches use the *Gardiner Street jetty* daily, from where they chug around the harbour or take to the sea — parallel to the shoreline. The harbour ferry leaves from the *New Small Craft Harbour* on Victoria Embankment. Used mainly by harbour folk, the ferry is good fun.

A slow drive south along Maydon Wharf will bring you to the *Prince Edward Graving Dock*, where ocean-going ships are brought in and left high and dry for repairs. Driving around the bay edge towards Salisbury Island, you will find the *Floating Dock*, where vessels are raised out of the water for reconditioning.

The three sugar terminals at the junction of Maydon Wharf and Canal Road store and move large quantities of Natal's sweetest export. Entire shiploads of sugar can be loaded in a day. Public tours operate three days a week (tel. 313994).

Victoria Embankment, landing site for many an early seaborne settler, has a number of historical features. Graced by the *Old Supreme Court* building, a national monument, the Embankment is the site of the first railway in South Africa, which was built from Durban to the Point in 1859.

On the Embankment, known also as the Esplanade, there is a statue of Dick King, commemorating his historic ride of 1 000 km to Grahamstown in 1842 to fetch aid for the British soldiers besieged in the Old Fort by the Boers. Another brave rescue mission, by the young boy John Ross, is honoured by a statue in front of the imposing John Ross House. In 1826 Ross walked 1 000 km north to Delagoa Bay to obtain medicines for the fledgling Port Natal settlement.

Stepping back into the past

The *Local History Museum* in Aliwal Street (tel. 3048694) offers a good introduction to Durban's past and its peoples. Backing on the museum is the *City Hall* (tel. 3040111), pivot of the city's historic centre. The majestic building, resembling the Belfast City Hall in Northern Ireland, was opened in 1910, and now houses a first-rate natural history museum and art gallery (entrance on Smith Street).

The City Hall faces Francis Farewell Square, named after one of the British naval men who established the first white settlement at Port Natal in 1824, and believed to be the site of Farewell's camp. Also overlooking the square is the *Post Office*, which started out in 1885 as Durban's town hall. Now a national monument, along with the square and the City Hall, it has a plaque on its eastern steps commemorating a speech made there in 1899 by the young war correspondent — and later British Prime Minister — Winston Churchill.

Church Street Plaza next to the Post Office is the home of the Durban Publicity Association — in the double-storey building next to the flower-sellers. Guided historical and 'Oriental' walks set off from here regularly (tel. 3044934). The underpass from the Plaza brings you out on the former site of Durban's railway station where Victorian railway sheds have been converted into a shopping centre, a hotel, and an exhibition centre.

A historical gem is the *Old House Museum* in St Andrew's Street (tel. 3040111, ask for extension 321). Built in 1849 by John Goodricke, a former mayor of Durban, the tiny house is crammed with the accoutrements of early colonial homes.

Another relic from the past is the *Old Fort*, on the corner of NMR Avenue and Old Fort Road (tel. 329619), the site of the British camp during their 1842 Battle of Congella against the Boers. Some earthworks, a small chapel, and barracks that

The sparkling jewel of the South Coast reflects its holiday lights on the bay.

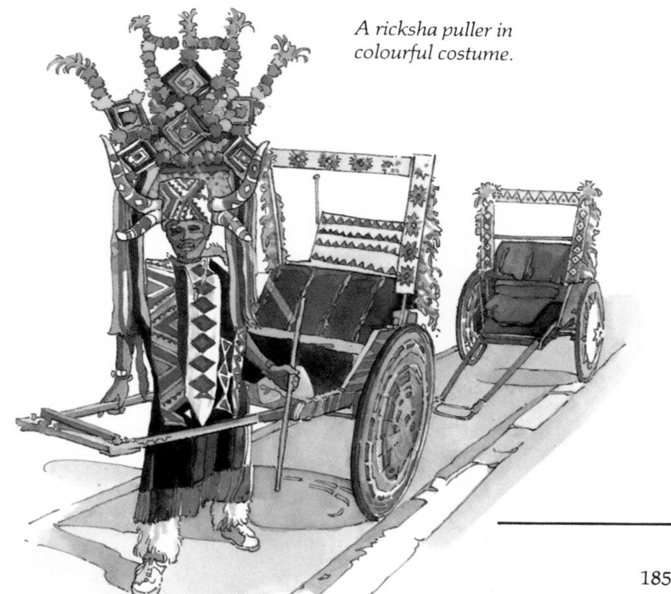

A ricksha puller in colourful costume.

Surf-fishing offers splendid rewards for anglers with patience and stamina.

Durban's ornate old City Hall is a copy of the City Hall in Belfast.

have been converted into quarters for war pensioners, are surrounded by informal gardens. War memorabilia are on view at Warriors' Gate, a small building modelled on a Norman gatehouse. The building is also headquarters for the ex-servicemen's organisation, the Memorable Order of Tin Hats (MOTH).

The *Killie Campbell Museum* (tel. 285311), situated high on the ridge known as the Berea in a gracious house that belonged to the famous sugar family of Sir Marshall Campbell, holds an acclaimed Africana library, and collections of furniture and Zulu art and crafts. Medical memorabilia are on display at the *Addington Hospital Centenary Museum* in Prince Street (tel. 324360). Photography buffs can focus on the *Whysalls Camera Museum* (tel. 371431) in Brickhill Road — noted for old and rare cameras.

Orientation and viewsites

The multi-sensory *Durban Experience Show* offers an audio-visual perspective on the city's past, present and future. There are five shows daily at the Durban Exhibition Centre in Walnut Road (tel. 3017763).

Viewing spots reached by bus or car include the University of Natal, on King George V Avenue on the crest of Berea ridge, and a number of points along South and North Ridge roads. A drive around the crown of the Bluff gives views of the city, the bay and the Indian Ocean. And a stroll to the end of North Pier provides a shoreline panorama — close enough to passing ships to feel you can reach out and touch them.

A more extravagant way to get your bearings is with a 20-minute air flip from Virginia Airport, organised by the Natal Flight Centre (tel. 844720). A number of hotels also offer excellent views of the city.

Culture and the arts

Several cultural and arts venues are to be found in Durban and its outlying areas. Focus of the performing arts is the *Natal Playhouse* (tel. 3043631), an ultra-modern complex run by the Natal Performing Arts Council (Napac). This venue for opera, ballet, contemporary theatre, and the Natal Philharmonic Orchestra, is housed on Smith Street in the refurbished shells of two former cinemas — hence the eccentric facade.

Open-air theatre is often staged on the parkland slopes of the University of Natal campus (tel. 8163133). The *Elizabeth Sneddon Theatre* (tel. 814544), also on the campus, features local theatre, and is the venue for the Durban International Film Festival.

The Durban Arts Association in Silverton Road, telephone 212711, is an excellent source of information on all aspects of the arts, including music in city parks.

For visual arts, the *Durban Art Gallery* in the City Hall offers one of the best-patronised formal galleries in the country (tel. 3040111). It houses a permanent collection of South African and international works, as well as covering the applied arts.

The *Natal Society of Arts Gallery* (tel. 294934) at Overport City, Ridge Road, regularly exhibits works by local painters and sculptors, as does the *Elizabeth Gordon Gallery* (tel. 3032914) in its historic Victorian house in Windermere Road.

On a smaller scale, the *Grassroots Gallery* (tel. 866263) in Westville also

Tall palms and other sub-tropical plants line Victoria Embankment.

Catamaran sailors take to the water at the start of a regatta at Vetch's Pier.

Marine Parade — a tourist's paradise and a fun-filled world for children.

Medwood Gardens, a tranquil spot to escape the bustle of the city centre.

displays works by Natal artists in a building that is part of an Islamic religious complex built last century. *The African Art Centre* (tel. 3047915) off Gardiner Street has excellent works by black artists, and sells beadwork, baskets, woven goods and woodcuts.

The *Mariannhill Monastery* (tel. 7004288), in its rural setting on Durban's outskirts, houses church and religious artefacts, as well as an ethnological collection of art. The mission complex, founded in 1882 by Trappist monks, is equally interesting.

A unique collection of 150 pieces of Buddhist sacred art dating from the 3rd to the 19th century can be viewed in the city by arrangement. Telephone owner Molly van Loon at 231954 for a guided tour.

Indian settlers have brought much of their culture and traditions to bear on the local environment since the arrival of the first 341 indentured labourers in Natal in 1860. Their varied creeds have added a number of exquisite buildings to the city landscape. The *Juma Mosque* in Grey Street, said to be the largest in the southern hemisphere, may be visited by arrangement.

A number of Hindu temples adorn the city — some eye-catchingly ornate, others simple and flower-strewn — and the Hindu religious calendar brings many colourful festivals, including firewalking, processions and acts of penitence.

The most accessible temples are those in the Umgeni Road complex, another in Somtseu Road, and the Bellair temples west of the University of Natal.

Still another religious venue open to visitors is the *Hare Krishna Temple of Understanding* in Chatsworth, with its dazzling architecture set in spacious gardens.

Nature trails and parks

A number of parks, gardens and protected bush areas add to the general effect of a lush, green Durban, and provide havens from the city bustle and hot beaches. Closest to the beach are the formally and attractively landscaped *Amphitheatre Gardens* between North Beach and the snake park. *Medwood Gardens* and tea kiosk offer a pleasant breather for city strollers, and *Albert Park* has a restaurant/roadhouse, and an exercise track for the energetic.

The *Botanic Gardens* (tel. 211303), which started as an agricultural research station in 1849, offer a pretty, tranquil setting, and a tea kiosk serving refreshments. The gardens are well-known for their orchid house and rare collection of cycads, and the *Natal Herbarium* (or Botanical Research Institute) is tucked away in the St Thomas Road corner of the gardens (tel. 224095).

A popular family destination is *Mitchell Park* with its playgrounds, displays of animals and birds, and open-air cafe. *Jameson Park* next door specialises in roses.

The Metropolitan Open Space System (MOSS) has established self-guided walking trails not far from the city centre at Pigeon Valley, Burman Bush and Virginia Bush. Excellent guidebooks are obtainable from the Durban Publicity Association. Also nearby are walking trails and picnic sites at the *Kenneth Stainbank Reserve* in Yellowwood Park; at *Paradise Valley* on the Umbilo River; and at *Krantzkloof Nature Reserve* (see pages 178-9). The *Japanese Gardens* in Durban North, laid out in delicate Oriental fashion, make a popular picnic and photography spot; and the *Umgeni River Bird Park* (tel. 841733) offers aviaries of exotic and indigenous birds (see pages 182-3).

Umhlanga's *Scarlet Tanager Bird Park* is a favoured tea-and-scones halt, with its birds and pony rides for children. The *Umhlanga Lagoon Nature Reserve*, administered by the Natal Parks Board, has a lagoon trail through the Hawaan Forest to picnic and braai sites.

Inland from Umhlanga, on Umhlanga Rocks Drive, is the headquarters of the *Natal Anti-Shark Measures Board*, which runs guided tours of its modern complex.

Shoppers' delight

For those who enjoy shopping for arts, crafts and bargain items, there are sprawling fleamarkets in the Marine Parade Amphitheatre on the second and last Sundays of the month. Shoppers unfamiliar with Durban should make a point of exploring the many arcades that run between Smith and West Streets in the centre of the city. And for shopping — and haggling — for fish, meat, spices, ornaments, curios and knicknacks, in an exotic Oriental environment, the *Indian Market* in Warwick Avenue is the place to go on weekdays ●

For further information:

Durban Publicity Association Church Square, Durban 4001 Tel. (031) 326946
Amanzimtoti Publicity Association 47 Louis Botha Drive, Amanzimtoti 4125 Tel. (031) 932121
SA Tourism Board Suite 520, Southern Life Centre, 320 West Street, Durban 4001 Tel. (031) 3047144

City skyline above the yacht harbour.

Vasco da Gama Clock, the Esplanade.

Palms, wild bananas and golden sands adorn the 'Strelitzia Coast'

The wild bananas that grow profusely in the dune forests south of Durban have given this popular holiday area its name: 'Strelitzia Coast'. We make our way to idyllic beaches lapped by the warm Indian Ocean, and also venture inland — to visit the domain of the deadly crocodile, and explore a gently winding country road.

Durban
Umgababa
Clansthal
Crocworld
Pennington
Scottburgh
Amanzimtoti
210—230 km

LEAVE DURBAN BY travelling south on Victoria Embankment (the Esplanade), passing the yacht basin and harbour on your left. At the end of the embankment, exit left for 'South Coast/M4'. After about 13 km the road merges with the south-bound N2 — note your kms here.

After 17,8 km on the N2, exit left for the R78 to Pietermaritzburg and Winkelspruit. At the end of the off-ramp turn left, then 100-200 m later turn right at the T-junction for Winkelspruit and Illovo Beach. 300-400 m later turn right onto the R102, noting your kms.

The R102 runs parallel to the N2 on your right for a short distance, with a large sugar plantation on its far side. After roughly 1,5 km you cross the wide Lovu (Illovo) River. Soon afterwards you pass a turn-off on your left to Illovo Beach. After just over 7 km on the R102 you have a view on your left of the lagoon formed by the uMgababa River (Zulu for 'place of jealousy'), with dense bush on its far bank.

Soon afterwards you cross the river, and after 8,4 km on the R102 turn left into the Umgababa Curio Centre, a market that sells fresh sub-tropical fruits, baskets, beadwork, pottery, carvings and other curios.

Umgababa to Crocworld

From the curio centre turn left onto the R102, noting your kms. 1,5 km later there is another craft and fruit market on your right — the Iminwe Zulu Craft Association.

The road closely follows the coastline for a while, and 3,2 km beyond the second craft market you cross a bridge high above the wide mouth of the Mkomazi River — before entering the town of Umkomaas.

Note your kms as you pass the turn-off on your left soon afterwards to Umkomaas (which also leads to the tidal pool, the beach and the river mouth). After 3,8 km turn left for Clansthal Caravan Park. 200 m later you cross the railway line, with Claustal station on your right (see opposite). Go right immediately afterwards onto Greenpoint Road, and after 400 m park on your left — for a short walk south along the beach towards the aptly named Greenpoint, with its lighthouse high up on the hill (allow 30-40 minutes).

Retrace your route to the R102, turn left and note your kms. After 2 km turn right for Crocworld, which lies a further 400 m along this side-road. (There is an entry fee, and the centre has a restaurant and snack bar. Visitors may watch the crocodiles being fed at 11 am and 3 pm; enquire at the gate about which enclosure. A shady 3 km trail leads through the forest.)

Crocworld to Pennington

Return to the R102, and turn right. After 1,8 km you cross the pretty lagoon of the Mahlongwa River. Soon afterwards you cross the Mpambanyoni River on the outskirts of Scottburgh.

Remain on the R102 through the settlements of Scottburgh and Park Rynie, and note your kms as you pass a turn-off on your left to the N2 and the R612 to Umzinto. After 6 km you cross the wide Mzinto River. 2,6 km later turn left into Pennington Drive, an attractive tree-shaded road that leads to the beach. After 400 m go right at the fork, and 600-700 m later go straight where the larger road curves sharply to the left. Cross the railway line, and stop in the parking area alongside the shaded picnic spot (with braai place and toilet). There is a tidal pool here, and the beach offers a lovely walk along an unspoilt stretch of coast backed by indigenous bush.

Pennington to Scottburgh

Return to the R102, and continue south. The road winds its way inland through attractive rural scenery. 3,2 km after rejoining the R102 you cross the attractive Mkumbane (Inkabana) River. You cross the N2 soon afterwards — 200 m later turn left for Bazley to remain on the R102, and note your kms.

Soon afterwards you cross the Sezela River (named after a legendary man-eating crocodile whose reign of terror over the Malangeni people was ended when Chaka ordered it killed for its skin). The road traverses rolling green hills, covered with sugar cane, traditional huts, mealie fields, banana trees and patches of forest. You are likely to spot troops of vervet monkeys in the bushes alongside the road.

After 6,2 km on this road you cross the lovely Fafa (Zulu for 'sparkling') River. 1,3 km later turn left onto gravel for Ifafa Beach. After just over 1,8 km turn left for Club Marina, and 1 km later turn right into a viewsite for a view over a bend in the Fafa River, with its dense indigenous forest on the far bank.

Return to the tarred R102, and turn left. After 1,5 km you pass a turn-off on your left to the N2, Ifafa Beach and Elysium, then the road begins to descend towards the Mtwalume River. You cross the river over a single-lane steel bridge. (The river is named after a tree whose bark is believed by Zulus to be a cure for dysentry.) Just over 1 km beyond the river turn left for Mtwalume, Scottburgh and Port Shepstone, and after a further 3,3 km turn left onto the N2 for Durban, noting your kms.

After 24,8 km exit left for the R612. At the end of the off-ramp turn right, and 1,4 km later turn left onto the R102 for Scottburgh, noting your kms. After 4,2 km turn right into Scottburgh's Airth Street. Turn left into Scott Street (the main road), then turn right into Cordiner Street. At the T-junction 200 m later turn left, and cross the railway line to reach the parking area at the beach, tidal pool, river mouth and miniature railway.

Scottburgh to Inyoni Rocks

Retrace your route to the R102, and turn right. After 1 km you cross the Mpambanyoni River, and 500 m later turn left for Dududu and the N2 to Durban. After roughly 1,2 km turn right onto the N2.

Roughly 30 km from Scottburgh, you pass the exit for 'Amanzimtoti/Adams Road'. After a further 2 km exit left for Umbogintwini/Athlone Park/Adams Mission. At the end of the off-ramp, turn right and note your kms. At the T-junction turn right for Amanzimtoti. Just after 1,4 km turn left for Inyoni Rocks, then turn

Crocodiles laze in the sun — safely behind fences.

THE GENTLENESS OF DEADLY JAWS

The Nile crocodile, one of the oldest creatures still surviving, has a powerful jaw that can exert 40 tons of pressure per square cm. Yet a mother can gently roll an egg between her teeth to crack the shell if her hatchling is having difficulty emerging into the world. The first journey the young make to the water is also in the mouth of their mother. This is the safest place for them, since in spite of the immense power of adults the young are extremely vulnerable to predators — out of a clutch of 40-80 eggs a mere one or two will survive to adulthood in the wild.

Vervet monkeys abound in the coastal forests.

left immediately. At the bottom of the hill (1,8 km after noting your kms) turn right into Beach Road. 700 m later park on your left next to the Visitor's Bureau for a late-afternoon stroll along the beach at Inyoni Rocks.

Inyoni Rocks to Durban
From the parking area, turn left, noting your kms. After 1,1 km you pass a parking area on your left alongside the lagoon, where boats may be hired. 500 m later turn left, then immediately go left again. After a further 150 m turn right for Durban/Adams Road. After crossing the N2, turn right again and follow the signs onto the N2 for Durban ●

AA Office AA House, 537 Smith Street, Durban 4001 Tel. (031) 3010341
Durban Publicity Association Church Square, Durban 4001 Tel. (031) 326421
SA Tourism Board 520 Southern Life Centre, 320 West Street, Durban 4001 Tel. (031) 3047144

Colourful Zulu crafts tempt shoppers at Umgababa.

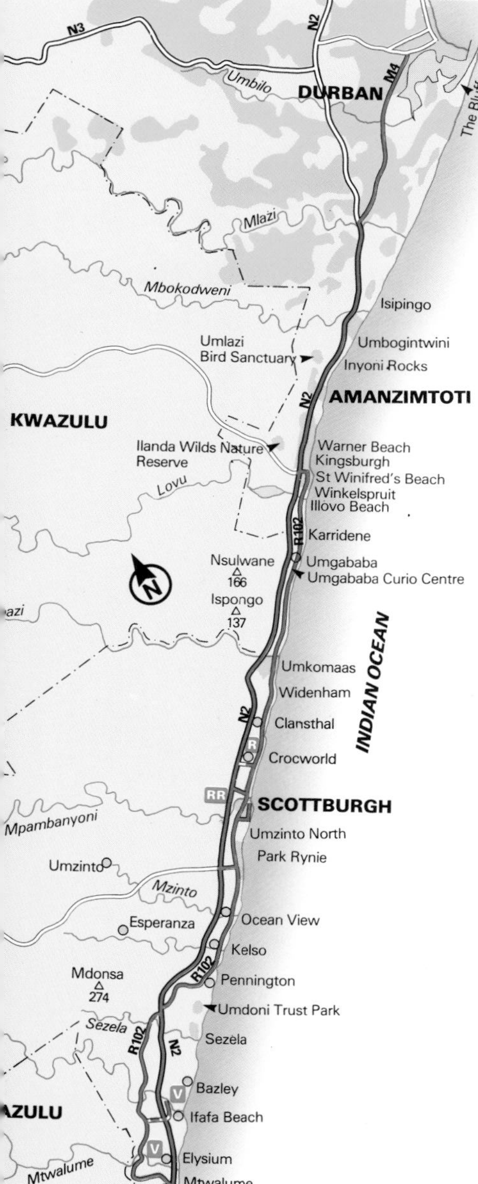

SCOTTBURGH
This popular holiday resort was founded in 1860 and named after the governor of Natal, Sir John Scott. The little bay known as Scott's Bay was once used as a precarious port for the export of sugar, and at the beginning of last century Chaka's warriors are believed to have drawn water from a spot near where the present water slide has been built next to the river.

Apart from the tidal pool near the river mouth and protected surf swimming, Scottburgh offers rides on a miniature railway, angling, and several amusements for children.

WHERE THE WATERS ARE SWEET
The resort and residential area of Amanzimtoti takes its name from a remark attributed to the Zulu king Chaka when he was given water from the river: 'Kanti amanza mtoti' (So, the water is sweet). There is a tidal pool at Inyoni Rocks, from where a promenade leads along the beachfront. The lagoon is popular for boating, and there is good surf and rock angling. Other attractions in the area include the Ilanda Wilds Nature Reserve and the Amanzimtoti Bird Sanctuary.

The pretty lagoon of the Amanzimtoti River.

CLANSTHAL AND GREENPOINT
The beautiful, unspoilt beach at Clansthal takes its name from the nearby farm Clausthal, which in turn was named after a German town. Although the misspelling is now official, the railway station of Claustal retains a name closer to the original.

Overlooking Clansthal beach is the Greenpoint lighthouse, built in 1905 to warn seamen against the offshore Aliwal Shoal, on which many a ship has come to grief. Greenpoint is now a popular surfing spot.

The tranquillity of Clansthal's unspoilt beach belies the danger of this coast for passing ships.

Where endless river valleys reach down to a golden shore

The rivers that rise in the Drakensberg have carved steep valleys that zig-zag towards the golden sands of the Natal coast. Our route through this lovely land includes visits to a hill-top nature reserve, a historic mission station, the attractive settler town of Ixopo, and several delightful beaches. More than two-thirds of the route is on tar.

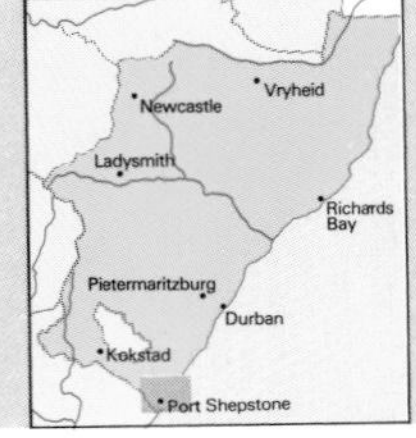

Scottburgh
Vernon Crookes Nature Reserve
Ixopo
St Faith's
Umtentweni
Umzumbe
310 – 330 km

LEAVE SCOTTBURGH BY turning inland from Scott Street (the main road) into Airth Street, between the library and the post office. 750 m later turn left onto the R102, noting your kms. After 4,2 km you pass on your right the R612 to Umzinto and the N2. Just over 1,8 km later turn left onto gravel for Rocky Bay Caravan Park. A further 250 m brings you to a parking area alongside Park Rynie's old whaling station jetty (now used as a fishing pier). The unspoilt stretch of beach offers a lovely early-morning walk (allow 30-40 min).

Park Rynie to St Michael's

Return to the tar and turn right onto the R102. Retrace your route for the 1,8 km to the R612, and turn left towards Umzinto, noting your kms. Soon afterwards you cross the N2, and after 12 km on the R612, turn right onto the gravel D145 for Vernon Crookes Nature Reserve, noting your kms. Where the road branches into three take the extreme left road. After 350 m on gravel go right at the fork, and 650 m later go left at another fork. The road climbs steadily through hills covered with sugar cane and forests, and after 5,6 km you enter the nature reserve (small entry fee). Ask for a map at the gate, and follow the signs to the picnic area at the summit of the hill, beyond the dam wall (roughly 5,8 km from the gate). The road and picnic area offer good views and you are likely to spot zebra and impala.

Retrace your route to the tarred R612, and turn right. The road climbs through sugar country, and after 9,2 km you can see far away on your right the As-Salaam Islamic seminary with its exotic tower. 6,3 km later you can see Himmelberg Mission, also on your right.

The scenery changes gradually to grassy cattle country, dotted with traditional huts and mealie patches, and with large tracts of forest in between. 31,7 km after rejoining the R612 turn right onto a gravel track for St Michael's Mission and Ndonyane Weaving Centre. (The 2,9 km road to the churches at St Michael's may be treacherous after heavy rain.) Park near the churches, and walk along the 200 m path behind the old church to visit the weaving centre.

St Michael's to Ixopo

Retrace your route to the tarred R612, and turn right, noting your kms. After 3 km you pass through Jolivet, named after C C Jolivet, Catholic bishop of Natal and co-founder of the Mariannhill Mission near Durban. The road climbs ever higher through magnificent scenery, hugging the course of the old narrow-gauge railway for much of the way.

16,9 km after noting your kms turn left into the grounds of St James Anglican Church, Highflats. A track of about 200 m leads to the small stone church, from where stone steps lead to pretty falls on the Mtwalume River.

Continue northwards from the church on the R612. After a few kms you enter Highflats, an attractive town founded in 1863, where a few lovely old buildings survive. In the town you pass a turn-off on your left to St Faith's (our

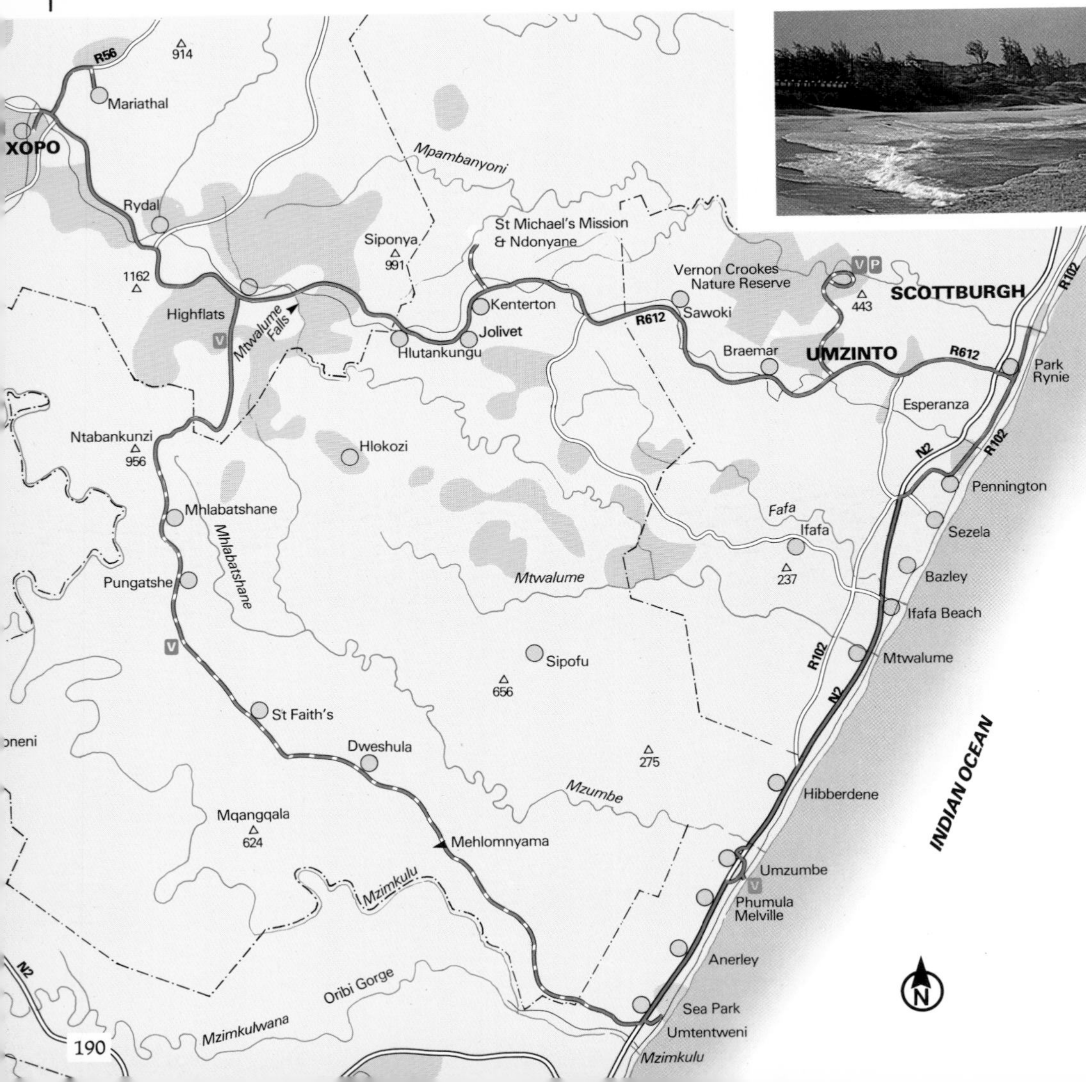

The beach at Park Rynie curves to the north beyond the old whaling jetty.

'A STRANGE, WEIRD TALE...'

St Michael's, founded in 1854 as the first Catholic mission in Natal, was soon abandoned because of its lack of success in converting the local people. Two missionaries who later returned to rebuild the church and make a fresh start had their daily building work quietly torn down each night while they slept. But now the mission has grown to such an extent that the 1894 stone church has had to be supplemented by a new, bigger building.

The out-of-the-way community made world headlines in 1907 with a personal account by Bishop Delalle of a 'strange, weird tale from the depths of darkest Africa', in which he told of an excorcism rite he performed to rid two adolescent African girls – Germana and Monica – of the demon 'Dioar'. The girls were reported to have great strength and cognitive powers under Dioar's influence.

Today the mission runs a weaving and spinning centre named Ndonyane after the nearby river.

return route).

Beyond Highflats the road climbs even higher in a richly forested area. Roughly 22 km after leaving Highflats go straight at the crossroads where the R56 leads right to Richmond and Pietermaritzburg and left to Umzimkulu. 1,5 km later turn left for Ixopo, which you enter on Margaret Street. (Two hotels in the historic town serve lunch.)

Ixopo to Umtentweni

After your visit to Ixopo, return along Margaret Street and the R612 to the R56, and turn left onto the R56 towards Richmond and Pietermaritzburg, noting your kms. After 4,7 km turn right onto a gravel track that leads after 200 m to Mariathal Catholic Church, a stately redbrick building decorated with magnificent paintings, statues and stained-glass windows.

Retrace your route along the R56 to the R612, turn left onto the R612 for Highflats noting your kms. After 22,3 km turn right for St Faith's, noting your kms again. After 15 km the road surface changes to gravel, and after roughly 3 km more you can see across the undulating Mzimkulu (home of the rivers) valley towards the faraway Drakensberg. Soon afterwards you can also look out over the attractive hills of the Mzumbe valley on your left.

After 28,2 km on this road, pull onto the wide shoulder on your left for a view over the Mzimkulu valley on your right. You will see the prominent double hump of Nkoneni rising from the valley. Continue from here along the scenic St Faith's road, which roughly follows a ridge of hills between the Mzimkulu and Mzumbe rivers. The mission village of St Faith's lies 40 km from Highflats, and commands a lovely view of the cliffs above the Mzimkulu.

From St Faith's the road winds through magnificent countryside, with other views over the cliffs of the Mzimkulu valley on your right. Eventually, after 51,1 km of gravel, the road surface changes to tar, and you begin to glimpse Port Shepstone on your right, and the sea ahead of you. 82,7 km from Highflats you reach the N2. Cross over the N2 for Umtentweni, noting your kms. After 300 m you cross the railway line. Immediately afterwards turn left, then turn left again immediately for North Beach. 800 m from the N2 you reach a parking area alongside a tearoom and changerooms (with toilets). The beach here offers a pleasant walk towards the south — although you may prefer a walk a little later at Umzumbe.

Umtentweni to Scottburgh

Retrace your route to the N2, and turn right onto the N2, noting your kms. The road makes its way through a string of lovely holiday resorts, and you cross a number of pretty river mouths. Just after 10 km on the N2 you can see an attractive sweep of unspoilt beach ahead of you, with St Elmo's Convent silhouetted on the hillside above a rocky point. Opposite the convent, after 11,8 km on the N2, turn right for Umzumbe, noting your kms.

After 400 m turn right into 'Stebel Beach Road', and cross the railway soon afterwards. Pass a parking area on your left, and follow the road where it curves to the right. 600 m after leaving the N2 turn left into a parking area and walk onto the outcrop known as Stiebel Rocks for a beautiful view of the coast. The beach here offers a delightful late-afternoon walk.

Leaving the Stiebel Rocks parking area, turn right, noting your kms. After just under 300 m turn right at the T-junction, and after just over 1,1 km further turn right for Port Shepstone and Scottburgh. A few hundred metres later turn left onto the N2 for Scottburgh and Durban, noting your kms.

18 km after rejoining the N2 you cross the wide mouth of the Mtwalume River, then enter countryside lush with fields of sugar cane, banana plantations, and tracts of dense indigenous bush. After 28 km exit left for Sezela and Esperanza, and at the end of the off-ramp turn right onto the R102 — an attractive country road that winds its way leisurely back to Scottburgh ●

AA Office 35a Wooley Street, Port Shepstone 4240. Tel. (0391) 22503
SA Tourism Board Suite 520, Southern Life Centre, 320 West Street, Durban 4001 Tel. (031) 3047144

The sparkling blue lagoon at the mouth of the Mpambanyoni River is part of Scottburgh's appeal.

SOUTH COAST SILVER

The waters off the stretch of coast we travel along are the scene of an extraordinary annual event — the sardine run. Every year at the beginning of autumn hundreds of millions of sardines make their way from the Cape up the Mocambique Current to spawn in the warm East African coastal waters. The current keeps the sardines out to sea for much of the journey, but sweeps them close to the shores for a 250 km stretch from Port St John's to just south of Durban. Apart from the thousands that people catch along the way — sometimes by the bucketful — the little fish are also prey to larger fish, and the run provides excellent game-fishing in its wake.

The Mzumbe River makes its way through hilly land to the sea.

IXOPO

The novel *Cry the Beloved Country* by Alan Paton begins in the beautiful hill country of the Ixopo area. Established as a colonial town in 1878, Ixopo was at first named Stuartstown by the settlers in honour of a local magistrate, but eventually reverted to the original Zulu name for the river and area. Spelt eXobo in Zulu, the name imitates the noise made when walking through marshy ground. A number of interesting old buildings date from the town's early settler history, and the town has become an important centre for timber and dairy farming.

Left: *Burchell's zebra and wildebeest at Vernon Crookes Nature Reserve.* **Right:** *Typical landscape near Ixopo.*

The stark beauty of Oribi Gorge and a lush, sun-drenched coast

Natal's South Coast offers a string of golden beaches, hidden away amidst lush forest, sugar-cane fields, and plantations of bananas, mangoes and pawpaws. Our route includes stops at several coastal resorts, and leads through the spectacular Oribi Gorge, famed for its magnificent rock shapes. Almost the entire route is tarred.

Margate
Uvongo
Oribi Gorge
Umtamvuna
Nature Reserve
Port Edward
Southbroom
180 — 200 km

LEAVE MARGATE by travelling north along Marine Drive and turn right on to the R61 coastal road just outside the town. You pass through Manaba, and about 2 km from Margate you enter Uvongo. After crossing the Vungu (Uvongo) River, turn right at the first intersection into Forster Street, then turn right again at the stop street into Uvongo Beach Road. Park 200 m later for an early-morning walk on the beach, alongside the lovely lagoon. You may hire boats here, to paddle a short distance upstream to a 23 m waterfall (allow 30-40 min).

Uvongo to Oribi Gorge

Return along Uvongo Beach Road, and turn right into Marine Drive, noting your kms. The road passes through St Michael's On Sea and Shelly Beach, offering fine views over the sea and inland hills. After 3,6 km turn left for Gamalakhe and Izotsha.

After a further 3,6 km turn right towards Port Shepstone onto a pretty country road that winds through cultivated farmlands and clusters of banana trees. The industrial area of Marburg on the outskirts of Port Shepstone soon comes into view ahead of you.

After 5 km on this road turn left onto the N2 for Izingolweni and Harding, noting your kms. The N2 climbs steadily through hills covered with sugar cane, and after 5,2 km you ascend a pass with views left to the coast and right over the valley of the Boboyi River. Soon after the road levels out (after 8,2 km on the N2) turn right for Oribi Gorge, noting your kms.

Almost immediately you have views of rolling hills in the valleys of the Mzimkulwana and Mzimkulu rivers — many of the hillsides intensely cultivated despite their steepness. After 4,2 km the road begins to descend into the Mzimkulwana valley, and 1,3 km later you can see the high Four Men's Hill on your left at the southern end of Oribi Gorge. After a further 1,8 km you cross the river, then begin to climb steeply towards Oribi Flats.

12 km after leaving the N2 turn left onto gravel for 'hotel viewsites'. 1,3 km later there is a gate at which an entry fee is charged — a map of the viewsites area is obtainable here. The drive along the edge of the gorge for roughly 4 km to the panoramic view of Oribi Heads is particularly worthwhile, and there are a number of spots along the way offering breathtaking views. (There are picnic and braai sites, and the hotel serves lunches and teas.)

Oribi Gorge to Wilson's Cutting

Return to the tarred road and turn left, noting your kms. 5,6 km later turn right onto the gravel D419 (opposite 'Whistling Pines'). After a further 1,5 km stop alongside the road and walk to your left for a magnificent view of the cliffs on your left known as the Walls of Jericho, which tower above a classic horseshoe bend in the Mzimkulu River and locked-in farms far below on the fertile river banks. 800 m further along the D419 (opposite the trading store) there is another view into the spectacular Mzimkulu gorge, with the prominent Gibraltar Rock standing like a sentinel above it.

Return to the tarred road, and turn right, noting your kms. After 1,5 km turn left for Oribi Gorge Nature Reserve. The road descends a steep pass into Oribi Gorge amidst dense natural forest and towering sandstone cliffs. 5 km after turning onto this road, turn left into a parking area alongside the river at the foot of Oribi Heads — this makes an ideal lunch spot (with braai and picnic sites, and toilets).

100 m beyond the parking area you cross the river on a narrow bridge, then begin the steep ascent out of the gorge. After a further 3,7 km you pass a turn-off right to the Natal Parks Board hutted camp. 300 m later turn right at the T-junction onto the N2 for Izingolweni and Harding, noting your kms.

Roughly 4 km later you pass through the small farming community of Paddock. Beyond the town the views open out over a gentle landscape scattered with huts, with the Transkei mountains in the distance. 11,7 km after rejoining the N2 you begin to descend a pass — 300 m later turn left into the Wilson's Cutting viewsite, which gives excellent views over the Mbizane River valley and the surrounding countryside.

Wilson's Cutting to the Mtamvuna River

Note your kms at the far side of the viewsite parking area as you continue down the pass on the N2. After 800 m you pass KwaCele tribal village on your right, and on your left here you can see back towards the rocky mountainside you have just crossed. The road winds amongst the crests of hills, offering fine views over KwaZulu on both sides.

After 4,8 km — on the outskirts of Izingolweni — turn left, then 100 m later turn left again for Port Edward, noting your kms. The road now descends along a spur of land between the Mbizane and Mtamvuna rivers — through beautiful countryside, and offering views towards the distant Indian Ocean.

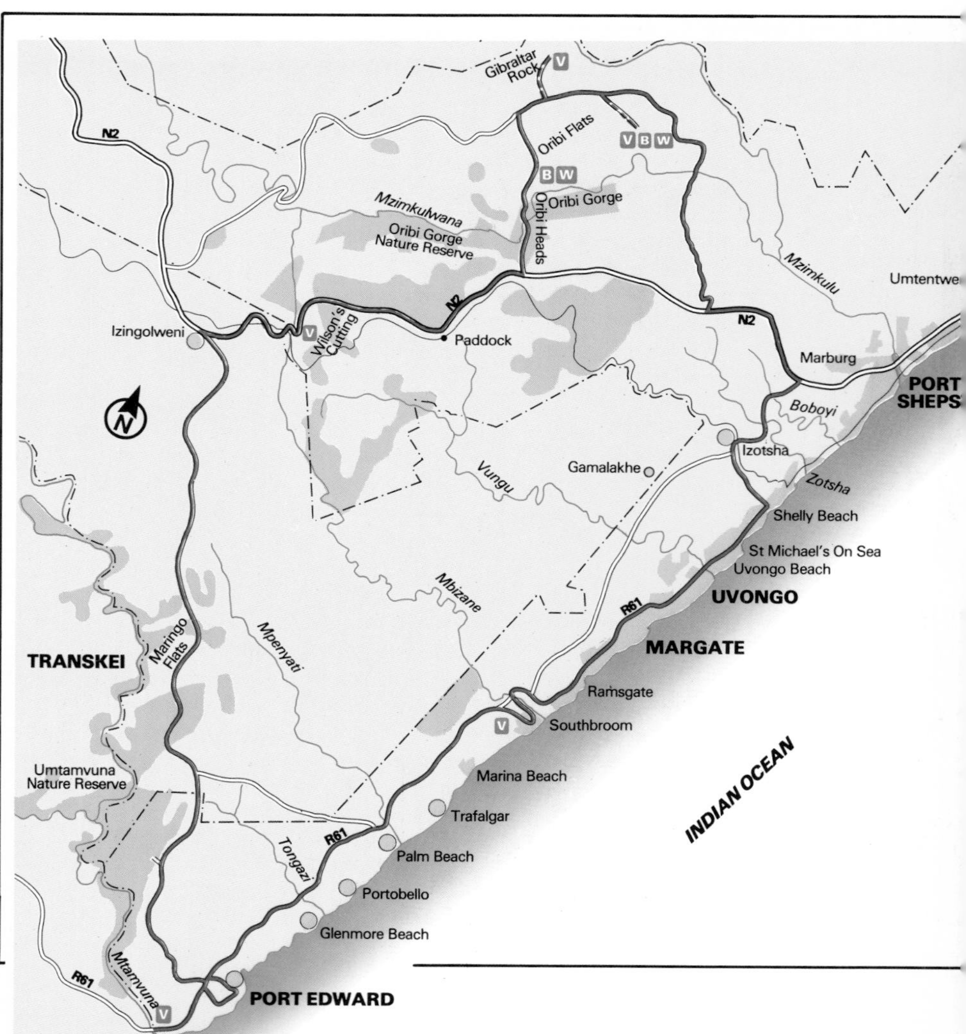

Roughly 29 km after noting your kms turn right into Umtamvuna Nature Reserve. You reach the gate after 200 m (small entry fee), and the parking area after a further 250 m. A short walk to the top of a rocky knoll near the parking area gives excellent views over the nature reserve, with the sea in the distance on your left (allow 30-40 min).

Return to the tarred road and turn right, noting your kms. After 6,5 km you pass a turn-off right to Old Pont Road, which leads to the old river crossing and the lower section of the Umtamvuna Nature Reserve. 1,7 km later turn right onto the R61 for Bizana. 3,9 km later you cross the Mtamvuna River — park on the far bank and walk back onto the bridge for a view of the river and mouth. (You are in Transkei, and should carry identification.)

Mtamvuna River to Margate

Return along the R61, and 3 km beyond the bridge turn right (where left leads to Banner's Rest Retirement Village), noting your kms. The road leads into the resort of Port Edward. After 1 km turn right into Portsea Avenue, and 200 m later turn left into Newport Street. 600 m later, where the tar curves left into Gloucester Road, continue straight on gravel, past the lighthouse on your left. Park at the end of the road for a walk on the beach at the interesting rocks known as The Gully.

Return past the lighthouse, turn right onto tar into Gloucester Road, and 700 m later turn right into Owen Ellis Drive. Turn right into Beach Road, which leads to a parking area at the foot of Tragedy Hill (see below).

Return along Beach Road and Owen Ellis Drive to the R61, turn right for Margate and Port Shepstone — and note your kms. After 19,7 km turn right for Southbroom, noting your kms as you turn. After 1,5 km you reach a small traffic circle where you bear left on Imbezana Drive. Follow this road for 1 km until you reach a parking area on your left overlooking a magnificent stretch of Southbroom beach at the mouth of the Mbizane lagoon. After taking a few minutes to enjoy the magnificent view, drive out of the parking area and turn right to return along the same route to the R61 coastal road.

Turn right on to this main road for the short journey to Margate ●

AA Office 35A Wooley Street, Port Shepstone 4240 Tel. (0391) 22503
Margate Tourist Information Bureau Beach Office, Main Beach Terrace, Margate 4275 Tel. (03931) 22322
SA Tourism Board Suite 520, Southern Life Centre, 320 West Street, Durban 4001 Tel. (031) 3047144

The magnificent, forested Oribi Gorge, from the top of Lehr Falls.

ORIBI GORGE

The Mzimkulwana River has carved a 24 km ravine known as Oribi Gorge through Natal's hilly interior, creating a unique gallery of sculpted sandstone cliffs. From the cliff-top vantage point of the privately owned Fairacres Estate one can view formations such as Baboon's Castle, The Pulpit, The Needle, Overhanging Rock and Oribi Heads, which tower above the river 400 m below. There is also a hotel on the estate, and braai and picnic sites have been laid out along the panoramic drive that leads along the lip of the gorge.

A reserve of 1 800 ha in the gorge preserves dense indigenous forest, where trails and climbs bring visitors close to the bushbuck, blue and grey duiker, monkeys and people-wary leopards that make their homes here. There are picnic and braai sites in this idyllic setting, and the Natal Parks Board has a camp with bungalows overlooking the head of the gorge. Details on the walks and climbs in the area are available from the camp superintendent.

A boardsailer makes the most of the end of the day at Southbroom.

A TRAGIC RUMOUR

Tragedy Hill, overlooking Port Edward's main bathing beach, was the scene of a massacre in 1831 sparked by a false rumour of war. The Zulu king, Dingane, had received a report that the fledgling British community at Port Natal (now Durban) was about to attack him. A party of settlers led by Frank Fynn, fleeing from Dingane's army, was cornered and killed on this pyramid-shaped hill by a group of Zulus who believed the settlers were stealing Dingane's cattle. When Dingane discovered the report of the planned attack had been false, he ordered the man who had started the rumour to be shot — an execution performed by one of the settlers.

UMTAMVUNA NATURE RESERVE

The old pont across the Mtamvuna River between Natal and Transkei operated just downstream from the border of the present Umtamvuna Nature Reserve — a 3 100 ha sanctuary for wildlife and birds that is also noted for its impressive riverine forest. Endangered Cape vultures make their home in the steep cliffs of the river gorge, and the call of the fish eagle is also heard here. The reserve has a bird list of 80 species, and hikers may also see baboon, black-backed jackal, large spotted genet, reedbuck, blue and grey duiker, bushbuck, monkey, oribi, serval and leopard.

The Horseshoe Bend, Oribi Gorge.

Above: *Rock-anglers at Uvongo Beach.*

Below: *Umtamvuna Nature Reserve.*

TRANSKEI

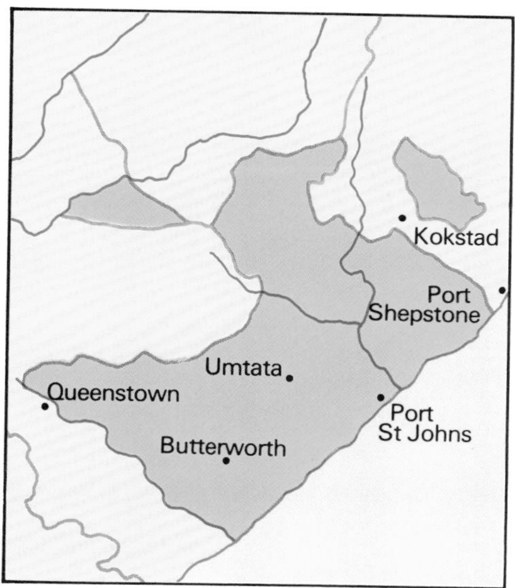

The wreck of the Jacaranda — one of the victims of the Wild Coast.

Above: *Mist shrouds the mouth of the Mzimvubu River at Port St Johns.*
Left: *Typical undulating landscape of rural Transkei.*

The timeless magic of Umngazi Mouth and Port St Johns

This drive from Umtata to Port St Johns leads east through the hills and valleys of central Transkei. We pass Mhlengana Rock and visit Umngazi Mouth along the way. Over half the route is tarred. Arrange to stay the night in Port St Johns — or switch the order of drives down to the coast so that you end the day at Umngazi Mouth.

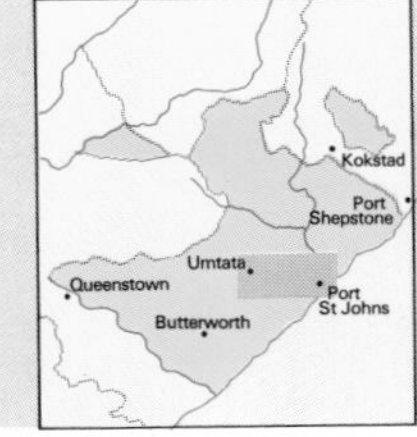

Umtata
Libode
Mhlengana Rock
Umngazi Mouth
Port St Johns
Silaka Nature Reserve
130—150kms

LEAVE CENTRAL UMTATA by driving east along Sutherland Street. Cross Madeira Street, and note your kms immediately after the traffic lights. Continue out of town on Sutherland Street, which becomes the R61. After 2,7km you cross the Mtata River and enter the restful, undulating landscape of central Transkei — with rustic villages, small maize fields and cattle kraals flanking the road. After 13,9km stop on the left shoulder of the road and walk across the road for a fine view back the way you have come over the Mtata Valley.

From here the road leads into progressively greener country, with small stands of eucalyptus and wattle dotted about the grassy hillsides. 27km after leaving Umtata you cross the Mdlankomo River, and 900m later you reach a turn-off left into the small town of Libode. The town is worth visiting, especially on a Friday or Saturday, when the local Pondo and Mpondomise people trade beadwork here. Whether or not you drive into the town, note your kms at this junction as you continue on the main road towards Port St Johns.

Libode to Umngazi Mouth

After travelling some 12km from Libode, just after passing the St Barnabas Mission Hospital, the road surface changes to gravel. Roughly 5,7km later you begin the descent through the Mhlengana Cutting into the magnificent Mngazi Valley — the cutting includes some sharp curves and requires slow, careful driving, especially in rainy weather. 20,5km from Libode, stop on the shoulder of the road for a good view over the Mngazi Valley and eastwards to the distant Indian Ocean. 800m later, stop again to see in front of you and to your right Mhlengana Rock — where offenders were formerly executed. Looking down from here into the Mngazi Valley, you can see rows of white huts perched above the river as it snakes towards the sea. Another 1,7km brings you to the base of Mhlengana Rock.

Driving on from here, you pass hillsides thickly covered in aloes. A little over 26km from Libode the cutting ends, and you drive past picturesque Xhosa settlements. At 31km the road surface changes back to tar, and after a further 12,9km you reach a parking area on your right. Stop here for a good view west over the tranquil Mngazana River. Note your kms as you leave this parking area.

After 3,6km the tar ends again and you find yourself on a bumpy track that leads down again into the Mngazi Valley. You cross the Mngazi River, then climb out of the valley on the eastern side. After driving 11,6km from the parking area, turn right, following the signs to 'Umngazi River Mouth'.

This narrow side-road twists and turns as it follows the eastern bank of the river, and you pass through an assortment of banana plantations, patches of dense indigenous forest, and fields of pumpkins and maize. Just under 12km after turning onto this side-road you pass through the gate of the Umngazi Bungalows Hotel (which offers lunch), and a short distance further brings you to a parking area at the river's edge. Park here for an attractive 500m walk along the banks of the river to the sea.

Umngazi Mouth to Port St Johns

Retrace your route to the main road and turn right for Port St Johns, noting your kms as you turn. After 3,7km the road descends quite sharply into a valley blanketed in thick riverine forest, and shortly after this you emerge from the greenery to your first view of the Mzimvubu (hippopotamus) River. After 12,5km the road surface changes to tar, and you pass on your left the bridge that carries the main road over the river to Lusikisiki, Kokstad and Port Edward in southern Natal.

Follow the course of the river until you enter Port St Johns, and note your kms as you enter the town. After 900m stop on the left side of the road and walk down onto the beach at the point where the Mzimvubu reaches the sea. Behind you are the famous 'Gates', the two headlands

Mhlengana (execution rock) on the road to Port St Johns.

The Mngazi River meanders through rural Transkei.

Huberta the divine hippo.

HIPPO ON THE MOVE

One of the great legends of Port St Johns concerns Huberta the hippo, who strolled into the town one day and found it so much to her liking that she stayed for six months. Huberta's incredible journey started in November 1928, when she left her muddy swamp in what is now KwaZulu, and ended three years and 1 600km later. She wandered at a very leisurely rate along the coast, stopping in Durban, Port St Johns and East London. The Pondos of Transkei's Wild Coast believed that she was the reincarnation of a legendary diviner, and worshipped her wherever she went. In Port St Johns she was the first hippo to wallow in the Mzimvubu River for almost one hundred years. At night she ambled through the streets of the town, venturing into private gardens for food.

From The Wild Coast, Huberta's wanderings took her south to East London, which she reached in March 1931. She was spotted asleep on the main railway line, and gently nudged out of the way by a kindly engine driver.

Huberta's wanderings ended, suddenly and sadly, when she was shot while bathing in the Keiskamma River — by hunters who claimed to know nothing of her special status.

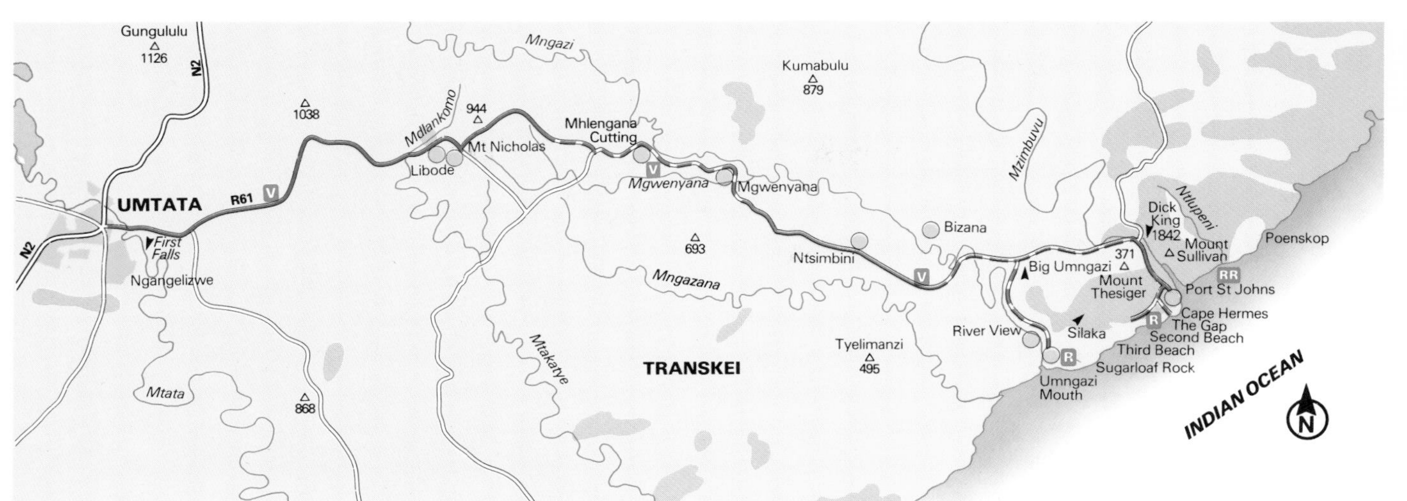

THE ILL-FATED *SAO JOAO*

Transkei's shore is littered with wrecks, dating back to the days when the first European navigators edged gingerly along this treacherous, uncharted coast, on their way to seek the riches of the Orient. Port St Johns is thought to owe its name to one of the earliest of these wrecked vessels, a Portuguese sailing ship, the *Sao Joao* (Saint John).

The *Sao Joao* came to grief on the rocks just south of the Mzimvubu River on 5 June 1552. Miraculously, of the 540 people on board, 440 passengers and crew reached the shore alive — and faced a 700 km walk to Lourenco Marques (Maputo). Hunger and sickness, and hostile natives, all took their toll as the survivors painfully made their way along the coast. After three months of hardship the straggling party reached Lourenco Marques, only to discover that the annual trading ship to Portugal had just left. The disappointed band continued their journey northwards, losing many lives, until just 25 survivors eventually reached the island of Mocambique, roughly 1 600 km from the wreck of the *Sao Joao*.

PORT ST JOHNS

The story of Port St Johns began in 1846, when the British schooner, *Rosebud*, became the first vessel to cross the sandbar at the mouth of the Mzimvubu River — proving that this was a viable harbour. It became a busy trading port, supplying ivory, maize, hides and other goods to the outside world. But the traders who settled here and the soldiers of the British garrison established in 1882, lived a very isolated existence — albeit surrounded by some of the world's finest scenery. The majestic gates of Mount Thesiger and Mount Sullivan, named after General Thesiger and Commodore Sullivan who hoisted the Union Jack here, bore mute witness to many drinking parties under the wild fig trees.

Life is more orderly today, but the town retains its isolated atmosphere and is a favourite retreat for holidaymakers seeking peace and tranquillity. This stretch of coast has some of the best fishing spots in southern Africa, and the bathing facilities are good. There are numerous walks through beautiful riverine forests, and along uncluttered sandy beaches.

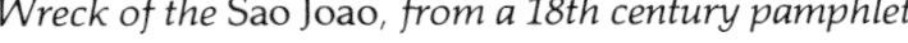
Wreck of the Sao Joao, *from a 18th century pamphlet.*

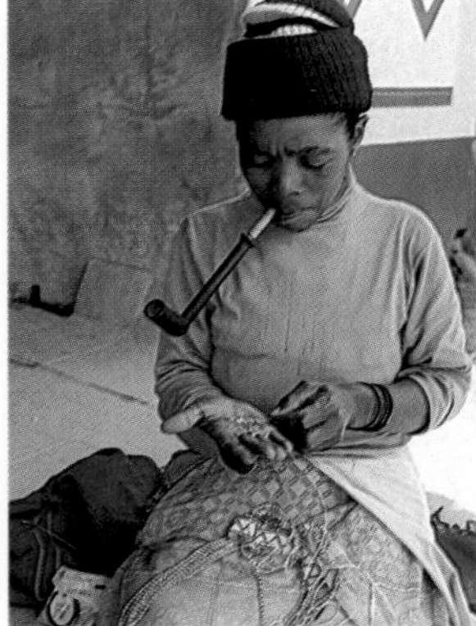
Beadwork in Transkei.

Wide estuary of the Mzimvubu River near Port St Johns.

that flank the river mouth — Mount Thesiger to the west, and Mount Sullivan to the east.

Port St Johns to Silaka Reserve

Return to your car and retrace your route for 300 m. Take the second turn-off to your left (the road to Second Beach), noting your kms as you turn. This road leads west out of the town. After 2,5 km turn left onto a dirt track, which twists up and around a steep hillside. Eventually this track leads along a high, narrow ridge, and brings you after 1,5 km to a grassy hilltop from where there is a splendid view over the coast. To the west the Indian Ocean thunders down on Second and Third beaches, where dense sub-tropical vegetation seems to tumble down the cliffs into the sea. By now you will also have noticed a difference in the climate in the sub-tropical coastal region.

Return to the tarred road and turn left towards Second Beach, noting your kms. After 2,6 km you pass a turn-off to the Second Beach bungalows, and a short distance after this you reach a sign pointing the way to Third Beach. Turn onto this track to Third Beach, which leads through dense bush and up a hill to the entrance to Silaka Nature Reserve and Third Beach. Drive down the hill towards the beach, cross a small stream, and take the first track leading to your left. 200 m along this track brings you to an attractive picnic site. Blesbok, wildebeest, steenbok and vervet monkeys are protected here in the reserve, and over 200 bird species have been recorded.

Retrace your route to Port St Johns. When you reach the main road in the town, turn right, then turn right again at the next opportunity. Follow the signs to the Cape Hermes Hotel, and walk down to the rocks in front of the hotel for a magnificent coastal sunset ●

Department of Commerce, Industry and Tourism cnr York Road and Victoria Street, Umtata, Transkei Tel. (0471) 25191
Cape Hermes Hotel Port St Johns, Transkei Tel. (04752) 35
Coastal Needles Hotel Port St Johns, Transkei Tel. (04752) 11
Umngazi Bungalows Hotel Umngazi Mouth, Transkei Tel. (0020) ask for Umngazi Mouth 3

• TRANSKEI TRADITIONS •

In the land of *uthikoloshe* and the giant Lightning Bird

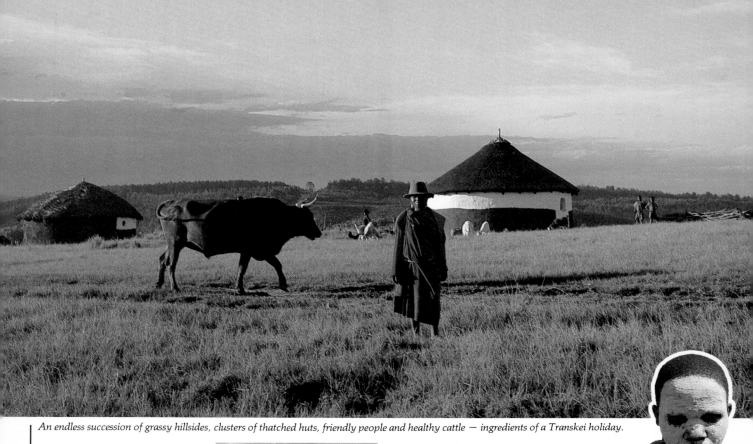

An endless succession of grassy hillsides, clusters of thatched huts, friendly people and healthy cattle — ingredients of a Transkei holiday.

ALTHOUGH 'TRADITIONAL' South African history tells of southward-migrating Nguni peoples who clashed with Cape colonists moving north and east in the 18th century, the Transkei — the land beyond the Kei — has been occupied by the Nguni and their ancestors for many centuries. Their presence has been confirmed by archaeologists, and was recorded by shipwrecked Portuguese mariners who trudged wearily along the Wild Coast beaches, leaving behind them shattered caravels and broken dreams of the route to the Indies. Inland, had they but known it, lay abundant food in a smiling land of green hills and clear rivers, like the Great Kei itself — the 'sand' or 'shining' river of the earlier Khoikhoi.

Although they were doughty opponents in a century of frontier wars, the people of Transkei did not possess the rigid and merciless militarism with which Chaka was to infuse the Zulu nation to the north. Wars between clans were fought by no more than a few dozen warriors, casualties were slight, and by the end of the day the quarrel was considered as settled. The men went back to admiring their Sanga cattle — a longhorn-zebu cross, now extinct as a result of interbreeding with European strains — and the women returned to tilling the fields. This idyll was ended by the coming of the white man and the *difaqane* — a state of continuous war — unleashed by Chaka.

Xhosa women in traditional dress.

Early last century, Transkei was already settled by a number of different tribes, the largest of which was the Xhosa, named after their 16th century founder, the son of Mnguni. The Xhosa were — and are still — divided into two main groups, stemming from the followers of Gcaleka and his grand-nephew Ngqika (Gaika). Other tribes include the Thembu, Mpondo, Mpondomise and Bomvana. Relative newcomers, fleeing from the *difaqane*, were the Mfengu, made up of numerous destitute tribes. Their name is derived from the word *ukufenguza* — to beg for food. The Mfengu were settled by the Cape Government on land belonging to the Gcaleka in the southern part of Transkei — an act that created great resentment and led eventually to the outbreak of 'the last frontier war' in 1877.

'National suicide' of the Xhosa

The coastal strip for some 32 km north of the Mbashe (Bashee) River is known as Bomvanaland, home of a people who had originally sought refuge among the Gcaleka, but who moved to this region in 1856 after refusing to take part in the cattle-killing that was to become known as 'the national suicide of the Xhosa'.

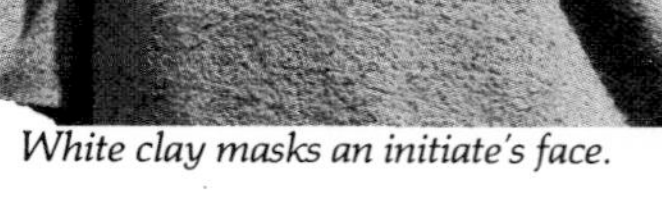

White clay masks an initiate's face.

A young girl, Nongqawuse, who was a niece of a powerful *isanusei* (priest-diviner) named Mahlakaza, claimed to have been spoken to by ancestral spirits and to have seen visions at a pool on the Gxara River. If the people killed their cattle and destroyed their crops, she said, their warrior ancestors would arise and assist them in driving the whites from the land on an appointed day, believed to have been in February 1857. The people did as she instructed — but then the day passed, and no ancestors appeared, neither did the promised crops nor the cattle miraculously return. As a result, at least 25 000 people are believed to have starved to death.

In about the year 1500 two sons of a chief, Mpondo and Mpondomise, formed two separate clans, which are known today by the names of their founders. Pondoland, the region in which they live, is the section of coast north of the Umtata River. Here high hills sweep down to a shore that has claimed innumerable ships, of which the East Indiaman *Grosvenor* is the best known.

All Transkei tribes speak dialects of isiXhosa — the Xhosa language. Customs and traditions differ, however, and each tribe proudly preserves its own special identity.

A red and gold dawn silhouettes the 'hole-in-the-wall' formation, a short distance south-west of Coffee Bay.

uthikoloshe and _impundulu_

Even today, witchcraft and superstition play a large part in the traditional way of life, and there is widespread belief in the hairy and mischievous goblin known as *uthikoloshe*. As a rule, *uthikoloshe* can be seen only by children who, unaware of his evil reputation, accept him as a playmate. He becomes a danger only after he has been captured by a witch who makes him the instrument of evil. *Hili*, as he is also known, may cause disease in humans and animals, but is said to show mercy sometimes, especially when the intended victim is a child.

Another creature who inspires fear is *impundulu* — the huge lightning bird, believed to cause death and disease. Standing, *impundulu* is as tall as a man, and when the creature flaps its wings the roar of thunder is heard. When it spits, so the superstition goes, lightning flashes across the sky.

Rivers are believed to be the home of *aBantu bomlambo* — the people of the river. These are kindly creatures, closely resembling humans, except that they have flipper-like appendages instead of hands and feet. There should be no mourning for a person who has drowned and whose body is not recovered, because he has been accepted into a family of *aBantu bomlambo*.

Despite widespread acceptance of Christianity, traditional religious practices flourish. There is veneration of a supreme being, who may be umDali, Qamata or uThixo — creator of the world and of life.

An important member of the community is the *igqirha*, or diviner, who mediates between the world of the living and that of the spirits. Failure to satisfy the spirits will inevitably bring misfortune, and professional advice must be obtained on how to placate the dead. Most of the diviners are women who have spent a long period of apprenticeship to an older practitioner.

Outside the towns, life is concentrated in the family settlement-unit known as *umzi* — a collection of huts grouped around the cattle enclosure. Typically, those who live here consist of the head of the family, wife or wives, and children — including the married sons.

Huts were formerly made of grass and reeds plaited around a framework of sticks, but during the past century this style has been replaced by a round, mud-walled hut with cone-shaped thatch roof. The traditional floor is of cowdung or the crushed soil of an ant-heap, tightly compressed and easily swept.

A hut with two similar-sized euphorbia trees growing close by is probably the birthplace of twins. Among many tribes twins were once regarded as unlucky and either one or both would be killed. Today in Transkei the birth of twins is welcomed, and the trees are planted to grow up with them. The death of a tree foretells the death of the twin with whom it is associated.

Education and Initiation

Traditionally, Transkeian children had no formal education, but would learn from their elders the work that would occupy their adult life. From an early age, boys herded cattle, and girls helped their mothers with housekeeping, cooking, and gathering water and firewood.

Hunting and war games have been regarded as important to a boy's development, and stick-fighting is an advanced art in Transkei. A boy's standing in youthful society is based on his skill with the fighting-sticks — a stout knobkerrie for attack, and a stave for defence.

Before boys and girls are accepted as adults they must undergo initiation. With the exception of almost all Mpondo clans, circumcision is regarded as an essential step towards manhood. The youth's departure for the initiation lodge is a significant event, which may be marked by the sacrifice of a goat. Initiation schools may consist of only a few boys, and it is considered important to be a member of a school attended by a chief's son. The school is held in a remotely-situated hut, usually near a stream, and specially built for the purpose. Initiates are instructed by a 'father', assisted by 'guardians', and, before circumcision, must sit in the stream, ritually cleansing themselves while confessing misdeeds to the adults. The circumcision itself is expected to be borne unflinchingly.

Throughout the period of initiation, the boys must go naked beneath the particular pattern of blanket of their initiation lodge, with their bodies and faces smeared with white clay to conceal their identities and as protection against evil. For a month after circumcision, while the wound is healing, initiates must remain in their lodge. After this, a goat is slaughtered, and initiates may venture from the hut in search of food.

At the end of the initiation period the new adults wash the white clay from their bodies, and the lodge is burnt, together with every article used during the initiation period — symbolizing the end of the child-life.

In their colourful traditional garb, the peoples of Transkei make fascinating subjects for the photographer. However, before you photograph an individual or a group, always ask permission, even if you have to do this by means of sign-language. Gifts to the subjects are always appreciated ●

Above: *Dress varies from region to region.*

Right: *White water on the 'Wild Coast'.*

High green hills sweep down to the cliffs of the Wild Coast

This route leads from bustling Umtata through the rural heartlands of Transkei to the sea. We stop to view the Mtata River valley, and take a side-road to the fascinating 'Hole-in-the-Wall', then continue to the tranquil resort of Coffee Bay. The main road to Coffee Bay is almost all tarred, but side roads are gravel.

Umtata
Viedgeville
Mqanduli
Hole-in-the-Wall
Coffee Bay
Mapuzi River
Mtata Mouth
140 – 160 km

THIS IS AN ATTRACTIVE drive, but includes time-consuming stretches of winding gravel road, and we recommend that you spend the night in or near Coffee Bay before attempting the return journey.

Leave Umtata by driving south on the N2 (towards East London) and note your kms as you pass the Holiday Inn on your right. After 16 km turn left onto tar at a road signposted 'Mqanduli/Coffee Bay' — and note your kms again as you turn. Drive with care as the road is flanked by many small unfenced communities, and cattle and other livestock wander freely across the road.

You pass through the small trading centre of Viedgeville, then the road begins to wind through undulating hills towards the coast — a fine drive, highlighted in early winter by the magnificent crimson blooms of aloes, and in summer by green fields of maize. After 8,4 km you descend into a cool eucalyptus forest and shortly after this you can just see the sea appear mistily through the green rolling hills. After 14,2 km you cross the Manqondo River and climb to the little town of Mqanduli (the maker of grind-stones).

Mqanduli to Hole-in-the-Wall
Continue along the main tarred road, which crosses countryside deeply scarred by soil erosion. After 31 km, park on the left side of the road to see a cairn erected to commemorate the historic ride of Dick King from Port Natal to Grahamstown in 1842. 1,8 km after this you pass a Xhosa Village on the opposite side of the road, then a deep, tree-lined valley.

You pass the Lutubeni Mission (signposted 'Mission Hospital') after just under 40 km, and

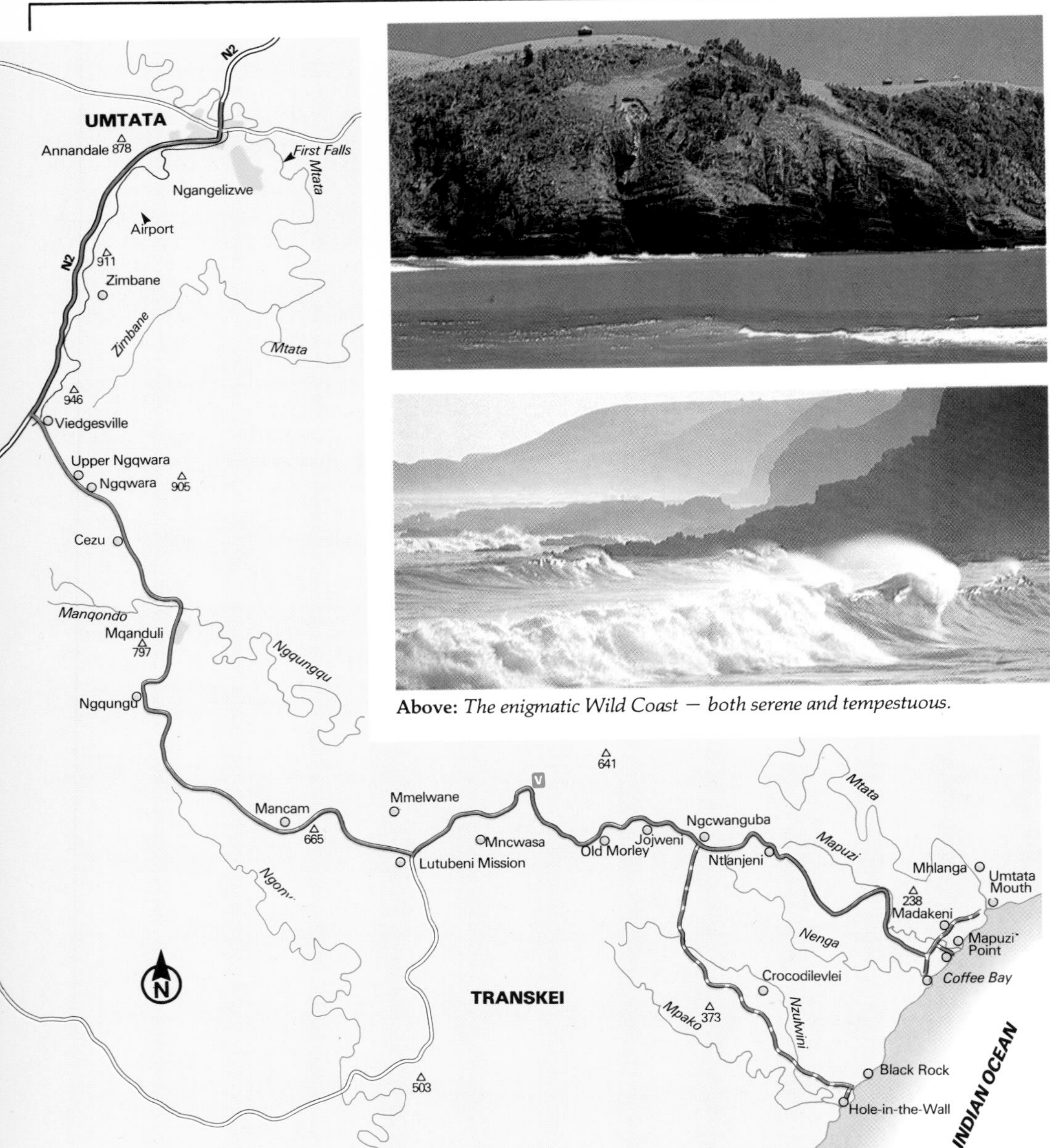

Above: *The enigmatic Wild Coast — both serene and tempestuous.*

HOLE-IN-THE-WALL
One of southern Africa's most interesting natural formations is the massive outcrop of rock that rises from the sea some 8 km south of Coffee bay. Referred to by local people as esiKhaleni (the place of sound), it is more widely known as Hole-in-the-Wall. The huge tunnel through the centre of the cliff has been eroded over the millenia by the constant pounding of the waves, and is large enough to accommodate a fair-sized fishing boat. Many people have been tempted to climb the cliff faces, but most have had to be rescued from the grassy top. There are also local tales of people who have drowned or been dashed against the rocks when trying to swim through the tunnel. Fishing in this area is excellent.

WILD COAST SHIPWRECKS
This wild stretch of coast has long proved treacherous to ships, and beneath the restless waves lie the remains of many vessels — plus their cargoes and their passengers. Most of these ships were Portuguese, including the *Sao Bento*, one of the largest ships of the 16th century, which foundered at the mouth of the Mtata River on 21 April 1554 with the loss of 150 lives. The *Santo Alberto*, a merchant ship, was wrecked near the Hole-in-the-Wall on 24 March 1593, losing a valuable treasure and 63 lives. Those who survived such wrecks had to face a dangerous journey overland to Lourenco Marques. One particularly unfortunate gentleman, Manuel de Castro, survived one shipwreck and the subsequent trek to the north, was taken from Lourenco Marques to India, and was then put aboard the *Sao Bento* for Portugal. He died in despair when that ship also perished on the same stretch of coast and he was faced with the prospect of a second overland trek.

now the road begins its long and winding descent to the coast through a succession of river valleys densely covered with sub-tropical vegetation. After 50km turn left onto a narrow gravel track that follows the ridge of a steep mountain. 200m along this track, park your car and look east for a magnificent view over the Mtata River valley — a wild, unspoilt landscape.

Return to the main road and turn left to continue your journey, noting your kms as you turn. After 9,2km turn right onto a gravel road for Hole-in-the-Wall, noting your kms again.

The road descends gently through thick forest and curls around small settlements of thatch-roofed huts. After 8km you reach a fork. Take the road on your left, which leads into the country of the friendly Bomvana people. After 14km you descend sharply into a valley, and after a further 2,5km you cross a bridge. Almost immediately after this you reach a second fork — take the road on your right here, which leads into another valley.

After 19,8km you reach the Hole-in-the-Wall Hotel (which offers lunch) — metres from the crashing surf and white sands of the Indian Ocean. Pass the hotel and continue up the hill for a beautiful view overlooking the geological formation known as the Hole-in-the-Wall.

Hole-in-the-Wall to Coffee Bay

Retrace your route to the tarred road and turn right towards Coffee Bay, noting your kms as you turn.

You now descend through a series of loops and bends into a particularly attractive part of Transkei, with huts sprinkled across the rolling hills. After about 14km palm trees come into view, and shortly after this you cross the Mapuzi River. After 18,3km turn left onto a gravel road for Coffee Bay. (The tarred road will eventually continue to Coffee Bay). The road now climbs, and after a short distance you reach a fork. Take the road leading right, and continue for 600m, when the small settlement of Coffee Bay comes into view. Drive through the village, pass the Ocean View Hotel, cross the bridge over the Nenga River, and park next to the Lagoon Hotel on your left. From here a short sandy path on your right leads under a canopy of indigenous trees to the wonderfully tranquil beach. (Both hotels offer lunch.)

Coffee Bay to Mtata Mouth

Retrace your route, noting your kms as you pass the Ocean View Hotel. After 1,1km go right where the road reaches a fork, and 400m later go right again where the road forks for a second time. You now drive along the ridges of green hills with fine views across the coast. After 2,5km the road descends sharply towards the sea and you reach the lush, sub-tropical valley of the Mapuzi River. After 2,9km park on the side of the road and walk to your right down a narrow path. The path leads around the base of a steep headland and offers attractive views along the coast. (If you wish to climb the headland, the top offers even grander views, east to Mapuzi Point and west to a line of mighty, precipitous cliffs.)

Return to your car and retrace your route, but turn right at the first fork you reach — onto a bumpy gravel road. Note your kms as you turn. The road crosses the Mapuzi River and penetrates indigenous bush. After 4km turn right onto a road that takes you to the summit of a hill overlooking the Mtata River and its generous expanse of white-sand beach. You may wish to park your car at the side of the road here, and walk down the steep, grassy slopes to the river. (There is a ferry service, that carries passengers to the other side.)

Return at your leisure to Coffee Bay, where there is a choice of accommodation. (And note that this stretch of coast is renowned for its beautiful sub-tropical sunsets.) ●

Department of Commerce, Industry and Tourism cnr York Road and Victoria Street, Umtata, Transkei Tel. (0471) 25191
Lagoon Hotel Coffee Bay, Transkei Tel. (0020) ask for Coffee Bay 6
Ocean View Hotel Coffee Bay, Transkei Tel. (0020) ask for Coffee Bay 7

Sub-tropical aloes dot the hillside above the mouth of the Mapuzi River.

Anglers try their luck at Hole-in-the-Wall.

COFFEE BAY

It is believed that the restful resort of Coffee bay received its name when a large cargo of coffee beans was washed up at the mouth of the Nenga River after a shipwreck. Many of the beans took root and grew into small coffee plants, but they all died and today the only coffee found here is imported. Nestling snugly between the rolling green hills of the Transkei coast, this small village has two hotels, caravan and camping areas, and various sports facilities. The beach is popular with surfers, and the lagoon offers safe swimming.

Near Coffee Bay the Mapuzi River reaches the sea in a spectacular curve, passing steep sandbanks and high, wooded hills dotted with huts.

Donkey power in Transkei.

Densely forested valleys and idyllic Wild Coast beaches

Our route leads from Butterworth across fertile hills to the historic village of Centane. From here we drive to the palm-fringed beaches of Qolora Mouth, and to Mazeppa Bay. Almost the entire route is on gravel roads. Arrange to stay the night in Mazeppa Bay — or change the order of drives from Centane to end your day at Qolora Mouth.

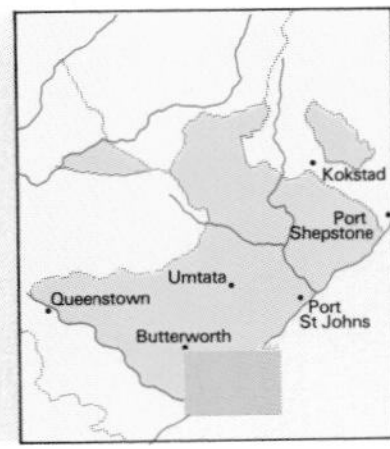

Butterworth
Tutura
Centane
Qolora Mouth
Kobonqaba River Valley
Mazeppa Bay
130 – 150 km

TRAVELLING NORTH ON THE N2, just after the town centre of Butterworth, turn right for Centane (Kentani) — roughly 200 m after crossing the Gcuwa River on the outskirts of the town noting your kms as you turn. The first 2 km of this road takes you through the industrial fringes of Butterworth, the oldest town in the Transkei and main trading centre for the southern part of the territory. It grew up around a Wesleyan mission school built in 1827. 4,5 km after turning the road surface changes to gravel. You now enter typically rural Transkei, with tall grass and dense groves of acacia trees flanking the road.

After 7 km the road descends into a small valley and 1,8 km later you cross a bridge. You now pass through farming country, with maize fields, cattle kraals and clusters of huts scattered across the hillsides. After 13 km you drive through the small settlement of Tutura, and after a further 3 km you enter an area that is relatively densely populated — be watchful here for the livestock that wanders freely around the huts and onto the road. After travelling 21 km from the N2, stop on the left side of the road for a panoramic view of the countryside stretching down to meet the sea. To your right you can see the distant valley of the Great Kei River snaking southwards. This part of Transkei is rich cattle country, with grassland covering the rolling hills. In spring and summer, after good rains, the country is emerald green, while in autumn and winter — the dry season — the grass fades to a drab brown.

Continue along the main road, and at 24,5 km stop again for a view left over the mighty valley of the Kobonqaba River. Note your kms as you drive on from this spot.

Just 700 m later you pass the Centane Hills Forest Reserve, and from here the landscape becomes greener. After 7,6 km you enter Centane (Kentani). The village contains several shops, as well as being of historical importance (see below).

Centane to Qolora Mouth

Retrace your route out of Centane, and on the outskirts of the village turn left, following the sign for Qolora Mouth and Kei Mouth. Note your kms at the turn.

MAZEPPA BAY

If you don't catch a fish at Mazeppa Bay, you won't catch one anywhere — so say the residents of this beautiful coastal resort. The fishing here is so good that people come from all over the world hoping to catch 'the big one'. Shark fishing is the main attraction — particularly hammerhead sharks — and every August heralds the arrival of hundreds of fishermen in the grips of 'shark fever'. Great white sharks, ragged-tooth sharks and hammerheads are caught in abundance — the largest of all being a 791 kg great white that was caught in April 1981 off the rocks at the Boiling Pot. The following year a dusky grey, weighing 564 kg, was caught at the same place.

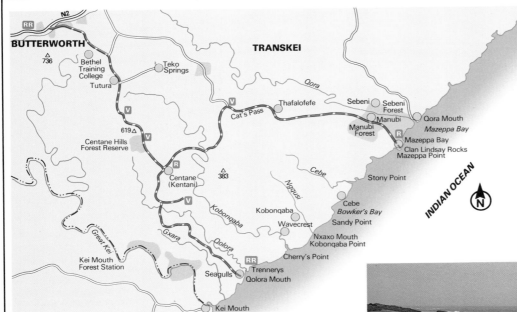

Wave-kissed mouth of the Kobonqaba River near Qolora.

Wild Coast graveyard: Wreck of the Jacaranda *near Qolora.*

ATTACK ON CENTANE

In February 1878, some 5 000 Xhosa warriors, led by the great chiefs Kreli and Sandile, mounted an attack on the British garrison of 700 men stationed at Centane. Despite assurances from the spirit diviner, Xito, that the white man's bullets would not harm them, 300 brave warriors lost their lives. Kreli and his soldiers disappeared, hiding in the forests and valleys of Gcalekaland, until eventually they surrendered and went into retirement near Elliotdale. Sandile and his followers fled south to the Kei River.

The road winds down a small mountain pass — and it is worth stopping after 2,4 km for another good view over the coastal hills. You then begin the steep descent to the coast, passing through grasslands and thick acacia forest. 6,1 km after noting your kms you reach a fork — take the road leading right. (The road left leads to Kobonqaba Mouth, and we drive part of the way along it later.) A short distance after this fork you cross the Qolora River, and later there are views to your right over the valley of the Gxara River (see opposite). After travelling 20,2 km from Centane, continue straight where a road branches right to Kei Mouth.

A little over 27 km from Centane, palm trees appear, and shortly after this you enter Qolora, in an attractive sub-tropical coastal setting. You come to a sign that points the way to the Trennerys Hotel and the Seagulls Hotel (both of which offer lunch) — continue straight here, and roughly 300 m later park on the grass overlooking the beach. From here you can take a short walk eastwards to the mouth of the Qolora River (allow 30-40 minutes).

When you leave Qolora, to drive back towards Centane, note your kms at the sign that points the way to the hotels. 20,7 km later you reach the fork where the road to Kobonqaba Mouth leads off to your right. Turn onto the road to Kobonqaba Mouth, but stop after driving 4,4 km along it — for a breathtaking view of the Kobonqaba River Valley with its deep green sub-tropical forests. Retrace your route to the fork, and turn right to return to the town of Centane.

Centane to Mazeppa Bay

When you reach Centane, drive straight across the main road onto the road for Mazeppa Bay and Nxaxo Mouth — noting your kms. The road leads north-east, and descends into the broad Kobonqaba Valley, dotted with rural settlements. After 8 km you cross the Kobonqaba River, and after 9,7 km you pass a road on your right that leads to Wavecrest and Nxaxo Mouth. After travelling 20,2 km from Centane you begin the descent of Cat's Pass. Stop here at the beginning of the pass for a fine view northwards over the valley of the Qora (place of clay) River.

You now penetrate the heart of Gcalekaland, and after 25,6 km you pass the Dutch Reformed Mission Hospital of Thafalofefe. A further 14,4 km brings you into the Manubi Forest — noted for its indigenous yellowwood and stinkwood trees, and a rich variety of orchids.

47,8 km after leaving Centane you reach Mazeppa Bay, with one of the most idyllic beaches on the whole of the Wild Coast. Follow the main road down the hill and into the grounds of the Mazeppa Bay Hotel — the only hotel at this resort. Park in front of the reception area, and walk 100 m, under a canopy of rustling palm trees, to the gently sloping white-sand beach. If you then walk 500 m eastwards along the beach, you will come to a suspension footbridge linking the mainland to a small island, and you can end your day with a walk across the bridge while the Indian Ocean foams beneath your feet ●

Royal Hotel Centane, Transkei Tel. (0020) ask for Centane 17
Trennerys Hotel Trennerys, Transkei Tel. (0020) ask for Trennerys 4
Seagulls Hotel Seagulls, Transkei Tel. (0020) ask for Seagulls 9901
Mazeppa Bay Hotel Mazeppa Bay, Transkei Tel. (0020) ask for Mazeppa Bay 4

End of the road: suspension bridge at Mazeppa Bay.

Finely chiselled rocks tumble into the sea at Mazeppa Bay.

Xhosa youth during period of initiation.

SUICIDE OF A NATION

There is a small pool in the Gxara River where a legend was created that led to the tragic deaths of more than 40 000 people. In 1856 a 14-year-old prophetess, Nongqawuse, claimed that she had seen faces of her ancestral spirits in the pool, and that they had warned her that the Gcaleka people should destroy their crops and cattle before a specified date. If they did this, the sun would rise blood red, the white people would be driven from the land, and all the cattle pens and grain bins would be filled. For 10 months the Gcaleka engaged in a frenzy of cattle killing and crop burning, until the day of deliverance — 18 February 1857 — ended without anything extraordinary happening. The Gcaleka starved to death in their thousands. Nongqawuse fled to King William's Town and sought sanctuary with the British there until her death in 1898.

Traditional dress is still very much an important part of rural Transkei.

EASTERN CAPE

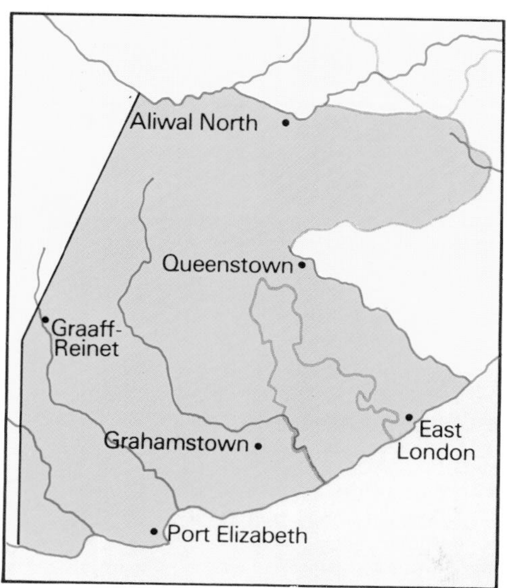

Above: *Rich cultivated fields cover the floor of the Gamtoos River valley.*
Left: *The scenic lagoon formed where the Krom River opens into St Francis Bay.*

Exploring a romantic coast of sandy shores and lazy lagoons

East of the Buffalo River the warm Indian Ocean washes gently into a succession of tranquil lagoons and glittering river estuaries. Inland the rounded hills are dotted with traditional African huts in a peaceful green landscape unexpected so close to a major city. A little more than half this drive is on tarred roads, the rest is on gravel.

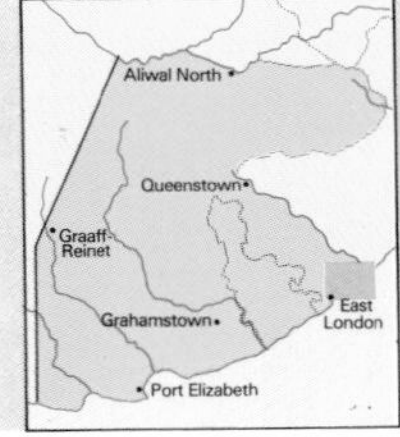

East London
Cintsa East
Cefane Mouth
Morgan Bay
Double Mouth
Gonubie
210–230 km

LEAVE EAST LONDON on the North East Expressway. Immediately after crossing the Nahoon River, turn right onto the N2 towards Umtata, noting your kms. After 3,9 km exit left for 'East Coast Resorts/ Gonubie'. At the T-junction go left, and immediately afterwards turn right onto the R102 for East Coast Resorts, noting your kms.

After 5,4 km turn right onto the Schafli Road for East Coast Resorts, noting your kms again. You pass a number of turn-offs on your right. After 18,7 km turn right onto a gravel road for 'Cefane Mouth/Cintsa Mouth East', and note your kms.

This pleasant rural road crosses a single-lane bridge and several cattle grids. You pass a turn-off on your left to Cefane Mouth, and after 5,6 km on the gravel road turn left. The road now descends directly towards the sea, and soon changes to a tarred surface. 400 m later turn left at the T-junction within the resort of Cintsa East, and park alongside the restaurant. There are braai sites here, and a shady 100 m path leads along the lagoon to the broad, gently shelving beach.

Cintsa East to Morgan Bay

Retrace your route out of Cintsa East, and roughly 3 km from the resort turn right for Cefane Mouth. Within a further 2 km the road leads along the wide and placid Cefane Lagoon, with wooded hills on its far bank. Park at the end of this road — a short walk brings you to the beach and lagoon mouth.

Return to the tarred Schafli Road, and turn right. 7,4 km later, turn right at the T-junction onto the N2 towards Umtata, noting your kms. You pass an intersection with turn-offs to Kei Mouth and Haga Haga, and to Bluewater. After 20,5 km on the N2 turn right onto gravel towards Kei Mouth. 2,4 km later turn right at the T-junction towards Kei Mouth, noting your kms (the road on the left leads to Komga).

At the fork after 18,8 km go left for 'Kei Mouth/Morgan Bay', and turn right 14 km later for Morgan Bay. A further 7 km brings you to Morgan Bay, with its wide beaches and tranquil lagoon. (A hotel in the resort serves lunch — booking is advisable.)

Beyond the hotel you reach a small road — follow this past a beach, across a stream, and uphill towards the Double Mouth Reserve. There is a gate across the road (please close it behind you), and beyond it a second fence, from where two sets of tracks lead to the left. Follow either of these, and park where convenient. Footpaths criss-cross the four headlands between Double Mouth and Morgan Bay, offering magnificent views of the sea and cliffs. The grassy hillside offers a splendid place to picnic, although there are no facilities.

Continue along the road towards the reserve. Just before the reserve entrance there is a white beacon on a low hill — a short walk uphill towards the beacon gives good views of the two broad river channels below.

Beyond the beacon the road descends to the camping and fishing spots at the beach, which offers a pleasant walk along the sea shore.

Morgan Bay to Gonubie

Retrace your route, noting your kms as you pass the Morgan Bay Hotel. After 7,3 km turn left at the oblique T-junction where the road from Kei Mouth joins from the right. After a further 14 km turn left towards East London and Haga Haga.

Continue on this road for 22,7 km — past a turn-off to Haga Haga, across a number of narrow causeways, and through a number of minor intersections. Opposite the Moria Church and a signpost to Mooiplaas, turn left onto the tarred N2 towards East London, noting your kms as you turn.

Shortly after the N2 becomes a double-lane freeway — roughly 30 km after re-joining it — turn left for 'Beacon Bay/Gonubie'. Turn left at the T-junction, noting your kms. After 7 km turn left into Riverside Road for Gonubie Mouth Caravan Park. Less than 1 km along this road, turn right outside the caravan park onto the beach parking area — for a pleasant late-afternoon walk along the sandy edge of the lagoon. Return to East London on the N2 ●

AA Office AA House, 3a Terminus Street, East London 5201 Tel. (0431) 21271
Greater East London Publicity Association Tourist Information Bureau, City Hall, Oxford Street, East London 5201 Tel. (0431) 26015
SA Tourism Board 4th Floor, NBS Building, Terminus Street, East London 5201 Tel. (0431) 26410

The broad sweep of the Nahoon River curves between low hills near East London.

Cintsa Mouth bay forms a backdrop to rustic farm buildings.

EAST LONDON

The first ship to unload and accept a cargo at the mouth of the Buffalo River was George Rex's brig *Knysna*, and the little anchorage became known as Port Rex. Abandoned by the British for several years, the port was revived later with the creation of British Kaffraria, and named first London, then East London.

It was exposed to storms for many years, and the early name was recalled by some cynics who suggested that the anchorage should be renamed Port Wrecks.

The headlands at Double Mouth offer superb walks overlooking rivers and sea.

THE RAUCOUS HADEDA

The coastal area east of East London, with its varied habitat and plentiful water, is particularly rich in birdlife. At Morgan Bay, close to 200 species have been recorded in a relatively small area. Among the most common of the larger birds in this region is the hadeda, a type of ibis named for the raucous sound it makes when startled, and often also when flying. These short-legged wading birds hatch their chicks in early summer, high in trees along the river banks, in nests built of platforms of sticks lined with grass.

The intimate resort of Morgan Bay nestles at the mouth of the Ntshala River.

MORGAN BAY

The idyllic resort at Morgan Bay with its hotel grew up at the spot named after A F Morgan, sailing-master of the ship Barracouta in which Captain W F Owen surveyed the coastline in 1822. From adjacent Cape Morgan a tall light-tower flashes its message far out to sea. Nearby are the abandoned workings of the Cape Morgan titanium mine, first exploited in 1958.

Four rivers reach the sea within a few kilometres of each other on this stretch of coast. Northernmost is the Great Kei, and south of it is the Ntshala River, which forms the lagoon at Morgan Bay. Further south the Gondwane and Quko rivers join to form the lagoon at Double Mouth.

Rare shells are often found along these beaches, and fragments of ancient Chinese porcelain are sometimes washed out of forgotten wrecks to lie scattered on the sand.

THE SHIP OF BRIDES

Perhaps the most eagerly awaited ship to cast anchor in the river port of East London was the Lady Kennaway in 1857. Her cargo consisted of 157 young Irish girls who had left their homeland to seek a new life — and husbands — on the Cape frontier. The men they came to marry were of the British-German Legion, disbanded after the Crimean War, who had been settled as farmers along the frontier. The severe shortage of eligible women had led the British government to import brides for the men. Lady Kennaway was wrecked, but by then her precious cargo was safely ashore.

A lazy afternoon on a broad sweep of the Gonubie River.

Glittering river estuaries and the silent sands of an unspoilt coast

West of East London, along the fringes of the Indian Ocean, our route explores a pretty coastline with lagoons, winding rivers and wild sweeps of shining sand. We then swing inland to the rolling country of the Ciskei, with a visit to the cold-blooded world of reptiles. More than half the route is tarred, the rest is good gravel.

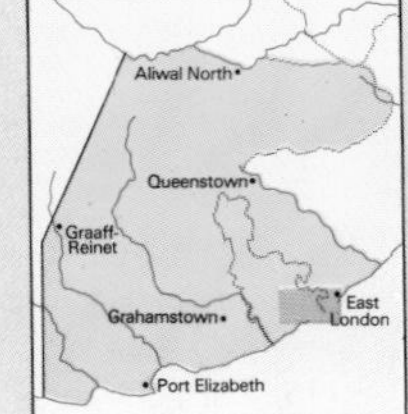

East London
Igoda Mouth
Kidd's Beach
Ciskei
Hamburg
Buffalo Pass
220 – 240 km

LEAVE EAST LONDON by driving west along Fleet Street. Go right at the fork, following the airport sign onto the R72. The road crosses a bridge over the railway line, then the John Vorster Bridge over the Buffalo River. At the end of the bridge, turn left into Nuffield Road, and turn right a few hundred metres later at the T-junction. Turn left at the next T-junction into Bank Street (where Military Road goes right), and turn right at yet another T-junction into Strand Street following the sign for 'Coastal Resorts'.

After roughly 3,5 km on Marine Drive follow the larger road to the right – (the road ahead leads to a shooting range). This stretch of road was once part of the international Grand Prix motor racing circuit (see opposite), and you soon pass between the grandstand and control tower, with the pit lane and pits on your left immediately afterwards.

Marine Drive to Igoda Mouth

Continue on this road across two narrow bridges, and turn right at the oblique T-junction where a smaller road joins on your left from Cove Rock. Within 2 km you reach the intersection between the Cove Rock road and the R72. Continue straight across the R72, and 1,8 km beyond the intersection turn right towards King William's Town and Buffalo Pass. You pass a turn-off on your right to SANTA, and 100 m after this turn left towards King William's Town, noting your kms.

Immediately after the turn you pass an agricultural research station on your right. After 8,4 km turn right into Reptile World – open weekends and public holidays 10 a.m.-5 p.m. and on weekdays by appointment at tel. (0431) 462605.

Return to the Cove Rock road/R72 intersection, and turn right onto the R72 towards Port Elizabeth and Kidd's Beach, noting your kms. You pass Ncera Road on your left, and soon afterwards – after 4,1 km on the R72 – turn left onto gravel for Igoda Mouth, Winter Strand and Hlozi Beach.

Pass a road on your right leading over the hill, and after 3,1 km on the gravel turn right for Igoda Mouth. Park where the road ends, overlooking the mouth of the lagoon, for a pleasant stroll along the beach or lagoon bank.

Igoda Mouth to Kidd's Beach

Return to the R72, and turn left towards Port Elizabeth and King William's Town, noting your kms. You soon cross a bridge over the Igoda River, and then a bridge over the Gulu River. After 7,3 km there is a turn-off on your left to Gulu Beach. (To reach the beach along this road, turn right at the T-junction on the river bank, and left after the old bridge. This brings you to a small parking area with changing rooms and toilets, next to the lagoon and the wide beach.)

Continuing on the R72, you cross the Mcantsi River 4,5 km beyond the Gulu Beach turn-off. After a further 800 m turn left for Kidd's Beach. The road leads to a parking area near the resort's tidal pool, and there are long stretches of unspoilt beach to walk on. (A hotel in the resort offers lunch.)

Kidd's Beach to Hamburg

Return to the R72, and turn left towards Port Elizabeth and King William's Town, noting your kms. You cross the Ncera River, and soon afterwards – 5,3 km after re-joining the R72 – you pass a gravel road on the right leading to Calgary Farm and Museum (the road on the left leads to Kayzer's Beach). Note that Calgary Farm has been sold to the Ciskei Government and is closed to the public.

You are now in the Ciskei ('this side of the Kei River'), the name given to the area between the Keiskamma and the Kei to distinguish it from Transkei, an area north of the Kei.

The road passes two turn-offs on your left to the Chalumna (Tyolomnqa) River mouth, then winds through the attractive scenery of the Keiskamma River valley.

You pass a turn-off on your right to Peddie after 41,4 km. After a further 4,3 km turn left onto the gravel R345 to Hamburg. Stop at the parking area at the extensive and magnificent beach.

Return to the R72, and turn right for East London. Follow the R72 for 66,5 km to the Cove Rock/R72 intersection you crossed in the morning. Turn left here for Buffalo Pass (right leads to Marine Drive). 1,7 km later turn right for Buffalo Pass and King William's Town. Soon afterwards you pass on your left the turn-off to Reptile World. The road passes through indigenous forest, and traverses the scenic Buffalo Pass. As you begin the descent into the pass there is a parking area on your left with a view over a classic horseshoe bend in the Buffalo River. Continue through the pass into East London ●

AA Office AA House, 27 Fleet Street, East London 5201 Tel. (0431) 21271
Greater East London Publicity Association Tourist Information Bureau, City Hall, Oxford Street, East London 5201 Tel. (0431) 26015
SA Tourism Board 4th Floor, NBS Building, Terminus Street, East London 5201 Tel. (0431) 26410

Professor J L B Smith identifying the Coelacanth.

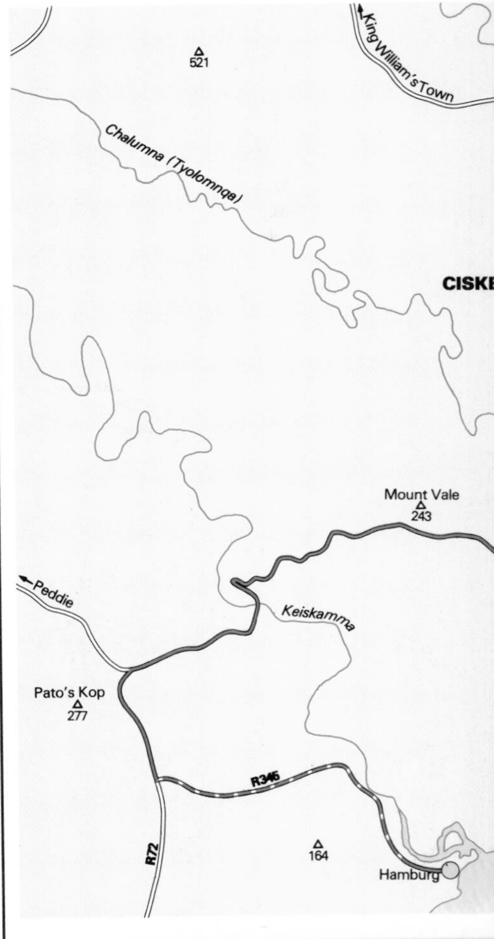

The curve of unspoilt coast at Kidd's Beach.

THE LIVING FOSSIL

The seas around East London have yielded many surprises, but perhaps the most astonishing was tipped from a trawler net off the mouth of the Chalumna River in 1938. It was a fish the likes of which none of the trawlermen had seen before, with fins like stumpy, rudimentary legs and a curious pointed tail. The fish was familiar, though, to palaeontologists — as the coelacanth — but they knew it only from fossil imprints, of which the youngest was about 80 million years old.

Since then other specimens have been found off east Africa.

GRAND PRIX GLORY

For more than 30 years East London was the 'capital' of motor-racing in South Africa. In 1934 the track near the Buffalo River was the scene of the first international race in this country — the 'Border Hundred', won by Whitney Straight of the United States. From then until 1967, with a break during World War II, the world's leading drivers were seen here regularly, doing battle for championship honours. Costs of bringing the stars to East London became prohibitive, and in 1968 the newer Kyalami took over as the country's motor-racing centre.

East London's rocky shore — a lure for anglers.

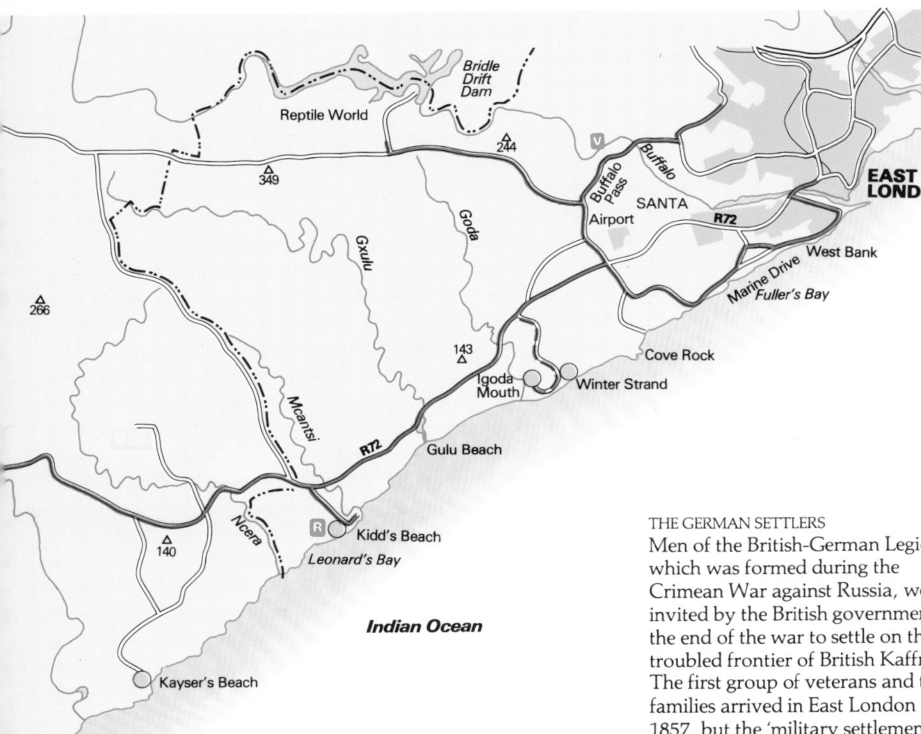

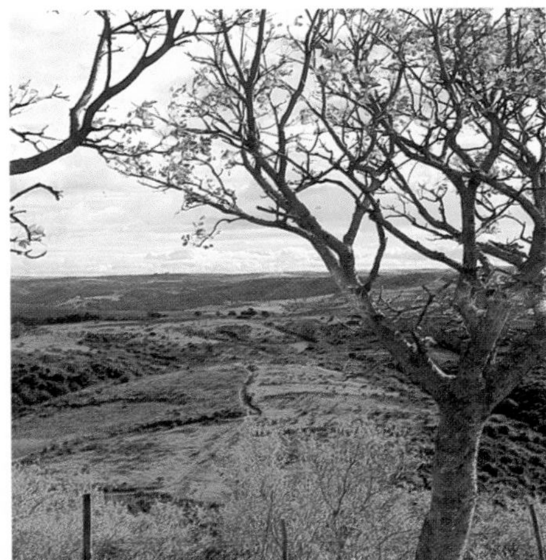

A view over hills and forests from Buffalo Pass.

THE GERMAN SETTLERS

Men of the British-German Legion, which was formed during the Crimean War against Russia, were invited by the British government at the end of the war to settle on the troubled frontier of British Kaffraria. The first group of veterans and their families arrived in East London in 1857, but the 'military settlement' of the area was not very successful, and German civilians were recruited in the latter half of the century to supplement dwindling numbers. Many of the towns in this part of the country bear the names of these German settlers' home towns, such as Hamburg, Berlin and Potsdam.

The tranquil charm of the lagoon at Igoda Mouth.

THE KIDD'S BEACH PHANTOM

Kidd's Beach has long been a popular resort. A shop established here during the last century did good business trading with the Xhosa and providing for the needs of the summer campers. One day the owner inspanned his oxen and set off for East London to replenish his stocks before the summer 'rush' — and vanished, along with the entire team, wagon and leaders.

Since then, some locals believe, if you visit the beach on the night of the last full moon before Christmas, you can hear the bellowing of oxen and shouts of men as these lost souls re-enact their frantic and futile battle to free themselves from quicksand.

The wide Gulu River lagoon between Winter Strand and Kidd's Beach is ideal for swimming and walks along its banks.

The Magistrate's Court clock tower with its distinctive weather vane dominates the view along Taylor Street.

Memorial to the dead of World War I.

Solid stone buildings from the days of the frontier wars

KING WILLIAM'S TOWN, a former garrison town and capital of the short-lived Province of Queen Adelaide, and later of British Kaffraria, is steeped in history, much of it reflected in the mellow stonework of its gracious old buildings. This leisurely stroll explores the heart of the old Borough of King William's Town — an area that retains many reminders of its strong colonial and military past.

Our walk begins on the lawned expanse of Maclean Square at the *statue of Queen Victoria* **(1)**, which was unveiled in 1899. A few years later the four smooth-bore, muzzle-loading cannons that stand around the statue were presented to the town, after the obsolete pieces had been found among military stores.

At the northern end of the square, on the corner of Taylor Street, is the ornate building of the *British Kaffrarian Savings Bank* **(2)**. This bank is one of the few survivors of the many financial institutions established during a boom in the 1860s. If you look past the bank along Taylor Street, you will see the double-storeyed facade of *Lonsdale Chambers* **(3)** next door, with the entire street dominated by the tower of the *Magistrate's Court* **(4)**.

The 'Military Reserve'

Walk north-west along Maclean Street until you reach the historic *Town Hall* **(5)** on your left. Built in 1867, it has the borough arms in relief on the gable. Turn right at this corner into Downing Street, then turn left into Alexandra Road.

Some distance along Alexandra Road, beyond Smith Street, you will see on your left the *Holy Trinity (Anglican) Church* **(6)**, begun in 1850 as a military chapel. Behind it is the old rectory.

Turn left into Berkeley Street. Set into the pavement, opposite Alfred Street, on your right, is a large, round-topped grey stone with the letters 'B.O.' and the British Army 'broad arrow' cut into it. This Board of Ordnance beacon is one of several that once marked the bounds of the 'Military Reserve' that the British established in the town.

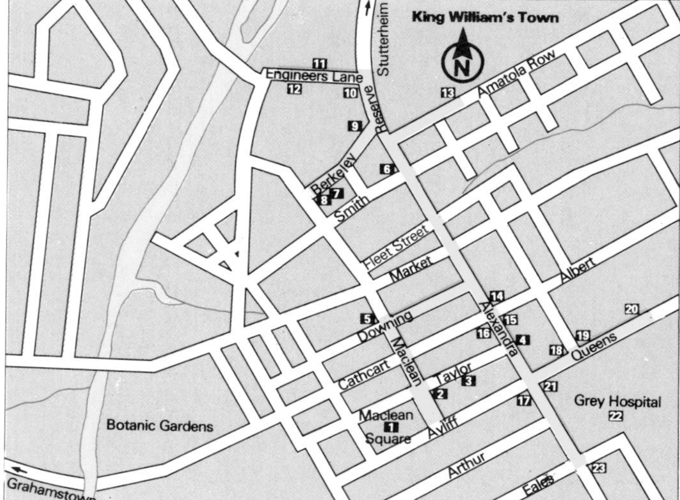

On your left is the *South African Missionary Museum* **(7)**, which is housed in a former Methodist Church building of 1855. You also pass the old double-storeyed Methodist manse, before reaching the town's synagogue **(8)**. This building, originally part of the Methodist complex, was the first venue for the Borough Council, and was converted into a synagogue in 1908.

The Old Residency

Return to Alexandra Road, passing the prominent stone monument to the German Settlers. Turn left into the continuation of Alexandra Road, known as Reserve Road.

On your left, set back slightly from the pavement, a stone plinth with a bronze plaque records the history of the *Old Residency* **(9)**, the thatched building behind the plinth. On this site the man dubbed the 'father of King William's Town', the Reverend John Brownlee of the London Missionary Society, built his original mission house in 1826 on the banks of the Buffalo River.

Sir Harry Smith lived at the old Residency 10 years after it was built, while he was military governor, and it was here that he announced somewhat melodramatically to thousands of Xhosa tribesmen that Governor D'Urban had annexed their territory as the Province of Queen Adelaide. Seven months later the British Government under Lord Glenelg repealed the proclamation of the province and returned it to its inhabitants. In 1847, when Sir Harry had been appointed governor of the Cape, he again annexed the area, this time as British Kaffraria.

Just beyond the Residency turn left into the shady, gravel avenue known as Engineers Lane. You pass on your left the former *Royal Engineers officers' mess* **(10)**, and on your right the old *Military Hospital* **(11)**, both dating from the 1840s.

Major General Eardley-Wilmot's gun.

Workmen's legacy

Beyond the officers' mess on your left is a square building with a curious roof — this was once the blacksmiths' shop **(12)** where the British Army farriers did their sweltering work. The roof rises to a central peak, surmounted by a smaller canopy — the space between the roof and the canopy allowed the hot air of the smithy to escape.

A little further along the lane you will come across neatly built, stone rainwater channels on both sides of the road — also the work of the versatile Royal Engineers. Turn around here, return to Reserve Road, and turn right.

Turn left into Amatola Row at the small Dick King Memorial. About 100 m along this road is a pair of grey gateposts **(13)** on your left, which once marked the main entrance to the Military Reserve. Pass through the gate, into what is now a trade school, to view the bronze cannon under its roofed shelter. As you walk towards the cannon, you pass on your right the long stone building of 1849 that was the Commissariat Store.

The little cannon belonged to Major General Frederick Eardley-Wilmot. It is thought that he presented it in memory of his younger brother, who was killed in action in the Fish River bush during the war of 1850-3. The gun was taken to war in 1877 by the Grahamstown Volunteer Horse Artillery.

The Kaffrarian Museum

Return to Alexandra Road, and turn left. Pass Downing Street on your right, before reaching the *Roman Catholic Church and presbytery* **(14)** on your left.

Cross Albert Road to reach, also on your left, the main entrance to the *Kaffrarian Museum* **(15)** through its Thomas Daines Wing (which was previously the public library). The buildings in the museum complex include the old post office, which lies next to the Thomas Daines Wing on Alexandra Road and houses the museum's Xhosa section, and the 1898 Natural History Museum building around the corner in Albert Road.

Huberta the Hippo

The Kaffrarian Museum contains many exhibits relating to early settlers, with a section devoted to the Germans who settled in the area in the middle of last century. There are also many military items on display, and a famous natural history section.

The charming entrance to Grey Hospital, built by Sir George Grey in 1859.

Among the natural history exhibits is Huberta the hippopotamus, who made headlines around the world from the end of 1928 when she began a journey southwards from Natal that lasted several years. Huberta turned up in many unusual places, and was once found fast asleep on a busy railway line. She was eventually shot illegally by three hunters while she was bathing in the Keiskamma River.

An impressive insurance company building completed in 1904.

Leave the museum through the Thomas Daines Wing on Alexandra Road. On the opposite corner is the elaborate, domed building **(16)** erected for an insurance company in 1904.

Continue south-west on Alexandra Road. Opposite Taylor Street is the Magistrate's Court, dating from 1877, with its elegant clock tower and brass plaque commemorating the Reverend John Brownlee. The bronze plaque in front of the court building outlines the history of the town, and shows profiles of King William IV and Queen Adelaide.

Across the road, on the corner of Ayliff Street, is a monument to Sir Henry Timson Lukin **(17)**, who commanded the South Africans at the battle of Delville Wood in 1916.

War memorial

Turn left into Queens Road. On your left you reach the neo-classic *Victoria Drill Hall* **(18)** built in 1897, *Sutton House* **(19)**, a school property dating from 1877, and the *Convent of the Sacred Heart* **(20)**, also of 1877. Return to Alexandra Road, passing the soaring memorial to the dead of World War I **(21)** on your left as you turn left into Alexandra.

Our walk ends at the corner of Eales Road. As you reach the corner, look left at the lovely facade of *Grey Hospital* **(22)**, which was built in 1859. The long, stone building on the corner of Eales Road that now houses the School Board offices was originally the town's *railway station* **(23)** from 1877 to 1933. There was only a single spur line, and trains reversed all the way from the main line outside of the town to the station so that they would be facing the right direction for departure ●

HUBERTA

Huberta — the hippo who won hearts around the world.

Turn-of-the-century elegance in a 1908 bank building.

The high road over the wild and solitary southern Drakensberg

Eastwards from the old river-crossing of Aliwal North our route winds through the awesome southern Drakensberg — crossing Naudesnek, at 2621 m the highest road pass in South Africa, and Barkly Pass. This long drive takes a full day, and should be avoided in wet or snowy weather. Roughly two-thirds of the route is on tar, the rest is gravel.

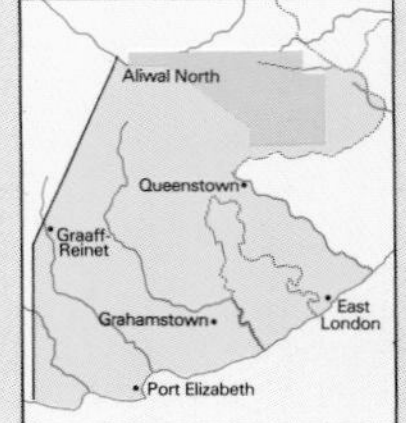

Aliwal North
Lady Grey
Barkly East
Rhodes
Maclear
Elliot
510 – 530 km

TURN OUT OF ALIWAL NORTH'S Somerset Street into Young Street — towards Lady Grey and Barkly East on the R58 — and note your kms. After 44,7 km you pass a turn-off on your left to Sterkspruit. 3,8 km after this, turn left for Lady Grey, which you reach about 3 km later (see opposite).

Return to the R58, and turn left for Barkly East and Elliot. After 3,1 km you pass a turn-off on your right to Jamestown, and roughly 12 km later you cross the Karnmelkspruit. After a further 5 km the road begins to wind up the scenic Benjaminshoogte, and within the next 2 km you pass a turn-off on your right to Dordrecht. Roughly 4 km later you pass on your left a turn-off to Lady Grey via Joubert's Pass.

Soon afterwards on your right you pass the prominent Motkop (drizzle hill), and at its foot the railway siding known as Drizzly. This apparent reflection of the prevailing weather is soon reinforced by signs that warn of ice and slippery road surfaces.

After passing a turn-off on your left to New England and Sterkspruit via 'Lundeansnek', the road soon begins to descend into the Kraai River Pass, which crosses two rivers. The road passes another turn-off to Dordrecht, then continues into Barkly East.

Barkly East to Naudesnek

You enter the town on Molteno Street. Turn left into De Villiers Street, then turn right into White Street (onto gravel), noting your kms. There is a very short experimental tarred section before the road surface turns to gravel again. After roughly 14 km you reach the Rebelshoogte pass.

After several kms more, you pass a turn-off to Elliot, and 100 m later you cross a single-lane bridge over the Kraai River. Within the next 1 km the road passes a turn-off on the left to 'War Trial', and crosses a narrow girder-bridge across the willow-lined Bell River.

After roughly 43 km on the gravel road, the route traverses a ridge, giving wide views of mountains and valleys on both sides. About 3 km later there is another narrow causeway.

At the fork 52,4 km from Barkly East, go right for Rhodes where the road on the left leads to Maartens Hoek. The road crosses a narrow causeway after 400 m, and enters the little settlement of Rhodes 6,2 km later.

Turn left for Maclear and Naudesnek at the

Poplars cast their slender shade across a road near Motkop (drizzle hill).

A class 19D steam locomotive stands in the town square of Barkly East.

LADY GREY

The town of Lady Grey, centre of a sheepfarming district, was named after the wife of Sir George Grey, who was governor of the Cape from the end of 1854 to 1861 (except for an interruption of one year), and who is recorded as a man of achievement and distinction.

His married life was less successful, however, although it started happily enough when he married in Australia. Unreasonably, Sir George blamed his wife for the early death of their only child. Lady Grey remained loyal but, on a voyage from England to South Africa, Sir George suspected her of committing some indiscretion with a naval officer. She was put ashore in South America, and the two were estranged for 37 years. Well-meaning friends brought them together in their old age, but the attempt at reconciliation failed, and Lady Grey died sad and misunderstood.

A TOWN OF CHILLY NIGHTS

Barkly East's temperature drops to below freezing point on an average of one night in four, giving this pretty town the reputation of being one of the coldest in South Africa.

Named after Governor Sir Henry Barkly, the little town at an altitude of 1 800 m presented problems to the railway-builders. They solved it by building a line with an average gradient of 1 in 36, with eight reversing stations. The local museum specialises in early transportation.

T-junction, noting your kms. After 12,2 km there is a small riverside picnic area on your left (with braai place) at the foot of the spectacular Naudesnek Pass. A plaque here records that two brothers who farmed nearby, Stefanus and Gabriel Naude, had found a way out of the isolated valley over the mountains in 1896, and that the pass was built along their original route.

The steep road twists its way upwards from the foot of the pass, which is at 1 920 m above sea level, to reach the summit at 2 621 m. After 8 km on the pass, the road levels out for a while, before beginning the long and gradual descent. (If you are running out of time, or if you wish to shorten the route, Naudesnek Pass makes a turning point.)

Naudesnek to Maclear

There are a number of causeways, and the road passes two turn-offs to the left (the second to Mount Fletcher). Roughly 50 km from the summit of Naudesnek the road reaches the Pot River Pass — which is mostly downhill.

The road surface changes to tar after a further 30 km. On the outskirts of Maclear, follow the road as it bends sharply to the left, then turn left at the T-junction for Elliot. 300 m later turn right at the T-junction. (A number of establishments in the town provide lunch.) After 800 m turn right onto the R56 for Ugie, Barkly East and Aliwal North.

Maclear to Barkly East

About 19 km later the road enters Ugie, named after a stream in Scotland, overlooked by the Prentjiesberg (picture mountain). The route then continues to Elliot.

In Elliot, turn right at the second stop street into Lloyd Street (R58). After 9,2 km you reach the start of the scenic Barkly Pass. The road passes a turn-off on your right to Rhodes and Sterkspruit after 19,4 km, and reaches Barkly East after a further 40,4 km.

Turn right into De Villiers Street, then left into Molteno Street, and retrace your route on the R58 to Aliwal North ●

AA Office AA House, 3a Terminus Street, East London 5201 Tel. (0431) 21271
Aliwal North Municipality Barkly Street, Aliwal North 5530 Tel. (0551) 2441
Barkly East Municipality Molteno Street, Barkly East 5580 Tel. (04542) 73/123
SA Tourism Board 4th Floor, NBS Building, Terminus Street, East London 5201 Tel. (0431) 26410

The Kraai River cuts a gorge through arid land.

Wild countryside in the Barkly East district.

RHODES AND MACLEAR

The tranquil little village of Rhodes is noted for its cold, bracing climate, and the nearby ski slopes, as well as for trout-fishing in its many willow-lined streams.

It was originally named Rossville, after the Reverend David Ross of the Lady Grey Dutch Reformed congregation. The name was changed to honour Cecil John Rhodes, who arranged for the planting of the stone-pines that still spread their generous shade over the town's main road.

Separated from Rhodes by the wild beauty of Naudesnek is Maclear, established in 1876. The town was named after Sir Thomas Maclear, the Queen's Astronomer at the Cape for almost 40 years until his retirement in 1870.

Trained as a medical doctor, Maclear was an amateur but very gifted astronomer at the time of his appointment, and eventually made many valuable contributions to the science. Travelling with him from England to the Cape was his servant, Thomas Bowler, who went on to achieve fame as one of the Colony's leading artists.

Naudesnek Pass — highest road in the country.

ELLIOT

Major Henry Elliot, after whom this attractive little town was named, resigned from a distinguished career with the British army because of ill health. He came to South Africa in 1870 to recover, and was about to return when he was appointed Chief Magistrate of Tembuland.

He had a unique method of keeping the peace among the local communities — when he heard that trouble was about to break out, he would set off with a single black trooper to reason with the antagonists. He gained a reputation as a peacekeeper, and was eventually appointed Chief Magistrate of the whole of Transkei.

The waters of the Orange River bring life to a thirsting land

The first sight of the vast expanse of the Hendrik Verwoerd Dam comes as a surprise in the arid Karoo landscape. Our route traverses the shores of this impressive man-made lake, passes two nature reserves, and takes in the historic towns of Bethulie and Burgersdorp. All but 58 km of the drive is on tarred roads.

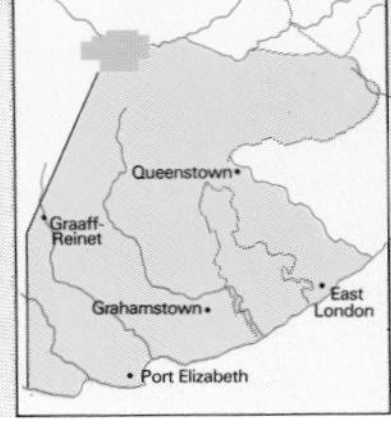

Aliwal North
Bethulie
Norvalspont
Venterstad
Burgersdorp
320 – 340 km

TURN WEST OUT OF Aliwal North's Somerset Street into Barkly Street. Go right at the fork, following the signs for Bloemfontein and Johannesburg. Cross the Orange River over the iron General Hertzog Bridge, and 200 m later turn left for Goedemoed and Bethulie.

After 25 km the road surface changes to gravel as you pass a road on your right leading into Rouxville. Continue straight on, crossing the Caledon River after 18 km. 6,6 km after the river, the gravel gives way to tar as you pass a turning to Smithfield on your right. Continue straight on for Bethulie. 25,7 km later turn left into Bethulie on the R391.

At the intersection outside the town, where the road on the left leads to the railway station and the road on the right to Bethulie, continue straight to visit the D H Steyn Bridge over the Orange River. This is the longest bridge in South Africa, measuring 2 993 m if one includes the approaches. The concrete bridge section is 1 121 m long and is supported on 26 arches.

Return to the intersection on the outskirts of the town, and turn left. After 100 m there is a gravel road on your left that leads to the site of the Bethulie concentration camp and the old cemetery dating from the Anglo-Boer War.

Cross the single-lane bridge at the start of the town's main road, and turn right at the four-way stop street 1 km later. After 100 m you will see on your right the Pellissier House Museum, in what is believed to be the oldest settler-built structure north of the Orange River. Continue on this road (which changes to gravel after a few hundred metres) to reach the caravan park on the shores of the Bethulie Dam (braai places, toilets, water).

Bethulie to Norvalspont

Return to the four-way stop street, and turn right — noting your kms. 3,2 km later turn left onto the R701 towards Verwoerd Dam and Donkerpoort. After a further 46,6 km turn left at the T-junction for Verwoerd Dam and Norvalspont (where the road on the right leads to Donkerpoort and the N1). 3,5 km later turn left

THE FIRST CONCENTRATION CAMPS

The name concentration camp was first coined during the Anglo-Boer War, when the British forces 'concentrated' Boer women and children at points close to water and the railway line. Many of these people had become homeless as a result of the British tactic of destroying land off which the Boer armies lived so successfully.

Close to 28 000 people died in these concentration camps, many of them from a particularly virulent form of measles. Victims originally buried in the camp cemeteries at Norvalspont and Bethulie have been re-interred in gardens of remembrance.

Concentration camp relics, Norvalspont.

TUSSEN-DIE-RIVIERE AND OVISTON

The Tussen-die-Riviere Game Farm, which lies between the Orange and Caledon rivers, is unusual in that it is opened to hunters for part of the year. From September to the end of April it operates as an ordinary game reserve, with visitors admitted during daylight hours. The reserve is on land that was expected to be flooded when the Hendrik Verwoerd Dam plans were first drawn up.

Across the dam is the Oviston Nature Reserve, which supports large herds of game and is used as a breeding place for restocking other reserves. It is open to the public on weekends and public holidays.

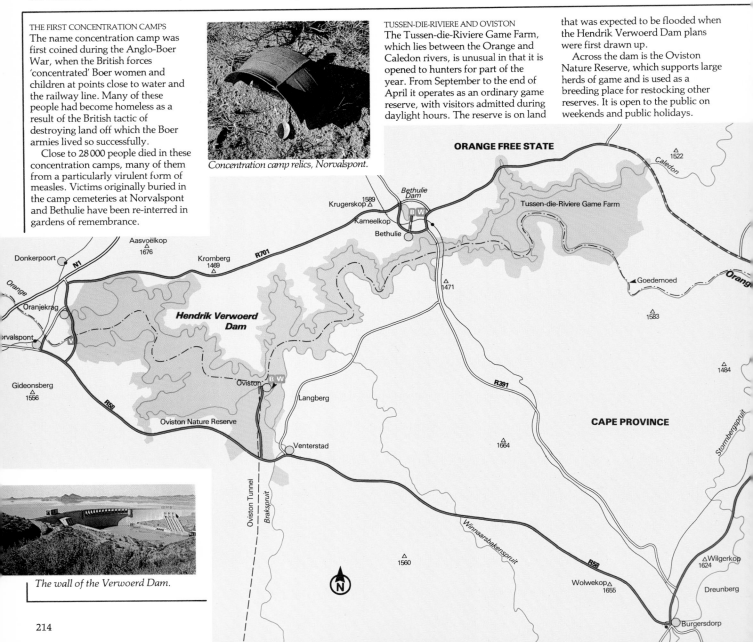

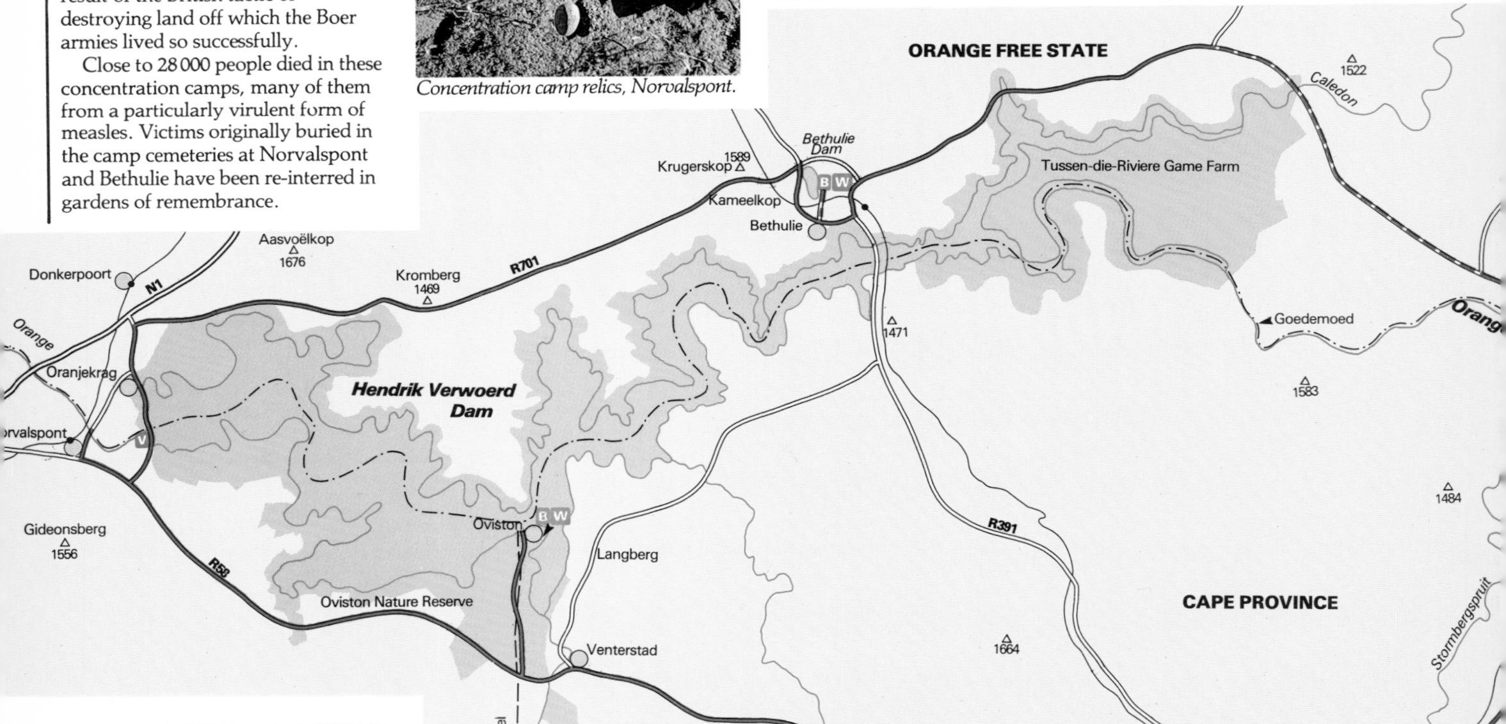

The wall of the Verwoerd Dam.

again, onto the R58 towards Venterstad via Verwoerd Dam.

The R58 leads past the Hendrik Verwoerd Dam Motel, which serves lunch, and several kilometres later it runs along the top of the dam wall. (Before the road reaches the wall, there is a fork to the right that leads to the Department of Water Affairs offices, from where there is a good view of the dam wall.)

Cross the dam wall to the south side. Turn right onto a road signposted 'Viewsite', and continue straight for just over 1 km. A footpath of about 100 m leads around a small hillock to the viewsite.

Leave the viewsite, and turn right onto the R58, noting your kms. After 2,6 km turn right onto tar towards Colesberg. 4 km later turn right onto the R701 towards Norvalspont and Oranjekrag.

The road enters Norvalspont, and passes the Glasgow Pont Hotel (which serves lunch by prior arrangement). Soon afterwards, on your right, there is a blockhouse dating from the Anglo-Boer War, which has been converted to a house and is now almost hidden by trees. Immediately afterwards there is a long, single-lane bridge over the Orange River, with a railway bridge alongside. Turn around here, and retrace your route back through Norvalspont to the R58.

Norvalspont to Burgersdorp

Turn left onto the R58 for Venterstad. After 900 m there is a gravel road on your right that leads to the Norvalspont concentration camp site and cemetery.

After a further 3,1 km you pass the road on which you arrived earlier from the Verwoerd Dam wall — note your kms here.

Continue straight, and after 31,8 km turn left off the R58 for Oviston (where the road on the right leads to Steynsburg). 3,6 km later turn left at the T-junction for Oviston. Follow the signs to the right where the road ahead is blocked by the gate to the nature reserve (open weekends and public holidays; small entry fee).

The road passes the offices of the Department of Nature Conservation on your left, and a turn-off to picnic sites on your right (braai places, toilets, water). Continue straight to the edge of the dam, where a parking area overlooks the intake tower of the Oviston tunnel. This tunnel links the Orange and Fish rivers — hence the name, from the Afrikaans Oranje-Vis Tonnel. It is the longest tunnel of its kind in the world, and runs for 82,8 km from Oviston to Teebus in the south.

Return to the R58, and turn left for Venterstad. Follow the signs through Venterstad for Burgersdorp and East London. The historic town of Burgersdorp, birthplace of one of South Africa's Afrikaans universities and home of the first taal monument, is reached after a further 57,8 km.

When you leave Burgersdorp, follow the signs for Aliwal North, which lies just over 52 km further along the R58 ●

AA Office AA House, 56 Church Street, Bloemfontein 9301 Tel. (051) 76191
Aliwal North Municipality Barkly Street, Aliwal North 5530 Tel. (0551) 2441
Bethulie Municipality Voortrekker Street, Bethulie 9992 Tel. (05862) 333
SA Tourism Board 2nd Floor, Penbel Building, 29 Elizabeth Street, Bloemfontein 9301 Tel. (051) 71362

A railway bridge arches above the tree-lined road to the Bethulie Dam.

The moon rises over grain silos as sunset tints the Aliwal North sky.

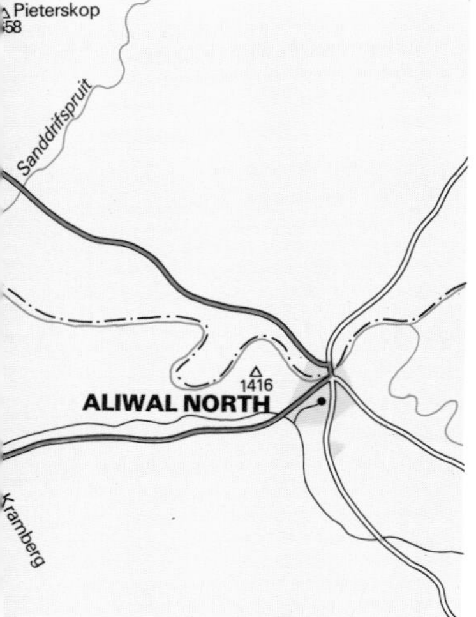

The head of the Oviston Tunnel — 82,8 km from its outlet in the Fish River.

ALIWAL NORTH

This town on the banks of the Orange River was named to honour Sir Harry Smith's victory in 1846 over the Sikhs at Aliwal in India. The 'North' was added because Mossel Bay had been renamed Aliwal South.

Two thermal springs at Aliwal North provide more than 3 million litres of water a day, at a temperature of 34,4°C. The waters are credited with curative properties, and the springs have been visited by invalids for many years.

During the Anglo-Boer War the town was the site of a concentration camp, and a garden of remembrance has been made on the edge of the town at a well-preserved blockhouse from the same war.

THE HENDRIK VERWOERD DAM

Covering 374 sq km and with a storage capacity of 5 958 million cubic metres, this dam has harnessed the life-giving waters of the Orange River to the benefit of not only the surrounding arid land, but also of valleys further afield. The dam is part of the Orange River Project, and supplements the Fish River via the 82,8 km Oviston tunnel. Another tunnel feeds the faraway Sundays River with valuable additional water for irrigating the citrus groves and other farms on its banks.

The Hendrik Verwoerd Dam and the P K le Roux Dam together supply 455 million litres of water per day, and generate 600 000 kilowatts of hydro-electric power.

TOWN OF CITIZENS

Burgersdorp, meaning simply the town of citizens, is the chief town of the old Division of Albert. The town housed the country's first Dutch Reformed theological college, which later moved to Potchefstroom. The original college buildings now house a museum.

The town was also the site of the first Taal (language) Monument, unveiled in 1893 to commemorate the use of Dutch in the Cape Parliament. It was damaged during the Anglo-Boer War, moved, and finally lost. A replica was erected, but about 35 years later the original was found, by accident, buried at King William's Town. Both original and replacement are in Burger Square.

Where traditional villages shelter beneath dramatic peaks

From Queenstown our route enters Transkei, passing traditional African villages dotted among rolling hills. The road then crosses the wild southern Drakensberg via the soaring Otto du Plessis Pass, before returning through wooded kloofs and the town of Dordrecht. A little more than half the route is on tar, the rest is on gravel.

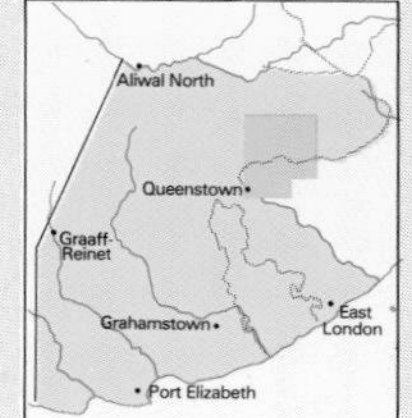

Queenstown
Lady Frere/Cacadu
Indwe
Otto du Plessis Pass
Rossouw
Dordrecht
310–330 km

DRIVE NORTH ALONG Queenstown's Kingsway, which becomes Hangklip Road as it veers left, to the Lawrence de Lange Nature Reserve. 2,4 km after the start of the gravel surface turn left into the reserve, and follow the road for 4,8 km to reach a viewsite that offers a splendid panorama.

Retrace your route along Hangklip Road and Kingsway, but turn left out of Kingsway into Livingstone Road — this becomes the main road to Lady Frere/Cacadu and Dordrecht. You pass the Bonkolo Dam on your left, and shortly afterwards turn right for Lady Frere/Cacadu (the road straight ahead is your

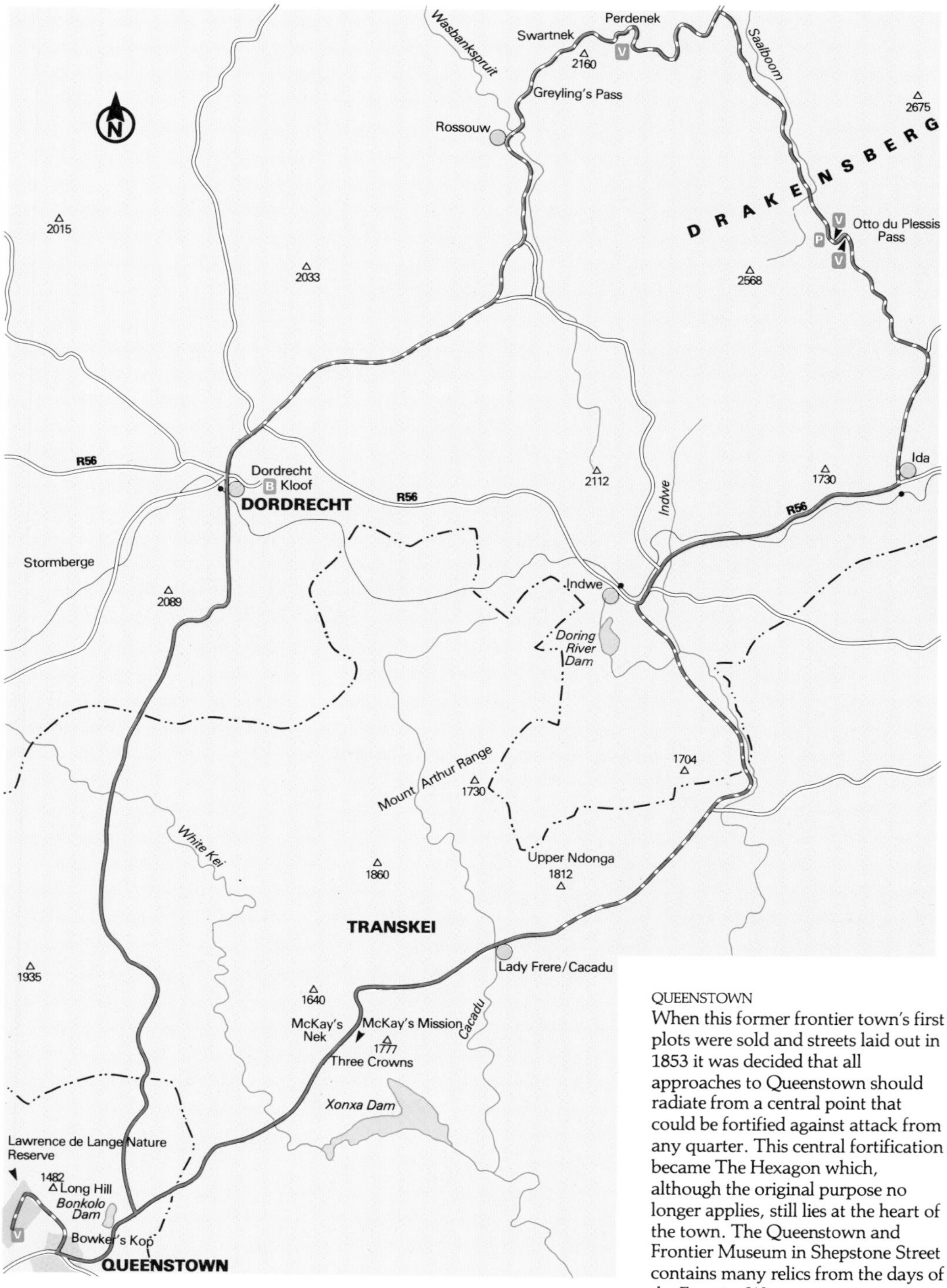

Perdenek
Swartnek
2160
Wasbankspruit
Saalboom
Greyling's Pass
2675
Rossouw
DRAKENSBERG
Otto du Plessis Pass
2015
2033
2568
R56
Dordrecht Kloof
DORDRECHT
R56
2112
Indwe
1730
Ida
R56
Stormberge
2089
Indwe
Doring River Dam
Mount Arthur Range
1730
1704
White Kei
Upper Ndonga
1812
1860
TRANSKEI
Lady Frere/Cacadu
1935
1640
McKay's Nek
McKay's Mission
1777
Three Crowns
Cacadu
Xonxa Dam
Lawrence de Lange Nature Reserve
1482
Long Hill
Bonkolo Dam
Bowker's Kop
QUEENSTOWN

Rural scene beneath the Three Crowns.

The picturesque McKay Mission.

LAST BASTION OF A HUNTED PEOPLE

Deep among the wooded kloofs where the Stormberg and Drakensberg ranges merge, the San people, hunted and harried from the plains, established their last strongholds.

Their stone implements and many other artefacts are still to be found throughout the area, and in many places San artists have painted the rocks with enduring scenes from their day-to-day lives.

QUEENSTOWN

When this former frontier town's first plots were sold and streets laid out in 1853 it was decided that all approaches to Queenstown should radiate from a central point that could be fortified against attack from any quarter. This central fortification became The Hexagon which, although the original purpose no longer applies, still lies at the heart of the town. The Queenstown and Frontier Museum in Shepstone Street contains many relics from the days of the Frontier Wars.

LADY FRERE/CACADU

This little town was originally named after the wife of Sir Henry Bartle Frere, the High Commissioner for South Africa who was later recalled after the disastrous Anglo-Zulu War in 1880. Since its incorporation into Ciskei, the town has been officially renamed Cacadu, after the nearby river, but many of the inhabitants — and the road signs — still use the old name. The town, which serves as the centre for the Glen Grey agricultural district, has several old churches, as well as a quaint prison building.

return route from Dordrecht). Roughly 4km after turning, you pass through the South African border control post, and 1km later the Transkei border control post. (Identity documents will be needed.) Soon after this the Xonxa Dam comes into view on your right.

Roughly 16,5km after leaving the Transkei border post you pass a road on your right to McKay Mission, and begin to climb the McKay's Nek Pass, with a view eastwards to the peaks known as the Three Crowns.

The road continues through rocky countryside, and crosses a bridge before entering Lady Frere/Cacadu. 5km beyond the town the road turns to gravel. You cross several narrow bridges and causeways, then the road winds through the picturesque Indwe Poort.

Roughly 25km from Lady Frere/Cacadu you cross the border back into South Africa. 10km later turn right at the oblique T-junction. After a further 6,5km turn right at the T-junction, onto the tarred R56 for Elliot — noting your kms. (The road left leads into Indwe, which has two hotels.)

You pass a turn-off on your left to Barkly East via Barker's Nek. After 22,4km on the R56, at Ida, turn left onto gravel, noting your kms. You soon pass a church on your right — go left almost immediately at the fork.

You pass a turn-off on your right for Elliot, then a turn-off on your left for Tungela, and cross two narrow causeways. The road then climbs fairly sharply, with views back over fields and foothills. Soon afterwards, 12km after turning off the tarred R56, go left at the fork.

Within the next 21km the road crosses five causeways, then reaches a signboard on your left reading 'Dr Otto du Plessis Pass'. (This pass, named after an Administrator of the Cape, is not suitable for towing caravans or trailers.)

The road climbs steeply up the pass, and crosses a causeway within 1km. On the steep section roughly 3km after the sign there is space on your left to pull over and enjoy the view. Stop again 2km later on your right for a different view — of a mountain amphitheatre. After a further 1km there is an unshaded picnic site that also offers good views. Roughly 300m later you reach the summit of the pass at 2254m.

Tall shade trees and dappled sunlight combine to make Dordrecht Kloof an idyllic braai and picnic site.

A poplar turns to gold alongside the Doring River.

TOWN OF THE BLUE CRANE

In 1896 several companies were formed to exploit coal deposits in and around the Stormberg range, and the town of Indwe came into being near the towering sandstone cliff known as Xalanga (place of vultures). The seams proved to be patchy and the coal was of poor quality, so the mines were soon abandoned, but the town of Indwe (the Xhosa name for the blue crane) now flourishes as an agricultural centre.

CHILLY SLOPES OF THE STORMBERG

Dordrecht, now the centre of a sheep-farming area, was founded on the farm Boschrand in 1856 and named after the town in Holland where the historic 1618 synod of the Reformed Churches was held. Situated on the northern slopes of the Stormberg range, the town is often hit by snowfalls and bitterly cold weather in winter.

The Anderson Museum in Grey Street, housed in a long, stone-built shop that dates from the beginning of this century, contains varied exhibits relating to the history of the area.

Otto du Plessis Pass to Dordrecht

The road winds down the pass, crossing the Saalboom River and its tributaries seven times. 21km from the summit of the pass turn left at the T-junction, noting your kms. (The road to the right leads to Barkly East.)

A steep ascent soon brings you to the summit of Perdenek, after which the road descends again. After 6,8km go right at the fork (the road on the left leads to Kettingdrift). After a further 5,1km go left at another fork (the road on the right goes to Heuningneskloof). Roughly 1,5km later, just before a sharp left bend, pull off the road for a view back over a large irrigated valley locked in among the mountains.

After 5km the road begins to descend Swartnek, offering constantly changing views of rugged mountains. The road then descends further, following the old Greyling's Pass.

On the outskirts of the tiny settlement of Rossouw you cross the Jan Schoombee Bridge. 5,2km beyond the bridge, after crossing two narrow causeways, turn right at the T-junction, noting your kms. You pass roads on your left to Bonthoek and Indwe. After 13,8km go right at the fork for Dordrecht, and after a further 19,4km — in which you pass turn-offs to Barkly East and Lady Grey — turn right at the T-junction onto the tarred R56. A further 3,3km brings you to Dordrecht.

Dordrecht to Queenstown

To visit the beautiful picnic and braai sites in Dordrecht Kloof, turn left into Tower Street just past the stone Anglican church with its green roof. Turn right after roughly 100m (where a smaller track goes straight up the hillside). Turn left after another 100m, and follow this road for a few kms to reach the kloof.

Leave Dordrecht by travelling south on the R56. After roughly 20km this road enters Transkei and winds among pleasant hills with hutted villages dotting the cultivated valleys. After a further 40km you reach the junction at which you turned off to Lady Frere ●

AA Office AA House, 3a Terminus Street, East London 5201 Tel. (0431) 21271
Queenstown Municipality Town Hall, Cathcart Road, Queenstown 5320 Tel. (0451) 3131

Forest-clad mountains remain where territorial wars once raged

This drive from Fort Beaufort is as rich in history as it is in scenery. We head north along the fertile Tyume Valley, with its orchards and villages, then climb the spectacular Hogsback Pass towards Cathcart. We return by skirting the Amatole range, passing through picturesque Stutterheim. Half the route is tarred, the rest is good gravel.

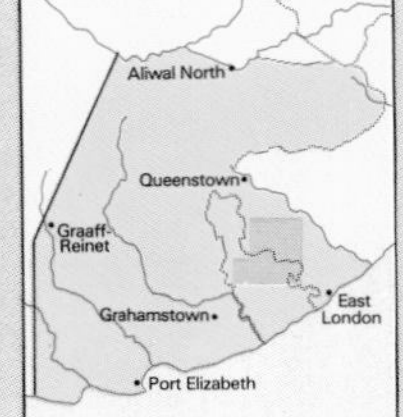

Fort Beaufort
Alice
Hogsback
Cathcart
Stutterheim
Keiskammahoek
210 – 240 km

LEAVE FORT BEAUFORT on the Alice road, and note your kms as you cross the white-walled bridge dated 1958 on the outskirts of the town. The road passes through thornbush-covered cattle-country, and as you approach Alice – roughly 20km from Fort Beaufort – you see the prominent Stewart Memorial on Sandile Kop (see pages 222-3).

20,8km after noting your kms, go right at the fork in Alice, and note your kms again. You cross a bridge dated 1955, and pass the buildings of Fort Hare University on your left.

Alice to Hogsback

After 3,7km from the fork in Alice, turn left onto the R345 towards 'Cathcart via Hogsback', noting your kms. You pass crossroads 3km later, with the village of Dyamala on your left. After a further 11,1km you pass a turn-off on your left to Seymour and Queenstown. The road then ascends the easily negotiated Hogsback Pass, offering spectacular views of the Tyume Valley and lush mountain scenery.

After 26,3km on the R345 the tarred surface gives way to gravel on the edge of the Hogsback State Forest at the Stormberg divisional boundary. The road now passes through the straggling settlement of Hogsback (see pages 220-1).

Hogsback to Cathcart

Roughly 5km beyond the police station, which is the first building you pass in Hogsback, you reach a T-junction. Turn left here towards Seymour via Michel's Pass, noting your kms. After 2,1km stop on the left for the magnificent view of the surrounding countryside.

Retrace your route, noting your kms as you pass the Hogsback turn-off, and keep straight for Cathcart. On your right here is the prominent Gaika's Kop (see opposite).

After 7,8km turn right at the T-junction for Happy Valley and Cathcart, noting your kms again. You cross several single-lane causeways, and after 18,5km on this road you pass a side-road on your left. Immediately afterwards you cross a narrow bridge and pass a little church and cemetery on your right. Many shady sites along the roadside offer attractive picnic places.

34km after turning onto the Happy Valley road, turn right at the T-junction for Cathcart. After a further 6,2km turn right at the T-junction onto tar. Soon afterwards turn left at another T-junction onto the R30, which leads into Cathcart. (A hotel here provides lunch.)

Cathcart to Keiskammahoek

Leave Cathcart by travelling south on the R30 through green and tranquil countryside to reach Stutterheim after roughly 46km. In Stutterheim turn right into Hill Street, following the sign for Keiskammahoek, and noting your kms.

This road becomes the R352, and changes to gravel after about 1,5km. Soon afterwards you pass a turn-off on your right to the indigenous Kologha forest and Eagles Ridge resort (there are many fine forest walks in the area). You cross a number of single-lane causeways, and after 14,6km from the turn in Stutterheim you pass a turn-off on your left signposted for Sandile's Grave and Evelyn's Valley (this road leads to the chief's grave after roughly 10km).

Roughly 3km beyond this turn-off, the Gubu Dam comes into view on your right, and after a further 3km you begin to descend through the pine-covered Dontsa Pass, first built in 1857.

The road passes St Matthew's College and Hospital, with several buildings dating from the 1850s, then passes a large sawmilling complex on your right, before you enter the town of Keiskammahoek. The road is tarred in the town and it veers left before it gives way to gravel again. Cross a bridge soon afterwards, then turn right for Middledrift and Alice.

Roughly 7km beyond Keiskammahoek you cross the wall of the Sandile Dam. Turn left at the far end of the dam wall, and about 5km later (after crossing two narrow causeways) go right at the fork.

A further 4km brings you to the village of Burnshill, and after another 7,6km turn right onto tar at the T-junction for Alice. From Alice retrace your route to Fort Beaufort ●

AA Office AA House, 3a Terminus Street, East London 5201 Tel. (0431) 21271
Fort Beaufort Museum Durban Street, Fort Beaufort 5720 Tel. (0435) 31555
SA Tourism Board 4th Floor, NBS Building, Terminus Street, East London 5201 Tel. (0431) 26410

The famous Gaika chief Sandile.

SANDILE

Sandile, son of Ngqika (Gaika) and his senior wife, was born about 1820, and succeeded to the chieftainship of the Ngqika tribe when he was only 20 years old. His reign was marked by violent clashes with the settlers and military – for which he was not entirely to blame. The most tragic event of his reign was the 'national suicide' of the Xhosa, a ritual cattle-killing and destruction of crops that Sandile was unable to prevent. It was also during his reign that the refusal to deliver the tribesman who had stolen an axe from a Fort Beaufort shop led to the War of the Axe.

The Ngqika tribe, subjected to a white, British-appointed paramount chief, took part in the uprising of 1877. Sandile was fatally wounded the next year in a skirmish with Fingo troops, and died in the thick bush of Isidenge Mountain. The local British commander ordered that his body lie in state before being accorded a military funeral. The grave is south of Stutterheim at Mount Kempt.

A finger of land reaches into the waters of the Sandile Dam.

FORT BEAUFORT

This town, now a centre for the citrus farms irrigated by the Kat River, was founded in 1822 as a defence post, and named after Governor Lord Charles Somerset's father, the Duke of Beaufort.

The Martello tower built in 1836 to replace the original fort still stands in Bell Street, and is believed to be the only Martello tower ever to be built inland. A short-barrelled cannon is mounted on its flat roof – on a wooden turn-table that allows it to be rotated to fire through a full circle. The old double-storeyed building nearby was built soon after the tower as a barracks for the garrison, and now houses a military museum. The town's museum is in the old officers' mess-house on Durban Street.

Fort Beaufort's Martello tower, built in 1836.

Gaika's Kop dominates this rural scene.

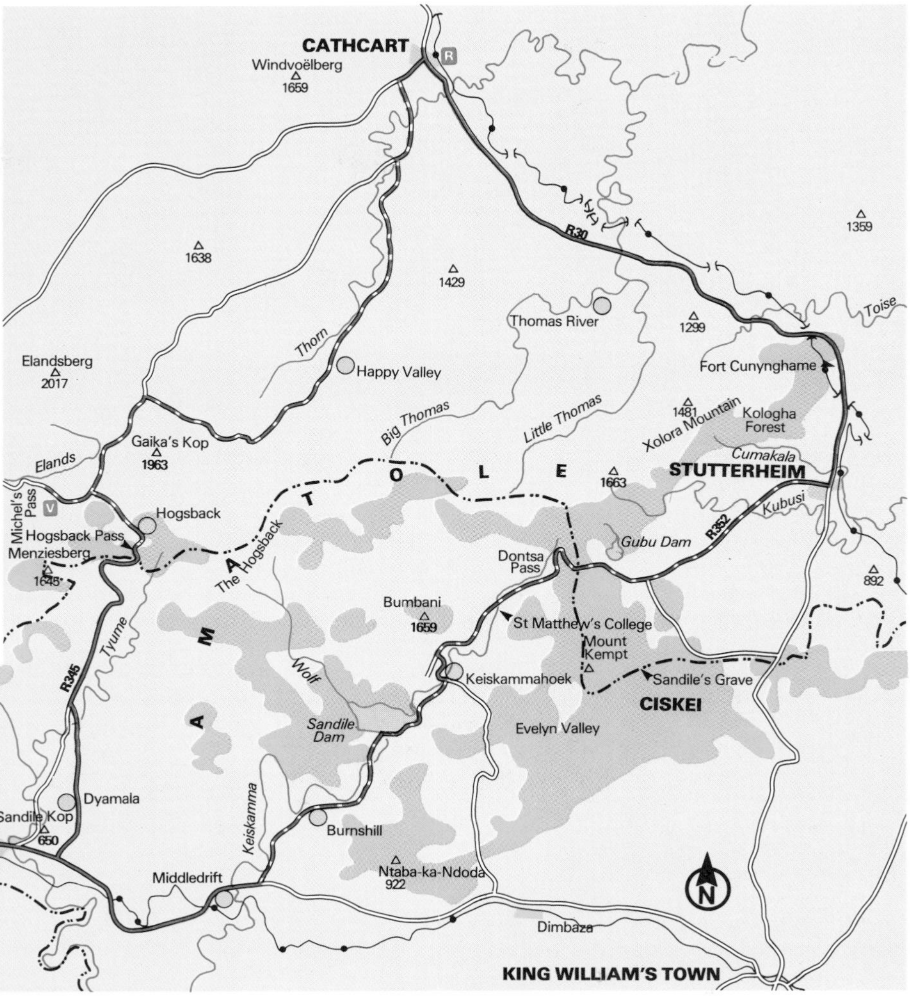

GAIKA'S KOP

This prominent peak in the Amatole range takes its name from Ngqika (Gaika), the warrior-chief and founder of a Xhosa tribe. Legend has it that he made his home under the frowning slopes of Gaika's Kop, and that death sentences were carried out by flinging the condemned from the precipitous cliffs near the 1963 m summit.

Another legend claims that Gaika's Kop was once the home of a renowned diviner or 'ngqira', and that the present name is a mispronunciation.

The cannon mounted on the roof of Fort Beaufort's Martello tower.

Young pines cast their mottled shade over a track near Stutterheim.

STUTTERHEIM

The richly forested mountainsides around Stutterheim not only provide a healthy timber industry, but are also the basis of the area's popularity with holiday-makers. The nearby Kologha State Forest — on a spur of the Amatole range — a favourite spot for weekend relaxation, and the Kubusi River offers fishing, swimming and boating.

The Bethel Mission north of Stutterheim was established in 1837 by Berlin missionaries. More German settlers arrived in the area after the disbanding of the British-German Legion in 1857, and the town they established was named after their commander, Major-General Richard von Stutterheim.

SIR GEORGE CATHCART — MAN OF ACTION

The town of Cathcart, under the slopes of Windvoëlberg, is named after a Cape Governor who showed himself to be fearless and incisive in action, and who died, disillusioned, far away from the frontier that he had successfully subdued.

As a young soldier, Sir George Cathcart took part in many battles against Napoleon, including the final slaughter at Waterloo. He was appointed Governor of the Cape in 1852 and, by personal leadership at the war front, ended the most disastrous frontier war to date.

He was immediately appointed to the British army which had just gone to Crimea to fight the Russians. The Crimean War is said to have been the worst-managed war in which Britain ever took part. In protest, Cathcart exposed himself with reckless gallantry at the battle of Inkerman, and the hill on which he died was later named Cathcart Hill.

The market bell in the town of Cathcart, which hangs near the back of the municipal building, is inscribed *'Orient'*. It was the bell of the Russian ship of that name that went aground at East London in 1907, giving Orient Beach its name.

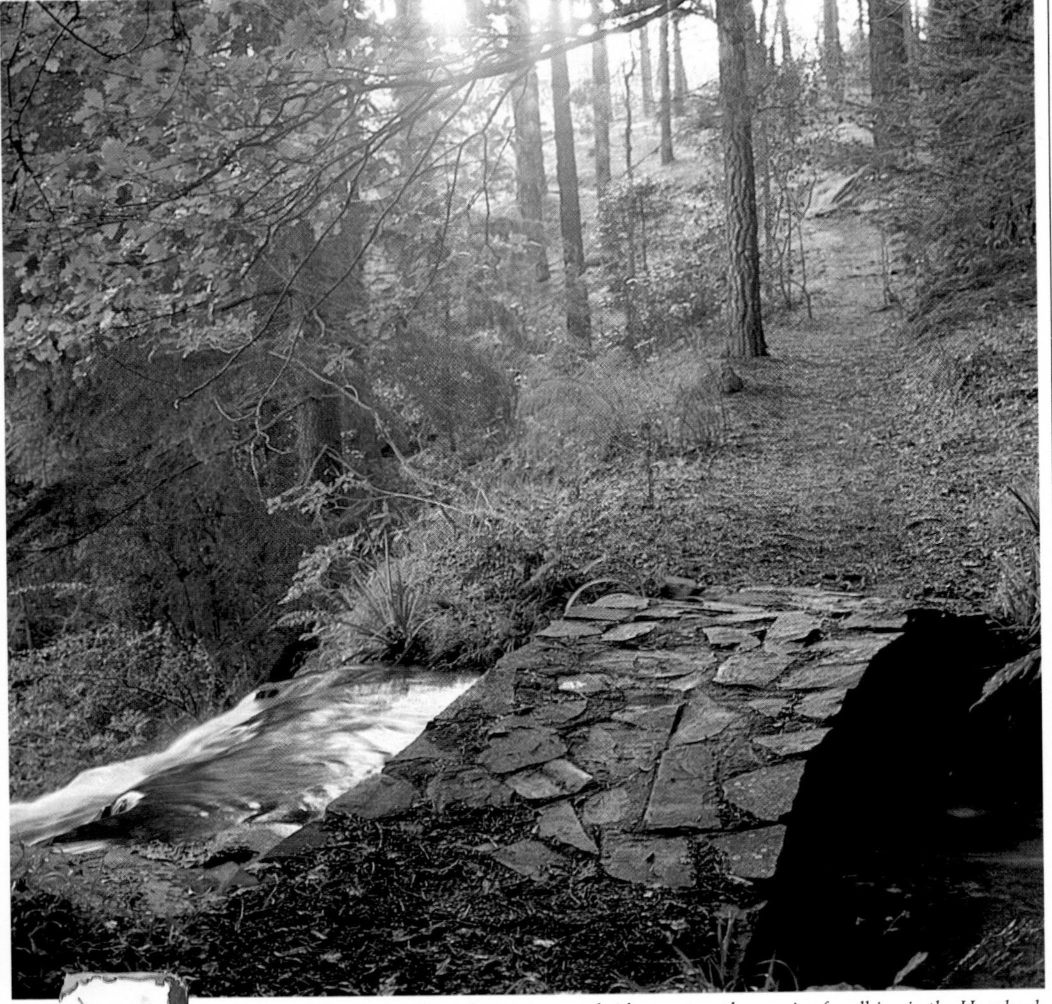

A forested walk and a rustic stone bridge capture the magic of walking in the Hogsback.

Mountain-top wonderland of forests, streams and waterfalls

AT THE WESTERN END of the Amatole range an escarpment falls away to the broad, green Tyume valley. Before reaching the fertile flats, the Tyume and its tributaries fall in showering cascades over silvery rocks in the cool depths of an ancient indigenous forest. This remote mountain resort area has been known for more than a century as the Hogsback.

The village of Hogsback, which lies a short distance from the three Hogsback peaks, straggles along a mountain slope with considerably varying altitudes — from the post office at 1 213 m above sea level, to the T-junction at the top of the village at 1 332 m. It is this high altitude that is largely responsible for the area's wonderfully cool summers, as well as the winter snowfalls that blanket the peaks, and often the village too.

A feature of the Hogsback is the 'Englishness' of many of the avenues and gardens, which flourish under a high annual rainfall of 1 270 mm. In summer there is a profusion of edible berries, which, served with cream, are a local delicacy. The berries, and many other plant species, were introduced by Thomas Summerton, a market gardener from Oxfordshire, England, who settled at Hogsback 100 years ago. He developed an orchard of apples, pears, cherries and nuts, and produced a cider that was tasty and potent.

Early visitors

The name 'Hogs Back' — as two words — first appeared in 1848 in the journal of the artist Thomas Baines, applied to the 'Great Amatola Peak'. There are several explanations of the name: that it was given because there were many wild hogs in the forest; that it was named after a Major Hogg; that the mountain is similar to a Hogsback in England; that it is named after a fairly complex geological concept. But the most generally believed explanation is that the name comes from the fact that the ridge known as the first Hogsback looks like the back of a hog, with the summit rocks resembling the bristles on the animal's back.

Xhosa herdsmen probably grazed their cattle here in the lush summer vegetation many years before the first soldiers arrived in the 1830s under Colonel Michel of the Warwickshire Regiment. The soldiers built a fort on the slopes of Tor Doone, where the earthworks still remain. The colonel's name has become corrupted to Mitchell, which is often applied to the fort as well as to the mountain pass that links the Hogsback to Seymour.

The Forestry Department started a pine nursery in the area in 1887, and two years later began large-scale planting. By then there were already a few permanent residents, and members of the farming community brought their cattle up the mountain to escape the valley's summer heat.

Today the area is reached most easily along the tarred route from Alice via Hogsback Pass (see pages 218-9) or the gravel road from Cathcart via Happy Valley. The gravel road from Seymour across Michel's Pass is very steep and narrow, and should be avoided when towing or when the surface is wet. The original old road from Keiskammahoek over Wolf Ridge is suitable only for four-wheel-drive vehicles.

Walking trails

The Hogsback is renowned for its many attractive walks. Several of the trails to the various beauty spots, such as waterfalls and contour paths, are marked with colour-coded hog emblems. These markers are maintained by one of the local hotels, and a key to their destinations is contained in a booklet sold locally and known as the 'piggy book'. Inquire locally before you set out, as some of the routes that cross private property may have been closed since the booklet was published.

A short walk leads along Redcoat Lane (opposite Oak Avenue), past the village library housed in its tiny rondavel, and along the path Colonel Michel's soldiers followed from Fort Hare to Hogsback last century. Eventually this pretty lane links up with the tarred Hogsback Pass.

The area's waterfalls are among the major attractions. Kettlespout Waterfall is well worth a visit when there has been rain and there is a wind blowing from the valley: this forces the water back, sometimes over the rim of the fall, giving the impression of steam coming from the spout of a

The church of St Patrick-on-the-Hill.

This bird's eye view captures the English feel of the Hogsback settlement.

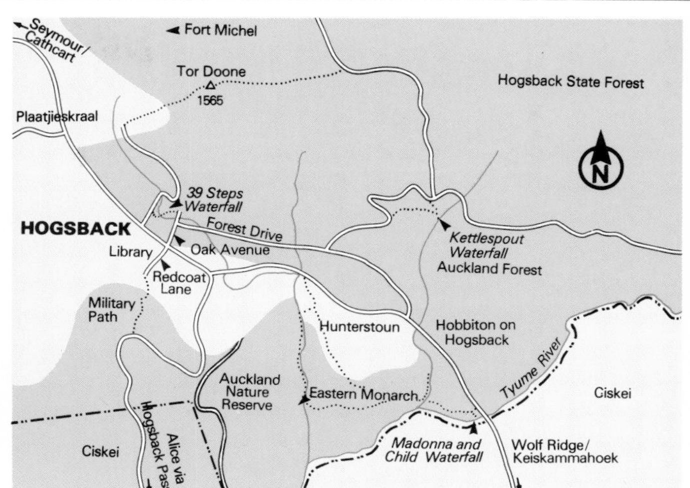

kettle. (A number of other pleasant walks also lead from the parking area near the Kettlespout.)

The Madonna and Child Waterfall, named because of the appearance of the rock formation over which the water falls, is reached off the Wolf Ridge road, along a footpath that also leads eventually to an enormous, ancient yellowwood tree known as the Eastern Monarch.

Scenic drives

A footpath leading off Oak Avenue leads to another waterfall, known as the 39 Steps. Oak Avenue, with its rows of logs placed on both sides of the road, serves as a lofty, open-air, inter-denominational church at Easter and Christmas, and the road forms the start of a circular drive known as Forest Drive.

Another scenic drive leads for 8 km along the Wolf Ridge road to a parking area at King's Nek, from where there are superb views over the Amatole range and the Tyume basin.

To the west of the village main road is the road to the Plaatjieskraal Forest. The left fork after the Forestry Department notice board leads for another 2 km to an area where there are several relatively easy mountain walks with good views.

Mists roll in over the upper Hogsback.

Travelling north on the village main road, 1 km beyond the Plaatjieskraal turn-off, you reach the little church of St Patrick-on-the-Hill on your right. One of the smallest churches in South Africa, it was built as a private chapel in 1935, but now serves as an Anglican-administered, inter-denominational church.

Hiking through the Hogsback forests, you may come across the Knysna loerie or the Cape parrot. In the indigenous sections some of the trees are numbered for easy identification. Enormous yellowwoods spread their crowns above the forest canopy, and are often draped with beard-like fungi or the ubiquitous 'monkey rope'. Other indigenous trees include the wild lemon *(Xymalas monosporo)*, the red-berried forest currant *(Rhus chirindensis)*, white ironwood *(Vepris undulata)*, assegaai-wood *(Curtisia dentata)*, and the cabbage trees *(Cussonia spicata* and *C. paniculata)*.

Lush ground cover

Among the most notable of the exotics are the Californian redwoods *(Sequoia sempervirens)* and holy cypress *(Abies religiosa)*, which is actually a member of the fir group.

Below the trees there are many ferns, mosses, berries and bracken, including the wild strawberry, and flowers abound — particularly agapanthus, arum lilies and the white blood flower, or haemanthus.

The weather patterns of the Hogsback are often described by locals as 'fickle', and it is advisable to take warm as well as rainproof clothing. Late afternoon mists in summer may form quickly, and can be a hazard on higher ground. It is therefore wise to ask local opinion on the weather before setting out on any hike, and to let someone know where you plan to go and when you expect to return ●

Forest Drive — the beginning of a scenic circular drive through the Hogsback, and popular venue for open-air church services at Christmas and Easter.

Past forts and forgotten frontiers to the sweeping heights of the Katberg

From Grahamstown the old Queen's Road leads to Fort Beaufort, and a magnificent scenic drive over the Katberg range. We return through the tranquil beauty of the Tyume Valley, and take the military road — still dotted with stone forts that once guarded a troubled frontier. Roughly half the route is on tar, the rest is on gravel.

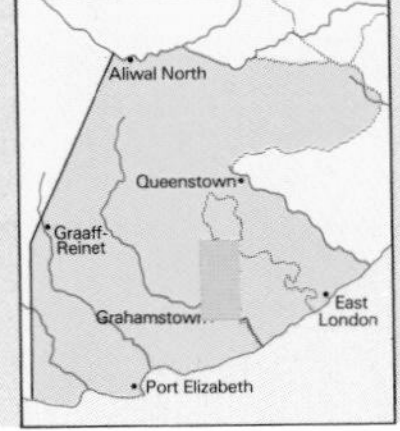

Grahamstown
Ecca Pass
Fort Beaufort
Katberg Pass
Seymour
Alice
300 – 320 km

LEAVE GRAHAMSTOWN ON the N2, following the signs for East London/King William's Town. Just outside the town you pass the tree-crowned hill known as Makana's Kop, with a monument at its foot (see opposite). 5,5 km outside town turn left onto the R67 for Fort Beaufort, noting your kms.

9,1 km later you pass a road on your right to Committee's Drift. A few metres beyond this on your left is a large parking area and a monument to Andrew Geddes Bain, who built the Ecca Pass, which you soon begin to descend (see below).

After 20,9 km on the R67 you pass on your right the turn-off to the Andries Vosloo Kudu Reserve. Within 1,5 km from here you reach Fort Brown on your right. The fort is now part of a South African Police post, and may be visited with the permission of the policeman on gate duty.

Continue on the R67, which immediately crosses the Great Fish River — note your kms at the start of the bridge. After 49,5 km turn right onto the R63 for Fort Beaufort. 600 m later turn right again at the T-junction onto the R63/67, which brings you to the town of Fort Beaufort (see pages 218-9).

Fort Beaufort to Katberg Pass

Leave Fort Beaufort on the R67 (signposted Seymour/Queenstown), and note your kms as you pass the R63 on which you entered (signposted for Adelaide/Grahamstown). After 20,2 km you pass the Toll Hotel on your right — formerly the site of the tollhouse known as Tidbury's Toll. 7,5 km later turn left onto gravel for Katberg and Balfour. You reach a T-junction almost immediately — turn right here (R351).

The road crosses one single-lane bridge, and passes a turn-off on your left to Post Retief. Continue straight for Katberg Pass at the intersection at a railway level crossing. 2,5 km later go left at the fork, and after a further 4,1 km go right at another fork.

After 800 m you pass a road on your left to the Katberg Hotel (which serves lunch), and reach the offices of the Department of Forestry on your right after a further 1,1 km — enquiries can be made here about the drives and walks through the local forests.

After a further 1 km go right at the fork for the road over the Katberg Pass (the road on the left is the scenic Forest Drive). Where the road levels at the top of the pass there are places on the side of the road where you can picnic, but no fires are permitted.

Katberg Pass to Alice

Turn back roughly 10 km from the fork, where a road on your left leads to Tarkastad. Return down Katberg Pass, and note your kms as you pass the Forestry Station on your left. After 8,4 km you reach the railway level crossing — turn left at the intersection immediately afterwards.

Roughly 4 km later turn right at the T-junction with another gravel road. Turn left onto the tarred R67 at the T-junction some 50 m later. The R67 passes a turn-off to the Kat River Dam. 3,2 km after this turn right into Seymour.

At the stop street in Seymour (with the old town hall on your left) turn right towards Alice and Hogsback. The tar surface gives way to gravel after 400 m. Note your kms at the start of the bridge immediately afterwards.

You cross a number of cattle grids. After 22,1 km turn right at the T-junction onto the tarred R345 in the Tyume Valley. 14,6 km later turn right again at the T-junction onto the R63, which leads into Alice.

Alice to Grahamstown

After passing Fort Hare on your right, veer left at the fork at the entrance to Alice. Immediately after passing the railway station on your left, turn left over the level crossing. At the T-junction in front of the hospital, turn right onto the R345, noting your kms. The tar gives way to gravel after 400 m.

Keep straight at the intersection after 14,9 km (where a small road leads to the right and a fork to the left leads to Junction). You pass a number of turn-offs to your right and left. 40,1 km from the hospital in Alice turn right.

After a further 15,5 km you cross the Great Fish River by a narrow bridge. On your left just after the bridge is a police post which incorporates parts of the old Committee's Drift fortifications. Across the road a few hundred metres later is the former Committee's Drift Hotel, now a private residence, and an 1888 church that was virtually destroyed by a tornado in 1972.

600 m after you pass the road leading to the church, turn left. After a further 20 km you reach a complex of buildings on your left at Trompetter's Drift.

Roughly 2 km later, at the T-junction, turn right onto the N2 for Grahamstown. (A gravel road on your left after 6,7 km on the N2 leads to the remains of the Fraser's Camp signal tower and fort — turn right at the T-junction to reach the stone building on your right after 2,5 km from the tarred road.) ●

Grahamstown Publicity Association 63 High Street, Grahamstown 6140 Tel. (0461) 23241
SA Tourism Board 310 Mutual Building, Mutual Arcade, 64 Main Street, Port Elizabeth 6001 Tel. (041) 27761

A gracious old bandstand in the grounds of Fort Beaufort's military museum.

An artist's impression of the 'Blinkwater Monster' and the skull Bain found.

THE BLINKWATER MONSTER'
Andrew Geddes Bain is honoured by a cairn on the heights of the Ecca Pass on the Queen's Road which he built from Grahamstown to Fort Beaufort from 1837 to 1845. While building the road Bain developed an interest in geology. In the course of blasting he worked out the stratigraphy of the Karoo System. Bain discovered the type skull of the fossil reptile group known as the dicynodonts, and also 'the skull of a huge animal with 56 fluted and serrated teeth'. This creature, one of the earliest animals known to have adopted an upright stance, he named the Blinkwater Monster. Bain achieved instant renown in the scientific world for his collection.

The gentle landscape of the Katberg stretches to a horizon of blue mountains.

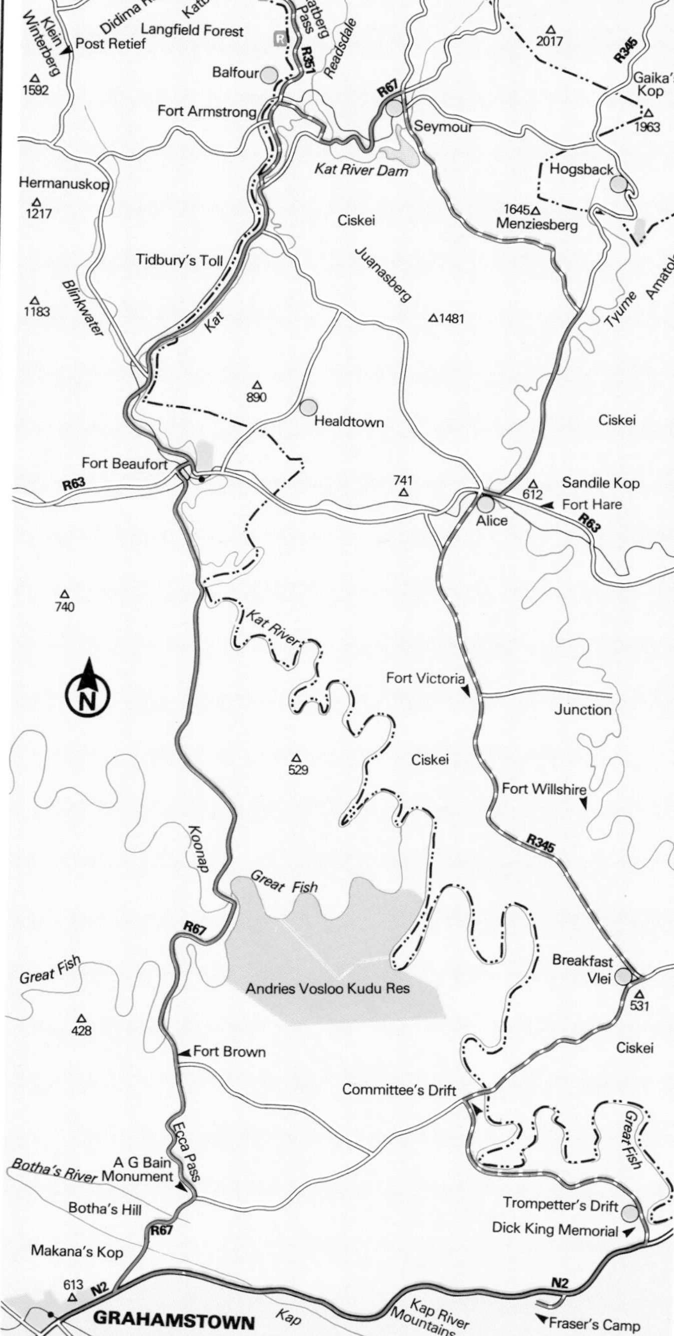

THE 'CAT MOUNTAIN'

The forests and hills of the Katberg (cat mountain) make this a popular holiday area for hikers and riders. The range is crossed by the Katberg Pass, a good gravel road which offers spectacular views.

Seymour and the Kat River Valley are distinguished in the history of the development of Afrikaans — Kaatje Kekkelbek, the character created by Andrew G Bain and John Rex in their humorous song, came from 'Katrivier'; and one of the earliest published works in Afrikaans, the *'Zamenspraak tusschen Klaas Waarzegger en Jan Twyfelaar...'* was written by a Seymour magistrate, Louis Henri Meurant.

St Bartholomew's Church in Alice.

ALICE

Governor Sir Harry Smith named this town to honour his sister, although publicly he diplomatically claimed to have chosen the name in honour of one of Queen Victoria's daughters.

Alice started as a mission station of the Glasgow Mission Society in 1824. Today it is an important educational centre, home to Lovedale College and the University of Fort Hare. East of the town is Sandile Kop, named after the famous Xhosa chief, and now surmounted by a memorial to the Reverend James Stewart, one of the early missionaries.

A Roman Catholic mission church shelters in a cultivated valley near Balfour.

MAKANA'S KOP

In the Battle of Grahamstown in 1819 about 10 000 Xhosa warriors under Makana poured down this hillside towards the small post defended — along the line of the present York Street — by some 30 civilians and 300 soldiers under Major 'Tiger Tom' Willshire. In spite of the disparity in numbers, the firearms of the defenders proved decisive, and the attackers were driven off.

Shocked by the defeat, Makana later surrendered rather than subject his followers to the risk of further disaster. Makana is often referred to as 'Lynx', a corruption of the Dutch word 'Linksch' (left) by which he was known because of his left-handedness.

TROMPETTER'S DRIFT

This drift, one of the oldest crossing places along the Great Fish River, was named not for some 'trumpeter' but after a Khoikhoi freebooter, Hans Trompetter. The Cape Governor, Lord Charles Somerset, established a fortified post here in 1817 as part of his system of frontier defence. During the war of 1835 a large pont was established here under an armed guard to ensure that supplies could reach Grahamstown, but a Xhosa attack captured the entire position.

After this war a more substantial fort was built, and this was the scene of fierce fighting in 1846. Today the watch tower and a few low walls are all that remain of the outpost.

Meander across gentle hills to the sparkling sands of the Settler coast

South of Grahamstown our route winds down to wide, sandy beaches and the old harbour of Port Alfred — now an attractive pleasure resort. Then we turn inland again, across hills dotted with Settler buildings that have grown old in a green land where time seems to stand still. More than half the route is tarred, the rest is good gravel.

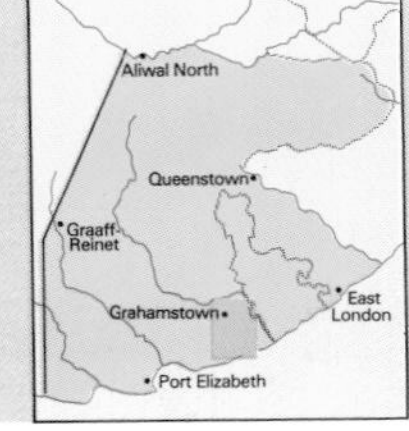

Grahamstown
Salem
Alexandria
Bushman's River Mouth
Port Alfred
Bathurst
180 — 200 km

DRIVE UP GRAHAMSTOWN'S Lucas Avenue to the 1820 Settlers National Monument on Gunfire Hill (see pages 226-7 for street map), which offers an excellent view over the town and surrounding countryside. Continue past the monument to the T-junction with the N2, and turn right, noting your kms.

The road soon begins a gradual descent through Howison's Poort. After 10,2 km turn left onto the R343 for Alexandria, Kenton on Sea, Thomas Baines Nature Reserve and Salem — and note your kms. (1,8 km later you pass a gravel road on your left to the nature reserve and Settlers Dam.) After 11,9 km on the R343 turn left into Salem to see the old Settler churches that still form the heart of the village.

Salem to Bushman's River
Return to the R343, and turn left for Alexandria. After a few hundred metres the road surface changes to gravel for roughly 15 km. Another 14,5 km brings you to Alexandria.

At the stop street after the shops, turn left into Voortrekker Street. Within 200 m turn right into Karl Landman Street, noting your kms — this becomes the road to Boknes and changes to gravel after a few hundred metres. After 17,3 km on this road turn right for Cannon Rocks, then turn left 1,8 km later to reach a parking area on a wide, secluded beach.

Return to the road from which you turned to Cannon Rocks, and turn right. After 700 m, now on tar, turn left for Boesmansriviermond (Bushman's River mouth). You pass a rough road on your right to Diaz Cross. 1,7 km later turn right at the T-junction onto the tarred R72 for Port Alfred. After a further 4,1 km turn right on to a road signposted 'Boesmansriviermond'. This brings you to a parking area at the mouth of the river. (Both river and beach are safe for bathing. The municipal camping site has braai sites, water, toilets.)

Bushman's River to Port Alfred
Return to the intersection with the R72, and turn right for Port Alfred. You pass turn-offs on your right to Kenton on Sea and Kasouga, and reach Port Alfred after 23,5 km. Keep straight where the road forks in the centre of town (the road on the left crosses the old Putt Bridge

The simple, puritan lines of the historic Methodist Church in Salem.

RICHARD GUSH OF SALEM
The name Salem means peace, yet the village of this name saw much strife during its early years. The little settlement, founded by a party of 1820 Settlers under Hezekiah Sephton, was besieged by Xhosa warriors in the war of 1834. One of those whose wife and children had found precarious refuge in the church was Richard Gush, a Quaker carpenter sternly opposed to the shedding of blood. He offered to go out of the stockade and reason with the warriors, despite the risks.

Unarmed, he strode out, followed at some distance by his interpreter, Field Cornet Barend Woest. Asked why they were attacking the settlement, the surprised Xhosa could say only that they were hungry. Gush returned to the village for loaves of bread as well as tobacco, and distributed them among the warriors who, true to their word, passed on without attacking Salem.

The lagoon at the Bushman's River mouth is a paradise for holiday-makers.

Settlers' Monument, Grahamstown.

towards Grahamstown).

Turn right just before the road crosses the concrete arch bridge, then turn left immediately into Beach Road. This road runs along the west bank of the Kowie River. There is a parking area at the beach, and another road leads off to the right past idyllic bathing and fishing beaches. (A number of establishments in the town provide lunch, and the municipal camping grounds on the riverbank offer braai and picnic sites.)

Port Alfred to Bathurst

Leave Port Alfred by crossing the Putt Bridge over the Kowie River. Turn left into Wharf Road, and follow this road out of town across gently rolling countryside to reach Bathurst.

At the intersection opposite Bathurst's Pig and Whistle Hotel turn left onto gravel for Bradshaw's Mill. Turn right after 400m to reach the mill after a further 900m.

Driving back from the mill, turn right at the first T-junction, and follow this road for 4km to an attractive viewsite above a classic horseshoe bend in the Kowie River.

Return to the Pig and Whistle intersection and drive uphill on the tar road. Follow the sign to your left along a gravel road for 400m to reach St John's Church on your right.

Turn around, return to the tar road and cross it, onto a 2,4km tar road that leads to the 1820 Settlers Toposcope.

Return to the tarred road (R67) and turn right, noting your kms. 3,7km later turn right towards Trappe's Valley and Clumber. Soon afterwards you pass a turn-off on your left to Clumber. 6,5km after this, turn left for 'Kaffir Drift', noting your kms. After 2,7km turn right at the crossroads. 100m along this road on your left are the substantial remains of Cawood's Post, one of the original fortified farmhouses built by the Settlers. Turn around, and continue straight across the crossroads.

The road crosses the railway line four times. After 24,7km turn right at the T-junction onto the tarred R67 for Grahamstown ●

Grahamstown Publicity Association 63 High St, Grahamstown 6140 Tel. (0461) 23241
SA Tourism Board 310 Mutual Bldg, Mutual Arcade, 64 Main St, Port Elizabeth 6001 Tel. (041) 27761

The site of the toposcope atop Thornridge.

1820 SETTLERS TOPOSCOPE

In 1820 Colonel Jacob Cuyler chose Thornridge near Bathurst — with its wide views over the surrounding coastal countryside — as a base from which to direct the newly arrived Settlers to their alloted farms. In 1968 a toposcope was erected here showing where the Settlers went.

Bathurst was intended to be the administrative centre of the new Settler Country, but this position was soon usurped by Grahamstown.

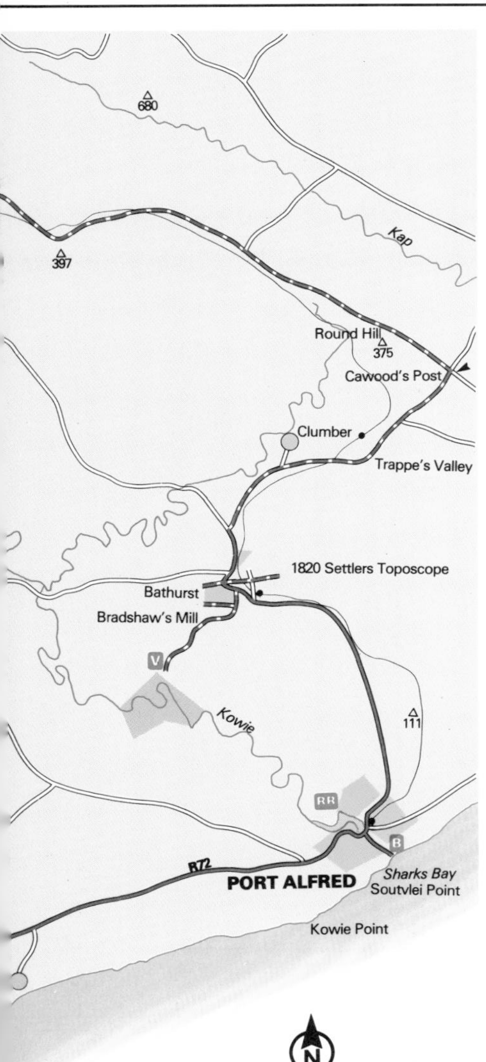

The sturdy little St John's Church in Bathurst.

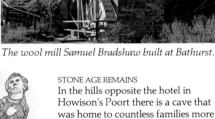

The wool mill Samuel Bradshaw built at Bathurst.

ST JOHN'S CHURCH, BATHURST

This little church, started in 1832, three times did duty as a shelter for Settlers during strife on the frontier — the first time even before the building was completed. St John's was opened for services in 1838, and during the War of the Axe (1846-7) it again served as a shelter, with as many as 300 people sleeping in the church at night. It sheltered the Settlers again, for the last time, during the war of 1850-3.

Kowie Museum figurehead.

STONE AGE REMAINS

In the hills opposite the hotel in Howison's Poort there is a cave that was home to countless families more than 100 000 years ago, during the period known in South Africa as the Middle Stone Age.

Archeologists have found in the cave a layer some 30cm deep containing the bones of small animals that had formed the meals of early man — as well as a new phase of stone-implement culture.

Wharf Street in Port Alfred bustles with holiday-makers.

'THE KOWIE'

The delightful holiday resort of Port Alfred lies at the mouth of the Kowie River, almost exactly midway between Port Elizabeth and East London. It was established as Port Kowie soon after the arrival of the 1820 Settlers, later renamed Port Frances, and given its present name after the 1860 visit of Queen Victoria's son, Prince Alfred. Faced with all these choices, the locals refer to the town, as well as the river, simply as 'the Kowie'.

Efforts to turn the Kowie into a profitable port were frustrated by the recurring problem of silting, although for 20 years last century as many as 100 ships used the port annually.

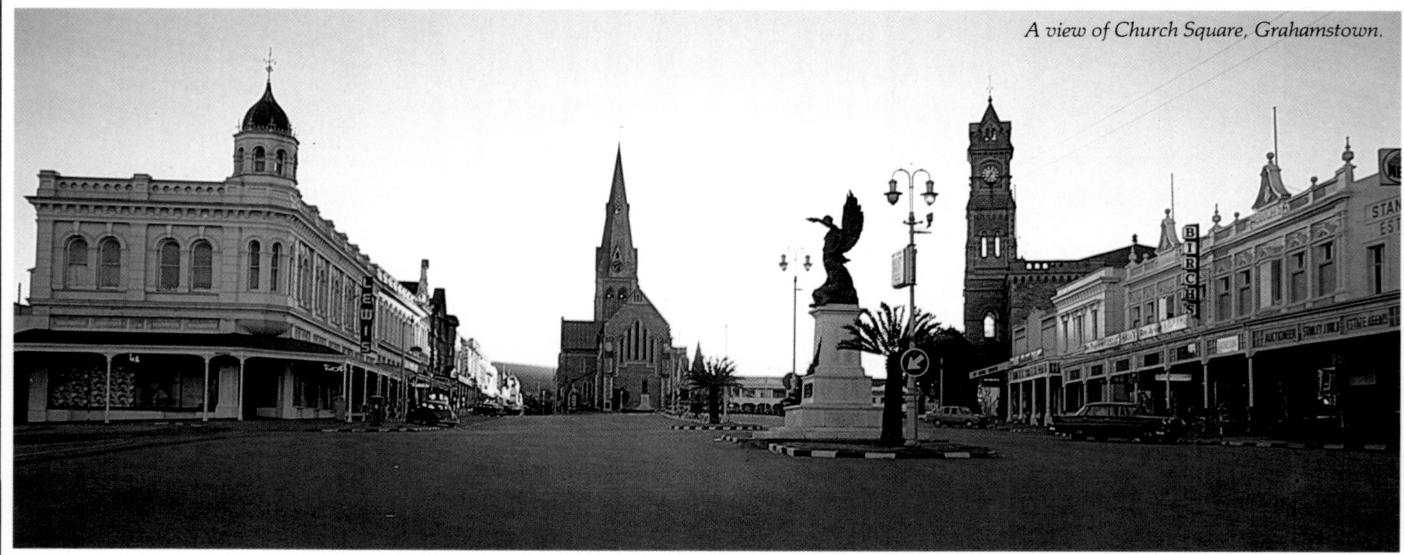

A view of Church Square, Grahamstown.

A rough outpost that became 'The City of the Saints'

ONE DAY IN 1812 a weary soldier dismounted from his horse near an abandoned farmhouse on the war-ravaged frontier. He hung his sword on the branch of a thorn tree, and looked around. This, he decided, was where he would establish a fortified post. The soldier was Colonel John Graham, and his fortified post was to grow to become Grahamstown, capital city of 1820 Settler country and home to many notable characters in the history of South Africa.

In gratitude for their survival in a strange land, many religious denominations built churches in the little town — and a total of close to 40 places of worship gave the place one of its nicknames: 'The City of the Saints'. In spite of the passage of years, Grahamstown still retains the dignity of the devotion that raised it, with its soaring stone spires and other historic 19th century buildings.

Retief's legacy

Our walking tour of historic Grahamstown begins at the south-western end of High Street, facing the *Drostdy Gateway* **(1)** that leads to the campus of Rhodes University. The gateway was designed by Major Charles Jasper Selwyn of the Royal Engineers, and was completed by men of his regiment in 1842. Parts of the original Drostdy (magistrate's residence) — which no longer stands — were built by the Voortrekker leader Piet Retief, who worked as a building contractor in Grahamstown.

Walk from the gateway along High Street. On the corner of Somerset and High streets is a double-storeyed home **(2)** that belonged to Andries Stockenström, who became Lieutenant-Governor of the Eastern Province.

On your right, beyond number 120, a single-storeyed stone house is *'The Yellow House'* **(3)**, dating from about 1814 and believed to be Grahamstown's oldest building. Originally built as the town jail, it soon became too small for this purpose, and was later used as a public library and meeting hall. The north wall of The Yellow House served as the line along which the new town's main thoroughfare, High Street, was laid out. A bas-relief now set into this wall depicts the 1820 Settlers arriving at Algoa Bay.

Continue along High Street. On your right, next to an imposing double-storeyed stone building, is the distinctly 'colonial' *Albany Club* **(4)**. Beyond this is *Bannerman House* **(5)**, which houses the South African Library for the Blind, founded in 1919. From here you can also view the Supreme Court building with its wooden turret.

Shortly before reaching the cathedral you come to a tall memorial marking the position of a tree under which Colonel John Graham met Captain Andries Stockenstrom in 1812 to discuss the establishment of the new outpost.

The cathedral

Turn left into Hill Street, and cross from here to the Anglican *Cathedral of St Michael and St George* **(6)**. The original church, simply St George's, was started in 1824 on the site of De Rietfontein, the farmhouse that had served as Colonel Graham's headquarters. When Grahamstown became the seat of a bishop in 1853, the church was elevated to the status of a cathedral and the building was enlarged considerably.

The cathedral contains many monuments and memorial tablets. Among them is a little-known 'horse memorial' recalling the campaign of the 9th SA Mounted Regiment in East Africa during World War I. The inscription from the troopers reads 'with thanksgiving for the help of their patient comrades'.

Walk away from the cathedral along the north side of Church Square — you will see on your left next to the Publicity Association Building a daintily designed building erected by an insurance company in 1901 **(7)**. The plasterwork is fes-

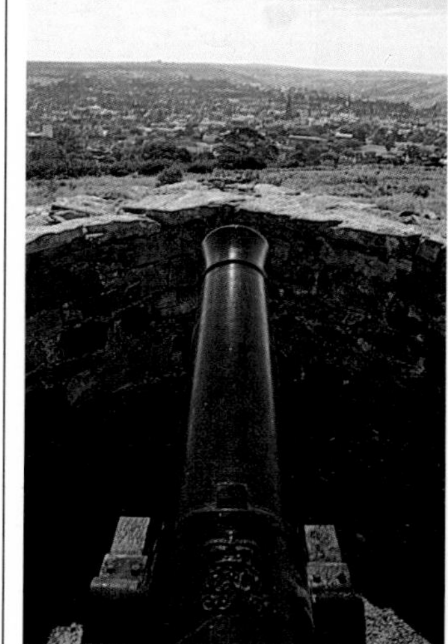
Fort Selwyn, above the city's spires.

The Commemoration Church, started 25 years after the Settlers' arrival.

The building in Huntly Street used as a school for more than a century.

Rhodes University lies behind the historic gates that once led to the Drostdy.

The Old Provost in Grahamstown.

tooned with flowers and faces, and the building has a soaring eagle on its roof, and an ornate tower.

A little further along is the stone *City Hall* **(8)**. Its impressive clock tower originally stood on its own when it was unveiled in 1870 to honour the Settlers, and the halls and Chambers were added later. The inaugural meeting of the National Press Union of South Africa — an organisation of newspaper proprietors — was held here in 1882.

If you look across Church Square from the City Hall, you will see a row of Victorian commercial facades **(9)**, which have been preserved in a group as a national monument.

Where Parliament assembled

Beyond the City Hall on your left, opposite Bathurst Street, is the *Commemoration Methodist Church* **(10)**, the foundation of which was laid in 1845. In the centre of the Bathurst Street intersection is a large Anglo-Boer War monument.

Further along High Street, on your right almost opposite Cawood Street, is *Shaw Hall* **(11)**, where Members of the Cape Parliament assembled before marching to the old military hospital for their 1864 session. This was the only time Parliament met outside Cape Town — a move intended to placate 'separatists' who campaigned for a separate administration for the eastern Cape Province.

Return to Bathurst Street and turn left. On your left is the *Observatory Museum* **(12)** — which has a small entry fee. This was the home of jeweller and watchmaker Henry Galpin, who made the first formal identification of a South African diamond here. Chief attraction amongst the fascinating exhibits is the camera obscura Galpin built into the roof, and which has been fully restored.

Continue along Bathurst Street, and pass the *Baptist Church* **(13)** of 1840 on your left. Turn left into Beaufort Street, and then turn right into West Street. On your right is the *Cathcart Arms Hotel* **(14)**, which is on a site that has been occupied by a hotel since the 1820s.

At the end of West Street, facing you on Market Street, is *Merriman House* **(15)**, the home of a former bishop of Grahamstown where the ill-fated General Gordon of Khartoum spent some nights. Turn right into Market Street. On your left is the *Church of St Bartholomew* **(16)**, built in 1860. Turn right into Bartholomew Street. On your left you pass *Chapel House* **(17)**, built in 1823 as the first Baptist chapel in South Africa.

At the intersection with Cross Street walk for a short distance to your right to look at the early Settler houses in this area — known as Artificers' Square. Turn around, walk along Cross Street to Hill Street, and turn right.

On your left is the *Presbyterian Trinity Church* **(18)** of 1842, and on your right is the double-storeyed old stone building that now serves as the *First City Regiment's headquarters* **(19)**, built in about 1860. Originally known as Albany Hall, this building later became the Drill Hall, and was the venue for the Settlers Jubilee Ball of 1870.

Continue up Hill Street. On your right, on the corner of Dundas Street, is the *Synagogue Hall* **(20)**. On your left is the stone battlemented *St Patrick's (Roman Catholic) Church* **(21)**, in which settler women and children sheltered during the war of 1846. Just beyond it, also on the left, is the *Public Library* **(22)**, in a mid-19th century building that once housed a steam mill.

Turn around, walk back downhill to Huntly Street, and turn right. On your left you pass the old stone building known as the *Huntly Street School* **(23)**, built in 1844 as a Sunday school for St George's Church.

Turn right into Somerset Street, then turn left into Lucas Avenue between the *1820 Settlers Museum* **(24)** and the *Albany Museum* **(25)** (a small entry fee admits you to both).

About 200 m along Lucas Avenue you reach the *Old Provost Building* **(26)** on your left. Built as a military prison in 1838, it had as its first inmates mutineers of the Cape Corps, who had shot and killed Ensign Crowe at Fraser's Camp. They were shot and buried nearby in unmarked graves in what is now the 1820 Wildflower Reserve.

Opposite the reserve, in the grounds of the university, is the stone building of the *old military hospital* **(27)** where the working sessions of Parliament took place during the heady three months of its sojourn in Grahamstown in 1864.

Our walk ends at the Wildflower Reserve. If time permits, a short drive along Lucas Street, which becomes Fort Selwyn Drive, will bring you to Fort Selwyn and the 1820 Settlers National Monument on Gunfire Hill. From the historic Fort Selwyn there is a magnificent view down over the steeples of the Settler City ●

The striking Observatory Museum.

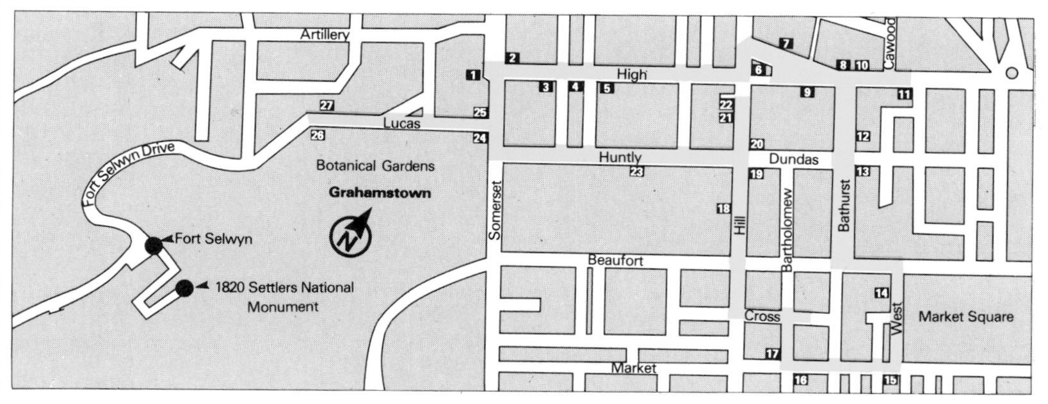

An unspoilt wilderness where the dry Karoo plains meet the mountains of the Eastern Cape.

A remote mountain sanctuary for one of the world's rarest animals

THE COOL, HIGH plateaux of the Mountain Zebra National Park, and the rugged Bankberg, rise abruptly and unexpectedly out of the surrounding Karoo landscape. The 6536 ha park is in many ways an area of striking contrasts. Stretches of grey Karoo scrub are splashed with the brilliant blue of the Karoo tulp. Four-metre-long earthworms move slowly through the soil as fleet-footed buck streak over the veld above. Soaring summer temperatures give way to snow-capped peaks in winter.

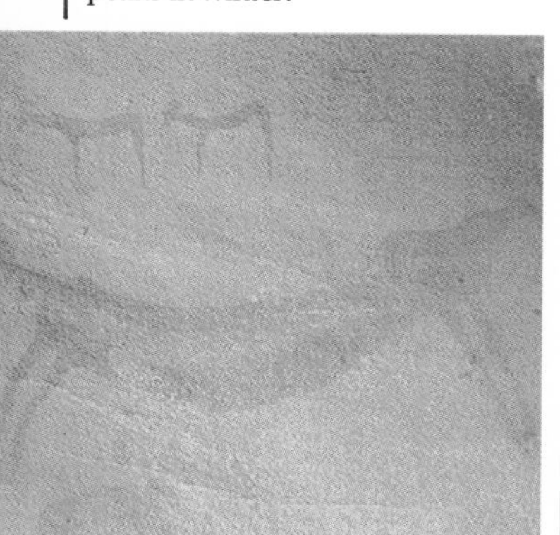

The San paintings are easily reached.

The park lies a short distance south-west of Cradock, and in addition to bracing mountain air, it offers a chance to view one of the rarest animals in the world: the once threatened Cape Mountain Zebra (*Equus zebra zebra*).

These distinctive animals, an easy target for hunters, narrowly escaped extinction in the first decades of this century. They were at one stage dismissed by a cabinet minister as merely 'donkeys in football jerseys', and it took a concerted fight by conservationists before the zebra were granted the safety of a park — established on the farm Babylons Toren in 1937. There are now over 200 zebra in the park, roughly the maximum population that the area can support, and a number of 'surplus' animals have been moved to the Karoo National Park outside Beaufort West and the Karoo Nature Reserve at Graaff-Reinet.

Mountain zebra
Equus zebra zebra.

Variety of scenery and wildlife

The mountain zebra is easily distinguishable from other zebra species by its conspicuous dewlap, white belly, orange-brown muzzle, and sharply-defined stripes that cover the entire leg down to the hoof. At about 1,25 m it is also the smallest of the zebra family.

The park created to protect these animals offers fine scenery and superb game-viewing for both the walker and the motorist. Deep ravines cut into the mountains — like the Grootkloof, which is clearly visible from the rest camp.

The park lies in a transition zone between the Karoo shrublands and the better watered grasslands to the east, and the vegetation is accordingly varied — including renosterbos, sweet thorn, Cape beech, wild olive, white stinkwood, mountain cabbage tree, Cape mistletoe, and the interestingly named bastard shepherd's tree.

The sweet grass covering the Rooiplaat plateau attracts the great majority of the grazing animals that live in the park and this is a particularly good game-viewing area. The plateau is easily reached by taking a steep but well-maintained gravel road, which leads from the rest-camp and completes a 14,5 km circuit of the plateau summit. From the top there are clear views in all directions as far as the eye can see.

It is here that the visitor is most likely to see the zebra, as well as eland, red hartebeest, kudu, black wildebeest and blesbok. Also found here are the smaller springbok, klipspringer, duiker, steenbok, mountain reedbuck, and the ubiquitous sun-loving dassie (rock hyrax). The mountain reedbuck and the dassies form much of the diet of the park's largest predator, the caracal (seldom seen by visitors because it is essentially a night prowler).

Seemingly lost in the wide African landscape, the administrative headquarters of the Mountain Zebra National Park and two important residents of the park.

The dassies are also preyed upon by the magnificent black eagles that nest in the park, and which are just one of the 200 bird species that will interest the birdwatcher. Also to be seen are martial eagles, tawny eagles, and the migratory booted eagle — which flies in from Angola every August and stays until April. Visitors can obtain from the reception office a checklist of all the birds in the park. The list includes the blue crane, cardinal woodpecker, Cape eagle owl, malachite kingfisher, the African hoopoe and the hamerkop.

The rest-camp in the park is modern and well-maintained. Its facilities include 20 fully equipped 2-bedroom cottages, a camping and caravan park with full ablution facilities, a swimming pool, petrol pumps, a restaurant, and a shop where basic foodstuffs, film and souvenirs may be bought. One of the original farmhouses in the area, meticulously restored, is also available for hire.

Hikes, drives and San paintings

From the rest-camp a number of short walks lead into the mountains, and the popular three-day Mountain Zebra Trail also starts here. This is a 31,5 km hike that climbs the slopes of the Grootkloof, descends into the valley formed by the Fonteinkloof stream, then climbs again to the high summit of the Bankberg — before returning to the camp. Two picturesque stone huts with fireplaces and water provide hikers with overnight accommodation.

For those who prefer to view nature from the comfort of a car, there are 37 km of good gravel roads, and two particularly attractive drives are recommended. The first leads to the top of the Rooiplaat plateau, as previously described, and the second leads from the crest of the plateau along the Wilgerboom River, eventually arriving back at the rest-camp. There are three well-marked picnic sites along this drive, each equipped with wooden tables and benches.

Although the modern rest-camp and the roads seem to imply that man is a recent arrival in the area, 30 archeological sites in the park prove the contrary. Primitive artefacts have been found, dating back to the Upper Pleistocene (38 000 to 10 000 years ago), and in a cave on the Rooiplaat plateau visitors can see San paintings — featuring antelope, baboons, and what appears to be a leopard. The cave containing the paintings is easily reached. Follow the road over the crest of the plateau, then watch carefully for the stylised sign on your left. The paintings are just a short walk from the road.

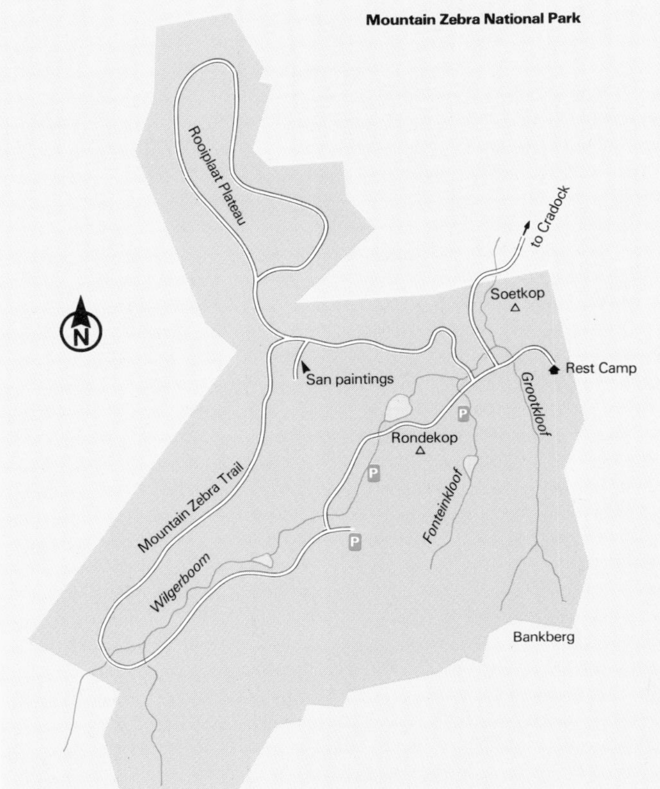

How to get there

The route to the Mountain Zebra National Park is clearly signposted from Cradock. You drive roughly 5 km out of town along the R32 towards Middelburg, then you turn onto the R61 towards Graaff-Reinet. After 7 km on the R61 you turn left onto the 16 km access road into the park.

A small entry fee is payable when you reach the gate. The park is open to day-visitors in the summer (1st October to 30th April) from 07h00 to 18h00, and in the winter (1st May to 30th September) from 08h00 to 18h00.

To book accommodation in the park, contact the National Parks Board at either of the following addresses: National Parks Board Reservations Office, Picbel Arcade, Strand Street, Cape Town 8001 Tel. (021) 4195365; or The Chief Director, National Parks Board, P.O. Box 787, Pretoria 0001 Tel. (012) 441191. Staff in the park itself can only accept 'last minute' bookings a day or two in advance of arrival ●

Among the world's rarest animals.

Adventure into Elephant country from the shores of St Francis Bay

In the course of this drive we savour a variety of Eastern Cape experiences — a barefoot walk on the golden sands of St Francis Bay; a visit to a historic Uitenhage manor house; a tour through the scented Sundays River Valley, and finally an afternoon among the elephants in the Addo Park. Over four fifths of the route is tarred.

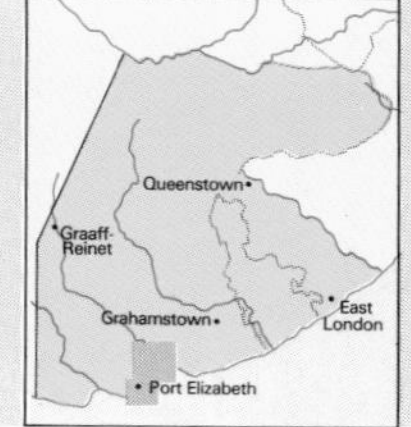

Port Elizabeth
Maitland Mouth
Uitenhage
Sundays Valley
Suurberg Pass
Addo Elephant Park
300 — 320 km

LEAVE PORT ELIZABETH on the N2, heading towards Cape Town. Take the exit left for 'R102/Greenbushes/Seaview', and at the end of the off-ramp turn left for Seaview, noting your kms. After 3,3 km you come to a fork — take the road leading left. You now pass several side-roads, and eventually the road on which you are travelling sweeps down towards the sea, leading through The Island Forest Reserve, then passing the Seaview Game Park.

At the bottom of the hill, turn right, following the sign to 'Maitland Mouth/Beachview'. The road winds along the rocky shore, begins to climb after passing Beachview Caravan Park, then descends to Maitland River Mouth. Turn left off the main road to reach a small parking area. This is a perfect place for a walk along the beach, but aim to leave by 09h30.

Maitland Mouth to Uitenhage

Continue on the tarred road, passing the Maitland Mines Nature Reserve on your left. The road climbs through a valley blanketed with dense indigenous forest, and eventually reaches a T-junction. Turn left here, noting your kms. After 3 km, turn left towards Van Staden's Mouth. After a further 3,6 km you come to crossroads — continue straight, following the sign to 'Old Cape Road', and note your kms.

After 1,8 km the road crosses over the N2, and 1,4 km later you cross an unfenced railway line. Immediately after this, turn right at the T-junction onto the R102 (the Old Cape Road). Almost 3 km later, where the R102 widens, turn left towards Rocklands, noting your kms. After 5,8 km you come to an oblique junction — turn right here for Uitenhage, noting your kms.

After 4,5 km there are views to your left over the Swartkops River Valley, and about 8,5 km later you cross the Swartkops River and enter Uitenhage (see below). Continue straight ahead on Cuyler Street until you come to Caledon Street (second set of traffic lights). Turn right into Caledon Street, following the sign to Port Elizabeth. Continue on Caledon Street, which changes its name to Union Street, then becomes the R333. Note your kms as you pass under the R75 on the outskirts of the town, and 2 km later turn right, following the sign to 'Uitenhage Historical Museum'. This short gravel road leads into the grounds of the Cuyler Manor. The manor house is open weekdays 10h00-13h00, 14h00-17h00, but may be closed at weekends and on public holidays.

Uitenhage to Kirkwood

Return to the R333 and turn left, to retrace your route for roughly 2 km. Immediately after passing under the R75, turn left to drive onto the R75, following the sign to Graaff-Reinet. A little over 3 km later you pass under the R334 — note your kms here. Stay on the R75 for a further 29,6 km, then turn right, following the sign to Kirkwood. The road now leads through dense fenced-in bush, and after 12 km you reach a T-junction. Turn left for Kirkwood, and almost immediately you cross the Sundays River (see opposite).

The road leads past citrus groves and rose plantations, and about 2 km after crossing the river you enter Kirkwood. Kirkwood's main street is lined with colourful bougainvillea and golden shower (in full bloom during May-June), and several establishments offer lunch.

Kirkwood to Addo

Retrace your route out of Kirkwood and re-cross the Sundays River — then continue on this road (R336), noting your kms as you pass on your right the road on which you arrived earlier. After roughly 16 km you enter the village of Summerville, and about 700 m later you pass on your left a quaint country church surrounded by trees. After a further 1,9 km you cross the Sundays River again — note your kms at the far end of the bridge.

After 700 m you cross the railway line. Turn left immediately after this towards Slagboom

The Maitland River broadens into a lagoon before emptying into the Indian Ocean.

An Addo elephant prepares to drink. Only the bulls have tusks.

A SANCTUARY FOR THE ADDO ELEPHANT

There are over 100 elephants in the 8 596 hectares of evergreen bush that form the Addo Elephant National Park, and visitors are allowed to drive through the park, following a route map issued at the gate. (Ask at the petrol pumps for the waterholes at which elephants have been seen earlier in the day.)

The Addo elephants are reddish in colour, smaller than equatorial elephants, and they have shorter tusks. In the past they had a fearsome reputation for raiding farms, and this led to their being hunted almost to extinction. The park was proclaimed in 1931 to save the few that remained.

Although the elephants are the main attraction, the park is also home to eland, bushbuck, kudu, steenbok, duiker, grey rhebok, oribi, grysbok, red hartebeest, buffalo and bushpig — and there are some rarely-seen black rhino. For bird watchers, some 170 species have been recorded, and there is an observation point at a dam near the entrance.

Accommodation is available in the park in self-contained thatched huts with electricity. There are also caravan and camping sites, with ablution blocks and laundry facilities. All have braai areas. There is a restaurant in the park, and a shop that sells curios and refreshments.

UITENHAGE

Set in the Swartkops River Valley at the foot of the Great Winterhoek Mountains, Uitenhage is an industrial town with a difference. Its streets are lined with jacarandas and oaks, and it is famed for its beautiful gardens.

4 km from the town's centre is the Cuyler Manor, the restored homestead of Jacob Glen Cuyler, a British officer of Dutch descent who made Uitenhage his headquarters during the frontier wars. There is a Railway Museum in Market Street.

and Tregaron. 2,5 km later you cross a small bridge and the road surface changes to gravel. Ignore the road to your right signposted 'Cemetery', and continue on the gravel for a further 1,3 km until a sign reading 'Look Out' indicates a track to your left. Park at the end of this track and walk through the white gates. Sir Percy Fitzpatrick and members of his family are buried here (see below) and there is a fine view from here over the fertile valley.

Retrace your route to the R336 and turn left. You now pass through the citrus and rose-growing centre of Sunland. A few kilometres later you cross the Coerney River, then you pass through the small settlement of Selborne. After this, as the road sweeps downhill, there are good views to your right over the valley, with farmhouses among the orange groves.

About 2 km after crossing the Coerney River you pass through the settlement of Hermitage. When you reach the T-junction soon after this, turn left onto the R335 towards the Addo Elephant National Park, noting your kms. After 11 km the road surface changes to gravel and you then reach a turn-off right into the Addo Park — drive on past this turn-off to continue towards the Suurberg Pass. The road dips as you approach the Suurberg, and roughly 7 km after passing the Addo turn-off you reach the start of the Suurberg Pass.

The pass includes a number of sharp bends that need to be taken at low speeds. Roughly 4 km after the start of the pass you can park off the road and look back over the Sundays Valley. A further 5 km brings you to the top of the pass.

Suurberg National Park

At the top of the pass, on your right, you will see the Zuurberg Inn (which offers refreshments and lunches). Immediately opposite the entrance to the Inn, turn left onto a narrow gravel track that leads for 750 m to a National Parks Board office. Park here and walk through the gate into the Suurberg National Park. A few metres after walking through the gate you come to a sign indicating that a 1 hr (2,5 km) 'circular walk' leads away to the right. The full walk would be too long if you plan to visit the Addo Park later, but just a few hundred metres along this path will bring you to a fine viewsite on the crest of a hill — overlooking grassy mountainsides and valleys filled with dense indigenous forest. (Two very rare plants that grow in the park are the Suurberg cushion bush and the Suurberg cycad.)

Retrace your route to the main gravel road and down the Suurberg Pass. After roughly 16 km turn left onto the gravel access road into the Addo Park (entry fee; see opposite). We recommend that you spend the remainder of the afternoon in the park, and note that it takes roughly 45 min to drive back to Port Elizabeth. When you leave the park, turn left onto the R335, and after some 50 km on the R335 turn right onto the N2 for Port Elizabeth ●

AA Office 2 Granville Road, Greenacres, Port Elizabeth 6001 Tel. (041) 341313
SA Tourism Board 310 Mutual Building, 64 Main Street, Port Elizabeth 6001 Tel. (041) 27761
Port Elizabeth Publicity Association Library Building, Market Square, Port Elizabeth 6001 Tel. (041) 521315

The Sundays River Valley is also tortoise country.

VALLEY OF FRUIT AND FLOWERS

The Sundays River rises in the Sneeuberg, then flows through the Suurberg range. Its waters are captured in the man-made Lake Mentz, which makes it possible to irrigate the lower reaches of the valley — filling the air with the scent of orange groves, and supporting a profusion of sub-tropical flowers.

The town of Kirkwood was named after an early pioneer of irrigation, James Somers Kirkwood, who settled in the valley in 1877. The creation of Lake Mentz in 1922 was largely the work of Sir Percy Fitzpatrick, author of the classic *Jock of the Bushveld*. Sir Percy settled in the valley after a successful career in the gold-mining industry. He and his wife and two sons are buried at the 'Look Out'.

Below: *Green carpet of the Addo forest.*

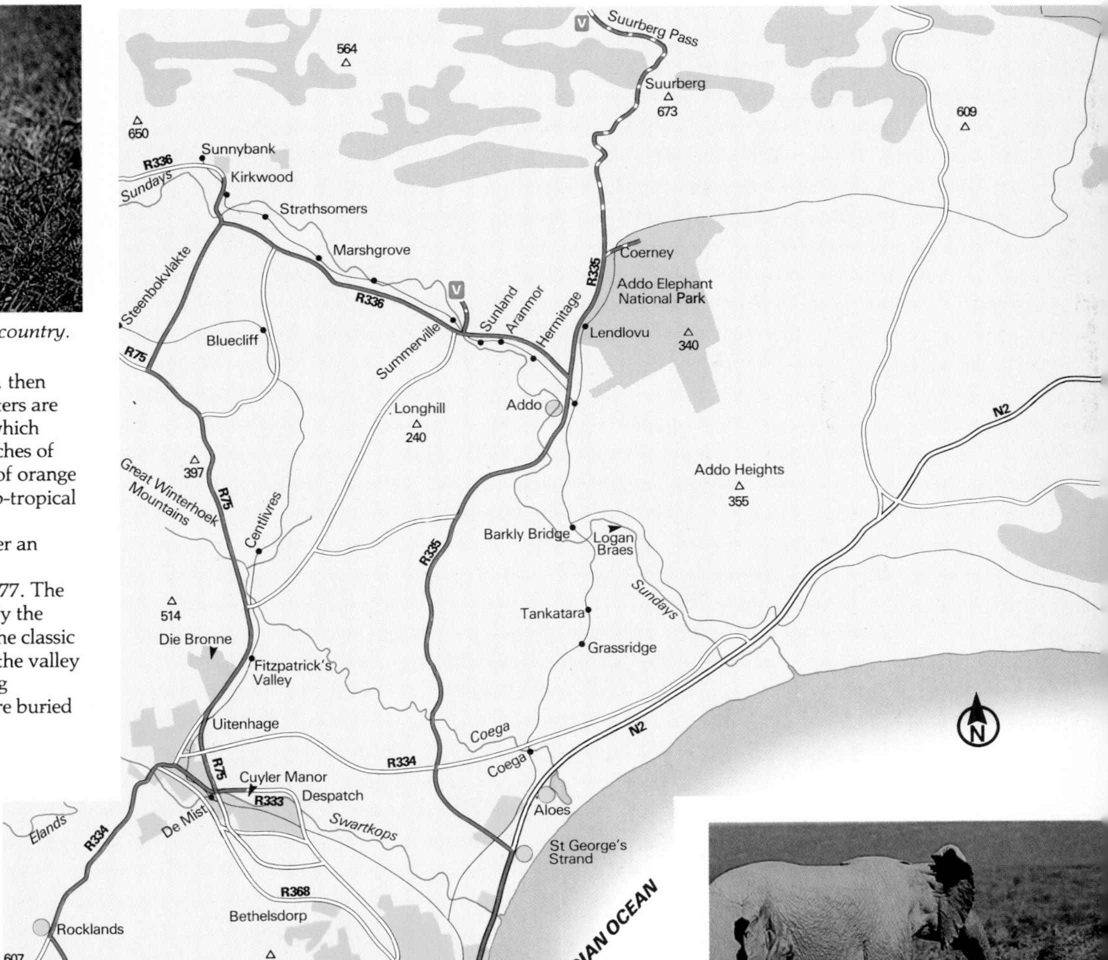

Family scene in the Addo Park.

Terraced houses climb up from the sea, recalling the heyday of Queen Victoria's empire.

A cluster of settler cottages on the coastal hills of Algoa Bay

IN 1576 the stretch of coast where Port Elizabeth now stands was given the name Bahia de Lagoa (bay of the lagoon) by the Portuguese navigator Manuel de Mesquita Perestrelo, but for generations it remained on the navigational charts as merely a 'landing place with fresh water'.

The story of Port Elizabeth began in 1799. The British had occupied the Cape, and they decided to protect their 'Algoa Bay' landing place by constructing on an overlooking hilltop a small stone fort — just 24 metres square. It was named Fort Frederick after the Duke of York, who was commander-in-chief of the British army at the time. A garrison was stationed here, and later barracks and a military hospital were built. The old fort ranks as the oldest stone building in the Eastern Cape, and it still offers a fine view over the harbour and along the coast.

PE's landmark: the Campanile.

After the landing of the 1820 Settlers under the supervision of the garrison's Captain Francis Evatt (whose grave is at the fort) the acting governor of the Cape, Sir Rufane Donkin, visited the growing settlement and named it Port Elizabeth in memory of his wife. The original settlement grew into a substantial town as more and more settlers built their homes on the slopes near the fort — and the slopes were quite steep, with the result that anyone now wishing to explore the old part of the city must be prepared for a few uphill stretches.

If you have come into the city centre by car, park near the fort in Fort Street or Belmont Terrace, and begin your walk by exploring the *fort* **(1)**. When you leave the fort, walk along Belmont Terrace for several blocks. After crossing Whites Road you have the Donkin Reserve on your right, and on your left the *Edward Hotel* **(2)**, built in 1903. Next on your left, one block further along, you will see the *Old Grey Institute* **(3)**, a Gothic-style building dating back to 1859. Sir George Grey commissioned the building to promote higher learning in the Eastern Cape, and by 1914 the Grey School had grown so large that it was moved to Mill Park. The old building is now a national monument.

Continue along Belmont Terrace and cross over Donkin Street to reach Alfred Terrace — on the corner to your left is the *Port Elizabeth Presbyterian Church* **(4)**, consecrated in 1865. Turn left and walk up Alfred Terrace into the part of the old town known as the 'Upper Hill Street' area. Many of the houses here have been extensively renovated and the area has again become a fashionable place to live. At the top of Alfred Terrace turn sharp right down Ivy Terrace, and after passing a few houses turn left into George Street. On the corner of George Street and Upper Hill Street is the Sir Rufane Donkin restaurant, housed in a restored cottage furnished in period style.

In Upper Hill Street, on an exterior wall, you can see a mural depicting the landing of the 1820 settlers, and also an old post-box front. Directly opposite the Sir Rufane Donkin rooms are cottages built in about 1858, notable for their attractive balconies that are now adorned with trailing bougainvillea. Walk downhill along Upper Hill Street, passing more restored cottages, until you reach Belmont Terrace once again.

Terraced houses

Turn right into Belmont Terrace, and walk past the Presbyterian Church again on your right. As you cross over Donkin Street you will see down to your left a row of *terraced houses* dating from 1870 **(5)**.

Follow one of the footpaths leading half-left into the Donkin Reserve, and walk through the small reserve to the *Pyramid* and *Lighthouse* **(6)**. From here you can see the bay over the tops of the buildings in the city centre. A few days after he had named the town in memory of his wife, who had died in India, Sir Rufane Donkin visited this hill overlooking the town and marked the spot where the memorial Pyramid now stands. The Lighthouse was built in 1861 and is still used as a beacon for ships in the bay. You can climb to the top for a magnificent view over the city and its harbour.

Leave the Donkin Reserve by walking back towards the fort, but turn left down Whites Road. After about 200 m you pass the *Opera House* **(7)** on your left. Built in 1892, this is the oldest functioning opera house in South Africa, and the country's only surviving example of a Victorian theatre. Opposite Chapel Street (which turns off to your left at the side of the Opera House) you can see *St Augustine's Roman Catholic Cathedral* **(8)**, slightly obscured by trees. The cathedral was built in 1866 under the direction of the parish priest, Father Murphy.

Continue down Whites Road until you reach an alley on your left. (There is no street sign but it is called St Mary's Terrace.) Walk into the alley, and take the first turn right. On your left you pass *St Mary's Anglican*

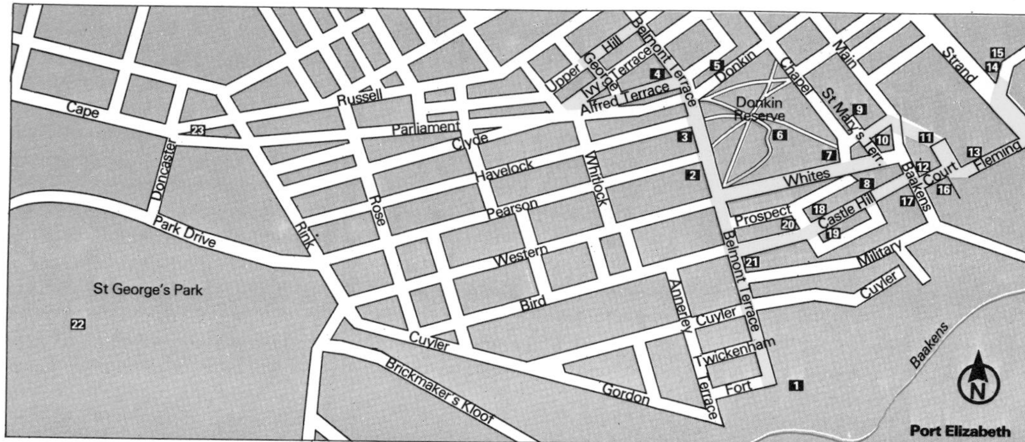

Church **(9)**, and on your right the old *Library Building* **(10)**.

St Mary's Anglican Church was established in 1824 by Captain (later Sir Francis) Evatt, who was buried there in 1854. The original church was destroyed in a fire in 1895 and rebuilt, and in 1956 Sir Francis Evatt's remains were re-interred at the fort, but the original tombstone can still be seen here in the church.

The present Library Building, a good example of Victorian Gothic, dates from 1902 and stands on the site of the original library (completed in 1848). Its stucco facade was manufactured in England and sent out in numbered pieces to be assembled here. From Main Street, at the bottom of the hill, you can view the front of the library, and a statue of Queen Victoria erected in 1903.

Historic Fort Frederick; oldest stone building in the eastern Cape.

Traditional flea market

Cross over Main Street, and walk onto the *Market Square* **(11)**. This was the commercial heart of Port Elizabeth in the early days, and there is still a traditional flea market on Saturday mornings. At one time a bell was rung to signal the start of the market's activities. (The same bell also served as the town's fire alarm.) *The City Hall* **(12)** stands on the southern side of Market Square. The original building was completed in 1862, but it was destroyed by fire in 1977 and has since been restored.

To reach the Campanile, walk down the steps to the left of the City Hall, then after a few paces turn left, and walk along Fleming Street. On the corner of Fleming and Strand Streets you pass the *White House* **(13)** on your left. The building dates from 1904, and is a fine example of Art Nouveau architecture.

From Fleming Street, turn left into Strand Street and walk under the flyovers. From here you can see the brick, 51,8 metre *Campanile* **(14)**, built in 1923 to commemorate the landing of the 1820 settlers on a nearby beach (the beach no longer exists). The Campanile has a spiral staircase of 204 steps leading up to a viewing platform, and a carillon of 23 bells. Just north of the Campanile is the *Railway Station* **(15)**, dated 1875.

Castle Hill Street

Retrace your route along Strand Street and Fleming Street, then walk along Court Street between the back of the City Hall and the *General Post Office* **(16)**, built in 1900.

Cross Baakens Street and walk up Castle Hill Street, which runs roughly parallel to Whites Road. Immediately on your left is the *Feather Market Hall* **(17)**, built in 1885 to accommodate auction sales of the ostrich feathers that were fashionable at the time — and also sales of wool, hides, skins and fruit.

As you climb the steep hill, you step into another era. On both sides of the road are charming settler cottages, and on your right is *Castle Hill No. 7* **(18)**, probably the oldest dwelling in Port Elizabeth. It was built in about 1830 by the Reverend Francis McLeland, the first rector of St Mary's Church. The house is open to the public, and is furnished in the style of the period.

Across the road are the two *Sterley Cottages* **(19)**, also built in the 1830s. As you reach the top of Castle Hill Street you pass on your right the *Drill Hall* **(20)**, opened in 1882 as headquarters of the Prince Alfred's Guard Regiment and now a regimental museum.

On the corner of Castle Hill Street and Belmont Terrace you pass on your left the *Athenaeum Club* **(21)** — formerly the Athenaeum Institute, founded in the early days to promote cultural activities. Turn left here and walk along Belmont Terrace to return to the fort.

To visit two further places of interest, drive along Fort Street away from the fort, turn right into Annerley Terrace, then after a short distance turn left into Bird Street. Continue along Bird Street until you reach St George's Park (see map), where you can visit the *Pearson Conservatory* **(22)**, dating from 1882. The conservatory was named after Henry Pearson, 16 times Mayor of the city, and it houses a magnificent collection of exotic plants.

From the conservatory, drive along Doncaster Road (see map). Park in Doncaster Road, and walk towards Cape Road to see the famous *Horse Memorial* **(23)**, erected in 1905 and moved to its present site in 1957. During the Anglo-Boer War, Port Elizabeth was the main port of entry for the horses used by the British forces. A resident of the city, Mrs Harriet Meyer, started a fund for this monument to the many horses that died in the course of the war. Its inscription reads: 'The greatness of a nation consists not so much in the number of its people or the extent of its territory as in the extent and justice of its compassion ●

The steep climb up Castle Hill Street is dotted with historic buildings.

An empire and its compassion.

Follow a river 'wily as a lion' to the Mountain of the Clouds

From Port Elizabeth we take a coastal road to Van Staden's River Mouth, then explore the Gamtoos River Valley and the scenic Groot River Gorge. Finally we climb the valley wall to confront T'Numkwa, towering 'Mountain of the Clouds'. Roughly two-thirds of the route is tarred, the rest is gravel. (Take food and drink with you.)

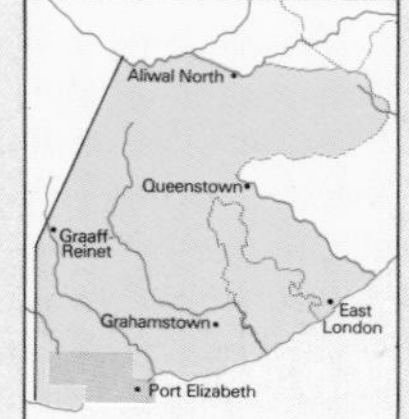

Port Elizabeth
Van Staden's River Mouth
Hankey
Groot River
Cockscomb Mountain
310 – 330 km

LEAVE PORT ELIZABETH by driving south on Beach Road. As the road winds through the coastal bush it becomes Marine Drive, and it soon offers attractive views of the rocky coast on your left. Follow this coast road until it ends on a low bluff known as Skoenmakerskop, where you can park and look out along an unspoilt shore towards Sardinia Bay.

Retrace your route for 1,2 km and turn left (up the hill). Just over 3 km later, turn left again for 'Sardinia Bay', and after a further 4 km turn right. 700 m later turn left at the T-junction for 'Seaview/Beachview', noting your kms.

After about 16 km the road turns inland and begins to climb. On the crest of the hill you pass on your right the Seaview Game Park, and 1,5 km later you pass on your right the entrance to the Island Forest Reserve (see pages 238-9). When you come to a crossroads, continue straight ahead for 'Greenbushes/Maitland Mouth' — but 100 m later turn left towards Maitland Mouth, noting your kms.

After a little over 5 km you pass on your left a turn-off to Maitland River Mouth. After a further 3 km turn left for 'Van Staden's Mouth', and at the crossroads 3,5 km later turn left again for 'Van Staden's Mouth'. The road now descends through high hills to the beautiful estuary of the Van Staden's River (see opposite; entry fee per car, per day).

Van Staden's River to Hankey

Retrace your route for 13 km to the crossroads, and turn left for 'Old Cape Road'. After 1,8 km you cross the N2, and 1,4 km later you cross an unfenced railway line. Immediately after this you come to a T-junction — turn left onto the R102 (Old Cape Road) noting your kms.

After about 8 km on the R102 you pass under the N2, and 1 km later you pass on your right the Van Staden's Wild Flower Reserve (see pages 238-9). Immediately after this you come to a fork — take the road leading right to stay on the R102, and note your kms. You now negotiate the old Van Staden's River pass. After 10 km turn right onto the R331 for 'Hankey/Patensie', noting your kms again as you cross over the N2.

The R331 sweeps over a succession of hilltops, offering views reminiscent of Natal's Valley of a Thousand Hills. You pass the little town of Loerie, and 26 km after crossing over the N2 you enter Hankey (see below). As you drive downhill into the town there is a sign on your left saying 'Enjoy View'. Turn off the road here and park. A path leads to the top of the koppie known as Vergaderingskop (meeting-place hill) from where there is a fine view over the Gamtoos River Valley.

If the time is right for your picnic, turn right on the far side of Hankey for Yellowwoods, and 1,2 km later turn left into the shady Yellowwoods picnic area — there are braai places, water and rustic toilets. (To complete the drive, leave here not later than 14h00.)

Hankey to Groot River Gorge

Leave Hankey by continuing on the R331 towards Patensie, and note your kms at the point where the road to Yellowwoods joins the R331. After 1,1 km turn left for 'Philip Tunnel'. Park on the side of this road after a further 1 km, just before descending into the valley. From here you can see Die Bergvenster (the moun-

The Groot River snakes through its magnificent, richly-coloured gorge.

The Gamtoos River valley from Die Bergvenster — a rewarding climb for the fit.

A MISSION IN THE VALLEY

The little town of Hankey on the Gamtoos River dates from 1822. It was founded by the London Missionary Society, and was named after the Society's treasurer of the day.

William Philip, son of the missionary Dr John Philip, saw the valley's potential riches — if only the flat alluvial floor of the valley could be properly irrigated. He employed Khoikhoi workers from the mission village to dig a tunnel from a high point in the river to lower-lying fields. Tragically, on the day the tunnel was officially put into operation in 1845, William Philip was drowned by the 'wily river' he had dared to tame — in one of the unpredictable flash floods for which it is notorious.

LAND OF THE KHOIKHOI

Before white or Xhosa people encroached on the Eastern Cape, the Gamtoos River Valley belonged to the Khoikhoi. Gamtoos is said to mean 'wily as a lion', and was not only the name of the river but of the people who lived beside it. There is another echo of the Khoikhoi language in Patensie, which is thought to mean 'a resting place for cattle'.

The distinctive peak that Europeans were to dub Cockscomb Mountain was known to the Khoikhoi as *T'Numkwa*, meaning 'mountain of the clouds'. At 1 759 m this is the highest peak in the Eastern Cape, and it dominates both the Gamtoos and Elands River valleys.

Distant view of Cockscomb Mountain.

tain window), a natural arch on the crest of the ridge ahead of you. Drive on across the river, and follow the gravel road leading to the Philip Tunnel (see below). A path near the tunnel leads up to Die Bergvenster, but this is a steep scramble over loose earth and stones.

Retrace your route to the R331, and turn left for Patensie — noting your kms. After 12 km you pass Patensie on your left. Note your kms again as you cross the small bridge on the far side of the town, and 2 km later turn left onto gravel towards Humansdorp. Note your kms as you cross the Gamtoos River, and 600 m later turn right towards Humansdorp. 2,6 km after crossing the river, go left at the fork. 7,9 km after the river turn right at the T-junction onto the R332 towards Willowmore. As you approach the river again the road forks — keep right, and re-cross the river. At the T-junction turn left onto the tarred road towards Willowmore (still R332) noting your kms.

The road leads up the Gamtoos River Valley. After 4 km you pass on your left a gravel road leading to the Paul Sauer dam. Immediately after passing this turn-off the road surface changes to gravel — note your kms here. Continue on the gravel road for 11 km before turning at the low ford across the Groot River. This short excursion gives you a good view of the magnificent Groot River Gorge.

Cockscomb Mountain and Elands River Valley

Retrace your route from the ford, and note your kms as you pass on your right the turn-off to the Paul Sauer dam (just after driving back onto the tar). Continue on the tar, passing on your right the gravel road on which you arrived earlier. 19,5 km after noting your kms, turn left onto a gravel road leading to the Elands River Valley — noting your kms at the turn.

The road climbs steadily, and you can look back over the Gamtoos River Valley to St Francis Bay sparkling in the distance. After 15,7 km on this gravel road, at one of its highest points, a road leads off to your left. Pass this turn-off, but after a further 150 m take the next road on your left — this road has a better surface. Drive about 1 km along this side road for a panoramic view across the green valley to *T'Numkwa*, or the Cockscomb Mountain (see opposite).

Turn where the road is widest, and return to the main gravel road. Turn left, to drive down the full length of the Elands River Valley. At Rocklands, drive across the X-shaped intersection onto the diagonally opposite 'arm' of the X. Roughly 6 km later you reach a stop sign — turn left here onto the R102. From here you can take any of the turns signposted 'National Road' to join the N2 to Port Elizabeth ●

AA Office 2 Granville Road, Greenacres, Port Elizabeth 6001 Tel. (041) 341313
SA Tourism Board 310 Mutual Building, 64 Main Street, Port Elizabeth 6001 Tel. (041) 27761
Port Elizabeth Publicity Association Library Building, Market Square, Port Elizabeth 6001 Tel. (041) 521315

VAN STADEN'S RIVER MOUTH

Sheltered by huge sand dunes and dense bush, Van Staden's River Mouth is one of the most attractive spots on the South African coast. A holiday resort has been established here, with thatched cottages, a caravan park, and camping and braai facilities. The quiet lagoon is safe for swimming but sea bathing can be dangerous. There are kilometres of unspoilt beach to walk along, and canoes can be hired for an interesting paddle on the lagoon.

Above: *Sea and sand at Van Staden's River Mouth.* **Right:** *The coast at Skoenmakerskop.*

A sweep of white sand where surfers await the perfect wave

This drive explores the western shores of St Francis Bay — a great curve of gently sloping white-sand beaches, famous to surfers throughout the world as the coast of the perfect wave. We then drive inland to the Groot River Gorge and Cockscomb Mountain on our way back to Port Elizabeth. Over two thirds of the route is tarred, the rest is gravel.

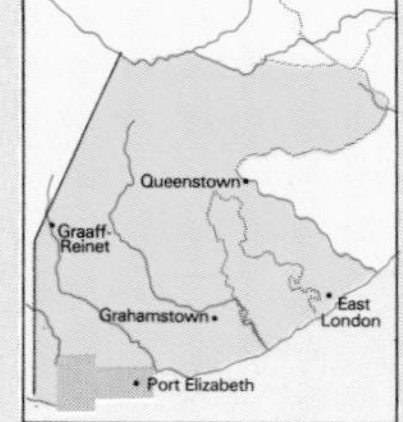

Port Elizabeth
Jeffreys Bay
Cape St Francis
Hankey
Groot River Gorge
Cockscomb Mtn
390 — 410 kms

DRIVE WEST OUT OF Port Elizabeth on the N2 (towards Cape Town) and note your kms as you pass the exit for 'Greenbushes/Seaview'. 6,3 km later you pass the 'Van Staden's River/St Albans' turn-off, and immediately after this you pass under a flyover. At 17,3 km take the exit for 'Uitenhage R102/Van Staden's Pass', and at the end of the off-ramp turn left for Van Staden's Pass.

After a little over 1 km you pass the entrance to the Van Staden's Wildflower Reserve on your right — note your kms as you pass. A short distance after this you come to a fork — take the road leading right, to stay on the R102 (the Old Cape Road).

Drive slowly as you follow this road through the old Van Staden's River Pass. The road surface is poor, and after heavy rains there may be places where washaways permit only one car through at a time. (As you cross the old bridge you can see the newer Van Staden's River Bridge towering high above you.)

Roughly 10 km after passing the Van Staden's Wildflower Reserve you reach a major turn-off right to Hankey and Patensie — continue straight ahead here on the R102. Soon after this the road passes under the N2, descends through cuttings to the old bridge over the Gamtoos River, then strikes out across the river's flood plain. Note your kms as you pass under the N2 once again. About 2,5 km later, as the road climbs the hills, park on the shoulder of the road for a good view to your left over the great lagoon at the river's mouth. After a further 7 km across the low hillsides you look down onto the much smaller lagoon of the Kabeljous River.

Note your kms as you cross the small Kabeljous River, and 1,2 km later turn left for 'Aston Bay/Paradise Beach/Jeffreys Bay'. Roughly 700 m later turn left again, and follow the road that leads left between the holiday houses until you reach a parking area alongside the Kabeljous River's lagoon — an attractive place for a short walk along the beach.

Note your kms as you leave the parking area, and continue along this road that you arrived on, for a drive along the shores of Kabeljous Bay. After 1 km turn left at the stop street into Da Gama Road, which will take you into the village of Wavecrest. 2 km after passing through Wavecrest you pass a yellow sign for 'Super Tubes', one of the world's most famous surfing spots. In the course of the next 2 km you cross through three stop streets. Note the third of these because we return to it. Immediately after crossing through this third stop street you enter Jeffreys Bay.

Jeffreys Bay to Cape St Francis

Retrace your route to the stop street you noted, and turn left (uphill) into De Reygers Street. When De Reygers Street ends at a T-junction, turn right for 'Humansdorp', noting your kms. 3 km later, turn left at the crossroads onto the R102 for 'Humansdorp'. After driving a short distance through rolling countryside you pass a road on your left leading to Paradysstrand (paradise beach), and 6 km later you enter the town of Humansdorp on Voortrekker Road (see opposite). As you reach the central area of the town, turn left into Hoofstraat (Main Street) and continue on Hoofstraat through two four-way stop streets. At the third four-way stop street, turn left, following the sign for 'St Francis Bay'. Cross through another four-way stop street, and at the next four-way stop street turn right into Saffery Street, following the signs for Cape St Francis and St Francis Bay. Roadworks here may necessitate a gravel detour, but within a short distance you will find yourself on the tarred R330, travelling almost due south towards Cape St Francis.

After travelling roughly 13 km on the R330 you cross the Krom River on a long, low bridge, and at the end of the bridge the road surface changes to gravel. Continue straight ahead on the main road, passing several side-roads. The road leads through coastal bush for roughly 10 km, and eventually emerges amid the cluster of holiday houses that make up Cape St Francis Village. Continue on the main road, which gradually swings to the left and becomes Seal Point Boulevard. Turn left when you reach a sign pointing left to 'Beach parking'. This short side-road leads to a parking area next to a small, pretty beach, known locally as 'Seals' and popular with surfers. (There are toilets near the parking area.)

Cape St Francis to the Groot River Gorge

When you leave this parking area, note your kms, and retrace your route for a fraction over 8 km, then turn right into Homestead Road. This leads down the hill into the attractive holi-

Smoothly breaking rollers welcome surfers to St Francis Bay.

SEA SHELLS AND SUPER TUBES

The popular holiday resort of Jeffreys Bay took its name from a trading store that was built on the coast in 1849 by a Mr J A Jeffrey. In those days no railway served the area, and cargo was loaded from and landed onto the beach in front of Jeffrey's store. When the holiday-makers discovered how sheltered and safe the beaches are along this stretch of coast, the little settlement blossomed into a popular place to build a holiday shack or a retirement home. Now the name has become synonymous with surfing, and Super Tubes and other famous beaches draw enthusiasts from throughout the world — especially during the winter months from May to September.

The rollers that put Jeffreys Bay onto the world surfing map also sweep in rich harvests of shells, and a magnificent collection of beautiful and rare specimens can be seen in the Charlotte Kritzinger Shell Museum.

ST FRANCIS BAY

In 1575, when Portuguese navigator Manuel de Mesquita Perestrelo named St Francis Bay after the patron saint of sailors, he could not have imagined that 400 years later the beaches along the bay's west coast would have become internationally famous for their majestic rollers — regarded by the sportsmen who ride on them as some of the finest waves in the world.

Seal Point, just to the south of Cape St Francis, is now the site of a 28 m lighthouse, built in 1876, and a short distance from the Cape along the shores of the bay lies the particularly attractive St Francis Bay village — all its houses have white-washed walls and thatched or dark-tiled roofs. This theme has now been continued at the marina nearby on the Krom River estuary.

Luxury homes line the marina at Krom River Mouth.

day resort of St Francis Bay — formerly known as Sea Vista — notable for its white-washed houses with thatched roofs (see below). Follow the signs to the beach, where you can park and walk along a short footpath to a 3km stretch of white sand, similar in form to the 'Seals' beach but on a larger scale.

When you leave the beach, drive northwards along St Francis Drive to explore the new marina where grand holiday villas have been set on the banks of canals — then retrace your route along St Francis Drive and follow the signs back onto the R330 for Humansdorp.

Drive back through the centre of Humansdorp on Hoofstraat, and cross Voortrekker Road, following the sign for 'Hankey R330'. After 3km you cross over the N2. Continue straight ahead on the R330 for Hankey. As you leave the coast and drive further inland the vegetation changes. The road descends from a line of low hills into the Gamtoos Valley, and in the distance to your left you can see the towering crest of Cockscomb Mountain.

Roughly 26km after leaving Humansdorp you cross the Gamtoos River on a low causeway, and 2km later you enter the small farming centre of Hankey (see pages 234-5). At the stop street in the centre of the town, turn left onto the R331 for 'Patensie'. On the town's outskirts you pass a road leading right to the Yellowwoods picnic area, and 1,1km later you pass a road on your left leading to the Philip Tunnel (see pages 234-5). Note your kms here.

The road leads up-river, and 7,6km after passing the turn-off to the Philip Tunnel you have a fine view over the fertile floor of the valley. Roughly 4,5km later you pass through the outskirts of the small village of Patensie. Continue on this road (R331), passing a number of side-roads and staying close to the river. Roughly 19km from Patensie you pass the R332 to Humansdorp on your left, and 4km later you pass on your left a gravel road leading to the Paul Sauer Dam. Immediately after this the road surface changes to gravel — note your kms here. Continue on this gravel road for 11km, then turn at the low causeway across the Groot River — this 22km there-and-back trip will give you excellent views of the colourful Groot River Gorge.

Groot River Gorge to Port Elizabeth

When you return from the Groot River Gorge, note your kms as you pass the turn-off (now on your right) to the Paul Sauer Dam — just after driving back onto the tar. After 4km you pass the road leading right to Humansdorp, and after a further 15,5km, turn left onto a gravel road leading to the Elands River Valley — noting your kms.

Follow this road as it climbs higher and higher, but stop periodically for fine views back over the Gamtoos Valley. After 15,7km you reach a road leading off to your left. Pass this, but turn left 150m later — this becomes the same road but has a better surface. Drive roughly 1km along this side-road and park, for a fine view across the valley to Cockscomb Mountain, known to the Khoikhoi as the 'Mountain of the Clouds' (see pages 234-5).

Retrace your route down into the Gamtoos Valley and turn left onto the tarred R331. You now retrace your earlier route past Patensie to Hankey, but drive straight through Hankey, staying on the R331. The road then leads along the crest of a line of hills, offering fine views to your right as far as St Francis Bay and to your left over a scene reminiscent of Natal's Valley of a Thousand Hills. Roughly 16km after leaving Hankey you pass the small farming centre of Loerie on your right. After a further 11km turn left, following the signs onto the N2 for Port Elizabeth ●

AA Office 2 Granville Road, Greenacres, Port Elizabeth 6001 Tel. (041) 341313
SA Tourism Board 310 Mutual Building, 64 Main Street, Port Elizabeth 6001 Tel. (041) 27761
Port Elizabeth Publicity Association Library Building, Market Square, Port Elizabeth 6001 Tel. (041) 521315

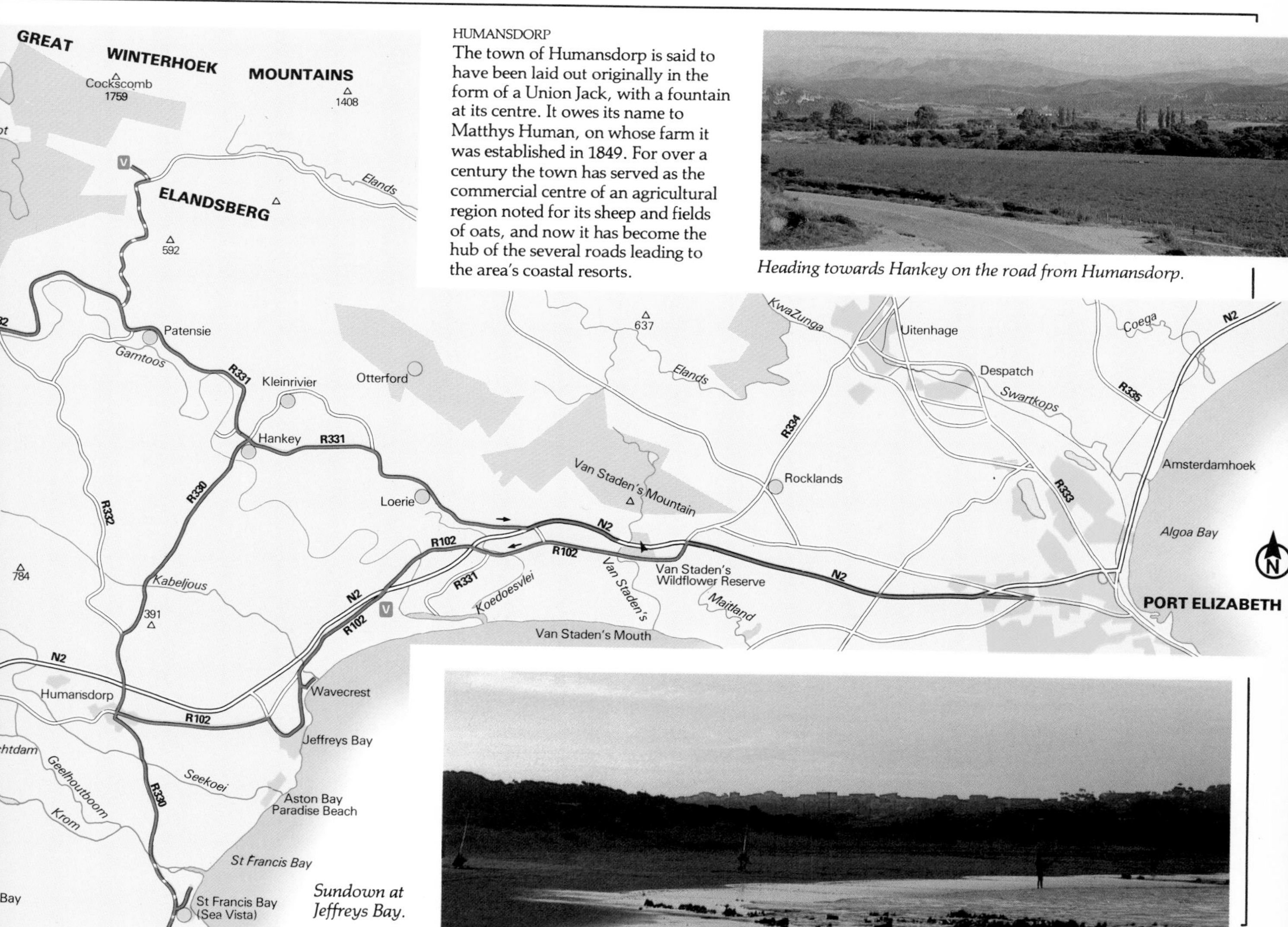

HUMANSDORP
The town of Humansdorp is said to have been laid out originally in the form of a Union Jack, with a fountain at its centre. It owes its name to Matthys Human, on whose farm it was established in 1849. For over a century the town has served as the commercial centre of an agricultural region noted for its sheep and fields of oats, and now it has become the hub of the several roads leading to the area's coastal resorts.

Heading towards Hankey on the road from Humansdorp.

Sundown at Jeffreys Bay.

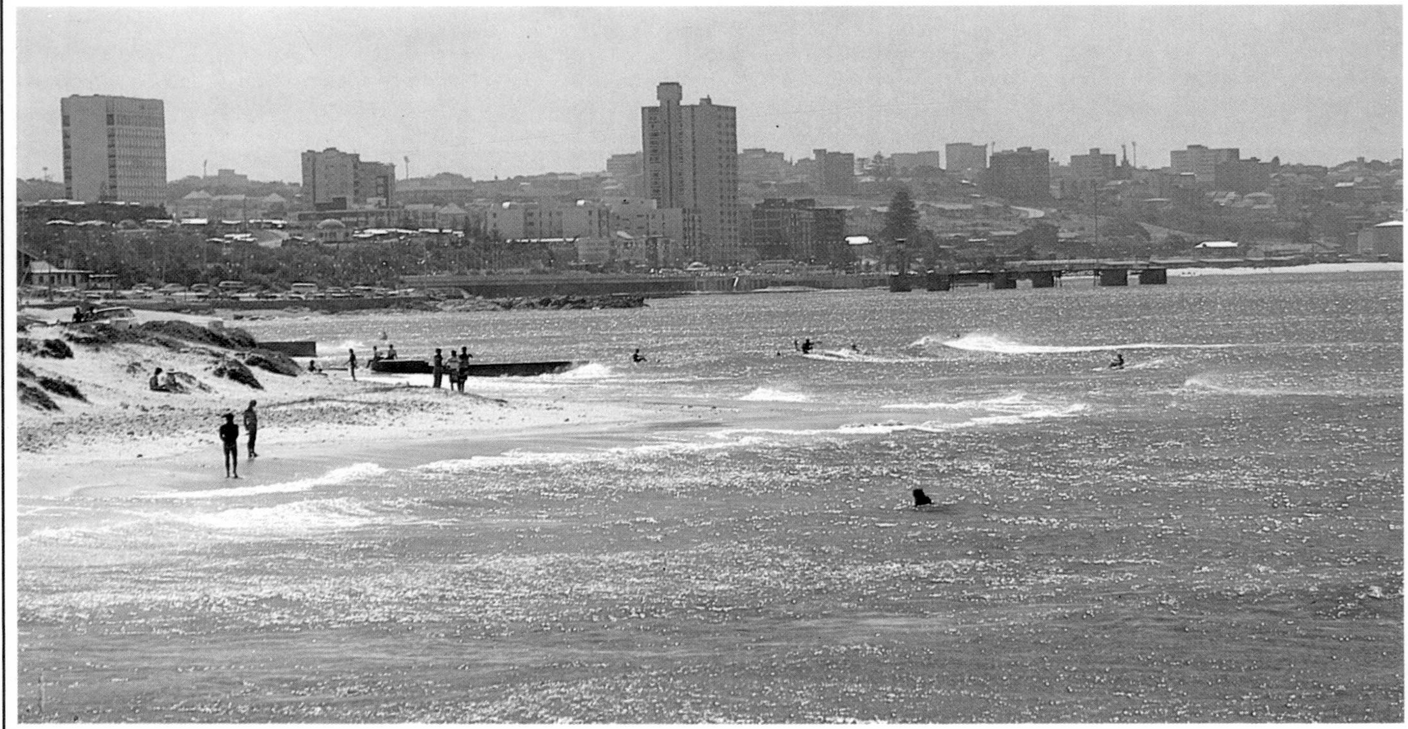

Port Elizabeth rises above the sparkling waters of the Indian Ocean. A view from Bird Rock.

Unspoilt forests and wild beaches surround the 'friendly city'

THERE ARE MANY places within easy reach of Port Elizabeth that offer fine walks and hikes through unspoilt natural surroundings. Even within the boundaries of the city, walkers who take to the *Guinea Fowl Trail* through *Settlers Park Nature Reserve* will be surprised by the wildness of the area.

Settlers Park contains some 160 different trees and shrubs, and is noted for its richly varied birdlife — which includes the Knysna loerie, giant kingfisher, fork-tailed drongo, gymnogene, herons, Guinea fowl and Egyptian geese. Also common are dassies *(Hyrax)*, tortoises and leguans. The Guinea Fowl Trail takes two to three hours to walk, but is relatively easy. Many shorter walks through the park are also possible, and the park has several entry points, making it easily accessible from almost any part of the city.

Also within the city limits is the start of an interesting beach walk, which leads along the shore from *'Bird Rock'* at Summerstrand to *Cape Recife* — approximately 10 km. Roughly half-way along the route, at 'Flat Rocks', there are fascinating rock pools that can be reached at low-tide. To drive into the *Cape Recife Nature Reserve* you need a permit, but if you are walking along the beach no permit is required.

A short distance west of the city there is a particularly beautiful beach walk that leads from *Skoenmakerskop* to *Sardinia Bay* (see pages 234-5). This stretch of coast is contained in two reserves, the *Sardinia Bay Sea Reserve* and the *Sylvic Nature Reserve*. Although Sardinia Bay now has a car park, toilets and a launching ramp for small boats, the aim is to maintain the whole coastal strip in as natural a condition as possible — one intention being to use this as a reference area for measuring the impact of civilization on dune life and coastal flora. The walk along the beach has a pristine, wild quality, and superb displays of wildflowers can be seen at various seasons.

A little further along the coast, perched atop a coastal hill — actually an enormous 282 m sand dune — there is the *Island Forest Reserve* (see pages 234-5). Although the entrance is on the eastern side of the road, the bulk of the reserve lies to the west, and contains for the most part indigenous sub-tropical coastal forest of the 'Alexandria' type. Living in the forest are bushbuck, the rare blue and grey duikers, bushpig and vervet monkeys. Prominent among the birds to be seen is the Knysna loerie.

Right: *The long arm of Cape Recife stretches into the Indian Ocean.*

Left: *The Island State Forest.*

Bushbuck trail

A circular 16 km path has been established in the forest and is known as the *Bushbuck Trail*. Apart from exploring the depths of the forest, this also offers some fine views over the great sweep of St Francis Bay.

Just a few kilometres further west there is another, shorter forest trail through the *Maitland Mines Nature Reserve* (see pages 230-1). The trail is a little over 3 km, and for part of its route it follows an old wagon road

through the area. The forest is noted for its rich birdlife.

Moving inland from here, and slightly further west, there is the *Van Stadens Wild Flower Reserve.* This 400 ha area offers attractive river-gorge scenery in addition to a profusion of indigenous flowering plants. There are two short trails through the reserve for walkers, and there are numerous picnic sites — but there is no water except near the main gate.

A completely different kind of inland vegetation can be found at *Die Bronne* (the springs) — a holiday resort and nature reserve just a few kilometres north of Uitenhage. The reserve is centred on the 'eyes' (springs) of the Uitenhage Artesian Basin, and it offers several walks through a much drier landscape, dominated by aloes and other Karoo-type succulents.

Still further north, some 80 km from Port Elizabeth, the slopes of the Suurberg range are covered by the *Suurberg National Park* — offering two attractive walks. The shorter takes roughly one hour, the longer covers some 12 km and takes a good four hours to complete. The scenery in this area is attractive, including large expanses of indigenous forest and mountain-tops covered with fynbos and grass. See pages 230-1 for instructions on how to get there, and for additional information contact The State Forester, Suurberg National Park, Private Bag X6052, Port Elizabeth 6000 Tel. (04252) 106.

Alexandria Forest

Slightly further from Port Elizabeth, eastwards along the coast, a new hiking trail has recently been established through the *Alexandria Forest Nature Reserve.* The reserve comprises roughly 60 km of coastline from the Sundays River mouth past Cape Padrone to Cannon Rocks, plus a broad belt of land lying behind the coast. Part of this area is covered by the Alexandria Forest, a subtropical coastal forest reminiscent of the indigenous forests of the Garden Route, and quite distinct from the surrounding countryside. For details, contact The Forester, Alexandria State Forest, P O Box 50, Alexandria 6185 Tel. (04652) 1103.

Dolphins show their paces at the Oceanarium.

The wildest tract of country that is easily accessible from Port Elizabeth is *Groendal Wilderness Area* — nearly 22 000 ha of mountain slopes and forested valleys, lying at the feet of the Great Winterhoek Mountains and surrounding the Groendal Dam. The forests here include fine specimens of Outeniqua yellowwood, real yellowwood and white stinkwood, and are home to bushpig, bushbuck and duikers — and also leopard and caracal. These remote valleys were among the last parts of the eastern Cape to be inhabited by the San, and many rock overhangs and caves in the area contain San paintings.

There are two fairly long hikes through this area. The shorter of the two is the Blindekloof walk — its fairly easy 16 km take roughly six hours. The longer walk is to Emerald Pool — this is a strenuous hike that takes at least ten hours, and an overnight camp is recommended. In the course of this hike you climb high into the mountains and pass several caves containing San paintings. For details of the walk, contact The Forester, Groendal Wilderness Area, P O Box 445, Uitenhage 6230 Tel. (0422) 25418.

Catwalk through the Seaview Game Park.

Lions and dolphins

In addition to these many wilderness areas and nature reserves for walkers, lovers of animal life have several fascinating places to visit. The most obvious of these is the *Addo Elephant National Park* (see pages 230-1). Here the Addo elephants can be seen living in their natural habitat, and if you are fortunate you may spot black rhino, buffalo and eland.

West of the city, very close to the entrance to the Island Forest Reserve, there is the *Seaview Game Park* (for instructions on how to get there, see pages 230-1 or 234-5). The game park has been laid out in a scenically attractive stretch of countryside, amid hills overlooking the coast, and in this natural environment you can see lion, cheetah, giraffe, rhino, and several antelope species that are relatively rare, such as nyala and lechwe. A particular attraction is the 'catwalk' which takes you through the cheetah enclosure, and there are also 'walk-through' aviaries.

Surprisingly, one of the most interesting places to visit for anyone interested in animal life is right in the heart of the city — at the *Oceanarium* complex in Beach Road. The Oceanarium is best known for its dolphin displays, but also houses seals, turtles, sharks, and many other fish. Next to the Oceanarium is the city's principal *Museum,* a *Tropical House,* a *Night House,* and a *Snake Park.* The Tropical House contains a lush jungle of exotic plants, inhabited by equally exotic birds. The Night House is home to many species of nocturnal animals. Here day and night are artificially reversed, so that the animals can be viewed when they are active instead of asleep ●

Peering into the depths of the tropical house in the Port Elizabeth Museum.

The 19th century labourers' cottages of Stretch's Court — beautifully spruced up for luxury hotel accommodation.

'Gem of the Karoo' in a spacious mountain setting

LYING IN A LOOP of the Sundays River, beneath the distinctive dome of Spandau Kop, the old town of Graaff-Reinet is progressively being restored to the glory that earned it the title 'Gem of the Karoo'. Another title, conferred by a Cape Town newspaper last century, was 'Athens of the Eastern Cape' — a reflection of the town's reputation as a cultural centre.

The citizens of Graaff-Reinet took some time to attain this status — the town was first no more than a straggling lane of mud huts. These nevertheless constituted one of the capital cities of the world when Graaff-Reinet declared itself an independent 'republic' only 10 years after being established.

The town was founded in 1786 on instructions from the Governor of the Cape, Cornelis van de Graaff, and named after him and his wife, Hester Cornelia Reinet. A frontier spirit prevailed in the new town, and the hardy pioneers took little notice of the regulations posted by the landdrost (magistrate). The Dutch East India Company, on the verge of bankruptcy, was unable to enforce its laws on this remote community, and could not spare a garrison to protect them from cross-border raids.

Matters came to a head in 1795 when a band of citizens and local farmers formed a committee, dismissed the landdrost and officials who opposed them, and then proclaimed a Burger Government. They appointed their own officials, including a new landdrost, Dawid Gerotz, who was also head of the National Assembly. Thus was born South Africa's first 'republic', which lasted only a few months until the burgers reluctantly submitted to the new British rulers at the Cape.

The lovely old Drostdy

Our walk through old Graaff-Reinet begins at the historic official residence of the landdrost, the *Drostdy* **(1)**, near the northern end of Church (Kerk) Street. The building was completed in 1806 to a design by Louis Thibault, although the local artisans departed from his original plans to some extent.

By 1847 it was decided that the Drostdy had become too dilapidated to be worth repairing, so it was sold. But, not only did the building not fall down, it withstood the stress of the addition of a second storey, and had served as a hotel for almost a century when restoration began in 1975.

Accommodation at the Drostdy Hotel is in the attractive historic cottages in Drostdy Hof, also known as *Stretch's Court* **(2)**, after Captain Charles Lennox Stretch, the surveyor who bought the land in 1855. The land was subdivided for houses for labourers, possibly former slaves.

A lamppost of bygone days still serves historic houses on Parsonage Street.

From the back door of the Drostdy, look through the softly lit interior and the elegant front doorway to the serene facade of the *Reinet House Museum* **(3)** at the far end of Parsonage (Pastorie) Street.

Walk along Parsonage Street on the southern (right-hand) side. The *John Rupert Theatre* **(4)** on your right was once the church of the London Missionary Society, and later the Congregational Church. It was known as 'die groot Londen kerk' (the big London church) to distinguish it from its smaller sister in Middel Street. The adjacent rectory, built in about 1840, has been reconverted into a home after serving for many years as a school.

Next on your right is a row of houses now used as a home for the aged. The best of the group is number 17, Williams House, although the addition of an iron roof has resulted in the 'clipping' of the front and end gables. Much of the external woodwork is believed to date from when the house was built — around 1860.

Firearms through the years

At the corner of Murray Street, on your right, is the old *Residency* **(5)**, built in the 1820s. The irrigation furrows in front of the building are a relic of a system laid out in the 1820s by Andries Stockenström, who succeeded his father as landdrost of Graaff-Reinet in 1815.

The Residency, an impressive thatched and gabled house typical of the Cape Dutch style, has an unusually ornate fanlight. The building now houses the Jan Felix Lategan memorial collection of historic firearms which traces the development of firearms used in South Africa. (As with a number of the places that we visit, there is a small entry fee here.)

Leave the Residency and cross Murray Street to visit Reinet House, which, as the Dutch Reformed parsonage, was occupied for 82 years by the Murray family. The Reverend Andrew Murray served as minister from 1822 until his death in 1866, and was succeeded by his son, Charles, who died, still in service, in 1904.

The building, completed about 1812, was altered dramatically through the years. After the Murray family's departure, it became a girls' hostel. The gables were removed and, by 1950, the old parsonage was unrecognisable.

A meticulous restoration was started in 1953, based on old photographs and a careful study of old building techniques. Stone steps with

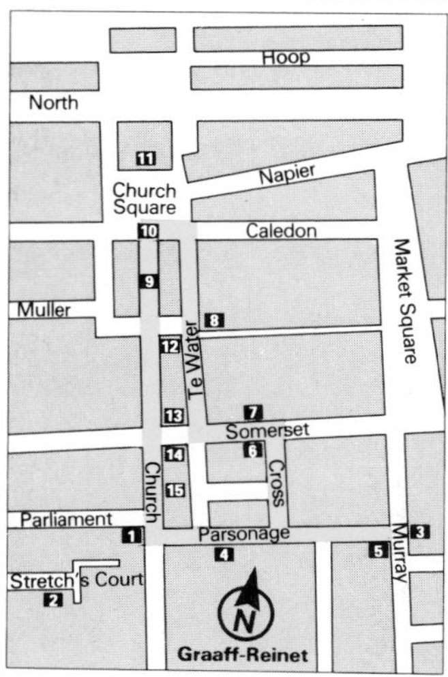

An aerial view of the pretty town that lies in a crook of the Sundays River.

their original iron railing sweep up to the stoep, above which the gable bears a winged hourglass to remind passers-by that 'time flies'.

Reinet House is now a superb period house museum, containing some of the personal possessions of the Murrays, and many fascinating domestic items. There is also a display on the town's Reinet dolls. These were first made during World War I when many luxury imports, including dolls, could not be obtained.

In the back yard of Reinet House there is a reconstructed water mill, which can be operated by inserting a coin, and nearby is the old Black Acorn vine planted in 1870 by Charles Murray — believed to have been the thickest in the world until dead wood was removed in 1983.

From the front door of Reinet House you can see the classic facade of the old Drostdy with the Camdeboo Mountains behind. Return to Parsonage Street, looking right as you cross Murray Street to see the old gunpowder store on Magazine Hill, which was carefully sited outside the town limits in 1831.

Walk along the northern side of Parsonage Street, where most of the little houses as far as Cross Street date from the mid-19th century. Number 18, at the corner of Cross Street, has a curiously 'detached' gable, and small-paned windows with old glass that produces distorted reflections.

The stately Dutch Reformed Church.

Turn right into Cross Street, which contains a number of simple, old buildings. On the corner of Somerset Street, on your left, is the *St James (Anglican) Church* **(6)**, consecrated in 1850. The original church forms the nave of the present building, and is the portion under the higher section of the roof. The church contains beautiful woodwork, and many memorials dating from the Anglo-Boer War.

Victorian beauties

Turn left into Somerset Street. Next to the church is the parish hall and the rectory — which has something of a doll's house quality — both of which date from 1895. Opposite is a long, two-gabled building **(7)** with a verandah with ornately fretted woodwork, and windows with elaborate glazing.

Cross Somerset Street towards numbers 22 and 24, which form a single unit with three doors and rounded windows on the street frontage. Number 26 shows fretted wooden railings and pillars, with much tracery-work below the eaves; while number 28, on the corner of Te Water Street, is a much-altered Victorian double-storey with a hoisting beam to raise goods to the attic.

Turn right into Te Water Street, a short street of small cottages. At the end of the street you emerge on to Church Square, passing the building of the *Graaff-Reinet Club* **(8)** on your right. This rather grand building was built in 1881 as a social club after the town authorities refused permission to open a 'smoking parlour' in Parsonage Street.

About three metres before you reach Caledon Street you can see to your left the chimney protruding from the *Dutch Reformed Church* **(9)** between the main and end sections. Chimneys rarely form part of ecclesiastical architecture, but the church elders required a fireplace in their consistory.

Before crossing to the church, walk north towards the *Mayor's Garden* **(10)**, with its war memorial, and beyond it the stone *Town Hall* **(11)**, built in 1910 and known as the Victoria Hall.

The Dutch Reformed Church is open to visitors during normal business hours and, on request, the collection of valuable Cape silver will be unlocked for viewing. In the consistory there are portraits of all the clergymen who have served the congregation, starting in 1792 with the Reverend van Manger. The church, consecrated in 1887, was built in the Gothic Revival style, and is known as the 'groot kerk' (big church) to distinguish it from the 'nuwe kerk' (new church).

Leave the church and walk along the left (eastern) side of Church Street. You pass a bank **(12)** on your left, that was originally the Standard Bank of British South Africa in 1874. Beyond this is a long row of newspaper offices.

Karoo fossils and San art

On the corner of Somerset Street, also on your left, is *Te Water House* **(13)**, built in 1818. It was formerly thatched, but now has an iron roof and clipped gables. It is one of the few old South African houses with an underground wine cellar, and was once the homestead of a wine estate.

Cross Somerset Street, and pass on your left the *Information Office* and *Reinet Museum* **(14)**, housed in the town's first library of 1847. On display are collections of period costume, fossil remains of Karoo reptiles of 200 million years ago, and carefully executed reproductions of San rock art.

Also on your left in Church Street, is the *Hester Rupert Art Gallery* **(15)**, in a cruciform building of 1821, built as a school and mission church. Like the similar institution in Swellendam, it was known as 'die oefeningshuis' — the house of (religious) practice or service — to comply with a regulation that stated that, in the country districts, no church should be built within three days' ride of an existing church of the same faith.

Cross Church Street and look along Parliament Street, where a number of the houses are national monuments, before returning to your starting point ●

The gracious old Reinet House, restored to the splendour of its earliest days.

Pillars of rock tower above the Valley of Desolation near Graaff-Reinet.

A desolate valley perched high in a thirsty mountain wilderness

Looking over the dry Karoo.

THE KAROO Nature Reserve all but surrounds the historic Karoo town of Graaff-Reinet (see pages 240-1), and the town serves as the ideal centre from which to visit the reserve. The reserve was established in 1975 by the South African Nature Foundation, and it encompasses 14 500 ha of Karoo plains and mountains, including the Van Ryneveld Pass Dam. This great tract of countryside, once fertile and covered with vegetation, had become badly over-grazed and had begun to show signs of consequent erosion, but today it is recognised in South Africa as a model of conservation and correct land management.

The reserve is effectively split into three sections by the roads to Middelburg and Murraysburg. The western section is the most accessible, and by far the most visited. The eastern section of the reserve is maintained as a natural wilderness — rough tracks do exist, but no good roads, and visitors who wish to hike through this part of the reserve must be accompanied by a member of the reserve staff.

Between the eastern and western sections lies the Van Ryneveld Pass Dam, which constitutes virtually a third section. This is an open area accessible only on foot, and the paths are rough — but the rich birdlife makes it well worth visiting. Among the most notable birds to be seen are large numbers of South African shelduck, Cape teal, yellow-billed duck, grey herons, Egyptian geese, spurwinged geese, white-breasted cormorants and flamingoes. A particularly good spot for viewing the flamingoes is the marshy area created by the Sundays River where it enters the dam.

Valley of Desolation

The western section of the reserve contains the most spectacular area — known as the 'Valley of Desolation'. Unexpectedly for a valley, this lies high above Graaff-Reinet. To reach the Valley of Desolation, drive out of Graaff-Reinet on the R63 towards Murraysburg, pass the Van Ryneveld Pass Dam on your right, then turn left to enter the reserve.

Butterflies seek Euphorbia nectar.

A good tarred road leads up the steep mountainside. Shortly before reaching the valley you pass a toposcope set on the summit of a small koppie known as 'The Lookout'. From here there is a magnificent view over Graaff-Reinet, and one can clearly see the ox-bow formed by the Sundays River as it curls lazily around the town.

The Valley of Desolation itself, noted for its grotesque and bizarre dolerite formations, offers a marvellous illustration of the processes of erosion. Jumbled dolerite pillars, which have weathered more slowly than the sedimentary rock surrounding them, now rise to heights of 120 m above the boulder-strewn valley floor. Cobbled paths lead to the edges of the valley, where convenient safety walls enable one to lean over and admire the confusion of rocks below — thought to be the product of some 200 million years of erosion.

You can also look across from here to Spandau Kop, standing guard over Graaff-Reinet rather like a towering fortress. (Spandau Kop is said to have been given this name by an early Prussian settler, who found that the mountain reminded him of Spandau Castle, a fortress situated near Berlin.)

Flora and fauna

It is interesting to note the changes in vegetation that one passes through as the road to the Valley of Desolation climbs up from the plains. The reserve contains several distinct vegetation zones. The plains are covered with thorny succulents and aromatic shrubs. The lower slopes of the mountains are sprinkled with spekboom, also known as 'elephant's bush' *(Portulacaria afra)* — a fleshy grey-green shrub that is a major source of food for grazing animals such as the kudu. Higher up the slopes the spekboom is gradually replaced by mountain veld or grassland — the home of klipspringer and mountain reedbuck. Finally, at the highest level, there is savannah grassland, dotted with stinkwood and karee trees.

This last type of vegetation covers much of the eastern section of the reserve, and is the favoured habitat of the Cape mountain zebra *(Equus zebra zebra)*, which were reintroduced into this area from the Mountain Zebra National Park near Cradock (see pages 228-9).

In addition to offering a home to mountain zebra, kudu, klipspringers and mountain reedbuck, the reserve contains black wildebeest, blesbok, springbok, steenbok and the common duiker — and there are many smaller mammals, including the caracal, the silver jackal and the bat-eared fox. Large leopard tortoises can often be seen in the summer months. The plan is to re-introduce other species eventually, including hartebeest, black rhino and buffalo, all of which once roamed the area freely.

The reserve also supports a wide variety of birds — quite apart from the water birds to be seen on the dam.

A distant view across the Karoo to the waters of the Van Ryneveld Pass Dam.

On the plains there are ostriches, blue cranes, bustards and secretary birds. High in the mountains black eagles build their nests on the towering cliffs and feed on the ever-present rock hyraxes, or 'dassies'.

There are few walks in the reserve that can be undertaken without being accompanied by a member of the reserve staff. However, you may if you wish walk up the plateau that overlooks the Valley of Desolation, and there are the various paths around the dam. There is also a steep walk to the top of Spandau Kop — where the adventurous will be rewarded with splendid views.

If you are planning any of these walks, make a point of taking drinking water with you. The Karoo takes its name from a Khoikhoi word meaning 'dry' or 'barren', and the area, which is classed as semi-desert, becomes extremely hot in the summer. If you are visiting the reserve in summer, you should confine any walking you do to the early morning and late afternoon — not only will you find the walk more pleasant, but the animals are also more active during these cooler periods.

A rich storehouse of fossils

This region was not always the semi-desert that it is today. The soil and the rock strata that have been exposed by erosion are rich in fossil reptiles — evidence that the area was once an extensive marsh, probably very hot and humid. These fossils are of international importance, and there is an excellent collection to be seen in the Reinet Museum in the town.

The reserve offers no overnight accommodation, and no camping is allowed within its boundaries except on guided hikes. However, there is a caravan park outside the town on the banks of the Sundays River, with a number of bungalows that can be rented, and there are several fine hotels in the town. The reserve is open to visitors every day from sunrise to sunset. Anyone wishing to take part in a hike through the wilderness areas of the reserve should contact the Officer-in-Charge, Karoo Nature Reserve, P O Box 349, Graaff-Reinet 6280 Tel. (0491) 23453 ●

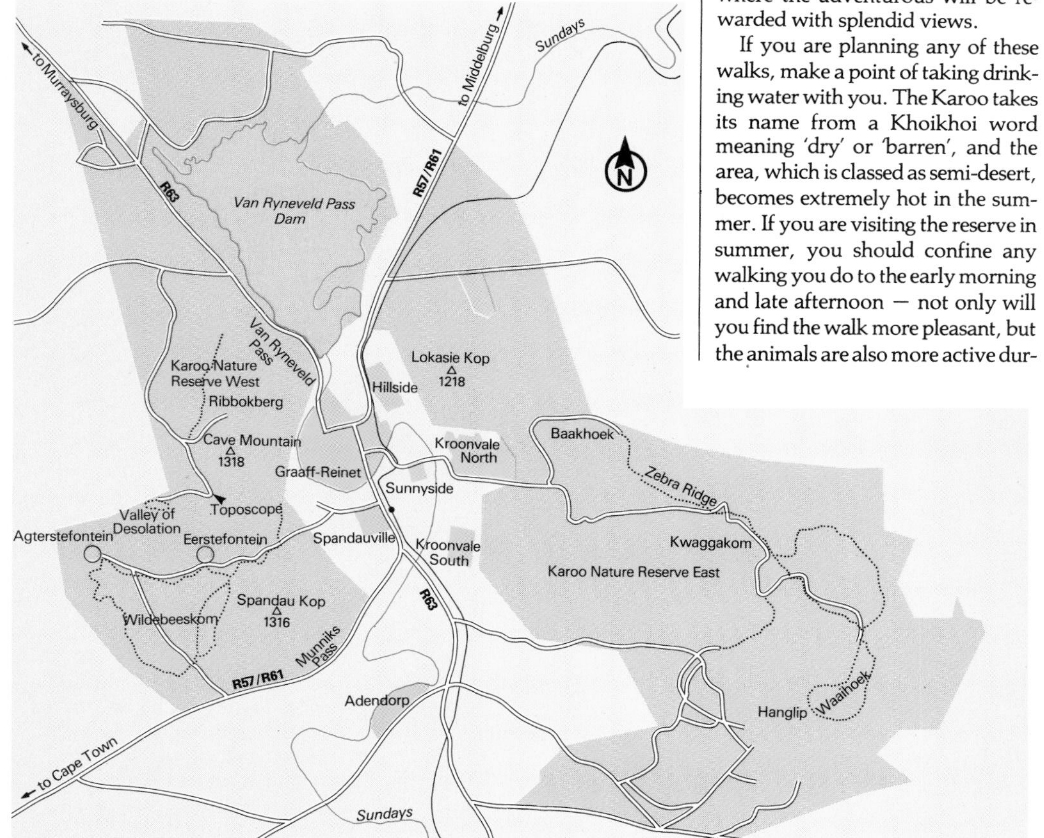

Insects feed off wild hibiscus.

SOUTHERN CAPE

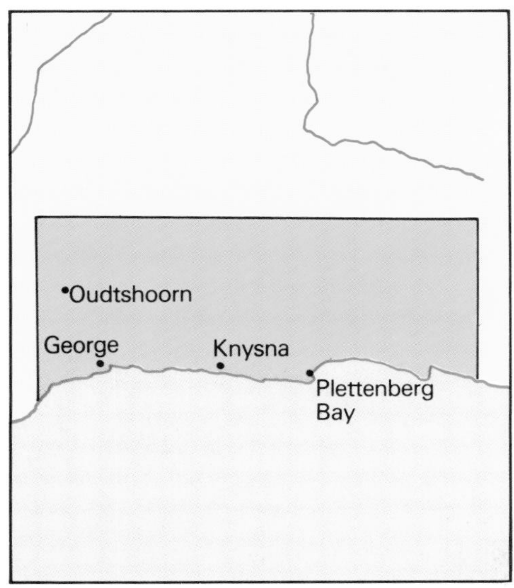

Above: *Sailing on the calm waters of Plettenberg Bay.* **Left:** *Two sandstone cliffs — The Heads — flank the entrance to the beautiful Knysna Lagoon.*

Through a giant's garden of dense forests and precipitous gorges

East of Plettenberg Bay the Tsitsikamma (sparkling water) Mountains crowd in towards the sea, ensuring a rich rainfall throughout the year. Our route leads along the coastal plateau at the foot of the mountains, through a quiet world of high, primeval forest, and deep gorges rushing clear mountain streams to the sea.

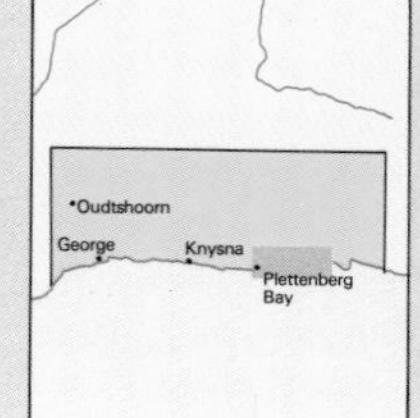

Plettenberg Bay
Keurbooms River
Nature's Valley
Tsitsikamma Nat. Park
Storms River
180 — 200 km

LEAVE PLETTENBERG BAY by driving past the beach and across the Piesang River, then turn right into Piesang Valley Road. Turn left after 200 m into Robberg Drive — noting your kms. After 3,4 km turn left and follow this side-road to the parking area at the beginning of the Robberg peninsula.

Walk 100 m along the path on the southern side of the peninsula for a view of the coast below. Then walk from the car park just 25 m through the fynbos to the northern side of the peninsula, for a grand vista over the entire Plettenberg Bay region to the Tsitsikamma Mountains in the distance — the particularly beautiful stretch of country that you are about to explore.

Robberg to Nature's Valley

Drive back towards the town, but turn left into Piesang Valley Road. Pass by the road to the Country Club, then turn right onto the N2 at the T-junction. The N2 offers fine views over the Keurbooms River lagoon.

Cross the Bietou River, then the Keurbooms River, and turn left at the far end of the Keurbooms River bridge, into the Keurbooms River Nature Reserve. An old track leads up-river, offering a pleasant walk (allow 45 min).

From Keurbooms River the road climbs fairly steeply and turns inland. Several parking areas along the route offer attractive views back over the bay and the lagoon. Turn right onto the R102 for Nature's Valley (there is a huge sign), avoiding the N2 toll road.

The R102 winds down through indigenous forest to the Groot River lagoon. At the bottom of the downhill stretch, turn right for Nature's Valley. After 1 km the road forks — take the left road to a large parking area. From here it is a short walk to the gently shelving beach and along the side of the lagoon. (Strong currents make it unsafe to swim near the river mouth.)

Nature's Valley to Storms River Mouth

Return to the R102 and turn right. There are shaded picnic sites where the road crosses the Groot River. After this the road climbs steeply out of the Groot River valley. At the top of the

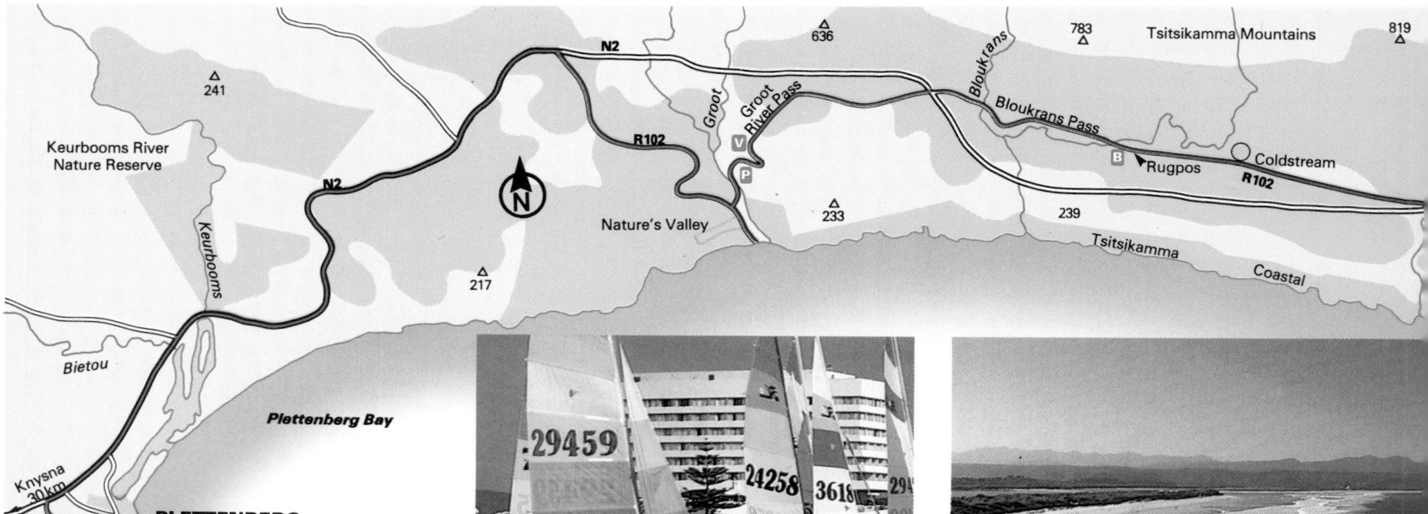

Water sports at Plettenberg Bay's Central Beach.

Lookout Beach and the Keurbooms River lagoon.

SEAL MOUNTAIN

Robberg or Robbe Berg (seal mountain) took its name from the many seals that once basked on its shores. The peninsula is now a nature reserve, noted for its varied coastal vegetation, its rich inter-tidal life, and its many bird species.

Archeological excavations in a large cave on the southern shore of the peninsula have revealed that this was once the home of prehistoric Strandlopers.

Fishing from the rocks is permitted in the reserve, and generations of fishermen have criss-crossed the peninsula with footpaths that hikers can use to reach numerous viewsites.

Die Eiland (the island) juts out into the sea from the southern shore of the Robberg peninsula.

PLETTENBERG BAY

Baia das Alagoas (bay of the lagoons) and *Baia Formosa* (beautiful bay) were among the names the Portuguese gave to this bay that Governor Joachim van Plettenberg subsequently renamed after himself. This was the site of the first European 'settlement' in South Africa. A Portuguese vessel, the *Sao Gonzales*, anchored here in the year 1630 and was wrecked during a gale. The survivors lived here for six months, building two small boats out of the wreckage. One boat reached Mocambique, and eventually Portugal. The other was picked up by another Portuguese vessel, the *St Ignatius Loyola*. Ironically, the *St Ignatius Loyola* was wrecked in the river Tagus, within sight of Lisbon, and most of the *Sao Gonzales* survivors were drowned.

uphill stretch, as the road swings to the right, park in the small area on your left for a view back over the valley and lagoon.

Continue on the R102, passing over the N2 toll road, down into the Bloukrans Pass. The road is narrow, and twists through dense indigenous forest. Looking up from the bottom of the pass you will see the Bloukrans Bridge (part of the toll road) high in the sky above you.

On the final pull up out of the pass, soon after the white-walled hairpin bend, a poorly defined road on your right leads to the shady Rugpos picnic site on the forest's edge. There are braai places here and short forest walks.

The R102 continues past the sawmilling centre of Coldstream, which has a shop and a petrol station. When you reach the T-junction turn left. 6,8 km after this, turn right for Storms River Mouth and the Tsitsikamma National Park. This side-road leads through plantations and into the National Park (small entrance fee), then winds through indigenous coastal forest to Storms River Mouth. The road ends alongside a restaurant, noted for its fresh line fish. There is a short walk from the restaurant along the shore and through indigenous forest to a suspension footbridge across the river mouth (allow 1 hr 30 min).

Storms River Mouth to Paul Sauer Bridge
Return to the N2 and turn right, noting your kms. After 5,2 km park off the road on your left at the sign to the 'Big Tree'. There are two parking areas, one near the road and a second deeper in the forest. An interesting 15 min walk, the Big Tree Trail, leads from the first parking area to the second. The 'Big Tree', an Outeniqua yellowwood, is just a few metres from the second parking area.

Continue along the N2 for 1 km before turning right onto a gravel road signposted 'Picnic spot'. Drive past the picnic sites near to the road and when the road forks, turn left. You are now on the original Storms River Pass road, built by Thomas Bain more than a century ago. It winds down through dense indigenous forest to a low bridge across the Storms River, and next to this is the shady Oubrug (old bridge) picnic site.

Retrace your route to the N2, watching carefully for the fork where you turned left — it looks quite different when you are coming from this direction. Turn right onto the N2, and after roughly 2 km, as you approach the Paul Sauer Bridge, park in the large parking area on your left. There is a restaurant here, also a shop and a petrol station. From the restaurant there is an attractive circular forest walk known as the Tree Fern Trail (allow 1 hr). Along the route there is a gigantic fallen yellowwood and a reconstruction of an old-fashioned saw-pit.

Return towards Plettenberg Bay on the N2. Take the toll road if you are in a hurry, or follow the signs onto the R102 if you have the time to retrace your outgoing route through the Bloukrans Pass and past Nature's Valley. If time allows, return to your first stop of the day, the beginning of the Robberg peninsula, and walk to the north-facing viewsite to look out over the bay in its evening colours ●

Plettenberg Bay Publicity Association Sewell Street, Plettenberg Bay 6600 Tel. (04457) 32050
SA Tourism Board 310 Mutual Building, Mutual Arcade, 64 Main Street, Port Elizabeth 6000 Tel. (041) 27761

Knysna loerie (Tauraco corythaix).

Surf pounds the rocky shore of the Coastal National Park — scene of the Tsitsikamma Underwater Trail.

THE TSITSIKAMMA PARKS
The Tsitsikamma Coastal National Park stretches for roughly 75 km along the southern Cape coast. It comprises a wild, unspoilt and rugged belt of land, much of it blanketed in dense indigenous forest, and fragmented by winding river valleys.

There are numerous walks and trails through the park, ranging from strenuous five-day hikes (The Otter Trail, and the Tsitsikamma Hiking Trail) to easy one-hour strolls. A particular attraction is the Tsitsikamma Underwater Trail designed for swimmers and scuba divers. The boundary of the reserve lies 800 m offshore and the marine segment of the reserve is notable for its rich variety of both warm-water and cold-water species.

The Tsitsikamma Forest National Park lies a short distance inland from the Coastal Park and is noted for its fine yellowwoods and stinkwoods. It has three short trails running through it, the 15-minute Big Tree Trail, the one-hour Tree Fern Trail, and the slightly longer Bushpig Trail that links the other two together.

Both the Knysna loerie and the relatively rare Narina trogon inhabit the forest, and in addition to the well-known yellowwoods and stinkwoods there are many impressive ironwoods to be seen.

A mighty yellowwood in the Groot River valley.

STORMS RIVER MOUTH
The Storms River divides the Tsitsikamma Coastal National Park in half, and the principal access road into the park brings visitors to a point within a few hundred metres from the river's mouth. Several paths lead off from here, one leading to a suspension footbridge over the river and to a small Strandloper cave.

The suspension footbridge over the Storms River.

A wild, rocky coast and quiet forests of mighty trees

Between Plettenberg Bay and Knysna the N2 winds through pine and eucalyptus plantations and patches of indigenous forest. Today's drive, much of it on gravel, follows several side-roads, two of which lead to the coast — then turns inland to explore the depths of the primeval forest, where the last of the Knysna elephants live their secret lives.

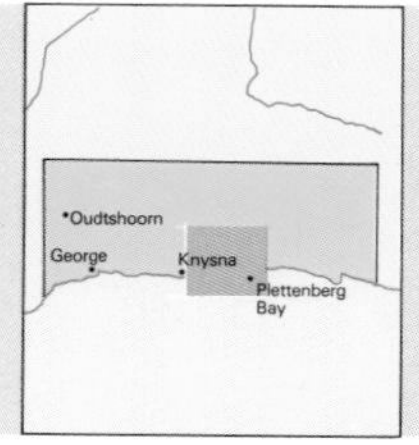

Plettenberg Bay
Kranshoek
Noetzie
Spitskop
Diepwalle
Dieprivier
140—160km

LEAVE PLETTENBERG BAY on the N2 towards Knysna, and note your kms as you pass the Stromboli Motel on your left. After a further 3,7km turn left onto a good gravel road signposted 'Harkerville'. 1km later turn left, and after a further 500m, at a small group of houses, turn right, passing picturesque cottages before entering indigenous forest with ferns crowding the roadside.

The road eventually emerges from the forest onto high cliffs covered with fynbos. There are two large, lawned picnic areas, the first by the Kranshoek River (with toilets, braai places and water) and the second (with toilets and water, no braai places) a few hundred metres further, on the edge of the cliffs, with a magnificent view over the rocky coastline. From the first site there is a short walk to a point from where the Kranshoek River can be seen falling ovei the rock face in an almost sheer drop. (Children must be held here, as the cliff top is unfenced.)

Kranshoek to Noetzie
Return to the N2 and turn left. After 7,5km on the N2 turn left onto a gravel road for Bracken Hill Falls, passing a signposted 'Big Tree' on the left (a Karri Gum, 67m tall). Keep right at the fork, to reach the Bracken Hill Falls viewsite (with toilets). Here the Witels River takes a spectacular tumble into a bushy gorge.

Return to the N2 and turn left. At the crossroads for Uniondale/Noetzie turn left onto the gravel road to Noetzie. This road offers outstanding views of the Knysna lagoon, then descends past rocky cliffs to a parking area above Noetzie, 5km from the N2.

From the parking area, walk down the concrete strip road towards the river mouth. When the strip road forks, keep right. Near the bottom, walk down the stone steps on your left. The Noetzie River has a small lagoon and a wide sandy beach at its mouth. There are no refreshments available on the beach, but there is a small toilet block tucked away in the bush near the lagoon, and water is available here.

Noetzie to Dieprivier
Return to the N2, and drive straight across the N2 onto the tarred road to 'Prince Alfred's Pass/Uniondale/Avontuur'. The tar ends after roughly 5km. There are several picnic sites along the road, located at or near 'Big Trees'. Some sites have water and toilets. All have tables and benches.

The first picnic site is on your left, just over 14km from the N2. Across the road there is a 600m path to a giant Outeniqua yellowwood, 620 years old and 38m high.

Any of the picnic sites along this forest road will make an ideal spot to break for lunch. One of the most interesting sites is near the King Edward VII Tree at Diepwalle. The tree marks the start of the Elephant Nature Trail.

Go left where a minor road keeps straight for Kransbos. 5,6km after this fork a 1,5km road leads off to the left to the Spitskop viewpoint. This road is steep, narrow and rough, and you cannot turn until you reach the top. There are also enormous drops over the unprotected edge. Park and walk if you prefer. The walk to the top will reward you with a wonderful 360-degree view and is highly recommended.

Return to the main road towards Avontuur and drive on, noting your kms. Pass a second turn-off to Kransbos. After 15km you will reach the Dieprivier picnic site, with braai places, a pleasantly shady expanse of lawn, and the river flowing past. A stone cairn and plaque commemorate Thomas Bain, who built the road on which you have been travelling.

(More adventurous drivers may continue north over the precipitous but spectacular Prince Alfred's Pass to Avontuur, returning to the Dieprivier picnic site by the same route. However, this should not be attempted unless the weather is completely clear and you have at least two hours of daylight left. This pass must never be attempted if you are towing.)

Dieprivier to Plettenberg Bay
Retrace your route from Dieprivier, but turn left at the fork at Kruisvallei, towards Kransbos and Keurbooms River. The road passes through farmlands and forests, with the rugged gorges of the Keurbooms River on your left.

About 7km after Kruisvallei the road passes below Perdekop, closely following the route of a track built almost two centuries ago. As you reach the summit about 9km from Kruisvallei there are fine views on all sides.

A little over 18km from Kruisvallei you reach the tarred road. 8km later you pass a turn-off to the right towards Wittedrif. 5km further on, after passing the wide flats of the Bietou River on your right, you reach the N2 at Keurbooms River mouth. Turn right for a short drive back to Plettenberg Bay on the N2 ●

AA Office Millwood Building, cnr York/Victoria Sts, George 6530 Tel. (0441) 3041
Plettenberg Bay Publicity Association Sewell St, Plettenberg Bay 6600
Tel. (04457) 32050
Knysna Publicity Association 40 Main St, Knysna 6570 Tel. (0445) 21610
SA Tourism Board 124 York St, George 6530
Tel. (0441) 5228

The delightful, unspoilt beach at Noetzie.

NOETZIE
Noted for its modern 'castles', Noetzie is one of the prettiest little places on this scenically magnificent southern coast. It was also the scene of an unsolved mystery. In 1881 a three-masted schooner, the *Phoenix*, was washed onto the rocks near the river mouth. No trace was ever found of her crew, and the last entry in her cargo book had been made five years earlier.

A rare photograph of one of Knysna's elephants.

ELEPHANTS OF THE FOREST
The extensive forests of the southern Cape were originally the home of large herds of elephant, but persistent hunting throughout the 18th and 19th centuries greatly reduced their numbers.

The hunting seems also to have made them very wary of mankind, with the result that it is now difficult to locate and count the few that survive. A count carried out in 1982 found only three, but there may well be others living in remote parts of the forest.

One of the most celebrated elephant hunters to pass this way was Queen Victoria's second son, Prince Alfred, after whom Prince Alfred's Pass was named. Another renowned hunter by the name of Marais is said to have accounted for exactly 99 elephants. He boasted that before killing his hundredth he would first pluck a hair from its tail. He did indeed pluck the hair, but No 100 succeeded in killing him in the process.

Occasionally the elephants have killed people other than their hunters. A recent instance was in 1963 when an angry cow elephant caught and killed a labourer in the forest near Veldmanspad.

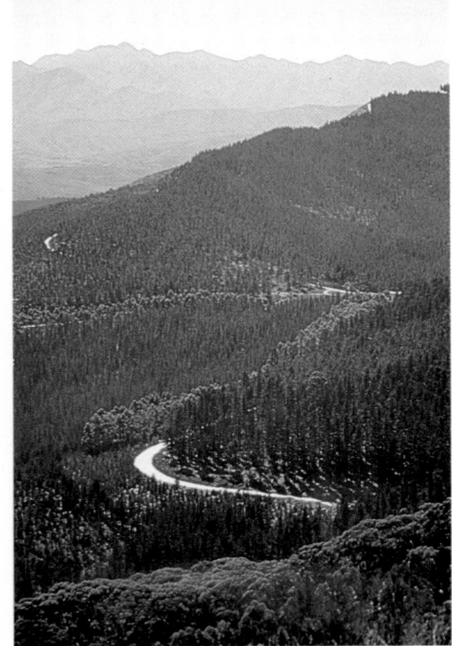

A section of Thomas Bain's road through the forests from Knysna to Avontuur.

The magnificent coastal vista — looking west from the second Kranshoek picnic area.

The massive trunk of an Outeniqua yellowwood, undisputed monarch of the southern forests.

THOMAS BAIN AND PRINCE ALFRED'S PASS

From our turning point at the Dieprivier picnic site, the road to Avontuur continues north over Prince Alfred's Pass. This is a narrow pass and dangerous in bad weather, but it offers magnificent views over some of the wildest scenery in southern Africa. The pass and the landscape have changed little since the building of the road was completed in May 1867.

The route was originally worked out in 1856 by the Scottish-born road builder Andrew Geddes Bain. However, it was left to his son Thomas to complete the building of the road, with a work force of 270 convicts.

During the building, Bain lived with his family in the farmhouse known as Die Vlug — which you pass on the way on the left side of the road.

MONARCH OF THE FORESTS

The grandest of the many species of indigenous trees that grow in these southern forests is unquestionably the Outeniqua yellowwood (*Podocarpus falcatus*).

Many of the giants were felled by woodcutters before controls were introduced in the 1920s, but some fine specimens were left standing. One of these is the King Edward VII Tree that you pass on this route, standing 46 m high and with a girth of 9,5 m — and estimated to be at least 700 years old.

The yellowwood was a boon to the early colonists. Its timber is as light as Oregon pine but far stronger, which made it ideal for furniture, ceiling beams and floor boards. Early examples of yellowwood furniture are now much sought-after by collectors, and fetch very high prices.

Jewel-like lakes, and gold hidden in the forest's streams

This drive explores one of the most romantic regions in southern Africa — the emerald-green landscape of Knysna, the old gold mines that can still be visited in the forests nearby, and the string of glittering lakes that stretches eastwards from Wilderness. More than half of the route is tarred, and the rest is good gravel.

Oudtshoorn
George
Knysna
Plettenberg Bay

Knysna
Brenton-on-Sea
Millwood
Wilderness
Sedgefield
200 — 220 km

AT THE EASTERN END of Knysna turn off the N2 onto George Rex Drive towards the Knysna Heads. As you approach the Heads, take the left fork, uphill, following the sign to the 'view point'. This road climbs for 1 km to a car park on top of the eastern Head. There is a viewsite a few metres downhill from the car park, but young children must be held, as the cliff edge is only partially fenced.

Knysna Heads to Millwood

Return to the N2, turn left, and drive through Knysna. The road skirts the lagoon, then crosses a concrete bridge. At the far end of the bridge turn right, and take the road towards Brenton, which swings around and passes under the bridge. 1,6 km after the bridge, turn left onto a narrow road that winds down to Belvidere Church (see opposite).

Return to the road for Brenton and turn left. Note your kms as you cross the railway line. After 1,5 km park in a small area on your left (not very visible from this direction). Beware of sticking in the soft sand. From here there is a splendid view over the whole Knysna region.

Drive on to Brenton-on-Sea. There is a hotel here, and you can walk down wooden steps for a short stroll along the beautiful beach.

Return to the N2, and turn right towards George. After 2 km on the N2, turn off right for Rheenendal. 1,1 km along this road, park on your left, and walk across the road for another fine view over the Knysna Lagoon.

Pass through the little settlement of Rheenendal, then turn right onto a gravel road for 'Millwood/Goldfields'. Follow this road past the forestry offices on your right and later a 'Big Tree' picnic site on your left (braai places, water, toilets). Keep right here, following signs to Jubilee Creek. Where the road divides into three, keep left for 'Millwood Hut via Jubilee Creek'. At the next fork keep left again, and follow the road down into Jubilee Creek to the picnic area (toilets, braai places, water from the river).

Driving back from Jubilee Creek, turn left at the fork for Millwood. 3,7 km along this road you pass a turn-off to the old town's cemetery on your right. Just after this, the road forks. The left road used to be Millwood's main street, but nothing of the town remains, except for a few fruit trees and flowers.

Unless you wish to explore the site, take the road to the right, then at the next fork go right again. Follow this road, formerly 'St Patrick Street', until you see the boiler of an old steam engine in a clearing on your left. This was the site of the stamp battery of the Bendigo mine, worked by a party of Australians.

A sign points to a mine below the road. This is the main Bendigo Tunnel, which reaches 200 m into the hillside and now houses a large

The unspoilt sweep of sandy beach at Wilderness makes a splendid walk.

MILLWOOD GOLD AND JUBILEE CREEK

In 1876 gold was discovered in the Knysna forests. Fortune-hunters began pouring into the area and the mining town of Millwood sprang up amid the many claims. In its heyday, Millwood could boast a post office, a periodic court, three competing newspapers, numerous shops and six hotels. Most of the houses in the town were built of corrugated iron, erected on a stone foundation.

The gold reefs proved thin, and difficult to work, so the miners gradually drifted away, many to the goldfields in the Transvaal. By 1900 only a few pioneers remained, and the goldfield was deproclaimed in 1924. All that remains are the cemetery, traces of old workings scattered about the forest, and a lingering dream.

Jubilee Creek is one of several sites where alluvial gold was panned. As you approach the picnic site, to the right of the causeway across the river, a pleasant footpath leads through the forest and along the bank of the river to an abandoned gold mine. The mine consists of just a single adit, but you will need old clothes and a torch to explore it.

A few hundred metres beyond the mine there is an impressive waterfall and a deep pool in the river.

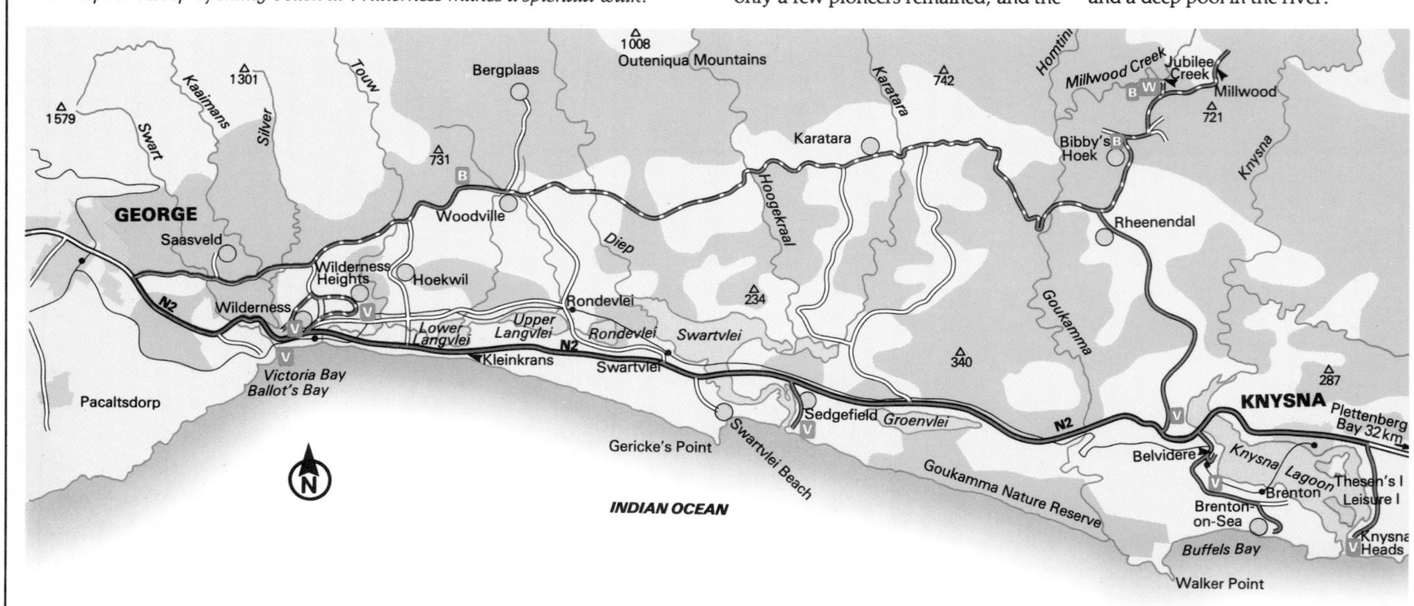

bat population. (It can be reached by car — retrace your route and take the first left turn.)

From Millwood through the Passes

Retrace your route past the forestry station and turn right onto the tarred road. The tar soon gives way to gravel, and the road winds down to an iron-girder bridge across the Homtini River. After the bridge, the road climbs out of the gorge, passes through farmlands, then drops again to the Karatara River.

After crossing the Karatara River on a single-lane bridge, the road passes the Karatara forestry settlement. The next pass leads through the gorge of the Hoogekraal River, and the one after this takes you across the Diep River.

You reach the tar again roughly 35 km from Rheenendal, and soon after this you pass the small settlement of Woodville. Turn right onto the gravel road signposted 'Big Tree and Picnic Spot'. The picnic site to which this leads has braai places and toilets. From the car park a short path leads across a wooden bridge to the Woodville Big Tree, an Outeniqua yellowwood roughly 800 years old.

Return to the tarred road and turn right, noting your kms. After a little over 3 km, turn right onto a gravel road for 'Saasveld'. The road now negotiates three more river-valley passes. Note your kms as you cross the Touw River, and 4,6 km later keep straight, onto the tar, for 'George'. You then cross the Silver River, and after this the Kaaimans River. The old stone bridges over the Silver and the Kaaimans rivers have been proclaimed national monuments.

After climbing out of the Kaaimans valley you pass Saasveld on your right. This is the country's only training school for foresters, and it is worth driving into the grounds to appreciate its beautiful setting. 5 km after Saasveld you reach the N2, shortly before entering George. Unless you wish to stop in George, turn left onto the N2 towards Knysna.

The N2 crosses the Swart River, and immediately afterwards the Kaaimans River. It then swings around the hillside overlooking the Kaaimans River mouth, presenting a splendid view of wild beaches and lakes stretching far into the distance. Stop in the parking area alongside the road to appreciate the view.

At the bottom of the hill, turn left into the village of Wilderness. After passing the Wilderness Hotel, turn left at the T-junction. Turn right almost immediately onto the narrow White's Road, and follow this road as it climbs the hills north of Wilderness. Turn right onto the tarred road, then turn left, following the sign to 'Map of Africa'. This side-road leads to a viewsite overlooking the Kaaimans River. A twist in the river encloses an area of wooded land that resembles the map of Africa as viewed from the south.

Drive back down White's Road, stopping part-way down for a fine view over the lakes. Retrace your route to the N2, and turn left towards Knysna.

When you reach Sedgefield, turn right into the road signposted 'Police'. Drive around the traffic circle and continue straight towards the sea, with Sedgefield Lagoon on your right. Park in the parking area next to the lagoon mouth for a walk along the beach.

As you walk towards the sea, a path on your left, with a few broken steps, leads around to the top of a weathered bluff. There are views from here along the beach. (Archeological research has shown that this was for many centuries a favourite Strandloper camping site.)

Return to the N2 and turn right for Knysna. You will pass Groenvlei on your right, the only fresh water lake in this region. If time allows, return to the 'soft sand' viewsite on the road to Brenton-on-Sea, to look out over that same vista in its evening mood ●

AA Office Millwood Bldg, cnr York/Victoria Sts, George 6530 Tel. (0441) 3041
Knysna Publicity Association 40 Main St, Knysna 6570 Tel. (0445) 21610
S A Tourism Board 124 York St, George 6530 Tel. (0441) 5228

A tranquil evening vista typical of the lake country to the west of Sedgefield.

BELVIDERE CHURCH

'The little church dreams on in quietness,
Its ancient peace more vocal than a psalm.'
— from *Memories of Belvidere* by O R Bridgman *ca* 1935.

In 1833 a Captain Thomas Henry Duthie of the Seaforth Highlanders married Caroline, daughter of George Rex, and purchased from his father-in-law a large tract of land on the western shore of the Knysna Lagoon. On a gentle slope, a few paces from the lagoon, Duthie built this church, with the help of several other families living in the region.

The church took five years to build, and is a miniature in the Norman style of the 11th and 12th centuries.

Belvidere Church at Knysna.

Scene of the Emu's *foundering — the brightly coloured Knysna Heads watch over the dangerous but navigable channel leading into Knysna Lagoon.*

THE 'STRAIGHT DOWN' PLACE

The name *Knysna* is believed by some authorities to be a Khoikhoi word meaning 'straight down' — a reference to the sheer cliffs known as The Heads.

Knysna's most celebrated settler was George Rex, who arrived in 1804. Legend has made him an illegitimate son of George III of England, but this has never been proved. Rex worked hard to develop Knysna as a port. In 1817 the brig *Emu* struck a rock as she entered the channel between The Heads, but a second vessel, the *Podargus*, sent to salvage the *Emu*, entered and left the lagoon successfully. From then on Knysna served as a port for small to medium-sized vessels, and Rex's own boat, the 127-ton *Knysna*, traded along the coast.

Pleasure boats laze at their moorings in Knysna Lagoon.

A ride through the Lake District on the 'Outeniqua Choo-choo'

WHEN THE RAILWAY reached George in 1907, after years of delay, the entire town turned out to watch the first train puff into the station. During the festivities, the archdeacon observed that its arrival would be like the kiss of the handsome prince that woke the Sleeping Beauty. Perhaps he was right — there is certainly a fairy-tale quality in a journey by steam train through this fascinating part of the southern Cape.

The 'lakes route' between George and Knysna is one of the last stretches of rail in the country still traversed regularly by a steam locomotive, and the 'Outeniqua Choo-choo' that works this line is known to steam enthusiasts worldwide.

Emerging from the second tunnel to cross the Kaaimans River mouth.

The choo-choo makes no special concessions for visitors — it is a goods train with usually just a single passenger coach attached at the end. The train leaves George early in the morning and arrives in Knysna well before midday — stopping on the way at a host of quaint little places, such as Bleshoender (bald chicken) and Mielierug (mielie ridge). (Passengers may board and disembark at any of the stations along the line.) After a leisurely lunch break in Knysna, the train sets off along the same route back to George — arriving home in mid-afternoon.

A hidden treasure chest

From George station, the line runs along the valley of the Meul (Mill) River, with views down to the sea at Ballot's Bay — where a treasure chest is said to lie wedged in the rocks awaiting recovery. The first stop is Victoria Bay, immediately above the tiny beach. This is a popular surfing spot, with a small fishing jetty and a children's paddling pool.

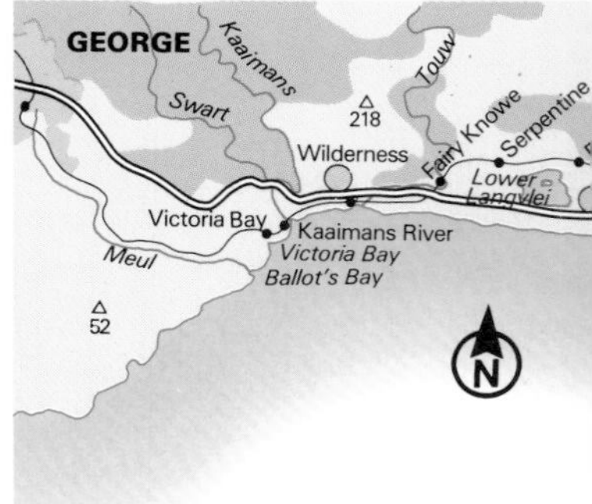

Soon after Victoria Bay the train enters a pair of tunnels, then emerges onto a bridge across the mouth of the Kaaimans River. The railings on the bridge are below the height of the carriage windows, and the train seems to be floating high above the river. From the bridge there are superb views, both up the river and out to sea. Soon afterwards there is a magnificent view on your right over the Wilderness beach, stretching away far into the distance.

Island of the camel's hump

The line descends gradually to the pretty Wilderness station, then crosses the mouth of the Touw River on an iron bridge. Soon after this it crosses the Touw a second time and passes (on your right) a small rounded hill known as Fairy Knowe.

You cross the Touw River a third time, on a combined road and rail

The 'choo-choo' steams out onto the long bridge over Knysna's Lagoon.

bridge, then travel alongside the Serpentine — a meandering waterway that links the Touw River to Lower Langvlei, also known as Island Lake. As you pass the lake you will see the island that gives it this name, known as Dromedaris Island (dromedary island) because of its likeness to a camel's hump.

Meandering among the lakes

A narrow canal links Lower Langvlei to Upper Langvlei, which is linked in its turn to Rondevlei by yet another canal. The line passes along the northern shores of these lakes, offering tranquil views of small-scale farming scenes, then turns south-east, through pine forest, and runs between Rondevlei and Swartvlei.

Swartvlei is by far the largest of the lakes in the region. The line runs along its shore, then crosses it at its southern end, shortly before arriving at Sedgefield. After Sedgefield you travel the full length of Groenvlei, the only freshwater lake in the region, then climb through forest, and wind down steeply into the vivid green of the Goukamma valley.

The climb out of the Goukamma valley involves a series of loops — leading to Keytersnek. After this you begin to catch glimpses of Knysna Lagoon. The train stops at Belvidere, and again on the very edge of the lagoon at Brenton. After skirting the western shore it then swings out over the water and crosses the lagoon on a long wooden bridge, with Knysna station waiting at the far end ●

IN HOLIDAY SEASONS the workaday choo-choo is sometimes replaced by 'Tootsie', a glamorous passenger train for the tourist and the enthusiast — travelling a longer route from Mossel Bay to Knysna. To make enquiries or reservations for either train, contact any South African railway station, or Sartravel, Market Street, George 6530. Tel. (0441) 68202.

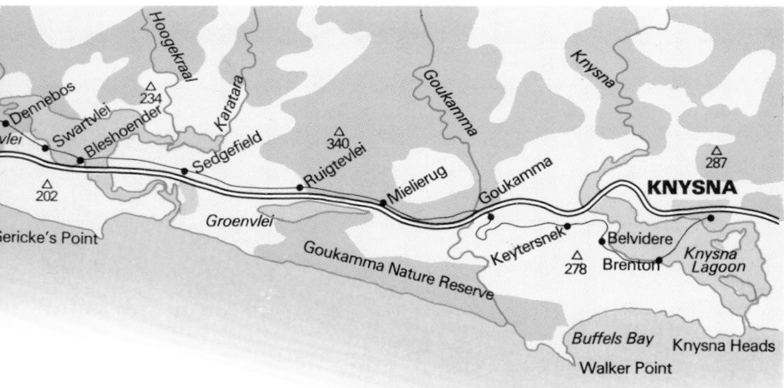

Huffing and puffing out of Wilderness station in a blaze of early morning sun.

'Choo-choo' maintenance is an art.

Across the Touw River a second time — the third will be on a narrow bridge where cars must share the railway line.

Over the Outeniqua Mountains to the Little Karoo and Kango Caves

Heading west from George, our route leads through the lush coastal garden of the southern Cape to the sandy shores of Mossel Bay, then turns inland, over the Outeniqua Mountains to the Little Karoo — a dry land of ostriches and scattered white-washed farmhouses — and the Kango Caves. All but some 36 km of the route is on tar.

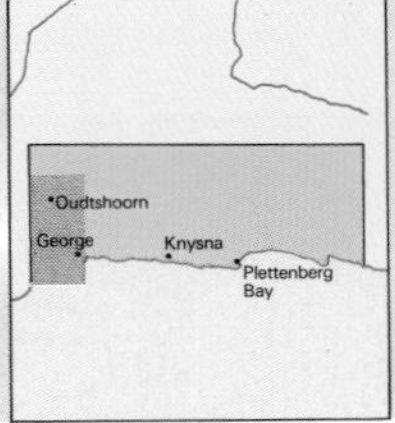

George
Great Brak River
Robinson Pass
Oudtshoorn
Rus-en-Vrede
Kango Caves
Outeniqua Pass
250 – 270 km

LEAVE GEORGE ON C J Langenhoven Street, heading towards Oudtshoorn. After passing the golf course on your left, turn left into Witfontein Road towards Blanco, and turn right at the next signpost for 'P W Botha Airport via Blanco'. After a few hundred metres the road crosses the Malgas River, with a picturesque old stone bridge to your left. At the far end of the village of Blanco, take the road that veers left, and continue past hop plantations to the old national road (R102).

Drive straight across the R102, and after driving around the airport, turn right onto the N2 towards Mossel Bay. The N2 sweeps down over the coastal hills, offering splendid views over the sea to Mossel Bay and Cape St Blaize.

As the N2 descends to sea level it crosses a bridge over the Great Brak River. At the far end of the bridge, turn left for 'Great Brak River/Route 102', and immediately turn left again. Drive back over the river on the old bridge, then turn right and cross the railway line. Pass the station, then turn right to reach 'The Island' by driving across one channel of the lagoon on a single-lane bridge. Park where convenient on the island (or park on the mainland and walk across the bridge).

Several lanes between the holiday houses lead down to the beach — an attractive 30-40 min walk. (If the water level is too high for this, you can reach the sea by driving around the lagoon to the western side.)

Great Brak River to Robinson Pass
Retrace your route across the old bridge to the western side of the Great Brak River, noting your kms at the end of the bridge. Do not turn right onto the N2, but continue straight on the R102 towards the Little Brak River.

After 8 km turn right and cross over the N2, then at the T-junction turn right again, towards Oudtshoorn. 1,3 km after the T-junction the road forks — take the left road here. Drive past a road on your right to Gonnakraal 2,2 km later, and take the next turn to your right 200 m after this, keeping to the tar. After another 200 m the tar ends — note your kms here. The road continues to climb, offering views over the Little Brak River.

The road now winds among hills and farmlands, and offers increasingly spectacular views as it approaches the Outeniqua Mountains. After 13,2 km on the gravel there is a road on your right to Leeukloof — drive 200 m along it, just over the hill, for the view, then return to the junction and continue on the main gravel road.

3 km later, turn right onto the tarred R328. After 2,5 km on the R328 you reach the Eight Bells Mountain Inn — the official entry point for the Ruitersbos Forest (see below).

From the Eight Bells Mountain Inn, continue on the R328 over the Robinson Pass. Viewsites and picnic spots dot the roadside, and it is interesting to note how the fynbos changes in character as the road climbs higher. This present Robinson Pass road follows the original Attaquas Kloof road built by Thomas Bain in 1869, and climbs to 860 m above sea level.

Robinson Pass to the Kango Caves
From the summit of the pass the road descends steeply into the Little Karoo, and the landscape becomes drier, with aloes dotting the hills. 1,5 km after the summit there is a picnic site on your right with fine views. As you descend into the Little Karoo you can see the Groot Swartberg range shimmering on the horizon.

You are now in ostrich country, and it is possible to visit an ostrich show farm. You pass two as you drive towards Oudtshoorn. The first is the Highgate Ostrich Farm, 2,3 km along the second tarred road to your left signposted Volmoed. The second is the Safari Farm, set just off the main road (R328) on your right. Both farms date back to the days of the ostrich-feather boom at the turn of the century.

Shortly after the turn-off to the Safari Farm you reach a T-junction — turn right for Oudtshoorn (see pages 256-7). At the second set of traffic lights turn left into Baron van Reede Street. As you turn you will see on your left a gracious old stone building that now houses the C P Nel Museum — noted for its ostrich exhibits. Park nearby to visit the museum. (Several establishments in Oudtshoorn offer lunch.)

Continue out of town on Baron van Reede Street, which becomes the main road to the Kango Caves. Note your kms as you leave Oudtshoorn. The road passes a crocodile ranch and the Greystone Wildlife Park, then leads through Schoemanspoort, along the shady banks of the Grobbelaars River, where there are picnic sites on your left.

For an especially attractive picnic spot, turn right onto a gravel road roughly 20 km after leaving Oudtshoorn. 10 km along this road you reach the Rus-en-Vrede picnic area (small entry fee, braai places, water, toilets). From the picnic area a 2,5 km road, and then a short footpath, lead to the Rus-en-Vrede waterfall, which plunges 80 m into a series of pools. (The path includes steps and narrow bridges, and is not recommended for small children.)

Retrace your route to the tarred road and turn right for the Kango Caves. The road leads directly into the Kango Caves parking area after roughly 6 km. Regular tours of the caves are conducted through the day. You can ascertain the latest starting time before setting out on your journey by telephoning the Oudtshoorn Tourist Bureau (04431) 2221, or the Kango Caves office (04435) 7410.

Kango Caves to George
Return through Schoemanspoort to Oudtshoorn. Drive the full length of Baron van Reede Street and continue on this same street where it veers left slightly and changes its name to Langenhoven Street. Langenhoven Street eventually becomes the R29 to George.

31 km after leaving Oudtshoorn, turn right at the fork for George (the left road leads to Uniondale and Port Elizabeth). As you approach the Outeniqua Pass the road again leads through plantations of hops, and also numerous orchards of apples and pears.

The road rises steeply to the summit of the Outeniqua Pass (799 m) then winds down the southern slopes to the coastal plateau and George. There are beautiful vistas over the whole George area and the sea shimmering in the distance. Several parking areas along the route offer opportunities to enjoy the view ●

AA Office Millwood Building, cnr York/Victoria Sts, George 6530 Tel. (0441) 3041
Oudtshoorn Tourist Bureau Civic Centre, Voortrekker Road, Oudtshoorn 6620 Tel. (04431) 2221
SA Tourism Board 124 York Street, George 6530 Tel. (0441) 5228

'The N2 sweeps down over the coastal hills...'.

EIGHT BELLS INN AND WALKING TRAILS
The Eight Bells Mountain Inn on the southern side of the Robinson Pass is the official start and finish of the Ruitersbos Forest Walk, laid out by the Department of Forestry. Entry is permitted between 08h00 and 16h00 (no dogs, vehicles, smoking or fires) and visitors must sign at the reception desk before starting the walk. The paths, marked in yellow for 'young and old' and white for fitter walkers, lead through fynbos particularly rich in proteas, and through patches of indigenous forest along the banks of the Perdeberg River — many of the trees are identified by their national tree numbers. Details and maps are available from the reception office at the Inn. Outside the main building of the Inn there is an enormous oak tree reputed to have been planted in 1817, when the original title deeds were granted by Lord Charles Somerset.

Visitors are dwarfed by the crystal wonderland lying hidden in the Kango Caves.

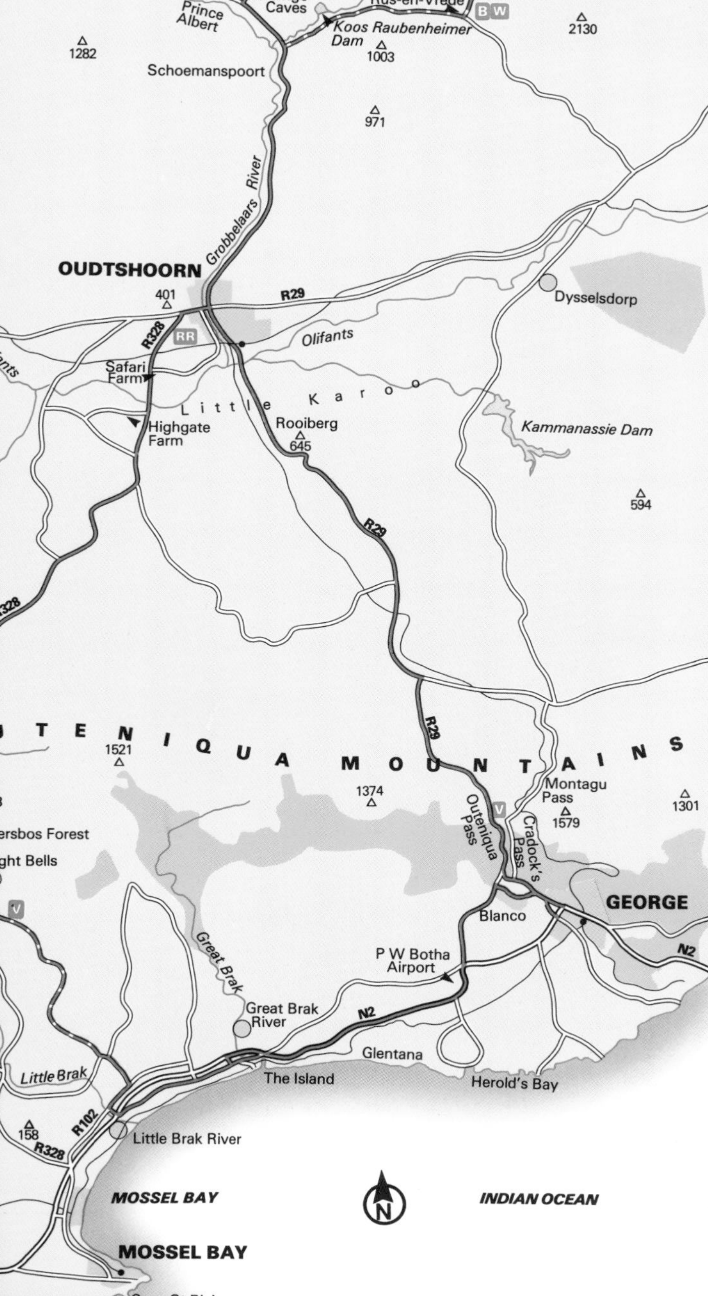

THE CAVES OF THE KANGO MOUNTAINS

The Kango Caves are regarded as one of South Africa's foremost natural wonders. They owe their origin to a geological fault in the Swartberg mountains (which were known to the San as the *Kango*). Water seeping through the limestone rock, over hundreds of thousands of years, created the present display of grand caverns ornamented with dripstone formations — stalagmites reaching up from the floor, and stalactites hanging from the ceiling.

The cave sequence known as Kango One was discovered by a herdsman in 1780. Two large extensions of this original sequence were discovered relatively recently, Kango Two in 1972 and Kango Three in 1975, but neither of these is yet open to the public.

Looking east from the Outeniqua Pass, you can see the Montagu Pass of 1847.

BIRDS OF A FEATHER

Standing 2,4 m high and weighing up to 135 kg, the commercially bred ostriches of the Little Karoo around Oudtshoorn are remnants from the great ostrich-feather boom of the late 19th and early 20th centuries. At its height, there were more than 750 000 domesticated ostriches in the Little Karoo — a good breeding pair could fetch what was an enormous sum for those days: R2 000.

The boom lasted from 1870 until the start of World War I, when the wearing of ostrich feathers did not fit the austere image of the war years. Many farmers went bankrupt, although the ostrich industry revived somewhat with a demand for ostrich skin, biltong, eggs and feathers. At present there are about 90 000 ostriches in the region.

'Ostrich derby' in the Little Karoo.

Harvesting hops in the Blanco district.

GEORGE

George is a holiday town with a history. The tens of thousands of holidaymakers who crowd through its busy main street every summer follow in the steps of early British administrators who established the settlement in 1811 to provide a base for more effective control over the · area. The town was named after the reigning King of England at that time, George III.

The George Museum, housed in the old *Drostdy*, includes a splendid collection of Victorian bric-a-brac. About 100 m from the museum, in York Street, there is a huge oak known as 'the slave oak'. Embedded in its trunk is a length of stout chain and an antique padlock. Legend has it that slaves were chained to this tree to await auction, but there is some doubt as to whether this is true.

Across the Swartberg and through the brightly coloured Meiringspoort

The Grootrivier (great river) sculpted the colourful Meiringspoort gorge through the barrier of the Swartberg range, and our route follows the road that now winds along the river's banks. First, however, we cross the mountains from south to north by means of the soaring Swartberg Pass. Four fifths of the route is tarred, the rest is gravel.

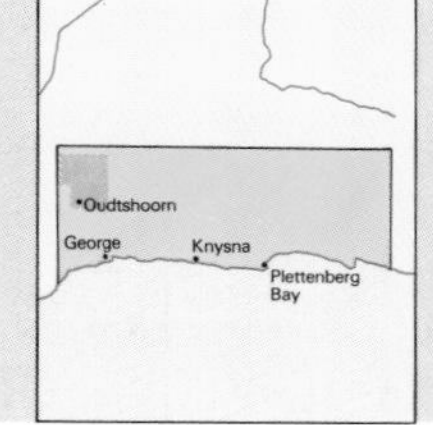

Oudtshoorn
Swartberg Pass
Prince Albert
Meiringspoort
De Rust
180 — 200 km

IF YOU ARE CONSIDERING this drive in winter, first check with the AA in George (see opposite) that the Swartberg Pass has not been blocked by snow.

Drive along Oudtshoorn's Baron van Reede Street, following the signs towards the Kango Caves. A number of houses in this street, particularly on the left-hand side, are relics of the ostrich feather boom, and show ornate cast-ironwork, turrets and balconies.

The road out of town is lined by jacaranda and blue-gum trees, and on both sides there are tobacco-drying sheds, loosely built of poles to allow for ventilation. A little later the road winds alongside the Grobbelaars River through Schoemanspoort.

The Grobbelaars River bridge marks the end of Schoemanspoort. 3,4 km beyond the bridge, turn left onto the R328 for 'Prince Alfred/ Swartberg Pass'. (To continue straight would bring you to the Kango Caves — see pages 254-5.)

Soon the road passes the De Hoek caravan park and holiday resort, and after a further 9,5 km the tarred road ends. The steep gradients and sharp turns of the pass dictate low speeds, but the gravel surface is almost always in excellent condition.

Swartberg Pass to Prince Albert

1,5 km after the start of the gravel you pass the barely visible ruins of two buildings on your right, and soon after this you reach the first picnic site on the pass, in a cluster of pine trees. About 1 km after the picnic site, the road approaches a left-hand bend beyond which you can see a steep ascent marked by a dry-stone wall. At the apex of the bend there is a built-up section to carry the road across a ravine. As you approach the bend you can see the date 1887 chiselled into a rock on the culvert. (The date 1886 may be seen about 3,7 km further on, where the road crosses another ravine — showing that the pass was built from north to south.)

Fields and fynbos form a rural patchwork amid the foothills of the Swartberg.

THE SWARTBERG PASS

This is one of the most spectacular of South Africa's mountain passes, climbing over the Swartberg range in wide loops and reaching a height of 1 585 m. The pass was completed by Thomas Bain in 1887 after years of difficult work and numerous stoppages in the winter months due to heavy falls of snow and hail.

The appearance of the pass has changed little since its construction, and the mountain slopes along which it makes its way are richly covered in indigenous wildflowers.

Before attempting the pass during winter weather, inquire locally in case the road has been closed.

The road snakes over the Swartberg Pass.

OSTRICH CAPITAL OF THE WORLD

Oudtshoorn was founded in 1847 and named after Baron Pieter van Rheede van Oudtshoorn, who had been appointed governor of the Cape in the 18th century but who had died on his way to take up the appointment. The town is now the principal centre of the Little Karoo — the 250 km long sunburned plain that lies between the Swartberg in the north and the Langeberg and Outeniqua ranges in the south.

Oudtshoorn is also claimed to be the ostrich capital of the world, and many grandiose houses — the so-called 'ostrich feather palaces' — date from the days of the ostrich feather boom. The C P Nel Museum in the heart of the town is noted for its many ostrich-related exhibits.

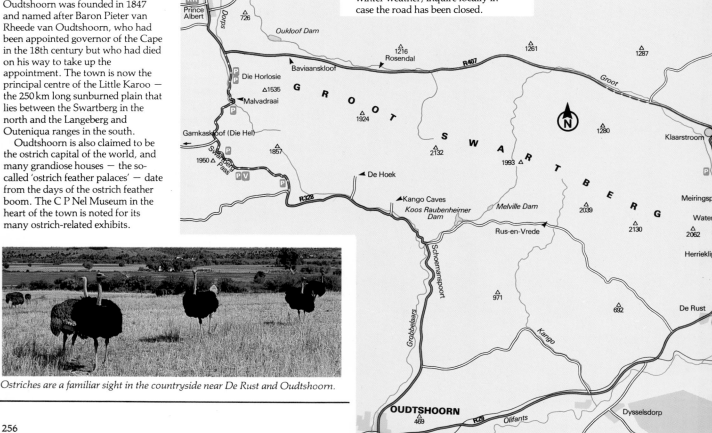

Ostriches are a familiar sight in the countryside near De Rust and Oudtshoorn.

Prince Albert
Dorps
726
Oukloof Dam
1216
Rosendal
R407
1261
1287
Beaufort West
Baviaanskloof
Die Horlosie
1535
Malvadraai
GROOT SWARTBERG
1924
Groot
1280
Klaarstroom
Gamkaskloof (Die Hel)
1857
2132
1993
1950
Swartberg Pass
De Hoek
R328
Kango Caves
Koos Raubenheimer Dam
Melville Dam
2039
Meiringspoort
Water
2130
2062
Rus-en-Vrede
Herrieklip
Schoemanspoort
971
692
De Rust
Grobbelaars
Kango
OUDTSHOORN
469
R29
Olifants
Dysselsdorp

2km later you come to picnic sites with magnificent views over the Kango valley.

As you reach the summit of the pass you will notice on the left side of the road a stone cairn surmounted by a bronze plaque. This records the story of the construction of the pass (see opposite).

1km beyond the summit you will see a clump of pine trees and the ruins of fairly large buildings. These served as a convict station, and later as the toll-house and the toll-keeper's residence. There are also picnic sites here.

2,7km from the summit you pass the turn-off to Gamkaskloof, also known as 'Die Hel'. (This is a daunting road of 57km and is not recommended unless you are determined to explore more deeply into the mountains.) There is a picnic spot on the right at Malvadraai, named for the *Abutilon sonneratianum* (wildemalva; butter-and-cheese) which puts out its bright orange and yellow flowers in early spring.

The road passes stone quarries, then runs along the foot of towering cliffs, to reach a picnic site near the Tweededrif (second drift) causeway. After a further 600m you come to a second picnic site at Eerstedrif (first drift). If you study the rocks to the left of the road here you will see, just below the highest point, the feature known as 'Die Horlosie', or the clock-face.

At the T-junction with the tarred road, turn left for Prince Albert, a particularly attractive country village (see pages 258-9). The Hotel Swartberg and a restaurant, both in Church Street, offer lunch.

Prince Albert to Oudtshoorn

Retrace your route out of Prince Albert, but drive past the road from the Swartberg Pass on which you arrived. Follow the tarred road for 'Klaarstroom/Beaufort West'. A little over 5km from the junction you pass the farmhouse and cemetery of Baviaanskloof. The date on the gable reads 1837, but the house is believed to be even older.

Be ready for a sharp left-hand bend — just before you reach a T-junction with the road from Beaufort West (see map opposite). At the T-junction turn right for 'Klaarstroom'.

Just over 1km after passing the village of Klaarstroom on the right, the road enters Meiringspoort, where there are frequent picnic sites (with toilets) on both sides. 8,2km into the pass there is a parking area with shady picnic sites on your left, sign-posted as 'Waterfall'. The waterfall (with rock pools) is reached after an easy 300m walk from the parking area.

2,7km beyond this parking area, on the right side of the road, you can see the 'Herrieklip', on which CJ Langenhoven chiselled the name of his famous elephant — joking at the time (1929) that this rock would be his memorial.

After leaving Meiringspoort the road passes through De Rust, and 34,5km later you enter Oudtshoorn on Voortrekker Street ●

AA Office Millwood Building, cnr York/Victoria Sts, George 6530 Tel. (0441) 3041
Oudtshoorn Publicity Office Civic Centre, Voortrekker Road, Oudtshoorn 6620 Tel. (04431) 2228
SA Tourism Board 124 York Street, George 6530 Tel. (0441) 5228

On a country road near Klaarstroom — a 19th century pace of progress.

The brilliantly coloured and fiercely twisted rock strata of the Swartberg.

THE 'HERRIEKLIP'

In his book *Sonde met die Bure*, C J Langenhoven wrote of the bizarre exploit of Herrie the elephant pulling an old tramcar from Oudtshoorn to Meiringspoort.

In a gentle tilt at town councillors he described a confrontation in the street between the mayor on the one hand and the elephant plus tramcar on the other.

Herrie is commemorated at both the start and the finish of his immortal journey — in Oudtshoorn by a statue of him, and in Meiringspoort by the Herrieklip, a sandstone rock on which Langenhoven himself carved the elephant's name.

Langenhoven's Die Stem van Suid-Afrika, *and his 'Herrieklip' in Meiringspoort.*

MEIRINGSPOORT

It was Petrus Meiring of the farm De Rust who, in 1854, followed the Grootrivier gorge through the colourful Swartberg range to emerge eventually on the southern edge of the Great Karoo.

For many years this remained the sole link between Prince Albert and the Little Karoo — a rough track through the gorge that forded the river some 30 times and was often washed away. The present tarred road was constructed only recently.

A feature of the Swartberg range is the dramatic folding of the composing sandstone strata — clearly visible both in Meiringspoort and along the Swartberg Pass.

The 1850 water-mill of the Alberts family — millers for more than a century.

A town of quaint gables and a forgotten gold rush

ON THE SOUTHERN edge of the thirsty land of the Great Karoo lies Prince Albert — an enchanting little oasis watered by mountain streams from the Swartberg range. Here the peaceful atmosphere of the 19th century lingers on, preserved along with the town's unique and quaint architecture.

Settlement in the area dates back as far as 1762, when a few loan-farms were granted at what was described as 'agter de Roggelandsberg in de Koup'. (Koup, also spelt gouph, is a Khoikhoi word believed to mean 'flat, open plain'). In the same year, Samuel de Beer — 'father' of Prince Albert — was born in faraway Drakenstein. When he was 37, he trekked here with his wife, Anna de Villiers, and settled on the farm Kweekvallei. A congregation of the Dutch Reformed Church was formed here in 1842, and the settlement became known as Albertsburg, later changing to Prince Albert, in honour of Queen Victoria's consort.

A convenient place to begin a walk through the little town is at the *Hotel Swartberg* **(1)** on Church (Kerk) Street, where there are shady trees under which to park. The hotel dining room contains an enormous and ornate Victorian sideboard that evokes memories of the great Prince Albert gold rush of 1890-1.

Two coach lines — the Welcome Line and the Fuller and Coetzee's Line — brought eager diggers from the railhead at Fraserburg Road. There was a butchery and a few buildings, and there was even a newspaper — the Gouph Gold News. But for the most part the gold-rush settlement was a tent-town that sprang up in the inhospitable veld north of Prince Albert. The easily won gold was soon worked out, and the adventurers drifted away. A few persevered with steam-driven drills, but the reef eluded them, and peace returned to Prince Albert.

The 'Prince Albert gable'

Opposite the hotel is 56 Church Street **(2)**, set unusually far back from the road. Its pedimented gable is dated 1841 — the year before the town was officially established — and the design of the end gables is atypical of Prince Albert.

A feature of the town is the great number of gabled houses that have survived, including a number of so-called 'Prince Albert gables'. These 'holbol' (convex-concave) gables, sometimes supported on short pilasters and with characteristic horizontal mouldings, are thought to be the work of Carel Lotz, an artisan who had worked in Tulbagh.

Typical Prince Albert gables grace 52 Church St (left) and 4 De Beer St.

Head south along Church Street. On the corner of Deurdrif Street is number 52 **(3)**, which has a typical example of the Prince Albert gable, dated 1850 and bearing the letters ACT. These are possibly the initials of a member of the Theron family, who bought Kweekvallei from Samuel de Beer.

Cross Deurdrif Street and pass Chaplin Street on your right. The Fransie Pienaar Museum **(4)** is at 16 Church Street. This building was once the home of the Haak family, and also served for a while as the town's hospital. The museum contains relics of the Prince Albert gold rush, a collection of family bibles, Cape furniture, domestic items, firearms, old vehicles and farm implements. The most bizarre exhibit is a coffin, only some 30 cm long, complete with brass fittings. It was found, firmly sealed, in the loft of a former cabinet-maker in the town — and

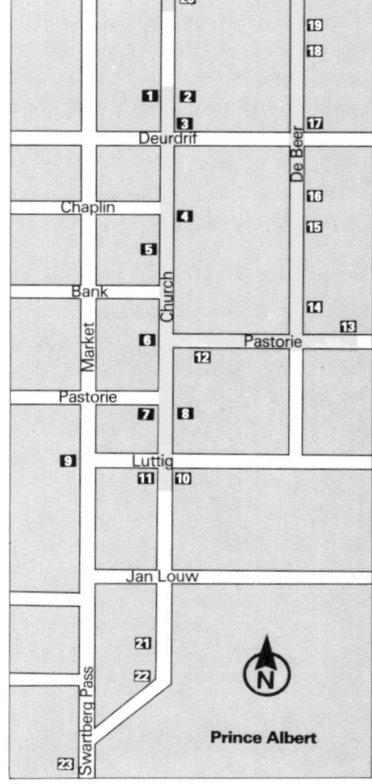

The museum's horse-drawn hearse.

The old cinema on De Beer St contrasts with gabled 19th century homes.

remains unopened to this day.

Diagonally opposite the museum there is an interesting group of old houses **(5)**, starting with 53 Church Street. This building has no front gables, but it has end gables with little waisted pediments. Number 51, dated 1858, is linked to number 49 and to number 47, which is thatched and has a gable dated 1852.

Pass Bank Street on your right to reach the handsome *Dutch Reformed Church* **(6)**, also on your right and facing Pastorie Street. Built in 1865 in the form of a Greek cross, it has battlemented gables and tower, and originally had a thatched roof. During the Anglo-Boer War a sandbag 'fort' was built in its grounds.

Lovely fanlights

Continue along Church Street to number 23 **(7)**, on your right. This L-shaped house has undergone some modernisation, but has retained its typical Prince Albert gable. Opposite it is number 24 **(8)**, a double-storeyed Georgian building known as Huis Krige. The stoep has an end-seat, and a fine fanlight surmounts the front door. It is thought that this was originally a single-storeyed building, but since the 'new' floors and ceilings are of yellowwood, it was probably converted at an early date.

As you reach Luttig Street, look right to see the old double-storeyed warehouse **(9)** on Market Street. Across Luttig Street, on your right, is 20 Church Street **(10)**, a fairly plain double-storeyed Victorian home of 1885. Number 15 **(11)**, on the opposite side of Church Street, dates from 1858, and is known locally as 'die doktershuis' (the doctor's house). Each of the three doors facing the street has an attractive fanlight, and the gable is quite unlike any other in the town, although it still has traces of the Prince Albert elements.

The museum's cool, tranquil interior.

A Victorian double-storey of 1885.

The Dutch Reformed Church building.

Victorian parsonage

Turn around here, return to Pastorie Street, and turn right. The first house on your right is the *Dutch Reformed parsonage* **(12)**, a late-Victorian building dated 1892, with three tall chimneys of red face-brick. Ornamentation is of wood rather than iron, and it shows the vogue for rustication — 'the imitation of rough rustic work' — in the projections cut to resemble massive stonework at the corners and around the doors and windows.

Cross De Beer Street to reach, on your left, a fine example of the smaller Victorian house **(13)**. It has retained all its original cast iron, including ornamentation along the ridge-line of the roof, which was intended to discourage birds from perching.

Return along Pastorie Street to De Beer Street and turn right. Number 4 **(14)** has a gable dated 1854 and has retained its thatch — but this is now covered by an iron roof. The house was once occupied by a man known as 'Swartbaard' (Blackbeard) le Grange. Number 8 **(15)** has a typical Prince Albert gable (dated 1860), as does number 12 **(16)**, which dates from about 1850. The verandahs of these houses are all later additions. The little building adjoining number 12 once served as the town cinema.

The lovely Dutch Reformed parsonage with its late-Victorian embellishments.

Cross Deurdrif Street to reach, on your right, an interesting TT-shaped house **(17)** which, unlike most of the houses in the town, does not face the street. Instead it faces north, with its back on Deurdrif Street. Its gable, with the date 1851 and the letters WJC, can be seen clearly from De Beer Street.

Number 22 **(18)**, also on your right, is just one room deep, and has a tall gable that seems to owe nothing to the influence of the builder Carel Lotz. Number 24 **(19)**, also just one room deep, has a thatch roof.

Turn left into Leeb Street, passing two old thatched cottages on your right, then turn left into Church Street. You pass number 68 **(20)** on your left, a charming cottage with elaborate fretwork on its verandah.

If time permits, continue your exploration of Prince Albert's historic buildings by car, driving south along Church Street past a number of other interesting houses. Particularly worth noting is number 5 **(21)**, on your right, which has been described as having 'one of the purest examples of the Prince Albert gable'. It was once the parsonage of the Dutch Reformed mission church.

Number 1 **(22)** also on your right, has an unusually complex Prince Albert gable dated 1856. It was one of a number of houses built by Jan Luttig, a Member of the old Cape Parliament who campaigned for the right to use Dutch in the House, and whose name has been recorded on the old Taal Monument at Burgersdorp (see pages 214-5).

Where Church Street meets up with Market Street, turn left into Christina de Wet Street. On your right is 29 Market Street **(23)**, which was the home of the miller. It formerly had a thatched roof, and retains its brandsolder (fire attic) — formed by a ceiling of poles and clay which, it was hoped, would be a fireproof layer if the thatch caught fire.

The old water-mill

Prince Albert's best-known landmark is its water-mill, just to the left of the road (which is the route to the Swartberg Pass road) on the outskirts of the town. Built in 1850, the mill has been in the possession of the Alberts family for more than 100 years. If the mill is locked, the key can be obtained, at reasonable hours, from the house on the opposite side of the tarred road. The mill's wheel, 2,4 m in diameter, is of the overshot type — turned by the action of water falling onto it. To save wear on the restored machinery, the water is led to a point just beyond the wheel ●

The building that is now Prince Albert's museum was once the town hospital.

SOUTH-WESTERN CAPE

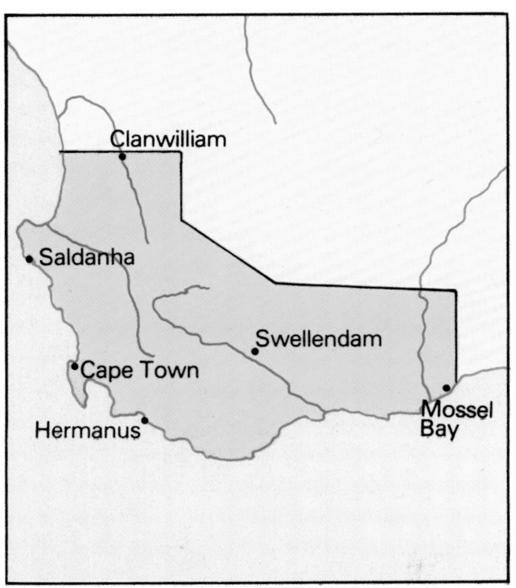

Above: *A view of Lion's Head from below the Twelve Apostles.* **Left:** *The historic Boschendal farmstead beneath the Groot Drakenstein mountains.*

To the 'magic mountain' through the Seven Weeks Pass

South of the Karoo plains around Laingsburg, rolling hills swell into the sandstone peaks of the Klein Swartberg range. Rivers have etched their way through the seemingly impenetrable rock, and the slow erosion has exposed contorted strata that tower high above our winding route into the Little Karoo. About half the route is tarred.

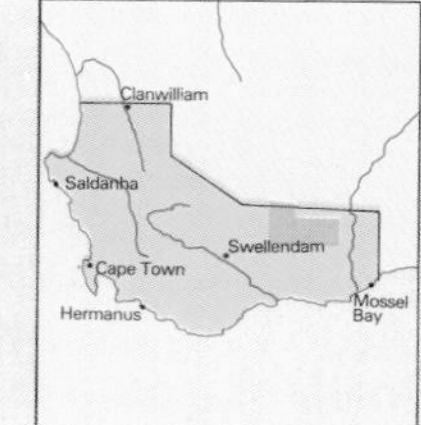

Laingsburg
Seweweekspoort
Amalienstein
Zoar
Hoeko
Ladismith
200 — 220 km

TURN SOUTH OUT OF Laingsburg's main street between the buildings of the Standard Bank and the Co-operative, and note your kms. Pass under the railway bridge 700 m out of town, and continue straight.

You pass a turn-off on your left to Floriskraal Dam (the entrance is reached after 7,5 km along this gravel road), and later you pass a gravel road on your right to Ladismith. Soon afterwards the road crosses a river bridge in an area of intensely folded rock strata.

The road surface changes to gravel about 29 km from Laingsburg, and soon emerges from among the hills, giving clear views of the Klein Swartberg range. After a further 23 km the hills and mountains close in again. Just short of 2 km later there are some spectacular rocky outcrops on the left.

Roughly 15 km beyond this — 69,2 km from Laingsburg — the road forks: go right here for Seweweekspoort and Ladismith. The ruins of the original tollhouse are on the left at the fork. Individuals used to tender for the 'farming' of a toll, but traffic through this poort was so infrequent that the Cape government was obliged to place one of their own employees here. The ghost of this lonely man is said to haunt the spot.

Seweweekspoort to Hoeko

Immediately after the fork the road enters Seweweekspoort (seven weeks pass). This follows the river between towering walls of sandstone, which in many places almost shut out the sun. On the left after 2 km are the ruins of one of the convict stations which housed the labourers who built the original road.

After a further 1,7 km on the right is a picnic site (with toilets). On the left 2,2 km later there are braai sites, and 400 m beyond, also on the left, there is another picnic site in front of a large rock overhang. More picnic sites dot the roadside throughout the poort.

Shortly after the road emerges from the poort, you pass a number of ruined buildings.

Laingsburg's handsome Dutch Reformed Church — unscathed by floods.

SURVIVOR OF THE FLOODWATERS

Laingsburg was laid out on the farm Vischkuil along the banks of the Buffalo River in 1881 and named after John Laing, Commissioner for Crown Lands at the Cape. Growth has never been great in Laingsburg and much of the town was devastated by a flood during its centennial year, but here and there in the side streets there are clusters of quaint Victorian buildings with much curved corrugated-iron and ornamental cast-ironwork.

The original Dutch Reformed Church, behind the present church building, dates from the earliest years of the town, as does the Lutheran Mission Church.

There is a small museum of local history in Laingsburg's public library in Van Riebeeck Street.

An isolated cottage lies beneath fantastic rock strata typical of our route.

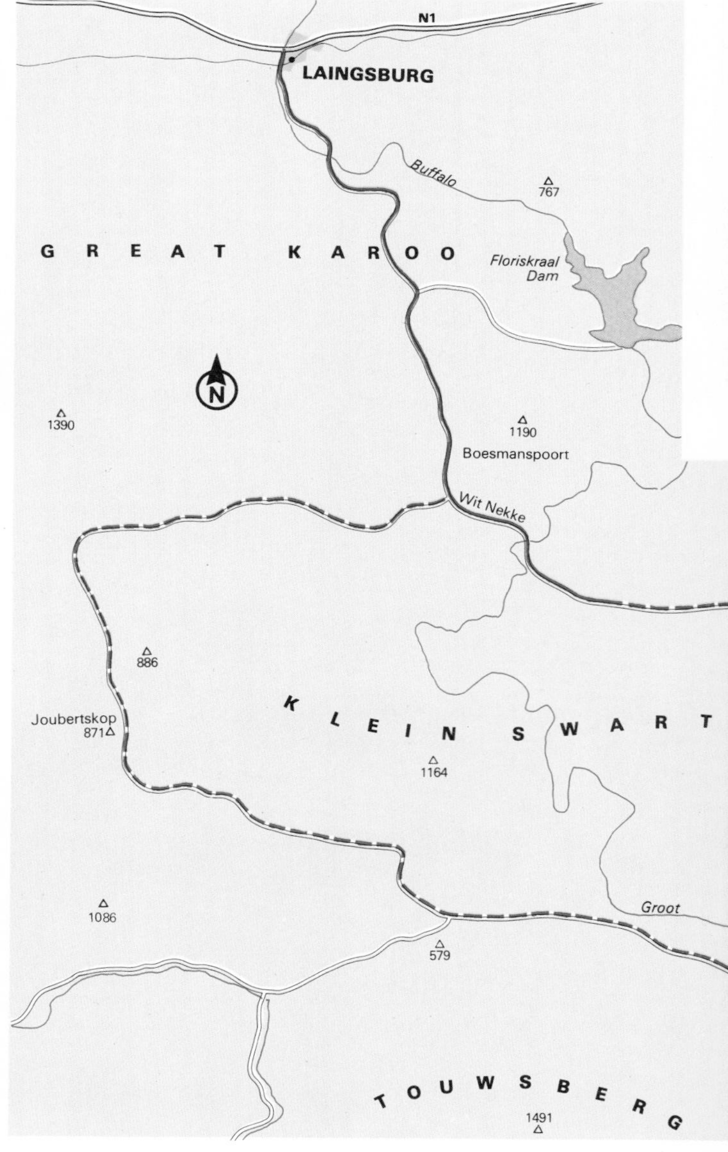

At the T-junction opposite the old mission village of Amalienstein, turn right onto tar (R62), noting your kms. A few kms further you come to the still older mission village of Zoar on your left (see below).

9,3km after the Amalienstein T-junction, turn right for Hoeko. 2,2km later on your right is the house in which the poet C J Langenhoven was born. The T-shaped farmhouse on your right 500m beyond is believed to have been the original Hoeko homestead, dating from about 1810.

Hoeko to Laingsburg

The road soon changes to gravel, and enters Ladismith roughly 9km later. At the stop street, turn right into the tarred Church Street. (There are a number of hotels in the town, as well as a public swimming pool.)

Turn right into Van Riebeeck Street, and drive west out of the town. After about 100m on your right is the old Jewish synagogue — a reminder of the role Jewish immigrants played in developing the ostrich industry.

The road passes vineyards and irrigated fields before entering an area of rocky, scrub-covered hills, with the cleft peak of Towerkop (magic mountain) on your right at the edge of the Klein Swartberg range. Approximately 18km after leaving the town of Ladismith you reach a T-junction — turn right here.

Cross a bridge over the Groot River. After a further 7,4km the road surface changes to gravel. Continue on this road, past a turn-off on your left to Montagu, through a number of cattle grids and sharp right turns. The road eventually enters a gorge in which the rock strata are almost vertical on your right, yet horizontal in other places.

Turn left for Laingsburg at the T-junction with the tarred road on which you travelled south in the morning ●

S A Tourism Board Level 3, Golden Acre, Adderley Street, Cape Town 8001 Tel. (021) 216274
AA Office AA House, 7 Martin Hammerschlag Way, Box 70, Cape Town 8000 Tel. (021) 211550

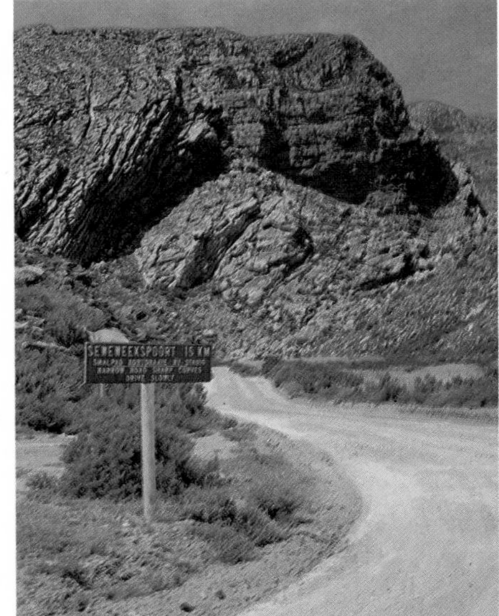

Seweweekspoort — a geological marvel.

A tree-lined lane leads up to the church in Amalienstein mission village.

ZOAR AND AMALIENSTEIN

Zoar, named after the Biblical city of palms, was founded in 1817 by the South African Missionary Society. It was taken over for a while by the Berlin Missionary Society in 1843, but many members of the congregation protested about, among other things, the introduction of crucifix and candles, so the Berlin Missionary Society established another mission at a nearby site. They named it Amalienstein in honour of their chief patron, Baroness Amalie von Stein. The mission at Zoar eventually came under the control of the Dutch Reformed Mission Church.

THE SEVEN WEEKS PASS

There are several explanations of the name of Seweweekspoort (seven weeks pass), including the quaint notion that brandy smugglers used the route to evade revenue collectors — the detour taking them seven weeks to negotiate by ox wagon.

The likeliest theory is that the name is a corruption of 'Zerwick se poort', after the Reverend Zerwick, one of the founders of the mission station at the nearby village of Amalienstein.

The rocky gorge is overlooked by the 2325m Seweweekspoort Peak, highest in the Swartberg ranges, and the road is lined by fantastically curved and broken rock strata that tower high above.

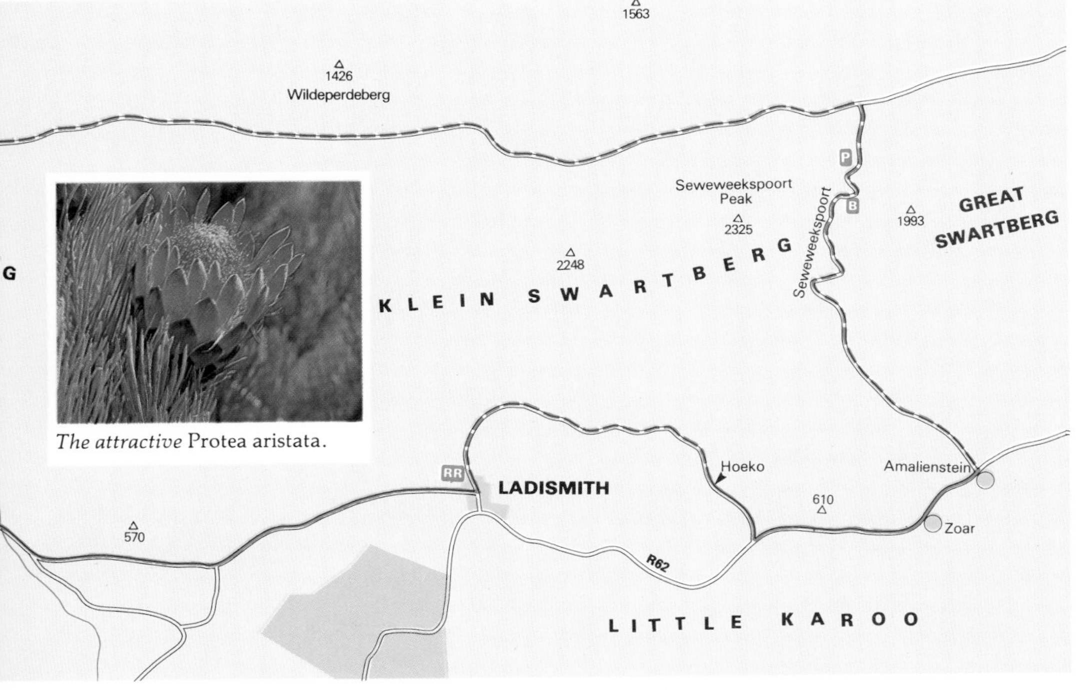

The attractive Protea aristata.

A RARE BEAUTY

The *Protea aristata*, discovered only in 1928, was later believed to be extinct, as no further specimens were found for 25 years. But then a clump of five of the plants was found close to the road in Seweweekspoort, and several others have now been sighted higher up the mountain slopes.

LADISMITH AND THE MAGIC MOUNTAIN

Dominating the Little Karoo town of Ladismith are the twin pinnacles of Towerkop (magic mountain). Legend has it that one night a heks (witch) cleft the towering rock in two with her magic wand when she found to her fury that she was unable to cross the mountain top.

Ladismith was the second town to bear the name of the wife of Governor Sir Harry Smith. Ladysmith in Natal was founded two years earlier, in 1850, and the spelling of the Cape town was later changed to its present form to distinguish the two. There are many quaint and beautiful old buildings in the town, particularly in Church Street.

Two ancient and colourful passes through the Langeberg

The Langeberg form a natural barrier between the fertile farmlands of the Breë River valley and the sunburned rock garden of the Little Karoo. Our route straddles this rocky divide, passing through two rugged gorges, closely following ancient paths of the San and Khoikhoi. Almost the entire route is on good tarred roads.

Swellendam
Bonnievale
Cogmanskloof
Montagu
Tradouw Pass
200 – 220 km

FOR A VIEW OVER Swellendam and the rolling countryside to the south, turn out of Voortrek Street into Andrew Whyte Street, driving towards the mountain (see pages 268-9 for a town map). After 1 km, turn right for 'Swellendam State Forest'. Go right at the fork, then turn right towards the concrete dome of the reservoir. Park at the reservoir and walk around the reservoir fence to the south side, from where the view is uninterrupted.

Return to Voortrek Street and turn right. At the end of the town, turn right out of Voortrek Street onto the R60 for Ashton and Montagu, noting your kms. About 5 km later on your right there is an old water mill. Soon afterwards the road begins to ascend Bakoondshoogte (oven height).

Roughly 20 km from the turn out of Voortrek Street, turn left onto gravel for Middelrivier, then 2,3 km later turn left at the T-junction. Keep straight, passing through the settlement of Drew and crossing the railway within the next 1 km.

Cross the Breë River and turn right at the T-junction onto tar — noting your kms. Stop after a few hundred metres for a view back of the river and bridge.

After 9,4 km, turn right at the T-junction. Continue into Bonnievale and turn left at the T-junction. Call at the municipal office (opposite the hotel on your left) to collect the key to the Myrtle Rigg Memorial Church. If you intend visiting the church on a public holiday or at the weekend, telephone the Town Clerk at (02346) 2105 to arrange to collect the key.

Turn right out of the main road, following signs for 'Police' into Forrest Road. After about 1 km, turn right into Myrtle Rigg Avenue. The church is on your right after 100 m (see opposite).

Bonnievale to Montagu

Return via Forrest Street to Main Road, and turn left. At the first road past the municipal offices turn left for Montagu and Ashton. Follow the road left around the church, and continue straight. Note your kms as you cross the railway, and roughly 7 km later turn left at the T-junction onto the R60. A little over 5 km later turn right at the T-junction for Montagu.

As you approach Cogmanskloof, about 1 km after the T-junction, there is a shady picnic spot on your left near the river (no facilities). Close to Bain's Tunnel it is possible to see the Anglo-Boer War blockhouse, Sidney Fort, on the hill — slightly to the left of the top of the tunnel. It is difficult to spot because it is built out of the local sandstone. From the bridge approaching the tunnel mouth you can also see the old road on your right.

Soon after the tunnel there is a picnic site on your right (no facilities), with a bronze plaque recording the building of this road by Thomas Bain. 500 m further on your right is the Keurkloof campsite, where there are braai and picnic sites close to the river (small entry fee at weekends and on public holidays; water, toilets). From here there is an attractive short walk along the Keurkloof into the mountains.

Just short of 2 km after the campsite, the road crosses a bridge and enters Montagu. 1 km beyond the bridge, turn left into Barry Street, then turn right into Badstraat (the information office is on your right after 100 m; a number of establishments in the town serve lunch). Continue on Badstraat for roughly 3,5 km, then turn left at the 'hot springs' sign, and immediately turn right into Uitvlugt Street.

There is an attractive 2,5 km 'lover's walk' from the springs along Badkloof to an old mill ('Eyssenhuis'). While some members of the party walk, one person can drive the car around to meet them — drive back along Badstraat, right into Barry Street, left into Meulstraat, past

LITTLE MYRTLE RIGG'S LAST WISH

Early this century, gold-seeker-turned-farmer Christopher Forrest Rigg bought a tract of land in the Breë River valley known as Bosjemansdrif. He transformed it by building a canal to bring water from the river, and he renamed his acquisition Bonnievale.

The Riggs' daughter, Myrtle, who is said to have been a considerate and deeply religious child, was only seven years old when she became ill with meningitis. Realising that she was going to die, she asked her father to build her a little church. Myrtle died in 1911, and work on the church stretched over several years, with only the best materials being used, including imported Italian marble.

Consecrated in 1921, the church was initially used regularly by the Bonnievale community, but eventually it fell into disuse and became derelict, until the Bonnievale municipality restored it in 1978. Mystery surrounds the locked safe in the porch. The key was lost many years ago and the contents — if any — are unknown.

The old Sidney Fort above Bain's Tunnel in Cogmanskloof.

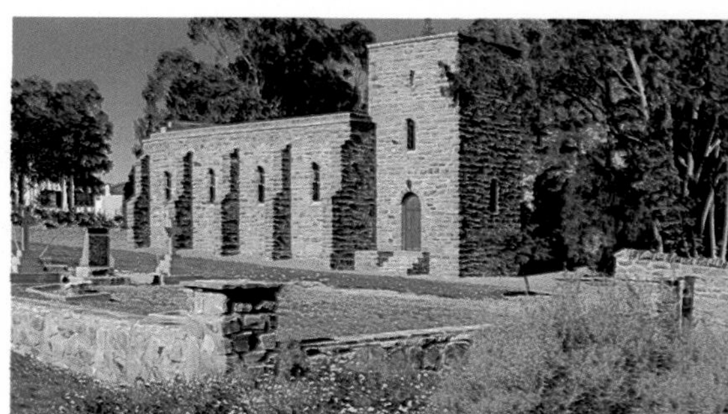

Now a museum, this quaint church in Bonnievale stands as a memorial to seven-year-old Myrtle Rigg.

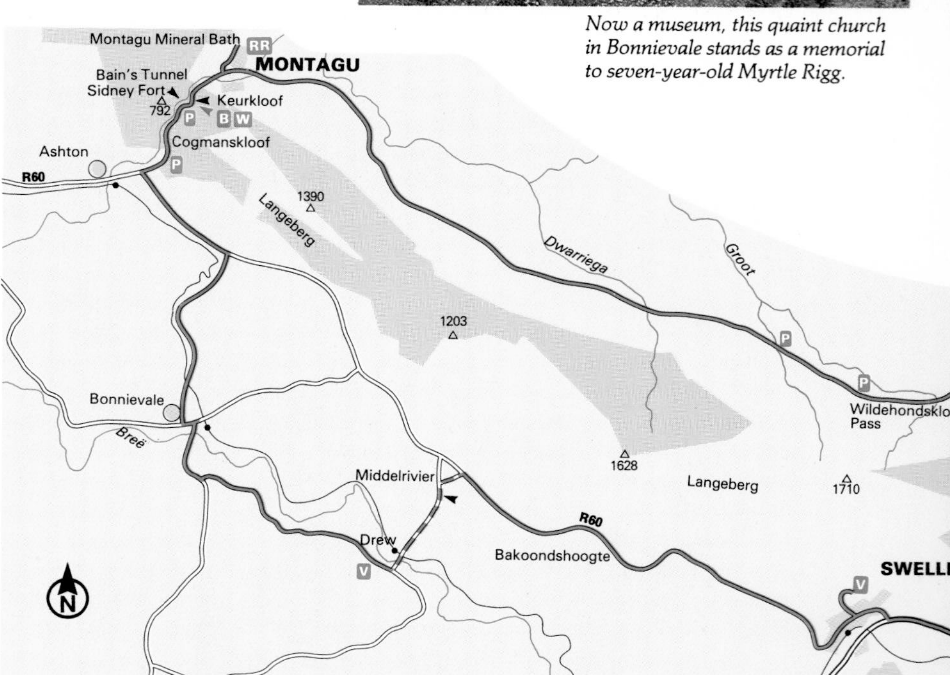

a suspension footbridge over the river, then right into Tanner Street. The road ends at the old mill.

If it is springtime, visit the Centenary Nature Garden — turn from Badstraat into Kerkstraat, cross Langstraat (the through-road) and turn left into Van Riebeeck Street. The entrance to the garden is on your right 700m from the turn.

Montagu to Swellendam

Drive east out of Montagu on Langstraat and follow this road (R62) towards Barrydale.

There is a shady riverside picnic site on the left after about 29km, and another just over 7km later, roughly 4km up the Wildehondskloof Pass.

On the outskirts of Barrydale, turn right onto the R324 for the Tradouw Pass — noting your kms as you turn. 4,6km from the turn, stop at a large picnic site set back from the road, next to a small stream that flows under the road. There are braai places here, and on the far bank of the stream a steep path leads up to a rock shelter containing San paintings. (Some of the paintings have been damaged, but a few remain in good condition.)

About 4km beyond this picnic site, two loops of the old road can be seen on your left. There are braai sites here near the water. Roughly 3km after the summit of the pass the road crosses the Andries Uys bridge. To your left you can see the old Letty's Bridge.

At the T-junction at the end of the pass, turn right. 4km later the road enters the straggling mission village of Suurbraak, which stretches along the roadside for the next 2,1km.

A further 2,1km after leaving Suurbraak, on your right, is the entrance to the farm Rooipoort. 400m beyond, also on your right, is a small cement campanile set in a field about 10m from the roadside. A plaque records that this was the site of an outpost established in 1734 by the Dutch East India Company as a protection against marauding Khoikhoi and San. The fort itself was close to the solitary house in the middle distance as you look directly past the campanile towards the mountain.

Roughly 5km beyond the campanile, turn right at the T-junction onto the N2 ●

AA Office AA House, 7 Martin Hammerschlag Way, Box 70, Cape Town 8000 Tel. (021) 211550
Montagu Municipal Information Office Badstraat, Montagu 6720 Tel. (0234) 42471
Swellendam Public Library Voortrek Street, Box 20, Swellendam 6740 Tel. (0291) 41755
SA Tourism Board Level 3, Golden Acre, Adderley Street, Cape Town 8001 Tel. (021) 216274

COGMANSKLOOF'S SUNSET COLOURS

This kloof takes its name from one of the Khoikhoi groups of the area. The Cogmanskloof road, with its tunnel driven through the russet-coloured rocks, is an example of the work of Thomas Bain. His road, opened in 1877, was replaced by the present one only in 1952, and during the floods of 1981 it was Bain's road that remained passable while the modern route was unusable.

Sidney Fort, built during the Anglo-Boer War, was named after the district commandant.

Farmlands shelter at the foot of the Langeberg range near Bonnievale.

One of Montagu's historic cottages.

blossoms colour the hills of Swellendam.

MISSION VILLAGE AT SUURBRAAK

Hans Moos, chief of a branch of the Attaqua Khoikhoi, asked to have a missionary sent to his people at their settlement in a tranquil valley east of Swellendam. In 1812 a Mr Seidenfaden of the London Missionary Society arrived, and the village began to grow from that date — virtually all of it along a single main street that stretches over more than 2km.

A feature of the Suurbraak cottages is that a number of them are double-storeyed, with tiny upper windows. The church, which was taken over by the Dutch Reformed Mission Church in 1857, is believed to date from around 1835.

An outside staircase adds charm to this attractive old homestead in Montagu.

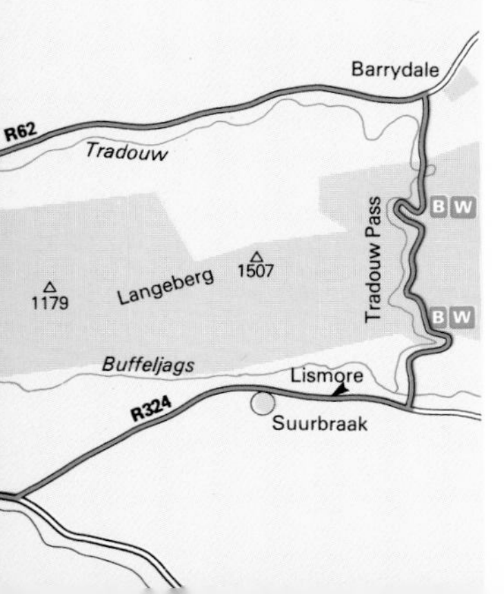

THE PATH OF THE WOMEN

The Tradouw Pass through the Langeberg (long mountains) was given its name, meaning 'the path of the women', by the Hessequa Khoikhoi. A roadway which closely followed the gorge cut by the Buffeljags River was built by Thomas Bain between 1869 and 1873. This new road was officially named Southey's Pass, but it soon reverted to its old name.

Letty's Bridge, built of teak in 1879, still stands, in good condition, beside the modern tarred road.

TINY CAPITAL OF THE LANGEBERG VALLEY

Montagu, founded in 1851, was named after John Montagu, the Colonial Secretary who did much to advance the building of good roads at the Cape. Today it is a centre for wine and fruit production.

There are many beautiful and historic houses in Langstraat, including the museum and its annexe. The Dutch Reformed Church parsonage in Rose Street, which has been described as resembling a miniature Groote Schuur, was built in 1911 for the Reverend D F Malan, who became South Africa's Prime Minister in 1948.

The radio-active Montagu hot springs are situated in an impressive kloof overlooked by walls of rugged rock. A 'lover's walk' leads from here into Badkloof. Other walks can be taken in the Centenary Nature Garden (renowned for its profusion of flowers in spring) and in Keurkloof and the Montagu Mountain Reserve.

Through rolling hills to the Southern Cape's wild shores

Like the Breë River that winds its way south from Swellendam, this route meanders through the rolling countryside of the Rûens and Duineveld to the sea. It includes the National Bontebok Park and the De Hoop Nature Reserve, and a crossing of the Breë River by pont. Most of the route is on well-maintained gravel roads.

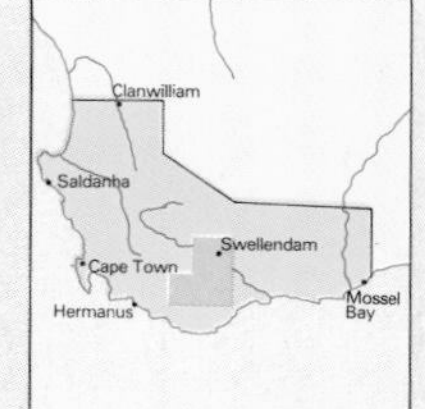

Swellendam
Bontebok National Park
De Hoop Nature Reserve
Malgas
Witsand
200 – 220 km

THE RESERVOIR ABOVE Swellendam makes an ideal starting point, as it offers an excellent view south towards the countryside through which this drive leads (see pages 264-5 for directions). From the reservoir, drive down to Voortrek Street and turn left. Turn right at the fork into Swellengrebel Street.

Cross the N2 for the Bontebok National Park (the road surface changes to gravel within 100 m). 3,7 km from the start of the gravel, the road takes a sharp right-hand bend, and 1,2 km later you reach the entrance to the park (see below; small entry fee).

Bontebok Park to De Hoop

After your visit to the park, return to the N2 and turn left. The road crosses the Breë River after about 7 km. 1,4 km beyond the bridge, turn left for Malgas and Infanta, noting your kms (the surface changes to gravel within 100 m).

The route now passes through rolling wheatlands, with particularly broad vistas as you crest the appropriately named Aalwynkop (aloe hill) 15,8 km after turning off the N2. About 5 km later you pass the equally appropriately named Witklipkop (white stone hill) on your left. Roughly 22 km after turning off the N2, turn right for Ouplaas and De Hoop. About 13 km further, turn right at the T-junction, pass the tiny settlement of Ouplaas on your left, then 2,1 km later turn left for De Hoop Nature Reserve.

After 1,5 km, as the road crosses the cattle grid, you pass an immense and laboriously constructed stone farm-wall stretching away over the hill ahead of you — a relic of the days before fencing wire had reached the country. You reach the entrance to De Hoop Nature Reserve just short of 5 km later (small entry fee).

Follow the main road into the reserve. Turn right after 4,3 km, following the signs to the administrative 'office'. The administration of the reserve is housed in the old De Hoop homestead overlooking the De Hoopvlei.

There is an attractive walk leading from the homestead along the vlei towards the sea (this outing allows time to walk only a short distance along it). Another walk leads along the beach for 5 km on both sides of Koppie Alleen — a 14 km drive from the homestead. Near the homestead there are picnic sites (braai places, toilets, water).

De Hoop to Witsand

Drive out of the reserve and turn right at the T-junction. A short distance beyond Ouplaas you pass on your left the road on which you entered from Swellendam — note your kms here. After 2,3 km turn left for Malgas and Infanta. (The road from which you have turned reaches the old homestead and environment centre of Potberg after some 9 km.) After a further 11,9 km turn right at the T-junction, and 1,4 km later turn left for Malgas.

The road that winds down the short distance

A herd of bontebok graze beneath the grandeur of the Langeberg range.

Lesser flamingoes add a dash of pink to the tranquil stretch of De Hoopvlei.

A FIGHT FOR SURVIVAL

The bontebok (*Damaliscus dorcas dorcas*) came close to suffering the same fate as the little bluebuck (*Hippotragus leucophaeus*), which was hunted to extinction almost 200 years ago. But a group of Bredasdorp farmers banded together in 1850 to ensure the bontebok's survival.

The present Bontebok National Park outside Swellendam, opened in 1961, is in the heart of the natural 'home' of the bontebok and bluebuck — a strip of coastal plateau from Bot River to Mossel Bay. Bontebok tend to remain near their water holes, and are usually easy to spot.

COASTAL SANCTUARY FOR WILDLIFE

De Hoop Nature Reserve is sited in an area rich in coastal fynbos. Well over 200 bird species have been observed in the reserve and the Potberg area has the southernmost breeding colony of the endangered Cape vulture. The major game species are bontebok, zebra, eland and daintier buck such as the klipspringer.

The Sout (salt) River is blocked on its course to the sea to form a lake in the midst of the reserve. Known as De Hoopvlei, it is roughly 14 km long, and there is a beautiful walk along its edge.

Saved from extinction — two Cape mountain zebras enjoy De Hoop's fynbos.

to the pont at Malgas is tarred. Cross the river on the pont (small fee). Sound your hooter if the operators are not visible.

On the east bank, after just under 3 km, turn right for Heidelberg. Note your kms as you turn, and after 3,7 km turn right again. At the inclined T-junction with the main Swellendam-Witsand road, turn right again.

Keep straight on this road for 24,4 km through several intersections until you reach a parking area at Witsand beach. (To reach the old jetties and hotel, drive back from the beach for about 3 km, and after passing the lone-standing church turn left towards the river.)

Retrace your route to the junction just under 3 km from the pont, and turn right, away from the pont, towards Swellendam. Note your kms as you turn. Pass a road to Michielskraal on your left and keep straight past a number of other roads on your left and right. After 27,8 km turn right at the T-junction.

Soon after crossing the railway, turn left onto the N2 for Swellendam ●

AA Office AA House, 7 Martin Hammerschlag Way, Cape Town 8001 Tel. (021) 211550
Swellendam Public Library Voortrek Street, Swellendam 6740 Tel. (0291) 41755
De Hoop Nature Reserve Private Bag X16, Bredasdorp 7280 Tel. (02922) 782
S A Tourism Board Level 3, Golden Acre, Adderley Street, Cape Town 8001 Tel. (021) 216274

Countless wheatfields turn Swellendam's rolling hills to gold.

The wool merino — pride of the southern Cape farmers.

SWELLENDAM'S MERINO COUNTRY

The foundations of South Africa's merino industry were firmly laid on farms to the south of Swellendam. The first merinos were imported from the Netherlands in 1789, and this stock was later successfully crossed with the indigenous fat-tailed Cape sheep. Today the sheep of this district produce the country's highest yield of high-quality wool.

New grazing-crops have increased the carrying capacity of the land. Some winter crops shed highly nutritious pods and seeds which the sheep eat in summer — the sight of sheep apparently devouring stones in what seem to be barren fields has puzzled many visitors.

MALGAS – RELIC OF A RIVERBOAT ERA

The little river port of Malgas was founded in the middle of the last century to alleviate the laborious trek of more than 60 km across the hilly Rûens (ridges) from Swellendam to Port Beaufort.

On the west bank of the Breë River, on the farm then known as Mallegaskraal, there is a deep channel where ships could draw alongside a convenient stretch of level ground. A jetty was built there, just upstream of the site of the present pont crossing.

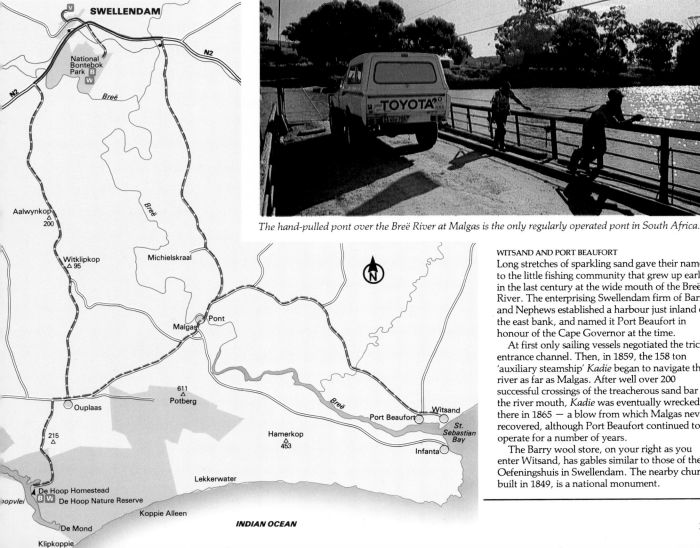

The hand-pulled pont over the Breë River at Malgas is the only regularly operated pont in South Africa.

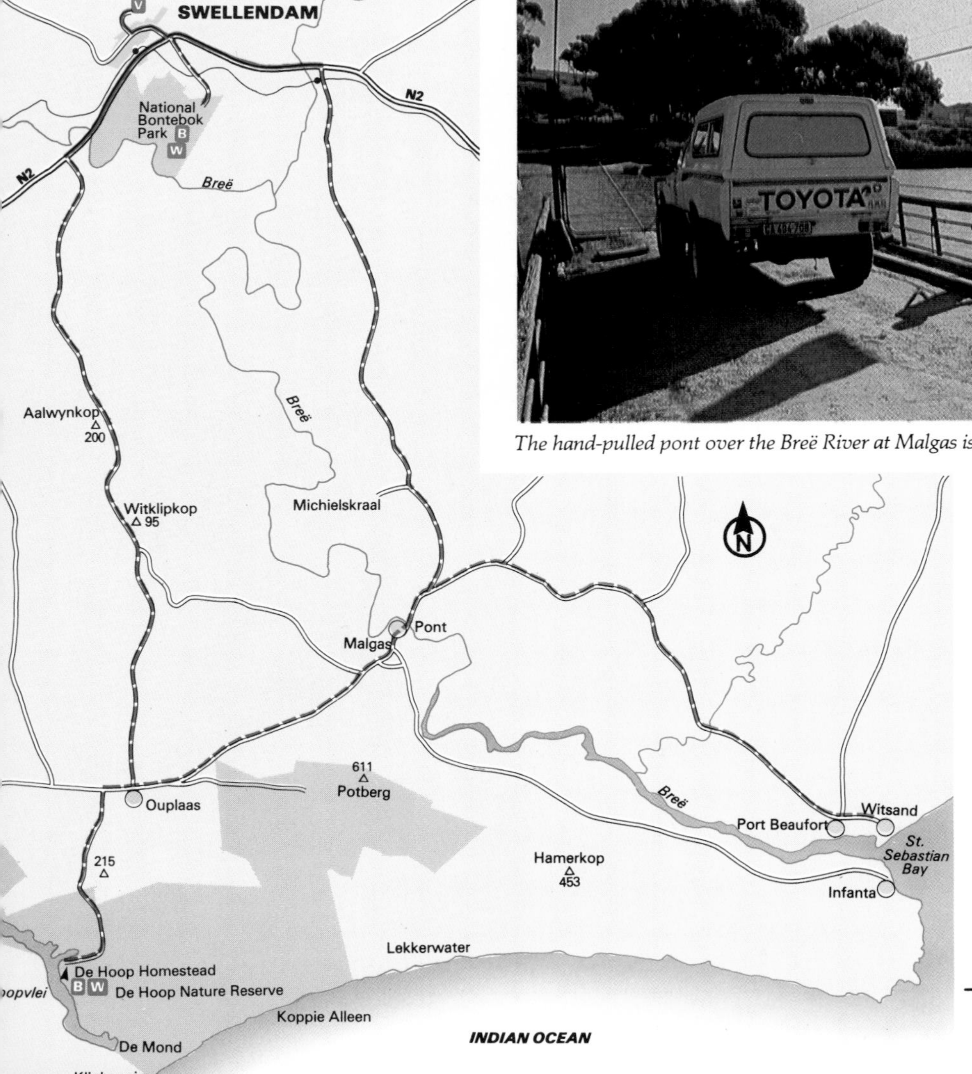

WITSAND AND PORT BEAUFORT

Long stretches of sparkling sand gave their name to the little fishing community that grew up early in the last century at the wide mouth of the Breë River. The enterprising Swellendam firm of Barry and Nephews established a harbour just inland on the east bank, and named it Port Beaufort in honour of the Cape Governor at the time.

At first only sailing vessels negotiated the tricky entrance channel. Then, in 1859, the 158 ton 'auxiliary steamship' *Kadie* began to navigate the river as far as Malgas. After well over 200 successful crossings of the treacherous sand bar at the river mouth, *Kadie* was eventually wrecked there in 1865 — a blow from which Malgas never recovered, although Port Beaufort continued to operate for a number of years.

The Barry wool store, on your right as you enter Witsand, has gables similar to those of the Oefeningshuis in Swellendam. The nearby church, built in 1849, is a national monument.

For ninety-one days a rebellious colony

LYING ALONG THE banks of the Cornlands River at the foot of the Langeberg Mountains, Swellendam is one of the oldest and most gracious of South Africa's historic towns. The site is perhaps the prettiest in the whole of the 'Overberg' — the name given by the Dutch settlers at the Cape to the land lying to the east of the Hottentots Holland Mountains.

A dignitary of the Dutch East India Company, visiting the Cape in 1743, chose this tranquil site for the establishment of a new drostdy (magisterial district), and the new settlement was called Swellendam in honour of the Governor of the Cape, Hendrik Swellengrebel, and his wife, Helena ten Damme. Work on the Drostdy building began in 1746, and the town grew slowly around it.

By 1795 the burghers of Swellendam had become disenchanted with the Company, and they formed their own National Convention, electing one of their number, Hermanus Steyn, 'president' of the convention. (The burghers did not claim complete independence. They rejected the Company's authority, but chose to remain under the Dutch flag. Just 91 days later, however, British forces occupied the Cape, and the days of independent government in Swellendam were over.)

Three years atter the burghers' rebellion, in 1798, a congregation of the Dutch Reformed Church was established in the town, with services being held in the Drostdy until the first church was built in 1802. It was the church that was responsible for building the quaint *Oefeningshuis* in Voortrek Street.

A £5 note issued by the firm Barry and Nephews last century.

Our walk through the old heart of the town starts here, at the Oefeningshuis **(1)**. Built in 1838 as a church for the education of freed slaves, its name was derived from the fact that religious instruction (godsdiensoefening) was practised there. The plaster clock-face in the west gable had a real clock set in the wall just below it.

The historic Oefeningshuis with its quaint plaster clock in the end gable.

It is believed that when the 'real' hands matched the plaster clock, it was time to assemble. Like many of Swellendam's old buildings, the Oefeningshuis seems to lie well below the road. In fact the road has been raised to a height far above its original level by repeated reconstructions.

Diagonally across Voortrek Street from the Oefeningshuis is the quaint double-storeyed shop built by *Buirski and Co.* in about 1880 **(2)**. The attractive little *Church of St Luke* **(3)**, directly opposite Buirski's shop, dates from 1865.

Cross the road and enter the grounds of the *Dutch Reformed Church* **(4)**. The old gateway, on your right, formed part of the original church wall of 1840, while the present ornate building dates from 1910. A door on the right side is usually left open from 9 am to 5 pm for visitors (except on Saturdays). The original pulpit is still in use, but has been considerably altered.

Turn left as you leave the church grounds. You reach the oak-shaded Church Square on your left at the next intersection, with its row of simple double-storeyed houses **(5)**. This square was where farmers outspanned their wagons when they trekked into town for the periodic Nagmaal (Communion) services, and these 'tuishuisies' — little townhouses — were built for their use.

In front of the tuishuisies, facing onto Voortrek Street, is a thatched house now known as *The Cottage* **(6)**, which was built in about 1832. Next to it, standing well back from the road, is a little house that appears on a map of Swellendam of 1808 as the *'house of Constable Oomse'* **(7)**.

The Barry 'empire'

Across Voortrek Street from The Cottage is the *Auld House* **(8)**, built in about 1802. It was bought in 1826 by Joseph Barry, founder of the firm Barry and Nephews. This was the dominant commercial enterprise in the Overberg for half a century, even issuing its own banknotes.

The Auld House was enlarged after a fire in 1834, and retains the appearance it was given then. For many years it belonged to Barry descendants, and contained many relics of their 'Empire', including the dining table and benches from the Steamer *Kadie* — now in the Drostdy.

The main road, which pre-dates the town and is part of the early Cape Wagon Road, still bends to the south past the Drostdy, just as it did in 1776

Buirski and Co.'s shopfront features an attractive cast-iron verandah.

A quiet corner of Mayville's garden.

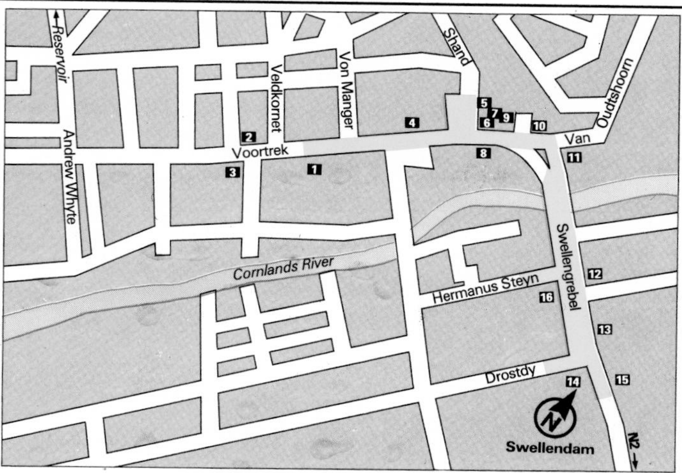

Filligree cast-ironwork has turned Schoone Oordt into a Victorian beauty.

when the artist Johannes Schumacher set up his easel somewhere near the Cornlands River to record the scene. Where the road forks, continue straight, slightly uphill, into Van Oudtshoorn Road.

On your left, set back from the road, is number 23 **(9)**, one of the few houses to have retained its original small-paned casements and wooden shutters. It dates from 1820, the same period as number 21 **(10)**, which was remodelled in the Georgian style in about 1855.

Turn right into Swellengrebel Street, passing on your left the double-storeyed *Schoone Oordt* **(11)**, built in 1853 in the Cape Georgian style. The elaborate cast-ironwork was added in the Victorian period.

Across the river on your left is number 18 **(12)**, which houses the offices and library of the *Drostdy Museum* (visitors permitted). This was originally a single-storeyed thatched house, but was converted in the mid-19th century to the Cape Georgian style.

Swellendam's museums

A little further, also on your left, is a starkly simple but very attractive row of buildings that can be seen in the Schumacher drawing of 1776. This was the *Swellendam jail* **(13)**, and also the home of the jailer and other Drostdy officials. It is now part of the Drostdy Museum. (There is a small fee at the entrance, and keep your admission ticket, as it will admit you to the other two museum buildings open to the public — the Drostdy and Mayville. All three open daily except Sundays and religious holidays.)

In a wing of the old jail building are the cells — including a 'black hole' with no windows. Behind the jail an 'ambagswerf' (trades yard) has been built. Around a grassy square with a charcoal furnace there are small buildings in the local style, each containing the tools and products of a particular trade. The coppersmith, leatherworker, wagon-builder and wheelwright are represented — also nearby are a replica of an undershot water-mill, a horse-operated mill and a threshing floor.

The Langeberg range forms a majestic backdrop for Swellendam's old jail.

Cross Swellengrebel Street (in which many of the oaks are national monuments) to the *Drostdy* **(14)**. Before entering, look back, across Swellengrebel Street, at the handsome farmhouse of *Zanddrift* **(15)**, dating from 1768. This farmhouse originally stood near Drew, in the Bonnievale district, and after standing empty for a number of years was carefully moved to its present site, where it serves as a restaurant.

The Drostdy, which served as court and residence for the magistrate for 100 years until 1846, was originally a T-shaped building. Later it was enlarged and turned into an H-plan with two short wings. At the same time the main entrance was moved from Drostdy Street to where it is today. The charming little wine cellar, with its plaster oak leaves and vines, is thought to have been added around 1825.

In the foyer of the Drostdy are large reproductions of paintings of Swellendam and Breë River scenes painted by Thomas Bowler in 1860, and a collection of Cape silver in the wall cupboard (muurkas).

On the right, the sitting room has had its lime-sand floor restored to the pattern shown in a sketch of 1798 by Lady Anne Barnard. The Drostdy floors vary considerably in composition, but all are traditional — from the cow-dung finish of the kitchen floor to the peach pips laid in clay in another part of the building.

The kitchen in the Drostdy is particularly well-equipped with the many implements — from oven rakes to sausage-fillers — needed to supply the family with food in the days before electricity.

A Victorian treasure

In an outbuilding of the Drostdy is a small collection of animal-drawn vehicles, including a hearse, the country's oldest ox-wagon (made in 1795) and a replica of a mail coach.

When you leave the Drostdy, cross Drostdy Street and walk down Swellengrebel Street, turning left into Hermanus Steyn Street. Number 4, *Mayville* **(16)**, was built as a private home in 1853, and now houses another section of the museum.

Mayville was built on land cut off from the Drostdy and formerly stood on a plot which extended to the Cornlands river. The stumps of the oaks which lined the walk to the river can still be seen in the garden on the opposite side of Hermanus Steyn Street.

Perhaps the most charming feature of Mayville is its garden, laid out in formal Victorian style, complete with gazebo. Only 'old' strains of flowers are grown here, and a slow stroll through this quiet garden of yesterday is an experience appropriate to a town which preserves so much of a more gracious era ●

Wintry sunshine casts long shadows over the entrance to the old Drostdy.

Land of timeless villages and the 'river without end'

This route leads through a land of wild mountains, and remote river valleys that have been bypassed by the clamour of commerce. Villages retain their appearance of a century or more ago, except perhaps that their oak trees have grown larger and more noble. A little more than half of this route is on good gravel roads — the rest is on tar.

Robertson
McGregor
Stormsvlei
Riviersonderend
Greyton
Genadendal
Villiersdorp
230 — 250 km

AT THE SOUTH-EAST end of Robertson's railway station, turn south out of Voortrekker Street towards McGregor. About 2 km later, the road crosses the Breë River on the Victoria Bridge. Immediately after the bridge, turn left.

This road passes the Vrolijkheid Nature Reserve on your left. Also on your left is the McGregor Co-operative Winery, which is open to the public during the week for tasting and sales, and makes an interesting stop. Beyond the winery, the road crosses a bridge before entering McGregor, 18 km from Robertson. The picturesque architecture of the town merits a short walk through its streets (see opposite).

To leave McGregor, turn left from Voortrekker Street into Van Reenen Street (this is a gravel road). After about 2 km the road takes a sharp left bend. On the right here is the old Rhebokskraal homestead, with a gable dating from 1874.

At the T-junction 1,6 km later, turn right, noting your kms. 18,5 km later, turn right onto gravel for Stormsvlei, then turn right again 6 km later at the T-junction. After a further 3,3 km turn right onto tar at the T-junction.

The road winds down through the scenic Stormsvleipoort. Towards the end of the pass, broad vistas suddenly open out before you — pull to the side of the road for the view over the fertile valley of the Riviersonderend.

Continue through the poort, cross a narrow bridge over the Riviersonderend (river without end), and enter the tiny settlement of Stormsvlei. There is a hotel here, and a holiday resort on the river bank that caters for picnickers (small entry fee, braai places, water, toilets)

Stormsvlei to Greyton
At the T-junction 1,3 km beyond the river, turn right onto the N2. Continue on the N2 for 19 km to the town of Riviersonderend. Roughly 2 km beyond the town, turn right from the N2 onto gravel for 'Lindeshof, Greyton, Genadendal', and note your kms as you turn.

After 5,3 km go left at the fork where the road to the right leads to Lindeshof School. Pass another road to Lindeshof School on your right, and 16,2 km from the N2 go right at the fork, immediately passing a road on your right.

As you crest a hill just over 2 km later, there is a sign on your left that reads 'Historical Monuments'. When clear of the hill, pull off the road. On the right side of the road, opposite the signboard, there is a small brick pillar with a plaque. This denotes Ziekenhuis (hospital), a cave that provided shelter for invalids on the old road to the interior. Among the initials carved on the rock are 'OB', believed to be those of the 17th century explorer Oloff Bergh.

Turn right at the T-junction about 500 m later. After a further 1,6 km, in which you cross three narrow bridges, turn left at the T-junction. About 3,3 km later, on the left, is the homestead of The Oaks, dating from 1792.

Roughly 10 km later you cross a bridge on the outskirts of Greyton. 400-500 m later turn right at the fork into High Street. Turn right onto the tarred main street at the Central Hotel. (The hotel and one or two other establishments in the town serve lunch.) Where the tar ends, turn left, following the sign for the 'nature reserve', and turn right at the T-junction. Continue to the gate of the nature reserve and park under the oaks. There is an attractive walk into Noupoort (narrow gorge) — allow 40-60 minutes. You can picnic at the entrance to the park, but there are no facilities.

Greyton to Villiersdorp
Return to the main street and drive towards the

The historic bell tower in Genadendal — built in 1798.

THE VALE OF MERCY
Genadendal was the first mission station established in South Africa. In 1737, Georg Schmidt of the Moravian Mission Society settled here at Baviaanskloof to preach to the remnants of the Hessequa Khoikhoi tribe. However, his baptism of his converts annoyed the church authorities, as Schmidt was not ordained. He returned to Germany in 1744, and work lapsed for almost 50 years until three other missionaries from the society arrived.

A village soon grew up, with school, church, mill, and a small factory for making sheath knives. The name Genadendal (vale of mercy) became official in 1806.

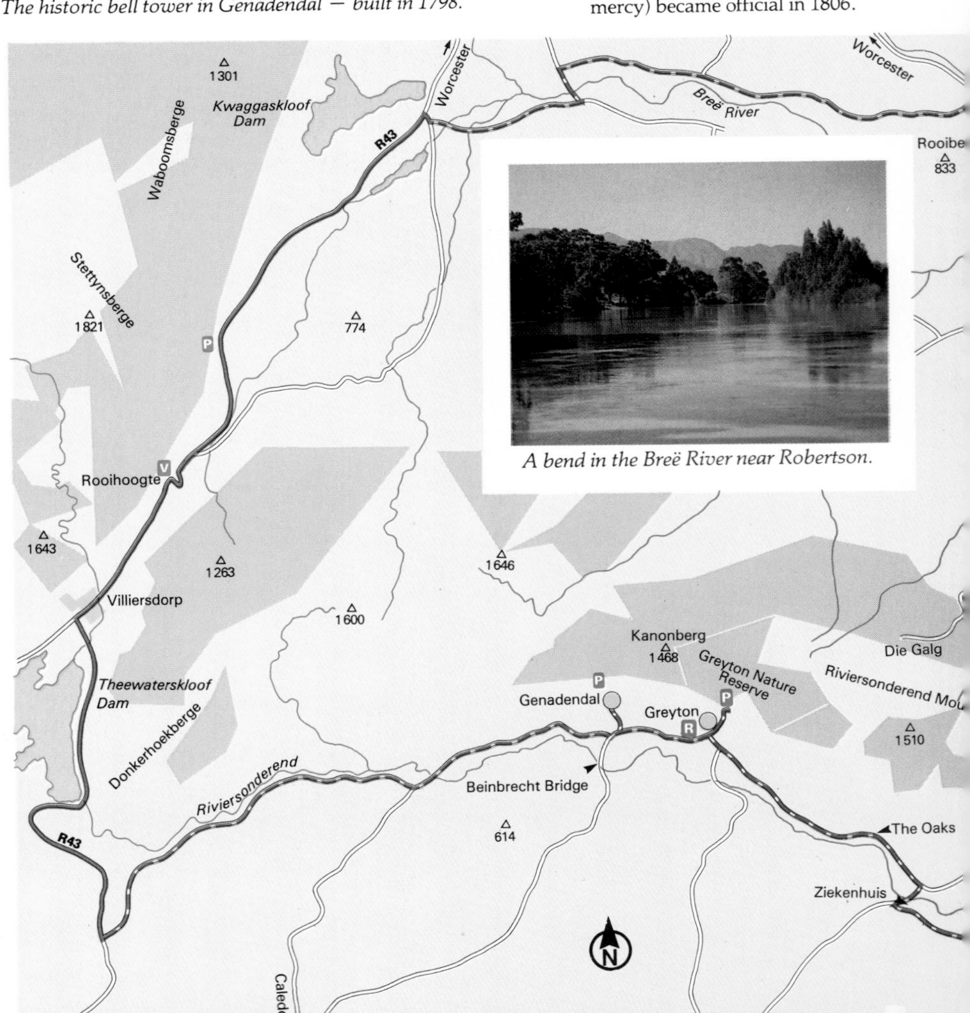

A bend in the Breë River near Robertson.

south-west end of town. Note your kms as you pass the hotel. The road surface changes to gravel after 600 m. After a further 4,1 km turn right for Genadendal. After a few hundred metres you pass the police station on your left, and 1 km later you pass the post office, also on your left. Turn left 100 m later, and after a further 300-400 m turn right to park near the church for a stroll around the historic mission complex.

Retrace your route and 1 km beyond the post office turn right next to the police station. 200 m later turn left, and 600 m later turn right at the T-junction — noting your kms. After 11,2 km (after crossing the Riviersonderend) turn right for Villiersdorp. The route runs alongside the Riviersonderend and passes the entrance to the large Helderstroom prison complex on your right. After 18,7 km on this road, turn right at the T-junction onto tar (R43). The road climbs for 3 km, then descends Floorshoogte to cross the wall of the Theewaterskloof Dam.

After 18,9 km on the R43 turn right at the T-junction with Main Street in Villiersdorp, noting your kms. After 1,6 km (at the road that leads on your left to the Co-operative) there is a large, old-fashioned steam-engine on the corner. Roughly 6,5 km later you reach the crest of the Rooihoogte (red heights) pass, and as you descend there are good views ahead over the Breë River valley. Roughly 9 km later on your left there is a large picnic site under oaks.

Roughly 15 km later turn right onto tar for Doornrivier and Scherpenheuwel, and 500 m further turn left onto gravel, noting your kms. 7,5 km later, turn left for Worcester. A few hundred metres beyond the turn, the road crosses the Breë River over a long causeway.

1,4 km later, there is almost a 'reverse fork' — turn right here for Eilandia. 7 km later you can see that the road ahead narrows and crosses a cattle grid — take the road that curves to the right here.

Just short of 14 km later, turn right at the T-junction onto tar. After 12,2 km a road on your right leads to the river resort of Silver Strand on the outskirts of Robertson ●

Robertson Municipality Town Clerk, Church Street, Robertson 6705 Tel. (02351) 3112
SA Tourism Board Level 3, Golden Acre, Adderley Street, Cape Town 8001
Tel. (021) 216274

THE VICTORIAN VILLAGE OF McGREGOR

Time seems to have stood still in McGregor, which was founded in 1861 to benefit from the passing trade that was expected to stream over the new pass linking the Breë River Valley to the coastal plateau. But the road was never finished — although you can drive for some 16 km south from Voortrekker Street to the point where the roadmakers finally downed tools when bureaucratic bungling lost them their jobs.

It is one of the best-preserved Victorian villages in South Africa, but without the Victorian embellishments that would have been added to the simple Cape lines had prosperity materialised.

Rich farmlands lie tucked away beneath the Riviersonderend Mountains.

THE MUSCADEL CAPITAL

The peaceful town of Robertson — the 'Muscadel capital' of the wine world — is also renowned for its enormous brandy distillery, and its jacaranda-lined streets.

The 35 wineries in the vicinity form the Breë River Valley Wine Route, and the KWV brandy distillery here, with its 128 potstills under one roof, is believed to be the biggest in the world.

There is a large cactus garden 8 km out of town on the Ashton road, and a smaller one — the Malherbe Memorial Garden — at the Ashton end of Voortrekker Street. The river resort of Silver Strand is just 600 m out of town on the Worcester road.

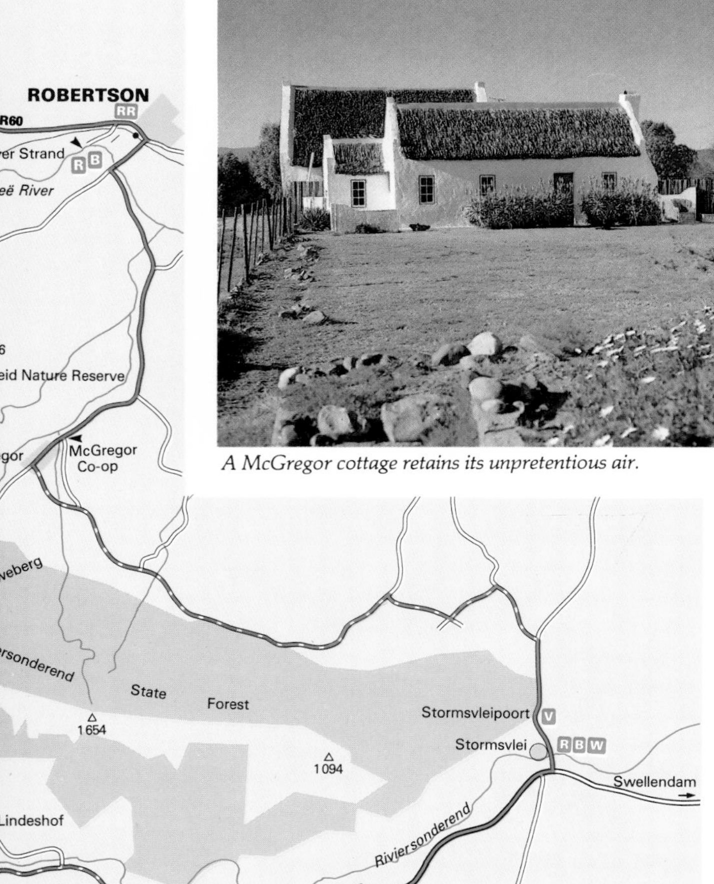

A McGregor cottage retains its unpretentious air.

The little village of Greyton preserves the tranquillity of a bygone era.

RIVER WITHOUT END

Riviersonderend, the town that bears the name of the 'river without end', was established in 1925 to serve the farming community of the river valley — which produces mainly fruit, wool and wheat.

The river itself was named by the earliest explorers — some say because it seemed to wind on without end. In fact it joins the Breë River just south-west of the present Swellendam, on a route well known to the old travellers. A more likely explanation for the name arises from the impression which the traveller has, even today, of endless streams feeding into the river.

The Strandveld — exploring the southernmost shores of Africa

Lying at the southernmost tip of Africa, the Strandveld is an isolated land of sun-bleached sand dunes and beautiful bays. Popular holiday resorts now dot a coastline feared by generations of sailors and littered by countless shipwrecks. About two-thirds of this route is on tar and the remainder is on good gravel.

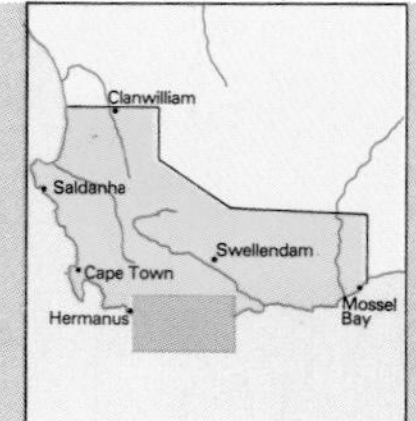

Hermanus
Elim
Cape Agulhas
Waenhuiskrans/
Arniston
Bredasdorp
260—280 km

AT THE WESTERN END of Hermanus, turn inland from Main Road into Rotary Way, and follow this scenic mountain drive for some 3,7 km to the point where it forks. Park near the benches on the right, from where there is a fine view over the town and the full sweep of the Walker Bay coastline.

Return to Main Road, turn left, and follow this road (R43) through the town towards Stanford and Gansbaai. After passing the Hermanus Lagoon on your right, cross a bridge over the Klein River (which feeds into the lagoon), and enter Stanford 300 m beyond.

Keep straight for just over 17 km, then turn right (on tar) for Die Kelders (the cellars). Park after 400 m outside the hotel, where admission tickets may be bought for the caves — the 'cellars' which gave the place its name. An underground stream forms deep pools as it flows through a series of caverns below the cliff.

Return to the T-junction with the R43, and turn right. The road enters Gansbaai after 2,6 km. 100 m after passing the Gansbaai sign on your left, turn right out of Hoofstraat. After a further 300 m turn right at the T-junction with Park Street — this becomes Coast Road as it bends left towards the sea, and the surface soon changes to gravel.

The road passes a tidal bathing pool with changing rooms on your right. Turn right immediately after the pool to stay on the shore, and pass the entrance to the harbour. Return to Hoofstraat (R43) and turn right.

Gansbaai to Agulhas

Note your kms 700 m out of Gansbaai as you pass the road on your right leading to Danger Point. Keep straight for 17,9 km, then turn left onto gravel at the intersection where the road on the right leads to Pearly Beach (after some 2,2 km). Note your kms as you turn.

The road climbs Groenkloof, an area noted for its proteas, then reaches a T-junction 9,6 km after leaving the tar road. Turn right, and go right at the fork 6 km later. After a further 9,6 km the road enters Elim (see opposite).

A monument built in 1938 near the Elim church commemorates the centenary of the liberation of slaves at the Cape. Drive along the right side of the church to a grassy clearing just beyond to visit the old water mill.

Drive back past the church and turn right towards Bredasdorp/Agulhas, noting your kms. The surface changes to gravel after about 100 m.

Continue on this road, passing a number of side roads. Clumps of milkwood trees become a feature of the landscape after roughly 20 km. About 10 km later you pass on your left the entrance to the farm Soetendals Vallei, with a homestead dating from around 1816.

34 km after noting your kms turn right onto tar at the T-junction. Pass the residential area of Molshoop (mole hill) on your left just short of 2 km later, and the traditional old fishermen's cottages of Hotagterklip (left-rear stone) about 1 km beyond. As you enter Struisbaai, turn left into Duiker Street to reach a parking area at the wide beach. Return to the main road (Marine Drive), and turn left. Stop roughly 7,5 km later, after passing the Agulhas lighthouse near the southernmost tip of the continent.

Agulhas to Waenhuiskrans

Drive back through Struisbaai and note your kms as you pass the last cottage on your right in Hotagterklip. Pass on your left the road on which you arrived from Elim.

After 14,9 km turn right onto gravel for Waenhuiskrans/Arniston. 6,9 km later turn left at the T-junction. Cross a cattle grid after 300 m and immediately turn right for Waenhuiskrans/Arniston. After 6,5 km turn right onto tar and enter Waenhuiskrans/Arniston 5,5 km later.

At the four-way stop street, the road on your left leads to the slipway, hotel (which serves lunch), old fishing village, and the Arniston memorial. Turn right here for Waenhuiskrans cave, passing a number of cottages that have been proclaimed national monuments. This road changes to a gravel surface after 700 m, and reaches the parking area above the cave after a further 700 m. The mouth of the cave faces the sea, and can be reached at low tide by walking across some 200 m of sand and rocks — in which there are many fascinating pools — and going right when you reach the shore.

Waenhuiskrans to Stanford

Return to the four-way stop street, and retrace your route out of Waenhuiskrans/Arniston. Pass the Struisbaai road on your left, and continue straight. After 15 km from the four-way stop, the road passes a turn-off on your right to the farm Nachtwacht, with a homestead dating from around 1835. Immediately afterwards you cross the Kars River.

Enter Bredasdorp on Kerkstraat, and continue straight to the T-junction. Turn right and park as soon as possible to visit the Bredasdorp Museum on your left.

Continue down the hill on Independent Street to the traffic lights, and turn left. This tarred road will bring you to Napier after 13,7 km. Drive straight through, passing the Dutch Reformed Church — a national monument — on your left. Note your kms as you pass the sign to 'Napier Stn', at the intersection with Wesstraat, and keep straight.

After 26,4 km turn left onto tar for Stanford (R326). This road leads through the Akkedisberg (lizzard mountain) Pass, which follows the gorge of the Klein River. At Stanford turn right for Hermanus ●

AA Office AA House, 7 Martin Hammerschlag Way, Cape Town 8001 Tel. (021) 211550
Hermanus Publicity Association Main Road, Hermanus 7200 Tel. (02831) 22629
Bredasdorp Museum 6 Independent Street, Bredasdorp 7280 Tel. (0284) 41240

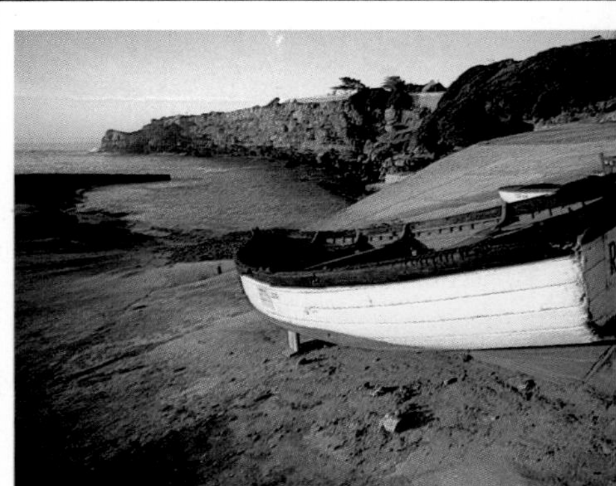
Early morning sun washes over weathered fishing boats at the old harbour in Hermanus.

A street scene in the quaint old mission village of Elim — virtually unchanged in 100 years.

A rocky outcrop at Gansbaai, battered by waves.

ELIM MISSION

The main street of this Moravian mission village has been described as 'one of the finest historic street-scapes in the Cape', lined as it is by ancient white-washed cottages with black thatched roofs.

The parsonage, just below and to the left of the church, is dated 1796, and the church itself dates from 1834. The clock mechanism is over 200 years old and was installed in 1914.

The water-mill building has been restored, and still houses the mill machinery. Much of the machinery was replaced in 1881, and continued to be used until 1972.

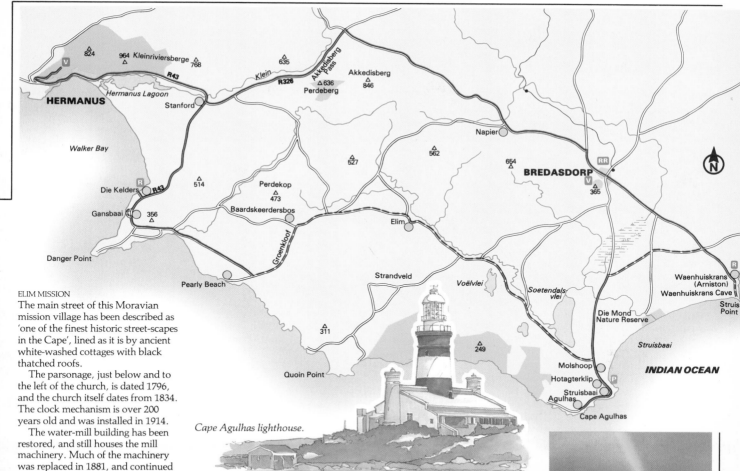

Cape Agulhas lighthouse.

Struisbaai fishermen row in to the beach after a day out at sea.

BREDASDORP'S SHIPWRECK MUSEUM

The Bredasdorp Museum in Independent Street has as its theme the shipwrecks of the southern Cape coast. The fascinating relics date from the wreck of the *Haarlem* in 1647 and include elaborately carved figureheads, gold and silver coins, and handsome shipboard furniture. The restful garden of the museum contains a number of ancient cannons, including a rare bronze mortar, and the coach-house shelters a display of old vehicles.

The Bredasdorp nature reserve is reached via Van Riebeeck Street, which leads off Independent Street, and preserves local fynbos — including many proteas and ericas. The hill in the reserve offers good views over the town and surrounding countryside.

THE SOUTHERNMOST TIP OF AFRICA

The name Agulhas, meaning 'needles' in Portuguese, is said to have been given to the southernmost tip of Africa because here the needle of a compass points true north with no deviation.

The lighthouse at Agulhas was designed by Colonel Charles Michell in the middle of the last century. It originally looked like a fortress when seen from the sea. The old light served faithfully for more than a century until its task was taken over by a more modern light in 1962. The building is now an extension of the Bredasdorp Museum.

A pair of historic fishermen's cottages at Waenhuiskrans.

A RESORT WITH TWO NAMES

A gaping cavern in the cliff gave Waenhuiskrans (wagon-house cliff) its official name — the shape reminded early visitors of a wagon-house. The cave is easy to reach at low tide, and may yield exciting discoveries cast up by the sea.

For many years this little resort was also known as Arniston, the name of a troopship that ran aground in 1815 on its way from Ceylon (now Sri Lanka) to England, with the loss of 372 lives. Only the ship's carpenter and five sailors survived. Many roofs in the Strandveld are still held up by massive beams that once formed the ribs of the ill-fated *Arniston*.

Waenhuiskrans cave — gouged out of the rock by pounding waves.

Salt spray and wildflowers where the Cape mountains meet the sea

This drive leads east from Gordon's Bay, along a magnificent, moody coastline where the colourful Cape mountains, blanketed in wildflowers, run directly into the sea. It then reaches inland and returns to Gordon's Bay through the rolling wheatfields of Caledon and the orchards of Elgin and Grabouw. All but 37 km of the route is tarred.

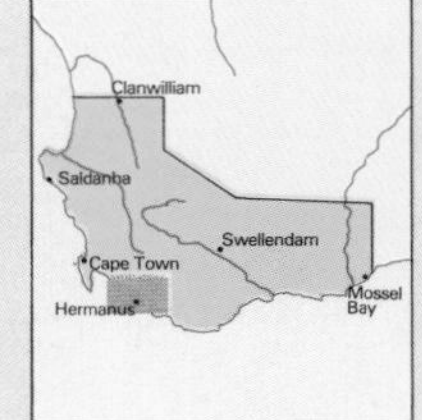

Gordon's Bay
Kleinmond
Hermanus
Caledon
Houhoek
170 — 180 km

START FROM GORDON'S BAY, 53 km from Cape Town on the N2. Drive along the beachfront towards the nearest mountains. Pass the harbour entrance and turn right at the T-junction onto Faure Marine Drive.

1,5 km after the T-junction, turn left onto the tarred road to Steenbras Dam. This road climbs the mountainside and offers outstanding views over Gordon's Bay, Strand and Somerset West, and across False Bay to the mountains of the Cape Peninsula.

Turn back at the entrance to the dam area, 3,6 km from the turn-off.

Drive back to Faure Marine Drive and turn left. After 3 km you pass a holiday resort with accommodation, swimming, braai area and tea room. 300 m after this the road crosses the Steenbras River, with a view to your right of the rocky river mouth. There is a picnic area on the right just after the bridge. From here the road (R44) is known as Clarence Drive.

Steenbras River Mouth to Kleinmond
More picnic and braai sites dot the side of the road as it leads to Koeëlbaai, a long white beach with rows of breaking waves. Nearly 2 km beyond the beach a gravel road on your right leads to Sparks Bay, where there are more braai sites (no water, no dogs, no camping). Ahead of you now is the prominent outcrop known as Klein Hangklip, overlooking the resort of Rooiels, which you reach after crossing the Rooiels River. Bathing in the river is safe.

Continue along the coast through Betty's Bay, which has a shop and a petrol station. Immediately after Betty's Bay, turn left to enter the picturesque Harold Porter Botanic Garden (you can picnic on the lawn; no dogs or fires).

Continue on the R44 for Kleinmond, noting your kms as you turn left out of the Harold Porter Garden. After 6 km stop on the side of the road and look up the mountainside to see the rock formation known as 'the elephant'. After 6,2 km you pass the Kleinmond Coastal Nature Reserve (the entrance is on the right). There are picnic sites along the road, which crosses the Palmiet River before entering Kleinmond. Kleinmond has several restaurants and a lawned picnic area with toilets, water and braai places.

Kleinmond to Hermanus
11 km beyond Kleinmond, turn right towards Hermanus at the T-junction with the R43. The road crosses the Bot and Afdaks rivers and passes roads to Hawston, Vermont and Onrus, before entering Hermanus. 800 m after entering the built-up area, turn left onto a tarred scenic drive called Rotary Way, which leads for 3,7 km through unspoilt fynbos with excellent views over the town and coast.

Return to the main road, turn left, and drive into the town, passing the road to the New Harbour. Continue straight at the traffic lights in the town centre until you reach a T-junction. Turn left and park in the parking area on your left in Marine Drive, across the road from the war memorial (flanked by two 12-pounder guns).

To the left of the war memorial a short path leads down to the Old Harbour and its museum. (A little further to the left of the memorial there is the start of a pleasant 'cliff walk' that can be followed for many kilometres along the seashore.)

After exploring the Old Harbour, drive back to the traffic lights in the centre of the town and turn right, noting your kms. After 3,4 km turn left, and follow the signs to Fernkloof Nature Reserve. Here you can take your time strolling through fine expanses of coastal fynbos, including roughly 50 species of erica, and can visit the herbarium, which has over 700 specimens.

Hermanus to Caledon
Retrace your route out of Hermanus, and turn right onto the R320 towards Caledon. This is a gravel road, but it is usually kept in excellent condition. The R320 passes through the Hemel-en-Aarde Valley, which has the southernmost vineyards in Africa — lying roughly 35 km further south than those at Groot Constantia in the Cape Peninsula.

The gravel gives way to tar after 24 km, at the start of Shaw's Mountain Pass. Pause at the summit of the pass for panoramic views over rolling wheatfields, sparkling dams, mountains and patches of forest.

Continue past a turn-off to the right for Bredasdorp and Napier, then turn left in front of a cluster of grain silos onto the R316 for Caledon.

Follow this road into Caledon (where it becomes Kerkstraat) until the intersection with Prince Alfred Road in the centre of the town. Turn left here, passing on your right the small sandstone Anglican Church of the Holy Trinity, consecrated in 1854.

Turn right into Joubert Street (second right after the filling stations), then take the second turn left into Krige Street, to reach the town's museum and information centre on the your right at 11 Krige Street.

Return to Prince Alfred Road and turn right towards the N2. At the T-junction with the N2 turn right for the Caledon Wildflower Garden, 1,3 km along the road on the left side.

GORDON'S BAY
Gordon's Bay was first known as Visch Hoek Baay, after a fishing station was erected there in the early 1700s. The name was changed to Gordon's Bay in honour of Colonel Robert Jacob Gordon, a soldier of Scots-Dutch descent who was the last commander of the Dutch East India Company garrison at the Cape. (He committed suicide after the Dutch capitulated to the British in 1795.) On the slopes above the town are the letters GB and an anchor, picked out in white-painted stones.

Gently shelving beaches make Gordon's Bay a safe bathing resort. The coastline from here to Cape Hangklip offers excellent angling, but many anglers have fallen off the rocks or have been swept to their deaths by exceptionally large waves. Yachts and fishing boats are moored in the sheltered harbour, which has launching facilities.

A lazy late afternoon in Gordon's Bay harbour.

Caledon to Sir Lowry's Pass
When you return to the N2 after visiting the Wildflower Garden, turn right and follow the signs towards Cape Town.

After 23 km, turn off left and cross the N2 towards Bot River on the R43 for a short detour through this picturesque town, the centre of an onion-growing district. Follow the main road past the town's hotel and rejoin the N2.

This stretch of the N2 has been known since wagon days as Langhoogte, the 'long slope' up to the 340-metre Houhoek Pass. 2,5 km past the summit of the pass there is a crossroads, with the Houhoek Hotel on your right.

Continue on the N2, passing the R321 to Grabouw. The road winds through tall forests in the Palmiet and Steenbras river valleys to the 450-metre Sir Lowry's Pass. At the summit of the pass, turn into the parking area on your left for the view (picnic site; no fires, no water). Below you is the sweeping curve of the False Bay coast, with Table Mountain in the distance. To your right is the picturesque valley of the Lourens River. Down to your left is your starting point at Gordon's Bay ●

AA Office AA House, 7 Martin Hammerschlag Way, Cape Town 8001 Tel. (021) 211550
Hermanus Publicity Association Main Road, Hermanus 7200 Tel. (02831) 22629
Caledon Museum & Information Centre 11 Krige Street, Caledon 7230 Tel. (0281) 21511
S A Tourism Board Level 3, Golden Acre, Adderley Street, Cape Town 8001 Tel. (021) 216274

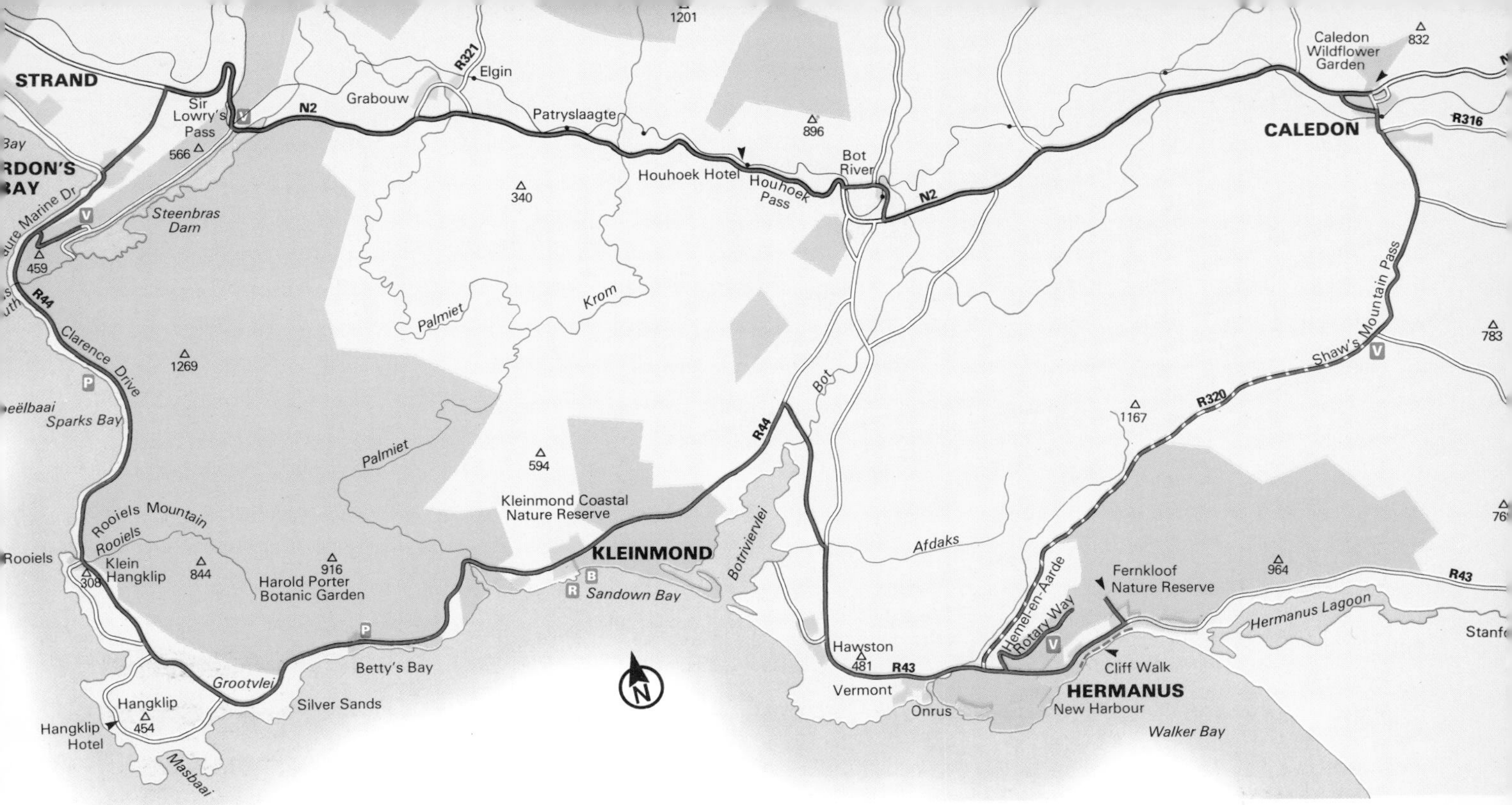

STRAND
Sir Lowry's Pass
566
Grabouw
Elgin
R321
1201
N2
Patryslaagte
896
Houhoek Hotel
Houhoek Pass
Bot River
340
Caledon Wildflower Garden
832
CALEDON
R316
Steenbras Dam
459
R44
Clarence Drive
1269
Sparks Bay
Palmiet
Krom
Bot
Shaw's Mountain Pass
783
R320
1167
594
Kleinmond Coastal Nature Reserve
KLEINMOND
Botrivierviei
Sandown Bay
Rooiels Mountain
Rooiels
Klein Hangklip
308
844
916
Harold Porter Botanic Garden
Afdaks
Hemel-en-Aarde
Rotary Way
Fernkloof Nature Reserve
964
R43
Hermanus Lagoon
Hawston
481
R43
Vermont
Onrus
Cliff Walk
HERMANUS
New Harbour
Walker Bay
Betty's Bay
Grootvlei
Silver Sands
Hangklip
454
Hangklip Hotel
Masbaai

Gentle colours, gentle textures, where the pretty Rooiels River reaches the sea.

The Houhoek Inn — 150 years of history.

Caledon's velvet fields.

KINGDOM OF THE FLOWERS

This area of the Western Cape is one of the world's richest floral kingdoms. One showpiece is the Harold Porter Botanic Garden at Betty's Bay, famous for its ericas, proteas and bulb plants.

The nearby Kleinmond Coastal Nature Reserve contains a rich mixture of riverine, kloof-living and seashore plants, many indigenous trees, and over 1 200 different wildflower species. An 8 km coastal walk leads past rock pools and inlets. The Fernkloof Nature Reserve at Hermanus ranges in altitude from 63 m to 842 m, with a wide variety of flora to match.

The Caledon Wildflower Garden owes its existence to three young men who in 1892 held a wildflower show, with prizes worth £60. The show became an annual event, leading in 1927 to the establishment of the Wildflower Garden.

THE OLD HARBOUR MUSEUM, HERMANUS

For over a century the Old Harbour at Hermanus served the fisherfolk of the town — until the New Harbour was eventually opened shortly after World War II.

The Old Harbour now has a museum building situated in a row of fishermen's cottages.

The museum contains numerous relics from the old whaling days, the WR Selkirk Collection of shark jaws (fearsome), together with various angling trophies, old photographs, boat building tools, pieces of deep-water diving apparatus, ship models, boats, blocks, sheaves, old fishing rods and reels, and a display of unusual mounted fish (plus a sea snake).

Outside the museum there is an interesting collection of old fishing boats. One of these, the five-oared 'Deppie', is believed to have been built as long ago as 1907.

LAST OF THE COACHING INNS

The original name of the Houhoek Pass, a route 'much dreaded by those who have to pass it in wagons', is thought to have been 'Hout Hoek' (wood corner). Alternatively, 'Hou' (hold) may refer to the steepness of the old road.

There have been four passes over the Houhoek mountains, apart from the present one, all passing close to the Houhoek Inn. Dating from 1834, this is claimed to be the oldest coaching inn in the country.

The Old Harbour at Hermanus, with the Kleinriviersberge in the distance.

Four passes that link together the pastoral patchwork of the Boland

The Boland mountains, long an obstruction to the pioneers, are crossed today by several easy, scenic passes. The passes overlook fertile valleys blanketed with vineyards, fields and orchards, where gracious homesteads nestle beneath craggy peaks. Our route through this region is on good tarred roads, and passes a number of attractive picnic sites.

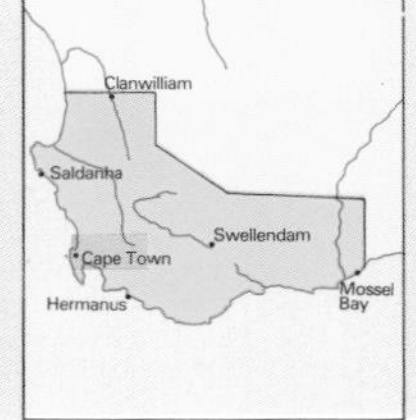

Cape Town
Sir Lowry's Pass
Grabouw
Franschhoek
Stellenbosch
250 – 260 km

BEGIN THIS DRIVE AT Rhodes Memorial (see pages 282-3 for directions). From here you have a view across the Cape Flats towards the distant mountains through which our route meanders.

Drive down to the M3 and head towards Muizenberg. At the end of the M3 after 13,7 km, exit left, and at the end of the off-ramp 600 m later turn left. At the T-junction, turn right onto the old main road.

After 3,4 km turn left at the robot-controlled intersection into Atlantic Road, Muizenberg. Follow this road past the pavilion and amusement area on your right, and turn right across the bridge over the Sandvlei river mouth.

Drive around the traffic circle and continue straight for Strandfontein and Mitchell's Plain (R310). Known as Baden-Powell Drive, this road runs along the sandy coast of False Bay, offering splendid views, then veers inland. After roughly 25 km on this road, turn right onto the N2 towards Somerset West.

Continue on the N2 up Sir Lowry's Pass. As you approach the top of the pass move into the central lane, and at the crest of the pass turn right into the parking area. From here you look over the Lourens River valley to your right, and across False Bay to the Peninsula mountains.

(Across the road from the viewsite entrance is the start of the Boland Hiking Trail that leads past the old Gandou Pass — see alongside.)

Sir Lowry's Pass to 'Purgatory'

Return to the N2, and after 8,1 km turn left for Grabouw and Elgin (R321). At the stop street in Grabouw, continue straight. Cross the bridge over the Palmiet River, then turn left at the sign for Villiersdorp and Franschhoek (R321).

The start of Viljoen's Pass is reached about 5 km later. When the road begins to descend, there are wide views of tree-bordered fields in the valleys below.

About 6 km from the start of the pass there is a hairpin bend to the right. Stop here in the parking area on your left to enjoy the view over the fertile upper reaches of the Riviersonderend (river without end).

From here the road descends into the valley, and you pass through the settlement of Vyeboom. Soon there are good views over the Theewaterskloof Dam, with the Franschhoek Mountains on its far side.

Cross the bridge over the dam and immediately turn left for Franschhoek (R45). 2,8 km later, on a right-hand bend, park on the left side of the road for a view of the dam and the road bridge. After a further 7,6 km you reach the tree-shaded 'Purgatory' picnic site (braai places, toilets, drinking water).

Shortly after the picnic site, the road begins to ascend the Franschhoek Pass and crosses a bridge over the Du Toit's River. A few hundred metres past the bridge you can see traces of the old pass, marked by a row of stones on the hillside to your right.

Over the Franschhoek Pass

Immediately after crossing the Jan Joubertsgat Bridge, stop at a parking area on your right. Steps lead down to the river on the mountain side of the road on both sides of the bridge. This allows you to examine the bridge — the oldest road bridge still in use in South Africa.

Continue up the pass, stopping just after the first hairpin bend at a parking area on your left, for a view back down the pass to the valley below with its rocky walls and deep kloof. Continue through another hairpin bend to the summit of the pass.

As the road begins to descend, turn left into a parking area. From here there are magnificent views of the Franschhoek Valley below, with its

From the lower reaches of Sir Lowry's Pass the Hottentots Holland mountains stretch to the east.

THE FRUIT OF DRAKENSTEIN

Until 1892, Cape fruit farmers were prevented by the lack of refrigerated cargo-holds from exporting their surplus fruit. But in that year the ship *Drummond Castle* safely delivered delicate peaches to London, changing the fruit farmers' fortunes.

A few years later C J Rhodes bought up a number of Drakenstein farms. These formed the basis of Rhodes Fruit Farms, today run by a large corporation.

Springtime sees Elgin apple country in blossom.

GANDOU PASS AND THE FAR-SIGHTED SIR LOWRY COLE

The Khoikhoi and San knew the animal track over the Hottentots Holland Mountains as *Gandou* (path of the eland). The early European settlers used this same steep track to haul their wagons over the mountains — until the traffic to and from the farms beyond became so heavy that pressure mounted for the building of a properly graded pass. Sir Lowry Cole, Governor at the Cape in the early 19th century, invoked the displeasure of the British Government — but the gratitude of the farmers — when he authorised the use of local funds to build the new pass that bears his name.

Luxuriant pastoral scene alongside the Theewaterskloof Dam.

farmlands, vineyards, forests, shimmering dams and ribbons of road.

The road winds down the mountainside into Franschhoek, reaching the Huguenot Monument almost immediately on your left. Park here to visit the monument and the adjoining Huguenot Museum. (Franschhoek has several restaurants offering lunches and teas.)

Franschhoek to Boschendal

About 100 m beyond the main museum building, turn right into Huguenot Road for Paarl, Stellenbosch and Cape Town. Drive along this road, passing the historic Dutch Reformed Church on your right.

At the fork 200 m beyond the church, take the left road. The road passes through the village of Groendal (green dale), crosses the railway, then leads through the vineyards of many of the original farms established by the first French Huguenot settlers.

After passing a picnic area on your left, the road crosses the railway again, then crosses the Berg River on a single-lane bridge.

About 5 km later, turn left for Pniel and Stellenbosch (R310). Immediately after the turn you cross a double set of railway tracks. 1,5 km later, turn off left to visit the historic Boschendal homestead (see pages 280-1).

Boschendal to Cape Town

After leaving the Boschendal estate, the road leads through the tree-shaded mission village of Pniel, with its picturesque church on your right, then winds gently uphill through the adjoining village of Johannesdal.

Keep right at the fork where Kylemore Road leads left. Continue on the R310 as it winds over the Helshoogte Pass, and down through Ida's Valley on the outskirts of Stellenbosch.

Keep straight, and at the stop street at Ryneveld Street, turn left. At the robot-controlled intersection turn right into Merriman Street. At the next robot-controlled intersection turn right into Bird Street.

Continue straight on this road (R304) for 14,7 km, then turn left onto the N1 towards Cape Town ●

AA Office AA House, 7 Martin Hammerschlag Way, Cape Town 8001 Tel. (021) 211550
Stellenbosch Visitors Bureau 30 Plein Street, Stellenbosch 7600 Tel. (02231) 3584
Huguenot Memorial Museum Lambrecht Street, Franschhoek 7690 Tel. (02212) 2532
S A Tourism Board Level 3, Golden Acre, Adderley Street, Cape Town 8001 Tel. (021) 216274

The view west from the Franschhoek Pass over the fertile Berg River Valley.

THE PARADISE THEY CALLED PURGATORY

The Franschhoek Pass, among the highlights of this scenic drive, replaces a number of earlier roadways. One of these was built in 1822 by the 'irregular and desperate' men of the Royal African Corps. Toiling in the alternating heat and cold on the Villiersdorp side, they named the place Purgatory. Lord Charles Somerset had sent them there not only to build a road but also so that they could 'be prevented from committing violence and depredation' on innocent citizens. The road they built replaced an earlier one made by a local farmer, S J Cats of Ida's Valley.

The Jan Joubertsgat Bridge, which is believed to take its name from an early traveller who drowned in the river that it crosses, was built in 1823.

Huguenot Monument, Franschhoek.

APPLE COUNTRY

The lucrative Elgin apple industry is relatively young — it was started only after World War I on the initiative of medical man and member of the Cape Legislative Council Sir Antonie Viljoen, after whom the pass was named. Viljoen planted the first apple trees in the area, but died before his dreams of a large apple-growing venture became reality. Although the apple capital is actually Grabouw, the industry has become known by the name of the nearest railway despatching point, Elgin, built on Glen Elgin farm.

HUGUENOT MONUMENT AND MUSEUM

This complex, commemorating the Huguenot settlers who fled persecution in 17th century France, is laid out among lawns and flower beds in the fertile bowl of the mountains. The main building, Saasveld, once stood in Kloof Street, Cape Town, and was moved piece by piece to its present site.

The museum houses fine collections of Cape silver, old crockery and furniture, and relics of the early fruit and wine industries. Staff members specialise in tracing Huguenot ancestry.

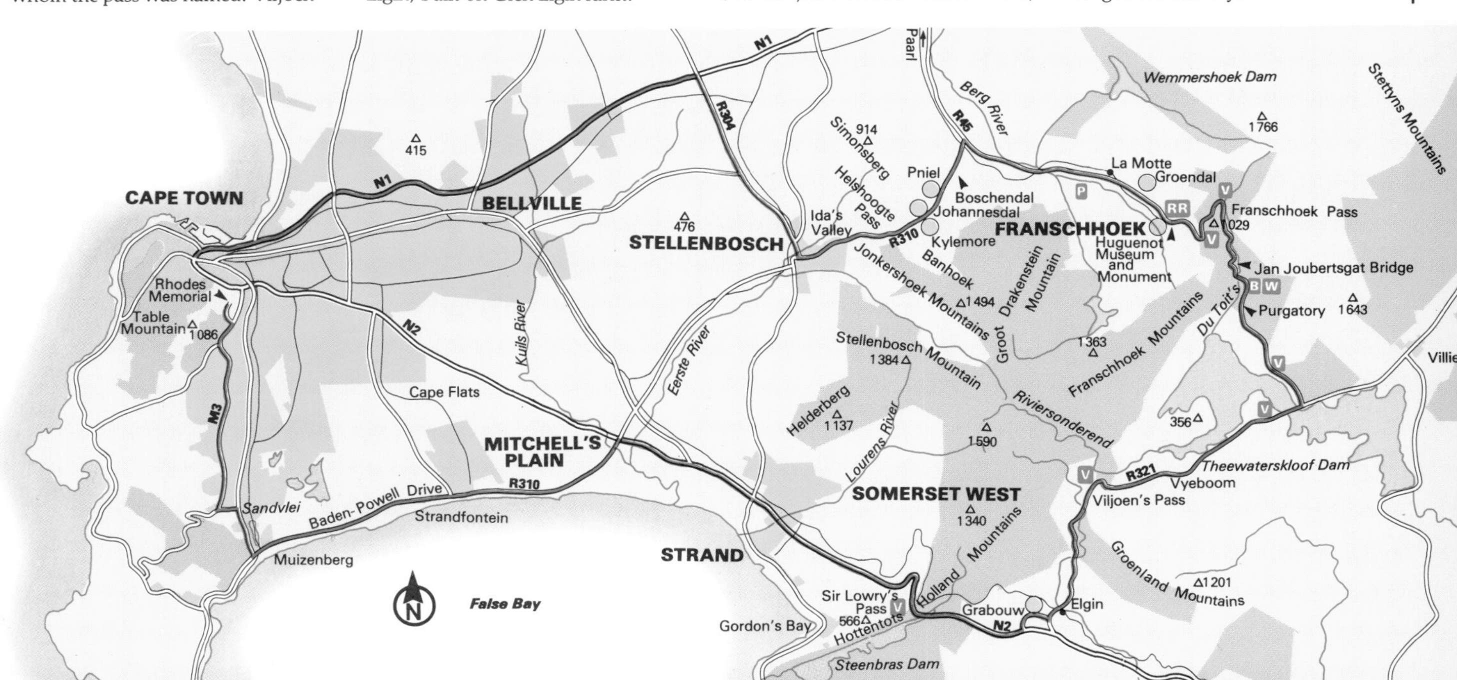

Elegant buildings and stately old oaks line Stellenbosch's Dorp Street.

Oak-shaded avenues and historic homes

IN THE SPRING of 1679 Simon van der Stel, governor of the Dutch settlement at the Cape, set out on a 'venture into the wilderness', to explore the settlement's immediate hinterland and assess its usefulness. In his journal he recorded his discovery of the Eerste River valley:

'... a level valley comprising several thousand morgen of beautiful pasturage. It is also ideal for agriculture, being drained by a particularly fine, clear river, along whose banks grow handsome, tall trees, suitable for timber and firewood.'

Van der Stel's encampment alongside the river was referred to as *Stellenbosch* (Van der Stel's wood) and this became the name of the village that subsequently grew here when settlers arrived and established farms in the area.

The older part of the town lies close to the river, and in a leisurely exploration on foot it is possible to visit many well-preserved homes, and other buildings of interest, dating from various periods in the town's nearly 300 years of history.

If you are arriving in Stellenbosch by car, turn into Old Strand Road at the western end of Dorp Street. Cross the small bridge over the Eerste River and park on the left.

Across the road from where you have parked there is a group of whitewashed cottages thought to have been designed by Sir Herbert Baker for labourers working on Cecil Rhodes's farm *Vredenburg*. Today these house a restaurant and the *Oude Meester Brandy Museum* **(1)** (open to the public).

Walk back along Old Strand Road, crossing the bridge over the river. Looking up-river from the bridge, one can imagine the scene almost 300 years ago, as the first few settlers began erecting their simple cottages within convenient water-carrying distance from this sparkling mountain stream.

Where Old Strand Road meets Dorp Street there are several interesting buildings. On your left is *Libertas Parva* **(2)**, which now houses the Rembrandt van Rijn art collection, and its adjacent wine cellar, now the *Stellenryck Wine Museum* **(3)** (both open to the public). Across the road is 50 Dorp Street **(4)**, formerly owned by a Mrs Ackermann, where Jan Smuts boarded while studying at Victoria College (now the University of Stellenbosch).

Living in Libertas Parva at that time were a Mr and Mrs Krige, with their daughter Sybella. Jan and Sybella met, in the vicinity of this crossroads, eventually married, and

Labourers' cottages designed by Sir Herbert Baker, in Old Strand Road.

went forward together to a destiny that was to hold them for many years in the international spotlight.

A rich collection of historic buildings
As you walk east along Dorp Street you pass through one of South Africa's richest collections of historically interesting buildings.

Opposite the Ackermann house there are the *Krige cottages* **(5)**, built by Mr Willie Krige in a Victorianised Cape style. A short distance further along, set back from the street, is the old farmhouse *Vredelust* **(6)**, now a restaurant. In earlier days Vredelust was known as *Libertas Oos*, and the farm was originally granted to a Jan Cornelisz in 1689. Cornelisz must have been quite a character, for he was generally known as Jan Bombam, and was even referred to by this name in official documents.

84 Dorp Street, on the left side of the street, is *Oom Samie se Winkel* **(7)**, a village shop that retains the charm of a more leisurely way of life. At 95 Dorp Street, on the right, we come to *La Gratitude* **(8)**, with a fine Cape Dutch facade.

La Gratitude was built in 1798 by the Rev Meent Borcherds. He and his family supervised the building and brick-making themselves, and his son later recorded that, despite these duties, he was still expected to keep up with his Latin lessons. It is still possible to see from the street the 'all-seeing eye of God' that Borcherds had carved above the gable window.

Further along the street, on the left, there is the old *Lutheran Church* **(9)** of 1851 — now housing the University of Stellenbosch Art Museum.

Exploring the Village Museum
Continue along Dorp Street, then turn left into Ryneveld Street. You now pass on your right the *Kolonieshuis* **(10)** (a name often given to the official residence erected in each new *drostdy*, or magisterial district). The present building incorporates parts of the original house of 1694. The new congregation's first permanent minister, Hercules van Loon, lived here for four years from 1700, until he committed suicide by 'cutting his own throat with a pocket knife'. Nobody could discover 'the cause of his profound despair' but it may have had something to do with the serious social problems then plaguing the church, involving fraud, drunkenness and immorality.

A 'fine, clear river, along whose banks grow handsome, tall trees... .

The Village Museum's Berghhuis — once home to Oloff Marthinus Bergh.

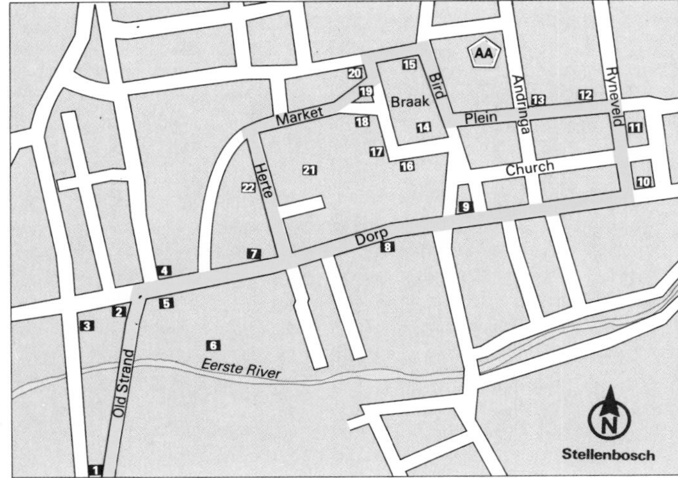

The very simple but warm interior of the early 18th century Schreuderhuis.

Cross Church Street and enter the Village Museum on your right at 18 Ryneveld Street **(11)** (small entrance fee). The Village Museum incorporates a section of the old town, and includes several distinct houses representing various periods in the town's history.

One of these, the *Schreuderhuis*, is probably the oldest restored town house in South Africa. It is clearly recognisable in the oldest known drawing of Stellenbosch, dated 15 February 1710. The interior is striking in its simplicity. In the early 18th century only the wealthy could have glass panes in their windows and use wooden planks for their floors and ceilings. Here the window frames are covered with cotton rubbed with beeswax, the ceilings are made of sticks and reeds, and the floors are simply compacted earth.

Next in the complex is the *Blettermanhuis*, built in the last quarter of the 18th century and furnished in the style characteristic of a wealthy burgher *circa* 1780. A third house in the complex is *Grosvenor House*, furnished in a style characteristic of the early 19th century. A fourth is the *Berghhuis*, former home of Oloff Marthinus Bergh, now furnished in the style of affluent townsfolk at about the middle of the 19th century.

Leave the museum complex through the Ryneveld Street entrance, turn right into Ryneveld Street, then turn left into Plein Street. In Plein Street, on your right, is the *De Witt House* **(12)**, dating from the second quarter of the 19th century. It now houses the Stellenbosch Visitors Bureau, where you can get up-to-the-minute information on where to have lunch as well as the latest news regarding current renovations and historical research.

The *Braak* and the *Kruithuis*
From the *De Witt House*, continue along Plein Street. In front of the City Hall complex on your right you will see the old furrow of the mill stream **(13)**, believed to date back to the founding of the town.

Cross Andringa and Bird streets to reach the *Braak* **(14)**, the 'village green'. Over the centuries this has served as fairground, sports venue and military parade ground.

To your right, at the north end of the Braak, there is the thatch-roofed *St Mary's Anglican church* **(15)**. Along the southern and western sides of the Braak you can see the handsome collection of buildings known as the *Rhenish complex*, including the elegant *Rhenish church* **(16)**, the *Rhenish Institute* **(17)**, now an arts centre, and the 1905 building **(18)** that housed the Rhenish High School and the Rhenish Primary School.

Cross from the Braak to the small triangular traffic island at the head of Market Street. Here you can see the old *V O C Kruithuis* (arsenal) of 1777 **(19)**. It now houses a collection of weapons and military uniforms, including examples of the heavy match-lock weapons with which Van Riebeeck's men were armed.

Across the northern arm of Market Street from the *Kruithuis* you can see the *Burgerhuis* **(20)**, built in 1797. Part of this building is now open to the public as a museum, and houses displays of furniture, glassware and ceramics.

Walk along Market Street away from the Braak, passing on your left several more buildings of the Rhenish complex, including the old parsonage **(21)** dating back to 1815. Turn left into Herte Street. Along the right side of Herte Street, behind a line of oaks, you will see a row of cottages **(22)** believed to have been built in 1834 as homes for newly freed slaves.

Continue along Herte Street, then turn right into Dorp Street. Turn left into Old Strand Road to arrive back at the point where you parked your car ●

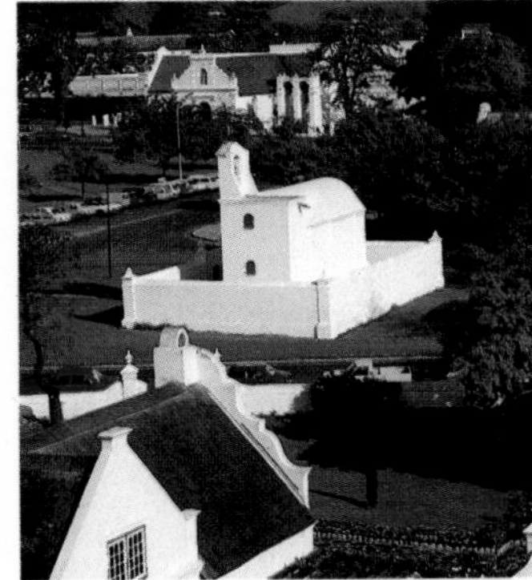

The V O C Kruithuis with the Rhenish Church in the background.

Sip fine wines under ornate gables and rugged peaks

The fertile soils of the Eerste and Berg river valleys were first cultivated 300 years ago when pioneering farmers planted vines and fruit orchards. Today many of these historic farms are open to the public, and we visit several on this drive, with their fine farmhouses and their wines. The entire route is tarred, except for short access roads.

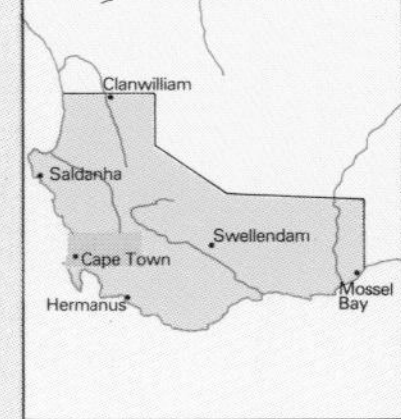

Cape Town
Muratie
Stellenbosch
Blaauwklippen
Helshoogte Pass
Boschendal
Taal Monument
170 – 190 km

FROM CAPE TOWN'S FORESHORE, drive towards Paarl on the N1, noting your kms as you pass on your left the large red-brick power station with its two tall chimneys.

After passing through extensive built-up areas, you enter a stretch of attractive undulating countryside, with the Slanghoek, Du Toit's and Drakenstein ranges in the distance.

34 km after passing the power station, take Exit 15, then turn right at the T-junction onto the R304 towards Stellenbosch. Note your kms as you cross over the N1. After 1,2 km turn left onto a tarred road towards 'Muldersvlei' and 'Klapmuts'. You are now travelling on the R101, the old Great North Road from Cape to Cairo. 3,3 km along it, turn right, following the sign to 'Muldersvlei/Elsenburg'. Soon you pass the small settlement of Muldersvlei on your right, and shortly after this you pass on your left the Elsenburg Agricultural College building. Continue until you reach a T-junction with the R44, then turn right onto the R44 towards Stellenbosch — noting your kms. After 2,3 km turn left onto a tarred side-road. Follow the tar until the road changes to gravel and enters the gates of the Muratie estate (see opposite).

Muratie to Spier

Retrace your route to the R44 and turn left towards Stellenbosch. As you enter Stellenbosch, continue straight ahead through the first set of traffic lights, and stay on this same road as it runs parallel to the railway line. When the road swings away from the railway line, turn right into Adam Tas Street, and continue travelling parallel to the railway line. Adam Tas Street becomes the R310. Note your kms as you pass the huge white-painted cellars of the Stellenbosch Farmers' Winery on your left.

After 2,6 km turn left, to stay on the R310 (towards Lynedoch/Faure). 2,2 km later you pass on your left the Van Ryn Brandy Cellars. These are open to the public, and offer a tour on weekdays. 200 m beyond the road to the Brandy Cellars, bear left to stay on the R310. 1,3 km later turn left into the Spier estate.

Spier is one of the largest and oldest wine

MURATIE — AGE AND ELEGANCE

Muratie (the name means 'ruins' in Dutch) ranks as the oldest privately owned estate in South Africa, having been established in 1685 when the virgin land was granted to Lorenz Kamfer. After changing hands many times, it was purchased early this century by the artist Georg Canitz — who was the first person in the region to plant Pinot Noir vines. Fine wines are made from these grapes.

The charming old buildings are surrounded by tall oaks, palms and cypresses, and Georg Canitz's studio and an old swimming pool lie to one side of the cellar. A plaque near the main homestead lists some of the estate's previous owners.

The wines here are still made by hand in the old-fashioned way, even the bottling and corking being done manually. Visitors may taste the estate's wines from bottles set out on a rough-hewn table in one corner of the cellar, and the same wines may be bought on the estate during normal business hours. Cellar tours can be arranged on Thursdays by appointment with the wine-maker.

Tall trees cast welcome shade on the lawns around Boschendal.

A GRAND ESTATE

The Boschendal estate was originally granted to one of the first Huguenot settlers assigned to the Franschhoek Valley. In 1715 it was acquired by Abraham de Villiers whose descendants ran the farm for nearly two centuries — until it was bought by Cecil Rhodes in 1896.

There are conducted tours through the manor house with its beautiful antique furniture on weekdays, and the farmyard buildings now house a restaurant that specialises in Cape Dutch and French Huguenot cooking (booking is essential). The wine cellars are a short distance from the main farm buildings, and wines from the estate may be purchased here during normal business hours.

Unusual goat 'castle' at Fairview.

Shuttered windows add to the charm of Muratie.

Stark lines of the Afrikaans Language Monument.

Wine Routes of the South-Western Cape

Over 40 wine estates in the Eerste River and Berg River valleys are open to the public. For detailed information about these estates contact the following:
Stellenbosch Wine Route: The Stellenbosch Wine Route (Co-op) Ltd, Doornbosch Centre, Old Strand Road, Stellenbosch 7600 Tel. (02231) 4310.
Paarl Wine Way: Paarl Publicity Association, cnr Main and Auret Streets, Paarl 7646 Tel. (02211) 24842
Franschhoek Wine Route: Kontrei Toere, Oude Stellen, 19 Huguenot Road, Franschhoek 7690 Tel. (02212) 3118

farms in South Africa. The estate's main cellars have been moved to the nearby farm Goedgeloof, but the wines from the farm can be tasted here for a small fee, and may be bought during normal business hours. The farm buildings house an art gallery and two restaurants.

Spier to Boschendal

When you leave Spier, turn left onto the R310 and note your kms. After 1,5 km turn left onto Annandale Road. Follow the Annandale Road for 5,4 km through farmlands until you reach a T-junction with the R44 (linking Stellenbosch to Somerset West). Turn left onto the R44 towards Stellenbosch — noting your kms.

After 3,5 km, turn right across the right half of the freeway, onto the gravel access road to the Blaauwklippen estate. Follow the signs to the cellars, passing on your right a small farmyard.

The Blaauwklippen farm buildings include a coach house containing a collection of old horse-drawn vehicles, and a museum. There is also a small farm shop selling farm produce, and the estate wines may be bought during normal business hours on weekdays. In the summer an open-air restaurant provides a pleasant 'coachman's lunch'.

Drive out of Blaauwklippen and turn right onto the R44 towards Stellenbosch, noting your kms at the turn. As you enter Stellenbosch, continue straight through three sets of traffic lights. You will find yourself on the road you travelled along earlier, but now going in the opposite direction. 4,5 km after turning onto the R44 from Blaauwklippen, turn right into Merriman Avenue. Continue straight ahead through the traffic lights at Bird Street, then turn left into Andringa Street. Take the first turning to the right, into Banhoek Road, and continue on Banhoek road (which becomes the R310) as it leads out of Stellenbosch and winds up the Helshoogte Pass towards the Drakenstein Valley and Franschhoek. As the road climbs, you have lovely views on your left to the slopes of Simonsberg — over a landscape of farms, forestry plantations and dams.

Over the summit of the pass, the road winds down into the Drakenstein Valley. You eventually pass through the small hamlet of Johannesdal, then the old mission settlement of Pniel — dating back to 1843. Note your kms as you pass through Pniel, and 1,2 km later, turn right into the Boschendal estate (see opposite).

Boschendal to the Taal Monument

Drive out of the Boschendal estate and turn right onto the R310. After 1,5 km you cross a double railway line. Immediately after this, turn left onto the R45 towards Simondium and Paarl — noting your kms. After 9,8 km, immediately after passing under a railway bridge, turn left onto the R101 towards 'Klapmuts/Cape Town' — then after 650 m turn right towards 'Suid Agter-Paarl', and cross over the N1. 2,2 km after crossing over the N1, turn right through the white gate-posts into the Fairview estate. In addition to making wines, Fairview specialises in the making of goats' milk cheeses. Visitors are welcome at the cheese factory and at the goat enclosure (milking time 16h00), and tours of the cellars may be arranged.

When you leave Fairview, turn left — back the way you came. Immediately after crossing over the N1, turn left, back onto the R101. 900 m along the R101, turn left, and note your kms as you recross the N1. The road takes a sharp bend to the right, and 900 m after crossing the N1, turn left at the 'Taalmonument' sign. The road now climbs the lower slopes of Paarl Mountain, bringing you eventually to a large parking area. Before visiting the monument (see opposite), walk to the edge of the parking area for a splendid view over the Berg River and Drakenstein valleys.

From the monument, retrace your route down the mountain, turning right at the T-junction at the bottom, left at the sharp bend, and crossing over the N1. Turn left when you reach the R101, and after just 400 m turn left for the N1 — heading back to Cape Town ●

Mountains of the south-western Cape form a romantic backdrop to the Wine Route.

MONUMENT TO A NEW LANGUAGE

Dominating the southern slopes of Paarl Mountain, the Afrikaans Language (Taal) Monument was designed by architect Jan van Wijk and opened to the public in 1975. The three columns on the west side of the structure symbolise the contribution of Western languages and cultures to Afrikaans, the three rounded shapes on a podium represent the influence of the African languages and cultures, and the wall flanking the steps represents the effect of the Malayan tradition. The main column in the centre represents the Afrikaans language and soars 57 metres over a fountain symbolising growth and new ideas. The smaller column to the right of the main column is a symbol of the Republic of South Africa — many cultures but one nation.

Floodlit gable at Spier.

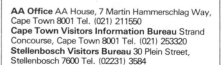

AA Office AA House, 7 Martin Hammerschlag Way, Cape Town 8001 Tel. (021) 211550
Cape Town Visitors Information Bureau Strand Concourse, Cape Town 8001 Tel. (021) 253320
Stellenbosch Visitors Bureau 30 Plein Street, Stellenbosch 7600 Tel. (02231) 3584

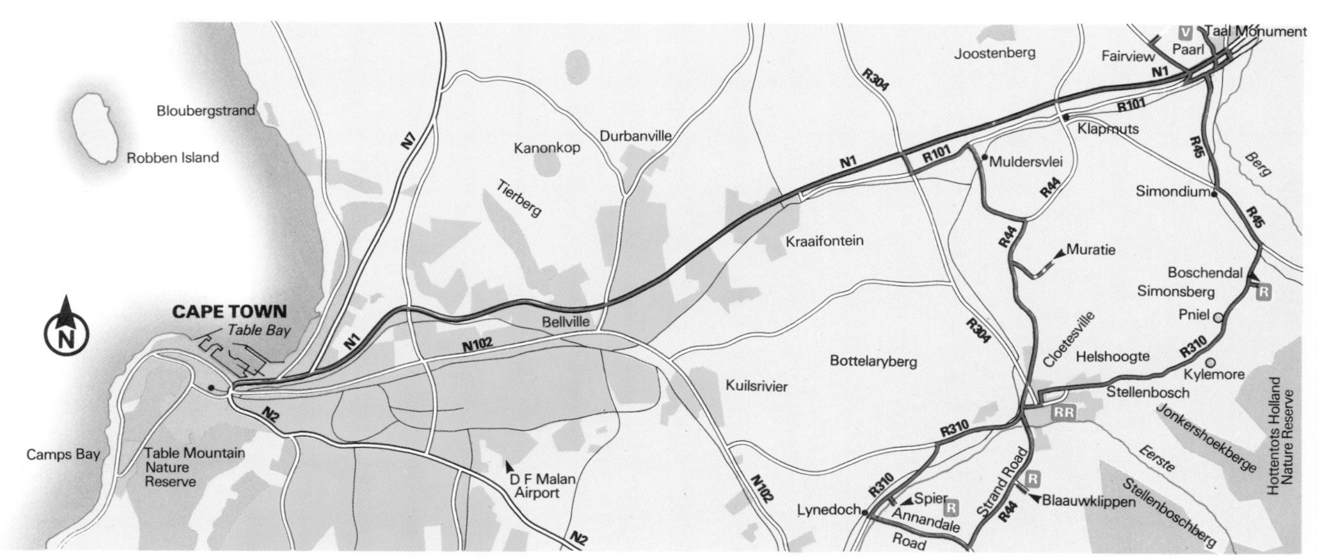

The Cape Peninsula — along the unspoilt shores of two mighty oceans

The Cape Peninsula is much like an island — a ridge of high mountains jutting into the sea, linked to the African mainland only by the sandy, low-lying Cape Flats. This drive explores the peninsula's scenic shores, where the waters of the Indian and Atlantic oceans meet, creating gentle bays, beautiful beaches and wild, wave-pounded headlands.

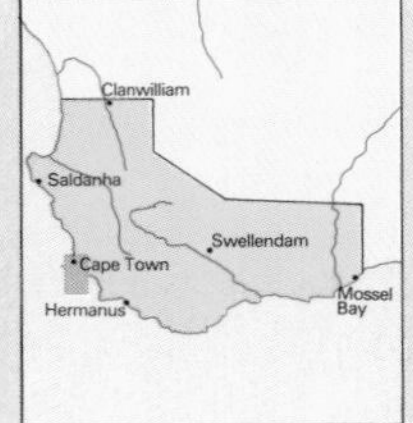

Cape Town
Fish Hoek
Simon's Town
Cape Point
Chapman's Peak
Clifton
150-160 km

LEAVE CAPE TOWN'S city centre on the N2. As the road dips, behind Groote Schuur Hospital, move to a right hand lane for Muizenberg (M3). Soon you pass Mostert's Mill on your left — note your kms as you pass.

You next pass the university on the slopes of Devil's Peak to your right. 1,5 km after Mostert's Mill, exit left, then turn right, under the highway, and drive up the mountainside to Rhodes Memorial (see opposite).

Rhodes Memorial to Kalk Bay

Return to the M3 (turn right immediately after passing under the bridge) and continue towards Muizenberg. When the M3 ends 12,5 km later, exit left and turn left at the top of the off-ramp. At the traffic lights (T-junction) turn right onto the old main road. 600 m later, turn right onto Boyes Drive and note your kms. Boyes Drive sweeps across the side of the Steenberg. Park after 2,1 km for the view (see opposite).

Drive on for 2,2 km, then park in a small parking area on the right. Cross the road for a view over False Bay to Hangklip (left) and Cape Point (right). A small iron gate and stone steps lead down to Sir Abe Bailey's grave.

Drive on until Boyes Drive dips to the left into Kalk Bay. At the T-junction with the coast road, turn right.

Kalk Bay to The Boulders

Drive past Kalk Bay harbour, around the headland, and into Fish Hoek. At the traffic island at the far end of Fish Hoek's main road, turn left, then park. Walk down any of several short paths to Jager's Walk, an attractive path along the rocks from Fish Hoek beach to Sunny Cove (allow 40-60 minutes).

Drive on along the coast road, passing Glencairn. Just before entering Simon's Town, turn right onto Red Hill Road (M65), which zigzags to the crest of the mountains. Park at the top for a magnificent view over Simon's Town harbour and across False Bay.

Drive back to the coast road, and through Simon's Town. As you leave Simon's Town, turn left into Bellevue Road. At the bottom of Bellevue Road turn left into a parking area. From here a path leads back towards the town, skirting the pretty Boulders Beach.

Cape of Good Hope Nature Reserve

Return to the coast road and drive on past the picnic area at Miller's Point. The road climbs the mountainside then turns inland. Take the first turn left and enter the Cape of Good Hope Nature Reserve (small entrance fee).

7,4 km along the main road through the reserve, turn left for Buffels Bay — an attractive lunchtime picnic area with braai places, water, toilets and a tidal swimming pool. The reserve also contains a restaurant (see map) and many other picnic sites.

Return to the main road, turn left, and drive to the parking area at Cape Point. There is a refreshment kiosk here, and a track to Cape Point Peak. You may walk up, or take the bus, 'the Flying Dutchman'. (Allow 60-80 minutes.)

Cape Point to Hout Bay

Returning from Cape Point, turn left after 2,5 km. Follow this side-road along the coast to a small parking area behind Cape Maclear and the Cape of Good Hope. A path leads up the back of Cape Maclear to the cliffs overlooking Diaz Beach. (Allow 40 minutes.)

On leaving the reserve, turn left. Turn left again 8 km later where the road forks. Drive through Scarborough (note 'camel rock' on your left) and past the village of Kommetjie. At the intersection with the M6, turn left, then left again after 900 m, following signs to Chapman's Peak.

The road leads through the Noordhoek valley, then hugs the cliffs as it rounds Chapman's Peak. Park in the small parking area at the highest point in this stretch of road, where it takes a sharp bend to the right and Hout Bay comes into view. A short path leads to a magnificent viewsite.

Drive on into Hout Bay village and turn left into Princess Street. At the T-junction, turn right into Victoria Avenue. (A left turn leads to the harbour, see pages 286-7.)

Hout Bay to Cape Town

Victoria Avenue climbs the side of Little Lion's Head to Hout Bay Nek. 800 m after driving over the Nek, park in the parking area on your left for a view over Llandudno.

Drive on along the coast road beneath the Twelve Apostles, through Bakoven and Camps Bay, then park again where the road swings to the right into Clifton. Walk down any of the several flights of steps leading to the beach. The crowds have left by this hour, leaving you one of the world's most beautiful beaches to stroll along in the evening light, before driving on through Sea Point into the city ●

AA Office AA House, 7 Martin Hammerschlag Way, Cape Town 8001 Tel. (021) 211550
Cape Town Visitors Information Bureau Strand Concourse, Cape Town 8001 Tel. (021) 253320
S A Tourism Board Level 3, Golden Acre, Adderley Street, Cape Town 8001 Tel. (021) 216274

The setting sun bathes Clifton beach in a soft pink light.

Lion's Head from below the Twelve Apostles.

CHAPMAN'S PEAK AND HOUT BAY

The road around Chapman's Peak is cut into the cliffs overlooking the sea, creating one of the most spectacular sea-cliff drives in the world. All the Cape mountains are composed of strata of colourful sandstone laid on top of a granite base, and Chapman's Peak drive, for much of its length, follows the natural join between these two rock formations.

From the recommended viewsite you can look out over the whole of Hout Bay, from the impressive Sentinel on your left, jutting forward from the Karbonkelberg peninsula, to the steep slopes of the Constantiaberg on your right. Further along the route, immediately before entering Hout Bay village, you can see, perched on one of the boulders overlooking the beach, a 295 kg bronze leopard — the work of the sculptor Ivan Mitford-Barberton.

Fishing boats at their moorings in Hout Bay Harbour.

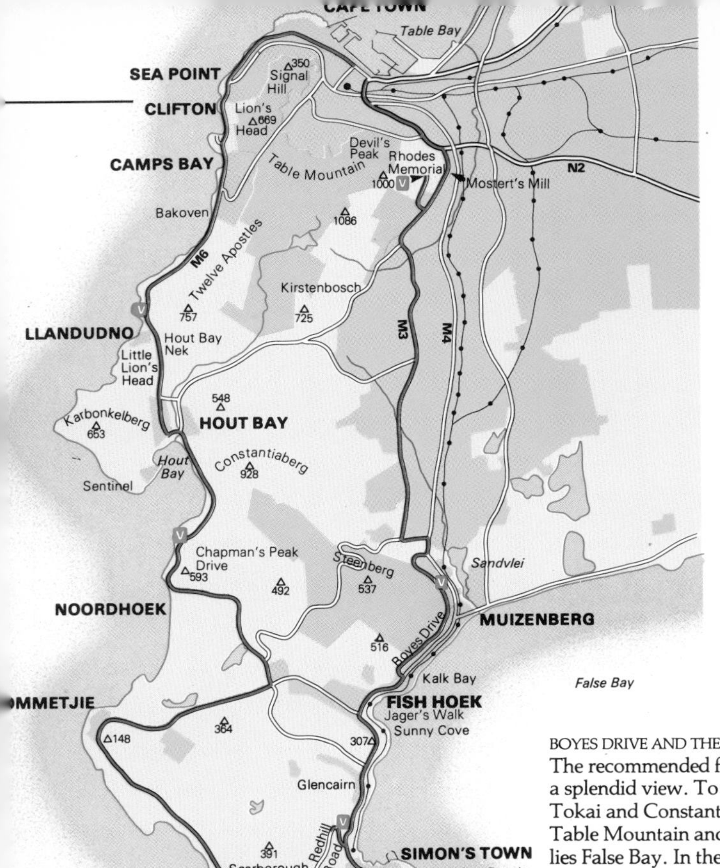

The impressive memorial to C J Rhodes, on the slopes of Devil's Peak.

REMEMBERING AN EMPIRE

Rhodes Memorial is set amid clusters of umbrella pines on the eastern slopes of Devil's Peak, and commemorates one of the most colourful personalities in South Africa's history — Cecil John Rhodes (1853-1902). Rhodes is said to have often enjoyed the view from here.

The focus of the neo-classical granite structure, designed by Sir Herbert Baker and Francis Masey, is the massive bronze statue *'Energy'* conceived by G F Watts. From the stone-paved apron in front of the statue you can look out as Rhodes did to the enticing mountains of the interior — the Groot Winterhoek range far away to your left, the Slanghoek and Drakenstein ranges and Simonsberg in the centre, then the Helderberg, and the Hottentots Holland range running away to the right. It is also possible to look out from here over two oceans at the same time. On your left is Table Bay (Atlantic) and far away to your right is False Bay (Indian).

BOYES DRIVE AND THE BATTLE OF MUIZENBERG

The recommended first stop on Boyes Drive offers a splendid view. To your left you look over the Tokai and Constantia valleys to the backs of Table Mountain and Devil's Peak. To your right lies False Bay. In the distance, beyond the Cape Flats, you can see the Drakenstein and Hottentots Holland mountain ranges.

The stretch of water immediately below you is Sandvlei, now a popular weekend venue for sail-board enthusiasts and dinghy sailors, but in 1795 the scene of the Battle of Muizenberg. Dutch forces under a Captain C Kemper had established themselves on the northern side of the vlei, down to your left, and were firing cannon across at the British, who were advancing around the foot of the mountain to your right. Superior numbers led eventually to a British victory.

Fishing and pleasure craft shelter in Kalk Bay Harbour, with Simon's Town in the distance.

Chacma baboon Papio ursinus.

CAPE OF GOOD HOPE NATURE RESERVE

Established in 1939, the reserve is home to eland, Hartmann's mountain zebra, bontebok, springbok, baboon and porcupine. Many bird species can also be seen, including ostrich, fish eagle and several species of albatross.

The low-lying 'fynbos' vegetation is rich in proteas, ericas and many other wildflowers — the total number of indigenous plant species in the reserve exceeds that of the entire British Isles.

WHERE TWO OCEANS MEET

Geographers are apt to treat Cape Agulhas, the most southerly point on the African continent, as marking the division between the Indian and Atlantic oceans. However, there is some common sense support for the popular notion that the two oceans meet off the rocky cliffs of Cape Point.

For much of the year the strong Mocambique Current sends its warm Indian Ocean waters around the southern tip of the continent and into False Bay. Eventually this great mass of warm water meets the cold South Atlantic at Cape Point.

The results are dramatic. The fish populations are quite different on the two sides of the peninsula, and the two distinct masses of water often have a totally different colour. What is of greatest importance to most holiday-makers is that bathers along the eastern shores have warm water in which to swim, while sea temperatures along the western side are many degrees colder.

The wild and rocky promontory of Cape Point.

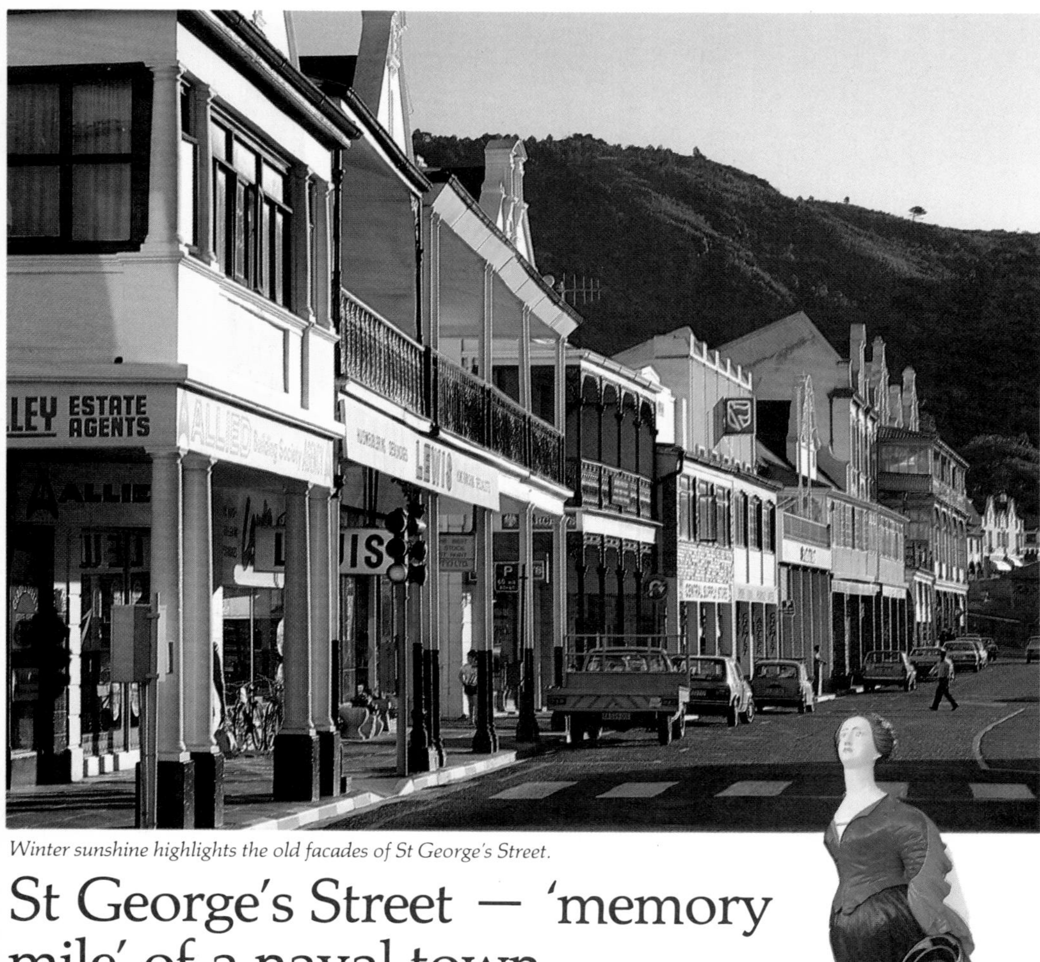

Winter sunshine highlights the old facades of St George's Street.

St George's Street — 'memory mile' of a naval town

THE BUILDINGS that rise in steep terraces above Simon's Bay look down on a harbour that sheltered square-rigged warships with muzzle-loader guns, and today protects the deadly submarines of the South African Navy.

Between the houses and the sea runs Simon's Town's St George's Street — a thoroughfare that has echoed to the tramp of marching feet for many generations. Countless sailors from throughout the world have a memory-filled corner of their hearts reserved for what is known today as 'the historic mile' — the central section of St George's Street.

To the memory of Tom Cockroach
Park at the railway station, and walk towards the town centre on the sea side of the road to get the best view of the town's historic features. This side of the road also offers more shade, especially in the morning. There are restaurants and cafeterias along the route. Allow at least two hours for the complete walk.

The beginning of your walk is slightly uphill, and you pass on your right a fine double-storey building with a central pediment. This is known as *Palace Barracks* **(1)** and is now naval property. Built early in the last century by John Osmond, it was originally named 'Mount Curtis', but soon became known as 'The Palace' in tribute to Osmond, known in his day as 'the king of Simon's Town'.

Some 400 m further, on the left, in the gardens of *Admiralty House* **(2)**, is the figurehead of HMS Flora, a 36-gun frigate which served as the Simon's Town guardship for 20 years until 1891. Although Naval Headquarters moved to Pretoria in 1977, Admiralty House, which dates back to about 1740, is the official residence of the Naval Officer-in-Command, Simon's Town, and is used by the Chief of the Navy when he visits the Cape. The 40-roomed building was acquired by the Royal Navy in 1814, and housed successive British admirals until 1957, when it was handed over to the South African Navy together with the naval base.

After passing the gates of Admiralty House you will see on the right an old building known as *Studland* **(3)**, built in about 1800 as a wine house and later serving as a home for the manager of the brewery that stands alongside it (dated 1830).

The figurehead of HMS Flora.

Turn left into Court Road, at the corner of which stands the Church of *St Francis of Assisi* (Anglican) **(4)**. Simon's Town is the oldest Anglican parish in South Africa, dating from the first British landings in 1795. The present church, consecrated in 1837, houses some very fine memorials, including one to the men of *HMS Boadicea*, listing names such as 'Tom Cockroach', 'Jack Ropeyarn', 'Bottle of Beer' and 'Blackwhale'. These were West African 'kroomen' who served with the Royal Navy and whose proper names were unpronounceable to the British sailors.

A grog barrel and a slave-ship gun
100 m down Court Road is *The Residency* **(5)**, which now houses the Simon's Town Museum. Built in 1772 to house the Governor on his visits to Simon's Town, it later served as a home, a school, and a post office, before being bought by the Cape Government in 1814. Since then it has been a customs house, port office, prison — with slave quarters below serving as cells — and a magistrate's court. Museum exhibits include a 'grog' barrel donated by the Royal Navy, a model of Lord Nelson's *HMS Victory* (Nelson visited Simon's Town as a young lieutenant) and a rare brass-barrelled flintlock swivel gun taken from a slave ship early last century. A corner of the museum is devoted to Able Seaman Just Nuisance, the Royal Navy's canine mascot during World War II.

Return to St George's Street and turn left, looking out for a number of plaques set in the white-painted wall on your left that record the history of various buildings in the dockyard. One of these historic buildings is the *Dockyard Church* **(6)**, or sail loft, used since 1801 and easily recognised because of its clock tower. It is now known as St George's Church.

You now pass on your right a number of the short, steep streets that

Admiralty House, a reminder of two and a half centuries of imperial history.

The stately lines of Palace Barracks.

are so typical of central Simon's Town. After a short distance you come to a small restaurant on your right, in a building **(7)** that was designed by Sir Herbert Baker for Cecil John Rhodes. Immediately after this is the *British Hotel* **(8)**, a three-storey building with elaborate cast ironwork — originally built in 1819 and renovated in 1898.

On the left side of St George's Street you now come to the West Dockyard Gate, where a plaque records the building of the first slipway in 1859 over a granite outcrop known as Sober Island. (The public may enter the harbour area at Wharf Road, a few metres further along on the left, but no dogs are allowed.)

Outside the Post Office, on the corner of Wharf Road, are a blubber pot from whaling days and two large cannons. Opposite the second cannon is Union Lane, from where you can see a small white-washed building, originally the *Union Tavern* **(9)** and dating back to 1806.

Near to the Post Office, on the left, is a small stone cairn commemorating the many people uprooted from their homes in Simon's Town in 1967 by the Group Areas Act. Opposite this is Rectory Lane, with an ancient flight of steps leading to the site of the town's first Anglican church.

From Jubilee Square to 'Black Town'

Jubilee Square **(10)**, on the left, commemorates King George V's Silver Jubilee in 1935. By coincidence, the drinking fountain in the square commemorates an earlier jubilee — that of Queen Victoria in 1897. It was moved here recently from its original position near The Residency. A statue of Able Seaman Just Nuisance was unveiled nearby in 1985.

About 50 m beyond Jubilee Square you will see Alfred Lane to your right. A short way along the lane you can glimpse a mosque, originally a private house, in which religious services were first held in 1888.

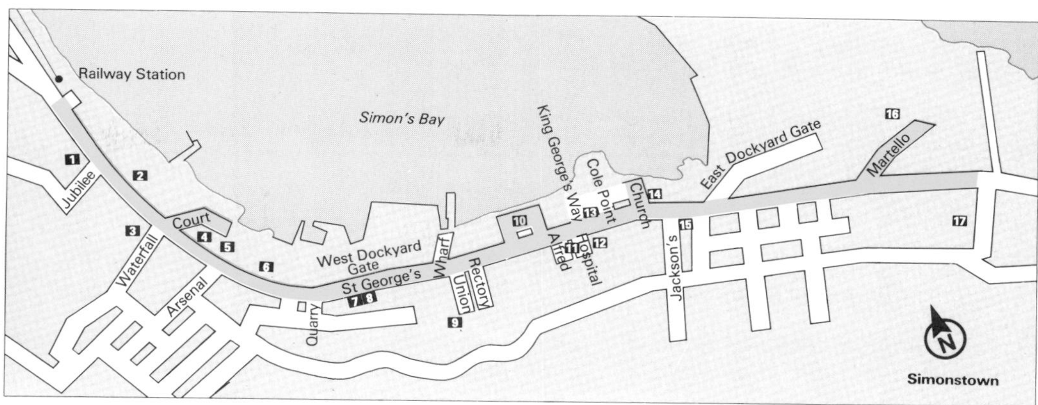

1837 Church of St Francis of Assisi.

(Opposite Alfred Lane, in St George's Street, there is a ladies' toilet.)

On your right, after passing Alfred Lane, you will see *Bayview House* **(11)**, which once served as a tavern and lodging house for sailors. A former resident of the house papered some of the walls with postage stamps, including rare Cape of Good Hope triangulars. A little further on, behind the stone wall on the right, is the *Old Hospital Terrace* **(12)**, built in 1812-1813. Used as a hospital until 1915, it is now a naval residence.

On the left side of the road, after crossing King George's Way, you come to the imposing *Phoenix Hall* **(13)**. Dated 1860, its street gable features a phoenix rising from the flames, and the Masonic emblem. You are now entering 'Black Town', as this part of the town was known over a century ago. It was here that blacks, freed from slavers by the Royal Navy, awaited resettlement.

Die Stem van Suid-Afrika

Cross Church Street to the Dutch Reformed Church (1856) and the adjacent parsonage, built in 1899 and known as the *Stempastorie* **(14)** (now the Museum for National Symbols), where the Rev M L de Villiers composed the music for Langenhoven's *'Die Stem van Suid-Afrika'*. De Villiers was born in Paarl in 1885 and

'Pub corner' in Simon's Town Museum.

studied at the Theological College, Stellenbosch, moving to Simon's Town in 1918, where he stayed until his retirement in 1930. Langenhoven rejected De Villiers' first melody in 1919, but accepted a second melody in 1922; and when the new South African flag was raised for the first time on 21 May 1928, De Villiers conducted a performance of his own composition.

In the Stempastorie the sitting room has been arranged as in De Villiers' day, including the piano on which *Die Stem* was first played. Upstairs, the study where he composed the music has also been preserved. Also of interest are the flag room, with examples of all the flags that have flown over South Africa,

The formidable Martello Tower.

and the heraldry room, where the country's various coats of arms are displayed. The flag room has a collection of some 200 designs, some of them bizarre in the extreme, submitted during the competition to find a new flag.

Walking on a short distance from the Dutch Reformed Church, you will see the Catholic Church of *Simon and Jude* **(15)** on your right, a handsome stone building with adjoining presbytery dating from 1855. The bell, dated 1871, was cast in the dockyard, complete with silver coins thrown into the molten metal to sweeten the bell's tone. The large St Joseph's Convent, adjoining the church, is now a boarding house.

Victory today at Trafalgar

Pass the East Dockyard Gate on your left, and after walking a short distance further, turn left into Martello Road to reach the historic *Martello Tower* **(16)** — which houses weapons, a newspaper of 1805 reporting the British victory at Trafalgar, and a large collection of South African naval uniforms and bells from South African ships. Exhibits in the grounds include a buoyant mine, a torpedo, and an old ship-board fire-fighting unit. The tower itself was built during the Napoleonic Wars to protect the town and harbour from a feared French landing.

Return to St George's Street and cross to the *old cemeteries* **(17)**. Among the graves is a monument to the men of *HMS Nerbudda*, which put out from Port Elizabeth in 1855 and was never seen again. An enormous stone near the St George's Street boundary commemorates Adriaan de Nys, *'onder Coopman en Hooft van de Baay Fals'*, the Dutch East India Company's 'postholder' at Simon's Bay who died in 1761.

To return to your starting point, walk back along St George's Street, stopping for a longer look at anything that caught your interest ●

Through the historic heart of the Cape Peninsula

The Cape Peninsula has a rich history. Here is a short drive that allows time to savour it. Our route leads through avenues of ancient oaks, past vineyards nearly three centuries old, to several places that share a peaceful, old-world charm — from the cool of Groot Constantia's cellars to the romance of small fishing boats in Hout Bay Harbour.

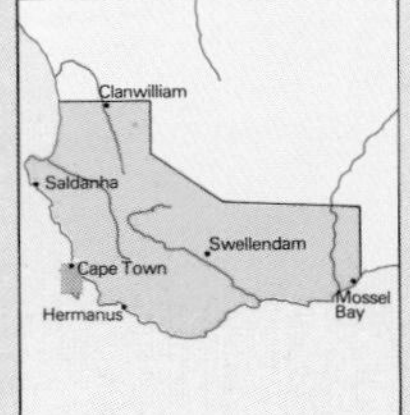

Cape Town
Mostert's Mill
Kirstenbosch
Groot Constantia
Silvermine
Hout Bay
70—80 km

THE LOW BRIDGE OF land between Table Mountain and Lion's Head is known as Kloof Nek. Drive to here from the city centre (see map on page 289) by driving along Adderley Street towards the mountain, turning right at the end of Adderley Street into Wale Street, then taking the 6th left turn, into Buitengracht, which becomes Kloof Nek Road.

Driving clockwise around the Kloof Nek traffic islands, take the 4th exit (uphill). Follow this road along the 'lion's back' to Signal Hill, from where there are fine views in all directions.

Return to the city centre and turn right at the harbour end of Adderley Street, taking the N2 towards the airport. As the road dips, behind Groote Schuur Hospital, move into the second-from-right lane. The two right lanes veer right and become the M3 towards Muizenberg. Immediately after this, take the first exit left, to reach Mostert's Mill (see opposite).

On leaving Mostert's Mill, drive downhill along Rhodes Avenue and turn right at the traffic lights into Main Road. After 600 m turn right, uphill, into Woolsack Drive, then follow the signs back onto the M3 towards Muizenberg. As soon as you rejoin the M3 you will see the University of Cape Town on the mountainside to your right, and after 1,2 km you pass the Groote Schuur Estate on your left.

The road runs along the edge of Newlands Forest, then dips to the left. Select the right lane and turn right at the first traffic lights into another Rhodes Avenue. 1,7 km later, turn right into Kirstenbosch (small entrance fee).

Kirstenbosch to Silvermine Reserve

Leaving Kirstenbosch, turn right into Rhodes Avenue, then right 700 m later at the T-junction. The road winds up the mountainside to Constantia Nek. At the traffic circle, turn left into Constantia Main Road (first exit) and note your kms. After 3,3 km turn right, and follow this side road into the Groot Constantia estate. (Two restaurants here offer lunch.)

Leave Groot Constantia and turn right into Constantia Main Road — noting your kms. After 900 m turn right into Ladies Mile Road Extension. 1 km later, turn right at the traffic lights into Spaanschemat River Road, noting your kms. Follow this road for 6,9 km (it keeps changing name) then turn right onto the Ou Kaapse Weg (old Cape road), which leads up the Steenberg mountainside.

There is a straight stretch of road at the top of the pass. If you have already lunched, turn right at the end of this stretch into a large parking area. There is a splendid view from here over the Tokai and Constantia valleys, and the backs of Table Mountain and Devil's Peak. If you plan a picnic, ignore this turn and take the first left turn, 600 m further, into the eastern section of the Silvermine Nature Reserve (small entrance fee). In the reserve, follow the gravel road leading to the left of the small pine forest. It leads past several picnic spots with splendid views. (Braai places, water and toilets.)

Silvermine to Hout Bay

Retrace your route to Constantia Nek, then drive straight on past the traffic island, noting your kms. The road winds down into Hout Bay valley through cool green tunnels of oaks. After 5,6 km you pass the old Kronendal homestead on your left. 1,1 km after this, turn right into Princess Street. (To continue straight will bring you after 5,7 km to a magnificent viewsite at the highest point on Chapman's Peak Drive — see pages 282-3.) Turn left at the T-junction into Hout Bay Harbour Road. Park after 300 m, to walk into the harbour area — usually full of picturesque fishing boats and yachts.

When you leave the harbour, drive back along Hout Bay Harbour Road, pass the T-junction, and follow the road you are on, now called Victoria Avenue, as it climbs up the side of Little Lion's Head and over Hout Bay Nek. 800 m after driving over the Nek there is an attractive view from a parking area on your left.

Drive along the coast road beneath the Twelve Apostles. As you enter Bakoven (the first built-up area you reach) turn right into Houghton Road. When this ends in a T-junction, turn right into Camps Bay Drive, which leads you back to Kloof Nek. At the Kloof Nek traffic islands turn right (uphill) onto Table Mountain Road. Note your kms as you pass the cableway station. After 2,1 km, park on the left — for a fine view of the face of Table Mountain, Kloof Nek and Lion's Head, and the city spread out below.

Drive back to Kloof Nek, and now take the second exit left (Kloof Road). After 2,1 km turn right at the T-junction and follow the road as it winds behind Clifton. 1,2 km later, just before turning the headland and leaving Clifton, park in the narrow area on your right. Cross the road for a splendid evening vista — before driving on through Sea Point into the city ●

AA Office AA House, 7 Martin Hammerschlag Way, Cape Town 8001 Tel. (021) 211550
Cape Town Visitors Information Bureau Strand Concourse, Cape Town 8001
Tel. (021) 253320
S A Tourism Board Level 3, Golden Acre, Adderley Street, Cape Town 8001
Tel. (021) 216274

Table Mountain, Twelve Apostles and Lion's Head.

SIGNAL HILL

This 350 m hill abutting on Lion's Head was once known as Vlaeberg (Flag Mountain) and it has been used as a signal station from the earliest days of the Cape settlement.

On its eastern slopes stands the Lion's Battery. Gun salutes are fired from here on ceremonial occasions, and the gun is also fired automatically at noon every day except Sunday.

Along the road to Signal Hill you pass on your left the domed *karamat* (tomb) of Mohamed Gasan Gaibie Shah — one of several Muslim shrines that encircle Cape Town.

Fishing boats in Hout Bay Harbour.

The high, whitewashed walls of Groot Constantia.

RELIC OF AN OLD CAPE INDUSTRY

Built in 1796 for the farm Welgelegen, Mostert's Mill, on the lower slopes of Devil's Peak, was one of the first windmills in the country. The owner of the farm, Gysbert van Reenen, subsequently sold both the farm and the mill to his son-in-law, Sybrandt Mostert — hence the name. Wheat-milling was one of the first industries to be established in South Africa, and Mostert's ancestors had been the first millers at the Cape.

Cecil John Rhodes bought the farm in 1891, but the mill was no longer in working order. It was fully restored in 1936, and the mill and its adjoining threshing floor were proclaimed a historical monument four years later.

The farm had meanwhile become part of Rhodes's bequest to the nation, and part of it is now the site of University of Cape Town residences and administrative buildings.

Mostert's Mill, survivor of nearly two centuries.

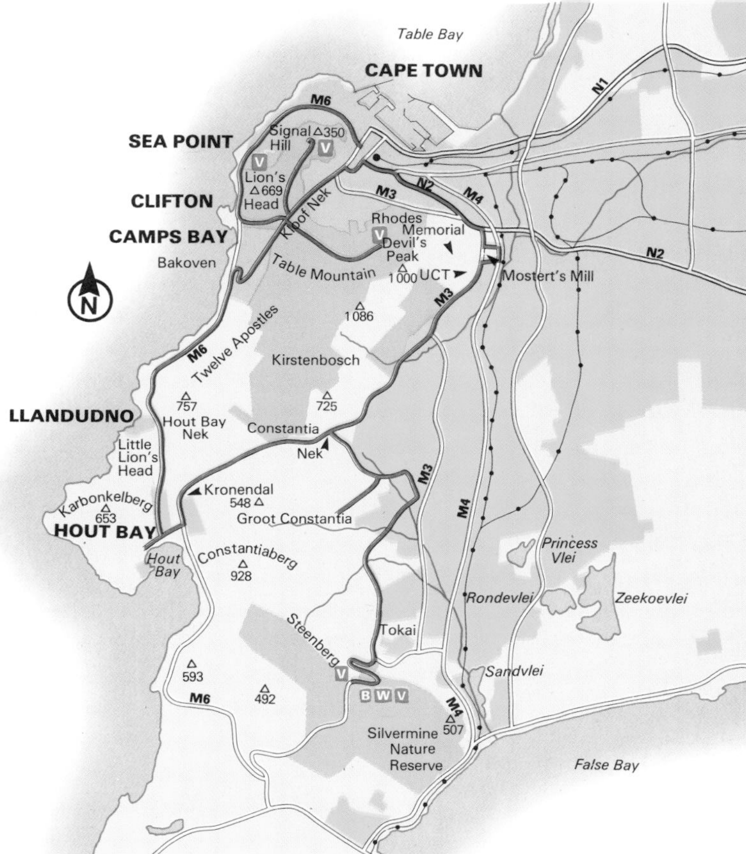

KIRSTENBOSCH BOTANIC GARDEN

The National Botanic Garden at Kirstenbosch covers 560 ha of land, stretching up the slopes of Table Mountain to its highest point — Maclear's Beacon. There are several walks that lead through the garden, where staff cultivate 9 000 of the 21 000 southern African flowering plants in a setting of mountain streams, pools and rolling lawns.

The land was a bequest from Cecil John Rhodes, who had bought it in 1895. In 1911 the site was chosen for a national botanic garden, and this was proclaimed two years later.

Professor Harold Pearson, the first director of Kirstenbosch, is buried in the garden. His epitaph reads: 'All ye who seek his monument, look around.'

Remains of Jan van Riebeeck's wild almond hedge around the first Dutch settlement can still be seen in the garden, and another relic from the past is a sunken bath at one of the springs of the Liesbeek River. This quaint structure is popularly known as Lady Anne Barnard's bath, but it was actually built by a Colonel Christopher Bird early in the 19th century.

The grounds of the garden also contain a lecture and exhibition hall, the Compton Herbarium (housing more then 250 000 specimens), the offices of the Botanical Society of South Africa, and a popular restaurant.

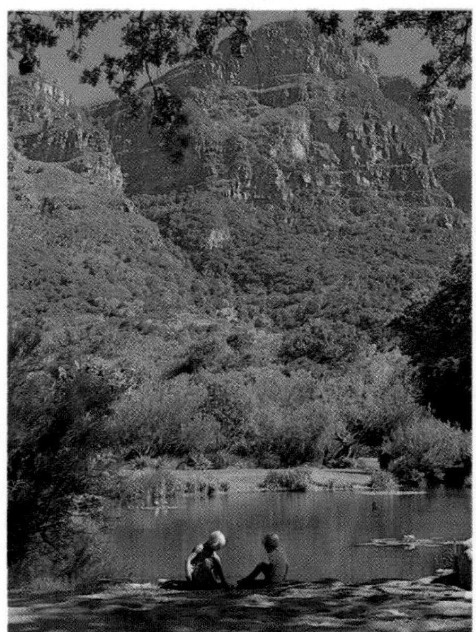

A quiet pool in the Kirstenbosch botanic garden.

GROOT CONSTANTIA ESTATE

In 1685 Governor Simon van der Stel could choose almost any part of the Cape for his private farm. He chose the site of Groot Constantia — fertile, well-watered, with beautiful views over False Bay and what is now Tokai, and towards the mountains of Stellenbosch and Paarl.

Van der Stel's original homestead was no doubt impressive for its time, but it was not the classic Cape Dutch manor house that we see today. The present manor house and the old wine cellar date from the 18th century and were the work of architect Louis Thibault and sculptor Anton Anreith — employed by Hendrik Cloete, who had bought the farm in 1778.

By the late 18th century the wines of Constantia had achieved world fame. The farm was bought by the Cape government in 1885, and it is now run as a model wine estate. Tours are conducted through the new cellars.

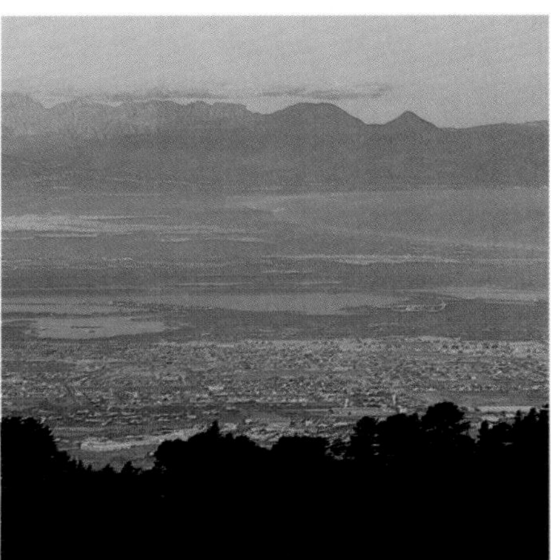

A view east over the Cape Flats from Silvermine.

ON THE SPINE OF THE PENINSULA

The 2 151 ha Silvermine Nature Reserve on the mountain spine of the peninsula extends from the boundaries of Muizenberg, St James and Kalk Bay in the east to Noordhoek Peak in the west. It provides numerous walks through wild mountain scenery and countless magnificent views — in the east over the Cape Flats and False Bay, in the west over Chapman's Bay, Hout Bay and the Sentinel. The reserve owes its name to an unsuccessful attempt to mine silver here in 1687.

The vegetation in the reserve consists of fynbos, including colourful species of protea, erica and leucadendron; pine plantations; and areas of indigenous forest with yellowwood, rooiels, sagewood and boekenhout trees.

Birdlife includes the long-tailed Cape sugarbird, the Cape robin, and the orange-breasted and malachite sunbirds. The mammals in the reserve include rhebok, porcupines and civet cats.

The Great Synagogue towers above Sydney Harpley's controversial statue of J C Smuts in the Company's Garden.

Morning flea market on the Grand Parade – Wednesdays and Saturdays.

The imposing Houses of Parliament.

Grace and stately beauty of the 'Mother City'

CAPE TOWN, THE oldest city in South Africa, has retained many features of its historic past amid all the bustle of modern development. Efficient skyscrapers rub shoulders with elegant, centuries-old buildings.

In a leisurely stroll through the heart of the city, you can follow in the steps of the early settlers. Our walk starts at the *Castle of Good Hope* **(1)**, which lies to the east of the Grand Parade. The Castle was built between 1666 and 1679 to replace Jan van Riebeeck's original mud-walled fortress. The Castle's main entrance at first faced the sea, which in those days almost lapped at its walls. The present main gateway with its elaborate stonework was built by Governor Simon van der Stel.

Admission to the Castle is free and by guided tour only. Tours begin on the hour from 10am to 3pm, except at 1pm, when the Castle closes for an hour. The buildings contain a military and maritime museum, and part of the William Fehr Collection of antiques and pictorial Africana.

As you leave the Castle, turn right and cross the road at the traffic lights to reach the *Grand Parade* **(2)**. Walk across the Parade to the north-western end (towards Plein Street). The impressive brown stone building on your left on Darling Street is the old *City Hall* **(3)**. It is the venue for the Cape Town Symphony Orchestra's performances, and now houses a lending library.

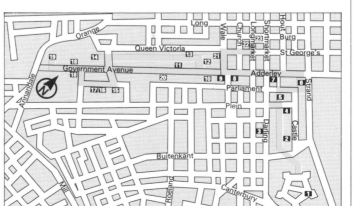

At the north-western end of the Parade there are green-roofed fruit and refreshment *kiosks* **(4)** – these stand on the site of Van Riebeeck's original fort.

Cross Plein Street at the intersection with Darling Street. On your right is the granite *General Post Office* **(5)**. Walk through the first entrance on the Plein Street side, which takes you through the lofty central hall to Parliament Street.

Turn right, pass the flower sellers in Trafalgar Place, and enter the Golden Acre shopping centre. On the lowest level is *Wagenaer's Dam* **(6)**, built by Zacharias Wagenaer, Van Riebeeck's immediate successor, on what was then the beach of Table Bay. Walk up the steps next to the dam – on the landing is a display showing Table Bay as it was in the time of Van Riebeeck.

Walk out of the Golden Acre into Adderley Street and turn left. Pass the flower sellers again, and then the imposing *Standard Bank building* **(7)**, built in 1882.

Stately old church

Cross Darling Street and continue up Adderley Street. On the left, on the corner of Bureau Street, is the stately *Groote Kerk* **(8)**, with its impressive vaulted ceiling and 18th century pulpit by Anton Anreith. Consecrated in 1704, the church was altered a number of times until 1840, but the tower and much of the east wall are part of the original structure.

The next building on your left in Adderley Street is the *Cultural History Museum* **(9)**. The building started out as a slave lodge in 1680, and later housed the Supreme Court. Its overall appearance dates from about 1810, when Louis Thibault and Anton Anreith remodelled it. Today the building houses the cultural and Africana sections of the South African Museum.

Beyond the museum is the Ivan Mitford-Barberton statue of General J C Smuts. Behind the statue you can see the *Houses of Parliament* **(10)**, which were opened in 1885.

Enter the *Company's Garden* **(11)** on Government Avenue to the right of Parliament. The establishment of a garden was the main reason for the existence of the European settlement at the Cape, although over the years the emphasis has changed — from the vegetable garden for scurvy-stricken sailors to a botanical haven for indigenous and exotic plants.

Tuynhuys — restored to its appearance of about 1780.

Tranquil avenue of oaks in the Company's Garden.

Away from the bustle

After about 150 m walk half-right through the entrance gate to the gardens. The white building on the right here is the *South African Library* **(12)**, a national reference library with some 400 000 books. It is also a 'copyright' library, and a copy of every work published in South Africa must be lodged here. (The library is open to the public, and displays are held in the exhibition room.)

The *restaurant* **(13)**, further along the path into the Garden, offers an idyllic setting for lunch or tea. Nearby are a statue of Cecil John Rhodes, aviaries, a reconstructed slave bell, a fountain set in a fish pond and public toilets.

From the restaurant, walk towards the mountain. Go up the steps beyond the rose garden to the Delville Wood Memorial Garden above. On your right is a statue of General Sir Henry Lukin, who commanded the South Africans at the Delville Wood battle in 1916. On your left a howitzer of that era serves as a memorial to the men of the South African artillery regiments.

Walk up the steps beyond the memorial garden to the *South African Museum* **(14)**. The museum has displays of reconstructed dinosaurs, lifelike casts of San people, and extensive natural history collections on mammals, reptiles, birds, fish, insects and whales. It operates a planetarium, and is an important centre of research. (Open 10am — 5pm daily except Good Friday and Christmas Day; small entry fee.)

Leave the museum through the front gates, turn right, and cross Government Avenue. You will see another statue here of General J C Smuts — this one by Sydney Harpley. Its unveiling caused a public controversy which eventually led to the commissioning of the one by Mitford-Barberton that you passed at the foot of the Garden.

At the far end of the lily ponds, walk up the steps to the *South African National Art Gallery* **(15)**. The gallery houses the works of many South African artists, and works by Romney and Gainsborough, and artists of the Dutch school and later periods. (Open daily except Monday mornings, Good Friday and Christmas Day; small entry fee, gift shop.)

Leaving the gallery turn left, walk up Paddock Avenue, and pass the white arch and wall on your left. The next building on the left is the *Jewish Museum* **(16)**, housed in South Africa's oldest synagogue, which was opened in 1861. The imposing *Great Synagogue* **(17)** next door, built in 1905, dwarfs its tiny predecessor.

Beyond the synagogues is an attractive terrace of double-storeyed houses dating from the 1890s, which are now part of a school. Turn right at the T-junction then left into Government Avenue.

Georgian grace

A few hundred metres later you reach a *pair of gateways* **(18)** flanking the avenue. These once led to paddocks of a zoo. On the left is the Lion Gateway, originally sculpted by Anreith but later replaced. On the right is the Lioness Gateway (although Anreith may have intended these animals to represent leopards).

Continue up the avenue, and turn right through a small gate at the sign for *Bertram House Museum* **(19)**. This Georgian brick townhouse of about 1820 is run by the Cultural History Museum as a Regency period display. Several interesting buildings of the Orange Street Campus of the University of Cape Town surround Bertram House, including the pillared Egyptian Building of 1841, which was the first building in South Africa built for the purpose of higher education; the Little Theatre, built in 1881 as a chemistry laboratory; and six buildings designed by Sir Herbert Baker around the turn of the century.

Return to Government Avenue and turn left. On your way back to Adderley Street you pass on your right a gateway to *Tuynhuys* **(20)**, the residence and offices of the State President during sessions of Parliament. Governor W A van der Stel built a lodge here in 1700 for housing important guests. This was gradually extended until Tuynhuys became the official residence of the governors.

At the foot of the Garden turn left. On your left is *St George's Anglican Cathedral* **(21)**. Work on the present cathedral, designed by Sir Herbert Baker, began in 1901. The building replaced the 'old' St George's, of which the copper cross still remains — now standing above the old steps.

Turn right into St George's Street, cross Church Street, and turn left into Longmarket Street. On the left, with its steps jutting out into the street, is the *Old Town House* **(22)**, also known as the Burgher Wachthuis. Built in 1755, it was used by Cape Town's earliest police force and the Burgher Senate, and later the Cape Town Municipality. Today it houses the Michaelis Collection of old Dutch and Flemish paintings.

The Old Town House faces onto *Greenmarket Square* **(23)**, where an open-air market is held daily (except Sundays), weather permitting ●

Wagenaer's 17th century dam, Golden Acre.

Flower sellers ply their colourful trade in Trafalgar Place.

Visitors to the top of Table Mountian have magnificent views from the cable car over 'the mother city' and Lion's Head.

A cable car ride to the mountain top and the romance of the 'penny ferry'

CAPE TOWN is famous throughout the world for her majestic mountain setting, and the many places and sights that both the city and the Cape Peninsula offer the tourist. Over the centuries visitors have marvelled, not only at the peninsula's natural splendour, but also at the cultural diversity of the 'mother city' — the blending of Eastern, African and Western ways of life, which is constantly evident in architecture, dress and local customs.

Many interesting and scenically striking parts of the peninsula have been mentioned in the preceding pages (pages 282-9). Here are a number of further attractions to tempt the holiday-maker — a rich assortment of mountain walks, glittering beaches, and various artistic and cultural venues.

A leisurely row in the 'penny ferry' across the entrance to the Alfred Basin.

Nature reserves and mountain walks
The whole of Table Mountain is a nature reserve and there are countless footpaths leading up and along its slopes. An alternative to climbing to the summit is to take the cable car, which sweeps visitors to the mountain top from the *cableway station* **(1)** on Table Mountain Road. There is a tearoom at the top, and footpaths criss-cross the summit, leading to various viewsites. The cable car operates every day of the week, but is closed in bad weather.

Lion's Head, connected to Table Mountain by the saddle of land known as Kloof Nek, has a path spiralling to the summit — with chains to help the walker over steeper parts near the top. Devil's Peak, at the eastern end of Table Mountain, offers several walks.

Newlands Forest offers a number of pleasantly shaded walks, as does Cecilia Forest, just south of Kirstenbosch. From Constantia Nek there is a long but easy walk to the top of Table Mountain. Further south there are shaded walks (and picnic sites) in Tokai Forest, and the Silvermine Nature Reserve offers high mountain walks with splendid vistas (see pages 286-7). On the western side of the peninsula there are walks along the mountain slopes above Camps Bay and Hout Bay. Virtually all these walks will take you through scenery far wilder than you would expect to find so near a major city.

The nature reserves on the peninsula contain baboon, porcupine, and various antelope — but none of the larger game animals that tourists come to Africa to view. A greater variety of animals can be seen at *Tygerberg Zoo*, which can be reached by driving out of the city on the N1 and taking the Klipheuwel exit. Nearby, in Brackenfell, is the *Aromaland Animal Park*, containing over 200 species of animals and birds.

For bird-lovers the Cape has several places of note. The *Rondevlei Bird Sanctuary* near Zeekoevlei is one of South Africa's leading ornithological research stations, and visitors are free to use several observation platforms and waterside hides. (Hippos have also been reintroduced here.) Many bird species can be viewed at the *Rietvlei Bird Sanctuary* in Milnerton, while the *World of Birds* **(2)** in Valley Road, Hout Bay, contains a huge collection of birds from throughout the world — many housed in enclosures through which visitors may walk.

A necklace of beautiful beaches
The peninsula is edged on both its eastern and western shores with numerous superb beaches — but if you are planning to swim, note that the water on the False Bay coast is many degrees warmer than that on the Atlantic seaboard.

There are several small beaches alongside the Sea Point promenade, used more for sun-bathing than swimming. More swimmers will be found in the large sea-water swimming pool at the *Sea Point pavilion* **(3)**. Moving south along the Atlantic coast you come to the Clifton beaches (particularly photogenic), the small Glen Beach (popular with surfers), and the grand white-sand sweep of Camps Bay beach. Several small beaches can then be found tucked away along the coast before you come to the scenic beaches of Llandudno and Hout Bay. South of Chapman's Peak stretches Noordhoek beach, a favourite with walkers, and this eventually runs into Long Beach at Kommetjie, which is recognised as one of the finest surfing spots in South Africa.

North of the city, but also on the cold Atlantic coast, there is the popular Bloubergstrand, with its world-famous view across Table Bay to Table Mountain. Between Bloubergstrand and the city lies the wild stretch of Milnerton beach, a place for long walks and shell-collecting.

The False Bay coast has a string of popular beaches, preferred by many bathers because of the warmer water. Muizenberg has Sunrise Beach and Surfer's Corner — where many a young Capetonian first learned to ride the waves. Here too there is the *Muizenberg Pavilion* **(4)** and amusement park. Another favourite swimming spot on this side of the peninsula is Fish Hoek beach. At Miller's Point **(5)**, St James **(6)** and

'The mountain slopes above Camps Bay'.

The Baxter Theatre in Rondebosch.

Dalebrook **(7)** there are natural sea-water swimming pools suitable for children, and a small, well-sheltered beach that is also safe for children can be found among the rocks at Boulders (see pages 282-3).

Places of cultural interest

Three hundred years of history have left Cape Town richly endowed with elegant old buildings. Many of these interesting places are included in the city walk described on pages 288-9, but there is more than can be visited in a single day.

One of the oldest thoroughfares in the city is Strand (beach) Street, and it contains several important buildings. At the upper (western) end there is the *Lutheran Church* **(A)** of 1776, which has many carvings by Anton Anreith. Adjoining the church is the *Martin Melck House* **(B)**, which was the church's original parsonage. Also in Strand Street, a short distance down the hill, is the *Koopmans De Wet House* **(C)**. This dates from 1701 and houses a priceless collection of Cape Dutch furniture.

On the slopes of Signal Hill, the heart of the Malay Quarter **(D)** is now a national monument — an area bounded by Rose, Wale, Chiappini and Shortmarket streets — and in Wale Street there is the *Bo Kaap* (upper Cape Town) *Museum* **(E)**, preserved as a typical 19th century Cape Moslem house. Two other buildings of note are the *S A Sending-gestig Museum* **(F)** in Long Street, and *Rust-en-Vreugd* **(G)** in Buitenkant Street. Rust-en-Vreugd houses part of the William Fehr Collection of water-colours and prints — the rest of the collection is held at the Castle.

A number of other places of historical and cultural interest can be found in the city's outlying suburbs. On the coast road between Muizenberg and Kalk Bay, *Rhodes's Cottage* and the old *Post Huys* are both open to the public. The Post Huys dates from 1673 — a year earlier than the first occupation of the Castle. Closer to the city, off Spaanschemat Road in Constantia, there is the *Nova Constantia* manor house **(8)**, which was originally part of Simon van der Stel's farm Constantia. In Cecil Road, Rosebank, there is the *Irma Stern Museum* **(9)**, housing a collection of works by Irma Stern and various other South African artists.

Of the several cultural venues that merit special mention, perhaps the foremost is the *Nico Malan* complex **(H)** on the foreshore — comprising opera house, theatre and restaurant. In Rondebosch there is the *Baxter Theatre* **(10)**, with a concert hall and two theatres. In Wynberg there is the open-air *Maynardville Theatre* **(11)**, renowned for its summer-evening Shakespeare productions.

Boat trips large and small

Cape Town had its origin as a sea port, and one attraction for visitors is the excitement of a boat-trip on the ocean waves. Several trips may be taken from Hout Bay Harbour. One trip visits the seal colony on Duiker Island. Another is a sunset cruise to Table Bay Harbour — offering magnificent views of the Twelve Apostles. From Kalk Bay there are launch trips to Seal Island.

More extravagant than any of these boat excursions is a helicopter tour of the peninsula. The helicopters leave from the heliport **(12)** in Grainger Bay — within the Table Bay Harbour area. But perhaps the quaintest outing is a ride on the *'penny ferry'* **(13)**. Ideal for children, this is a rowing boat that carries passengers across the entrance to Alfred Basin. Where the ferry moors alongside the East Quay there is a small museum in the old clock tower ●

Additional information concerning the places and events mentioned on these pages may be obtained from the following:
Visitors Information Bureau Strand Concourse, Cape Town 8001
Tel. (021) 253320
S A Tourism Board Level 3, Golden Acre, Adderley Street, Cape Town 8001
Tel. (021) 216274

Boardsailors at Bloubergstrand.

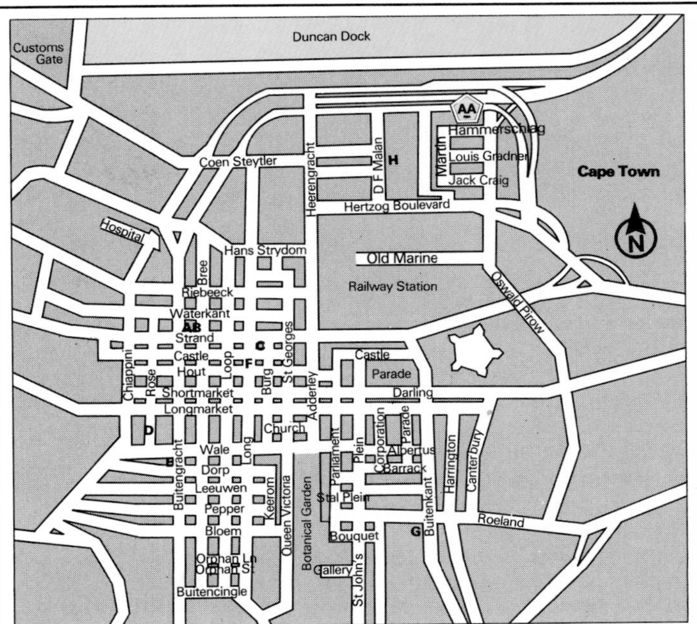

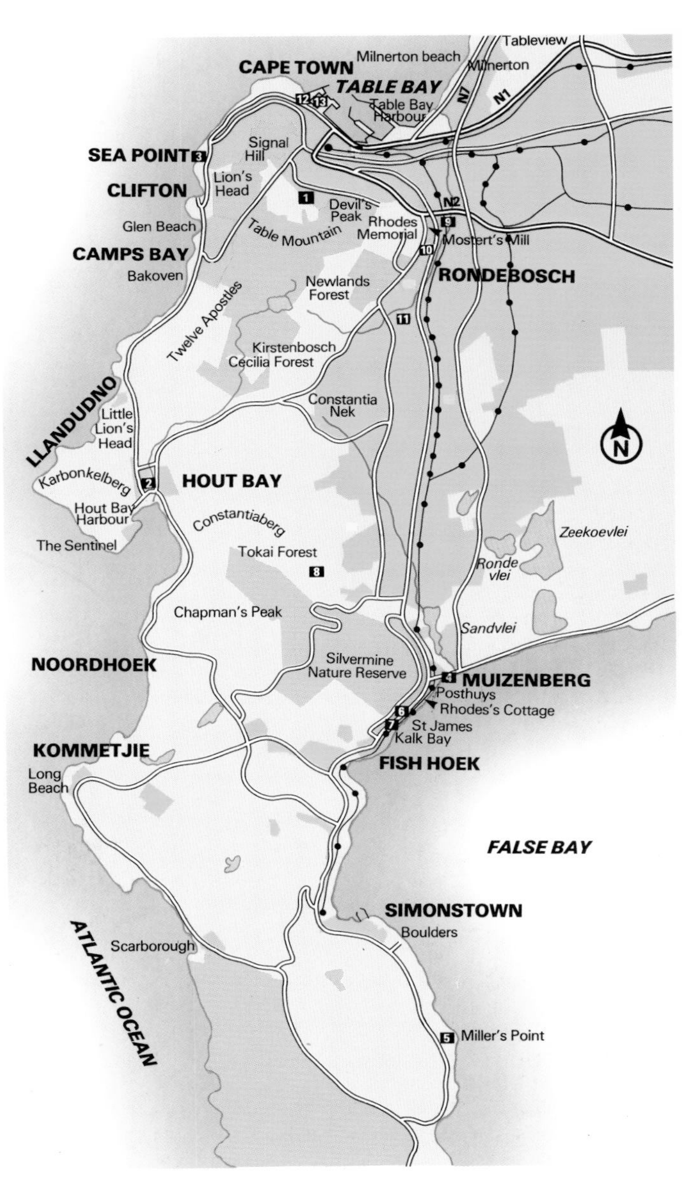

The 'Land van Waveren' and the wild beauty of Bain's Kloof

This drive starts with the famous view of Table Mountain from across Table Bay, then heads north in the footsteps of early searchers for the fabled treasure of Monomotapa. The wealth they found was in the soil — rich farmlands flank our route to the 'Land van Waveren' beyond the mountains. The entire route is on good tar.

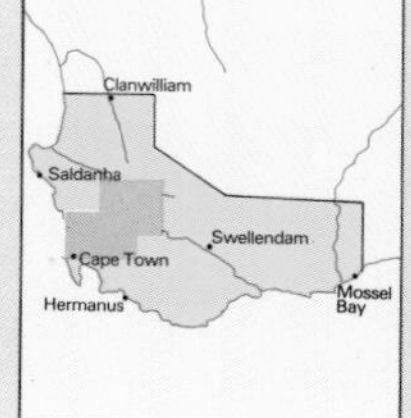

Cape Town
Bloubergstrand
Malmesbury
Nuwekloof Pass
Tulbagh
Bain's Kloof
Wellington
260-280 km

TURN OFF TABLE BAY BOULEVARD (N1) onto Marine Drive (R27). Drive past Milnerton, with the lagoon on your left. Soon after passing Rietvlei on your right, turn left for Bloubergstrand, noting your kms. There are a number of parking areas along the beachfront which afford magnificent views of the sweep of the bay and Table Mountain.

After 3,6 km turn left into Sir David Baird Drive, then turn left into Stadler Road to reach a parking area on the beachfront. The small restaurant here is housed in an old thatched building which is a national monument. The wide beach offers a pleasant short walk — and at low tide it is possible to walk across a sand bar to an outcrop of rocks in the sea.

Bloubergstrand to Tulbagh

Follow the painted arrows from the parking lot, and turn left at the T-junction onto Sir David Baird Drive — then turn left again at the next T-junction towards Melkbosstrand. Continue on this road as it turns inland, and cross the R27. After a further 8,3 km turn left at the T-junction onto the N7, noting your kms.

The road now passes through rolling farmlands. After 33,9 km turn left onto the R315, and follow the signs into Malmesbury. Turn left into Voortrekker Street at the traffic lights. After 100 m turn right into Rainier Street, then after 200 m turn right into Piet Retief Street. After a further 3,9 km turn left onto the R46 for Riebeek-Kasteel/Hermon, noting your kms.

Roughly 11 km later, the road reaches the summit of the Bothmaskloof Pass. After driving just a short distance down the pass, turn left to reach a parking area from where there is a splendid view over the town of Riebeek-Kasteel and the surrounding countryside. A monument here records the passage of a party of explorers sent out by Jan van Riebeeck in 1661 (see below). Return to the R46, noting your kms as you turn left.

Pass roads on your left to Riebeek-Kasteel and Hermon. After 12,3 km turn left at the T-junction onto the R44. Pass a road on your right to Voëlvlei Dam after a further 11,5 km.

About 8,5 km later the road crosses the Klein Berg River in the Nuwekloof Pass, built by Thomas Bain in 1873. An older road, which led to the valley known then as the 'Land van Waveren', can be seen clearly on the right. Roughly 4,5 km after entering the Nuwekloof

The best-known view of Table Mountain — from the flower-covered dunes at Bloubergstrand across Table Bay.

CAPITAL OF THE SWARTLAND

Malmesbury is the chief town of the wheat-rich Swartland (black country), so named not for the colour of its soil — which is reddish brown — but probably for the dark renosterbos (rhino bush) which formerly covered the area.

A warm sulphur spring was discovered in the region in 1744, and a few people settled nearby. The place became the venue for periodic Nagmaal (Communion) services, and three wells were sunk for fresh water. One of these, a national monument, may be seen inside the furniture store on the corner of Hill and Piet Retief streets. Malmesbury was named by Governor Sir Lowry Cole in 1829 in honour of his wife's family.

The view from Bothmaskloof Pass near Riebeek-Kasteel.

SEARCHING FOR MONOMOTAPA

Pieter Cruythoff led an expedition from the Castle in Cape Town early in 1661, under orders from Commander Jan van Riebeeck, to find a route to the legendary and fabulously wealthy kingdom of Monomotapa. They failed in this objective, but they did discover a way to the north as far as the edge of Namaqualand — and they made contact with new trading partners, the Nama.

On the way they encountered a great isolated ridge which Cruythoff loyally named Riebeek-Kasteel. Today the name applies only to the village at its foot, and the mountain is known as Kasteelberg (castle mountain).

In this vicinity the party found many hippopotami, rhinoceros, herds of buck, and even lions. The lions attacked them near the present Bothmaskloof Pass, which winds downhill towards Riebeek-Kasteel.

BAIN'S KLOOF PASS

This picturesque road above the Wit River, winding through rugged peaks of eroded sandstone and granite, was built by convict labourers under Andrew Geddes Bain. In places the pass is carried on dry-packed stone walls more than 12 m high. More than half its 30 km length had to be blasted from solid rock with gunpowder, as this was before the invention of dynamite. Bridges have been reinforced and the road has been tarred, but otherwise it remains as it was built by Bain.

WELLINGTON — EARLY COLONIAL LIMIT

Limiet Vallei was one of the earliest names given to the Wellington district, when it marked the limit of settler expansion from the Cape.

The town of Wellington, founded in 1837, is the home of the Huguenot Seminary, started by the Rev Andrew Murray, and of South Africa's first teachers' college.

Cool, clear mountain streams tumble through the rocky Bain's Kloof.

Pass, turn left to reach the town of Tulbagh.

There is not enough time on this drive to explore fully the historic area of the town, but a drive along Church Street gives a glimpse of Tulbagh's beautifully restored 18th and 19th century buildings (see pages 294-5). Several establishments in Tulbagh offer lunch. On the corner of Church Street and Twee Jonge Gezellen Road there is a municipal picnic site (braai places, toilets, water), and on the banks of the Klip River there is the Tulbagh municipal holiday resort, which has a swimming pool as well as braai and picnic facilities — entrance on Van der Stel Street.

Tulbagh to Bain's Kloof

Leave Tulbagh by travelling south on Van der Stel Street for Wolseley. Note your kms as you pass the road on your right to Gouda and Cape Town. The peaks of the Witsenberg range on your left and of the Watervalsberg and Elandskloofberg ranges on your right are frequently snow-clad in winter.

After 13,2 km turn right for Wolseley and Worcester. Continue straight through the town of Wolseley. About 3,3 km beyond the town on your right there is a stone blockhouse of the Anglo-Boer War which, with the better preserved blockhouse on your left 400 m beyond, was built to guard the railway bridges.

Turn right (towards Worcester) at the T-junction 900 m later, noting your kms. Pass the R43 to Worcester on your left after 6,9 km. Cross a single-lane bridge over the Breë River 500 m later at the beginning of Bain's Kloof, and another single-lane bridge within 200 m, followed by a sharp left bend.

After a further 5,5 km there are picnic places on both sides of the road next to a small stream (no facilities). Cross a single-lane bridge after a further 2,2 km, and turn right 100 m later into the Tweede Tol (second toll) camp and picnic site (small entry fee, braai places, toilets, water). There is a short walk from here under the road to a group of beautiful natural swimming pools in the Wit River.

2,4 km beyond Tweede Tol the road is overhung by a mass of rock known as Dacres' Pulpit, after a clergyman who was a member of a party which explored the kloof. Pass the Bishop's Arch rock formation on your left 1,5 km later, and stop at the parking area 400 m beyond for excellent views along the gorge.

2,8 km later, at the crest of the pass, there is the Eerste Tol (first toll) campsite on your right, opposite a burned out hotel. A plaque on the right records the construction of the pass in 1853. Park at the viewsite on the right 1,5 km later for magnificent views over Wellington and the Berg River Valley.

Bain's Kloof to Cape Town

From the viewsite the road winds down the pass to Wellington. Turn right at the T-junction into Main Street. After 1,5 km turn left at the four-way stop street, and right at the T-junction onto the R44, noting your kms.

Continue straight at the intersection with the Paarl-Malmesbury road. After 12,3 km turn right for Durbanville (R312), and roughly 22 km later turn left at the T-junction.

The road enters Durbanville 5 km after this. Turn left into Main Road, and follow the signs onto the N1 for Cape Town ●

AA Office AA House, 7 Martin Hammerschlag Way, Cape Town 8001 Tel. (021) 211550
Cape Town Visitors Information Bureau Strand Concourse, Cape Town 8001 Tel. (021) 253320
SA Tourism Board Level 3, Golden Acre, Adderley Street, Cape Town 8001 Tel. (021) 216274

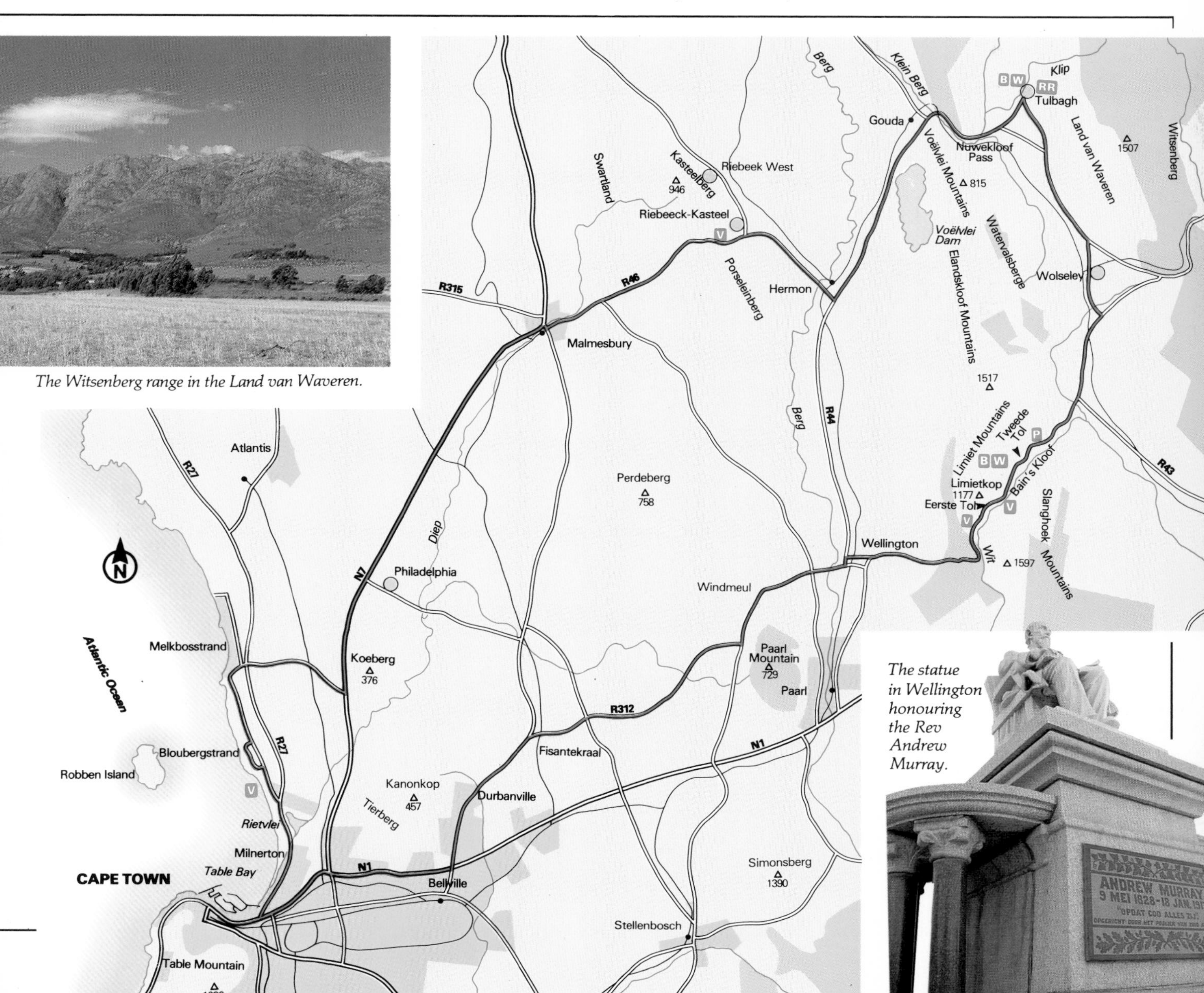

The Witsenberg range in the Land van Waveren.

The statue in Wellington honouring the Rev Andrew Murray.

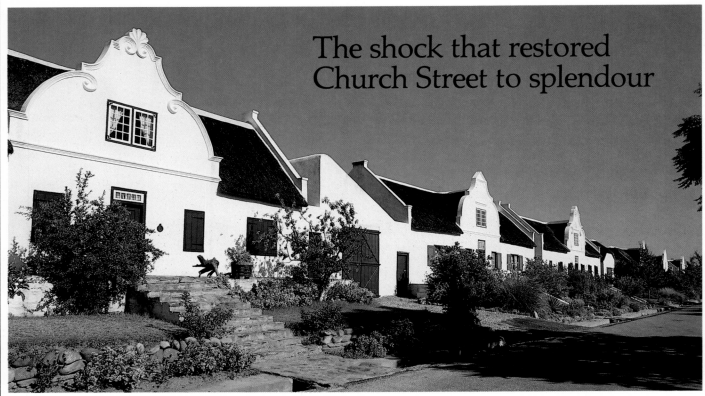

The shock that restored Church Street to splendour

Unspoilt by development, the row of perfectly restored buildings on Tulbagh's Church Street preserves the gracious atmosphere of the late 18th century.

TULBAGH LIES IN a valley sheltered by the Witsenberg and Winterhoek ranges, yet it is exposed to perhaps the most unusual of all natural hazards in South Africa — earthquake. On the night of 29 September 1969 a shift in the nearby Worcester geological fault brought widespread destruction to this peaceful town.

Ironically it was this threat of oblivion that mobilised efforts to restore Church Street — representing an almost perfect village of the late 18th century. Meticulous research and modern rebuilding techniques have combined to preserve a unique architectural treasure — the largest concentration of national monuments in South Africa.

Tulbagh once had the quaint nickname Tulpiesdorp (tulip town) because of the profusion of wild Cape tulips that grew in the area. The soil is now intensively cultivated, but the upper slopes of the mountains are still rich in wildflowers.

The existence of the valley was reported to Commander Jan van Riebeeck as early as 1658. In 1699 Governor W A van der Stel looked down on the valley and named it the 'Land van Waveren' after a wealthy Amsterdam family. Farmers were at once dispatched to the valley, where poor roads kept them isolated from the Cape settlement for many years.

Work on a church was started in 1743 and lasted until 1748. This building is now the *Oude Kerk Volksmuseum* **(1)** — old church folk museum — one of four buildings forming the museum complex. Our walk begins here at the Oude Kerk, at the southern end of Church Street.

A sexton's prophecy

The entrance to the church originally faced the old wagon road on the west side, but was changed to its present position during alterations in 1795, at the time that Church Street was built in a straight line to the parsonage.

For many years the church had an earth floor and, as burials took place within the building, collapses of the floor were fairly frequent. The sexton nonchalantly filled them in. There were no pews, and the members of the congregation brought their own chairs — or rather, the chairs were carried to the church by slaves.

One of the sextons, Leendert Haasbroek, was stabbed to death by a slave whom he had rebuked for failing to clean the church to his satisfaction. As he lay dying, Haasbroek prophesied that the slave would be brought to justice because 'even the crows would tell the story'. The killer escaped and remained at liberty for a long time, until one day he awoke beneath a tree and heard the crows chattering above. Convinced that they were proclaiming his guilt, he surrendered, was tried, and hanged on Tulbagh's Gallows Hill.

Behind the elegant lines of the Oude Kerk's entrance lies a fine museum.

The Oude Kerk Volksmuseum contains fine examples of early Cape chairs and other furniture, musical instruments, Cape silver, brass and copper articles, weapons, toys, porcelain and costumes.

Restoration photographs

When you leave the museum, cross the street diagonally to an old house **(2)** with a high stoep and an iron verandah painted in red and white stripes. This building, which also serves as an information centre for the town, houses a large collection of photographs that show Church Street — originally known as Onderstraat (lower street) — during various periods, including 'before-and-after' pictures of the restorations of earthquake damage.

Walk north along Church Street, away from the Oude Kerk. Number 12 **(3)** is believed to be the oldest house in Tulbagh. It was built in about 1754 — roughly 40 years before the street was made, which explains why its frontage is out of line with the street. The house became church property, and was gradually extended to serve as both a school and a house. Its pointed gable is typical of the Tulbagh district, and the house has been restored to its appearance of about 1861.

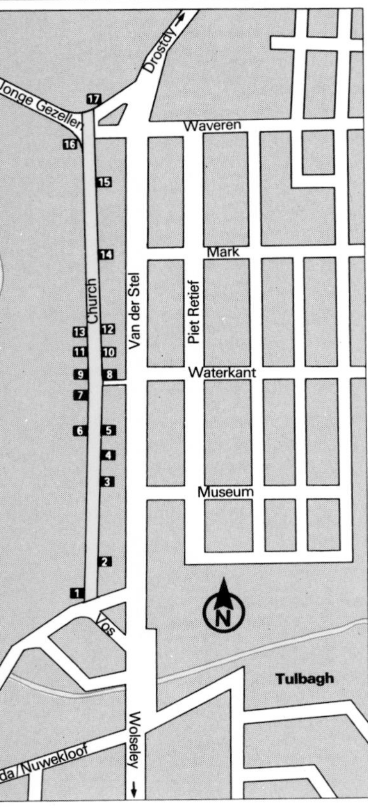

A wine press at De Oude Drostdy.

Next on your right is number 14 **(4)**, a late Victorian village house. The museum stages periodic exhibitions in it, but it is not always open.

Number 16 **(5)** is thought to have been an old wagon house, which had already been converted to a home by 1861. Its present yellow-ochre colour matches a shade found beneath layers of lime-wash when the building was restored. Across the street is number 17 **(6)**, probably built in 1852 by a bachelor Van der Merwe for himself and his mother.

A feature of Church Street is the narrow street-frontages of the houses. These are typical of the time when property taxes were charged on the basis of street-frontage.

Another unusual feature is that there are so few buildings on the west side of the street. This came about because all the original Church Street plots stretched down to the Klip River, allowing each occupant to irrigate his garden. On the west side of the street there is a stone-lined canal with steel sluices — a direct descendant of the early irrigation system.

Danie Theron's home

Among the first settlers at Tulbagh were members of the Theron family, and many Therons still live in the town, much as one finds many De Villiers families in Paarl. Just past number 18 on the right is number 21 **(7)** on the left, which was bought in 1877 by W W Theron — the father of the famous Boer scout Commandant Danie Theron, who fought to the death against overwhelming odds at Gatsrand near Potchefstroom. Comdt Theron, born in 1872, lived for much of his youth here.

Number 22 **(8)** , now a museum annexe, was probably built in 1803. It is furnished as a modest house of over a century ago might have been, and contains many of the ingenious implements people used to make their lives more comfortable.

Across the street is the entrance to Paddagang **(9)** (frog passage). This was either a store or slave quarters, but is now run as a restaurant by the KWV. (There are also a number of other restaurants in Tulbagh, and two municipal picnic sites. One picnic site is on the corner of Church Street and the Twee Jonge Gezellen road — with braai places, toilets and water. The other, in the Tulbagh Holiday Resort on the Klip River, has its entrance on Van der Stel Street with a swimming pool, braai places, toilets and water.)

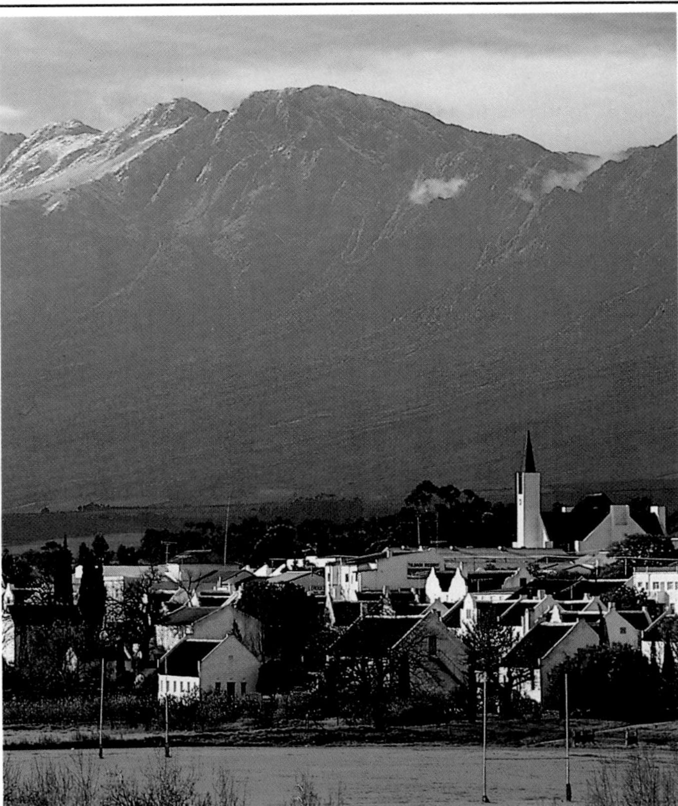

The Witsenberg makes a wintry backdrop to Tulbagh and the Land van Waveren.

Paddagang Restaurant in its verdant setting on the banks of the Klip River.

Rare H-shape

Continuing north along Church Street, you pass number 24 **(10)**, one of the few old H-shaped houses in Tulbagh, probably built before 1815, and occupied for many years by the local postmaster. The house across the street **(11)** was probably built at about the same time.

Number 26 **(12)** was once the mission parsonage, and number 27 **(13)** across the street from it served as its stables and coach house. If you stand in front of number 28 you can see a tree-shrouded hill across the little valley — this was once Gallows Hill.

Impressive and unusual in a street of gables and unpretentious single storeys is the double-storeyed Georgian appearance of number 36, known as *Monbijou* **(14)**. The design of the house is attributed to Thibault, and it was probably built before 1815.

Personal differences and fiery clergy led to the establishment of two parishes in the tiny settlement just after the middle of last century. Number 42 **(15)** was the parsonage of the rival Kruisvallei (cross valley) congregation, and the clergyman of the Oude Kerk therefore had to pass his rival's door on his way to his church from his own parsonage at the northern end of Church Street.

The last house on the left is *Ballotina* **(16)** , thought to have been built to a design of Thibault on land granted to the widow of the Reverend H W Ballot. The *Dutch Reformed Church parsonage* **(17)** still occupies its original position at the northern end of the street.

If time permits, drive along Van der Stel Street, which contains a few interesting old buildings, for some 3 km to reach on your right *De Oude Drostdy*. This building was planned after it was decided in 1804 to make Tulbagh a drostdy (magisterial district) separate from Stellenbosch, of which it was then a part.

After much controversy relating to cost, the Drostdy was formally opened in 1806. By then the British had already taken over at the Cape. (The new district was named after Ryk Tulbagh, a much-loved governor of the 18th century.)

Today the Drostdy serves as a museum, particularly rich in furniture and porcelain. 500 m beyond it, on your left, are the Drostdy Wine Cellars, which offer tours and wine- and sherry-tastings twice a day (except Sundays) ●

A sunburned haven for sea birds and hardy fishermen

Saldanha Bay and Langebaan Lagoon are the focal points of this drive through some of the finest west coast scenery. From Saldanha the route leads around the lagoon to the Postberg Nature Reserve — then heads north to the historic fishing harbours that dot the coast between Laaiplek and Paternoster. Roughly half the route is tarred, the rest is good gravel.

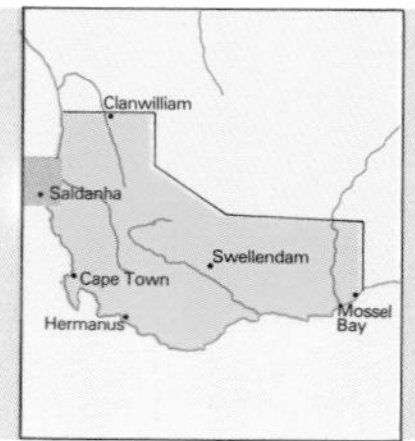

Saldanha
Langebaan
Postberg Nat. Reserve
Velddrif
Cape Columbine
160 — 180 km

BEFORE LEAVING SALDANHA, drive inland along Diaz Road. Turn right into Sea Bride Street, then left at the T-junction into Windhoek Street. After 200 m turn right into Panorama Drive, and now take all turn-offs leading uphill. This will bring you to a magnificent viewsite, 1 km from Windhoek Street. Away to your right is the entrance to the bay. At your feet lies the town, with Hoedjieskop rising among the streets and buildings. Beyond the town stretches the lagoon, an enormous expanse of sheltered water, with the ore-loading quay forming an unnatural, straight line across it. To your left the land stretches away flat and fertile, into a region renowned for the production of wheat and sheep.

Saldanha to Postberg

Leave Saldanha by driving along Kamp Street, which heads east along the north shore of the bay. You pass a caravan park and holiday resort on your right, and 6,2 km after leaving Saldanha you reach an intersection and a railway level crossing. Keep straight here, but if the railway crossing is blocked by an ore-train, turn left and use the level crossing a few hundred metres along the road.

Note your kms at the railway crossing on the main road, and drive on towards Langebaan. After 8,4 km turn right onto gravel, and note your kms. (You can see that the tar ends just after this turn.) You now pass beaches alongside the lagoon, and reach a T-junction with a tarred road after 4,6 km. Turn right onto the tar to reach Langebaan village.

The road changes to gravel as you leave Langebaan. Note your kms here, and after 17 km turn right for Churchhaven. Roughly 15 km after the turn, after passing the picturesque cottages of Schrywershoek and Churchhaven, you reach the Postberg Nature Reserve (entry fee). Although this is open only in September, the main road through the reserve can be followed at any time as far as the

Malgas Island — a favourite roost for many of Saldanha Bay's hundreds of thousands of sea birds.

CAPE COLUMBINE LIGHTHOUSE

The nine-million candlepower Cape Columbine lighthouse, first switched on in 1936, came none too soon; the area around Cape Columbine has long been a graveyard for unwary mariners.

Soldier's Bay, one of the indentations on this rockbound coast, is the site of two memorable shipwrecks. The troopship *St Lawrence* struck a reef here, and the Portugese mail steamer *Lisboa* ran aground here in 1910, with a cargo that included large casks of red wine. The *Lisboa* was eventually broken up by a gale, which stained the sea red with wine and washed many barrels safely onto lonely beaches where they were buried by locals — to be retrieved when the customs officials eventually left.

AN IMPENETRABLE CLOUD OF BIRDS

One of the unforgettable sights of the Saldanha Bay area comes at sunset as thousands upon thousands of birds — sea birds and waders — stream home in long, ragged lines over the water. The French naturalist Le Vaillant, visiting Saldanha two centuries ago, reported seeing an 'impenetrable cloud of birds of every species and all colours'.

Three islands in the bay — Malgas, Jutten and Marcus — are home to thousands of jackass penguins, and Skaap Island holds the largest known breeding colony of kelp gulls in southern Africa. In the summer months, up to 23 species of waders have been counted in the area, most of them migrants from far to the north, some of them coming from as far afield as Greenland and Siberia.

Meeuw Island (gull island) was named by the Dutch for the countless gulls that favoured it as a roosting place. These birds feed on the micro-fauna of the intertidal zone along the shores of the lagoon — and have left a treasure trove in their droppings, or guano. Malgas Island was 10 m deep in guano when it was first exploited for fertiliser in the 1840s.

Taking advantage of Langebaan's sheltered waters.

A weathered fishing boat on Churchhaven beach.

DAAR KOM DIE ALABAMA

Among the many famous ships to have dropped anchor in Saldanha Bay was the Confederate commerce raider, the *Alabama*, in 1863, during the American Civil War. Her Captain, Raphael Semmes, wrote: 'There is no finer sheet of land-locked water in the world than Saldanha Bay.' He was surprised that the unsheltered anchorage of Table Bay had been chosen above Saldanha. (The reason was that Table Bay had abundant fresh water, which was lacking at Saldanha.)

When the *Alabama* sailed, she left behind one of her crew, Third Engineer Cummings, who was accidentally shot and killed while hunting. His grave, on the farm Kliprug, just north of the town, is believed to be the only grave of a Confederate seaman in Africa.

The sun sets on a flotilla of yachts at Saldanha.

SADF security fence 5 km from the reserve entrance. Even when the reserve is closed, there is a good chance of seeing game from the road, and the views are attractive.

Postberg to Dwarskersbos

Retrace your route through Churchhaven, then turn right at the T-junction, towards Darling and Cape Town. At the T-junction with the tarred R27, turn left for Velddrif.

As you enter Velddrif you come to a stop street. Turn right here into Voortrekker Road. After 2 km you will see on your right a black and white gravestone, surmounted by a cross. 100 m after this turn right into Vyelaan.

Vyelaan winds along the river bank, past fisheries and old cottages, with bunches of bokkems' or Cape herrings hanging up to dry. At the first stop street turn right, then turn left at the intersection with Voortrekker Road and drive through the town. At the T-junction with Jameson Street turn left, then turn right into De Villiers Street to reach the entrance to Laaiplek harbour. (There are hotels and restaurants in Velddrif and Laaiplek, which are virtually opposite ends of the same town.)

After visiting Laaiplek harbour, turn left into Jameson Street, reaching Dwarskersbos after 10 km. Turn left here into Iris Road to reach a parking area on the beach. This is an attractive place for a walk, a swim, or a picnic lunch.

Dwarskersbos to Cape Columbine

Return to Laaiplek, turning left out of Jameson Street into Voortrekker Street, then turn right in Velddrif to cross the Berg River bridge. 1,5 km later, turn right onto the R399 towards Vredenburg and Saldanha. After 10 km on the R399 turn right towards St Helena Bay.

The road passes close to the sea at St Helena Bay, with views of fishermen's cottages, the harbour, and the first of a succession of fish-processing factories. A sign indicates the way to the Da Gama Monument, a few hundred metres to the right of the road. Immediately after the monument turn left onto a gravel road towards Vredenburg and Paternoster.

After a further 5,7 km turn right at the intersection. (The farm on the left is called Rondekop.) After a further 8 km turn right at the T-junction for Paternoster, where there is a hotel, a wide sandy beach, and many small cottages clustering on the hillside.

The road continues through Paternoster for 4 km, through the Cape Columbine Nature Reserve, past the lighthouse, and arrives eventually at the resort of Tietiesbaai.

Return through Paternoster, and pass on your left the road on which you arrived from St Helena Bay. You reach tar just before Vredenburg, a distance of some 15 km. Drive along Vredenburg's Main Street, and turn right at the second four-way stop street (there is a hotel on your right) into Saldanha Road — a 12 km tarred road back to Saldanha ●

AA Office AA House, 7 Martin Hammerschlag Way, Cape Town 8001 Tel. (021) 211550
Saldanha Municipal Information Office Cnr Bergstraat and Saldanhaweg, Saldanha 7395 Tel. (02281) 41277
S A Tourism Board Level 3, Golden Acre, Adderley Street, Cape Town 8001 Tel. (021) 216274

Cape Columbine light signals a treacherous coast.

A MAGIC CARPET OF FLOWERS

Langebaan Lagoon penetrates the rich floral kingdom of Namaqualand, and furnishes its own special kind of wildflower display, with the edge of the lagoon always richly blanketed in salt-marsh succulents.

The annual rainfall here is around 260 mm, and the display of colour is at its brightest in spring. Gazanias, forget-me-nots and buttercups are among the most abundant species, competing for attention with brilliant vygies. In the higher and drier patches, gnarled evergreens stand out among the granite outcrops.

Poppies cover the countryside near Vredenburg.

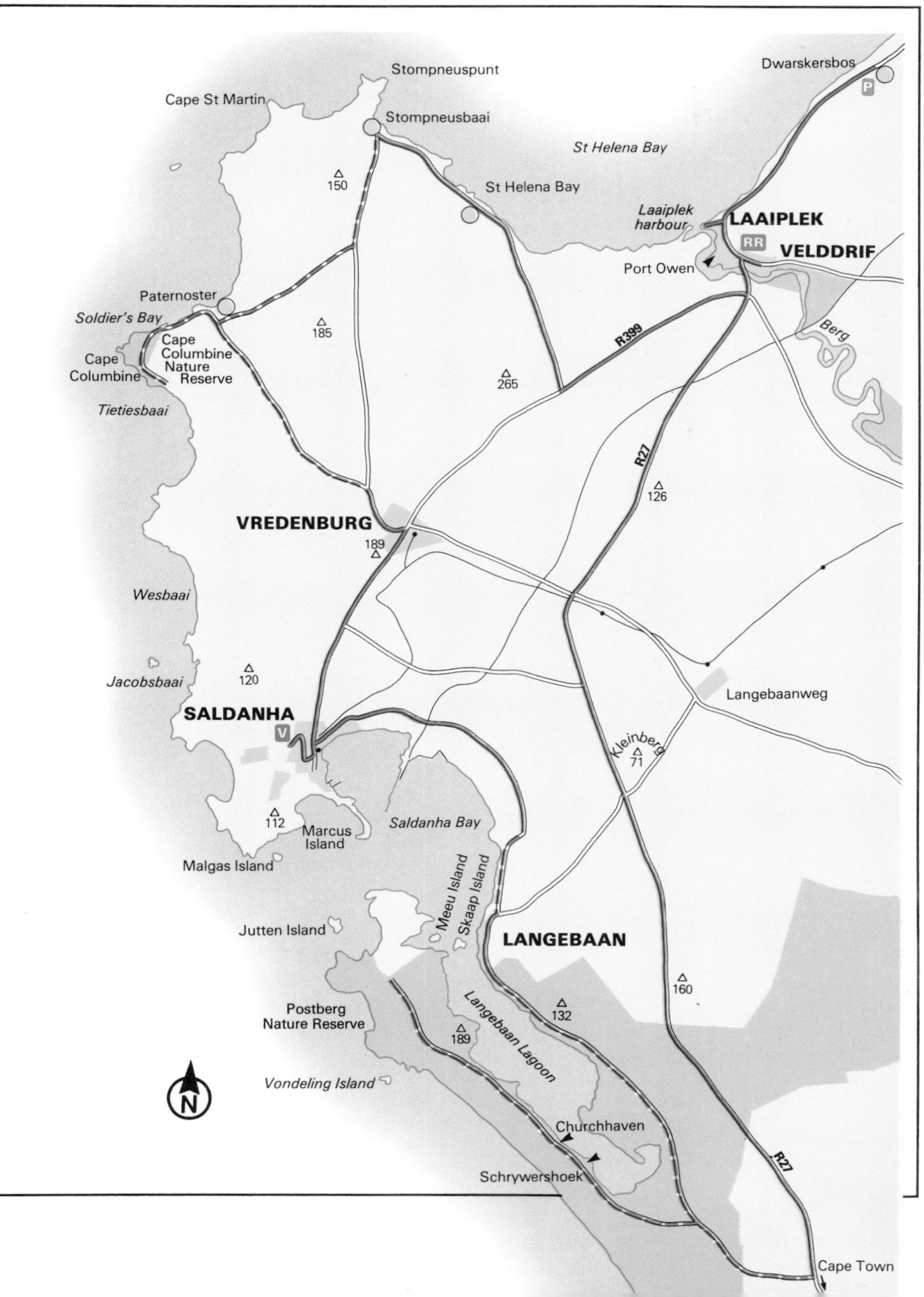

Traversing rugged mountains and sheltered, bountiful valleys

A series of scenic passes over stark and rocky mountain ranges forms a natural circuit — eastwards and southwards from the orange groves of Citrusdal to the gentle orchards of the Ceres valley, then west and north through Tulbagh and the wheatfields of the fertile Swartland. All but 40 km of the route is on tarred roads.

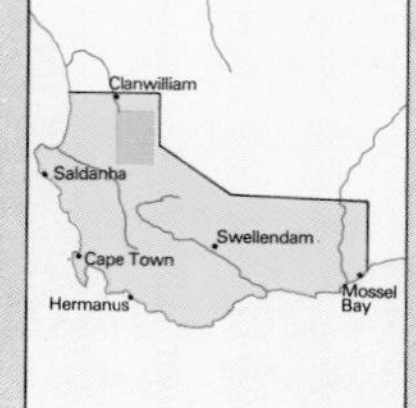

Citrusdal
Prince Alfred Hamlet
Ceres
Tulbagh
Porterville
240 — 250 km

TURN EAST OUT OF Citrusdal's Voortrekker Street into Paul de Villiers Street, noting your kms. After about 3 km there are fine views back over the town. The tarred surface ends 3,5 km later, and the road passes tangled rock formations.

The road begins the winding approach to Middelberg Pass after a further 5 km. At the fork 12,4 km from Voortrekker Street, go right on the larger road. Stop roughly 3 km later for good views into an isolated valley. The road now climbs steeply through a hairpin bend to reach the summit of the mountain. From here the pass is known as Buffelshoek Pass, and there is a descending hairpin bend after a further 200 m, where the road seems entirely shut in by the mountains.

In the valley below, on your right, you pass the thatched farmhouse of Tuinskloof, then cross a causeway 700 m later. Among the rock formations that you pass soon afterwards is one on your right that is said to resemble a weathercock on a steeple.

The road crosses a cement bridge dated both 1968 and 1961, and 4 km later the road is tarred for about 600 m as it climbs a steep hill.

The view changes from close mountain scenery to fields dotted with shimmering dams. Roughly 40 km from Citrusdal the road surface

Dutch Reformed Church, Porterville.

THE 'NARROW PASSAGE'

The little Swartland town of Porterville below the Olifants River Mountains was founded in 1863 on the farm Willemsvallei, and named after William Porter, the Attorney-General of the Cape. The gentle air currents that swirl around these craggy mountains make them ideal for hang-gliders. A favourite venue is the farm Cardouw, which takes its name from the old Khoikhoi word for 'narrow passage'.

Cardouws (or Kardouws) Kloof was once an important route across the mountains, although it was described by the traveller Thunberg as 'one of the most difficult roads that go across the African mountains'. The old pass can no longer be traversed by vehicle, and has not been used for more than a century. Even the section that can still be used (approaching close to the summit) is not for the nervous motorist.

A land of plenty — the fertile bowl of the Ceres valley below the Gydo Pass.

CERES — VALLEY OF THE CORN-GODDESS

The settlement in the Warm Bokkeveld was called Ceres after the Roman corn-goddess — an appropriate name for a fertile valley which has become known for its production of wheat and fruit.

The first stock farmers arrived in the Bokkeveld (goat or buck country) in 1727. More than a century later, after the discovery of diamonds in the northern Cape, nearby Michell's Pass became the main highway to the north, and the settlement entered a period of hectic prosperity. The pass collected a greater revenue than any other toll in the country, but this came to an end when the railway lines to the north bypassed Ceres. The Togryers (transport riders) Museum on the corner of Munnik and Oranje streets preserves many relics of the town's exciting history.

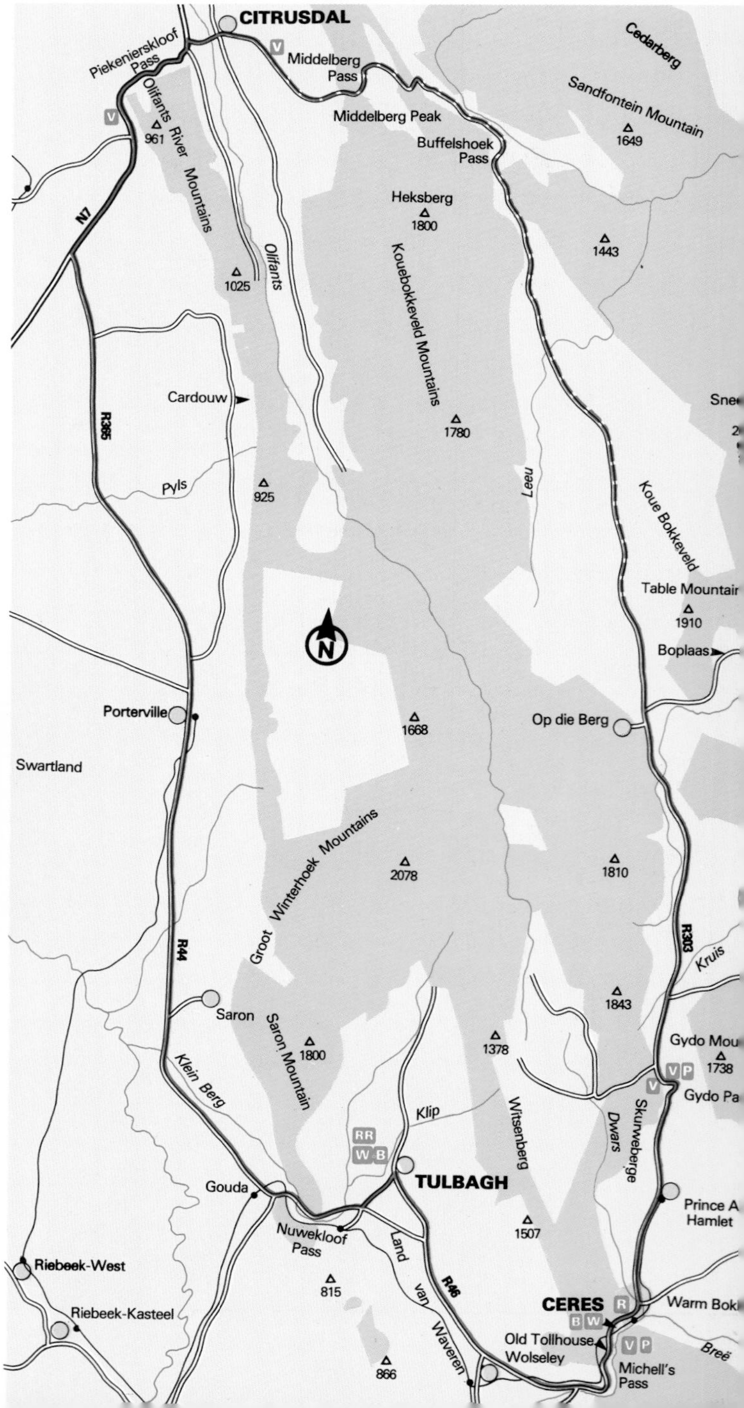

changes to tar. Note your kms as you pass a turn-off on your left to Boplaas, which was formerly the farm Moddervallei — birthplace of the poet Poerneef and historic home of 11 generations of Van der Merwes.

Soon afterwards you pass the turn-off on your right to the settlement of Op die Berg (on the mountain). After 23,1 km you reach the start of the easily negotiated Gydo Pass. After 3,2 km on the pass, stop on your left at a picnic site for a splendid view over the fertile Ceres valley (see opposite).

The road descends the pass, then continues through Prince Alfred Hamlet. After a few more kms you reach the outskirts of Ceres. (A number of establishments in the town provide lunch.) 300 m after the start of the dual carriageway in the town a caravan-and-campsite signpost to your right directs you to the Pine Forest Public Resort. (There is a small entry fee to the resort, which offers swimming, braai sites, water and toilets.)

Whether you have visited the resort or not, continue along the road on which you entered the town, and turn right at the traffic lights. After 1,4 km turn right and park at the entrance to the small Ceres Nature Reserve, where there is a delightful nature trail (allow 30-40 minutes).

Ceres to Tulbagh

Leaving the nature reserve parking area, turn right. The road immediately enters Michell's Pass. Stop after 900 m at the tarred loop of road on your left for an excellent view over the Dwars River (which becomes the Breë River after a few kms). There are picnic sites here, and on your left a waterfall tumbles down into a beautiful pool known as Koffiegat or Coffee Pot. After a further 1,5 km on your right is the old tollhouse, built about 1850 on what was then the main road to the mining towns in the north. Beyond the pass you drive past a road on your left to Wellington and Worcester (R43), two roads to Wolseley, and the road to Gouda and Cape Town.

Tulbagh to Citrusdal

You enter Tulbagh on Van der Stel Street passing a turn-off left onto Stasieweg for Gouda and Cape Town (see pages 294-5 for a street map and information on picnic sites and restaurants). After visiting the town, return to Stasieweg and turn right for Cape Town and Gouda, noting your kms. Turn right 3 km later onto the R46, to enter Nuwekloof Pass 2,3 km later. After a further 4,8 km turn right onto the R44 for Porterville and Piketberg.

Continue on the R44 through rolling wheatlands to reach Porterville's main street after 34 km. Leave the town by continuing northwards for Citrusdal, and note your kms as you pass the turn-off for Piketberg (R44) on your left. (A gravel road on your right soon afterwards leads to the farm Cardouw — a favourite launching site for hang-gliders.)

After 30,9 km turn right at the T-junction onto the N7, noting your kms. The road now heads directly towards the mountains, and soon you can see the line of the Piekenierskloof Pass ascending ahead and to the left. Below the present road are the old retaining walls of the original pass — known as Grey's Pass, and built by Thomas Bain in 1857. It was the first major construction task he supervised, and for almost a century was the only route over the Olifants River Mountains.

Stop on your left after 12,5 km on the N7 for outstanding views of the Swartland. Continue over the summit of the pass, and turn right for Citrusdal. (A gravel road on your right before you reach the town leads after 15 km to the hot springs.) ●

AA Office AA House, 7 Martin Hammerschlag Way, Cape Town 8001 Tel. (021) 211550
Ceres Publicity Association Voortrekker Street, Ceres 6835 Tel. (0233) 21177
S A Tourism Board Level 3, Golden Acre, Adderley Street, Cape Town 8001 Tel. (021) 216274

The stark and barren rocks of the Koue Bokkeveld mountains rise above the bounty of the plains.

DALE OF CITRUS GROVES

Although farms near Citrusdal have been worked for well over two centuries, the town dates only from 1916. The main road north reaches it through Piekenierskloof (pikemen's gorge) — a name dating from 1675 when the Dutch East India Company at the Cape stationed soldiers near here to protect one of their Khoikhoi allies from attack by a rival chieftain, Gonnema. Encumbered by heavy pikes and breastplates, the Dutch soldiers pursued their foes through the mountains in vain.

Citrusdal nestles in a tranquil valley along the banks of the Olifants River, surrounded by the deep green foliage of orange and lemon trees, which fill the air with the fragrance of their blossoms in spring. A 200-year-old orange tree on the farm Groot Heksrivier, near Citrusdal, still bears fruit and is a national monument.

The radio-active spa south of Citrusdal has been visited for its purported restorative powers since the days of the earliest explorers.

The Lovers' Bridge on Lyell Street in Ceres.

An inquisitive trio on a Ceres valley stud farm.

THE ORIGINAL HOME OF THE GRIQUAS

The countryside through which you travel after Porterville was once the home of a Khoikhoi tribe called the Grigriquas, encountered in 1661 by the surgeon Pieter van Meerhoff, who noted that some of them wore copper ornaments. It was a Grigriqua chief who later guided Governor Simon van der Stel on his expedition to the copper mines of Namaqualand.

One of the leaders of the tribe, Adam Kok (born in 1710) is said to have derived his surname from the fact that he worked as a cook (kok) to the governor. He later led his people northwards to settle at what became Griquatown. His descendant Adam Kok III headed the long Griqua trek that ended in the founding of Kokstad, thus creating a Griqualand West and a Griqualand East.

Middelberg Pass crosses wild mountain scenery.

Gargoyles and dragons — the magnificent rocks of the Cedarberg

A circular drive — almost all gravel — takes you through the rugged Cedarberg. But the section of 32 km from Wuppertal to Matjies River is a rough track suitable only for a sturdy vehicle with a high ground clearance. Without such a vehicle this should be treated as two there-and-back day trips from Clanwilliam — as we have described it.

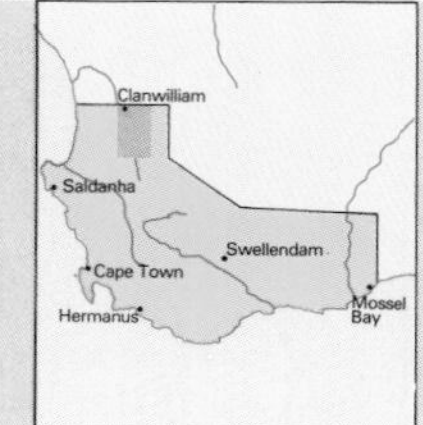

Clanwilliam
Wuppertal
140 — 150 km

Clanwilliam
Matjiesrivier
180 — 190 km

FOR THE NORTHERN DRIVE from Clanwilliam to Wuppertal, turn right at the northern end of Main Street for 'Vanrynsdorp via old main road', noting your kms. Keep straight past a road to Klawer on the left after 2,1 km. The tar surface ends soon after, and the road begins its gentle ascent amidst tumbled rock formations on both sides of the road — some of the rocks appearing to defy gravity by their top-heaviness.

After 16 km from Clanwilliam stop at the parking place on your left to visit the grave of Dr C Louis Leipoldt, the poet, author, journalist, physician and authority on Cape cooking. A sandy path leads for about 100 m to the simple grave, which is in a rock shelter once occupied by San hunters. There are faded paintings of an elephant and calf, and of human figures, which can be seen slightly to the left of the grave as you face the shelter.

Roughly 500 m further on the main road on your left is the entrance to the Rheeboksvlei picnic area (small entry fee, water, toilets). There are a number of attractive walks here — a permit may be obtained from the forester a few hundred metres further along the road.

Continue through rugged countryside, and pass a road on your left to Elizabethsfontein. Note your kms as you reach a cement causeway, and stop 5,8 km later, just before a sign that warns of a road to the right. On your right here is the Englishman's grave — almost entirely concealed by a large eucalyptus tree (see opposite).

100 m beyond the grave, turn right for the Biedou Valley and Wuppertal, noting your kms. Lonely farms in isolated valleys come unexpectedly into view as the road rises and twists. After 7,5 km the road begins the steep descent of Uitkyk (lookout) Pass. Stop after a further 100 m on the left in a parking area that offers magnificent views of smooth farmlands nestling among the craggy rocks.

The road crosses two cattle grids within the next 3 km, then crosses a low, narrow causeway. Soon after, on your left, you pass a road to the Biedou Valley and Uitspanskraal. (This side road is popular with visitors during the spring flower season.) On your right here is the farm Mertenhof, which has a homestead dating from the beginning of the previous century, and a stone-walled threshing floor that is visible from the road.

After a further 5,4 km the road crosses another narrow causeway, followed within 200 m by another cattle grid. Roughly 3,6 km later, on your right, a waterfall has created a smooth rock face that seems out of character with the ruggedness of the Cedarberg.

The final steep descent to Wuppertal down Kleinhoogte begins 3,3 km later, and offers frequent glimpses of thatched and whitewashed buildings in an oasis of soft green. The road passes the old cemetery on your right just before entering the village.

After your visit to Wuppertal, retrace your route back to Clanwilliam. (The rough track that links this route to Matjiesrivier leaves the village on the south side.)

Clanwilliam to Matjiesrivier

For the southern Cedarberg drive, turn southwest at the southern end of Clanwilliam's Main Street (opposite the old jail) onto the 'Kaapse Weg' (Cape road). The road surface changes to gravel after 900 m. After a further 200 m turn left at the Y-junction, noting your kms. (The road on your right leads to the wildflower garden, dam and caravan park.)

For several kms the road runs along the shores of the Clanwilliam Dam, offering many fine views. After 6,8 km turn right at the fork, and cross a narrow causeway immediately afterwards. Roughly 1,6 km later pull off the road at a picnic site for wide views of the dam.

Cross a concrete and iron bridge, and 4,3 km later pull off the road on your left to explore a large rock overhang and a number of smaller shelters containing old ochre hand-prints.

The gate across the road 2,3 km later opens towards you, and you leave the dam behind soon afterwards as the road passes citrus groves. At the crossroads roughly 7 km later turn left, away from the river, noting your kms.

The road soon ascends the Kriedouw Kloof Pass, and an Afrikaans road sign on the left warns of a 'smal kronkelpad' (narrow winding road). The road ascends even higher into the mountains over the Nieuwoudt Pass, offering spectacular views into remote valleys, before entering the area known as the Sederberg State Forest after 15,6 km.

After a further 400 m turn left for the Algeria campsite and office (small entry fee). There are toilets, water and braai places here — and firewood is for sale. The Rondegat River offers swimming, and there are several attractive walks from the camp.

As you leave Algeria, turn left and note your kms. Pass a road on the left to the Uitkyk Forest Station at the start of the Cedarberg Pass. After 5,6 km pull off the road for a fine view over the Driehoek River Valley, which stretches ahead.

The road crosses a number of causeways and cattlegrids before you reach a fork about 30 km from Algeria. Turn right for Kromrivier at the fork. The road winds down the steep mountainside to reach the entrance of the resort (small entry fee, braai places, toilets, water, swimming). Maps of the area are available here, as well as detailed directions for walks and sightseeing. Obtain a permit here for entering the Stadsaal area, and ask for instructions on how to open the locked gate there.

Return to the fork 4,4 km from Kromrivier, and turn right, noting your kms. After 3,5 km turn right towards the locked gate on a minor road. After passing through the gate and locking it, turn right onto a side-track about 600 m beyond. Stop before the track forms a loop, to visit the excellent group of San paintings of elephants and human figures in the large rock overhang on your right.

Return to the track on which you entered the locked area, and turn right. After about 1 km the road ends among the tumbled rock formations and caves of Stadsaal (city hall).

After your visit to Stadsaal, retrace your route to the main road, and after re-locking the gate turn right. Roughly 2 km later you cross a causeway. Stop on the right just beyond, where there is a shady picnic site next to the river. Nearby are the old farm buildings of Matjiesrivier, now more or less derelict, with the new homestead close by.

Retrace your route from here back to Clanwilliam. (The jeep track that leads to Wuppertal is reached by turning left at the T-junction 700 m beyond the picnic site.) ●

AA Office AA House, 7 Martin Hammerschlag Way, Cape Town 8001 Tel. (021) 211550
Clanwilliam Municipality and Divisional Council Main Street, Clanwilliam 8135 Tel. (02682) 28/215
Sederberg State Forest P O Citrusdal 7340 Tel. (02682) 3440
SA Tourism Board Level 3, Golden Acre, Adderley Street, Cape Town 8001 Tel. (021) 216274

Spring blooms at Clanwilliam Dam.

Lawns and shady trees at Algeria camp.

ROOIBOS CAPITAL

The town of Clanwilliam, established on the farm Jan Disselsvlei in 1814, was named by Governor Sir John Cradock after his father-in-law, the Earl of Clanwilliam.

Among the attractive old buildings in Clanwilliam are the Dutch Reformed Church, which was built in 1864, and the Anglican Church, consecrated in 1866. At the southern end of Main Street is the old jail, also dating from the 1860s. The road divides here, with many quaint buildings between the two.

The library in Main Street contains mementoes of C Louis Leipoldt and of Dr P le Fras Nortier, 'father' of the rooibos tea industry, of which Clanwilliam is the centre.

The wildflower garden on the outskirts of the town offers lovely spring displays. The Clanwilliam Dam is a major venue for water sports, and there are camping and picnicking sites along its shores.

Weathered rocks lie scattered across the landscape of Pakhuis Pass.

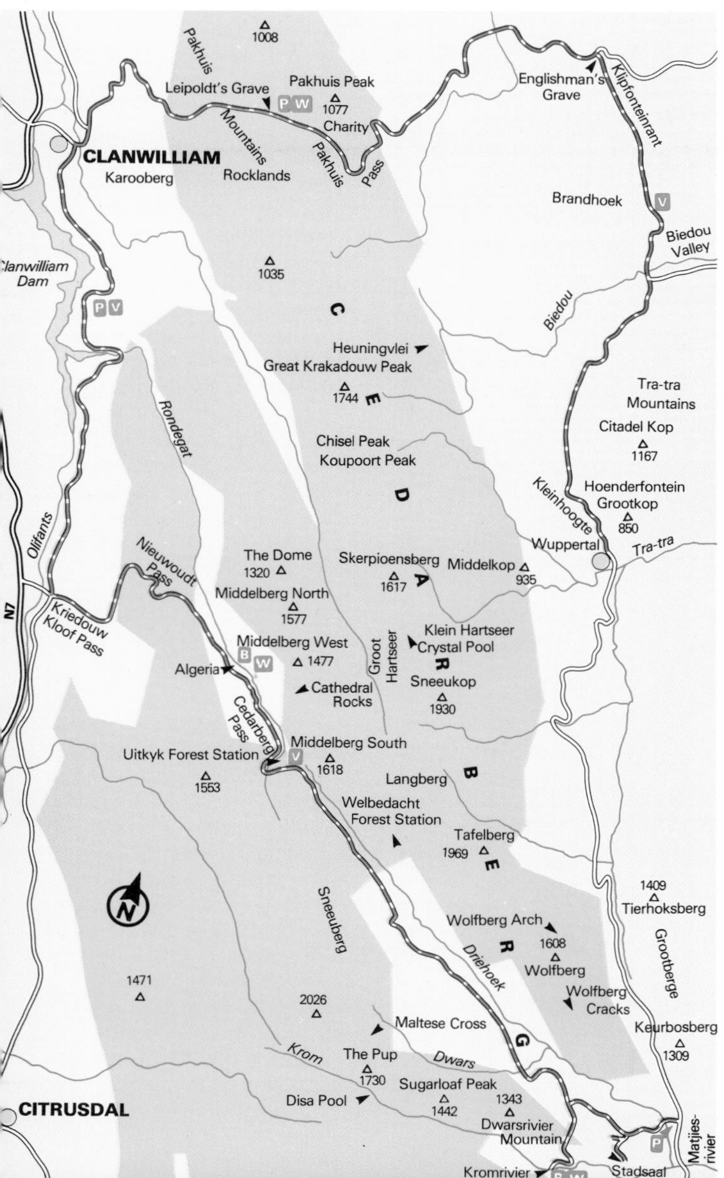

Wuppertal's quaint church — at the heart of this old-world village.

WUPPERTAL MISSION VILLAGE

This village was established in 1830 on an old farm known as Koudeberg (cold mountain) — an appropriate name in an area where the peaks are mantled with snow in winter. In summer the heat may be equally intense in these tucked-away valleys.

The settlement grew around the Rhenish church built on the banks of the Tra-tra River, and some 150 of the cottages on the terraced ground are more than 100 years old. On your right when you enter is the former school, built on a high stoep in about 1830 and now used as the village shop. If you turn right at the end of the shop, you will reach an old, unoccupied house which is believed to have been built for the first missionaries, Baron von Wurmb and Johann Leipoldt, who was C Louis Leipoldt's grandfather.

The church bells at Wuppertal.

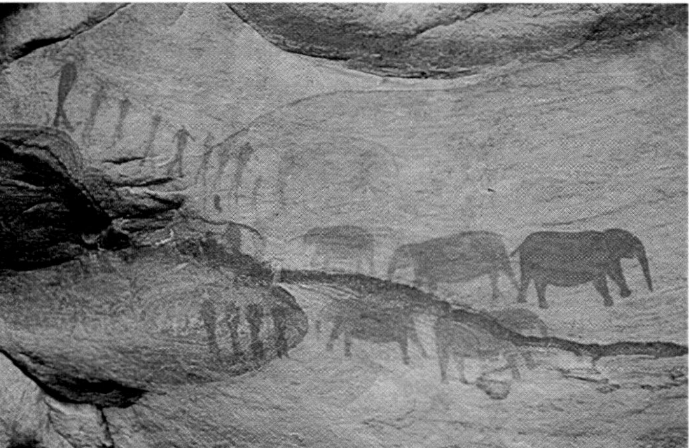

San artists left these enduring momentoes of their sojourn near Stadsaal Caves.

THE ENGLISHMAN'S GRAVE

During the Anglo-Boer War, 21-year-old Lieutenant Graham Clowes of the 6th Mounted Infantry set out from Clanwilliam with his batman, Trooper Clark, to ensure that horses could cover the ground towards the Boer headquarters in Calvinia. As they reached the Wuppertal turn-off, there was a flurry of shots, and the two men dropped from their horses — Clowes dead and Clark seriously wounded.

Clark was taken back to Clanwilliam, where he later died, and Clowes was buried close to where he had fallen. After the war, Clowes's widowed mother had the present monument erected here — plus a memorial at Eton School, where her son had sung in the choir.

In spring and summer visitors to this lonely grave may find small bunches of veld flowers laid upon its stones — the identity of the person who places them there is a mystery.

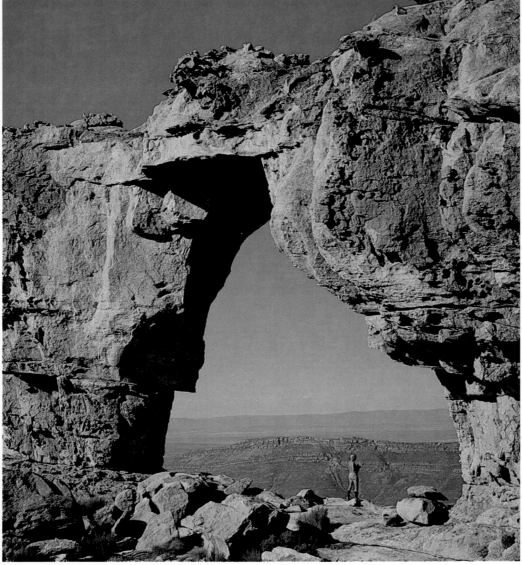

Wolfberg Arch epitomises Cedarberg magic — crisp air, spectacular rock formations and an unspoilt panorama.

The Cedarberg — a wilderness of sculpted rock and unspoilt valleys

Crystal Pool offers a refreshing swim after a hot hike in the mountains.

THE CEDARBERG REMAINED a little-known area for more than a century after the first European settlement was established at Cape Town — a mere 200 km away. Even today, in spite of the area's growing popularity with lovers of the outdoors, there are many spots among the craggy mountains that are known only to forestry officers or those hardy people who have made their home here.

The dual role that the area has as home and resort is clear in the many names that fill the map of the Cedarberg (see pages 300-1). There are the names that have been bestowed by the climbers and the visitors — names such as Frustration Peak, Maltese Cross, and Machine Gun Ridge. But no matter how descriptive they are, they lack the intimacy of such older names as Hartseer (heartache), Wegwaai (blow away), and Filander se Werf (Filander's farmyard) — the little farm where Filander, whoever he was, tended his crops in a majestic but lonely setting.

Hiking trails

The Cedarberg region covers some 130 000 ha. Just over half the area is State forest land, and of this a 71 000 ha portion was proclaimed a wilderness area in 1973. The mountains are criss-crossed with well-maintained hiking trails, and fantastic rock formations amidst the weathered sandstone peaks offer challenging climbs for mountaineers.

Hikers may set out from one of the several campsites in the Cedarberg on short walks, or they may spend a few days exploring the area. A number of overnight huts dot the range — including the Boontjieskloof Hut, Middelberg Hut, Sleepad Hut, Sneeukop Hut, Crystal Pool Hut and Sneeuberg Hut — some of them built more than 80 years ago by forestry officer George Bath. Caves are also popular for overnight stays, particularly the Sederkop and Welbedacht caves.

Walking in the northern Cedarberg, which can be reached easily from Algeria Forest Station and campsite, the hiker has access to the towering Middelberg peaks, Helsekloof with its waterfall, the craggy Cathedral Rock where weather-bleached cedars shelter from fire, and excellent views of the Sneeukop-Langberg massif. The path through Wildehoutdrif leads along the Groot Hartseer plateau to the natural swimming hole of Crystal Pool, while the track to Heuningvlei passes a number of the higher peaks — Great Krakadouw, Chisel Peak and Koupoort Peak. These northern areas can also be reached by car from Pakhuis Pass.

The cedar tree

In the southern area, where there are a number of campsites, popular excursions are to Tafelberg, the Wolfberg Arch, the Wolfberg Cracks (which are on private land and may be visited only with the owner's permission), the rock pinnacle known as the Maltese Cross, which lies on the eastern approach to Sneeuberg (at 2 027 m the highest peak in the range), the Disa Pool swimming hole on the Krom River, and the Stadsaal Caves, a series of smooth caverns worn out of the rock (also on private land).

The cedar trees (*Widdringtonia*

Wind-weathered rock takes on fantastic shapes high up in the Cedarberg range.

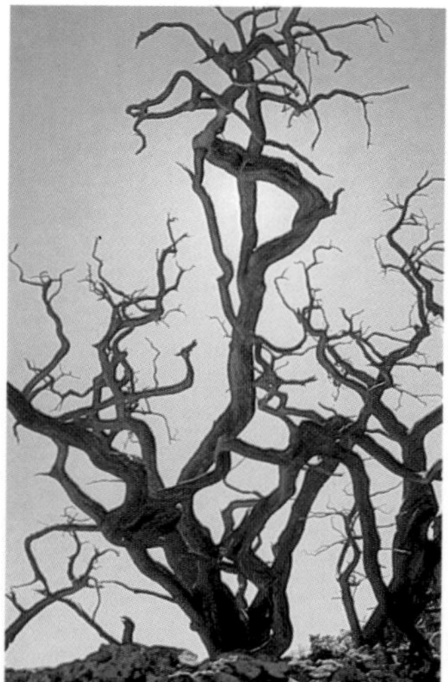

Bleached 'skeleton' of a cedar tree.

The Maltese Cross dwarfs hikers.

cedarbergensis) which are found at the higher levels of the mountain range, and after which the area is named, are not at all like the cedars of Lebanon, but rather like the cypress family. The excellent qualities of the local cedar wood were brought to the attention of Governor Willem van der Stel in 1700, and for more than a century the forests were recklessly exploited — in one instance in 1879 more than 7000 young trees were cut down to provide telegraph poles between Calvinia and Piketberg. Although the trees are now stringently protected, it is estimated that the slow process of restoring the forests to their former splendour will take a number of centuries.

A rare beauty

Another beauty to be found on the highest reaches of the Cedarberg is the snow protea (*Protea cryophila*), among the rarest of all proteas. It has an underground stem, which makes the flowers and leaves appear to sprout directly from the soil. The snow protea flowers between December and February — a bloom that is white and 'woolly' on the outside, and red and smooth on the inside. Less rare is the Cedarberg, or rocket, pincushion (*Leucospermum reflexum*), a popular garden plant that grows naturally only in the northern Cedarberg.

Two plants that are found in abundance here are the rooibos (*Aspalathus linearis*), from which a tea is made, and the buchu (*Agathosma butulina*), which has been renowned for its medicinal properties for many centuries. Both are important commercial crops for the area.

The number of wild animals in the wilderness area has increased in recent years since the introduction of stricter conservation measures. Among the mammals is the spectacled dormouse (*Graphiuris ocularis*), or namtap as the locals call the pretty, bushy-tailed rodent. The namtap has a reputation for rummaging in rucksacks during the night in search of food. The most common antelope are the grey rhebuck (*Pelea capreolus*) and the klipspringer (*Oreotragus oreotragus*), and baboons (*Papio ursinus*) are often seen.

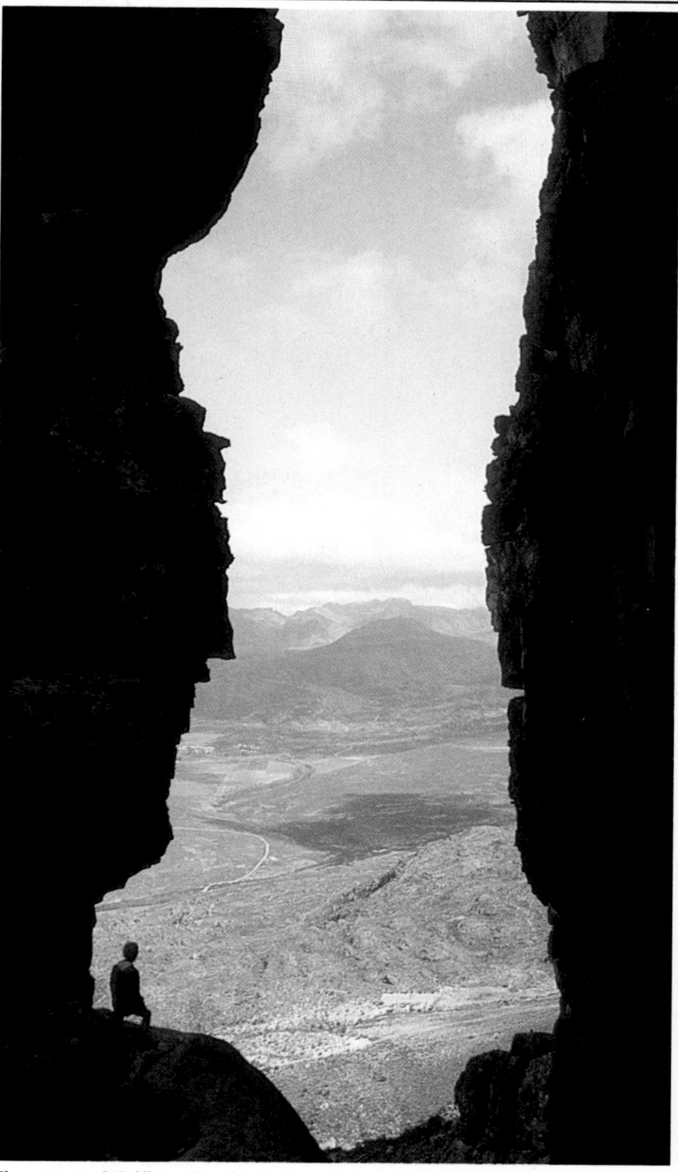

The majestic Wolfberg Cracks frame scenery typical of the wilderness area.

Leopards (*Panthera pardus*) still prowl the Cedarberg but are very rarely seen, and the old stone leopard-trap in the Sederberg Kloof is a relic of wilder days. An old legend from those times tells of a buchu-picker named Hans Möller whose wife died while the two of them were out in a remote kloof. Night fell, and soon Hans realised that leopards were stalking him. All he had with him was his violin, so, in desperation, he began to play. The leopards did not leave, but sat down to listen and, so the story goes, Hans was obliged to play all through the night until the big cats finally left him at dawn.

Maps are essential if you intend to undertake a long hike. An excellent map is available from the Forester at Algeria, and permits to walk in the wilderness area are obtainable in advance from the Forester, whose postal address is Sederberg State Forest, PO Citrusdal 7340, or tel. (02682) 3440. It is important to take warm clothes, as the nights can become very cold, and enough water for your proposed walk. No pets are allowed, nor may fires be made, except in the purpose-built braai places at the Algeria campsite ●

NORTHERN CAPE

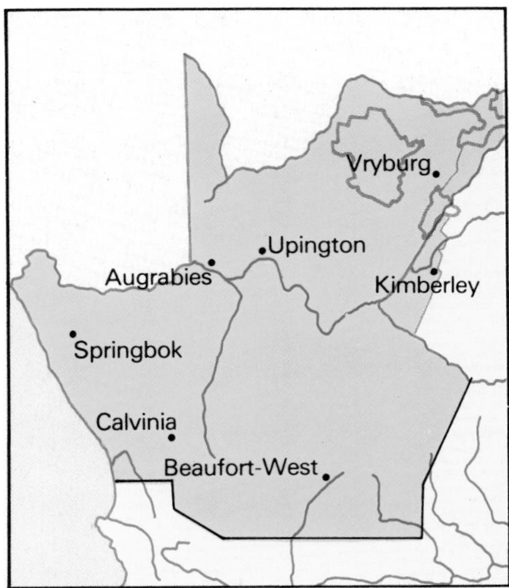

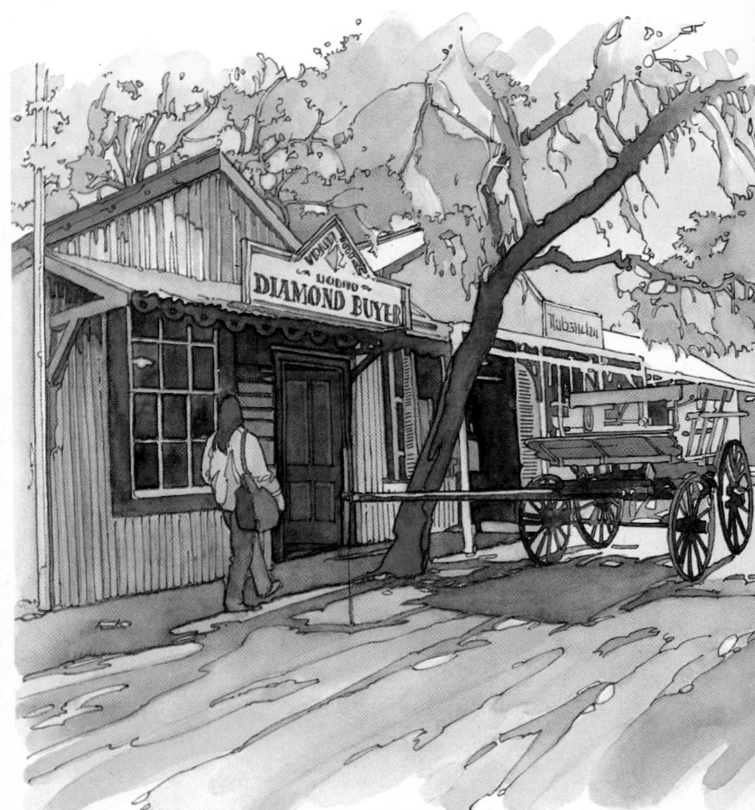

Above: *Kimberley's Mine Museum.* **Left:** *The dramatic Augrabies Falls — a stark landscape softened by the glow of the setting sun.*

Quaint old roads through the land of the copper mountains

This drive is most rewarding in the spring when the display of wildflowers is at its best, but the panoramic views over Namaqualand and the mountain passes — Spektakel Pass and the Messelpad — are memorable at any time of year. Note that two-thirds of the route is on gravel roads, and that you must take food and drink with you.

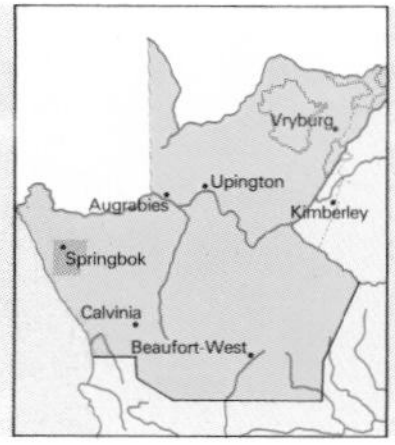

Springbok
Hester Malan Reserve
Okiep
Nababeep
Spektakel Pass
Messelpad
220 – 230 km

DRIVE NORTH-EAST ALONG Springbok's Voortrekker Street and turn right towards 'Airport/Cape Town', noting your kms as you turn. After 1 km turn right at the T-junction, and after a further 4,3 km turn left, noting your kms again. You pass the airfield on your right soon afterwards, and after 6,2 km you reach the entrance to the Hester Malan Nature Reserve on your left. The reserve is home to a number of Hartmann's mountain zebra, as well as many smaller mammals, and there is a shaded display of Namaqualand succulents alongside the administrative offices.

Retrace your route into the town and turn right into Voortrekker Street. Note your kms as you pass under the N7 road bridge about 200 m after turning. The R64 on which you are now travelling leads through a harsh granite landscape, and after about 4 km you will see on your right the Koperberg (copper mountain) with a number of old mines — including the fenced-in shaft dug in 1685 on instructions from Commander Simon van der Stel (see opposite).

After roughly 6 km you reach a crossroads. Turn right here, and after a further 500 m turn right again onto gravel. Pass the small mining settlement of Carolusberg and then turn right (7,3 km from the N7 road bridge). Go left at the fork 200 m later, to reach a parking area at the foot of the Koperberg after a further 800 m. A steep path leads from the parking area up to the Van der Stel mine, from where there are wide views over the sun-baked flats and the massive granite outcrops that characterise this region. (Allow 30-40 minutes.)

Van der Stel's mine to Nababeep

Return to the R64 and drive straight across it onto the private (mine-owned) road, noting your kms. After 9,8 km turn right at the T-junction to enter Okiep (see opposite). On your left after slightly less than 1 km you will see the Okiep mine's historic stone chimney stack, and behind it the stone building housing the 'Cornish pump'. 100 m after passing the chimney, turn left past the hotel. After a further 2,3 km you reach a T-junction with the N7. Turn left onto the N7, noting your kms.

After 2,3 km on the N7, exit left for 'Okiep/Nababeep', turn right at the crossroads, and cross the bridge over the N7. You pass a huge granite outcrop on your left after 2,5 km, and roughly 7 km later you enter Nababeep, passing great slag heaps and mine workings on your right. After about 1 km you reach a fork with a large 'go slow' sign. Turn right here, then park on the right after 100 m, outside the town's museum. The museum building is almost completely hidden behind the old locomotive and coaches (see opposite).

After visiting the museum, retrace your route out of town, noting your kms as you pass the 'go slow' sign. 3,7 km later, turn right onto gravel for 'Kleinsee via Spektakel', and after a further 7,8 km turn right at the T-junction onto the R355 — noting your kms.

Sandhoogte and Spektakel Pass

The R355 winds down Sandhoogte (sand hill) into the valley of the Eselsfontein (donkey spring) River, passing huge granite outcrops and boulders that have been split apart by the daily extremes of temperature. After a while the scene changes to one of bushy koppies and scrubby valleys. After 17,6 km on the R355 you reach the start of the Spektakel Pass.

After roughly 20 km on the R355 there are fine views over the plains far below, and at 21,2 km, just after a right-hand bend, there is space to pull off the road at a good viewsite. 10 km after this, after descending from the pass, turn left for Komaggas, noting your kms as you turn. (The Spektakel mine and its slag heaps are visible further along the R355.)

The first few kilometres of this road to Komaggas may be corrugated, but the surface soon improves. The road passes between rugged hills and irrigated fields, with a scattering of modern and traditional homes, then begins to wind in among the mountains. 8,5 km from the turn-off you cross a river bed, then the road narrows and climbs steeply. Copper salts and lichens give a range of subtle, sombre shades to the rocks in this area.

Komaggas to the Messelpad

20 km from the turn-off the road passes through Komaggas (the name is believed to mean 'brown clay'). In front of the Komaggas Ko-op building the road forks — take the road on your right, and 5 km later turn left at the crossroads — noting your kms.

The road you are now on has a good surface, but was constructed without any deep road-cuttings and undulates over the hills. There are four farm gates along the route that need to be opened and closed. A sign alongside the first of the gates prohibits the removal of wood — an indication of its scarcity in these parts. After 26 km turn left at the crossroads (the road to the right leads to Hondeklipbaai, and straight leads to Soebatsfontein) — noting your kms.

VAN DER STEL'S JOURNEY

In an elegant coach drawn by six horses, Commander Simon van der Stel set out from the castle in Cape Town on an exploratory expedition to the Copper Mountains of the Nama people. The party took 57 days to reach its destination.

On arrival at the Copper Mountains, an apparently rich vein of copper ore was discovered almost immediately. The eventual return was disappointing, however, and smelting was difficult because of the shortage of firewood. Eventually the mine had to be abandoned. Copper is still mined nearby.

Cultivated fields near the Messelpad (masonry road).

Spring covers the Namaqualand veld with wildflowers.

A TOWN WITH A WILD PAST

Springbok is the largest town in Namaqualand, and serves as the commercial centre for a vast region. The town began its career as the small settlement of Springbokfontein on the site of a copper mine that began operating in the early 1850s. It gained a reputation as a rough mining town, and one of the first acts of the local magistrate was to order a set of stocks for the detention of prisoners. A prison was built in 1856 and from then on was usually full of local convicts — the mining town having attracted a population of tough adventurers, few of whom knew anything about mining. The town has outgrown this wild youth, but many relics from the old days are preserved in its museum, a former synagogue built in 1930.

You can now see the road rising ahead of you, as it climbs towards the summit of the Wildeperdehoek (wild horses corner) Pass. After 7,6 km you reach an inclined T-junction. Turn left here, and you begin the ascent of the pass 100 m after this.

This road has a good surface, but is steep and narrow — extremely narrow in places. As you climb you have a succession of grand views on your right over the plains and low hills of Namaqualand far below. Once over the summit of the pass, the road winds among hills, following the courses of several rivers. As you round bends you can glimpse ahead of you the dry-stone support walls that gave this road the name 'Messelpad' (masonry road).

Just over 9 km after beginning the ascent of the pass you can see, down in the river bed, the extensive stone ruins of the old Koringhuis outspan (see below).

The Messelpad eventually emerges from the hills and you find yourself in a gentler landscape with extensive cultivated fields. Continue on this road for some 25 km until you reach the tarred N7. Turn left onto the N7, and after 7,6 km turn left again — to reach Springbok after a further 3 km ●

AA Office AA House, 7 Martin Hammerschlag Way, Cape Town 8001 Tel. (021) 211550
Tourist Information Springbok Cafe, Voortrekker Street, Springbok 8240 Tel. (0251) 21321
SA Tourism Board Level 3, Golden Acre, Adderley Street, Cape Town 8001 Tel. (021) 216274

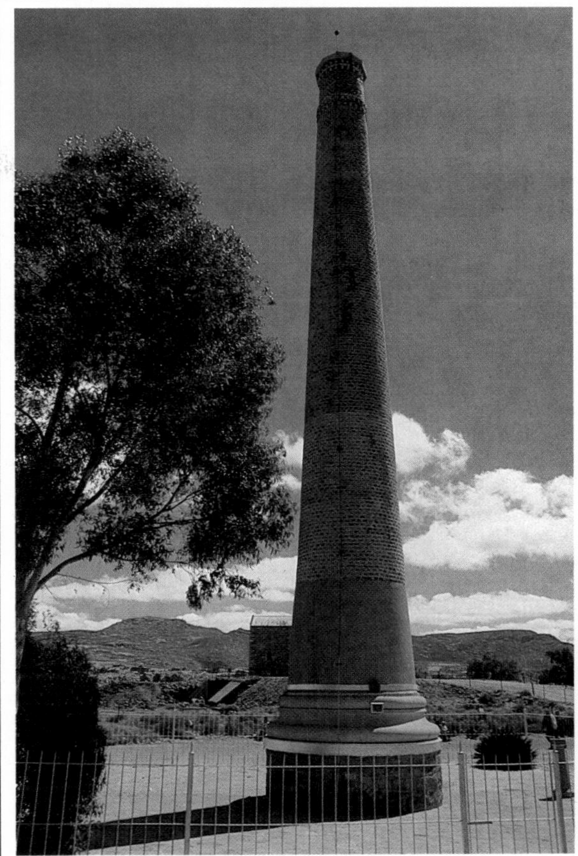

The historic chimney stack of the Okiep Mine.

MULE-POWERED RAILWAY TRAINS

The town of Okiep takes its name from a Khoikhoi word meaning 'large brackish place'. When the area was surveyed as a mine in 1856, there was just a single shaft, three metres deep. Within a few years it had grown into the most important mine in the region, worked largely by skilled Cornish miners.

When the railway was built to Port Nolloth, replacing the old Messelpad to Hondeklipbaai, it turned out that there was insufficient water to operate the steam engines, so teams of mules were used to pull the carriages. Eventually the water-supply problem was solved, and 'Clara', on display at Nababeep, is an example of the 'mountain type' locomotives that were put to work on this route.

The old stone pump-house at Okiep.

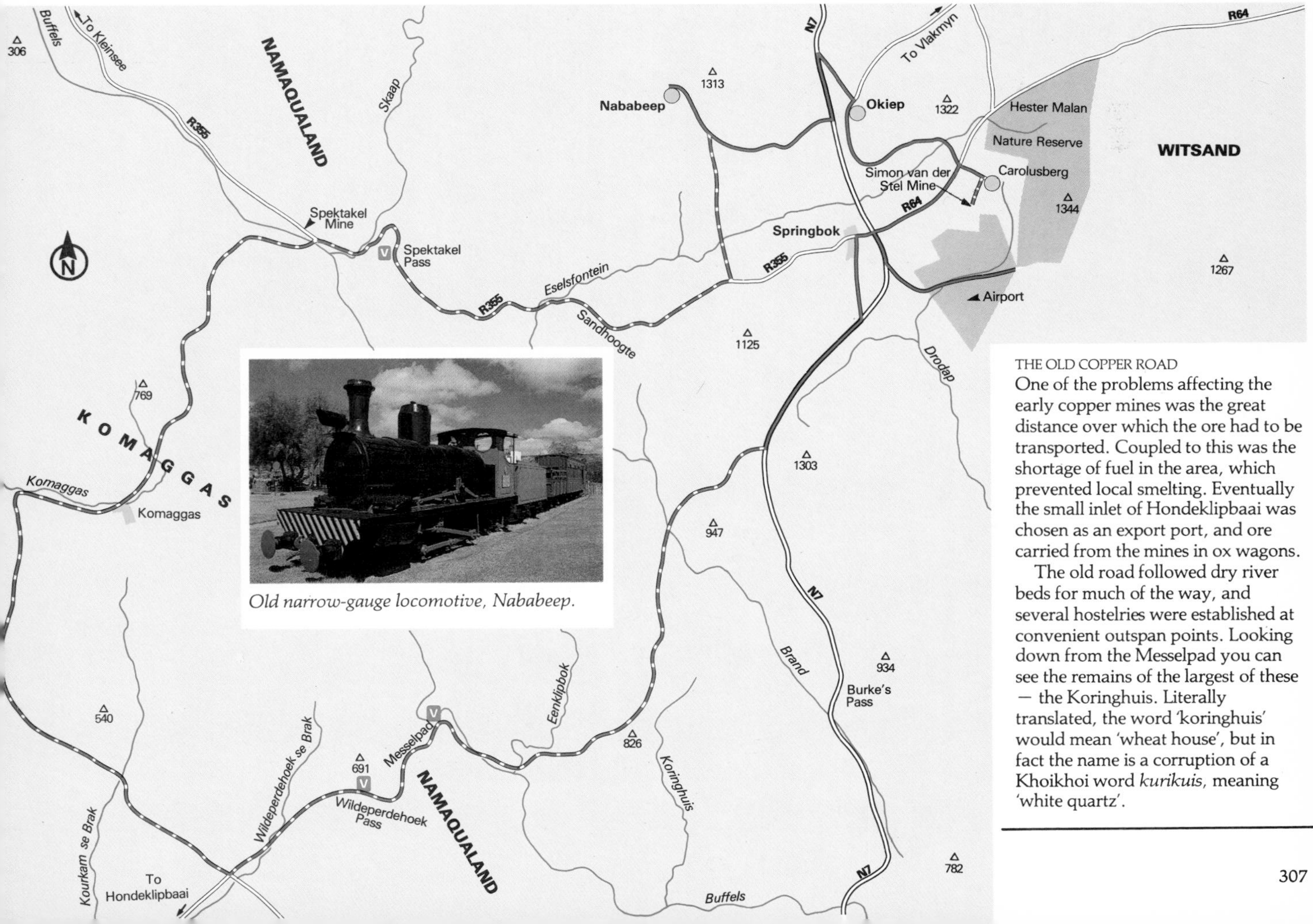

Old narrow-gauge locomotive, Nababeep.

THE OLD COPPER ROAD

One of the problems affecting the early copper mines was the great distance over which the ore had to be transported. Coupled to this was the shortage of fuel in the area, which prevented local smelting. Eventually the small inlet of Hondeklipbaai was chosen as an export port, and ore carried from the mines in ox wagons.

The old road followed dry river beds for much of the way, and several hostelries were established at convenient outspan points. Looking down from the Messelpad you can see the remains of the largest of these — the Koringhuis. Literally translated, the word 'koringhuis' would mean 'wheat house', but in fact the name is a corruption of a Khoikhoi word *kurikuis*, meaning 'white quartz'.

A sea of yellow Pentzia grandiflora *washes over the veld near Lambert's Bay.*

Where Nature paints the world with wildflowers

SWIRLING UP FROM the frozen South Atlantic, the Benguela Current chills a shore where the remains of dead ships loom ghost-like in the mist, and diamonds sparkle on lonely beaches. There is little lasting evaporation from these icy waters, and few winds to sweep the fragile clouds inland to the great plains of Namaqualand. This is a world of dry river-beds, threading their way through huge outcrops of granite that have been stained by the percolation of copper salts and glitter with fragments of quartz and mica. On the plains beneath the mountains sheep and goats range far in their search for grazing — across sandy, arid landscapes.

But if there has been rain, a miracle occurs with the coming of spring. Millions upon millions of brightly coloured flowers appear, seemingly from the very rocks, to spread their petals wide beneath the sun. Namaqualand is in flower.

It is said that more South Africans have visited Europe than have ever been to Namaqualand. But a visit to this wonderland during a good flowering season is an experience never forgotten.

The flower area — although not all of it can properly be called Namaqualand — stretches roughly from the Darling district in the south to the Orange River in the north, and inland to include Calvinia and Aggeneys. The region can be divided into many districts, each with its own character and mix of flower types.

Splendours of the Sandveld

In the south, one area that is particularly rich in flowers is the Sandveld, a 30 km-wide strip of low-lying sandy country running along the coast in the region of Lambert's Bay. The flora here consists mainly of semi-succulent scrub, the plants obtaining moisture from the mists that roll in from the sea. Here too you can see large patches of shimmering yellow grielum, or flat thorn, and wild flax *(Heliophila)* — the latter forming chains of azure lakes amidst the sands. A good route through this region leads from Clanwilliam to Lambert's Bay, then along the coast to Doringbaai and Strandfontein,

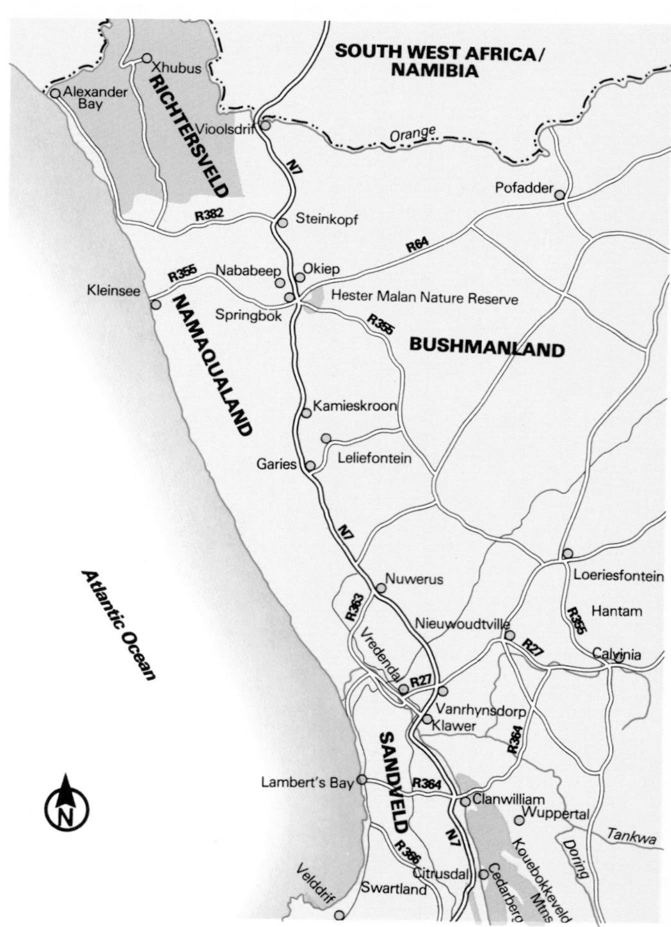

The flower-lined N7 near Steinkopf.

One of Namaqualand's kokerbome.

Ruschia extensa *forms brilliant mauve 'cushions' among the granite boulders.*

and back to Clanwilliam via Lutzville, Vredendal and Klawer. The section of this road that runs along the coast is sometimes in poor condition, but the flower displays at their best are splendid.

Inland from here, but still south of Namaqualand proper, lie the richly flowered landscapes of the Clanwilliam district and the Biedou Valley (see pages 300-1), and slightly further north there is the countryside around Nieuwoudtville (see pages 46-7). In these areas the various daisy species appear in great numbers and in a profusion of brilliant colours.

Kamiesberg and Springbok

North from here we enter the region properly called Namaqualand and the land rises to form the Kamiesberg range. The mountainsides support an evergreen fynbos flora, including Namaqualand's only protea species *(Protea sulphurea)*. Several rare wildflower varieties are to be found here, including the large-flowered, blazing orange *Gladiolus equitans*. The mission village Leliefontein (lily spring) takes its name from the *Androcymbium*, a ground-hugging plant with a deeply buried corm, whose white blossoms can be seen scattered thickly over the veld.

North of the Kamiesberg lies the boulder-mountain country around Springbok. The rainfall is higher here, and supports a greater variety of species. Springbok itself lies amid hills that are thickly clothed with blossoms.

Springbok is one of the best bases from which to take short flower-viewing trips. Alternatives are nearby Okiep or Nababeep — all three towns offer accommodation. The day-drive from Springbok described on pages 306-7 will take you past many excellent displays in a good season, in addition to providing outstanding panoramas from the Spektakel Pass and the Messelpad.

Dimorphotheca sinuata *(pink-orange) and* Ursinia speciosa *(yellow-orange).*

North of Springbok, and especially beyond Steinkopf, the quantity of wildflowers diminishes. But taking their place there are strange plants such as the *Pachypodium namaquanum*, or 'halfmens' (half man). The plant does resemble a man when seen from a distance or in poor light, and it is the subject of many legends among the Nama. It has a single trunk, swollen towards the base, and the head, which is always turned towards the north, is crowned by leaves that are shed during the scorching summer months. The tubular flowers are a delicate yellow tipped with red. Home for many of these 'halfmense' is the Richtersveld, stretching north from Steinkopf to the Orange River, and lying west of the N7 from the Cape to South West Africa/Namibia. This is an extremely arid region where only succulents can survive.

Desert displays surprise the traveller

East of the N7, sandy flats stretch away to Pofadder, and south from here as far as Loeriesfontein. The wildflower show is restricted in these regions by the low rainfall, but fine displays are occasionally encountered. Sometimes the fortunate traveller is greeted by huge expanses of the pastel-shaded *Arctotis canescens*, or may see the scorched veld completely blanketed in the blue flowers of the low-growing Karoo violet *(Aptosimum)*.

For anyone planning a springtime trip through the flower country, several practical tips may prove valuable. One is to book your accommodation early. Another is to find out in advance where the rains have been good and where fine displays are expected. (For sources of information, see the information panels on pages 68-9 and 306-7.) A third point to keep in mind is that many of the flowering species present their petals to the sun — sometimes, especially when you are driving northwards, you must remember to stop and look behind you to see the flowers at their best ●

The quintessential Namaqualand vista — a carpet of flowers stretches into the distance as far as the eye can see.

Following the Orange River to the 'Place of Great Noise'

Augrabies is a place of striking contrast. In a land of little rain the surging waters of the Orange River create a ribbon of life, then thunder over one of the world's mightiest waterfalls. This drive leads from Upington to the Augrabies Falls National Park, passing through Keimoes and Kakamas. All but a few kilometres of the route is tarred.

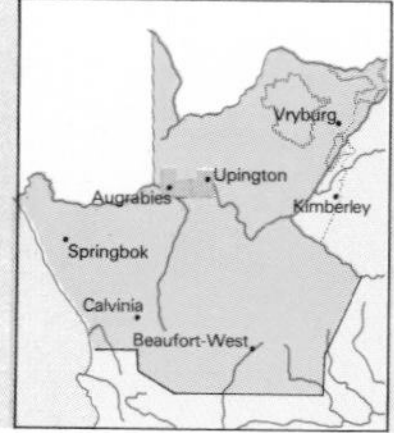

Upington
Kanoneiland
Keimoes
Kakamas
Augrabies Falls National Park
250 — 270 km

OUR FIRST STOP of the day is Upington's famous avenue of palms at the Eiland (island) holiday resort. To get there, drive south-west along Schröder Street, passing on your left the old mission complex that now houses the town's museum. Turn left at the stop sign, noting your kms. After some 200 m you pass on your left an irrigation canal and a bakkiespomp (bucket pump).

Cross a bridge over the northern channel of the Orange River and after 800 m turn left at the 'Research Centre' sign. Turn left again immediately to reach the entrance to the resort area (a small entrance fee may be charged at weekends and during holiday seasons). The main avenue through the resort is said to be the longest palm avenue in the world, and has been declared a national monument.

When you drive out of the resort area, turn left and note your kms. You cross the southern arm of the Orange, and at 1,2 km turn right onto the tarred R359 for Louisvale. The road leads after a short distance through irrigated fields and vineyards — this is the northernmost wine-making region of the Cape. After a little over 14 km you pass through the small farming settlement of Louisvale.

26,9 km after leaving the resort, turn right, staying on the tar. (The road ahead leads to Neilersdrif, and the surface changes to gravel.) You now pass on your left a Voortrekker centenary monument and a Roman Catholic mission, then cross the 400 m single-lane Eendragbrug (unity bridge) to Kanoneiland (see opposite). As you cross the bridge you can see the river tumbling over a prominent weir on your right.

Kanoneiland to Augrabies

At 28 km you reach a road on your left that leads to the village on the island. Unless you wish to call in at the village, drive on past this turn-off, crossing the Manie Conradie Bridge over the northern arm of the river and then two sets of railway lines. When you reach the T-junction with the R27, turn left for Keimoes — which you reach after a further 13 km.

As you enter Keimoes, turn right into Hoofstraat. On your left you pass a bakkiespomp at work in an irrigation canal, and on the opposite side of the road from this, just a few metres back, you can see the Dutch Reformed Mission Church that dates from 1889.

Continue along Hoofstraat, which becomes the R64 to Springbok. Roughly 5 km from Keimoes you pass a road on your right that leads to the Kalahari Gemsbok National Park. After this the road moves away from the river, the irrigated fields are left behind, and the country takes on a desolate appearance.

About 33 km from Keimoes the road draws close to the river again, as you approach Kakamas. Watch for a small sign on your right to 'The German War Graves 1914-18' (a few hundred metres before you pass a small cemetery set back from the road on your left). To visit the war graves and a monument commemorating the 1915 Battle of Kakamas, follow this sign onto a narrow gravel road and drive straight, crossing the cattle grid and following the main track. The monument soon becomes visible ahead of you and to your right, and you reach it after 1 km on the gravel road. There is a good view over the Kakamas Valley from the top of the hill.

Return to the tarred R64 and turn right, noting your kms. After 700 m you pass a road on your right that leads to South West Africa/Namibia and the Kalahari Gemsbok National Park. Shortly after this you cross a bridge over the Orange River and enter Kakamas (see opposite). 2,9 km after re-joining the tar you come to a crossroads. Turn left here to see, in the course of roughly 2,5 km, a number of the old-fashioned bakkiespompe still at work supplying the irrigation canals — making a picturesque scene.

Return to the crossroads and turn left to continue your journey on the R64/R359, noting your kms as you turn. After 8,2 km turn right on the R359. 4,5 km along this road you pass the small town of Marchand on your right. Here and there you will see some of the sloping cement 'floors' that are common in this region. They are used for drying fruit in the sun — mainly sultanas and raisins.

9,1 km beyond the turn-off into Marchand you pass the small Augrabies village on your right. Roughly 11 km later, turn right, and after a further 4,6 km, in the course of which you cross one of the channels of the Orange, you reach the entrance to the Augrabies Falls National Park (small entrance fee; no animals and no motor cycles allowed).

Augrabies Falls National Park

Close to the entrance there is an information centre where you can obtain a free booklet on the park. There is also a shop that sells a few tinned goods, firewood, refreshments, wine and beer — and petrol can be obtained.

There is a restaurant next to the shop, and picnic places nearby — set among trees along one of the river's channels. There are braai sites here, with water and toilets. (No drinking water is available elsewhere in the park.) There are also two swimming pools here, and a play pool for younger children.

There are several roads in the park leading to out-of-the-way corners (see pages 312-3). Two places worth visiting are Ararat and Oranjekom, and the road to both passes a 1 km side-road that leads to the base of the bare Moon Rock. At Ararat there are fine views up the rugged gorge, but there is little shade. At Oranjekom there is a roofed shelter with cement tables and benches — able to accommodate 30 to 40 picnickers — and there are also toilets. From

Bakkiespomp on an irrigation canal at Keimoes.

CHRISTIAAN SCHRÖDER'S LEGACY

One of the main crossing points on the Orange River became known to the early European explorers as Olyvenhoutsdrift (olive wood drift), and a missionary, Christiaan Schröder, established a mission station here in 1871. In 1884 the name of the small settlement that had grown around the mission was changed to Upington, in honour of Sir Thomas Upington, the new Prime Minister of the Cape Colony.

One year before the name change, the first of an intricate system of irrigation canals had been constructed, and Upington now serves as the centre of a rich farming district — thanks to the abundant waters of the Orange. Fruit, vegetables, cotton and wine are produced here.

The shady avenue of palms on Kanoneiland.

Augrabies — one of the world's most awesome waterfalls when in flood.

The Orange River gorge cuts through the Augrabies Falls National Park.

A BATTLE IN THE DESERT

World War I began in August 1914, and in September the government of the Union of South Africa decided to invade what was then German South West Africa. An invasion force was assembled near Upington, with 6 000 men encamped south of Kakamas.

The German commander, Major Francke, decided to attack rather than wait to be invaded. At that time the Orange River was crossed by means of two ponts which were heavily guarded by the South African forces. These ponts were the target of the leader of the German expedition, Major Ritter.

Shortly after dawn on 4 Feburary 1915, four German field guns opened fire, at a range of over 1 km, from a position near the site of the present monument. The rest of Ritter's forces, who had advanced closer to the river, opened fire on the troops guarding the ponts. The battle lasted six hours — the Germans being forced eventually to withdraw, with a loss of seven lives.

The simple monument was erected in 1960 by the Volksbund Deutschen Kriegs-gräberfürsorge, and the remains of the six soldiers whose graves could be found were re-interred here.

KANONEILAND

This is probably the best known of the many islands in the Orange River, and it has been occupied as an agricultural settlement since 1926. The island received its name during the Second Northern Border War of 1878-9, fought between the Cape Colony forces and the Koranna, led by Klaas Pofadder.

It is thought that the island takes its name from a cannon that Pofadder and his men constructed here from a hollowed-out aloe stem. This was loaded with gunpowder and stones, and pointed at the Cape Colony forces. When fired, the cannon exploded, killing several Koranna men.

THE GOLDEN PEACH FROM KAKAMAS

For many years experts at the Elsenburg Agricultural College near Stellenbosch struggled to find a variety of peach that would be suitable for canning — a potential fortune in fruit lay rotting on the ground unable to be preserved.

Eventually a former Elsenburg student, A D Collins, found a promising peach tree near Kakamas. Evidently a natural mutation — the peach proved to have all the qualities needed for successful canning. The newly discovered variety was carefully propagated, and from a single tree has come 75 per cent of all the peach trees now supplying South Africa's giant canning industry.

The mighty Orange River brings life to the desert near Kakamas.

Oranjekom there are wide views over the river 'kom' (basin), between towering cliffs.

Since the re-introduction of black rhino on the north bank, visitors are no longer permitted to cross the suspension bridge above the falls, but you are allowed to walk onto the bridge to obtain a good 'midstream' view.

Augrabies to Upington

Retrace your outgoing route as far as Keimoes, but when you reach the traffic lights in Keimoes, continue straight ahead instead of turning left towards Upington — noting your kms at the lights. After 900 m the road surface changes to gravel, and at 1,5 km you cross a single-lane bridge. At 2,4 km turn right for the Keimoes Nature Reserve.

Drive slowly from here, as the road is bumpy and becomes steep as it approaches Tierberg (tiger or leopard mountain). From the summit of Tierberg there are superb views over Keimoes and the irrigated lands nearby — the great expanse of green being in sharp contrast with the landscape near the Augrabies Falls, where the river is channelled into a rocky ravine.

Return from Tierberg to the traffic lights in Keimoes, and turn right. Stay on this main road (R27) the whole way to Upington, passing on your right the road on which you entered from Kanoneiland ●

Upington Tourist Bureau Civic Centre, Market Square, Upington 8800 Tel. (0541) 6911 ext. 2151
Tourist Officer, Augrabies Falls National Park Private Bag 1, Augrabies 8874 Tel. (0020) ask for Augrabies Falls 4.

The Orange River below the falls.

A thundering waterfall in a dry, desert landscape

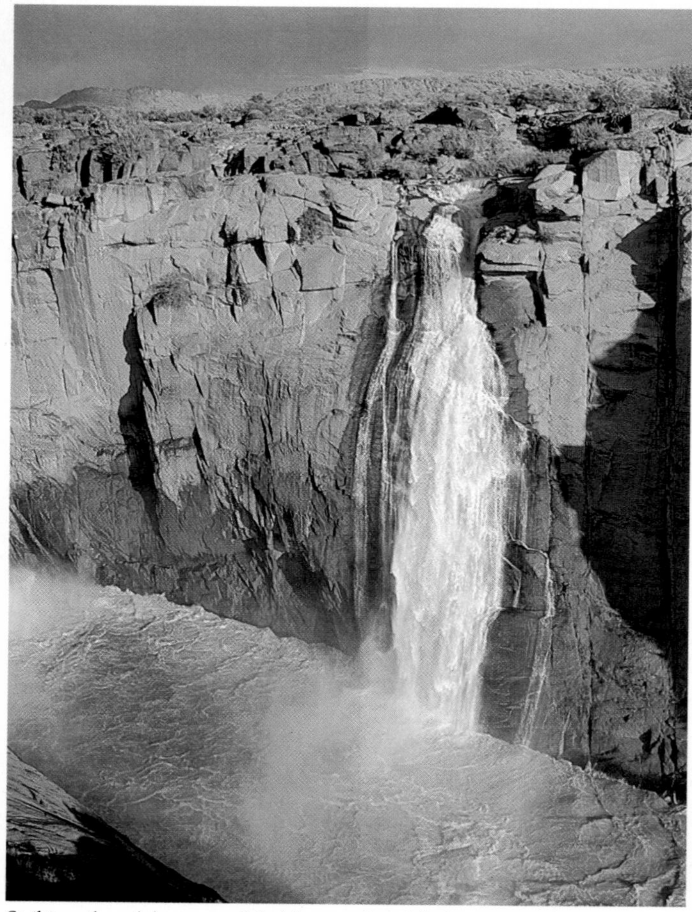
Striking, though less powerful, this secondary fall plunges into the gorge.

A bungalow in the park.

KNOWN TO THE wandering Khoikhoi as Aukoerebis (place of great noise), the Augrabies Falls thunder over a great granite slash in the barren bushveld of the northern Cape. Here the tumbling waters of the Orange River go mad in a series of deep ravines and dangerous, dizzying cliffs.

The first white man to see the falls was a Swedish-born soldier named Hendrik Wikar. Wikar deserted his post at the Cape in 1775 to escape an accumulation of gambling debts, and for four years he wandered through the uncharted country now known as the northern Cape describing in a journal, and sometimes also mapping, many of the places that he visited. Three years after leaving the Cape, he came to the verge of this immense granite gorge, with the full mass of the Orange River surging down over the ancient rocks.

Today visitors can share in Wikar's experience by viewing the falls from various observation points along the edge of the gorge. They may also view the river from a suspension footbridge that links the southern bank to the northern, just a short distance above the falls. From these sites one can see how the river, in the course of many million years, has worn through the granite-gneiss base-rock to form a 250 metre deep and 15 km long chasm. This erosion of granite by water is considered by many geologists to be the finest example of its kind in the world.

Contrasting scenery

The Augrabies Falls National Park covers a large area of land on both banks of the river, completely surrounding the falls. One of the most striking aspects of the park is the contrast in its scenery. The banks of the river are painted bright green by the lush vegetation, yet only a few metres away there is little but sand and rock, a virtual desert stretching away to the horizon. The falls themselves (see photograph, pages 304-5) are of course the centrepiece, mighty and harshly beautiful, with the river tumbling 65 metres over the edge of a massive granite barrier — into a mysterious pool, 92 metres across and believed to be 130 metres deep.

These falls are regarded as one of the six greatest waterfalls in the world. When the Orange River is in flood, up to 405 million litres of water crash over the granite shelf every minute in 19 separate falls. Best known of the secondary falls is the Bridal Veil Fall, which becomes part of the main falls when the river is in flood. The gorge at this time is shrouded in mist and the noise of the water is deafening.

The deep pool into which the falls plunge is surrounded by sheer cliffs, and is reputed to contain a fortune in diamonds — washed down the river and trapped in the gravel at the bottom. The pool is also claimed to be the home of a 'river monster', but sightings of this creature can perhaps be attributed to shoals of giant barbel, which grow to a length of two metres. During a severe drought in the 1930s, a group of thirsty cattle wandered up the dry river bed to the edge of the pool in search of water. A strong wind blew them into the pool and they were never seen again — which helped to convince many local people that a monster of some kind lurks in the depths.

Augrabies Falls National Park is centred on Klaas Island, just to the west of the main falls. Here there is a caravan park with picnic sites and swimming pools, several bungalows that can be hired, and also an information centre, a shop and a restaurant. In front of the restaurant there is a succulent garden containing roughly 100 species of aloe.

Walks and drives

From here there are a number of walks and drives that you can take to outlying viewpoints (see pages 310-11). One of the most popular walks is along the 2,5 km path leading to the Arrow Head viewsite. From here you can look out over the rapids that career along the bottom of the gorge far below. For the more energetic there is the Klipspringer Hiking Trail which runs for 26 km along the southern bank of the river. This is a three-day hike and walkers stay overnight in huts along the route. The trail passes Ararat, a granite rock that offers a magnificent view along the gorge, and also Moon

Sunset washes the grey boulders of the Orange River chasm with a pink hue.

Rock, which provides panoramic views over the whole park.

Walking through the park, you will discover that there is a far richer variety of animal and plant life than one would expect in such a barren landscape. Camel-thorn trees *(Acacia erioloba)* and kokerbome *(Aloe dichotoma)* are the most prominent plants, while the fauna includes the klipspringer, springbok, a number of smaller mammals and 150 bird species. The park is particularly rich in reptiles. At the edge of the gorge you can often see the beautifully coloured red-tailed rock lizard *(Platysaurus capensis)* and various geckos and agamas. In the hot summer months, you will frequently see snakes basking on the rocks — the Cape cobra *(Naja nivea)*, the spitting cobra *(Naja mossambica mossambica)*, or the ubiquitous puff-adder *(Bitis arietans arietans)*.

Springbok are easily seen on the bare rocks of the Augrabies National Park.

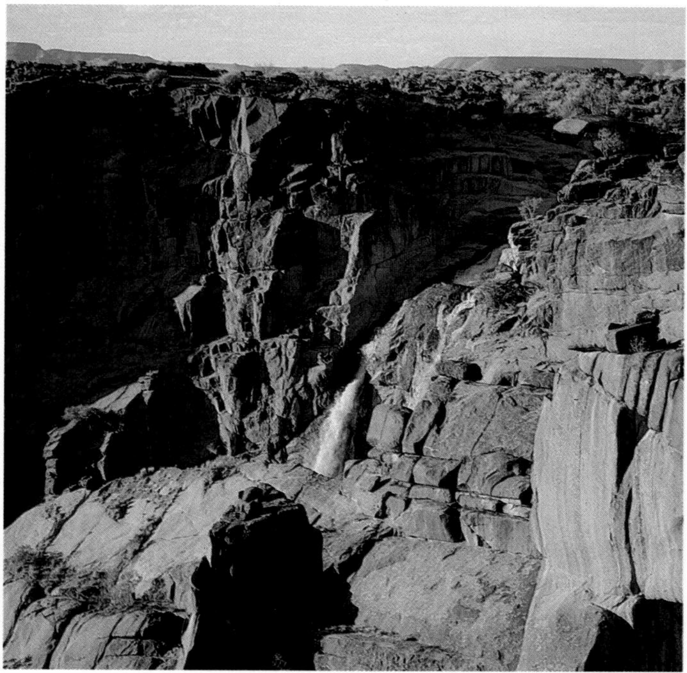

Granite rock, shaped over millenia by rushing water and extreme temperatures.

Treacherous granite walls

As a safety measure, chest-high fences have been erected at most of the popular observation points, but there will always be over-eager tourists who tempt fate by climbing over the fence for a slightly closer look. Since the proclamation of the park in 1966, some twenty people have died after losing their balance on the edge of the gorge and slipping down its steep erosion-polished granite walls.

To slip over the edge spells almost certain death, but occasionally miracles do happen. In 1979 a Scandinavian visitor lost his footing and slid the whole way down the rock face. The friction was so great that his clothes were ripped from his body. He suffered lacerations and broken bones, but was still able to clamber out of the river onto a rock. From this point he was saved by park wardens. Even his wallet containing R400 was found on a ledge.

The open nature of the countryside in the park, and the clear light, offer rich opportunities to the photographer, and eager cameramen have tried many stunts to capture the falls from a new angle. One of the first of these photographic adventurers was an acrobat named Lulu Farini, who toured the region with his stepfather Guillermo. He photographed the falls from many angles, but could find no way of capturing the main fall from the bottom of the gorge. Eventually he set his sights on an outcrop of rock about 100 metres down the sheer rock face — a point that could be reached only with ropes. After joining some kudu-hide ox-straps to the rope they had, the two men lowered the camera equipment, then climbed over the edge. From the outcrop below, Lulu made two exposures of the falls, before climbing back 'hand over hand, quicker than we had come down, for we were now sure of the rope's strength'.

Year-round attractions

The park can be visited at any time of year, and each season has its own particular attractions. Spring and autumn are the best seasons for hiking, as the temperatures in summer and winter are too extreme for comfort. The falls, however, are at their most spectacular in summer, between October and January, when the greatest flood of water rushes down from the highlands of Lesotho and the eastern Cape. (If you are planning to photograph the falls, note that they are best captured in the afternoon when the sunlight catches them — often creating a bright rainbow in the spray.)

Should you wish to book for the Klipspringer Hiking Trail, for use of a caravan site or camping site, or for one of the small number of bungalows that can be hired by the public, contact the Chief Director, National Parks Board, Box 787, Pretoria 0001 Tel. (012) 441191/98. If a booking is needed within 12 days, you can contact the Tourist Officer at the park: Private Bag 1, Augrabies 8874 Tel. 0020 ask for Augrabies Falls 4 ●

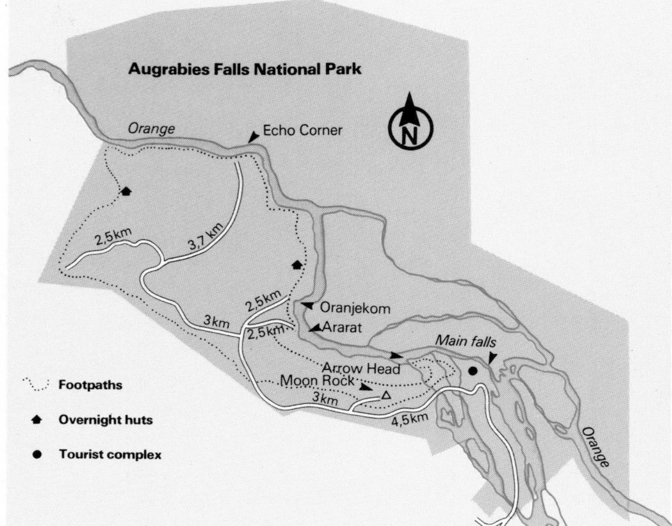

'Moon Rock' offers this fine view across the sun-baked hills of the park.

A pride of lions keep a watchful eye on a lone eland in a sandy stretch of the Kalahari Gemsbok National Park.

A wealth of wildlife in a world with little water

THE TRAVELLER IS greeted by an extraordinarily stark, sunburned landscape. Stretching away to a shimmering horizon are great waves of red sand, dotted here and there with camelthorn trees. The climate ranges from dry to very dry, and periods of extreme drought can be measured by the carcasses in the dry river beds. Yet there is abundant life in the harsh environment of the Kalahari — a primeval vitality that comes as a surprise amidst the seemingly inhospitable surroundings. For those who wish to see and feel an unspoilt Africa, this is perhaps the most rewarding place to visit. Here it is still possible to experience the wild excitement of a lion-kill, or to witness the lightning dash of a hunting cheetah — exactly as if mankind had never appeared on the scene.

A reserve between two rivers

The Kalahari Gemsbok National Park covers almost 1 000 000 ha of rugged desert country, sandwiched between South West Africa/Namibia in the west and Botswana in the east. An even larger game park adjoins it in Botswana, and animals roam freely between the two reserves — which together form the largest game park in the world.

The boundaries of the South African park are marked by the watercourses of two rivers — in the west the Auob ('bitter tasting' in the language of the San people) and in the east the Nossob ('big water'). The rivers rarely flow, but more than 40 boreholes have been sunk along the river beds, at intervals of several kilometres, and these make a small supply of water available to the game. The two principal routes in the park follow the courses of these rivers, and are linked by a road that switchbacks its way over the dunes that lie between them. (The roads in the park are untarred, but are usually in fairly good condition.)

Evocative names

Each borehole, with its attendant wind-pump, has an individual and often evocative name, ranging from 'Groot Skrij' and 'Kijkij' to the unexpected 'Montrose', and the no-doubt heartfelt 'Lekkerwater' (lovely water). The waterholes offer excellent vantage points for game viewing, especially in the early mornings and the late afternoons. It is here that cheetah, leopard and lion stalk the antelope that are attracted to the precious water, and few visitors leave the park without sighting one or more of the 'big cats'. Vultures, hyenas and black-backed jackals then clean the carcasses that the large predators leave behind — until a pair of horns and a few bones are all that remain of a once proud antelope.

Camouflage in the Kalahari

There are more than 10 000 springbok in the park, and visitors may be treated to the amazing sight of enormous herds of these agile animals flowing effortlessly over the dunes. Also to be seen are smaller herds of the park's namesake, the gemsbok, with their fearsome, rapier-like horns. Other animals commonly seen are blue wildebeest, eland (large numbers of which occasionally migrate across the park), kudu, red hartebeest, ostrich, bat-eared fox, silver fox and porcupine. Some 170 bird species have been recorded in the park. In addition to the ostriches, you are likely to see kori bustards, secretary birds, martial eagles, bateleur eagles, and various owls.

The most prominent trees in the park are the umbrella-shaped camel-

Sparse vegetation clings to the side of a sand dune.

Springbok drink at one of the few waterholes in the park.

Ostriches float across the harsh horizon of the Kalahari.

thorns (*Acacia erioloba*) — often supporting the huge nests of social weaver birds. The camelthorns provide a small amount of welcome shade, and their seed-pods are a valuable source of food for many species.

Adapt or die

The animals that live in the park have all had to adapt in one way or another to an almost waterless world. There are roughly 250 lion in the park, which are able to live for years without water, drawing moisture from the animals they kill. Gemsbok and other desert antelope can survive without water as long as tsamma melons and wild cucumbers are available. There are no elephants, giraffe or zebra in the park; they have not been able to adapt to the extremely dry conditions.

A lot of game can be spotted as you travel between the three rest-camps in the park. (Allow for one or two nights at each camp, if possible.) All the camps have fully equipped cottages and pleasant, albeit sandy camping sites. You can buy basic, non-perishable provisions at all three camps, including firewood and liquor, but no fresh produce or camera film is available. The camps have filling stations for petrol and diesel, but no repair facilities.

The largest of the three camps is Twee Rivieren (two rivers), situated at the southern entrance gate, where the Auob and the Nossob meet. This is also the administrative headquarters of the park. This is the only camp that stocks frozen meat, and it also provides simple meals in a 'lapa'. The smallest of the camps is Mata Mata (the very pleasant place), which lies on the Auob River at the entrance to the park on the South West African/ Namibian border.

Guidelines for visitors

In the northeastern area of the park is the Nossob camp. There is an interesting information centre here, and this is regarded as the best camp to head for if you wish to see lions.

The park is open throughout the year, but visitors are advised to avoid the months of December, January and February, because of the extreme heat during the summer. (And note that winter nights can be very cold, with the temperature often falling below freezing point.) There are several access roads leading to the park, all involving fairly long drives on sandy, untarred surfaces. One route leads from Kuruman, another from Upington, and several roads in South West Africa/Namibia converge on the entrance at Mata Mata.

Visitors to the park are advised to start a course of anti-malaria tablets before departure, and when driving to and through the park, always carry a plentiful supply of water. For further information, and for applications for accommodation or for camping sites, write to: The Chief Director, National Parks Board, P O Box 787, Pretoria 0001; or telephone (012) 441191/98

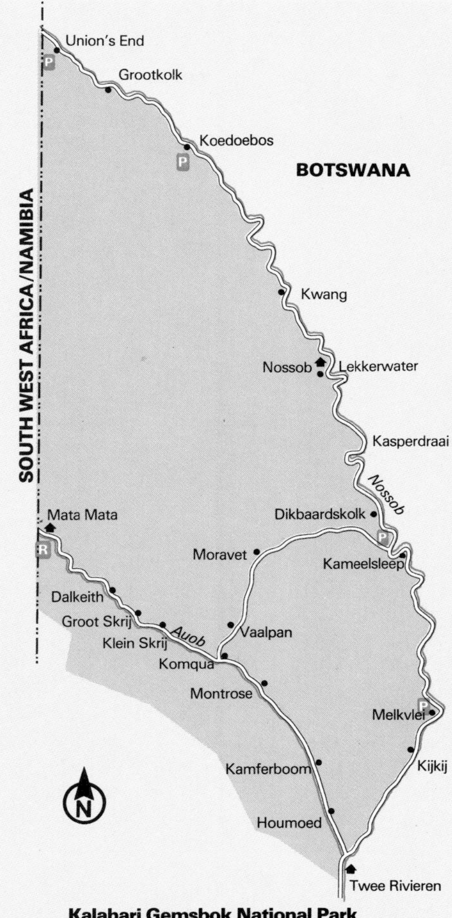

Kalahari Gemsbok National Park

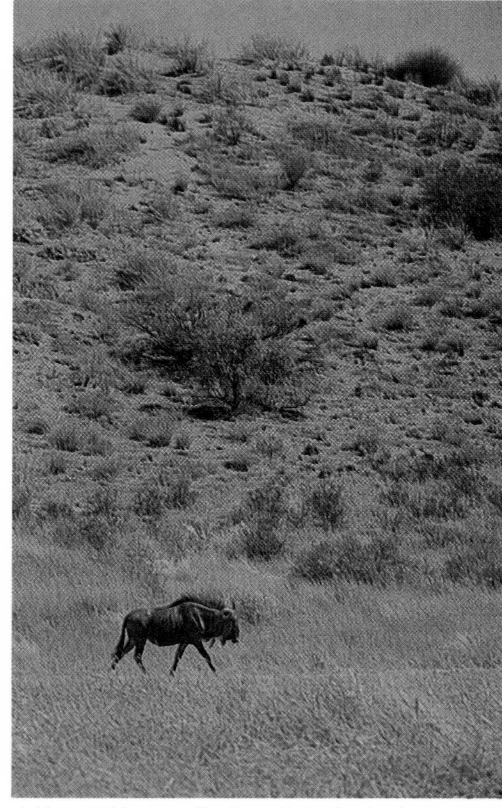

A blue wildebeest walks through the dry landscape.

Iron lace fronts the De Beers office in Stockdale Street; one of the many evocative buildings in the city.

Take a tram ride in the world's diamond capital

WITHOUT THE enthusiastic digging of an African cook — whose name is remembered only as 'Damon' — Kimberley might never have existed. It was Damon who first brought to light in July 1871 the riches that lay beneath a small hill known as 'Colesberg Koppie': three precious diamonds, the tip of an iceberg of glittering stones that within a few years were to be dug out of the biggest man-made hole in the world.

Today the Big Hole, as the mine is known, together with the restored diamond town nearby, forms the *Kimberley Mine Museum* **(1)**.

The best way to travel to the museum is by electric tram from the imposing *City Hall* **(2)**. Kimberley — known at first as 'New Rush' and later named after a British Colonial Secretary — was the first town in South Africa to have electric street-lighting (1882) and electric trams. The vehicle now in use dates from about 1910.

The museum is dominated by the great mine headgear, erected in 1892 and used until the mine closed in 1914. Nearby is 'Olive', an old locomotive once used to transport diamondiferous concentrates to the recovery plant, and a reconstruction of river-diggings, including the old-fashioned hoist, washing-table and sorting-table.

Highlight of the museum is the Big Hole itself — and at the entrance to the viewing platform are three fully-laden 'cocopans' representing the volume of diamonds (some 14,5 million carats) recovered from the mine. The Big Hole occupies 15,4 ha and has a mean diameter of 457 m. It was worked as an open-cast mine to a depth of 366 m, after which shafts and tunnels carried the depth a further 1 098 m. Water now fills the Big Hole to a level of some 260 m from the surface.

The De Beers Company, which eventually acquired control of the mine, took its name from the De Beer brothers, owners of the farm Vooruitzicht on which the diamond 'pipe' was discovered.

The old town

Not far from the Big Hole is a re-creation of a Kimberley Street during the diamond boom. Fronting the street, with its ornate cast-iron lamp standards, are the *St Martini Lutheran Church* of 1875, still with its original fittings and pews, and Kimberley's oldest house — a prefabricated structure consisting of little more than a front parlour and bedroom. To the many diggers living in tents and wagons in 1877, when the house was erected, it must have seemed the height of luxury. A diamond-buyer's office is furnished with a desk that once belonged to Sir Alfred Beit, one of the founding directors of De Beers. Among the framed shares and photographs on the wall is a diagram of a section through the Kimberley Mine as it was during the height of digging in 1890.

Of particular interest is the *Digger's Rest*, one of the 128 pubs that opened for business in the early days of the brawling mining camp. Next door is the original *Boxing Academy* run by Barney Barnato, who started his career on the diamond fields selling cigars and went on to become one of the world's richest men.

The nearby 'ballroom', a large iron building erected in 1901, contains a display of ladies' evening gowns of the period.

At the head of the street is *Transport Hall*, containing an earlier, steam-powered version of the present Kimberley tram and a home-made tricycle, powered by pedal and sail, on which a determined digger made his way from Plettenberg Bay to the diamond fields in about 1880.

Among motor vehicles on display is Kimberley's first car, a *Panhard et Levassor* of 1901 purchased for the General Manager of De Beers, and a 1906 Columbia Electric Victoria, which could run for only 13 km before its three 12-volt batteries needed recharging. A 1926 Chevrolet, converted for use as a hearse by the Jewish community, travelled only 2 900 km. Across the street is a very different form of conveyance: a specially-built Pullman railway carriage imported for the De Beers directors. Rhodes was among those who used this luxurious carriage, equipped with bathroom (rare on carriages of the time) and wine store.

Reconstructed shops, including a pawnbroker's, which provided an essential service in the uncertain early years of the diggings, form an arcade around an ornate cast-iron bandstand, with a restaurant nearby, close to a reconstruction of the original De Beer homestead.

The Mine Museum is by no means the only attraction in the Diamond City. In Atlas Road the *Alexander McGregor Museum* **(3)**, housed in a magnificent late-Victorian building used by Rhodes as his 'headquarters' during the siege, records the development of Kimberley and its numerous volunteer regiments. Among the exhibits is the Victoria Cross won at Delville Wood during World War 1 by Private W F Faulds of Kimberley Company of the 1st SA Infantry Brigade. Rhodes's rooms have been restored to record his occupancy during the siege, with life-like figures

Religion and commerce mix at the Mining Museum adjacent to the Big Hole.

Inside the recreated Digger's Rest.

Fountain tribute to the diggers.

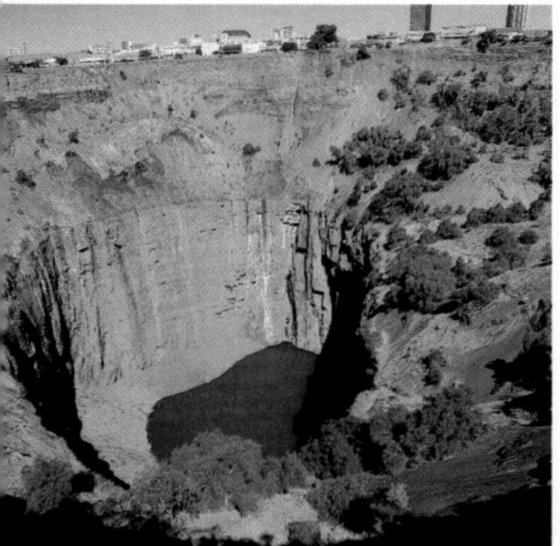

Kimberley's famous Big Hole.

re-creating his historic meeting with the leader of the relieving force, General French. Also in the museum is the Hall of Religions, detailing Kimberley's multi-ethnic origins.

There is a tea garden at the museum, and a short walk leads to the adjoining *Duggan-Cronin Gallery*, housed in The Lodge, erected in 1889, which records in photographs and artefacts the culture and lifestyles of the major indigenous peoples of southern Africa.

In Chapel Street the 'old' *McGregor Memorial Museum* **(4)** details southern Africa's natural history, geology and prehistory; while in Jan Smuts Road, the *William Humphreys Art Gallery* **(5)** with its statue of Queen Victoria outside, houses the town's art collection. Close by is the Ernest Oppenheimer Memorial Garden, with a striking fountain honouring the early diggers. In Loch Road *The Bungalow* **(6)**, which once belonged to a son of C D Rudd, Rhodes's great friend and business partner, is a good example of a typical mining magnate's home of the late 19th century. Another elegant residence is *Dunluce* **(7)**, in Lodge Road, built for a diamond-buyer in 1897 and still containing some of its original furnishings — including a coal scuttle damaged when a Boer shell penetrated the breakfast room during the siege. Arrangements to visit The Bungalow and Dunluce should be made at the McGregor Museum in Chapel Street.

One of South Africa's best-known monuments is the *Honoured Dead Memorial* **(8)**, designed by Sir Herbert Baker on the lines of a Greek tomb at Agrigentum in Sicily, which

Dunluce — hit by a Boer shell during the siege of Kimberley in 1899.

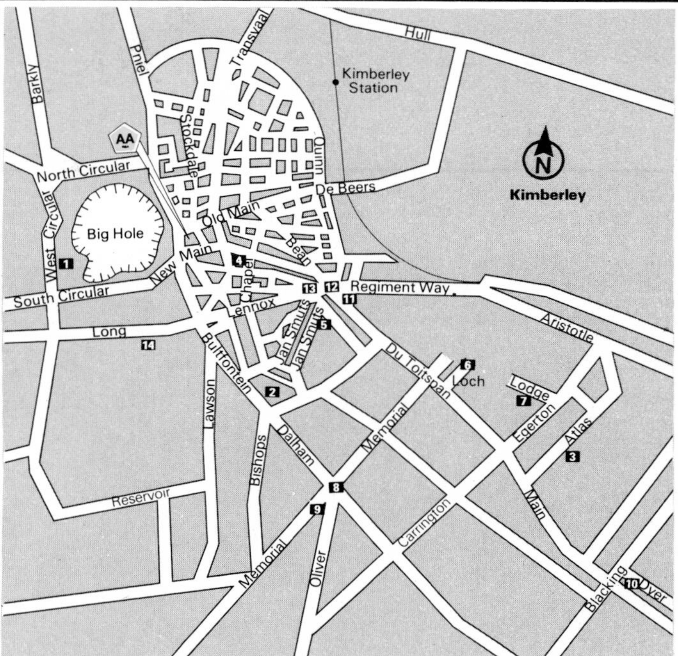

commemorates those who died during the siege. The memorial includes Long Cecil, built in the De Beers' Workshops in 24 days during the siege by men who had no previous experience of ordnance construction. The 4,1 inch rifled breech-loader was able to fling its shells 7,3 km.

Near the Honoured Dead Memorial, between Memorial Road and Oliver Street, is the *MOTH Garden of Remembrance* **(9)**, a tranquil garden that houses a Stuart light tank of World War 2 vintage, and a six-inch howitzer of 1917.

City of churches

Among Kimberley's churches is a modest iron structure **(10)** at the corner of Dyer and Blacking streets in Beaconsfield. This mother church of the Seventh Day Adventists in South Africa was founded in 1885 when a local farmer, Pieter Wessels, left the Dutch Reformed Church after a conflict over which day of the week should be 'kept holy'. *St Cyprian's Anglican Cathedral* **(11)** in Du Toitspan Road contains many interesting memorials, as well as flags — or colours — of diamond fields' regiments. The statue in the grounds, of Sister Henrietta Stockdale, is believed to be the world's only portrait statue of a nun in her habit. Sister Henrietta established professional nursing in South Africa at Kimberley's hospital just across the road.

In the town which he described as his 'foster-mother', Cecil Rhodes is honoured by a large equestrian statue at the corner of Du Toitspan Road and Regiment Way **(12)**. Opposite this, at the corner with Lennox Street, is a memorial **(13)** to Kimberley men of the Cape Corps: a German field gun captured from Turkish troops by men of the corps at the battle of Square Hill, at El Mughheir, near Jerusalem, in September 1918.

Kimberley's mother congregation of the Dutch Reformed Church is in Long Street (an extension of Lennox Street) **(14)**. The church building, dating from 1885, includes a memorial to those who died in the nearby concentration camp during the Anglo-Boer War.

Three old cemetries, Pioneers' Cemetery in Cemetery Road, West End Cemetery in Green Street and Gladstone Cemetery in Kenilworth, contain the remains of many Anglo-Boer War casualties reinterred from nearby battlefields.

Apart from buildings and memorials open to the public, Kimberley contains many old buildings — modest and magnificent — tucked away in quiet streets. In Stockdale Street is the dignified headquarters of the De Beers Company. Tree-shaded Armagh House in Memorial Road, with cast-iron and fretted verandahs, was built and named by an Ulsterman, R H Henderson, who started his business career as manager of a small store in Dordrecht and, by the outbreak of the Anglo-Boer War, was Mayor of Kimberley ●

Publicity Office City Hall, Market Square, Kimberley 8301 Tel. (0531) 22241
AA Office 13 New Main Street, Kimberley 8301 Tel. (0531) 25207

TOURING TIPS: 1
Defensive Driving

South Africans have an unenviable place among the world's most accident-prone motorists — and their poor reputation is largely deserved because all too many fail to apply basic safety rules. One of the most common failings among South African drivers is their apparent reluctance to acknowledge the rights or needs of other road-users, often driving too close to the vehicle ahead, or driving under the influence of alcohol. Statistics show that most accidents occur in urban areas, with more than half the fatalities being cyclists and pedestrians. In 1982, the most recent year for which figures are available, 15 persons died for every 100-million km travelled.

ANTICIPATING DANGER

The best way to avoid an accident is to be alert as to what might cause one, and to develop your powers of observation so that you can anticipate danger and react to it in time. Observation and aniticipation are the basic principles of the technique known as defensive driving. Here are some of the danger signals that an alert motorist will recognise in order to stay out of trouble on the road:

- Motorcyclists at a road junction ahead — if you see two ready to come out and one emerges safely, watch for the other. Will he follow?
- Pedal cyclist ahead — if he glances over his shoulder he is probably preparing to pull out to the right and may hesitate and wobble.
- Turning signal on a car ahead — never rely on the driver doing as he has signalled. He may have forgotten to cancel a previous signal, or may simply change his mind.
- Turning signal on a car to your right — if you are waiting to emerge from a side road onto a main road, never assume that it is safe to pull out just because an oncoming driver is signalling left. Wait until he slows down and is obviously going to turn.
- Brake lights coming on ahead — touch your own brakes to warn traffic behind. There may be an accident or obstruction ahead.
- Taxi ahead — it may slow down and move to the left with little warning. Keep an eye open for someone hailing it from the kerb.
- Bus ahead — beware of people running to catch it. Watch out for people jumping off.
- Siren sounding on police car, ambulance or fire engine — if you do not know where the sound is coming from, slow down and keep to the side of the road.
- Headlamp dazzle — if a car approaches with headlamps on full beam, do not look at them directly. Look slightly to the nearside and give a quick flash of your headlights to indicate that you are being blinded. Do not retaliate by switching your own headlamps to full beam. This is offensive rather than defensive driving and could cause an accident.

Roadside signs — watch for:

- Bus stops — people may run across the road, hurrying to catch a bus.
- School signs — children may run across the road, especially in the morning between 7.30 am and 9.30 am and in the afternoon between 12.30 pm and 2.30 pm. But look out for a lone child near the school at any time of day.
- Pedestrian crossings — scan the pavement on both sides to see if anyone is preparing to cross.
- Garage forecourt — vehicles are likely to pull in and out without signalling.
- Red traffic light — stop. Before starting off again, watch the cross traffic and pedestrians, in case someone tries to rush through just as the light is changing.
- Amber traffic light — be decisive. Slow down and stop unless you are almost at the lights. If you are almost at the lights, accelerate through; otherwise following traffic may run into you.
- Green traffic light — do not treat it as an open door; it may change. Reduce speed as you approach and look right and left to make sure that nothing is coming through.
- Roadworks sign — prepare to slow down or stop; the roadworks may be some distance ahead round a bend, or obscured by cars.
- Road-narrows sign — get into the continuing lane in good time, and watch for other drivers cutting across.

Making use of clues — watch for:

- Mud or straw on a country road — there may be a slow-moving tractor ahead.
- Droppings on a country road — there may be horses, cattle or sheep ahead.
- Telegraph poles — in country areas, the line of poles ahead of you can sometimes alert you to bends in the road that may be masked by hedges. Do not rely on them, however; the lines sometimes cut across fields, rather than go round them, and can mislead you.

Approaching a parked car — watch for:

- People inside — the door may be opened.
- Flashing indicator — the car may pull out into your path.
- Wisps of smoke from the exhaust — the car may be about to move off.
- Feet under vehicles — a child may run into the road.

DRIVING THROUGH FLOODWATER

Flooding is likely on many low-lying roads after heavy rain, posing considerable danger to motorists travelling at speed. Never assume that a patch of water on the road ahead is only a few centimetres deep: some roads have dongas that fill to quite a depth.

If you see a sheet of water ahead, slow down; if the water is obviously not very deep and other traffic is going through, there is no need to stop and check the depth. Wait until the car in front is clear, then drive through slowly.

Stop if you are uncertain of the depth. It is not advisable to drive on if the water level is higher than the bottom edge of the cooling-fan blades, because they will send a fine spray of water over the engine and could short-circuit the spark-plug leads or crack the hot engine block. In most cars, the blades are 25-30 cm above the ground — about as high as the centre of the wheels.

Enter the water on the crown of a cambered road so that you keep to the shallowest part, and drive slowly in first or second gear — on an automatic in L (low lock) or 1 (first gear) — so that as little water as possible is splashed on the

Driving carefully on country roads

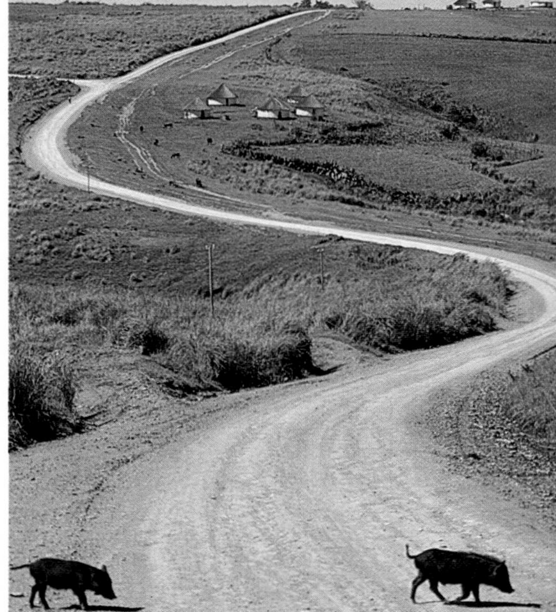

Keep a sharp lookout for straying animals.

- Drive at a sensible speed — this is dictated by the road surface, its width, the proximity of the shoulders, the depth of the wheel ruts and many other factors. If you are really in a hurry, choose a tarred route instead.
- Be aware of the increased risk from straying animals — both wild and domestic. If you see a herd of cattle or a flock of sheep on the road ahead, slow down in plenty of time — there may be strays.
- Do not swerve if you spot a pothole too late. It is better to suffer a shaking than roll your car by taking sudden avoiding action.
- If you are driving along a narrow road and see another vehicle approaching, do not assume there is enough room for it to pass you, and do not wait for the other driver to give you the right of way. Slow down.
- Deep sand drifts sometimes build up on bends in dirt roads — particularly after heavy rains. If you drive into this sand at high speed, it could cause you to swerve — with disastrous results. Learn to spot the likely places.

engine. But do not let the engine stall.

To keep the engine revs high at low speed with a manual gearbox, apply steady pressure on the accelerator (keep it about half depressed) and at the same time slip the clutch by pushing the clutch pedal a little way down. Avoid changing gear. If you alter the engine speed water may be sucked through the exhaust.

As soon as you drive out of the water, test the brakes. They are likely to be soaked and useless. To dry them out, drive slowly with your left foot pressing lightly on the brake pedal. Do not pick up speed until you have tested the brakes several times and are sure they are pulling evenly on all wheels.

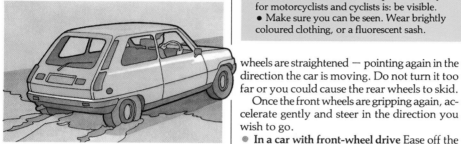

Once clear of the water, test the brakes.

CONTROLLING A SKID

A car skids because the tyres lose their grip and begin to slide over the road surface instead of rolling along it. What to do to control a skid depends on which tyres are skidding and whether or not the car has front-wheel drive. The 'natural' reaction — jamming the brakes on hard — is the worst thing you can do.

How to stop a rear-wheel skid

In a rear-wheel skid the back of the car slides sideways and the vehicle begins to swing round. This usually happens when you drive too fast round a bend or corner, but can also occur if you brake harshly on an uneven surface or a steeply cambered road. It is most likely to happen in a car with front-wheel drive.

Whether the car has front- or rear-wheel drive, the action to take is the same.

- Take your foot off the accelerator or brake. Do not push in the clutch pedal or grip the steering wheel hard.
- Turn the steering wheel in the direction the back of the car is sliding (for example, turn right if it is sliding to the right). Do not turn it too far or you may start a second skid with the back going in the opposite direction.
- When all four wheels are back in line, accelerate gently.

How to stop a front-wheel skid

In a front-wheel skid, the front of the car keeps straight on, even though you have turned the steering wheel to the right or left.

Front-wheel skids usually occur when the driver accelerates too harshly round a bend. What to do depends on whether the car has rear-wheel or front-wheel drive.

- **In a car with rear-wheel drive** Take your foot off the accelerator. Do not apply the brake or push in the clutch pedal.

Turn the steering wheel so that the front wheels are straightened — pointing again in the direction the car is moving. Do not turn it too far or you could cause the rear wheels to skid.

Once the front wheels are gripping again, accelerate gently and steer in the direction you wish to go.

- **In a car with front-wheel drive** Ease off the accelerator smoothly, but maintain enough pressure on the pedal to keep the car in motion. If you decelerate too fast the rear wheels may skid as well.
- Do not touch the clutch or brake pedals, and do not straighten the steering wheel.
- Continue steering smoothly in the direction you want to turn, but do not turn the wheel violently or too far.
- As the car moves back on course, straighten the wheels and accelerate gently.

Steer in the direction you want to turn.

How to stop a four-wheel skid

In a four-wheel skid — which usually happens during hard braking — the wheels lock and the car slides forward not seeming to lose speed. It may skid in a more or less straight line, or off to the side if the road is steeply cambered.

How to control a four-wheel skid

- Ease off on the brake pedal until the wheels unlock and start to roll again. Do not push in the clutch pedal.
- Once you have regained steering control, straighten the wheels.
- In order to stop the car, re-apply the brakes by repeatedly pushing them on and off with a pumping action — a technique known as cadence braking — which will help to avoid locking the wheels again.

DRIVING THROUGH FOG

In foggy conditions, being seen — particularly by drivers behind you — is as important as seeing. When fog is forecast, make sure all lamp glass on your car, front and rear, is absolutely clean. The film of dust and dirt that collects on a lamp from road spray can cut the light intensity of the beam by half.

- By day or night, drive through fog with dipped headlights. Sidelights are not bright enough and full-beam headlights will reflect from fog particles and may dazzle you.
- Use fog lights if they are fitted. If you have only a single fog lamp, this must be used in conjunction with headlights, or your car may be mistaken for a motorcycle.
- Switch on the windscreen wipers to keep the windscreen clear, and operate the washer as necessary. Use the de-mister to keep warm air blowing on to the inside of the screen.
- Keep your speed low. You should be able to stop within your range of vision.
- Drive with your window open. You may hear something coming, or hear a warning toot from a horn, even if you cannot see another vehicle because of the fog.
- Do not hunch over the wheel and peer forward. You will see better if you sit relaxed in your normal driving position.
- Try to drive in line with the nearside kerb or verge; if you have a passenger, ask him to keep you informed of the distance between the car and the roadside.
- Alternatively, use the reflective studs in the middle of the road as a guide. But do not drive on the central line, or you may collide with vehicles coming the other way.

STUCK IN SOFT SAND OR SNOW

Unless you are driving a four-wheel drive vehicle, it is very easy for your car's wheels to lose their traction in soft sand or snow.

Do not accelerate hard in an attempt to pull away, which will merely bury the spinning wheels even deeper, and ensure that the wheels are straight so that the treads are in the best position for gripping the surface.

Find something to pack under the driving wheels to improve their grip, such as rocks, branches or sacking; and to lessen the risk of wheelspin, start in a high gear ●

Safety on two wheels

Due to the relative lack of protection on a motorcycle, a motorcyclist is much more likely to suffer serious injury in a collision than the driver of a vehicle. Crash statistics show that motorcyclists are far more likely to be involved in a crash than a car driver. The most common motorcycle accident is a collision with a motorist turning on to a major road, and it happens because the car driver simply fails to see the machine in time.

The same circumstances account for most bicycle accidents as well. Four out of five serious cycling accidents that occur do so within a few metres of a junction.

For this reason the most important safety rule for motorcyclists and cyclists is: be visible.

- Make sure you can be seen. Wear brightly coloured clothing, or a fluorescent sash.
- Keep the headlight on constantly while riding, even during the day.
- Do not overtake on the inside. The car driver may not see you and could pull over towards the kerb or turn left in front of you.
- If the car in front of you turns left, beware of another vehicle pulling out across your path from the same side road. The driver may not have seen you behind the turning car.
- For a safe braking distance in dry weather, road safety experts recommend keeping as far behind the vehicle in front as you can travel in two seconds, which means allowing about 2 m for every 3 km/h. You can measure the distance using a roadside marker such as a postbox.
- In wet weather, braking distances may be doubled, so you need a four-second gap between your machine and a vehicle ahead.

TOURING TIPS: 2
Comfortable Driving

Before setting out on a day drive or longer journey, use this book to plan where you will go, how you will get there and how long it will take you to complete the trip. Planning ahead can make the difference between a pleasant outing and a disaster — and one of the essentials is a roadworthy vehicle. Ensure that the steering, brakes, tyres, windscreen wipers, indicators and all other lights are functioning correctly. If not, postpone your trip until everything is working as it should. Before leaving home, check that your insurance is fully paid up. If you plan to be away for a while, cancel milk and newspaper deliveries and leave a spare house key with a friendly neighbour. And take a spare ignition key (on a separate keyring). Ensure that your car's exhaust system is in good condition and check the spare wheel.

Adjust the seat and backrest until you are comfortable.

THE IDEAL DRIVING POSITION

Knees Knees should be bent at between 15° and 60°. Never stretch legs straight, even when operating foot controls, as after a short time at less than 5° the knees lock. The backs of the knees should not touch the front of the seat cushion.

Feet The angle between foot and shin is most comfortable at 100°, and should never be less than 90° or ankles will stiffen.

Hands Hands should be placed in the 'ten to two' position on the steering wheel rim.

Arms The upper arms should hang naturally from the shoulders. 'Straight-arm' driving is often tiring. Elbows must clear the body when steering, and be bent at an angle of about 120°, in order to obtain maximum leverage.

Neck The neck should be leaning slightly forward about 15° from the vertical.

Upper back Recline the back at between 15° and 30° from the vertical.

SITTING COMFORTABLY

Sitting properly in the driving seat is not simply a matter of sitting comfortably. The motorist who settles unthinkingly into his seat may be relaxed initially, but will find that aches and pains develop as the journey lengthens.

Slouching, sitting too close to the steering wheel, cramping the legs, failing to support the small of the back — all give rise to dangerous, distracting discomfort and lead to the early onset of fatigue.

The correctly seated motorist has the best possible view of the road ahead, has the car's controls within easy reach and is able to drive the vehicle with the minimum effort and the maximum efficiency for long periods.

After years of neglect, the design of car seats and the relationship of the driver to the hand and foot controls are at last being given attention by manufacturers.

But, even so, few seats have a means of varying the amount of lumbar support provided by the backrest, and it is unusual to find a car in which the position and angle of the steering wheel can be altered to suit the individual.

However, car seating with the minimum of built-in adjustment can often be modified to provide an improved driving position.

Seat runners can sometimes be reversed so as to give the seat greater rearward travel. Packing and wedges carefully placed beneath the runners can tilt the seat as necessary. Cushions and backrests can also help to make long-distance driving far more comfortable.

Ask yourself if your driving position permits a level gaze through the windscreen and if the angles of your elbows, knees and ankles are correct. There must be sufficient lumbar support.

Do not resign yourself to the seating position the manufacturer has given you if it does not suit you. There is almost always something that can be done to improve it.

Once you have experimented and found the ideal position, set the interior rearview mirror carefully. If on subsequent journeys the mirror appears to be wrongly adjusted, you will know that you are sitting sloppily and not taking advantage of the improvements you have made.

DRIVING INTO THE SUN

Many drivers like to wear tinted lenses on bright days. Eventually there may be an international standard for sunglasses. For the moment, the best protection is to buy glasses from an optometrist. Beware of non-neutral tints which can alter colour balance and perception.

Cheaper sunglasses with plastic lenses are much more prone to scratching than those with glass, and this in itself constitutes a hazard. A scratched lens will scatter light and give 'veiling glare', which reduces clear vision.

Sunglasses with polarised lenses cut down light reflected from horizontal surfaces, such as the car's bonnet, but they will tend to show the streaky pattern in toughened windscreens.

Night driving At dusk or night, colour largely disappears, depth perception blurs and range of vision decreases with speed; the normal daylight vision of 10-15 per cent of drivers declines so sharply at night that they are a positive hazard to other road users and themselves.

Some motorists with normal sight during daylight tend to become short-sighted at night. In the dark, eyes are drawn to the lightest areas; there is a danger that dark objects close at hand may be overlooked. It takes anything up to half an hour for a driver with good eyesight to become fully adjusted to night conditions. Night vision can be improved simply by sitting in the car for a few minutes before setting off.

IF YOU FEEL DROWSY AT THE WHEEL

If you find yourself beginning to nod off while driving, you must make an urgent effort to revive yourself until you can stop the car safely and wake yourself up.

Danger signs

Cruising for long periods in a warm car — particularly on a wide straight road such as a highway — can be more hazardous than negotiating busy urban streets. With little to do, you can be tempted to daydream and let your attention wander dangerously.

Since fatigue builds up only gradually, judging — in yourself or someone else — when it has reached a dangerous level can be very difficult. These are the symptoms to watch for:

- Continual yawning.
- Eyes feel heavy and are difficult to keep open.
- Difficulty in concentrating, especially on a monotonous stretch of road.
- Suddenly realising that you have no recollection of the last few kilometres you have travelled.

Making each litre count

Rising fuel prices make economical motoring a prime consideration for everyone, and there are a number of ways in which you can save petrol.

- Choose the right petrol octane rating for your car and the area in which you drive.
- Ensure that your car is fitted with the right tyres, inflated to the correct pressure.
- Replace faulty spark plugs (a misfiring engine uses more petrol) and check the exhaust system for leaks.
- Do not drive around with surf boards and other equipment permanently attached to the roof rack — they create considerable drag, which in turn burns extra fuel.
- Try to maintain a steady speed on the open road. Heavy-footed driving and over-rapid acceleration is another petrol-waster.
- Do not allow the engine to idle for unnecessarily long periods. Rather switch off the engine and re-start it when you are ready to drive off.
- Try to avoid stop-start driving. If possible, time your trips to avoid traffic jams at rush hours.

Dust-proofing your car

The propensity of many modern cars to admit choking dust when driven on South Africa's dirt roads suggests that they were designed for countries in which off-tarmac driving is of negligible importance.

Dust can easily spoil the enjoyment of a day drive — particularly when other motorists are intent on travelling the same dusty road at high speed. The problem is exacerbated by dry spells.

Try the following methods for keeping dust out of your car:

• Check the rubber seals at the windows. If they are broken or perished, replace them. Ensure that the tops of the closed windows make firm contact with the seals all around the edge.

• Open the boot lid and check for holes which might admit dust. Seal any openings with rubber grommets, a flexible sealing compound or strips of masking tape (temporary only).

• Use wide strips of masking tape to seal the undersides of the car doors — a common entry point for dust.

• Cover all ventilation outlets with fine muslin or another cloth and keep the material slightly damp. Clean the cloth at every stop.

• Open the bonnet and check for any holes in the firewall — such as the entry point for the bonnet release cable — which could admit dust to the car's interior. Close any openings with a flexible sealer or tape.

• Check the floor in front of the driver for any gaps around the clutch, brake and accelerator pedals. Seal as above.

• If another car is ahead of you on a particularly dusty road, and you are in no hurry, pull off the road for a while in order to allow the dust to settle.

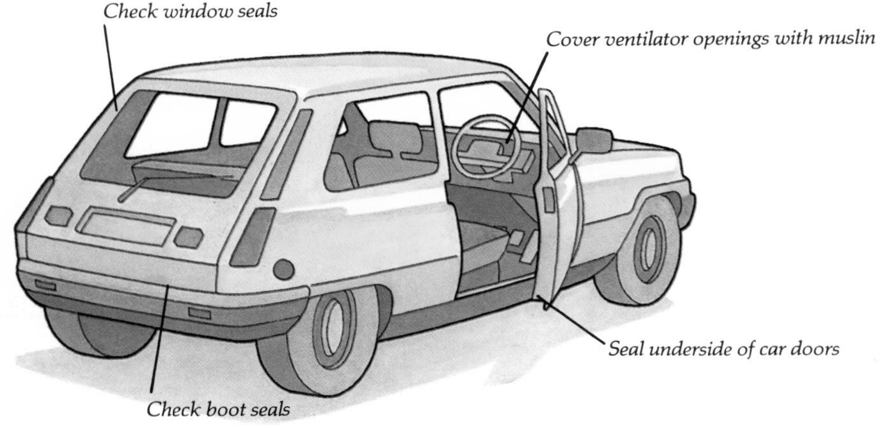

• A spasmodic jerk of the body, recalling you from the brink of sleep.

The car begins to wander off course and you have to correct the steering hurriedly.

• You have to take rapid action to avoid a hazard you had not noticed.

• You start at a shadow, reacting to an imagined hazard.

Reviving yourself at the wheel

• If you do find yourself becoming drowsy, pull off the road to a safe parking place as soon as possible. Do not stop on the tarred shoulder of a freeway — it is only for emergencies such as breakdowns.

• In the meantime, slow down.

• Direct the dashboard air vents onto your face. The blast of cold air will help to wake you up.

• Lick your finger and dampen your forehead and your eyelids — particularly at the inner corner of each eye. Let the air blow onto your face to cool it.

• Take a deep breath, purse your lips, and then breathe out again very slowly.

• Encourage passengers to chat with you.

• Wind down the window if the road is quiet and the weather dry. On a freeway or a busy road, however, let in blasts of fresh air only for short spells, because the extra noise increases fatigue.

• Play the radio or taped music only if it is something you will respond to positively. Some sounds can send you to sleep: others can irritate you and increase tiredness.

IF POLICE STOP YOU

The police can stop any motorist and question him — whether or not they suspect him of an offence. They may also search his car without a warrant — provided that they have reason to suspect that it is carrying an article that could be used as evidence in order to prove a crime.

• If a uniformed policeman stops you, give your name and address, when asked. If you are genuinely in a hurry — rushing to see someone seriously ill in hospital, say — explain your haste and ask to give the details later.

• If the policeman does not agree to this, he can insist on taking your name and address on the spot anyway.

• You are not obliged to carry such motoring documents as a driving licence. But if you have any, show them if asked. It will save time. If you do not show them, or do not have them with you, the police can insist that you produce them at a police station within 21 days.

• You must obey a policeman if he asks you to move your vehicle. Otherwise you can be prosecuted for obstructing the police — regardless of whether or not you were blocking the road and regardless of whether or not you were legally parked.

• If the police are looking for a stolen car, they may ask questions about your car, such as the registration number or the make of the tyres. Answer the questions as best you can — you will be helping to confirm that the car is yours.

• Be polite and co-operative, but do not answer any questions that you think might incriminate you. You are under no legal obligation to do so.

• If the police say they are going to arrest you, they must give you the reason for the arrest. Do not resist, even if you are innocent, or you could be charged with resisting arrest or obstructing the police. And you could be convicted of that even if the courts find you not guilty of the charge for which you were arrested.

• Telephone an attorney.

The breathalyser test

• The breathalyser is employed merely as a screening test, enabling traffic officers to decide with greater certainty whether a driver should be subjected to the definitive blood test.

• Results obtained with a breathalyser are not acceptable as evidence in court.

A driver is entitled to refuse to take a breathalyser test and is not obliged to give a reason for doing so. A refusal may, however, make the taking of a blood test more likely. It is illegal for a motorist to refuse to submit to a blood test if asked to do so ●

Preventing car sickness

Children between the ages of five and 15 are most susceptible to car sickness: excitement and energetic movement can lead to upset stomachs. Babies suffer less; the elderly rarely experience travel sickness in motor cars.

The car driver, fully occupied and firmly located in his seat, is the least prone to travel sickness. He can prevent discomfort among his passengers by thoughtful preparation for the journey and by smooth well-planned driving.

Children should be kept busy, but discourage them from reading or writing and restrict 'spotting' games to those that keep the eyes ahead: watching for objects flashing past the sides of the car can cause eye strain, giddiness and nausea.

Some travel-sickness preparations should be used with caution. Ask a doctor about the advisability of using them, especially in the case of children and expectant mothers.

The family dog can suffer even more from car sickness than human beings. Travel sickness pills for animals are obtainable from pet shops.

Do's and don'ts about car sickness

• *Do* take a travel-sickness tablet (*see* MEDICINES, 21) about 30 minutes-1 hour before starting out on a journey, but do not take tablets containing antihistamine which can cause the onset of drowsiness.

• *Do* take games, toys, puzzles, audio tapes or anything else that might be a distraction for a child sufferer.

• *Do* take some waterproof bags in case all else fails.

• *Don't* talk about the possibility of being sick in front of someone at risk, as this may cause him to be sick.

• *Don't* have a large meal or alcohol before setting out.

TOURING TIPS: 3

Emergencies on the Road

Every motorist must expect to encounter an emergency on the road during his driving career. It could be through his own action, through an act of commission or omission on the part of another driver, or simply a matter of chance. Whether this emergency has ill effects depends on your skill, your experience and your ability to anticipate situations. While it is not always possible to predict what will happen on the road, there is convincing evidence that a knowledge of what could happen has saved lives. Try to familiarise yourself with some of the emergency situations on this page — and how to get out of them.

BRAKE FAILURE AT SPEED

If the brakes fail when you try to stop a car at speed — perhaps on the approach to a crossroads — your only option is to use the engine and the terrain (such as an upward slope or thick hedge) to slow the car.

- Apply the handbrake smoothly and at the same time pump the footbrake — you may succeed in restoring brake pressure.
- Keep a firm grip on the steering wheel while you do this, because using the handbrake at speed may lock the rear wheels and cause the car to go into a skid.
- Do not switch off the engine, or you will be unable to use its power as a brake by changing down to a lower gear. Moreover, the car will take a long time to roll to a stop from high speed. On cars with power-assisted brakes, the brakes will not work properly with the engine switched off.
- With manual gears, change down to third gear as the handbrake slows the car and keep changing down as soon as you can. To engage lower gears at speed, try double-declutching.
- With automatic transmission, move the lever into L (low lock) or 2 (second gear) as soon as you have slowed sufficiently. In most cars, this is likely to be at about 30 km/h.
- If you cannot slow down or stop fast enough to avoid a collision, try to run the car up a slope or bank.
- You can also slow the car by mounting the kerb, if it is safe to do so, or by scraping the car along a hedge or fence. You may be able to drive straight into a hedge to stop, but you risk hitting a concealed tree or fence post — or someone unseen on the other side.

If the handbrake fails on a steep hill

If the handbrake fails when you stop on your way up a steep hill, you may experience difficulty in starting off again (in a car with manual gears) because, with your left foot on the clutch, you cannot move your right foot from the brake to the accelerator without the car rolling backwards.

- Swivel your right foot so that your toe remains on the footbrake while you place your heel on the accelerator.
- As you release the clutch pedal, ease your right toe off the footbrake and press your heel down on the accelerator. This should allow you to hold the car until you move forwards and can release the brake completely.
- If you cannot stop the car rolling backwards, turn the steering wheel so that the car backs into the kerb at the side of the road.

Why brakes fail

Complete brake failure is rare because modern cars have two separate circuits of hydraulic fluid operating the brakes. If one circuit is damaged, the other can operate the brakes on its own, though less effectively. Nevertheless, driving habits, inadequate maintenance and water can all cause brakes to become dangerously unreliable.

Brakes may become temporarily ineffective after driving through floods because the discs or shoes get wet.

They may also fail temporarily on a steep descent or after prolonged use because the fluid gets hot and may partially vaporise; if this happens, the pedal feels spongy when depressed.

Repeated pumping of the brakes usually restores pressure in these circumstances. Use a low gear on a long or steep descent and brake gently to prevent the brakes overheating.

Sometimes hard braking causes the brakepads to get so hot that they temporarily lose their stopping power. When this happens, the pedal does not feel spongy, and the brakes work again after a stop to let them cool.

Front tyre burst: try to stay on course.

WHEN A TYRE BURSTS

A burst tyre may be caused by a fault in the tyre structure, but it is much more likely to be caused by a puncture.

A punctured tyre does not always burst; it may deflate, giving the driver the impression he is travelling over a bumpy road, but the steering is affected in the same way as a burst. The main concern is to avoid slewing into other traffic.

If a front tyre bursts or deflates, the car pulls strongly to one side (the side on which the tyre has burst).

If a rear tyre bursts or deflates, the back end of the car may slide to one side.

- If a front tyre bursts, avoid braking if possible. Rather let the car roll to a stop and turn the steering wheel smoothly and gently to counter the sideways pull and keep the car on course.
- If a rear tyre bursts, brake gently — not suddenly or fiercely — and keep a firm grip on the steering wheel to keep the car on course.
- Do not change gear.
- Signal left, if you can, and steer the car to the side of the road.
- If you are on the outside lane of a freeway, it may be safer to pull onto the central island. Do not stop on the road.
- Try to stop on hard ground rather than a soft verge; you will need a firm base for changing the wheel.

WINDSCREEN SHATTERS AT SPEED

Most standard windscreens are made of toughened glass. However, if it does shatter it makes a crazed pattern of small pieces that can obscure the driver's vision. Zone-toughened screens break so that larger pieces remain immediately in front of the driver, giving him enough vision to be able to stop safely.

- If your windscreen shatters, do not follow the natural impulse to punch out an area of the glass with your fist as you drive. You risk cutting your hand or arm badly, or having a splinter blown into your eye.
- Instead, lean forward. It will help you to see more clearly through the shattered glass. Pull off the road and stop the car as soon as you consider it is safe to do so.
- Stuff rag or paper tissues into the demister slots on top of the dashboard and spread newspaper or cloth over the car bonnet. Pad your hand with a glove or cloth, get back into the car and push the glass outwards on to the paper.
- Remove as much of the glass as possible, or it may fall out while you are driving.
- If you have any adhesive tape, such as masking tape, apply a strip right round the windscreen so as to cover the grooved rubber flange which held the glass. This prevents fragments from being blown into your face.
- If you have no tape, wear sunglasses to protect your eyes. Alternatively, remove the rubber flange completely.
- Wrap up the glass in the newspaper. Dust any fragments off the top of the dashboard before removing the stuffing from the slots. Dispose of the glass in a suitable place — do not leave it at the roadside.
- Fit in a temporary windscreen, if you have one with you in the car.

Emergency screens are usually wrapped round the front door jambs so that they are held in place when the doors are shut.

- If you do not have a temporary screen, drive slowly and carefully to the nearest garage.
- Alternatively, you can get an emergency windscreen fitted at the roadside by a specialist firm (these firms are usually listed in the Yellow Pages).

Cutting the risks

A windscreen usually shatters because it has been hit by a stone flung into the air by the tyre of another car. There is no way of avoiding a stone, but there are ways to lessen the risks.

- Consider fitting laminated safety glass to your car. The glass — which is usually tinted — will not shatter, no matter how hard it is hit. It may crack or chip, however, and eventually need replacement.
- On a newly surfaced road with loose chippings, keep your speed low and maintain a bigger distance than usual between you and the vehicle in front.
- Take out insurance to cover windscreen damage, if your policy does not already include it. Ideally, the insurance should cover the whole cost of replacement, with no excess and no loss of your no-claim bonus.

FIRE IN YOUR CAR

About one-third of the fires in cars are caused by faults in the wiring system, and nearly as many by petrol under the bonnet catching fire. Others result mainly from collisions or are started by cigarettes.

A car fire must be put out very quickly because there is danger of the petrol tank exploding if the petrol vapour should ignite. As with any fire, the way to extinguish it quickly is to cut off its air and fuel supply.

- As soon as you notice smoke or flames, switch off the ignition but *leave the key in position* to avoid locking the steering.
- If the car is moving, coast to the side of the road if possible and stop.
- Get all passengers out and away from the vehicle.
- Disconnect the battery if you can, by pulling the wires off the terminals. But if the fire is under the bonnet do not open it wide, as air will fan the flames.
- If you do not have a fire extinguisher, try to smother the flames with a blanket, car rug or any thick material.
- If this is not successful, call the fire brigade to the scene.

A fire extinguisher for your car

An aerosol extinguisher of at least 1,5 kg capacity is effective for putting out most car fires. The extinguisher should be either of the type known as dry powder or one containing a liquid gas known as BCF. Both can be safely used on electrical equipment. However, BCF fumes are toxic in a confined space, so the car should be well ventilated once the fire has been put out.

A car fire extinguisher needs to be mounted in an easily accessible place, such as on the dashboard or in the driver's footwell — not in the boot.

Have the fire extinguisher serviced from time to time, even if it has not been used.

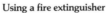

Using a fire extinguisher

- If the fire is under the bonnet, lift the lid just enough to direct the extinguisher through it.
- Direct the extinguisher at the base of the flames and work methodically from side to side and from the edge inwards.
- Do not leave a patch uncovered, or the flames may spring up again.

STUCK ON A LEVEL CROSSING

Your chances of surviving a crash with a train are minimal. If your vehicle stalls or breaks down on a level crossing, therefore, the priority is to protect yourself and your passengers — not the car. Even if the train driver can see you, he is unlikely to be able to stop in time.

- Get everyone out of the car and off the crossing as quickly as possible.
- If the engine will not start, release the handbrake, put the gear lever into neutral and try to push the car clear of the tracks.
- In a car with a manual gearbox, you can also use the starter motor to move it. Put the car in first gear with the handbrake off and your foot off the clutch, and turn the ignition key. The car will lurch forward as the starter motor turns.
- Telephone the signal box immediately. The driver and passengers in an approaching train could be injured in an accident as well — and the sooner you can alert the signalman, the more chance he has of stopping any trains before they reach the crossing.

Safety on crossings

Motoring experts recommend four rules for crossing a railway line safely.

- Approach at a moderate speed.
- At an open level crossing — one with no barriers or warning lights — treat the crossing as if it were a major road. Stop, look both ways and listen carefully before you cross, to make quite sure that no train is approaching.

Do not drive nose-to-tail over a crossing. Start to cross only when you can see that the road on the other side is clear.

- Do not stop on a level crossing for any reason. If you are already on the crossing when the lights start to flash or the alarms sound, carry on over the lines ●

Escaping from a car under water

If your car plunges into deep water, you may be able to escape through a door or window before it sinks — usually within a minute or so. But even if the car sinks with you inside, you can still escape because it may take 30 minutes or more to fill up with water. Precisely how long it takes depends on whether the windows are open, whether the car is well-sealed and the depth of the water. The deeper the car sinks, the higher the pressure of the surrounding water and the faster it will force its way in.

How to get out of a sunken car

- A car will generally sink engine-end first, and a pocket of air will form inside at the opposite end near the roof. Use this air to escape.
- Release your seat belt.
- If there is time, turn on the headlights and interior lights. They will enable you to see better and will help rescuers to find the vehicle once it has sunk underneath the water.
- Place yourself so that you can put your head into the air pocket and breathe. In a front-engined car, climb into the back seat.
- Close any open windows and ventilation ducts, if there is time, to retain air in the car.
- As the car settles, water will find its way in through cracks and holes until the pressure inside and outside the car equalises. Keep calm and wait until the pressures equalise — when the water level inside stops rising. Until then it will be extremely difficult to open a door — and failure to do so might lead to panic, which could be fatal.
- When the water stops rising, take a deep breath, open a window or door and, as the water fills the last air pocket, swim out.
- As you swim to the surface, allow air to bubble slowly out of your mouth. Because the air pocket in the car was under pressure, the air in your lungs will be as well — and will expand as you rise. If the excess is not allowed to escape, it could damage your lungs.

As the car settles, undo your belt.

Get everyone into the air pocket.

Take a deep breath and open the door.

As water floods in, swim out.

TOURING TIPS: 4
At the scene of an accident

If you are the first on the scene of a crash, do not dash headlong from your car to the aid of an injured person — you or your car may be struck by another vehicle. For this reason, the first thing to do at the scene of any accident is to protect the area from other traffic. Other drivers must be warned that an accident has occurred — otherwise a relatively minor incident could very quickly turn into a major pile-up.

WARN OTHER TRAFFIC

- Park your car well away from the accident — behind it, if possible. Turn on your hazard warning lights. At night, train your headlights on the damaged vehicles.
- Leave your car with its front wheels turned towards the kerb so that if another car runs into it, your car will be pushed off the road and not into you or the crashed vehicles.
- If one of the crashed vehicles is on fire, keep yourself and others well clear. Its petrol tank could explode without warning.
- Take charge of the accident scene if no one else has done so. If someone is already in charge, make yourself useful to him.
- Warn approaching traffic in both directions. If other traffic is coming up behind you, flag it down, keeping well to the side of the road; at night use a torch or light-coloured scarf. Ask someone to stop traffic coming the other way.
- Put a warning triangle, if one is available, about 90m behind the wrecked vehicles, towards the nearside edge of the road. Ideally, place another the same distance from the accident site in the opposite direction.

Send for the police

- Check the number of vehicles involved, and the number of victims, noting whether anyone is trapped.
- Ask a passing driver or anyone living nearby to call the police. Tell him how many people are injured or trapped. It does not matter if more than one person makes a call.
- If you make the call yourself, tell the police you are reporting an accident and give the telephone number in case you are cut off.
- Describe the accident location as exactly as you can. Say how many vehicles are involved, whether any vehicle is on fire, how many people are injured and whether anyone is trapped.

Immobilise the crashed vehicles

- Switch off the ignition of each vehicle, but leave the key in the ignition in case the steering locks — remember that the vehicle may have to be moved later.
- Check that the handbrake of each car is on. If it is not, put it on.
- Do not smoke, and warn others not to — even away from the cars. There may be petrol running in the gutter or leaking across the road from a ruptured fuel tank.

Help the injured

- Do not move anyone unless he is in immediate danger — if there is a car on fire close by, for example, or if he is lying in leaking petrol which you think might catch fire. If you move an injured person, you risk aggravating his injuries; that risk is worth taking only to protect him from a greater risk.
- Do not attempt to pick out glass from the victim's face or body wounds. If the glass is plugging the wound, you could make the bleeding worse by pulling it out.
- Check that each casualty can breathe freely. Loosen tight clothing around the neck.
- Do not give the injured anything to eat or drink. Hot, sweet tea is appropriate only for someone who has had an emotional fright. It should not be given to anyone who has been injured or who is suffering from shock.

Move the injured only if they are in immediate danger.

- See if the casualty can treat himself and show him what to do. He can stem blood coming from an arm or leg by gripping the wound with his hand, or by pressing on it with a clean handkerchief or tissue.

Treatment priorities

- Treat casualties in any accident in the following order:

1. Unconscious and not breathing.
2. Bleeding severely.
3. Unconscious but breathing.

- Then search the scene in case someone has left or been thrown from a crashed vehicle and is wandering around in shock — or has collapsed at a distance. If you find someone wandering around in a state of shock, persuade him to lie down.
- Cover each injured person lightly with a rug or coat.
- Reassure them that help is on the way. Tell them that any missing friend, relative or pet is being taken care of — even if you are not sure at that stage. The priority is to keep each casualty safe and as calm as possible until the emergency services reach the scene.
- If possible, do not leave the casualties alone after you have treated them. Get someone — a passer-by, say, or another motorist — to stay with each casualty until help arrives.

If available, set up a warning triangle.

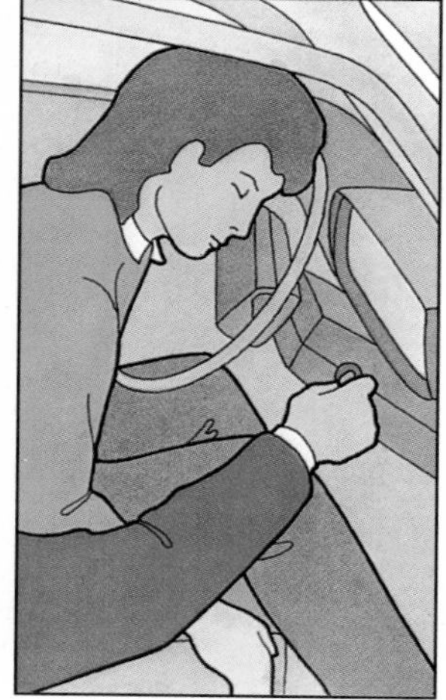

Switch off ignition of crashed vehicles.

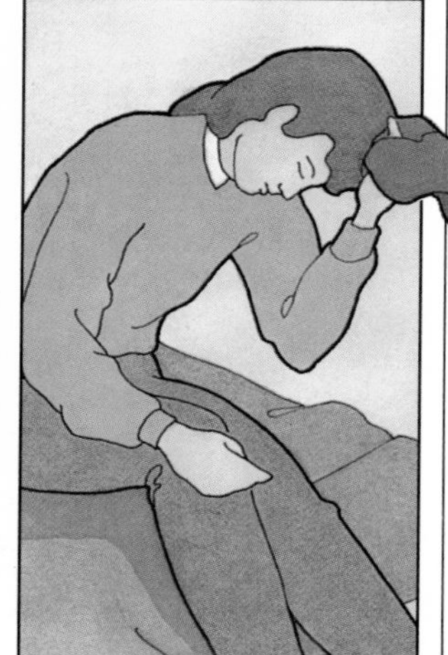

Encourage casualties to help themselves.

IF YOU ARE INVOLVED IN AN ACCIDENT

A traffic accident may involve only your vehicle and damage to property, such as a lamp post. Alternatively, it may involve other vehicles and perhaps injury to people or animals. Whatever the involvement, there are certain steps the law requires you to take, and other steps that are advisable for insurance purposes.

Try to remain calm and note down essential information, even though you will probably be feeling shocked and flustered by the incident.

At the scene

- Stop as soon as you safely can. You must stop even if your vehicle is undamaged but you have been indirectly involved — if, for example, one car collided with another after swerving to avoid you.
- Whatever the circumstances, do not become involved in arguments with other drivers or onlookers about what happened. Do not make

First aid kit

Thousands of South African motorists keep some sort of first aid kit in their cars. However, many of these kits contain either too much or too little. The ideal first aid kit should contain simple but essential items for dealing with injuries which may occur in a car crash.

Such a kit will enable even those who are unversed in first aid techniques to cope with emergencies until help arrives.

• Your kit might include the following items

Sterile eye pads
Large and medium open-weave bandages
Adhesive plaster strips
Adhesive tape
Safety pins
Burn dressings
Scissors
Pads for small wounds
Cotton wool
Gauze
Sal volatile
Tweezers
Triangular bandage
Disinfectant

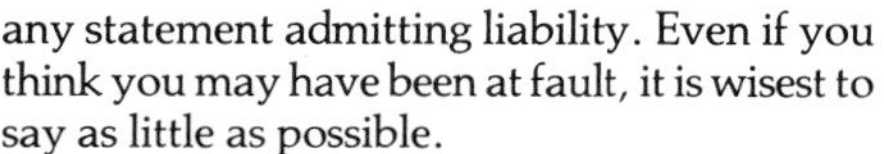

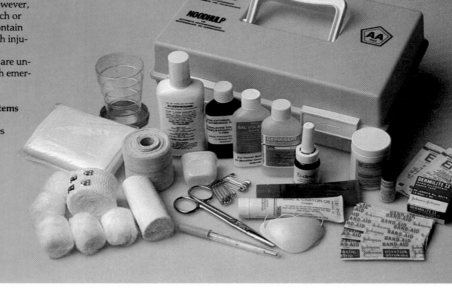

any statement admitting liability. Even if you think you may have been at fault, it is wisest to say as little as possible.

- If anyone has been seriously injured in the accident, call an ambulance.
- Before any vehicles are moved, make a sketch plan or note of their position in the road and in relation to the other vehicles involved. Note, for example, if any car has crossed the central white line. If any car has skidded, make an estimate of the length of skid marks.
- Examine your vehicle and the others involved and make a note of the damage each has sustained. Look, too, at the condition of the other cars involved in the accident. Were all their lights working at the time, for instance, and were their tyres in good condition?
- Give your name and address and the registration number of your car to other motorists involved and to anyone else who has reasonable grounds for asking, such as the owners of any damaged property. If you are not the owner of the car you are driving, give the owner's name and address as well.
- Collect the same information from other motorists involved. If anyone refuses, write down his car registration number (the owner can be traced through the number).
- If the police have not been called, try to find an independent witness (not someone travelling in your car) who is willing to make a statement about the incident.

After the accident

- If the accident involved serious damage to a vehicle or property, or if a traffic sign was damaged, it is advisable, though not legally essential, to report it to the police as soon as possible — certainly within 24 hours.
- If you hit and damage an unoccupied car — in a car park, say — report it to the police. If you fail to do so and are eventually traced, you could face not only a claim for repair of the damage you caused, but also criminal charges as a hit-and-run driver.
- Tell your insurance company of the accident within 24 hours, whether or not you or anyone else will be making a claim on your policy.
- Ask the company at the same time to send you an accident report and claim form on which you can fill in the details.
- Ask a garage to give you a written estimate of the cost of repairs to your car, but do not get any repairs done at once if you plan to claim the cost from an insurance company. The insurers will probably want the damage inspected.
- Send any bills or letters you get from other motorists involved to your insurance company. Do not write to or contact the other motorists or their insurers.
- Let your insurance company know if you receive a notice of intended prosecution from the police.

ANIMALS ON THE ROAD

If you suddenly find an animal in your path — a pet, a straying farm animal or a wild animal — there may be no time to avoid it. In heavy traffic or bad weather, there may be no choice but to hit it rather than to swerve and risk a serious accident.

- Pull over to the side of the road and stop as soon as you can after the impact. Find out whether the animal is dead or injured.
- If it is injured, try to restrain it so that its injuries can be treated.
- If the animal is dead or injured, call the police.
- If the animal is a pet or a farm animal, go to the nearest house or farmhouse as well and try to find the owner.
- If the animal is injured and small enough to handle, consider taking it to a vet at once. Tell the police if you plan to leave the scene of the accident to do this.

Approaching animals — watch for

- Dog not on lead — it may wander into the road or run across, especially if there is another dog (or a cat) on the other side.
- Cat crouching on footpath watching traffic — it may be intending to cross the road, and may dash in front of your car, relying on speed to get across.
- Horses ahead — slow down and give them plenty of room as you pass. Do not toot your horn or accelerate hard, or they may shy into your car.
- Herd of cattle or flock of sheep ahead — stop until they have gone round you or off the road. Do not sound your horn or rev your engine. If you startle them, they may take fright and blunder into your car.
- Wild animals ahead — slow down and drive on very slowly ●

Avoiding a head-on collision

If you see another vehicle coming towards you on the wrong side of the road, whose driver seems to be either unwilling or unable to get out of your way, you must act quickly and coolly to avoid a head-on collision. Head-on collisions are the most potentially dangerous of all road accidents.

- As soon as you see the hazard, sound your horn or flash your headlights as an early warning of your presence.
- Brake firmly but not violently. Otherwise the car may start to skid and you could very quickly lose control of the steering.
- As you reduce speed, scan the road ahead to see if there is anywhere to get out of the way safely — a verge, say, or a side turning.
- Start to pull left, but do not commit yourself until you see which way the other car is going. There is a danger that both of you could pull onto your nearside verge and collide there.
- As soon as you see which way the other vehicle is swerving, turn away from it — even if this means side-swiping another car travelling on the road. This type of accident is far less likely to kill you and your passengers than a head-on smash.
- If a collision is unavoidable, try to scrape the side of the other vehicle rather than have to collide with it head on.

INDEX

C

F

G

H

I

J

K

L

M

U

V

W

X

Y

Z

Acknowledgments

Many people assisted in the preparation of this book. The publishers wish to express their thanks to all who helped in any way, and feel that special mention is due to the following:

Julian Ardagh; Denyse Armour; Kevan Aspoas; Commandant O E F Baker; Mike Behr; Elizabeth Biggs; Daphne Carr; Barbara Castle; Keith Cooper; Colin Cochrane; Peter Coston; Petrus de Klerk; Max du Preez; Naas Ferreira; Rhoda Fourie; Jeff Gaisford; Richard Garstang; Sal Gerber; Danie Gouws; Isobel Grobler; Reg Gush; Martin Harvey; Frank Hollier; Bruce Hopwood; Lydia Johnson; Dick Jones; Bill Leppan; Theo Luzuka; Myles Mander; Guy and Jane Mathews; Corrie Middel; Paul Miles; Adrienne Millet; Theresa Moore; Barney Mostert; Dumisane Ngobese; Colin and Lynn Palmer; Pamela Paton; June Payn; Lena Payne; Derek Petersen; John and Cherise Pledger; Hugh Poulter; Elise Pretorius; Harry Pretorius; Sheryl Raine; Tony Rees; Dr John Rourke; Captain Tommy Ryan; the late Charles O Sayers; Derek Schaefer; Robert Schell; Grant Scholtz; Digby Schutz; Colleen Schwager; Anne Schwegmann; Paddy and Carol Smith; Cynthia Spurr; John and Rose Spurr; J J Stapelberg; Dr Pierre Swanepoel; Gwyn Taverner-Smith; Sally van Aardt; Erika van Greunen; Cynthia van der Mescht; Hannes van der Merwe; Dr John Vincent; Agnes von Bodenhausen; Ted Walsh; Denver A Webb; Alison Whitfield; Dr W G Winckler; John Wray; Terry and Kim Wray ●

Bibliography

The publishers acknowledge their indebtedness to the following books which were used for reference.

African Heritage by Barbara Tyrrell and Peter Jurgens (Macmillan); *Boot and Saddle* by H. Morin-Humphreys (George Robertson); *Bowler's Cape Town* by C Pama (Tafelberg); *A Cape Childhood* by Norah Henshilwood (David Philip); *Cape Colony Harbours: Knysna, Mossel Bay* by Sir John Coode (Waterlow and Sons); *Cape Drives and Places of Interest* by Jose Burman (Human and Rousseau); *Cape Town Guide* (Cape Town Directories); *Church Street in the Land of Waveren* by Gawie and Gwen Fagan (Tulbagh Restoration Committee); *Coastal Holiday* by Jose Burman (Human and Rousseau); *Connolly's Guide to Southern Africa* by Denis Connolly (Connolly Publishers); *Daar is maar net een... Elim, 1824-1974* deur J J Ulster (Elim Sendingstasie); *Descriptive and Illustrated Catalogue of the Fossil Reptilia of South Africa in the Collection of the British Museum* by Richard Owen (The Trustees of the British Museum); *Discovering Southern Africa* by T V Bulpin (T V Bulpin Publications); *The Drostdy at Swellendam* by M E and A Rothmann (Drostdy Commission); *Dynamite and Daisies: The Story of Barberton* by P G J Meiring (Purnell); *The Early Days of George* by D J J De Villiers (The George and Knysna Herald); *Everyone's Guide to Trailing and Mountaineering in Southern Africa* by Jaynee Levy (Struik); *A Field Guide to the Natal Drakensberg* by Pat Irwin, J Ackhurst and D Irwin (Wildlife Society of Southern Africa); *52 Daywalks in and around Johannesburg* by Brendan Ryan (Struik); *Gedenkboek Swellendam* deur L L Tomlinson (Swellendam Eeufeeskomitee); *Gleanings in Africa* (James Cundee); *Graaff-Reinet: A Cultural History* by C G Henning (T V Bulpin Publications); *Great Shipwrecks off the Coast of Southern Africa* by Jose Burman (Struik); *Guide to Lesotho* by David Ambrose (Winchester Press); *Guide to the Museums of Southern Africa* by Hans Fransen (Southern African Museums Association); *The Historical Monuments of Southern Africa* by J J Oberholster (National Monuments Council); *A History of Caledon* by Joy Edwards (Venster Printing Works); *History of Oudtshoorn* (Oudtshoorn Van Riebeeck Festival Committee); *Illustrated Guide to Southern Africa* (Reader's Digest Association South Africa); *Illustrated Guide to the Game Parks and Nature Reserves of Southern Africa* (Reader's Digest Association South Africa); *An Illustrated Social History of South Africa* by Alan Hattersley (Balkema); *Johannesburg Alive* by Heather Johnston and Judy Rowe (Map Studio); *Looking Back on George* by Charles O Sayers (Herald Phoenix); *Myths and Legends of Southern Africa* by Penny Miller (T V Bulpin Publications); *Official South African Municipal Yearbook 1985* (South African Association of Municipal Employees); *Overberg Outspan* by Edmund Burrows (Maskew Miller); *Pioneer Port: The Illustrated History of East London* by Joseph Denfield (Howard Timmins); *Pioneer Travellers of South Africa* by Vernon Forbes (A A Balkema); *Portrait of Plettenberg Bay* by Patricia Storrar (Centaur Publishers); *Riches of the Sea* by John R Grindley (Caltex); *Shipwrecks of the Southern Cape* by Brian Wexham (Timmins); *So High the Road* by Jose Burman (Human and Rousseau); *South Africa 1985: Official Yearbook of the Republic of South Africa by the Department of Foreign Affairs; South African Commercial Advertiser 1837-1848; South African Illustrated News 1884-1885; Standard Encyclopedia of Southern Africa* (NASOU); *Stellenbosch Three Centuries* by Francois Smuts (Stellenbosch Town Council); *The Stormy First Twenty Years of Graaff-Reinet* by Robin Blignaut (Graaff-Reinet Publicity Association); *The Story of Hottentots Holland* by Peggy Heap (the Author); *Thomas Bowler of the Cape of Good Hope* by Frank and Edna Bradlow (A A Balkema); *Thornton Cox Traveller's Guides: Southern Africa* (Geographia); *Timber and Tides* by Winifred Tapson (Juta); *Veld Express* by Harry Zeederberg (Timmins).

Use was also made of pamphlets from various local publicity associations ●

Photographic credits

PHOTOGRAPHIC CREDITS FOR each spread read from top to bottom, using the top of the picture as the reference point. Where the tops of two or more pictures are on the same level, credits read from left to right.

10-11 David Steele. **12-13** Walter Knirr; remainder Brian Johnson-Barker. **14-15** All, Walter Knirr. **16-17** Walter Knirr; David Steele; David Steele; Anthony Bannister; David Steele. **18-19** Walter Knirr; David Steele; Brian Johnson-Barker; Walter Knirr; Anthony Bannister. **20-21** Walter Knirr; David Steele; David Steele; Walter Knirr. **22-23** Herman Potgieter; Gerald Cubitt; David Steele; Gerald Cubitt; Gerald Cubitt. **24-25** Africana Museum; Brian Johnson-Barker; Brian Johnson-Barker;

Brian Johnson-Barker; Brian Johnson-Barker; Walter Knirr. 26-27 Walter Knirr; Chris Walton; Walter Knirr; Herman Potgieter; Walter Knirr. 28-29 Walter Knirr; David Steele; David Steele; Gerald Cubitt; David Steele. 30-31 Leo Braack; Jean Morris; Chris Walton; Anthony Bannister; Jean Morris. 32-33 Brian Johnson-Barker; Brian Johnson-Barker; Walter Knirr; Walter Knirr; David Steele; Walter Knirr. 34-35 Brian Johnson-Barker; David Steele; remainder, Brian Johnson-Barker. 36-37 All, Brian Johnson-Barker. 38-39 David Steele; Walter Knirr; Walter Knirr; David Steele; David Steele. 40-41 David Steele; remainder Brian Johnson-Barker. 42-43 All, Brian Johnson-Barker. 44-45 Brian Johnson-Barker; Brian Johnson-Barker; Gerald Cubitt; Brian Johnson-Barker; David Steele; David Steele. 46-47 Jean Morris; Brian Johnson-Barker; David Steel; Don Briscoe. 48-49 Riaan Wolhuter; remainder, Brian Johnson-Barker. 50-51 Emanuel Maria; Jean Morris; Herman Potgieter; Dr J B Poulter. 52-53 David Steele; David Steele; Gerald Cubitt; David Steele; Dr J B Poulter. 54-55 David Steele; Gerald Cubitt; David Steele; Gerald Cubitt. 56-57 All, David Steele. 58-59 David Steele; David Steele; David Steele; Brian Johnson-Barker; Brian Johnson-Barker; David Steele; David Steele. 60-61 Brian Johnson-Barker; Gerald Cubitt; Gerald Cubitt; Brian Johnson-Barker; Gerald Cubitt. 62-63 All, Walter Knirr. 64-65 All, Brian Johnson-Barker. 66-67 David Steele; David Steele; David Steele; David Steele; Walter Knirr. 68-69 All, David Steele. 70-71 Walter Knirr. 72-73 Walter Knirr. 74-75 Walter Knirr; Walter Knirr; Walter Knirr; Walter Knirr; Jean Morris; Walter Knirr. 76-77 Walter Knirr; Walter Knirr; Jean Morris; Jean Morris; Brian Johnson-Barker. 78-79 Walter Knirr; Brian Johnson-Barker; Walter Knirr; Walter Knirr; Brian Johnson-Barker; Walter Knirr; Walter Knirr. 80-81 David Steele; Gerald Cubitt; Herman Potgieter; David Steele; Brian Johnson-Barker. 82-83 Brian Johnson-Barker; Brian Johnson-Barker; David Steele; David Steele. 84-85 Both, Walter Knirr. 86-87 David Steele; David Steele; David Steele; remainder, Walter Knirr. 88-89 David Steele; David Steele; Walter Knirr; David Steele. 90-91 Walter Knirr; Walter Knirr; Brian Johnson-Barker; Gerald Cubitt; Brian Johnson-Barker. 92-93 David Steele; Transvaal Museum Services; Brian Johnson-Barker; Brian Johnson-Barker; David Steele; David Steele; Transvaal Museum Services. 94-95 David Steele; Walter Knirr; Walter Knirr; Brian Johnson-Barker. 96-97 David Steele; David Steele; Brian Johnson-Barker; Paddy Hartdegan; David Steele; David Steele; Paddy Hartdegan. 98-99 Brian Johnson-Barker; Walter Knirr; Brian Johnson-Barker; David Steele; Walter Knirr; Brian Johnson-Barker. 100-101 Walter Knirr; Brian Johnson-Barker; Government Archives; Brian Johnson-Barker; David Steele; David Steele; Africana Museum; Walter Knirr. 102-103 David Steele; Gerald Cubitt; David Steele; Brian Johnson-Barker. 104-105 All, Jean Morris. 106-107 Anthony Bannister; Anthony Bannister; Anthony Bannister; David Steele. 108-109 David Steele; Leo Braack; Anthony Bannister; David Steele; Anthony Bannister; Gerald Cubitt. 110-111 Gerald Cubitt; Gerald Cubitt; Leo Braack; David Steele; Gerald Cubitt; Gerald Cubitt. 112-113 David Steele; Gerald Cubitt; Gerald Cubitt; David Steele; Gerald Cubitt; Gerald Cubitt. 114-115 Gerald Cubitt; Leo Braack; Gerald Cubitt; Gerald Cubitt; Anthony Bannister; Anthony Bannister; Gerald Cubitt; Anthony Bannister. 116-117 Anthony Bannister; Gerald Cubitt; Gerald Cubitt; Leo Braack; Leo Braack; Gerald Cubitt; Anthony Bannister. 118-119 Walter Knirr. 120-121 Herman Potgieter; Walter Knirr; Walter Knirr; Herman Potgieter. 122-123 Walter Knirr; Walter Knirr; SA Tourism Board; Walter Knirr; Walter Knirr. 124-125 All, Walter Knirr. 126-127 All, Anthony Bannister. 128-129 All, Walter Knirr. 130-131 All, Walter Knirr. 132-133 All, Walter Knirr. 134-135 Walter Knirr; Walter Knirr; Walter Knirr; Walter Knirr; Herman Potgieter; Herman Potgieter. 136-137 Gerald Cubitt; Africana Museum; Walter Knirr; Walter Knirr; Gerald Cubitt; Gerald Cubitt. 138-139 Gerald Cubitt; Walter Knirr; Gerald Cubitt; Gerald Cubitt; Walter Knirr; Walter Knirr; Gerald Cubitt. 140-141 Walter Knirr; Dirk Schwager. 142-143 Walter Knirr; Alfie Steyn; Walter Knirr; Walter Knirr; Alfie Steyn. 144-145 Walter Knirr; Walter Knirr; Alfie Steyn; Walter Knirr; Walter Knirr. 146-147 Walter Knirr; remainder, Brian Johnson-Barker. 148-149 Dirk Schwager; Dirk Schwager; Neville Poulter; Dirk Schwager; Neville Poulter; Neville Poulter. 150-151 Neville Poulter; Neville Poulter; Dirk Schwager; remainder, Neville Poulter. 152-153 All, Dirk Schwager. 154-155 Walter Knirr. 156-157 Rob McCallum; Talana Museum, Dundee; Rob McCallum; Rob McCallum. 158-159 Gerald Cubitt; Gerald Cubitt; remainder, David Steele. 160-161 David Steele; David Steele; Gerald Cubitt; Gerald Cubitt; David Steele. 162-163 Felicity Harris; remainder, David Steele. 164-165 Alfie Steyn; David Steele; David Steele; Alfie Steyn; David Steele. 166-167 Gerald Cubitt; Walter Knirr; Walter Knirr; remainder, Martin Harvey. 168-169 David Steele; Herman Potgieter; David Steele; David Steele; Alfie Steyn. 170-171 David Steele; Marek Patzer; Alfie Steyn; Alfie Steyn; Alfie Steyn; Marek Patzer. 172-173 All, Walter Knirr. 174-175 Walter Knirr; Walter Knirr; Walter Knirr; Walter Knirr; Alfie Steyn. 176-177 David Steele; Alfie Steyn; Alfie Steyn; Alfie Steyn; Alfie Steyn; Alfie Steyn; Walter Knirr. 178-179 Walter Knirr; Walter Knirr; Gerald Cubitt; Walter Knirr; Walter Knirr. 180-181 All, Jean Morris. 182-183 All, Walter Knirr. 184-185 All, Walter Knirr. 186-187 All, Walter Knirr. 188-189 Pat Evans; Alfie Steyn; Pat Evans; David Steele. 190-191 Alfie Steyn; Emanuel Maria; Emanuel Maria; Gerald Cubitt; Gerald Cubitt. 192-193 Emanuel Maria; Emanuel Maria; remainder, Alfie Steyn. 194-195 Gerald Cubitt; Laura Parry; Laura Parry. 196-197 Jean Morris; Tim O'Hagan; Africana Museum; Herman Potgieter; Gerald Cubitt. 198-199 Jean Morris; Herman Potgieter; Jean Morris; Jean Morris; Jean Morris; Gerald Cubitt. 200-201 All, Herman Potgieter. 202-203 Tim O'Hagan; Gerald Cubitt; Tim O'Hagan; Jean Morris; Tim O'Hagan. 204-205 Both, David Steele. 206-207 Ethel Rosenstrauch; Ethel Rosenstrauch; Walter Knirr; Ethel Rosenstrauch; Ethel Rosenstrauch. 208-209 Prof M M Smith; Gerald Cubitt; Ethel Rosenstrauch; Brian Johnson-Barker; Ethel Rosenstrauch; Brian Johnson-Barker. 210-211 Gerald Cubitt; Brian Johnson-Barker; Brian Johnson-Barker; Brian Johnson-Barker; Gerald Cubitt; Gerald Cubitt. 212-213 All, Brian Johnson-Barker. 214-215 All, Brian Johnson-Barker. 216-217 All, Brian Johnson-Barker. 218-219 Gerald Cubitt; Africana Museum; Brian Johnson-Barker; Ethel Rosenstrauch. 220-221 Don Briscoe; SA Tourism Board; Gordon Douglas; Brian Johnson-Barker; Gerald Cubitt. 222-223 Gerald Cubitt; Brian Johnson-Barker; Gerald Cubitt; Brian Johnson-Barker. 224-225 Brian Johnson-Barker; Brian Johnson-Barker; Gerald Cubitt; Brian Johnson-Barker; Gordon Douglas; Brian Johnson-Barker; Gerald Cubitt. 226-227 Herman Potgieter; remainder, Brian Johnson-Barker. 228-229 Gerald Cubitt; Gerald Cubitt; Gerald Cubitt; David Steele; Gerald Cubitt. 230-231 David Steele; David Steele; remainder, Gerald Cubitt. 232-233 Herman Potgieter; remainder, David Steele. 234-235 All, David Steele. 236-237 All, David Steele. 238-239 All, David Steele. 240-241 Brian Johnson-Barker; David Steele; David Steele; Brian Johnson-Barker; Brian Johnson-Barker. 242-243 All, David Steele. 244-245 Walter Knirr. 246-247 Anthony Bannister; David Steele; David Steele; Walter Knirr; David Steele; David Steele. 248-249 Africana Museum; David Steele; David Steele; Wildlife Society of Southern Africa; David Steele; Herman Potgieter. 250-251 David Steele; Herman Potgieter; David Steele; David Steele. 252-253 David Steele; David Steele; Jean Morris; David Steele; David Steele. 254-255 David Steele; Gerald Cubitt; David Steele; Landbouweekblad. 256-257 Gerald Cubitt; David Steele; David Steele; Jean Morris; David Steele; University of Stellenbosch; David Steele. 258-259 All, David Steele. 260-261 Gordon Douglas; Jean Morris. 262-263 David Steele; Brian Johnson-Barker; remainder, David Steele. 264-265 David Steele; David Steele; David Steele; David Steele; Anthony Bannister; David Steele. 266-267 Gerald Cubitt; Gerald Cubitt; Gerald Cubitt; Ken Gerhardt; Gerald Cubitt. 268-269 David Steele; David Steele; David Steele; Swellendam Museum; remainder, David Steele. 270-271 All, David Steele. 272-273 Ken Gerhardt; David Steele; Herman Potgieter; Herman Potgieter; Ken Gerhardt; Herman Potgieter. 274-275 Jean Morris; Herman Potgieter; Gerald Cubitt; Gerald Cubitt; David Steele. 276-277 Will Till Inc; Jean Morris; Herman Potgieter; David Steele. 278-279 All, Dirk Schwager. 280-281 Herman Potgieter; Dirk Schwager; Dirk Schwager; Neville Poulter; Neville Poulter. 282-283 David Steele; Gerald Cubitt; David Steele; Gerald Cubitt; David Steele; David Steele. 284-285 All, Gerald Cubitt. 286-287 Gerald Cubitt; David Steele; David Steele; Herman Potgieter; Gerald Cubitt. 288-289 All, Gerald Cubitt. 290-291 All, David Steele. 292-293 Walter Knirr; Walter Knirr; David Steele; David Steele; Reader's Digest. 294-295 Walter Knirr; Gerald Cubitt; Jean Morris; David Steele. 296-297 Anthony Bannister; Gerald Cubitt; Gerald Cubitt; Herman Potgieter; Gerald Cubitt; Gerald Cubitt. 298-299 Brian Johnson-Barker; David Steele; Ethel Rosenstrauch; David Steele; Ethel Rosenstrauch. 300-301 John Yeld; Ethel Rosenstrauch; David Steele; John Yeld; John Yeld. 302-303 Gerald Cubitt; Gerald Cubitt; remainder, John Yeld. 304-305 David Steele. 306-307 Brian Johnson-Barker; Brian Johnson-Barker; Brian Johnson-Barker; David Steele; Brian Johnson-Barker. 308-309 Gordon Douglas; David Steele; Jean Morris; Walter Knirr; Jean Morris; David Steele. 310-311 Brian Johnson-Barker; David Steele; David Steele; Brian Johnson-Barker; David Steele. 312-313 Gerald Cubitt; David Steele; Gerald Cubitt; David Steele; Gerald Cubitt; David Steele; Gerald Cubitt. 314-315 All, David Steele. 316-317 Gerald Cubitt; Gerald Cubitt; Brian Johnson-Barker; Walter Knirr; Gerald Cubitt; Brian Johnson-Barker. 318-319 Herman Potgieter. 322-323 Kevin Rudham. 324-325 Kevin Rudham ●

Colour Separations by Hirt & Carter (Pty) Ltd. Cape Town.
Printed and Bound by CTP Book Printers (Pty) Ltd. Cape Town.